PR
5776   MacKenzie, Norman Ian
M3   H.G. Wells

H. G. WELLS

A Biography by

NORMAN AND
JEANNE MACKENZIE

SIMON AND SCHUSTER
New York

ACKNOWLEDGEMENTS

Many people and institutions have generously helped with this book. Our main debt is to Professor G.P.Wells for permission, on behalf of the Estate of H.G.Wells, to quote copyright material, and to the University of Illinois at Champaign-Urbana for unrestricted access to the Wells Archive in its Library. Our special thanks are due to Fred Nash and Mary Ceibert of the Library staff for their help, to Professor Harris Wilson who has long been associated with the Archive, and to Dr Gordon N. Ray, who has spent many years collecting Wells material and was responsible for establishing the Archive at the University of Illinois. Professor Asa Briggs read the whole manuscript and commented helpfully upon it.

We appreciate the kindness of all those who answered inquiries, drew our attention to unpublished documents, lent us letters, and provided valuable introductions. We thank in particular: Professor Daniel Aaron, Professor W.H.G.Armytage, Sir Arthur Bliss, Margaret Blunden, Vincent Brome, William Burns, Gordon Coucher, the Reverend Anthony Curry, Janet Dunbar, Lovat Dickson, Professor E.M.Eppel, Eric Ford, Dr Arnold Goldman, Sir Ronald Gould, Professor Richard Gregory, the Rt Hon Roy Jenkins, M.P., Dr Daniel Jenkins, Professor J.Kargalitski, Vincent Korda, Susan Lowndes Marques, the late Kingsley Martin, Professor John Maynard Smith, Doris Langley Moore, Anni Mygind, Tom Ponsonby, Reginald Pound, C.H.Rolph, Dr Darko Suvin, the late Lance Sieveking, Renée Tickell, Professor Jean-Paul Vernier, the late May Wallas, L.Watts, Jack Williamson and Alec Waugh.

The frankness and clear memory of Baroness Budberg, Lady Roderick Jones (Dame Enid Bagnold), Lord Ritchie-Calder, Sir John Elliot, Dame Margaret Cole, Nellie Guedalla, Félicie Goletto, Inez Holden, Odette Keun, Lucy Masterman, Malcolm and Kitty Muggeridge, J.B.Priestley, Berta Ruck, Frank Swinnerton, Dame Rebecca West, Anthony West, Amber Blanco White, Sir Clough and Lady Amabel Williams-Ellis and

Frank Wells filled in many gaps and evoked for us the vivid personality of H.G.Wells. We are grateful, too, for the hospitality of those now living in the houses once occupied by Wells, especially Paul and Mary Dixey of Easton Glebe, Robert and Anne-Marie Joriot of Lou Pidou and Mimi May of Spade House. Madeline Usher recalled Haldon Road; Sir Charles and Lady Shuckburgh permitted us to see Shuckburgh Park; and Lt-Col Courtis showed us over parts of Up Park which are normally closed to the public. The kindness of Professor Frank and Lela Costin, of Champaign, was spontaneous and sustaining.

The Society of Authors dealt helpfully with many tedious requests. The BBC Recorded Programmes Service made it possible for us to listen to broadcasts by Wells and those who knew him. Anyone who seeks Wells material can count on the knowledge and courtesy of A.H. Watkins, the Bromley Librarian, and his colleague Miss Plincke. D.A. Clarke, Librarian of the London School of Economics, gave us access to the Passfield Papers and permission to quote from the diary of Beatrice Webb, and his colleague Geoffrey Allen was unfailingly helpful. We wish to express our thanks to the Library staff at the University of Sussex, which also permitted us access to the unpublished papers of Kingsley Martin and Leonard Woolf; to the staff of the British Museum Reading Room; to the National Library of New Zealand, for information on William Pember Reeves; to the Smith College Library for the papers of Margaret Sanger; to Colby College for letters by Violet Paget, Cornell University for letters by Violet Hunt, the Bodleian for giving us access to the papers of Gilbert Murray, and Nuffield College for allowing us to inspect the Fabian Society papers. Other librarians who materially assisted us were those of the Royal Institution, Columbia University, the University of Virginia, Rutgers University, the Newberry Library and the University of Essex, as did M.W.Farr, the County Archivist for Warwick, Mrs Gill, the County Archivist for West Sussex, and Mrs Hay of Windsor Branch Library.

We thank all those copyright holders who have allowed us to quote published and unpublished material. The Society of Authors gave permission on behalf of the Estate of George Bernard Shaw, as did the Trustees of the Will of Mrs Bernard Shaw. Martha Gellhorn allowed us to use a letter to Wells, Jennifer Gosse permitted us to quote from letters by Sir Edmund Gosse, Sir Geoffrey Harmsworth released unpublished letters by Lord Northcliffe, Alexander R.James gave us permission to quote letters by William James, Sir Julian Huxley allowed us to use correspondence with Wells and quotations from his autobiography, *Memories*, May Wallas permitted us to quote unpublished letters by Graham Wallas, and Renée Tickell allowed us to use letters by E.S.P.Haynes. We acknowledge the quotations from the published works of Wells, whose publishers are listed with the titles in the bibliography at the end of this volume, and from the following works: Allen and Unwin, for Ford Madox Ford, *Mightier than the Sword*; Chatto and Windus and Mrs Cheston Bennett for the *Journals* of Arnold Bennett; J.M.Dent and the Trustees of the Joseph Conrad Estate for G.Jean-Aubry, *The Life and Letters of Joseph Conrad*; Faber and Faber for Sir Arthur Salter, *Personality in Politics* and, with Harcourt Brace and Jovanovich, for Geoffrey Keynes, *The Letters of Rupert Brooke*; Hutchinsons for Leo Amery, *My Political Life* and Frank Swinnerton, *An Autobiography*; Princeton University Press for Richard M.Ludwig, *The Letters of Ford Madox Ford*; the University of Illinois Press and Rupert Hart-Davis for Royal A.Gettman, *George Gissing and H.G.Wells*, Harris Wilson, *Arnold Bennett and H.G.Wells*, and Leon Edel and Gordon N. Ray, *Henry James and H.G.Wells*; and Rutgers University Press for A.C.Young (Ed.) *Letters to Eduard Bertz*.

The authors and publisher are grateful to Mr Frank Wells for permission to reproduce nos 1,2,4,11,12,13,14,15,17,18,19,22,23,24,25,26,27, 38 and 39; to the Radio Times Hulton Picture Library for nos 10,28,32, 35 and 46; to Popperfoto for no 34; to Bassano and Vandyke Studios for no 36; to Bromley Library for nos 3 and 6; to the University of Essex for no 37; to Baroness Budberg for no 40; to Mrs David Low for no 45; and to the William Allan Neilson Library, Smith College, for no 30.

There are always individuals who make a book possible by unstinting help. We are indebted to Sally Bicknell for undertaking the Index, and our final and warmest thanks go to Audrey Hunt, who typed much of the manuscript and looked after a complex correspondence with unfailing care.

For Janetta and Julia

CONTENTS

CONTENTS

ILLUSTRATIONS

'Tis not the times, 'tis not the sophists vex him;
There is some root of suffering in himself,
Some secret and unfollow'd vein of woe,
Which makes the time look black and sad to him.

Matthew Arnold: Empedocles on Etna

PART ONE
Little Bertie

I

DOWNSTAIRS PERSONS

"I dread my time so much", Sarah Wells wrote in her diary on 15 September 1866, when she was pregnant for the fourth time. Four days later she added, "please God soon to release me".[1] In the afternoon of Saturday 21 September she knew her time had at last come. She sent her eldest son Frank with a note to the local midwife, Emma Harvey, who arrived at three, followed by the doctor, Mr Morgan, at quarter-to-four. At half-past four Herbert George Wells was born.

Sarah and her husband Joseph were living in Bromley, a small Kentish town on the fringe of London, where they had been caught years before in a business that teetered always on the verge of insolvency. "A miserable half living" Sarah called it. Atlas House, at 47 the High Street, was their shop and home. It was an unpromising place to make a start in life, despite its pretentious name. The house, three small floors and an ill-lit basement, was in a row which faced towards the Market Square. The billheads, florid in the style of the period, were more presumptuous than the business. The "China Glass and Staffordshire Warehouse" announced "Goods Matched to Any Pattern" and "Parties and Balls Supplied on Reasonable Terms". But the shop, at whose door Joseph Wells spent much of the day lounging in talk with neighbours and passing cronies, was less a "warehouse" than a fairly small room lined with shelves which carried a miscellaneous collection of dying and dead stock. Its proprietor, indeed, would have been hard put to it to match up a complete dinner service, let alone supply a party or a ball. In registering his son's birth in the parish church, just behind Atlas House, on 17 October, Joe described himself as a "Master China Dealer", but his heart and skills were not in the trade. Behind the three panes of the front window, and under the centre display stand, the crockery was pushed aside to make room for the cricket goods which Joe found a more congenial line. When a new delivery came in from Duke's, his cousins at Penshurst who made cricket gear, bats and balls were even stacked in the

3

parlour behind the shop. To the right of the door, in a single window, stood the figure of Atlas bearing a lamp in the shape of the globe – the object which had inspired his predecessor to give the dingy house the high-flown name which was its one public claim to gentility.

There never was much trade and the rest of the house showed it. On each of the two upper floors there were two rooms and the twisted narrow stairs between were uncarpeted. The smell of paraffin – with which Joe Wells intermittently waged war against the vermin – hung always in the air. From the back windows there was a pleasant view of Bromley church and the fields beyond it that ran down to the river Ravensbourne, but immediately below lay the small yard with its outdoor earth closet and cesspool, the well that supplied the house with drinking water, an open refuse pit, and a soak-away for the household's drainage. This unhealthy space served as a playground for the boys, as a dump for odds and ends of earthenware, and as the last place in which Joe Wells could demonstrate his youthful training as a gardener by rearing a stunted bush of wigelia and a struggling vine. He was, in Wells's ironic phrase, "a gardener of some resolution". It was not a characteristic he displayed much in other aspects of his life.

Sarah Wells was forty-three years old when her youngest son, "little Bertie", was born. She had been married for thirteen years, and eleven of them had been spent in Atlas House in conditions far less comfortable than those she had enjoyed as a girl. Her father, George Neal, was an inn-keeper in Chichester and Midhurst. As Sarah grew up she helped her father to run the inn. By the standards of her day and class, Sarah Neal had an opportunity for youthful improvement. In 1834, when she was eleven, her father came into a little money, and sent her to a school for young ladies kept by a Miss Riley in Chichester. Her education for the next three years was not remarkable; it is merely remarkable that she had an education at all. She learned to read, write and do modest sums, and got a smattering of royal genealogy. French was an Extra she wanted, but her father baulked at paying for it; her religious duties, however, were not neglected, and Miss Riley's teaching reinforced the Protestant piety of her mother. By the time she was confirmed, Sarah Neal had acquired the little stock of talents and the ingrained evangelical view of the world which were to last her lifetime.

The situation at home became less congenial for the little girl who had been sent away to be schooled as a lady. Her father's family, who had come from northern Ireland, seem to have been somewhat feckless and prone to fortify themselves with drink. George Neal himself, still trying to make a living by providing post-horses at a time when the railways were beginning to compete for the custom of travellers, ran into money troubles. When he died in 1853 George Neal had nothing to bequeath to his two surviving children but a mortgage and a bundle of debts. Sarah got ten pounds from the sale when the lawyers were done. For several years it had been clear that Sarah would have to support herself and for six years she had served an apprenticeship as a dressmaker, and was trained in hairdressing. In 1842, without the prospect of a dowry and early marriage, a girl in her station of life had little option but to go into service. It was something of a comedown but it might have been worse. She already had the necessary accomplishments for a lady's maid: polite, devout, able to attend to the apparel and coiffure of her employer, she was probably a model servant. Her first post was at Liphook in 1842. Then, on 18 September 1845, she was engaged by Mrs Forde, wife of a Captain Forde.

For much of her life Sarah kept a diary, and the first surviving entry was made at a time when she was travelling in Ireland with the Fordes and recovering from some distressing emotional betrayal. In Ireland she wrote:

. . . How dear does this country appear . . . to one alas a voluntary exile from her dear native land to wander alone to brood over the wickedness the ingratitude of a faithless absent but not a forgotten lover . . . can man be happy who gains an innocent love and then trifles with girlish truthful heart may he be forgiven as I forgive him!!!

Sarah had already been away from home for a year, but the memory of the betrayal was still agonisingly fresh. Though she talked about forgiveness, and almost daily thanked her Heavenly Father for her blessings, she was obsessed by her grievance. "Lots of attention but cold stiff and distant my heart is frigid." She was tormented by the conflict between the humility of her religious faith and the pride of her feelings.

I hope this early trial will work good in me. I feel it ordered for the best and time will I think prove it to me how mercifully has Providence watched over me and for a wise purpose taught me not to trust implicitly to erring creatures how can I ever believe man again . . . burnt all the letters.

She left the Fordes three years later and returned to Sussex to be near her ailing mother. On 7 September 1850 she secured an attractive post as maid to a Miss Bullock at Up Park, near her Midhurst home. "The place is pretty and the house large", she wrote, "and a beautiful park with deer. This being a convenient distance from home I frequently go in to see dear Mother & Father, my brother is now at Mr E. learning the Baking." In a phrase that was to echo ominously in her later family life, she added that she "wished so much for him to be a Draper but he did not suit where we placed him at Petworth".

When Sarah Neal went to Up Park it was a country house still furnished and run in the high style of the eighteenth century, standing in beech woods on a sharp hill above the village of South Harting and looking southwards over the rolling Downs to the glint of the sun on the waters of the Channel.[2] A freak of family history had preserved it into the Victorian era. The house has had only seven owners since Lord Gray of Werke built it in the reign of William and Mary, and it has been in the hands of the Fetherstonhaugh family since 1747, when Sir Mathew bought it for £19,000. Sir Mathew was an amateur philosopher and a cultivated gentleman. He became a Fellow of the Royal Society, and experimented with electricity and magnetism. He was a Freethinker and built a fine and eclectic library.

It was Sir Mathew's son, Sir Harry, who changed the fortunes of the Fetherstonhaugh family and the fate of Up Park. He was a Regency buck, a friend of the Prince Regent; and a bachelor. Nearing seventy, Sir Harry lacked a wife and heir.[*] One day he impetuously married his twenty-year-old dairymaid, Mary Ann Bullock, and sent her to Paris to lose her slow Sussex speech and to learn how to be mistress of Up Park. There were no children but she made Sir Harry a kindly wife, living quietly with her younger sister Frances for companion. Sir Harry died at the age of ninety-two in 1846; Lady Fetherstonhaugh survived him until 1875, and Fanny Bullock lived until 1895. Through all the years the sisters lived after him they tried to "'ave everything as Sir 'Arry 'ad it". They lived in the house almost as caretakers, maintaining the fine public rooms but living much in the style of upper servants. Time stopped at Up Park because nothing happened to change it. There was only the slow turn of the seasons about an untouched rural microcosm remote from the factories and the urban squalor of Victorian England.

It was Fanny Bullock who hired Sarah Neal as her maid, and from the first Sarah seems to have been as much a friend as a servant. They were the

---

[*] Among the ladies he patronised was a pregnant girl of sixteen whom he brought for a time to Up Park. She was then called Emmy Lyon, but after several changes of name and patronage she became Emma, Lady Hamilton, and the mistress of Nelson.

same age, and Sarah's childhood background and education had been a cut above that of the dairymaid's young sister. The Bullock sisters could not put on airs with servants and villagers who knew every detail of their sudden elevation; and they had no desire to put on a false front. "It is a very good thing", Lady Fetherstonhaugh observed, "to be a Downstairs person as well as an Upstairs person."

Joseph Wells at that time was an Outdoor person. He was five years younger than Sarah, the youngest son of a large family, whose numerous relations were mostly tenant-farmers and upper servants. His father was head gardener to Lord de Lisle of Penshurst Place, the Tudor mansion in Kent which was the home of the Sydney family, and Joe had been brought up to the same job. He acquired a love of plants, but he somehow failed to acquire the disciplines of his trade. He was restless, given to spurts of enthusiasm of the kind that suggests a romantic rather than a practical personality, impatient to the point of being quick-tempered, and he had a taste for being his own master because he did not like to be told. Several times in his life he was seized by a fancy to emigrate, but his plans to dig gold in America or Australia never came to anything, for the whim passed when the moment came to turn the talk into action. It was a state of mind that persisted: Joe always seemed poised to flee when things got too difficult.

He was a country boy, who could swim and fish and use a fowling-piece; he learned to write, to do sums, and above all to read. He had a great liking for books, but his passion was cricket. Almost every village had a club which played on the green in the summer evenings and on Saturdays. His father's cousin, Timothy Duke, was a notable local player and had been on the Kent team for several years before setting up his own business in Penshurst to make bats, balls and stumps. When Joe had his first job, at nearby Redleaf, he would run a mile into Penshurst after the day's work was done to get half an hour of cricket before the twilight failed. He was a small man, only five foot eight, but he was a fast left-handed bowler – a round-arm "slinger" in the days when under-arm bowling was on its way out, and the cricket world was convulsed with debate about the legality of over-arm delivery.

The Redleaf job seemed to have suited Joe Wells, though none after it ever did. His employer was Joseph Wells, a namesake: he appears to have taken a paternal attitude towards his young gardener, lending him books on botany, encouraging him to draw and preserve specimens, and giving him an itch for improving himself. Joe had expectations from his patron, but unfortunately in 1847 old Mr Wells died without doing anything for him and Joe was out of a job. His employer's death seemed to have taken the heart out of him – he thought he had unfairly lost his chance to get "a start in life" – and for the next four years he wandered from one job to another. In June 1851, Sarah wrote in her diary "Mr Charlton the gardener left Up Park and Mr Wells came. On my return to Up Park I was introduced for the first time to him – thought him peculiar."

Almost nothing is known of their courtship. They would have seen each other often in that loosely-regulated household, and they would have met at the weekly dances in the Servants Hall and walked together in the procession that wound down the path through the Warren to and from South Harting Church on Sundays.

From an early letter written by Joe to Sarah, it is clear that they talked of serious matters. On 7 November 1852, over a year after Joe arrived at Up Park, he wrote to her pursuing a discussion they had had on the way home from the service that morning. "My own, my dearest Sarah", he began his letter: "it is through letters such as these that I feel more & more the value of that love and affection which oh! may God assist me to repay – with that affection and tenderness you so richly deserve.... I pray the day is not far distant when instead of thinking we differ upon the preachings of the preacher that by our own fire side we may for ourselves search the Scriptures."[3] Sermons such as those that he usually heard at Harting, he said, brought religion into contempt. Joe could not accept the idea of original sin that meant even a new-born child might be condemned to "everlasting perdition" on account of the sins of its parents. Joe had a different sense of humility from Sarah's evangelical rigour, for he reminds her that "we must beware of being righteous in our own eyes." "My own, my dearest Sarah", he concludes, "forgive me [for] this long reply but I earnestly wish to remove the impression that in my heart I evince a want of feeling of pure respect towards Religion – ... how happy I am in the thought that you love me well enough to correct me – may that gentle correction remain with [you] to the end of time. Oh – what hopes – what happiness. God bless you. Your own Joe."*

By this point Joe was certainly aware that religion was the dominant force in Sarah's life. Her Low Church piety (she had left one post because

---

* This letter (in part of which Joe makes an apt reference to the French philosopher Fenélon) and Sarah's diary show that both of them were unusually literate and articulate for their station. H.G.Wells was born of poor but not unlettered parents.

her employers were "almost Roman Catholics which made me uncomfortable") cramped her emotionally and directed her anxiety into feelings of guilt which she tried to relieve by a passion for churchgoing that verged on the obsessional. She seldom seems to have felt happy; and whenever she was prevented from attending divine service, the deprivation intensified the underlying depression which monotonously emerges from her diary entries. "I do not feel happy unless I can spend some part of the Sabbath at church", she wrote in a typical entry: "There is such a longing for that peace which the world cannot give."

In 1853, before there was any formal engagement, Joe and Sarah were separated. She left Up Park on 15 April and he went a month later – he may have given notice when Sarah decided to go, because he had no other post in view and went off to stay with his brother near Gloucester. Sarah had gone home to care for her sick mother, and then at the end of August her father died unexpectedly. Her mother became deranged, and "flew at me like a wild woman and declared I had put my father in prison . . . that time will never be effaced from my memory to see my poor mother hate what she had loved so much". By November she too was dead.

Joe hurried back from Gloucestershire and made the grand gesture. Within seventeen days, on 22 November 1853, Joseph Wells married Sarah Neal in St Stephen's Church, Coleman Street, just by the Bank of England in the City. They still had no home, though Joe had now found a post at Trentham in Staffordshire. Sarah, who was visiting around with relations, seems merely to have gone up there to see him. It was not until April 1854 that Joe found a suitable job with a cottage of his own at Shuckburgh Park, near Warwick. On 19 April Joe met Sarah off the train "and drove me to my house. Pretty cottage, in a dear little garden". The account books show that Joe was head gardener from 12 April 1854 until 11 August 1855, at a wage of twenty-five shillings a week. He had a staff of ten labourers under him, and the accounts were kept in his best copperplate hand.[4]

At first all seemed to go well, and Sarah was happy with her household duties and her churchgoing. Yet even after a month there was a sign of trouble to come: "Sir Francis very disagreeable. Felt low and anxious." The prospect that Joe might lose his place was particularly worrying since she now knew she was pregnant, though the first explicit reference to this occurred only in November when she coyly referred to being "busy making little shirts!!!" As her time came nearer she keenly felt the lack of family support and the embarrassment of her condition: "No mother, sister, had to see doctor alone, had to tell all myself." On 20 February a little girl, Frances, was born. Joe pleased Sarah, after the baby arrived, by going to church, but the situation was deteriorating. On 2 May, Joe wrote to a friend in Australia to enquire about the chances if they decided to emigrate.[5] In June he was offered a post at another mansion which, to their later regret, he refused, but he was already advertising for a place. He was, apparently, neither giving nor receiving satisfaction, for on 17 July the moment that Sarah had dreaded came. "Sir Francis gave Joe warning *to leave*. Oh what a sorrow! It struck to my poor heart to look at my sweet babe and obliged to leave my pretty *home*. May it please God to bless us with another happy quiet home in His own Good Time!"

In August they were homeless. They went to stay with Joe's relatives in Gloucestershire and Kent, and Joe went to London for interviews for posts he did not get. On 22 September Sarah wrote: "Felt very anxious about our unsettled condition. How often we both wished we had waited for brighter days before we married." Winter was coming on; they had no home and were separated while Joe searched for work. Finally, with nothing else offering, they decided to take over the Bromley china shop that belonged to Joe's cousin, George Wells. They had little capital, but Joe anticipated a hundred pounds he expected to inherit from his father, and on 9 October 1855 they arrived in Bromley.

It was only four days later that Sarah concluded that they had made a mistake. "I fear we have done wrong", she noted, and two weeks later she added that it was "a horrid business . . . no trade". Their experience of life so far had left them quite unprepared to become shopkeepers. They had both come from the regulated life of upper servants in country houses: provided that one knew and kept one's place, there were few uncertainties and one's living came on the same steady terms as one gave one's services. Suddenly, and literally, they were pitched into the market-place. It was a new pattern of life within which they had no assured living, for their daily bread now depended on the vagaries of trade, on the mysteries of holding stock, running credit, calculating profit margins and building goodwill. Joe's new occupation had an aura of independence but in fact the catch-as-catch-can life of the small shopkeeper was largely an illusory freedom – especially for a man without sufficient capital and a steady ambition. Sarah Wells thought they had been swindled. "How sad to be deceived by one's relations. They have got their money and we their old stock" she noted in her diary two weeks after they took over Atlas House.

There may have been good reasons for this harsh judgement, but there is some evidence that the relations tried to help the couple. George Wells seems to have given credit, because it was about three years before Joe finally paid off what he owed for the business, and Tom Wells, another cousin, helped with the groceries. And Joe continued to get help for years from the Duke relations back in Penshurst. They gave him a long line of credit on their cricket goods which increasingly supplemented the china and glassware as a source of income.

Town and country met in Bromley. So did early and late Victorian England. Midway through the nineteenth century much of the countryside was essentially the same as it had been for generations, but times were changing. As the cities grew, England was becoming the most urbanised nation in the world. By the time that Wells was born there were more than three million people herded into London, only a few miles to the north-west, and more than half the population lived in some thirty towns. The great railway boom had stitched a network of more than six thousand miles of line across the map; the telegraph wires looped across the fields, and the penny post brought letters and newspapers to the smallest hamlet. The English people were on the move, drifting from the great estates and the villages into the new factory towns and the great cities, losing the ties with their family and friends that had once woven them into a community, learning the disciplines of industrial toil and bearing the unhygienic meanness of urban life: there were now more labourers in factories than there were on the land. A nation that, by 1861, had a population of twenty millions, and was simultaneously experiencing a population explosion and its conversion into the foremost industrial power, was painfully coming to recognise that there were new problems which could not be accommodated within the old social framework.[6]

It was a confusing time in which to live, as one kind of society metamorphosed into another. Opportunities for getting on were matched by a fear of failing. "What is the hell of the modern English soul?" Carlyle had asked in 1843. "With hesitation, with astonishment, I pronounce it to be: the terror of 'Not Succeeding'." The Abyss yawned below everyone in Victorian society. The fear of falling into it was as terrifying as the fear of what might come out of it. Contemporary civilisation, Mark Rutherford concluded, was "nothing but a thin film or crust lying over a volcanic pit", and he asked "whether some day the pit would not break out through it and destroy us all". Such a fear was a sharp goad to effort, an explanation of the almost frantic search for respectability on the part of the new classes emerging by the middle of the century. It was a time of hope for the few and apathy for the many, of optimism and anxiety, of vast new productive powers and a growing doubt that individualism would necessarily harness them to the common good, of a sudden surge in knowledge and a haunting sense that it was pressing on a society poorly organised and educated to cope with it. The work of Darwin, Tyndall, Huxley, Mill and Arnold had not yet begun to shake the Victorians' complacent view of themselves as the chosen people located by Providence at the centre of a stable universe. In the next twenty years they were to spend much more on building churches than on building schools. Yet the century had turned on its hinge, and the modern age had begun. Rural England had become the world that was lost, and for millions the green fields beyond the smoke were soon to be little more than a nostalgic memory.

At the time that Joe and Sarah Wells took over Atlas House, Bromley was just beginning to revive after a period of decline.[7] The Hungry Forties had been a bad time. Rioters had looted bread from a baker's in the Market Square, many shopkeepers had moved away, the school had been closed and some of the local clubs had folded up. The village, it was said, was in a state of deep gloom bordering upon despair. But things had picked up in the Fifties. The population rose from four thousand in 1851 to five thousand five hundred in 1861, and when the Wells family moved into the High Street, there were over a thousand households. The houses themselves were improving. Thatch was giving way to slate; and round the edges of town substantial brick villas were being built. Though the streets were still unpaved, and lit only by a few oil lamps, the centre of the village had assumed the appearance it was to retain through the boyhood of Wells and almost until the end of the century. The High Street was busy enough. Coaches stopped at the Bell, a double-fronted stuccoed inn. Atlas House was just across the street, near enough for the Bell parlour to be Joe Wells's favourite evening retreat, where he could play a usually profitable game of Nap over a glass or two of beer. A hundred yards further on was Bromley's other post-house, the White Hart, behind which lay the recreation ground and the pitch for the Bromley Cricket Club, which Joe Wells had helped to revive soon after he set up in the High Street.

It was a township that was still small enough for everyone to know everyone else, yet big enough to contain all the subtle gradations of class which made Victorian society a social obstacle race. The people of Bromley could still look out to fields, or walk by the Ravensbourne, a small river which was clear enough for trout and peaceful enough for kingfishers to swoop over the fish-ponds, and yet they were fast becoming townspeople. They had a Literary Institute, a Literary and Discussion group and a Rate-payers' Association which met in rooms above John James, the baker's; there was a Philanthropic Society, which had been meeting in the Duke's Head since 1841; a Young Men's Christian Association had been formed. From 1850 the *Bromley Record* was the first of the three local papers that competed for custom through the years in which Wells was growing up. Though two horse-drawn carrier's carts left every weekday for London, and were to do so until 1884, it was the coming of the railway in 1861 that linked the village to the metropolis and turned it into a fast-growing suburb. The old way of life was on its way out, as the first season-ticket holders moved in, changing Bromley from a traditional community into a site for the speculative builders.

Around the Market Place, however, the local tradesmen were not yet greatly affected by the changes that were soon to come, when the growth of the "stores" in London and daily deliveries by train were to eat into their business. Next to Atlas House, in No 48, Mr Cooper the tailor kept a couple of men sewing in a workroom that looked into Joe Wells's yard – a cause of continual worry to Sarah Wells who suspected that they squinted out of the window to note the family's comings and goings to the privy. On the other side in number 46 there was Mr Edwin Mundy, the haber-dasher, in 45 Woodall's fishmongery, and just along the street was Covell's Corner, an imposing butchery which usually had twenty carcasses and a few score fowls hanging up outside to catch the eye and attract the flies. * Across from Atlas House, and almost next to the Bell, was Percy Oliver's Boot and Shoe Warehouse; Edward Isard was a tallow chandler, Edward Tuck an ironmonger, and Billy Bagnall at No 10 was the local rag-and-bone merchant. Around the Square there were more small shops, the police station and the Rose and Crown. As one swung back into the High Street, there was Hopton's coal agency and milkround. This was a "rough" family, on which Sarah Wells did not look favourably as neighbours across the street.

These were the men who made up the little business clique. Most of them had been born, and worked and died, around the Square which was

---

* Further down the High Street was Baxter the Chemist, whose son William was a con-temporary of H.G.Wells. His careful notes are the main source of information about Bromley in the second half of the century, and he is the primary reference – apart from Wells's own recollections and papers – on Wells's early life.[8]

the focus of their lives. But the Wells family was not really in this world. They lodged uneasily and uncomfortably on its edge, like birds of passage who have somehow lost their sense of direction and lack the strength to fly on.

THE BURDEN OF ATLAS HOUSE

The pattern of life in Atlas House was established long before Wells was born. The key to it was the conflict between Joe and Sarah, in a marriage which had never gone right over the years. In 1863, on the tenth anniversary of her wedding, Sarah looked back to find ill-omens even in the ceremony itself.[1]

What a novel my life has been to one who had to picture
everythink beautiful and what a marriage   no preparation
    alone at the Altar   no bridesmaid   the sombre
dress of black cast off for one hour   the solemn vows spoken
    once a faint glimmer to prophesy my future life   we
parted a few hours after   no more to meet that year   what
a wedding day!! [Sarah used gaps for punctuation and emphasis.]

The marriage was no more than a lingering disaster, and the birth of children was a source of worry rather than a blessing. Frank was born in 1857, Fred in 1862. By the time Bertie arrived in 1866 Sarah's fear of pregnancy really haunted her. Month after month in her diary she inserted a double asterisk, accompanied by the note: "Anxiety relieved". After Bertie was born, she and Joe began sleeping in separate rooms. Wells said later that "this was, I think, their form of birth control".

The word "anxiety" was significant, for it was Sarah's depression rather than poverty that left its enduring mark on the whole family. It permeated every aspect of life in Atlas House, feeding on adversity and deadening all pleasure. Sarah's fears numbed her capacity for love, and she was unable to create an atmosphere of emotional security in the home. The roles of wife and mother demanded too much from her, and she found refuge in masochistic self-pity and gloomy piety.

Joe also failed as a husband and father. He too was driven by resentment at his lost chances in life. Where Sarah reacted by dominating and managing the household, he dealt with the situation by running away from it and refusing to take any responsibility. Sarah insisted on order, duty and morality, while Joe exemplified disorder and self-indulgence. They responded to unpleasant reality in opposite ways so that their conflict and mutual resentment were the invisible threads that held the household together. The dialectic of martyrdom and self-indulgence in fact became the driving conflict of Wells's life.

The repetitive and mournful entries in Sarah's diary reveal what it was like for a child to grow up in Atlas House. The façade was one of austere respectability. Sarah's contemporaries in Bromley recalled her as a lady-like little woman who did her best to keep up appearances. In the afternoons she could sometimes be seen in her best bombazine dress with a cap and lace apron, sitting for hours in the parlour behind the shop sewing clothes for the boys and waiting – if Joe was out – to serve customers. The reality behind the appearance was less genteel. Sarah had become a complaining household drudge, shod in old slippers and wearing a stuff dress with a sacking apron. "Busy cleaning up Oh! this house is so large without a servant it wears me out", she wrote on 31 December 1858, "all this hard work and having visitors adds considerably to work and then my babies require great time and care." On Christmas Eve in 1862 Joe left for Gloucester, when both children had measles. "But what a Xmas alone with my Pets. Could I have left him as he has me?" she noted. "What happiness have I known as a wife?" she asked on 10 January 1865. "Morose unpleasant treatment shut in night after night *alone* my children in bed and I left to work, work is that what woman is destined for mans *slave*."

The task of keeping things together had fallen upon Sarah but her heart was never in it. Joe appears to have kept away as much as possible. He had even rigged up an ingenious semaphore device which raised an arm in the kitchen when the shop-door above was opened, so signalling to her the arrival of a customer. She and the children spent much of their time in that basement kitchen, where the light filtered through the pavement grating, and where, however hard the times, there was always coal for the fire they cooked on and sat by. There were some good reasons why Joe was so often from home, for an essential part of the family income came from his employment as a peripatetic cricketer; but Joe was generally happier when he was away from Sarah's moans about his inadequacy, whether he was off travelling or simply slipping across the road to the Bell. One entry after another recorded his absence. "J.W. went to London . . . J.W. went to Penshurst ... J.W. went to Buckingham .... J.W. went to Chisle-hurst"; and one note strikingly makes the point on 28 July 1861, "J.W. at home today   wonder!!!" Though much of their living came from cricket, Sarah always took a jaundiced view of Joe's enthusiasm. "What a life this cricket making me a slave", she wrote on 20 August 1863, "we cannot afford to keep a servant and this high awkward house to keep clean, mind, work and nurse 3 children   attend to the shop nearly every day and do all the needlework. Still I am not *appreciated*! What can man expect of woman." Cricket, she said flatly in June 1867, was "low, useless, merely for amusement". Even after ten years of this life she was not reconciled to it. "J.W. out as usual. Oh! How I am left!"

Wells was inclined to date his mother's depression from the death of his sister Frances in 1864. Certainly this tragedy provided a focus for her un-happiness, and for the remainder of her life she looked back on the child-hood of her darling "Possy" sadly and sentimentally. This fixated memory served the need to recriminate, so deeply rooted in her personality. "If only" was a recurring phrase: if only her mother's "life had been spared I think how vastly different our affairs would have been"; if only Joe had gone regularly to church, or been more considerate, or cared less for cricket; if only the relatives had not cheated them over the shop. Even when Fanny became seriously ill, Sarah blamed herself that she was resting and not with "my precious only first born child when she expired". The illness itself was a source of blame. Though she died of acute appendicitis, Sarah was convinced that she had eaten something unsuitable at a party at the Mowatts and continued to bear a grudge against these neighbours, refusing to speak to them or to allow their name to be mentioned in the house.

Fanny had been, at least in her mother's memory, one of those angelic infants who recur in the novels and poems of an age when childhood deaths were a tragedy few families escaped. She knew her Collect, sang hymns about the house and was in all ways her mother's treasure. When, two years later, little Bertie was born, Sarah fixed her fears as well as her hopes on the new baby. "My mother", Wells remarked, "decided that I had been sent to replace Fanny and to achieve a similar edification." It was a role he was unable to play, though not for want of effort on Sarah's part. "She wanted me to believe", he said, "in order to stanch that dark under-tow of doubt ... My heart she never touched because the virtue had gone out of her."

Sarah Wells found compensation for her despair in reveries – her son said that "there was indeed no reassurance for her except in dreamland".

17

When her work was done, she sat in the parlour musing about her lost "Possy", about the future of her sons, and about the days of her youth when she occupied a position with status and security as a lady's maid. She had never lost touch with Lady Fetherstonhaugh and her former mistress, Frances Bullock. Letters went off regularly to them and when little Fanny was alive she had occasionally been asked to spend holidays down on the Sussex estate. As she and Joe sank down through their Bromley misery she clung to this life-line resolutely. So much of Sarah's character had been formed in that rural past, and she found it so difficult to come to terms with the reality of the shop in Bromley High Street, that she seemed to believe that if only the right turn of luck would come she might somehow be translated back to Up Park, as in a magical transformation scene. There she had been "appreciated".

Sarah, like many upper servants, was also a snob. She saw the world as an ordained and unquestionable hierarchy and, though she had lost her natural "place" in it, this image was the only way to make sense of the social system. Over it all presided the omnipotent figure of God the Father, who demanded the deference of prayer but gave no assurance of response. Below him was Victoria, the very model on which Sarah Wells strove to pattern her life. The Queen, Wells recalled, "was in fact my mother's compensatory personality, her imaginative consolation for all the restrictions and hardships that her sex, her diminutive size, her motherhood and all the endless difficulties of life, imposed upon her". Sarah followed every detail of the Queen's public and family life. "I have no doubt about my mother's reveries", Wells said. "In her latter years in a black bonnet and a black silk dress she became curiously suggestive of the supreme widow." From these two fixed points in Sarah's firmament all the lower ranks descended. It was an order which seemed threatened only by the harassments of the Devil, the temptations of sin, and the dangers of falling into the hell-fire of Victorian poverty.

Sarah clung to her gentility the more strongly Joe derided it, and she tried hard to make her boys adopt it too. "*If only* your father had been a gentleman", she said to them regretfully. And the drive to present a front of respectability became more powerful as Sarah found herself forced to become the manager of the family's misfortunes. The more dishevelled their life became, the more strenuously she asserted her will. She was engaged in an unending, exhausting and joyless attempt to keep everything in its proper place – including her sons, who had to be chivvied and corrected, tutored in the subtle gradations of lower-middle-class society which dictated even minor points of protocol. Did one speak to that rough household of Hoptons who lived across the street? What was the proper way to hold a knife and fork, and how fast could one eat a pudding without seeming to gobble it? There was a great deal of irritable Pishing and Tushing in the kitchen of Atlas House.

Sarah's diary suggests that her temperamental differences with her husband were intensified by his carelessness about salvation, honest hard work, social deference and proper manners. He was no better at churchgoing than he was at shopkeeping, had no idea of his "place", and it seems that he was never a man to keep a civil tongue in his head when provoked. For Joe had lost his ambition. He was given to complaining that he had been denied his due expectations, with hints that his paternity might have been better than it appeared. When he was taken by an extreme fit of frustration, or his debts became pressing, he talked about "clearing off". Joe was clearly much less worried than his wife about keeping up with the Mowatts, Coopers and Mundys and, if possible, ahead of the Hoptons. Her nagging complaints that he was spending too much time on cricket and too little on minding the store seem only to have persuaded him to spend more time out of earshot. She could keep her sons indoors as much as she wished, insist that they never answered questions from other boys and neighbours which might reveal the petty secrets of the drudgery in Atlas House, and urge them to keep on their coats when playing; their underclothing "was never ragged but it abounded in compromises".

Sarah could not control Joe in the same way. He had come to take life as he found it, and one of the things that he had found was a slow but profound estrangement from all the values his wife was determined to uphold. Sarah was too rigid in her outlook, too stereotyped in her beliefs, for a husband who enjoyed small talk and whiling away his evenings with cards and draughts. He knew he had failed to provide her with the conventionally comfortable home for which she yearned, or even to play a more positive role as a husband and breadwinner. "He felt", Wells wrote, "her voluminous unspoken criticism of his ineptitude, he realized the justice of her complaints, and yet for the life of him he could not see what was to be done." Sarah was aware of his shortcomings rather than his virtues and he had gradually lost hope and confidence. The naturally insouciant manner that had made him an attractive young man had by now turned into a talent for sliding out of tight corners by visual conjuring tricks. It was only the sudden irrational fits of temper that broke through his easygoing humour that revealed his underlying anger at the way life had caught him. One contemporary described him as a "genial, gregarious man whose irritability led him to wander from one situation to another". Another noted that "Mr Wells was inclined to be irritable and occasionally used language which he afterwards regretted. Consequently he was not a universal favourite. But all who knew him intimately recognised that behind a rough exterior there was a kind heart." William Baxter observed that he "overawed his delicately made and lady-like wife". The neighbours could easily hear his voice coming up through the pavement grating when he was roused and berating his wife or bullying one of his sons.[2] *

The sale of cricket goods was just enough to keep the shop in business. For a number of years, moreover, Joe Wells earned a modest extra income as a professional bowler and coach. At Box's Brunswick Cricket Ground in Hove on 26 June 1862, playing for Kent against Sussex, he was the first player in first-class cricket ever to take four wickets with four consecutive balls. But within a year he went back to club cricket, earning about ten pounds a season for bowling at nets for members of the Bickley Park and then the Chislehurst clubs, and for several summers going off for a term to Norwich Grammar School as a resident professional. He was probably happiest when he hung up the sign in the shop window which read "Gone to Cricket. Back at 7.", and wandered across to the field behind the White Hart which had served as the Bromley pitch since 1751. There, by the Booze Tent, run by old Brazier, the barman from the Bell, this short, stocky man, with a ruddy complexion and a short crisp beard, could sit with his cronies – for a few hours a local worthy of modest but recognised status.

In the first months after little Bertie was born, Sarah's diary contains few references to him. When he was nearly a month old she noted "Baby so cross and tiresome", and "Baby very cross", and even a year later she

---

* Wells said his father "was never really interested in the crockery trade and sold little, I think, but jam-pots and preserving jars to the gentlemen's houses round about, and occasional bedroom sets and tea-sets, table-glass and replacements". Joe's sense of priorities in his business emerges clearly from his advertisement in the *Bromley Record* around the time Wells was born.

CRICKET! CRICKET! CRICKET!

Joseph Wells has an excellent selection of all goods requisite for the noble game, are of first class quality and moderate prices. His cane-handled Bats specially selected by himself are acknowledged to be unsurpassed in the trade. Youths' bats of all sizes, &c &c, at his

OLD ESTABLISHED CHINA AND

GLASS WAREHOUSE

High Street, Bromley, Kent.

remarks of him "never had so tiresome a baby as this one". On 28 April 1868, she recorded, "my precious baby fell out of bed and cut his eye. Oh how sad it is to be over-worried. No one to help. Joe out. Sent for doctor. Had to hold him myself while the cut was sewn up." Successive entries report her "full of anxiety and care" (on 1 May); "my precious child just running about so nicely. Quite made him baby again." "Sadly low and distracted" (on 3 May): "God help me." And on 5 May, "In sad care and sorrow about my child. Oh why did I use a nasty bottle? All my others did without it. How grieved I feel now. I wish I could recall the past. How disfigured my pretty sweet boy looks." The earliest photographs of Wells, taken when he was three, show a plump little fair-haired boy in a petticoat with puffed sleeves, the strong family features already marked in the face which peers suspiciously at the camera. Physically small, never robust in health, he became the spoilt youngest son of an anxious woman, a petulant child whom his schoolmates were later quick to identify as a "mother's boy".

Bertie was clearly a precocious child, and his precocity was encouraged by being petted and fussed. His contemporary, William Baxter, said that his gifts and mannerisms attracted the attention of his girl cousins, the daughters of Tom Wells, the grocer in the Upper High Street. They encouraged him to show off with childish recitations; "his drawings too were appreciated but they often shocked his mother by their unorthodoxy". When Bertie was thwarted, however, he was less winning. "Woe betide", said his brother Frank in later years, "if toys his highness wanted were denied him."[3] Wells himself remembered these tantrums:

My childish relations with my brothers varied between vindictive resentment and clamorous aggression. I made a terrific fuss if my toys or games were touched and I displayed great vigour in acquiring their more attractive possessions. I bit and scratched my brothers and I kicked their shins, because I was a sturdy little boy who had to defend himself; but they had to go very easily with me because I was a delicate little fellow who might easily be injured and was certain to yell.

At an early age he was learning how to have it both ways. His brothers were driven to desperation by his habit of throwing at them the nearest object to hand. On one occasion he threw a fork at Frank, which stuck in his forehead – and he also flung a wooden horse at Fred, which smashed the window when it missed. The brothers at last devised a means of silencing and punishing him.

21

They would capture me in our attic and suffocate me with pillows. I couldn't cry out and I had to give in. I can still feel the stress of that suffocation. Why they did not suffocate me for good and all, I do not know.

Through Wells's childhood, it was Frank – nine years older – who came out as the lively and adventurous member of the family. Fred was steadier, taking life more as it came and allowing his mother to model him in a way that Frank and little Bertie successfully resisted. All three boys were, in turn, apprenticed to drapers. Sarah Wells "certainly thought that to wear a black coat and tie behind a counter was the best of all possible lots attainable by man – at any rate by man at our social level". But Fred, bound to Mr Sparrowhawk, was the only one who stuck it, and eventually set up his own business in South Africa, the epitome of his mother's ambition. Frank was the rebel who found neither a cause nor a niche. He waged a guerilla war against tedium as the leader of a little gang of boys who roamed the fields, a mischievous lad who combined natural ingenuity with mechanical dexterity and inventiveness. He was capable of doing anything from repairing a clock to making a crude bomb to wake up the neighbourhood. "But oh! what larks we had", William Baxter recalled. "In any exploit our allegiance was given to Frank's orders only, and Master Bertie was regarded as a youngster. If he came with us we would have to get Frank's permission and I never remember it being granted." Frank was often in some kind of trouble and unable to settle to anything. Eventually, he threw up the drapery trade and wandered around Sussex and Hampshire as an itinerant clock-repairer, "appreciating character and talking nonsense". By the standards of an acquisitive society, Wells said, he was like his father, "a complete failure in life". The struggle "to acquire and keep hold and accumulate, to work for a position, to secure precedences and advantages was alien" to them both.

It was soon clear that Bertie was going to be different. When he was seven his leg was broken when a youth accidentally tossed him onto a peg of the scorer's tent on White Hart Fields. Though it was badly set, and had to be re-broken, he bore no grudge afterwards against young Sutton, son of the landlord of the White Hart, "for this fall was one of the luckiest events of my life". Because of this twist of fate, Wells wrote, "I am alive today and writing this autobiography instead of being a worn-out, dismissed and already dead shop assistant."

The accident meant that he was laid up for weeks on the sofa in the parlour the focus of attention, and pampered by the delicacies sent across from the White Hart kitchen with Mrs Sutton's apologies for the clumsiness of her son. "I could demand and have a fair chance of getting anything that came into my head", Wells said, "books, paper, pencils and toys – and particularly books." Whatever else was lacking in Atlas House it was not reading matter, or a concern about literacy. When Bertie was quite small, Sarah pasted up the alphabet in the kitchen in large letters and taught him how to count. The first word he ever wrote was 'butter" which he traced over her handwriting against a windowpane. When he was five years old he was ready to go to the little dame school which Mrs Knott kept at 8 South Street, only just over the road. There, under the immediate direction of Mrs Knott's daughter, Miss Salmon, he learned to read and do his tables.

The chance to read without interruption was a godsend. Joe brought books from the Institute Library almost every day, and Mrs Sutton sent more books – on natural history, travel, explorers, generals and great battles of the past. There were volumes of *Punch* and *Fun*, which stimulated his fascination with caricature, and whose cartoons turned politics into a cross between a circus and a zoo, with John Bull and Uncle Sam wandering among the Russian bears and Bengal tigers.

Sarah had many ways of dominating her family. She rejected Joe and scolded the boys. She martyred herself, inducing a sense of guilt by this emotional blackmail. But the most powerful means for preserving order was her insistent recourse to religion. Wells suggested that Sarah had a gentle faith in God the Father and a touching hope that before her ultimate salvation He would deal kindly with her. He also made it clear, however, that the God he knew in Atlas House was one of terror rather than of love and forgiveness, a God who scared him as much as His *alterego* the Devil, either of whom might be the Bogeyman who would snatch him away to the burning fires of Hell. The ambivalence may have been Sarah's as much as her son's. She came from a family of Ulster Protestants, given to a strain of belief much more severe than the body of the Anglican church in England and more inclined to a fundamentalist view of revealed religion. An apocalyptic tradition was undoubtedly transmitted to Wells, providing the unconscious pattern which cropped up again and again in his prophetic writings.

Books reinforced this view of life. Sarah made him read the Bible every Sunday, and he had a grounding in biblical texts at home and in the Bromley church which he attended each week with his mother. There may have been sermons and tracts about the house: other books may have come from the Institute Library, which included some mid-Victorian theology with a bias towards Low Church and Dissenting doctrine. Wells referred specifically to an old illustrated book called *Sturm's Reflections* which contained pictures of hell-fire and devils so horrific that Sarah obliterated them with stamp-paper. From John Bunyan's *The Pilgrim's Progress*, like other self-taught writers, he learned much about English style and narrative technique which persisted into his stories. From the same sources he absorbed the imagery and religious doctrines of Puritan England – ideas of the pilgrimage to salvation, the Last Judgement and the coming of the New Jerusalem which ran through everything that he wrote. The power with which millenarian symbolism worked within him was later reinforced by his extensive reading in utopian literature when he was about thirty years old.

The fundamental impress was that of a fearful religion upon a fearful child. The erratic temper of his father and his mother's brooding sense of sin and anxiety engendered intense and frightening emotions which haunted him. Some of his earliest memories were of terrifying dreams, the raw material from which he later spun his stories.[4] He had one recurring dream which was "a sort of geometrical nightmare as if an immense kaleidoscope charged down upon me, and this was accompanied by immense distress". In other nightmares he was pursued by giant spiders, or by images of monsters which he had seen in books. He claimed that one dream, triggered by a picture in *Chamber's Journal* of a man being broken on the wheel over a slow fire, "made me an atheist . . . if indeed there was an all-powerful God, then it was He and He alone who stood there conducting this torture". The idea of Nature as a force of mindless cruelty was to appear over and over again in his writings.

These fears were intensified by a feeling that he was weak and vulnerable. He even blamed his mother for his small stature by saying she kept him too long in a small bed. And he undoubtedly felt crushed by the emotional pressures on the youngest child in a family which was precariously held together by the dominating will of Sarah Wells: a love expressed in anxiety rather than by sustaining affection and understanding. The passion for reading, the capacity to learn, was a form of compensation, as if mental potency were a substitute for frailty. In that respect Wells internalised his mother's determination that he should at least sink no lower in the social scale, and prove capable of "getting on". She transferred her own disappointed hopes to him. Bertie began to carry "the burden of Atlas House" at an early age, to assume the role that his father refused to play, and to feel that the need to "get on" was in some mysterious way related to the threats that Joe made to decamp and abandon them all when he found the domestic situation intolerable.

The first step in Sarah's plan to make something of Bertie was to get him the best education she could. So he was sent to Mr Thomas Morley's Bromley Academy, a few doors along the High Street. As soon as Bertie had recovered from his fractured tibia, when he was still under eight, he was sent off in his holland pinafore and carrying a green baize satchel, to learn what he could from the irascible Scots schoolmaster of limited academic attainments.

The Academy's advertisements in the *Bromley Record* tell a little of its pretensions. Its object, one declared, "is to prepare youth for the various Mercantile and Professional pursuits ... The acquisition of the French language is greatly facilitated by the intercourse between the French and English pupils." Mr Morley laid stress on "writing in both plain and ornamental style, Arithmetic logically, and History with special reference to Ancient Egypt". It sounds like a Dickensian school, and in many ways it was. There had originally been a school in Bromley owned by a man named Robert Booth Rawes, who is said to have provided Dickens with the original for Mr Pickwick.[5] One of the assistant masters had been Thomas Morley, and when the Rawes school suddenly collapsed he set up on his own. He had a single room built out to accommodate some thirty boys, about half of them boarders who were the sons of London publicans and other parents unable to provide them with suitable homes. Morley was what passed for an educated man in the small world of the Bromley tradesmen, and he lorded it over them in style. What the drapers and grocers and innkeepers wanted from Morley's school was some sort of education which had the semblance of gentility – and private academies were virtually the only places which could offer this service. The upper classes had the old public schools; new ones were being founded and by a mixture of reform and almost brazen appropriation of many of the endowed grammar schools, these had been converted from their original charitable purposes to cater for the newly-prosperous as well as the gentry and clergy. The grammar schools, which had traditionally taken in the sons of tenant-farmers, tradespeople and upper-servants, were no longer adequate for this class.

In the middle of the nineteenth century the gap was filled by small academies, frail vessels that often made more sound than sense. They may have been a pedagogue's nightmare, run with brutal discipline by untrained teachers whose knowledge was at best patchy and whose methods were erratic, but they were schools which at least offered a ticket to a white-collar respectability. By a mixture of cramming and drills, boys (as in Mr Blimber's Academy at Brighton, which Dickens described in *Dombey and Son*) could be "blown upon" to learn a mixture of Euclid and book-keeping, to write reasonable English and – as Wells said of his years in Morley's school – have their French crippled for life and be made vowel-shy in any language. Wells, indeed, was so blown upon in the book-keeping line that at the age of thirteen he and another of Morley's pupils tied for first place in the examinations run by the College of Preceptors.

There was, of course, a National School in Bromley, and by 1869 this was so overcrowded that a hundred and fifty pounds had to be raised by local subscription to enlarge it. It would have been a matter of desperate last resort for Sarah Wells to send her sons to it, for such schools were very clearly on the wrong side of the crucial dividing line between respectability and the lower orders. The degree of class consciousness involved was highlighted by the running feud between Morley's pupils, known as the "Bull Dogs", and the National boys who were abusively entitled the "Water Rats" – an antagonism that occasionally broke out into a pitched battle with sticks on the waste patch at St Martin's Hill.

England at that time was poorly served by its schools, which at all levels were badly equipped, badly run and hopelessly inadequate to the demands being made upon them by industrial development, urbanisation and the enfranchisement of a million workers in 1867. About half of its children had no schooling at all before the Elementary Education Act of 1870. This was a turning point. By the end of the century the new schools were turning out a new class of semi-literates – the future market for North-cliffe's *Daily Mail* and the other halfpenny papers, and for the popular "railway novel" writers. But there is no gainsaying Wells's comment that, by and large, the effect of the Act was "to educate the lower classes for employment on lower-class lines, and with specially trained, inferior teachers who had no university quality". A witness in an official enquiry in 1888 observed that "it would be next to expecting a boy out of the London Board Schools to take wings as to expect him to advance by his own efforts to the university".[6]

The Bromley Academy tried to do a little better. Morley had "all the dignity, if little of the substance, of scholarship" and he did his best to make his pupils conscious that they were in some way marked out to be something different from the lower orders. His task was to make them members of the genteel class, however near its lower margins they hovered, and however limited the knowledge he erratically imparted to them. His indoctrination, reinforcing Sarah Wells's obsession with status, shaped young Bertie in the social attitudes of the lower middle class and ethnocentric Englishman. Wells was reading widely, but none of the new knowledge that he thus acquired did anything "to shake my profound satisfaction with the self, the township, the county, the nation, the Empire". He absorbed the current mythology of England's civilising destiny and fused it with the missionary zeal of the Evangelicalism which dominated his home and his religious upbringing.

Despite his shortcomings, Morley was not too bad a teacher, though the task of coping with thirty boys between the ages of seven and fourteen taxed his capacities. "He was like some very ordinary chess player who had undertaken to play thirty games of chess simultaneously", Wells observed, adding that by the standards of his day "this old-world pedagogue" was "by no means so contemptible. There was something good about old Morley and something good for me." That comment, when Wells was an old man, was more charitable than his bitter remark in 1892 that "I do not remember any teaching at all at school . . . we grew up dull."[7] But he filled in the gaps in Morley's pedagogy with the reading that went on by the oil-lamp in the evenings at Atlas House.

Words became a passport to experience – but to a special kind of vicarious experience in which Bertie's imagination could take flight and carry him away from Bromley to other lands and other times, as in *The Time Machine* where the Time Traveller was carried through the coming millennia without stirring from his seat. "I had just discovered the art of leaving my body to sit impassive in a crumpled-up attitude in a chair or sofa", Wells wrote of himself at the age of seven, when he had been caught by the magic of books, "while I wandered over the hills and far away in novel company and new scenes." But though he spent much time as a bookworm, Bertie was not a housebound delicate boy. While Sarah kept him closely under her eye, and restrained him from mixing with the "rough" boys, he loitered a good deal around the precincts of Bromley, sometimes alone, and sometimes with his close friend Sidney Bowkett, who later had a brief success as a light dramatist and provided Wells with the model for Chitterlow in *Kipps*. Bowkett, he said, "was one of those who see quickly and vividly, and say 'Look', a sort of people to whom I owe much, who could light up and colour and intensify an impression".

Wells himself had an excellent eye and ear, talents which launched him first as a reporter and then as an author. The power of convincing description later enabled him to carry his readers unnoticing from fact into fantasy. But his fascination with circumstance, with the senses rather than with sensibilities, was also a means of escape from depth of feeling. What emerged from the counterpoint of the absorbed reader in Atlas House and the observant boy idling through the meadows beside the Ravensbourne, was a distancing from real life, the projection of packaged ideas about history, geography, science and the cosmos into everyday experience as a substitute for strong but inexpressible emotions. Wells himself later gave some clues as to the nature of those repressed feelings. There was certainly a good deal of aggression and frustrated omnipotence about them, and one paragraph in his autobiography explicitly linked his destructive fantasies with his keen topographical sense – a link that he made repeatedly in his scientific romances. * He described how he, like his mother, was given to reverie, and how these fantasies would occupy his mind when he went out alone for walks. He would fancy he was Cromwell or Napoleon, and fight mock battles over the Kent fields.

I used to walk about Bromley, a small rather undernourished boy, meanly clad and whistling detestably between his teeth, and no one suspected that a phantom staff pranced about me and phantom orderlies galloped at my commands, to shift the guns and concentrate fire on those houses below, to launch the final attack upon yonder distant ridge. . . . Martin's Hill indeed is one of the great battlegrounds of history . . . I and my cavalry swept the broken masses away towards Croydon, pressed them ruthlessly through a night of slaughter on to the pitiful surrender of the remnant at dawn by Keston Fish Ponds . . . kings and presidents, and the great of the earth, came to salute my saving wisdom. I was simple even in victory. I made wise and firm decisions, about morals and customs and particularly about those Civil Service Stores which had done so much to bankrupt my father.

These dreams of glory, which all centre around a martial dictator dealing

---

* Topographical metaphors are a common means of describing social relationships. The environment of childhood provides something like a mental map of society whose outlines are filled in by later experience. The social and temporal dimensions of Bromley, located at the intersection of town and country, early and late nineteenth century, provided Wells with the co-ordinates within which he set much of his writing. His reliance on autobiographical techniques suggests that he wrote most spontaneously when he re-explored those earlier maps of childhood and adolescence.

death to his enemies and setting the world to rights with his subsequent benevolence, were a common and important feature of Wells's early adolescence. He plainly said so himself, and adds that "for many years my adult life was haunted by the fading memories of those early war fantasies". Wells did not connect these destructive obsessions with his own anger and rebellion. He thought that their subject-matter was simply an accident of his reading: "the only vivid and inspiring things that history fed me with", he wrote later, "were campaigns and conquests".

Wells was also putting his bellicose fantasies down on paper. In his last year at Bromley, apart from other pieces of juvenilia such as a boyish parody of *Punch*, he wrote and drew *The Desert Daisy*, a children's story which turned up among his papers after his death and was published in a facsimile edition in 1957.[8] It was an irreverent skit on royalty, politicians, generals and bishops, and the mock war which it described was very similar to the make-believe battles that Wells imagined as he wandered through the fields around Bromley. Some of the phrases already anticipated the manner of his later letters. The fake review of the *Naily News* declaimed that it "Beats *Paradise Lost* into eternal smash!", and the *Telephone* reported "Descriptions of the Battles sublime!" A curious feature of the little book was the fact that the drawings were in two distinct styles. The first was that of "Buss", the nickname that the family used for Bertie, and the more elaborate sketches were signed "Wells". The work was supposedly edited by "Wells", who said that he had completed the manuscript begun by Buss, "who has been obliged to retreat to Colney Hatch" asylum, "where he is forbidden to write again".

In these same years, moreover, he was also discovering the compensating power of sexual fantasies. "My own sexual life began", he wrote, "in a naive direct admiration for the lovely bodies, as they seemed, of those political divinities of Tenniel's in *Punch*, and . . . my first inklings of desire were roused by them and by the plaster casts of Greek statuary that adorned the Crystal Palace." It was from the stimulus of these mythical ladies that Wells began to construct his image of the ideal woman – the "Venus Urania", distant, unattainable, yet endlessly pursued, who by contrast made all his real relationships unsatisfying. It was difficult enough for any Victorian schoolboy to learn and cope with the facts of life – "a horrifying, astounding, perplexing individual discovery" that Wells made when he went to the Academy – but the split between fantasy and feeling was all the more acute for a child brought up in a home rigid with emotional tension and dominated by Puritan moralism.

In later years Wells summarised his state of mind at the end of his childhood. He was, he said, "a sentimentalist, a moralist, a patriot, a racist, a great general in dreamland, a member of a secret society, an immortal figure in history, an impulsive fork thrower and a bawling self-righteous kicker of domestic shins". This revealing catalogue of his postures and attitudes makes it clear that his early adolescence was a dress-rehearsal for much of his adult life.

When Bertie was eleven, the long grinding strain of life in Atlas House began to reach breaking-point. Disaster did not come quickly, but crept inexorably upon the family. In October 1877 Joe compounded his general incapacity as a breadwinner by falling off a ladder in the back yard and breaking his thigh. This laid him up for weeks, and led to bills for the doctor that the family could ill afford. It also finished him as a professional cricketer and put an end to the extra income that he had earned in this way. Times became hard. Meat meals gave way to bread and cheese, or half a herring. Mr Morley's bill once had to wait a year for payment. And when Frank, now a draper's assistant earning twenty-six pounds a year, once gave Sarah a week's wages to buy Bertie a pair of boots she wept with relief and pleasure.

The Wells family was beginning to fall apart. Bertie was almost of an age when he could finish school and be bound like his brothers to the drapery trade. If Sarah remained at Atlas House there was no prospect before her and Joe but an inexorable descent into squalor and bankruptcy. Somehow she managed, scraping enough from the shop to get Bertie through school. When Bertie was almost fourteen, and an opportunity came for her to leave, she showed little compunction about abandoning Joe to his own devices. She hurriedly thrust her son out into the world to fend for himself – a rejection that Wells bitterly resented, for it not only deprived him of the one source of security in his life and left him lonely and depressed, but it also cut off the one route of escape on which he had counted. For a boy in his class, education was the only ladder by which he could hope to climb out of it. When Sarah knocked it away, he felt betrayed. He realised that, for her, it had simply been the means to gentility and the drapery trade, while for him it had been the one alternative experience in his life that had a personal value and offered him a chance to make something of himself. For at the age of fifty-seven Sarah was offered the chance of a lifetime to escape from her burden. In the midst of her gloom, "suddenly the heavens opened", her son recalled, "and a great light shone on Mrs Sarah Wells". Down at Up Park, Lady Fetherstonhaugh had died in 1875 and her sister Frances had inherited the house and assumed the family name. She found it difficult to run the mansion and manage the servants, and her remembrance of her cordial relations with her onetime maid led her to the extraordinary conclusion that Sarah Wells was ideally suited to become her housekeeper. In 1880 she summoned Sarah down to Sussex and offered her the post. Sarah did not take long to make up her mind. It was a far superior form of servitude to that which she had endured in Atlas House, and she could revert to the world she had known and understood when she was a young girl, a situation which would give her status, security and enough income to smooth over the worst fluctuations in the fortunes of her husband and her sons.

In the summer of 1880, after she had taken steps to give little Bertie a start in life, she packed and left Bromley. She was done with Atlas House at last.

3

FALSE STARTS

When Bertie was almost fourteen he was hastily pitched out of his home and set to make his way in the world. Scarcely old enough to fend for himself, brought up in a family whose attitudes belonged more to the beginning than to the end of Victoria's reign, Wells was caught up by the whirling fringe of a social revolution and whipped away into a new phase of life full of uncertainty and fear. His memory of that time was of an invading and growing disorder. It was not merely that the disorder in the Wells household had finally broken it apart. At the same time Bromley itself had been invaded. The second railway station, at Bromley North, was built when Wells was eleven, and the new line quickly turned the village into a London suburb populated by white-collar commuters. The Ravensbourne, that central image of the undefiled stream of life, was no longer pure. It had become a dirty ditch. The jerry-built houses for clerks and working-men were run up along dead-end roads. And all round them was the cheap, nasty detritus of a sort of progress that had bolted. Wells felt that change had got out of hand, and that it was rushing nowhere in particular.

There was poverty and even squalor in Bromley, but Wells had no personal experience of the inhuman misery of slum life in London and the other industrial towns – nor of the appalling working conditions in which a new kind of trade unionism was being created. "My want of enthusiasm for the Proletarian ideal", he wrote, "goes back to the battle of Martin's Hill" between Morley's pupils and the boys from the National School. His radicalism sprang more from jealousy of those above him than from any identification with those below:

Just as my mother was obliged to believe in Hell, but hoped that no one would go there, so did I believe there was and had to be a lower stratum, though I was disgusted to find that anyone belonged to it. I did not think this lower stratum merited any respect. It might arouse sympathy for its bad luck or indignation for an unfair handicap. That was a different matter.

Wells was thus growing up in a situation which was socially and geographically on the margins of the extended urban experience that was transforming English life. Until he went to London in 1884, he moved from one false start to another in towns and villages around its edge, hovering between the older, rural and in some ways more secure world in which his parents had grown up and the machine civilisation, full of uncertainties, tension and relentless change.

The question was what to do about Bertie. Sarah Wells could see only one way to give her sons a start in the world. "Almost as unquestioning as her belief in Our Father and Our Saviour", Wells said, "was her belief in drapers." Sarah probably made contact with Rodgers and Denyer, a firm of drapers just opposite the Castle entrance in Windsor, through a second cousin named Thomas Pennicott, who kept a riverside inn called Surly Hall a couple of miles upstream from Windsor. He had been one of the witnesses when Sarah and Joe were married, and Sarah had kept in touch with him. He had always been willing to give her boys a healthy holiday by the Thames, and some of the happiest and most carefree moments of Wells's childhood were spent at Surly Hall, lazing about by the ferry and helping with the hired boats. He was, moreover, petted and spoilt by Pennicott's two daughters and the barmaids, who liked his bright Cockney talk and pretended to flirt with him. The improved "tone" that Bertie picked up on these visits greatly irritated his brothers.

It was the custom of the drapery trade to pay a premium of up to fifty pounds for the chance of learning the mysteries of the trade. For Wells this meant little more than sweating through a seventy-hour week in return for sixpence pocket-money and the dubious benefits of "living in". These were a bed in a scruffy dormitory, a poor diet and a strict "moral supervision" which in practice meant that even the limited free time must be used in a manner acceptable to the employer. Sarah somehow scraped together the money for the premium, though it was not far short of a year's cash income in Atlas House, but she was not called upon to put the money down until Bertie had completed a trial month and satisfied his employers that he had the makings of a gentlemanly assistant. Respectability was no doubt highly-prized in a shop in the High Street which was patronised by the Royal Family and described by its proprietors as the leading "silk-mercers, linen drapers, lacemen, court milliners and dressmakers" in the locality.

This period at Windsor turned out to be a month of trials, for Bertie

Wells and his employers. On Sunday 4 July, soon after he had been handed over by Uncle Pennicott, he wrote to his mother at Up Park.[1]

My dear Mother

Here I am, sitting in my bedroom after the fatigues of the day etc. Cough slightly better & I am tolerably comfortable.

I give you an account of one day's work to give you an idea what I have to do.

Morning

We sleep 4 together every 3 apprentices & 1 of the hands in one room (of course in separate beds).

We lay in bed until 7.30 when a bell rings & we jump up & put trousers slippers socks & jacket on over nightgown & hurry down & dust the shop etc.

About 8.15 we hurry upstairs & dress & wash for breakfast.

At 8.30 we go into a sort of vault underground (lit by gas) & have breakfast.

After breakfast I am in the shop & desk till dinner at 1 (we have dinner underground as well as breakfasts) & then work till tea (which we have in the same place) & then go on to supper at 8.30 at which time work is done & we may then go out until 10.30 at which hour the apprentices are obliged to be in the house.

I don't like the place much for it is not at all like home.

Give love to Dad & give the Cats my best respects.

I'm rather tired of being indoors but this morning I went to Clewer Church & then on to Surly which I found much better than I used to think it in fact its a perfect heaven to R & Ds.

I'm rather tired so excuse further writing.

yours
H.G.Wells

NB My washing will be 12/ a quarter.

The fact that Wells had done well in the book-keeping examination may have impressed his employers, but his success on paper did not prove to have much relevance to the practical task of looking after the cash-desk. There are a number of letters to Frank from these weeks. "Excuse my writing more as Mr R is wandering up & down like the Wandering Jew & I am not sure but he may light on me writing" . . . "and now I live amidst the heathen thou dost not write once a month . . ." In August 1880 one complained about his father "telling all the confounded gossips in the Beastly Old Town what boys he has got and what a disgrace they are to him".[2] As far as possible he dodged the morning rituals of dusting and window-cleaning, and while he sat at the cash-desk he either day-dreamed or used slack periods to read or work furtively at problems in Todhunter's *Larger Algebra*. When he could, he slipped away to read in the lavatory or behind the stacks in the store-room. Almost every day there was something wrong with the change and the accounts, and the deficit mounted with the weeks. Eventually Uncle Pennicott was called in. Wells was not formally accused of pilfering, for it was clear he was merely careless and inattentive in his work, but his general appearance, lack of refinement and propensity to be troublesome (there was a rough scrap with the junior porter) were too much for Mr Denyer and Mr Rodgers. He had to go.

By sullen resistance, Wells had won himself a respite from his mother's determination to make him into a respectable draper's assistant. He spent most of his free time at Surly Hall, "where there was something to touch my imagination and sustain my self-respect", and until a new start could be improvised for him he returned to Uncle Pennicott's. Sarah, still settling in at Up Park, was at a loss. His father made an ineffective attempt to persuade one of the cricketing gentlemen to take him on as a bank-clerk. But it was another distant relative who came to the rescue. This was the brother-in-law of Thomas Pennicott, an "Uncle" Williams, who had been a teacher in the West Indies and was about to become head of a village school at Wookey, near Wells in Somerset. He proposed to take on young Bertie as an "improver" – a pupil-teacher who would teach while continuing his own studies, and partially pay his way by the awards he earned – with the aim of entering a training college.

Alfred Williams was a grotesque. His appearance was odd – balding, yellow-faced with grey whiskers, and "a chin like the toe of a hygienic slipper"; in place of one of his arms he had a stump into which he screwed a fork at mealtimes. He had formed his own firm to market patent devices to schools, but an inability to manage its finances reduced him from its owner to its clerk; his ingenuity had also led him to forge the certificates and references he needed to add to his West Indian experience to persuade the education authorities that he was a fit person to conduct elementary education in a Somerset village. He was, in fact, a rogue, with the quick-spoken charm of the confidence trickster. He did not, of course, see himself in quite this light: deception seemed to him a quite reasonable way of evading the stupid exactions of authority, and facetiousness was a cover for sceptical and radical views. "He gave me a new angle from which to regard the universe", Wells said later; "I had not hitherto considered that it might be an essentially absurd affair, good only to laugh at." The contrast with the oppressive atmosphere of Atlas House was not only pointed by Uncle Williams's attitude to religion but also by his teenage daughter's attitude to sex. She took it upon herself to be instructive rather than edifying in this respect – lessons which left Wells "with a certain aversion": it seemed "hot, uncomfortable, shamefaced stuff".

Uncle Williams took over in October 1880, and within three months the irregularity of his affairs put an end to Wells's interlude at Wookey.[3] Government inspectors discovered that Alfred Williams's credentials were fraudulent. He was given notice and left in May 1881, but once Bertie's prospects were blighted there was no point in his staying on. The portmanteau was packed again, and Bertie was despatched back to Surly Hall, with instructions to the Pennicotts to post him on to Up Park as soon as Sarah had been able to beg permission for him to stay with her.

There are twenty pages in the first chapter of *Tono-Bungay* which brilliantly describe Up Park and the impact that this glimpse of a different, and grander, life made on Wells at the age of fourteen. It was, of course, life below stairs that made the first strong impressions. When Wells arrived, the servants' quarters in the semi-basement were busy with staff preparing for a houseful of guests over Christmas. Since his mother ranked with the butler as a head-servant, he had the run of the warren of still-rooms, store-rooms and pantries, as well as the eerie underground passages which linked the basement with the kitchen and stable blocks. All the food was prepared in the distant kitchen and carried through the tunnels on trolleys fitted with charcoal warmers. The grills on top of the ventilating shafts can be seen in the front drive.

Sarah's own accommodation was in two semi-basement rooms at the south-west corner of the house, lit by grilled windows. They were not far from the butler's pantry and close to the Servants' Hall, a high oblong room which was the only part of the house devoted to the servants that was sufficiently raised to enjoy full windows. Bertie, who was given a small attic bedroom, spent hours in his mother's room reading. When he was troublesome he was locked in it. On a later occasion, in a fit of pique, he took an air pistol and shot at an equestrian painting on the wall – the picture, which now hangs upstairs, has a hole drilled through the rear fetlock of the horse. Though life below stairs was as regulated by the hierarchies of status and custom as the life above stairs that it mirrored, the peculiar circumstances of the Up Park ladies gave their staff more latitude than was normal in the country house at this time. The family historian described it as "a paradisical era" for the servants. Sarah Wells was certainly not a woman who could run the staff firmly and raise the efficiency of the household. She looked the part of a superior housekeeper, the keys which were the symbol of her authority dangling down her black bombazine dress. She could keep up the stilted niceties of conversation which were expected when the upper servants withdrew for tea and cake in her room, but she had neither the capacity nor the training to supervise all the daily details to the degree that would have been expected in a house with higher standards. When Bertie first arrived at Up Park his mother had just established herself, and her precocious boy got a great deal of attention. The house was cut off for some days during the Christmas holidays by a great snowstorm, and during this time Wells produced a daily newssheet of gossip called *The Up Park Alarmist*. He also presented a shadow play to the maids in a miniature theatre he built.

Bertie was still a Downstairs person. The dark kitchen of Atlas House had been replaced by the basement in the Windsor drapery, and now by life below stairs at Up Park. But in all senses the last change was for the better. He now found himself translated into a world he had previously known solely from the memories of his parents. It was as if he was able to travel back through time, escaping from the hardships and bewilderment of the present into an earlier but still functioning and stable social system. For Up Park was not merely a museum of early nineteenth-century furnishings. It was equally a museum of manners and morals which left a lasting impression upon him. In later years Wells came to believe that "modern civilization was begotten and nursed" in houses like Up Park where "behind their screen of deer park and park wall and sheltered service, men could talk, think and write at their leisure . . . be interested in public affairs without being consumed by them".

Out of such houses came the Royal Society, the *Century of Inventions*, the first museums and laboratories and picture galleries, gentle manners, good writing . . . it has been far more through the curiosity and enterprise and free deliberate thinking of these independent gentlemen . . . that modern machinery and economic organization have developed so as to abolish at last the harsh necessity for any toiling class whatever. It is the country house that has opened the way to human equality, not in the form of a democracy of insurgent proletarians, but as a world of universal gentlefolk no longer in need of a servile substatrum. It was the experimental cellule of the coming Modern State.

This tribute was written more than fifty years after Wells first arrived at Up Park, and it reveals how the country house system became for him the model of an alternative order to set against the disorder that had come upon Bromley and upon his life at Atlas House. There was an element of snobbery in it: Wells absorbed something of his mother's deferent fascination with the life of the country gentleman. In later and prosperous years he lived as though he were the heir to the Up Park tradition, combining the intellectual interests of the Enlightenment with the morals of the Regency. But it also reflected his belief that the society which Sir Mathew Fetherstonhaugh exemplified was superior to the bourgeois, industrialised England in which he grew up, corrupted by complacency and torn by class conflict. The great estates, ruled by order and owned by enlightened guardians of scientific intelligence, provided him with the pattern for his utopian societies and the cultivated élites which were to control them.

Wells revealed this nostalgia clearly in the passages of *Tono-Bungay* in which, twenty-five years later, he described the Up Park system. It was Bladesover, he wrote, which

enabled me to understand much that would be incomprehensible in the structure of English society . . . all that is modern and different has come in as a thing intruded or as a gloss upon this predominant formula . . . you will perceive at once the reasonableness, the necessity, of that snobbishness which is the distinctive quality of English thought. Everybody who is not actually in the shadow of a Bladesover is as it were perpetually seeking after lost orientations.

And his regret at the passing of this system so coloured his prose that it produced the finest simile he ever wrote.

It is like an early day in a fine October. The hand of change rests on it all, unfelt, unseen; resting for a while, as it were half reluctantly, before it grips and ends the thing for ever. One frost and the whole face of things will be bare, links snap, patience ends, our fine foliage of pretences lie glowing in the mire.

When Wells wrote of the future, it was this past that he had in mind.

In those first weeks at Up Park, however, he was too young to build up his impressions into such a sophisticated shape. The immediate joy was the discovery of a fine collection of books. Some of them were rummaged out of an attic near his bedroom, in which Bertie also found the parts of Sir Mathew's Gregorian telescope which he assembled to gaze at the stars. Others were borrowed from the family library in the magnificent gilt and white salon below. There were volumes of engravings, works by Voltaire, Tom Paine's *Common Sense*, Swift's *Gulliver's Travels* and, above all, Plato's *Republic*. It is significant that it was these three books that he particularly recalled. They represent three themes – radicalism and agnosticism, utopian satire and the idea of a rational society ruled by men of intellect – which played a predominant role in his ideas and his writings. It was in the *Republic* that he found the notion that society was not immutable, but by the minds of men might be made anew.

Yet the winter weeks at Up Park were just an interlude of relaxation and mental stimulus before Sarah's drive to start him properly in life found a new outlet. This time her idea was to make him a chemist. He was to be employed by Mr Samuel Cowap, in Church Hill, Midhurst, only a few miles away from Up Park. The new post promised to be a pleasant situation, where Bertie might make amends for his poor showing at Windsor, and where the work itself was more interesting. Rolling pills and dispensing patent medicines was better than dreaming at a cash-desk and being hectored by a shopwalker.

Though Bertie was to stay only a few weeks with Mr Cowap, his new occupation led to the crucial contact which eventually lifted him out of the lowly world of articled apprentices. He did not have the smattering of Latin which he needed in order to qualify as a dispenser. It was arranged for him to remedy this deficiency by the aid of the headmaster of the local grammar school, which had been closed for twenty years and had just been re-opened. This master was Mr Horace Byatt, a Dublin graduate, who was not a great scholar himself but had the knack of helping rather than hindering a clever pupil. He had just come to Midhurst from being headmaster of the Endowed School in Burslem in the Potteries, where among the pupils of whom he thought highly was a young man of the same age as Wells called Arnold Bennett. Byatt was a "sallow-faced survival of the earliest Victorian days", wrote a schoolfellow of Bennett's. He had "a scruffy moustache and side-whiskers of baboon-like thickness".[4] Byatt seems to have noticed at once that his new part-time pupil had a gift for learning quickly, and that he might be a potential asset who could be set to earning awards for the school under the system of payment by results.

It was, however, impossible for Wells to stay on and study. Sarah had not realised how much work would be needed before he could pass the necessary exams, and the fees involved were more than she had anticipated. It became clear to Bertie that, although he liked his new prospects, his mother could not afford to support him through a long period of training, and he had no wish to stay on merely as an unqualified assistant. He therefore decided not to be articled after his trial month. Sarah could not have him back with her at Up Park, but no other situation offered. As a stop-gap she agreed to let Bertie stay on at Midhurst School, living in Byatt's house as a boarder while he tried to make up the leeway in his education. He became a full-time pupil on 23 February 1881, and he soon demonstrated that he was an unusually talented boy with an appetite for learning. Byatt realised that he might profitably be switched away from Latin to such grant-earning subjects as physiology and mathematics. In a school of thirty-three pupils, he was easily the most able and determined, capable of profiting from anything that Byatt could teach him.

This was the first chance that Wells had enjoyed to escape from his solitary dreamland and connect up his reading with the disciplines of knowledge. By the age of fourteen he had already acquired auto-didactic habits of learning which remained with him all his life – a roving curiosity, and impatience with parts of the work that he disliked or found difficult and boring, a bubbling excitement at discovering facts or making connections that were already known to the better-educated, and a passionate belief in the power of words to stir the imagination.

Sarah's selfish determination to impose her own design for her son's future blinded her to his potential. She saw no point in more education when there was a chance of security in "the drapery". After Bertie had been at Byatt's house for six weeks, she told him that she had prevailed on Sir William King, the Up Park agent, to "speak" for him – this time to Mr Edwin Hyde, owner of the Southsea Drapery Emporium of King's Road, Southsea. Bertie was dismayed at the prospect. He argued against his mother's tearful entreaties, but since he could not suggest any acceptable alternative he gave in and went off to Southsea for his trial month in May 1881. In June, his articles were signed. In both his autobiography and in the fictional version he gave of this apprenticeship in *Kipps* it is significant that Wells used the imagery of imprisonment to describe his plight "in the most unhappy hopeless period" of his life. He was "condemned", "caught" and "bound" to be one of the depressed class of shop assistants, a cramped and precarious existence. His fate seemed all the more unpalatable because he had had those few weeks of freedom at Up Park and at Mr Byatt's to tease him with a glimpse of a different world, in which books rather than bales were the stock in trade and ideas rather than prices were the currency.

At Hyde's Emporium the working day lasted thirteen hours, and the apprentices were harried from one tedious task to the next. Wells, who had no heart in what he was doing beyond the fear induced by the threat of losing his "crib", despised the irksome routines and did merely the minimum amount of work. "The unendurable thing about it", he complained, "was that I was never master of my own attention." The habit of reverie, which had led him to muddle the accounts at Windsor, was chased away by the continuous fuss and hurry, but Wells still snatched moments of reading in odd corners. In some ways the situation was a good one. There were many worse employers in the trade than Mr Hyde, and the dining-room and living quarters were a great improvement on those at Windsor. A contemporary of Wells at Southsea, named Maurice Camkin, wrote to him late in life recalling their time at Hyde's together. Hyde, he said, made a fortune of eighty thousand pounds by "saving the pins and never cutting the string from parcels". The "private mark" for prices was $\frac{1}{P}\frac{2}{T}\frac{3}{R}\frac{4}{A}\frac{5}{K}\frac{6}{Y}\frac{7}{S}\frac{8}{I}\frac{9}{O}$ remembered by the mnemonic Push The Remnants And Keep Your Stock In Order. And one can see where Wells caught his glimpse of the employer in *Kipps* in Camkin's description of Hyde "walking crab-wise to the counter and all the time washing his hands in invisible soap".[5]

Hyde provided his boys with a good housekeeper, reasonable food, and a collection of books for their use. The majority of these were improving novels, and Wells had already made it a rule not to be seduced by a good story. It was several years before a spell of illness gave him a run of fiction reading. He turned instead to the "popular educators" then in vogue – compact encyclopaedias which summarised philosophical doctrines, scientific ideas and historical events. These books, supplemented by others borrowed from the YMCA library, were more than a source of theories and facts. They had an important and lasting influence on the way Wells thought formal education should be supplemented for those who, like him, had to acquire their knowledge of the world the hard way, by solitary study.

Somehow, for the next two years, Wells stuck it out. Occasionally he got away to Up Park to see his mother, for it was less than an hour by train. On several Bank Holidays he went as far as Godalming in Surrey to see Frank, now in a reasonably pleasant job but as fundamentally dissatisfied with the drapery trade as his youngest brother. But social life was limited – for company there were only the other apprentices and assistants. Their trivial gossip was not very stimulating for Wells, who already felt himself cut out for something different. He struggled, under these cramping circumstances, to put a mass of new ideas and feelings into some kind of meaningful order. But he lacked a teacher to guide his learning, and he also lacked the kind of support from family and friends which might have sustained him and eased his loneliness and frustration. The change to this lowly and claustrophobic situation, moreover, was all the more painful because he had been spoilt as a child, and had usually got his own way by a mixture of tantrums and charm. Neither served to win him any special privileges at Hyde's shop. He was on his own for the first time in his life, and he was forced to confront his fears and ambitions.

The immediate form that this crisis of self-determination took was a conflict in Wells between the pressures of religion and the claims of science. By this time he had read enough to have picked up a smattering of geology and astronomy, and to have grasped the principle of evolution. The debate on Darwin's ideas had been public and continuous all through the years in which Wells had been growing up, and had been popularised down to the level of *Punch* cartoons and music-hall skits. So far as Wells understood this new scientific thinking he was impressed and influenced by it, but he was still unable to reconcile it with a deeper and less articulate sense that it did not ultimately explain the mystery of the cosmos. What was it? How had it begun? Where was it going? Was there a meaning in life? He found it hard to dismiss the simple but powerful concept, implanted by his mother's teaching when he was small, that "somebody must have made it all". The fear of an ultimate judgement had not been exorcised by his early rebellion against evangelical dogma. "I was still much exercised by what might happen when my earthly apprenticeship as a whole, was over", he wrote. "It seemed to me much more important to know whether or no I was immortal than whether or no I was to make a satisfactory shop assistant. It might be a terrible thing to be out of a crib on the Thames Embankment but it would be a far more terrible thing to be out of a crib for ever in the windy spaces of nothingness."

At the age of fifteen such a doubt about the prospects of salvation was bound to lead to a search for a satisfying faith which could take the place of Sarah's depressing puritanical beliefs, and yet leave room for the growing influence of science upon Wells's mind. This was a dilemma which was characteristic of the time, when the new science had dealt telling blows at revealed religion but offered no spiritually rewarding alternative to it. In search of answers and befriended by two clerks at Hyde's who had "found" religion, Wells began to spend his Sundays sermon-tasting in the local churches. In turn he attended Anglican, Catholic and Nonconformist services, but none of them kindled the fire of faith within him. Field, one of the clerks, was a strong evangelical. Cast in the same religious mould as

Sarah Wells, he touched Wells on a familiar nerve, but this advantage was offset by the fact that Wells had already been put off by his mother's dreary version of Christianity. Field could get him to join in lusty hymn-singing and wrestled with him in prayer, but the theological tracts that he gave Wells merely increased his doubts by presenting dubious refutations of "objections" which had not previously occurred to him.

Wells had already run into difficulties by offering facetious responses to his catechism in his Bromley boyhood, and his bumptious irreverence seems to have been provoked rather than over-awed by his experience of the Portsmouth and Southsea clergy and their various rituals. Even while he was racked by deep and barely expressible anxieties about the human condition, he would occasionally buy copies of the *Freethinker* and enjoy its agnostic mockeries. Whatever temporary settlement he made with his soul, his churchgoing in these two years set him against organised religion and especially against the Catholic Church. The fact of organisation oppressed him, and it was this, as much as the failure of the dogmas to satisfy him, that repelled him from the churches. He was unable to achieve a state of grace, and though this worried him profoundly he rallied his scanty resources of knowledge to defend himself against submission.

The pressures were strong. "The ideas I had on my side to pit against these great realized systems seemed terribly bare and feeble", he said, "but they possessed me. I felt small and scared but obdurate." The moment of decision came when Sarah pressed him to be confirmed. He did nothing about it. She then raised the matter with Mr Hyde, in *loco parentis*, who bluntly told Wells that he must visit the Vicar of Portsmouth to be prepared. When he went to see the vicar, some argument about the bearing of evolutionary theory on the doctrine of the Fall ensued – and was carried back by Wells to the dormitory where the other apprentices declared that a good dirty story was preferable to blasphemy. By this time Wells had almost made up his mind. He could no more see a hope of eventual salvation in the body of the Church than he could see any present hope for himself in the drapery trade. He was in a state of repressed rebellion, dissatisfied by the contrast between his station in life and his awareness of his own frustrated potential. Religion was rejected. So was his job, the family which had pushed him into it, and the class from which he had sprung. All of them had combined to give him an identity which he despised, and was forced upon him by the conventions of the society in which he found himself.

After nearly two years in Southsea, this inner struggle had brought Wells to the verge of a breakdown. His future seemed to be a choice between a miserable acceptance of his lot, suicide, or an escape from the suffocating situation which he found intolerable. Submission was out of the question. He contemplated suicide and could not bring himself to take it seriously. All that was left was a desperate bid to relieve his depression by breaking away to a new life. The decision was urgent, and it was also symbolic. It was the first occasion on which he tried to resolve a personal crisis by flight.

Wells now had to make a decision for himself, instead of being the victim of circumstances and his mother's will. He began to cast about for ways in which he could disentangle himself from the dismal trap of the Southsea drapery. He went to Godalming to talk things over with Frank. He had long talks with a friendly clerk named West who encouraged him in his fitful attempts to go on studying. And then he wrote to Mr Byatt. Was there a chance that he might be taken on at Midhurst School as an usher? After all, he had done well in his brief stay at the school. By now he was rising seventeen, well over the age at which most pupil-teachers were recruited. In May he wrote to Sarah to say that "Byatt half promises me a crib when I leave here if I pass a very stiff exam. It will require hard work and time but I can give that if I can but obtain books."

Sarah's reply was discouraging, but Wells persevered. He borrowed money for the fare and went over to Midhurst to see what Mr Byatt had to say.[7] Mr Byatt, he explained in a letter to Sarah,

informs me that I am too old to enter the teaching profession in the ordinary way as a pupil teacher in an elementary school and that my only method would be to obtain a position as an assistant teacher in a middle class school. In any case, for about nine or ten months I should have to maintain myself.

He offers to take me in his own school after the next holidays in September. I should have more instruction to receive than work to do for a little while and he could therefore give me no wages and I should have to keep myself.

There is an assistant master there and he informs me that he pays an old lady 3/- a week for a bedroom   share in her sitting room and to do his cooking   and he estimates his total expenses (including this 3/-) washing & food to be under 10/- a week.

(Of course the cost of clothes for a schoolmaster is half that of a draper)

Now I had a talk with this assistant master and he informs me that if I chose to come I can share his room & *old lady* for 2/6 a week

This in other words means that for a little while you would have to pay about 10/- a week for me   or estimating clothes to cost £10 a year you would have to pay for me about £35 in the year for one year more

But then, when the start is made   there is every prospect of rising to a good position in the world   while in my present trade I am a drapers assistant throughout life

But I must begin at once   if I start at all I must start next September.

Which would you prefer?

I leave the matter in your hands

I remain

Your aff Son

H.G.Wells

Matters came to a crisis in July. The whole family was convulsed by threats and counter-threats to such a degree that nearly fifty years later Frank still vividly recalled the middle of 1883. "My Gawd – what a time that was – to me of worry and gut-shrink", he reminded his brother in a letter. "You were pushing for the cancelling of Hyde's indentures and to go to Midhurst – & the old man, who was stony broke & was also in a mortal funk – that the fresh draw on the Damsey's nest-egg would be to his disadvantage, was keeping a sort of backhand & sending letters, which if they had ended as suggested (suicide) might have been a good thing all round."[8]

It was a tense situation. Part of Sarah's worry was undoubtedly financial. She had already paid Mr Hyde forty of the fifty pounds agreed for the premium, and this was liable to be lost if her son broke his indentures when only two of the four apprenticeship years had elapsed. Sarah wrote to her husband (who had originally written his son "a very kind letter") and, as Frank pointed out, Joe panicked and changed his mind when he found out how much money the change might cost.

Bertie wrote pleading letters all round. Frank's scarcely coherent recollections give a sense of the atmosphere they created.[9]

The masterly way you got things through with, one saying this and that, Father saying this & Frank that & Fred thinks this – if Miss Fetherstonhaugh Frances etc. Made a way undismayed & unflinching & that you HG the youngest – shed – those garments – that a loving mother almost on her knees – according to her lights – begged you to keep on & the steady march right-left-of – HG – towards a goal – is a most refreshing picture – of strength of will & purpose in a family of soft – incapable, incompetent – stupid – silly – hesitating degenerated people. Herbert – George – Wells it takes the cake. I remember your letters of reasoning from Hyde's, begging & suggesting, those words that eventually led to success. I often think how (if they had failed) different things might be today.

As Wells felt the chance of escape slipping from him, he became more rebellious. Told that some piece of rudeness was so serious that he was in for a dressing-down from Mr Hyde himself, he simply got up early one Sunday morning and walked the seventeen miles to Up Park. The servants were at church, and he walked on past the house to surprise the straggling procession as it toiled up the hill after the service in Harting.*

That afternoon, Bertie had it out with his mother. She was adamant that he must go back to Southsea. He threatened suicide if she would not agree to the cancellation of his indentures. At last on her promise to think things over, he agreed to go back and face Mr Hyde's disapproval. But nearly seventeen, with his determination hardened by two years of frustration and petty drudgery, he was not now content to leave matters to his mother's second thoughts – he knew that her mind ran too consistently in the direction of the virtue of "trying again", especially with the aid of prayer. He wrote again to Byatt, and sent more letters to his mother.[10] In one, on 10 July, he insisted that

Time here is wasted. I cannot study here in a room crowded with a set of noisy lads after twelve hours misery . . . A month lost absolutely lost now only means another month added on to the time I am to be a clog round your neck . . . I have been so foolish as to waste the greater part of 17 years more than $\frac{1}{4}$ of my life already . . . I have a fearful lot of lee way to make up & must get to work at once if you will let me.
I shall set a small value on my life   the fag End of my life I shall not enjoy it very much if I have to look back not on a success & well-earned rewards   but on so much time spent on half-hearted work . . .
June is lost   July is being spent on letter writing   Will you try & save August . . . You will not trust me   You ask Mr Hyde or Mr Byatt and do as they advise you & they may have other interests to consult than yours or mine . . .
. . . It would be the kindest & wisest thing you could do now to let me leave here very soon.

Sarah had almost capitulated – now she was simply holding out for Bertie to remain until the summer sale was over. If he was to go to Mr

---

* The much-quoted passage in which Wells described this episode in *Tono-Bungay* was said by him to have been the way it happened. The boy suddenly rises from the bracken and cries "Coo-ee, mother!" His mother, startled by this apparition, "looked up, went very white, and put her hand to her bosom".

Byatt at once it would mean borrowing money to float him. Wells sensed he had pushed her too hard, for two days later he wrote:

I felt sorry for my intemperate & incoherent letter almost immediately after I had despatched it & I hope that you will forgive my sending it. But here are many circumstances to irritate me   many little temptations to sharp speaking & unjust thinking at the place and you must not set too much value on the evil little snarls in some of my letters.[11]

The trouble now was his father, to whom he wrote two weeks later complaining about his opposition, and arguing that teaching was the only way he now had to make himself "a useful member of society".[12] Joe could behave cruelly if he wished "but the law of reaping as you sow is divine and unchangeable & you will have me in your last years a shame a disgrace & a curse instead of a support and a blessing". Three days later he was writing in the same angry mood to his mother, asking her to remind Joe "of all he has received from you in the last few years" and to insist he sign a cancellation of the indentures.[13] "He is now blocking my path in life & he will be a continual threat for the next two years unless he signs."

Joe was finally brought round, possibly because Byatt settled the issue by raising his offer. He proposed to pay twenty pounds for the first year, with an improvement promised to forty pounds thereafter. He had clearly come to the conclusion that Wells was a rare boy, sufficiently able and motivated to earn back in awards what it would cost to keep him. This money was almost enough for Wells to manage on without recourse to his mother, and it made him obstinate. He insisted on leaving Hyde as soon as the formalities for cancelling his indentures were completed. He would not even oblige his employer by staying on until the summer sale was over. He needed the four weeks before school began to catch up on his neglected reading.

In later years Wells admitted that the three hard years between his departure from Bromley and his appointment at Midhurst had been useful to him. It was, he said, "so bad a time as to stiffen my naturally indolent, rather slovenly and far too genial nature into a grim rebellion against the world – a spurt of revolt that enabled me to do wonders of self-education before its force was exhausted". He saw this as a training in will power, which enabled him to triumph over external circumstances. He gave Byatt credit for offering him this chance to climb out of the mire. Byatt, he said towards the end of his life in *The Fate of Homo Sapiens*, made him "suddenly wake up to the existence of a vast and growing world of thought and knowledge outside my ordinary circle of ideas altogether". As with Sarah's sudden chance to return to Up Park, he felt that "my heavens opened, and the world as I had seen it hitherto became a flimsy veil upon the face of reality". But Wells also conceded that he was driven as much by resentment as by ambition, and he recalled "my anger at the paltry sham of an education that had been fobbed off upon me; angry resentment also at the dismal negligence of the social and religious organizations responsible for me . . . I thought they had conspired to keep me down . . . They took my inferiority as part of the accepted order . . . I *hated* them as only the young can hate, and it gave me the energy to struggle, and I set about struggling, for knowledge."

Before Wells could close with Byatt, however, one last concession to the conventions was required of him. In order to hold any post at Midhurst he had to conform to the school statutes which required that every teacher must be an Anglican communicant. Wells baulked at the idea, but he realised that a refusal to be confirmed would put an end to his chances. He was prepared by the local curate, and went through with the ceremony. This greatly pleased Sarah, but he said that "the wound to my private honour smarted for a long time". He felt a deep shame at this betrayal of his conscience, because it undermined "the queer little mood of obduracy" which he felt to be vital to his sense of identity. Wells took up the offer of the room over the sweetshop kept by Mrs Walton. No sooner was he lodged in it than he pinned up on the wall a carefully worked out plan (a *Schema* which he later included in *Love and Mr Lewisham*) for the use of his time – to focus his energies more effectively, and to serve as a formal reminder that he was losing ground whenever he let his lively mind wander from the task in hand.

Byatt was a man of energy, and he was busy building up his school. While Wells had been at Southsea the new premises had been completed and there were now some sixty boys as well as two assistant masters. One of these, Harris, was the man who had found Wells his lodging and became his companion on energetic walks, timed to last one hour, on which Wells poured out his ideas in gasps while Harris mostly nodded and saved his breath. Wells had already acquired the knack of using his acquaintances as sounding-boards for whatever fancy was quick in his mind.

During these months at Midhurst Wells's fancies began to bubble faster than before. He was fascinated by Plato, sustained in his puzzlement at the difficult parts by some kind of intellectual snobbery. Plato was academically respectable, and yet there was something deeply radical about him that also appealed to Wells. Society, Plato appeared to be arguing, was not unchangeable, and it was legitimate to ask why it was so organised as to put the private before the public interest. Why, indeed, Wells asked, "was everything appropriated and every advantage secured against me before I came into the world?" He found one answer in a newspaper shop in Midhurst, where he bought a sixpenny paperback edition of Henry George's *Progress and Poverty*. George was not a socialist. His critique was based upon an attack on the appropriation of land by private owners, and his solution was the imposition of a single tax which would transform the unearned increment of the landlord into a collective rent for the common good. Yet his book, which swept through America and England at this time, probably turned more people towards the nascent socialist movement than any other. Wells (like Bernard Shaw) was one of them, and the socialist views that he advanced in his writings almost twenty years later still bore traces of that earlier mingling of Plato and George.

Wells had an insatiable desire for knowledge and a talent for self-expression. When he had first been at the Midhurst school, before he was despatched to Southsea, he had written and illustrated some comic histories and biographical sketches. The longest was a schoolboyish story called *The Battle for Bungledom*, rather like *The Desert Daisy*. He had produced the *Up Park Alarmist* during the Christmas of 1880, and while he was cramming at Midhurst he had been encouraged by Byatt to write a couple of longer stories. One was called *Potted Onions*. The other was about a Munchausen-like explorer called Otto Noxious. He was already beginning to play around with themes and a narrative style that are recognisably related to those of his published writings. There had not been much fun in his childhood, but he had somehow picked up a sardonic turn of humour and his keen eye and sharp ear serviced an extraordinary memory. Before he went to Southsea he had learned to see the comedy behind pretentious humbug. Even if the professional skill was acquired later, the ability to register his experience was already developed. All the time that he was struggling to disentangle himself from the swaddling constraints of his childhood, he seems to have been discovering the knack of observing those struggles as if from a distance, of separating his imagination from the unpleasant muddles of his real life.

During the winter months at Midhurst, Wells gave himself passionately to the task of catching up on the time he had lost. In the daytime he mostly taught the small boys in the big classroom under Byatt's supervision, but his real work began in the evenings when school was over. In an effort to train more teachers for science education, a national scheme had been launched which encouraged headmasters with university degrees to organise evening classes in some thirty subjects. Payment, as usual, was by results. The school received four pounds for each advanced pass in a subject, and fees on a diminishing scale for lower grades. Byatt had hitherto been running four classes with a dozen students. Now, with Wells on hand to be used like an academic milch-cow from whom awards could be wrung almost on demand, Byatt proceeded to offer a much larger number of classes. Most of these were bogus. Wells was the only pupil, and he knuckled down to the appropriate textbooks while Byatt sat at the other end of the room marking essays and writing letters. For several months Wells crammed, driven on by a hunger for knowledge and by an ambition to seize the opportunity Byatt had offered him. The essence of the scientific advances in the middle of the nineteenth century had been distilled into these textbooks on physiography, geology, physiology, chemistry and mathematics, and Wells was now imbibing it in great gulps. He had always shown a remarkable capacity to take in and retain facts, and he now acquired the technique of regurgitating them in the form required to pass written examinations. He could not have done better either for Byatt or for himself. When the results of the May examinations were announced, Wells had won several of the lucrative first-class passes. The money he earned for Byatt was more than Byatt had paid out to him in board and wages. But he had done too well for Byatt's interest. He had worked himself out of Midhurst.

As part of the training scheme for science teachers, a number of scholarships were provided by the government at the Normal School of Science in South Kensington for pupils who scored high marks in these examinations. Wells was among the small number who were invited to apply for one of these awards in 1884. He had not expected so much. When the blue form arrived, he was surprised, and he completed it without telling Byatt what he had done. Byatt, meanwhile, kept his part of the original bargain, and he offered Wells a full-time post at forty pounds, as well as additional "perks" which would bring him another twenty-five. He was too late. He had done all he could for his bright pupil. Wells soon heard that he had been given a place at South Kensington, with a maintenance grant of a guinea a week, and he regretfully told Byatt that he would take it. He could not turn down the opportunity, especially since he had been entered for a course of biological studies under Professor T.H.Huxley – after

Darwin, the greatest figure in British science. "Gloria in excelsis mei!" he hastily wrote to Frank. "I have now become a holy, a respectable person entitled to wear a gown . . . and to call myself an undergraduate of London University."[14]

At long last Wells had become free and self-supporting, and he no longer needed to refer decisions about his career to his mother. He now lightly dismissed her anxieties about the irreligious views of Professor Huxley by explaining that he was Dean of the Normal School – and went off to stay with his father at Bromley. For the first time in three years, while he waited for term to begin at the Normal School in September, Bertie was able to spend some time with Joe and to find a relationship with him that was uninhibited by the tensions that had riven Atlas House in his childhood. Joe was no longer fussed by the effort to keep up appearances. The shop was doing very little business.* He was making his living mainly by selling cricket gear which he peddled round the various pitches in the area. But he seemed indifferent to his reduced circumstances, especially as Sarah was no longer there to chide him. He had turned his hand to his hobbies. He still read a good deal, and he had taken up cooking, clock-repairing and bird-watching – a kind of second boyhood.

During this visit Bertie and Joe took long walks together, and camped agreeably in the bachelor disorder of Atlas House. As they rambled about the commons and woods of Kent, they came closer to each other than at any time in their lives: Wells had never before touched the hidden spring of imagination in his father. Joe talked of his youthful dreams. He told Bertie of his hopes and his disappointments, and how as a young man he used to lie on the green Downs at night looking up at the stars and speculating on what lay beyond them in the universe. And Bertie came to see and feel the open life his father had led before the shop and failure had trapped him.

* Joe managed to stay precariously in business until 1887, when he was sold up and went down to live in Sussex on a pension allowed him by Sarah. A neighbouring draper, Frederick Medhurst, gradually bought up the adjacent properties to found the department store which still bears his name and carries a plaque commemorating Wells's birthplace. When Medhurst bought Atlas House, he let the rent accumulate until Joe owed thirteen pounds, five shillings. Then, on 7 May 1887, he clapped a distress notice on the door. The inventory recorded on it reveals the pitiful stock Joe held at the end. He had 142 cups and saucers, 36 cream jugs, 125 pieces of dinnerware, 200 odd saucers, 142 assorted pieces of earthenware, 5 bedpans and some other oddments. The china and glass warehouse of more than twenty years earlier had been reduced to a collection of remnants, gathering dust.[15]

Joe had found his means of escape. He had dropped out. But Bertie wanted something better for himself. At the age of eighteen, he was about to start a new life which he had chosen for himself and made for himself by his own efforts. The means whereby he had achieved his independence left an enduring mark on his personality and his posture towards the world. To defend himself against his mother's rigid and persistent assertion of her authority he had been driven to develop a matching force of will. There had been no place for understanding and co-operation in Atlas House, and Bertie – copying his mother while he defied her – had learned to deal with adverse circumstances by escaping into fantasy or by imposing an authoritarian solution. When, in later years, he insisted that Will is stronger than Fact, he was merely putting into philosophical language the lessons of his childhood.

4

THE VISION OF SCIENCE

Wells never forgot the September morning in 1884 when he walked down Exhibition Road in South Kensington to enter the Normal School of Science. "I had come", he wrote later, "from beginnings of an elementary sort to the fountainhead of knowledge "[1] What he found there shaped the remainder of his life.

The Normal School was only five years old. This massive block, five floors of red brick topped by gothic towers and oriental minarets, was the temple of the new science which had begun with the geology of Lyell and Tyndall and developed into the evolutionary biology of Darwin. In 1881 Thomas Henry Huxley – the man they called "Darwin's bulldog" for the tenacity with which he fought for the idea of evolution – had managed to bring together a number of science departments originally based on the Royal School of Mines and establish the Normal School as a centre for science teaching. It offered, its prospectus announced, "systematic instruction in the various branches of Physical Science . . . to all classes", and among its fee-paying students were the scholarship holders like Wells, who received free tuition and a stipend of a guinea a week doled out each Wednesday morning.[2] It had been a hard struggle for the scholarship winners to get to South Kensington. Some of them had come from even poorer homes than Atlas House. Richard Gregory, who became the life-long friend of Wells, was the son of a Bristol bootmaker who was also a poet and a socialist, and at the time Gregory arrived at the Normal School his father was earning three shillings and sixpence a week.

This little group of scholars, pinching and scraping their way through college, had been selected to train as science teachers. At last, after a battle that had lasted nearly twenty years, a serious effort was being made to modernise English education. Religious dogmatism and social conservatism had fought a long rearguard campaign against popular education, and even against proposals to introduce new subjects into the curriculum at any level. There was not much room for science in contemporary notions of what was a fit upbringing for a Victorian gentleman, and none at all in what was thought a proper elementary education for the masses. The English were not only appallingly under-educated, but it had suddenly been realised that this weakness posed a real threat to social stability and industrial progress. The middle class found itself threatened by a barely-literate and poverty-stricken proletariat: one person in eight died in the workhouse. And yet the country was desperately short of trained man-power to support industrial expansion and maintain its position against new foreign competitors such as Germany and the United States. The working classes, one commentator observed, did not need religion to keep them quiet but science to make their work effective.

The years in which Wells grew up have been called the Age of Doubt. He reached manhood in what is best described as the Age of Anxiety. Things had gone awry. A long agricultural depression had been followed by widespread unemployment. There was squalor in the towns and fever in the slums. It was such anxiety that threw up the great Questions that domi-nated the last years of Victoria's long reign – the Industrial Question and the Irish Question, the Land Question and the Health and Housing Questions, the emerging Woman Question, the Imperial Question, and, slowly looming, the German Question. The search for answers stimulated an array of new organisations and campaigns in the Eighties, advocating remedies with missionary enthusiasm in an effort to replace what was lost when science snapped the thread of revealed religion. The idea of progress served for a time. The vulgarisation of Darwin's theories had fused with concepts of competition and free enterprise to make Englishmen feel that the Hidden Hand of Providence was guiding their improving destiny.[3] But by 1880 the Hidden Hand seemed less sure in its touch, and the aching doubt which lay behind the certainties of Protestant dogmatism was searching again for an assurance of salvation. That, after all, was the great anxiety for which all the lesser anxieties were merely vehicles. A generation which had grown up with the impress of evangelical fervour could not easily lose the will to believe, even if the object of belief had to be changed in the light of the new theories about the nature of the world and how man came to appear in it.

It was a time of substitution, of new names for old things and new things for old names. Contemporaries saw the conflict between science and re-vealed religion exemplified by the dramatic confrontation between

T.H.Huxley and Bishop Wilberforce about man's kinship with the apes,
and missed the way in which the new science slipped into the space left by
the rout of the old religion. The anxiety induced by the Protestant ethic
remained. What was the Plan of Salvation and what must a man do to
ensure that he was among the saved? Puritanism had taught that a man
might do nothing to change the mandates of God, but he could reinforce
them by his efforts. After Darwin and Huxley, the same might be said of
the mandates of Nature. But the sense of vocation, of being one of the
elect labouring against the powers of darkness, now derived from the
Idea of Science rather than from the Word of God.

When Beatrice Webb was a young woman she had known Huxley and
other eminent men of science, and in later years she recalled that they had
an "almost fanatical faith . . . that it was by science and science alone that
all human misery would be ultimately swept away".[4] In 1874 John
Tyndall, making his presidential address to a British Association meeting
in Belfast, had gone so far as to assert that science would eventually wrest
all cosmological theory from the province of religion. And in 1872 the
popular writer Winwood Reade, whose book *The Martyrdom of Man* had a
profound and enduring effect upon Wells, had gone even further:

When we have ascertained, by means of Science, the methods of Nature's
operation, we shall be able to take her place and to perform them for ourselves . . . men will master the forces of Nature; they will become themselves
architects of systems, manufacturers of worlds. Man will then be perfect; he
will be a creator; he will therefore be what the vulgar worship as a God.

The advancement of science had become a mission, as capable of arousing enthusiasm as any religious revival, and like such revivals it had its
counterpoint of pessimism and even despair. Darwin may have offered a
way of escape from the clutch of original sin, but if there was no Fall in
The Descent of Man what then distinguished this anthropoid ape from the
other animals? Evolution had destroyed the conventional theology. Could
it provide an alternative basis for morality and say whether human life
had any meaning? It took courage to ask that question, and it took more
courage to give a negative answer, as T.H.Huxley did in his famous
Romanes Lecture at Oxford on "Evolution and Ethics".[5] That question,
and that answer, however, provide a vital clue to the intellectual evolution
and personal ethics of Wells. They gave him the vital link between the
evangelical beliefs in which he had been brought up and the scientific
ideas which he absorbed as a student. For the remainder of his life he held

those two systems together in a dynamic relationship by means of the connection that Huxley made for him.

The popular and optimistic gloss on Darwin's theory of evolution had simply replaced the Divine Purpose by the processes of natural selection. Man remained the supreme achievement of genetic variation. It was by accepting this substitution that the Anglican Church managed to come to terms with the doctrine of evolution. But Huxley did not accept this benignly complacent view of Nature. Suppose, he asked, the emergence of the human species was merely an accident, and probably a temporary phenomenon. Suppose Nature were at best neutral and at worst hostile. Suppose the evolution of species could as easily lead to stagnation and regression as to progress. Then *Homo sapiens* might be damned as surely by the laws of evolution as by original sin. In both cases there would be a last judgement.

Was there therefore no hope of ethical and social progress – the equivalent, in Huxley's agnostic terminology, of the state of grace? Huxley, seeking to find some hopeful answer to his own question, argued that while the evolutionary laws of Nature were ethically neutral, they had produced a race with an ethical sense. How this happened, and why it happened, was unknowable, but once it had happened it must be fostered, since in this alone lay the means of grace and the hope of glory – increasing mastery over mankind's animal instincts and over his physical environment. Whatever the ultimate future of the race, or of the planet, men must strive for the good of society, and this act well might then produce a psychic evolution in which, by natural selection, the best would emerge.

Huxley put this point specifically in a key passage in "Evolution and Ethics":

Social progress means a checking of the cosmic process at every step and the substitution for it of another, which may be called the ethical process; the end of which is not the survival of those who may happen to be the fittest . . . but of those who are ethically the best.

Neither Darwin nor Huxley, nor Wells after them, therefore believed that progress was inevitable. It was simply urgently desirable. And both Huxley and Wells were plagued by haunting doubts whether in fact it would occur. Towards the end of his life in February 1889 Huxley wrote an article in the *Nineteenth Century* on "Agnosticism" – a term that he had invented. Its conclusion was so close to the position that Wells consistently took throughout his life that it can properly be taken as the text on which all his lay sermons were delivered.

I know of no study which is so utterly saddening as that of the evolution of humanity. Man emerges with the marks of his lowly origin strong upon him. He is a brute, only more intelligent than the other brutes, a blind prey to impulses ... a victim to endless illusions, which make his mental existence a burden, and fill his life with barren toil and battle.

This pessimism has to be set against the casual description of both Huxley and Wells as prophets of evolutionary optimism. Along with the vision of what science might do for mankind Huxley also passed on a much more depressing conception of man's place in Nature. This dualism lay at the heart of Huxley's belief, as it was subsequently to run through Wells's scientific romances, his novels and utopias, and his sociological and prophetic writings.

The ideological influence of Huxley on Wells was powerful, but its power was reinforced by personal and psychological factors which led Wells to model himself upon his teacher. In 1884, when Wells arrived at the Normal School, Huxley was ageing and ill, and spent from his brilliant campaign as Darwin's public protagonist and as an agitator for scientific education. Wells attended only one course of lectures given by Huxley.[6] He spoke to him but once, holding open the door and exchanging a simple "Good morning". But, Wells said, "I believed then he was the greatest man I was ever likely to meet, and I believe that all the more firmly today." * One lecture course and one casual contact seem thin threads to bind Wells to Huxley for a lifetime. They were enough. "The year I spent in Huxley's class", Wells wrote, "was, beyond all question, the most educational year of my life." It was not merely that Huxley was a great teacher, and that he could understandably arouse the students by the way he had pounded Gladstone and thumped the bishops. It was that Wells, in simple terms, was bewitched by Huxley – and remained so, emotionally and intellectually, to the end of his days.

On the face of it, Wells was an unlikely catch. He was eighteen, small, shabby, provincial, bright but mentally undisciplined, more crammed than educated, and with no definite aim in life except to get on and up as

* Speaking to the Oxford Philosophical Society in November 1903, Wells declared that Huxley's course was "the nucleus" around which he "arranged a spacious digest of facts", and at the end of his life he repeated that there "has been a lot of expansion and supplementing since then, but nothing like a fundamental reconstruction".[7]

best he could. Huxley was almost sixty, at the peak of his influence and reputation, the Grand Old Man of science. Yet there was more in common between them than the obvious contrast suggests. When Huxley taught that man must struggle for survival and that a mere slip of fortune might doom all his hopes, Wells could match that notion from his own experience. He had known what it was to scratch for his learning and to fight for his start in life with the ever-present fear that luck might fail. *
For Huxley, too, it had been a hard start. His father had not been a failing shopkeeper, but he had been an assistant master in a failing school, and it had taken grit and grind to get a medical training. The degree to which Wells identified with Huxley suggests a strong emotional affinity. There is a revealing comment on Huxley in Beatrice Webb's diary for 6 May 1887, only two years after Wells had taken his course. Huxley had been talking to her about his youth and how, "as a young man, though he had no definite purpose in life, he felt power; was convinced that in his own line he would be a leader". While he was a remarkable leader, she said, and had "the power of throwing himself into the thoughts and feelings of others . . . yet they are all shadows to him; he thinks no more of them and drops back into the ideal world he lives in". The same phrases could easily have been written about Wells, and the similarity was underlined by Beatrice Webb's summary:[8]

For Huxley, when not working, dreams strange things: carries on lengthy conversations between unknown persons living within his brain. There is a strain of madness in him; melancholy has haunted his whole life . . . None of the enthusiasm for what is, or the silent persistency in discovering facts; more the eager rush of the conquering mind, loving the fact of conquest more than the land conquered. And consequently his achievement has fallen far short of his capacity.

Huxley, in fact, had gradually given up his early success as a scientist to become a restless agitator and polemicist. He had abandoned his career as a zoologist, ostensibly to be Darwin's spokesman – a role he played with enormous verve and effect – but possibly, as Beatrice Webb implied, for deeper psychological reasons. "He might have done much more", Darwin noted in an unpublished passage of his *Autobiography*, "had he not been so much preoccupied with writing, education and public duties." There was

---

* This happens in what Wells called the "carefully done" short story "A Slip Under The Microscope", in which a science student at South Kensington finds his career ruined by chance.

another feature of Huxley's career which was reflected in that of his student. Huxley was an outsider who had forced the Establishment to accept him despite his heretical views. He had also become a key figure in the élite inner circle of scientists and public men who dominated English public life. He was a leading member of the select Metaphysical Society, which included such eminent men as Tennyson and Gladstone, Ruskin, Cardinal Manning and Walter Bagehot. The X Club, with nine members, was even more exclusive. With men such as Tyndall, Hooker, Lubbock and Spencer, Huxley virtually controlled British science. When Wells began to produce his recipes for setting the world to rights, he consistently assigned that task to an élite group, in which scientists always played a predominant part.

The course given by Huxley was in biology and zoology, and it lasted through the first of the three years assigned for the training of teachers of science. Wells worked hard and successfully in his first year, in an eager, lonely way. He had one friend, an older and more sophisticated student named A. V. Jennings, who once stood him a square meal when he noticed that by the eve of pay-day Wells had no money to buy food. It was a kindness that, out of delicacy for Wells's pride, he did not repeat. Jennings was also able, and, with Wells and one other student, was awarded first-class honours at the summer examination in 1885. Academically the year had gone well, and Wells went off cheerfully for the holidays at Up Park, and to stay with Joe at Bromley.

The beginning of the next academic year was an anti-climax. Wells found himself studying physics under Professor Guthrie, an indifferent teacher by comparison with the lucid and stimulating Huxley. Guthrie was already ill of undiagnosed cancer, and he "maundered amidst ill-marshalled facts" to the bewilderment of his students. Wells lost interest. He began to doubt whether he would stick out his training as a teacher. His performance deteriorated. He was naturally incompetent in the physics laboratory, and he made matters worse by insolent disregard of the practical work. One piece of apparatus that he constructed was so bad that it was preserved for some years as an exhibit. He behaved as though he was in a state of shock, and he recalled in his autobiography that he changed from an "extravagantly greedy and industrious learner" into a "facetious, discontented, restless and tiresome rebel". The new world he had glimpsed in Huxley's classes had faded like a dream. The spell had been broken, not merely by the transition to Guthrie's course but also by Huxley's departure from the School on sick-leave. The only serious work he did that autumn was to mug up the French, Latin and German he needed to pass his Matriculation examination for the London degree. He was warned by the registrar for cutting classes. By the end of the summer term it was touch and go whether he would do well enough to pass the annual examinations.

While he waited for the results he went down to The Elms at Minsterworth, a farm in Gloucestershire kept by his Uncle Charles, where he lounged about, reading, walking, and writing letters. When he heard the news he wrote at once to A.T.Simmons, who had become one of his closest friends. A first-class in geometrical drawing mattered little. More important was his poor showing in elementary physics, his failure in astronomical physics and his dreadful practical work. The scholarship seemed lost. He asked Simmons if he would immediately send him a list of employment agents. It was the "engaging season" for pupil teachers. Simmons sent back an encouraging reply, but it did little to reassure Wells. "Even if it is possible to get another year at South Kensington", Wells wrote back, "I don't think I shall come up. I am so disgusted with the extreme poverty in which we have to live. If I can get over £90 I shan't come. There!"[9]

Poverty had left its mark on him. His clothes were respectable but shabby, his celluloid collar and cuffs were yellow with washing. A photograph taken during his first year by a fellow student named J.E.Porter shows him looking strained and weedy, and during his student career his health deteriorated. He weighed less than 112 pounds, and he was "in a shocking state of bodily unfitness, very thin, under-exercised and with no muscular dexterity, loose in gesture, slow on the turn and feeble in the punch". In this poor condition he struggled on. The mood of chucking everything passed. He had not found a job. As his marks had been just sufficient to justify the renewal of his scholarship he had duly returned to study geology in a perfunctory way under Professor Judd, who demanded plodding note-taking and rote learning. He was not only habitually inattentive, as he had been under Guthrie. He now got into the habit of wandering off to other corners of the South Kensington complex – to read Carlyle in the Dyce and Foster Reading Room or look at Blake's engravings in the Art Library or stroll through the pictures in the Chantry Bequest. He had other things on his mind than the classification of minerals. It was all he could do to scrape a second-class at the Christmas examinations, and even his capacity for cramming failed in the end. In the summer of 1887 he failed the final in geology. He might still become a teacher, but the idea of a career as a research scientist was nothing more than the memory of a day-dream in Huxley's laboratory.

If that were all South Kensington had done for him it would have been a disaster. Yet those who knew him best, his friends among the students, had a much less negative impression. One of them, Elizabeth Healey, described the impact he then made on her.[10] He had remarkable blue eyes – something that struck everyone meeting him for the first time, and tumbling brown hair. "He was sociable, amusing, friendly, a most brilliant talker." * The quick charm that won people, and made them forgive the bouts of depression and petulance that went with it, was already evident, and it helped to win him good and steadfast friends. With two of them the tie was particularly intimate and enduring – A. T. Simmons and Richard Gregory. "All sorts of things happened to me", Wells wrote in 1931, when Gregory had just been awarded a baronetcy, "but nothing ever changed the steadfast friendship and helpfulness of Gregory."[11] And he was as grateful to Simmons, who died soon after the First World War. "I do not deserve a tithe of your praises", he wrote to Gregory in 1925: "if I have done anything in the world it is largely because you and Simmons did so much in the crucial years to make me believe in myself. I have had some stout friends and you have been chief among them." And with others of the group, such as William Burton (who became an industrial chemist in the Potteries) and A. Morley Davies (whose academic career took him back to a professorship at the Imperial College which grew out of the Normal School), he was on equally close terms as a student. For the first time in his life he knew what it was to have the support and stimulus of friends who were his peers in interest and ability.

Despite his high-pitched voice, small stature and unprepossessing manner, Wells was now making a mark in the Debating Society that met after hours in the gas-lit lecture theatre in the basement. "As a speaker", Elizabeth Healey recalled, "he never had an equal in my time. His wit was keen and swift. His sarcasm never wounded the victims of it, for it was tempered with humour and truth. He attacked conventions, shams and humbug . . . he loved 'cockshies' and smashing popular beliefs."[12] This was the "facetious, discontented . . . rebel" he had become in his second year. The more he was humiliated by academic difficulties that pricked "the

---

* This friendship, like some others that Wells made at the Normal School, lasted through life, though it was carried on largely by correspondence. It is a comment on the formality of the period that it was only in 1906, after they had known each other for twenty years, that she wrote to Wells saying "I prefer my Christian name to Miss".

immense self-conceit" he had brought up from Midhurst, the more he tried to find "compensating reassurances . . . in petty achievements and triumphs in other directions". He found that the role of a "philosophical desperado" helped ward off his depression.

After 1880 the socialist movement began to revive, and in London there were a number of new sects whose weekly meetings could be visited by young and impecunious radicals. Wells was in a phase of emotional revolt, more affected by Blake, Carlyle and Ruskin than by socialist theory, and the appeal of the socialist propagandists for him and his student friends sprang more from their rhetoric than the logic of their arguments. Their agitation, Wells said, offered "a congenial field for the mental energy" he so abundantly possessed but which he could not release on to the rigorous grind of his studies. With Simmons, Burton, and E.H. Smith, he began to attend socialist meetings as he had gone sermon-tasting with his fellow-employees at Southsea. Their favourite resort was the Sunday night meeting at Kelmscott House – the riverside home of William Morris at Hammersmith – where socialists, communists, Fabians and anarchists argued the present and the future into the night in a haze of tobacco smoke. There Wells had the chance to see, apart from Morris himself, artists such as Walter Crane and Cobden-Sanderson. There were writers such as Bernard Shaw, just beginning to make a name for himself as a brilliant debater, R.B. Cunninghame-Graham, the Scottish laird who was a poet and world-traveller, Annie Besant, on her pilgrimage from religious orthodoxy through socialism to spiritualism and theosophy, and Belfort Bax. Henry Myers Hyndman, the middle-class theoretician who introduced Marx to England without mentioning his name because Marx was a German, was the pillar of the Social-Democratic Federation. Among the Fabian speakers there were Graham Wallas and the two young civil servants, Sidney Webb and Sydney Olivier; and there were feminists, vegetarians and believers in the New Life to fill out the flamboyant and stimulating crowd.[13]

Their audiences were even more varied and fervent than the speakers, and their organisations had large ideas, small memberships and a tendency to split on minor points of doctrine. The new revolutionary journals, such as *Justice* and *Commonweal*, were as likely to attack their nearest friends as to denounce the landlord and the capitalist. But in this small world there was a common conviction that England might be on the verge of great changes. The memory of the Paris Commune was still fresh: there were old Communards among the audiences at Kelmscott House as well as fugitives from Bismarck's anti-socialist laws. In the depression of the Eighties, the socialists had been able briefly to link up with the unemployed demonstrations to create an illusion of hidden strength and, in a few clashes with the police, violent potential. Wells and his friends listened. They were too young and shy to join in the discussions themselves but they argued with each other as they walked home and carried the arguments over into the meetings of their Debating Society. The influence that this exposure to the socialist bohemia had on Wells was more one of styles and ideas than of practical politics. For several years after his student days were over he showed no serious interest in the socialist movement, and when he again picked up contact with it at the end of the century he came into it almost as a newcomer.

In the late Eighties, Wells and his friends were really more interested in student than in national politics. In September 1886, he wrote to Simmons about his plans for "a sort of advanced Political Mission down in the Debating Society".[14] With the sardonic humour that comes through his letters in this period, he suggested:

You will be made secretary . . . on the strength of your umbrella, the majesty of your behaviour & the gloomy solemnity of your visage . . . If we could . . . avoid being funny or pseudo-comic . . . we might really do something good to educate politically a lot of fellows who will presently be scattered all over the country in intellectually influential positions . . . Probably the best thing I could do in the cause of social improvement would be to take orders. It would irrecoverably damage the Establishment.

Already, too, there were signs that Wells conceived himself in a special role. All through his life he drew comic sketches in his letters or in presentation copies of books – there are hundreds of what he called "picshuas" surviving, and many of them express a mocking insight into his feelings about himself. Few are as revealing as the cartoon he drew in the depressed letter he wrote to Simmons from Minsterworth in the summer of 1886. It shows him dreaming on the farm, while around lie discarded scraps of paper on which are written such phrases as "How I Could Save The Nation", "All About God", "Secret of the Kosmos", "Whole Duty of Man" and "Wells's Design for a New Framework for Society".[15] The excitement of the Kelmscott House meetings and the little triumphs of the Debating Society were still in his mind, but larger and different thoughts were emerging – thoughts that had to be written down, rather than talked away.

63

Wells had, in fact, been writing odds and ends since early adolescence, and at South Kensington he began to think of writing for a wider audience. In 1885 he read a talk to the Debating Society on "The Past and Present of the Human Race" and during the summer of 1886 he drafted a formal paper on Democratic Socialism (which he read to the Debating Society on 15 October). By then he and a group of friends were already planning the *Science Schools Journal* which he was to edit.* It was launched in December 1886; on the fiftieth anniversary in 1936 Wells wrote an article in *The Phoenix* (which succeeded it) saying:

We thought the journal would do wonderful things for us. Most of us had been stirred by the socialist movement and we thought (not very clearly nor maturely) that there ought to be a distinctive science students' outlook on life and public affairs. That idea has clung to me ever since like the old man of the sea . . .

His term as editor was short. Reprimanded again by the registrar, he passed the nominal editorship to Burton, but he continued to be the key figure in the enterprise. Among the ephemera that appeared over his own signature and over such pseudonyms as Sosthenes Smith and Walker Glockenhammer, were three significant items which show that before his student days were over he had hit on the formula that eventually made his reputation – the mixture of romance, satire and scientific ideas. An early paper for the Debating Society on "The Past and Present of the Human Race", delivered in 1885 when he was only nineteen, was worked up into an article published in the *Pall Mall Budget* in November 1893 as "The Man of the Year Million", and then put out in the collection *Certain Personal Matters* in 1897. Darwin had linked Man to his evolutionary past; from Huxley came the idea of projecting Man's evolutionary future. Man, "unless the order of the universe has come to an end, will undergo further modification . . . and at last cease to be man, giving rise to some other type of animated being". It is likely that the distant descendants of *Homo sapiens* will have larger brains and diminishing bodies. In a passage that anticipates his descriptions of the Grand Lunar in *The First Men in the Moon* and the Martians in *The War of the Worlds*, Wells suggests that these great brains will float, under a crystal dome, in a tub of nutritive fluid.

* He recalled that his first sale was a "sloppy, sentimental, dishonest short story" he sold to the *Family Herald* for a guinea. Cosmo Rowe, an artist who shared his studio with William Burton and allowed it to be used as a meeting place for radical students, remembered that one evening Wells came through the door waving a cheque for ten shillings which was his first income from writing. He said he might be rich enough one day to ride in a hansom cab!

There is a vision of man, having mastered the techniques of photo-synthesis, living by chemicals and sunlight alone, on a planet where he has destroyed all other plants and animals. And as the sun cools, and the earth grows colder – for Wells had already realised that entropy, the second law of thermodynamics, would ultimately put a term to the most optimistic hopes raised by evolution – man's heirs would be driven underground, living in galleries linked to the surface by ventilating shafts – an image he later used both for the Morlocks in *The Time Machine* and for the Selenites in *The First Men in the Moon*.

In May 1887 he published, over the initials S.B., *A Tale of the Twentieth Century*,[16] which was a jocular story of what happened when a device for perpetual motion was applied to the underground railway in London. In June "Sosthenes Smith" wrote *A Vision of the Past*, a satire on Man's complacent self-image as the crowning glory of the evolutionary process. And he had had the basic idea for a tale which he worked up after he left South Kensington and published in the *Journal* issues of April, May and June 1888 – *The Chronic Argonauts*. After many revisions this story eventually became *The Time Machine*.

The quickness with which Wells seized on the notion of travelling through time illustrates the way he worked in his later scientific romances. He heard of some new concept or invention. He next set the novel theory in a conventional background. Then, having made the incredible acceptable by his attention to detail, his imagination was free to make what fantasies it pleased out of the resulting conflict. This trick-of-the-pen was a formula that he exploited repeatedly throughout his career and it accounts for much of the suspension of disbelief on the part of his readers. In the case of travelling through time, Wells had listened to a paper given at the Debating Society by a fellow-student named E.A. Hamilton-Gordon on the theory that Time was the Fourth Dimension. He fathered the idea on the inventor, Dr Nebogifel – more alchemist than scientist – who, in *The Chronic Argonauts*, finds himself in a village in North Wales. Like everything that Wells wrote for his magazine, *The Chronic Argonauts* was ponderous, jerky in style and very self-conscious. Yet the way he went on worrying at it in successive drafts shows that he sensed that he had laid hold of something original.

The discovery that perhaps he might make something of writing was a needed fillip for his self-esteem. Student politics and journalism had helped stave off the sense of doom about his academic career. He had found fun and companionship from his friends, who provided an outlet for the resilient humour that kept him bouncing back from his misfortunes. None of these compensations, however, could disguise the fact that he was steadily going downhill, and that there was no obvious way of escape from the fate which awaited him when all these supports were withdrawn at the end of the course. He was staving off a collapse all through his second and third years at South Kensington. The loss of Huxley had contributed to it. The involvement with student politics had been a way of coping with it. And his academic decline was the result of it.

The cause of the crisis was prolonged emotional strain in his private life. From the end of his first year at South Kensington he had become involved in a love affair which he could neither resolve nor bring to an end, nor even understand, and sexual anxiety became a gnawing distraction which slowly undermined his health as well as his work. When he first arrived in London, he was alone and friendless. As always, Sarah had done her best to arrange things and reaching out through her network of old connections she had found him a room in a lodging-house kept by the daughter of one of her girlhood friends. She had hoped that her son would be in the hands of pious evangelicals. She did not know that the lady had lapsed from her state of grace, that the manners and habits of the house were disorderly, and that the landlady and the wife of one of the lodgers were "entirely preoccupied with food, drink, dress and sex". It was a seedy setting for the gawky student, trying to read his Huxley notes by gas-light in a shared bedroom. Socially insecure, he was made more embarrassed when the landlady's sister was palmed off on him on Sunday afternoons for a fumbly sort of flirting. "I looked", he later recalled, "through a hole in my life of some weeks more or less, into a sort of humanity, coarser, beastlier and baser than anything I had ever known before." But he did not know how to get away from this place of "simmering hot mud". Inexperienced in city life, with only a guinea a week to support himself, there was no obvious means of escape. He was, in fact, rescued by a relative, who had been asked by his father to keep an eye on him. Janie Gall, a kindly girl who worked in a Kensington department store, had gone for occasional walks with him on Sundays, and to her he confessed his discomfort. She whisked him eastwards, to a gaunt decaying house at 181 Euston Road, where yet another relative let lodgings. Aunt Mary had been married to Joe's brother William, an unsuccessful draper who had died in the workhouse, and she and her sister had come up to London to make a marginal living by letting rooms. Aunt Mary was an affectionate woman: Wells found her "lovable", and within the limits of her means and her other duties as a landlady she did her best to provide him with something like a family home for a couple of years. It was spartan enough in winter. He worked in his room by candlelight, wearing his topcoat and putting his feet in the bottom drawer of the clothes-chest wrapped in his clean underclothing for warmth.

Aunt Mary also had a daughter Isabel, who was the same age as Wells. They met when Janie Gall took him along to Euston Road for tea to discuss the move. When Isabel came into the room Wells was immediately attracted to her. She was a dark-eyed girl, with "a grave and lovely face, very firmly modelled, broad brows and a particularly beautiful mouth and chin and neck". Her manner was shy and simple. She made a stunning impression on her cousin Bertie. At South Kensington, the women students were friendly but emotionally aloof: "they deliberately disavowed sex in their dress and behaviour", Wells remembered. The attractive women he saw on the streets or riding in the Park were distant and unattainable. Now, in Isabel, he found an object for his repressed feelings and romantic fantasies. "Proximity and isolation", Wells said, "forced upon us the role of lovers, very innocent lovers."

Isabel worked as a retoucher in a photographer's establishment in Regent Street, and when they left home early in good weather they walked to Oxford Circus. Wells then hurried on across Hyde Park to South Kensington. When there was nothing to keep him late at the Normal School, he walked back to meet her from work, or – when she was attending evening art classes at the Birkbeck Institute – he would stroll down through the Bloomsbury squares to escort her home. All the time he talked to her, and at her. He was bubbling with ideas and enthusiasms and not very experienced at small talk with young ladies. This smother of intellectual conversation also served as a means of muting emotional drives of which he was aware but did not know how to handle. So Isabel had to listen to rambling discussions of "atheism and agnosticism, of republicanism, of the social revolution, of the releasing power of art, of Malthusianism, of free love and such-like liberating topics", as Wells talked himself into believing that they "were passionate allies who would conquer the world together".

Isabel was a simple and conventional girl, affectionate but prudish, flattered by the attention that her clever cousin paid her. She bore up under this flood of talk without much idea of what it all meant. She read little, and had romantic tastes in fiction and fashion which were worlds apart from the ideas that Bertie brought back from South Kensington. But she enjoyed listening to him, and Wells never noticed that behind the flattery of her apparent interest there lay profound differences of attitude and feeling.

The passion for Isabel began to master him. It was increasingly difficult for him to concentrate on academic work that he found boring and sterile, and he began to spend more and more time with her, or waiting for her, or day-dreaming about her. But while he found this superficially comforting, the relationship was becoming an increasing psychological strain. He worried about his unattractive physique. He hated to look at himself in the mirror and compare his weedy frame with that of the muscular Apollos in the South Kensington museums. He began to lose weight, not so much from undernourishment, as from the strain of repression and anxiety. Feelings of guilt and inadequacy frustrated any attempt to push the relationship beyond the tantalising stalemate in which his passions were both aroused and sidetracked into romantic illusions about Isabel.

This conflict clearly began soon after he moved into the house on the Euston Road, and it gradually brought him to the verge of nervous and physical collapse. By the end of his three-year course he was in a dreadful state. "I had no outlook", he wrote, "no qualifications, no resources, no self-discipline and no physique." The bubble of ambition that had lifted him out of Midhurst had been pricked. All that he had saved from those three years were memories of the euphoria induced by Huxley's classes, a little reputation in the Debating Society, some scraps of writing, a patchy grounding in science, and an emotional relationship that was full of complexities and uncertainties.

He still recalled that sense of overwhelming failure fifty years later, when he described his feelings at the end of his college career. " 'And what is to become of me *now*?' I asked, in a real panic for the first time since my triumphant exodus from the draper's shop."

5

GRUB STREET

Wells had squandered his chances. He had left South Kensington with
wilted qualifications and a reputation as an inattentive and undisciplined
student. The dream that he might make a career as a scientist was shattered.
It was even doubtful whether he had any chance of appointment as a
teacher. He wrote answers to advertisements. He pressed the employment
agencies which served the private schools to find him a post. At last one
agency came up with a vacancy in North Wales, where he could start
earning at once. Wells packed his bag and left for Holt Academy, near
Wrexham. On paper the opportunity seemed a good one, but what he
found there was a devastating disappointment. The Academy was a group
of dingy buildings, catering to a handful of children of farmers and shopkeepers, and some candidates for the ministry who were "three lumpish
young men apparently just off the fields". It was much worse than Morley's
place in Bromley, not least because it was dirty, and its owner and his wife
were dirty, and they both let the affairs of the school slide while they drank.
The food was execrable, the little dormitories were crowded with boarders
sleeping two and three to a bed; there was no timetable and no plan for
teaching. There were two ushers, Wells and a young Frenchman. His
colleague, Wells wrote to A. Morley Davies, was an "atheist, socialist, a
cuckold maker, & all that is lovable in a comrade".[1] What their employer
expected of them was little more than fitful attempts at cramming punctuated by prayers to save the souls, and corporal punishment to curb the
bodies, of the loutish pupils. A few days after his arrival Wells sent a
dismal letter to Simmons (though full of the jocular errors in spelling he
used in writing to his friends).[2]

I am hier in this gloomy neighbourhood & I wish I was dead. The boys are
phoolish & undisciplined to an astonishing degree and the chemistry cupboard
is not worthy of the name containing mostly effloresced salts in cracked bottles
& broken test-tubes full of abominations left by the last science master in '74.

69

There is an absence an utter absence of coherent system in the whole damned affair.

For just over a month he managed, improvising lessons, teaching scripture on Sunday, and playing cricket and football with the boys. He discovered that, despite the unpleasant conditions, the school made no serious demands upon him. He had time to write a good many letters, and to draft some short stories. Most of these, like a much-rejected draft called *The Death of Miss Peggy Pickersgill's Cat*, were later burnt. On 23 August he wrote to A.Morley Davies.[3]

Just at present I am very happy but alas! foresee in the future multitudinous evil to grow out of this pleasant summer. I am, of course, doing no work here. That – how quickly bad habits grow! – has already become an essential to my happiness. I am a lounger in the schoolroom, teaching without effort through the disciplinarian habit of mind fostered by former masters ... I have a reputation for learning, nobody capable of finding me out, a dozen fortunate minor accidents, and the capacity for forgetting the future.

He had already told both Davies and Simmons the most important reason for his change of mood.[4] Soon after his arrival he wrote to Simmons on 13 August that,

... among these boors I have found a creature with a soul. She is a pretty girl, minister's daughter, teacher in a high school. When we met we were enchanted. She has read Ruskin, Eliot and an infinity of good novels. Now we meet surreptitiously & spend whole hours together by shady river banks, where I talk grotesque to her and she very intelligently to me.

On the same day to Davies:

Here the folk are Presbyterian, Radical and all that is altogether damnable, with an idiotic appeal to common repute under the misnomer common sense.

However I have a remedy. I have discovered a damoisel, beautiful, of extraordinary force of character & higher culture. Quite by accident I sent you her first note. The letters are getting warmer now as per enclosed specimen. If it was not for the suptil but exquisite excitement of this connexion I should even now be stagnating towards death ...

The flirtation with Annie Meredith developed rapidly into an Arcadian interlude, and towards the end of August 1887 he wrote of "an expectant catalogue of sensual delights – bright weather, perfect health, pretty girl in the foreground of a sunset by a pollard-bordered stream, football, success and so forth."[5] There was no mention of Isabel in his letters.

Wells himself was doubtful in later years whether he had even written to her from Holt: she "just went out of the scheme of happenings". He became very attached to Annie. Years later she wrote to his son G.P. Wells from Gravesend, where she was living in retirement:[6]

I have a history of his life written by himself and several love letters. I broke with him because he told me he was an atheist & socialist, that is why he describes me as "a creature with a soul". He wrote "I beseech you not to break with me now", and when I didn't answer he wrote, "I mean to win my way back to London & the big game somehow".

Wells then had no idea how this was to be done, but on 30 August the decision was made for him by an accident. He was badly fouled in a football match by a boy called Dick Gratton. Within a few hours he was passing blood, and in such a state that a doctor was fetched.

He spent his twenty-first birthday in the bleak bedroom he shared with two of the Methodist students, gloomily wondering about his future. Burton, now married and working as a chemist in the Potteries, came over to see him "in a spirit that was more than brotherly". But he resisted his employer's hints that he might take sick leave, unpaid. If he left Holt he had nowhere to go and no reserve to support himself. The news from home was bad. Joe Wells had at last been sold up, and Sarah – who now had to support her husband – had written to say that Miss Fetherstonhaugh was becoming difficult about the way her sons treated Up Park as a refuge when they lost their jobs.

Wells got on his feet, and went back to the unheated draughty classroom. Unless he could last out until after Christmas he would lose the twenty pounds due to him for a half of his annual wage. Within a week or so he was ill again. This time he was coughing blood, and the Wrexham doctors diagnosed tuberculosis.* He was clearly too ill to work, and he was filled with a fear and resentment of death. His reaction, whenever he scented danger, was claustrophobic: "I felt I was going to be stifled, frozen and shut up." He had to get away, and the only place to which he could escape was Up Park. Fortunately the consumptive was then an

---

* There is some doubt about these two illnesses at Holt, and their subsequent recurrences, which kept Wells a semi-invalid for the next twelve years. The Wrexham doctor diagnosed a crushed kidney and consumption. Doctors who treated Wells later were less sure, and one at least suspected a diabetic condition which developed unmistakably when he got older. Late in life Wells thought he had suffered at Holt from appendicitis. There is no question, however, that from Holt onwards he had a chronic pulmonary condition which frightened and debilitated him, and that stress seemed to precipitate an attack.

accepted object of charity and pity, and Sarah prevailed upon Miss Fetherstonhaugh once again to take in one of her troublesome sons. It was early November when Wells made a settlement with his headmaster and took the train to Euston. Ill and tired, he stopped overnight in London. Next afternoon he was back at the family's usual place of last resort.

To Wells it seemed likely that it might also prove to be his last resort. His first letter to Simmons, written soon after he reached Up Park, was headed: "The House of the Captivity: Valley of the Shadow of Death". Despite its bantering tone, the troubles listed in this letter – a kidney complaint, dyspepsia, a weak lung, possibly diabetes – show that his condition was serious, and that good nursing and medical attention had come just in time.[7] Wells continued to joke. He sent Simmons news of himself as a series of newspaper headlines.

> Illness of Wells!
> Thrilling Details!
> A Pint of Piddle Sent to London
> Examination by Council of Doctors

He also reported the more depressing news that the doctor "is sure I shall always be a chronic invalid". Dr William Collins, the Up Park family physician, was an unusually able and sympathetic man who later became professionally eminent. He seems to have had some idea of the psychic as well as the physical aspects of Wells's illness. Wells rested, relaxed, ate regular nourishing meals, and spent his time reading and scribbling, but he felt terribly frustrated. On 3 December he sent Morley Davies a long letter which concluded with the words "Damn, damn, damn, damn, damn, damn, God damn, God damn, God damn, God damn".[8]

Sarah was relieved when Bertie began to recover his strength. Christmas, when a house-party upstairs and the arrival of accompanying servants threw an additional strain on her limited capacity for organisation, was almost upon her, and in addition to Bertie she had Joe, Frank and Fred coming for the holidays. "All our people will be coming here during the festive three days", Wells wrote to Simmons on 13 December, "to the envy of all the other servants and heartburning universal . . . I'm all right again now comparatively and working a bit at the writing. There is a grand plan on foot for a new great undertaking but I haven't the arrant self-confidence to finance such speculation."[9]

The word "finance" was probably figurative. Though Frank always had plans for new ventures in the clock line, and every time that Fred was out of a job he talked of setting up in business for himself, the total cash resources of the Wells family at this time amounted to less than one hundred pounds. Almost all this money consisted of Sarah's savings. It is likely that Wells was referring to a substantial work of fiction that he was then planning – a successor to a lost romantic tale called *Lady Frankland's Companion*, which he had started at Holt and worked up to a total of thirty-five thousand words at Up Park during his illness. He was certainly writing a great deal, and for the first time he was reading a wide range of fiction and verse. What he read led to much flat imitation, but it also began to provide him with critical standards. He realised that he still wanted to write, but that an undisciplined talent was not enough. In these months he exhausted the Up Park library, he cadged books from the curate, he got Burton to send him parcels of reading matter, and he rushed through Keats, Shelley, Spenser and Heine, Whitman and Stevenson, Rousseau, Tennyson, Scott and Carlyle.

By Christmas he seemed to be making progress, and was allowed up for the feast in the Servants' Hall. Yet once the stimulus of the holidays was over his morale collapsed again. In writing to Simmons in January, he draws a "picshua" of the upper servants at table, and complains that the people are "all dead – purely automatic . . . Each of them has fifteen remarks to say over and they get through the lot each mealtime." Then, he adds in capitals which sound like the outbursts which made his mother collapse in nervous tears, "THEY ARE DAMNED PHONOGRAPHS, BLOODY TALKING DOLLS."[10] He was clearly not a comfortable person to have about the place, either for the Upstairs persons or the Downstairs persons, and he was anxious to get out. In a phrase taken directly from his mother (who used it frequently in her diary, with "dull" as a synonym for "depressed"), he cried to Simmons at this time: "O God how dull I am! O God how dull." If Sarah was on tenterhooks about his irritable tantrums, she was also getting on his nerves. "My mother", he wrote to Elizabeth Healey on 20 February 1888, "is an old lady of over sixty, very garrulous about a sister of mine who died in 1864, and certain great family events that mentally dwarfed her and her brothers, sisters, cousins to the third and fourth degree, in the decade 1820 to 1830."

Wells was at a loss what to do. Only one person seemed likely to help, and that was Dr Collins, who had many friends among the London intelligentsia. Wells swallowed his pride and asked him for aid. He must have given the impression that he "appreciated wine and oil above a consistent position and the prospects of self-advancement" because he got a rebuff from Collins. He tried again, in a pompously humble letter in February.[11] Collins knew "men like Harrison, Bernard Shaw, the Huxleys, who must from the active and extensive nature of their engagements of necessity employ numerous fags to assist in the more onerous and less responsible portions of their duties". In what Wells afterwards called his "Babu English", he pleaded that Collins was the only person who was "in a position to bring me into contact with that world of liberal thought in which alone the peculiar circumstances of my education render me capable of attaining to any degree of success". Collins, who had given friendly encouragement to his young patient and was aware of his talents, was still unable to help. It was difficult to intercede for a job on behalf of a young man who lacked both health and the social graces. Wells's friends were scarcely in a better position to help him. Simmons was scraping along as a schoolmaster in Portsmouth. Gregory was terribly hard up. Elizabeth Healey could do no more than provide a sympathetic answer to the stream of letters he sent her. Only Burton, now married, was in a better position, and he finally offered to take him in as a guest. It was an attractive offer because Stoke-on-Trent at that time had the reputation of having a climate suitable for consumptives.

By the end of February the arrangements were in hand. Wells broke the news gently to Elizabeth Healey – she disliked Burton – telling her why he could not simply move down the road to the cottage at Nyewoods, where his father and brother Frank were installed.[12] He intended to "visit the brigand-like establishment" of "that hoary Pagan, Old Silenus, my father" and "that changeling, my brother". But, as he wrote a few days later:[13]

I do not live with them two, because only by systematic poaching, garden-stye, and hen-roost raiding can they get food to themselves, and the home has only three rooms and there is a hole in the roof of one of them and one of the others is not boarded, and (NB I am inspired here) Old Silenus, that once powerful and promising youth (only he married early and poor) my father, is usually cleaning his gun with paraffin, smoking tobacco that reeks of the everlasting bottomless pit, or sleeping loose on the victual-strewn floor, while that misbegotten boy, my brother, studies clocks and musical boxes at a bench near the window with a view to constructing a patent machine to kill rats and suchlike pests by a method combining the maximum of row and expense with the minimum of effect.

The letters to Miss Healey in February struck a recurring note of depression.[14] On 20 February 1888 he wrote: "I have been experiencing lately what everybody has to experience who drops out of the marching column like I have done . . . I have been shedding my friends ever since my failures distinctly set in . . . I may drag on a maimed existence in this accursed land of winds, wet ways and old women for three or four years yet." Three days later he continued: "I shall never join the Marching Column again. My youth went long ago – my *life work* will be to give as little trouble as possible in an uncongenial universe while I stay therein and not to leave too big a hole in anybody else's world when my creation terminates." And with the self-pity went a continuing recognition of his irritable frustration. On 28 February, he replied to a letter from Miss Healey: "Two things were given for me to pitch stones at. Sometimes I fancy that that is the thing that gives me my profoundest pleasure – To chuck things at things and break them." But there were hopeful jests mixed with the gloom. On 2 March: "You say my poem has no feet! The humming bird has no feet, the Cherubim around the Mater Dolorosa have no feet" and "You say my lines are lacking in metre . . . Metres are used for gas, not the outpourings of the human heart."

Once the journey to Stoke was settled, he was much brighter. At the end of March he wrote a more self-assertive letter, headed "The 89th of the 21st year (Temporary) Centre of the Universe":

I am not a broken-down invalid. I have merely had a revolution in my constitution – on the principle that a man who would revolutionize the World
must first revolutionize himself – and I am now no longer an English person
flourishing freely in the open air, but an exotic – It is sad to think I shall never
grow in England again, but alas! too true. This last remark is jocquelar. . . . I am
sorry I cannot acceed to your rekwest about my litterery produckshons – I am
ashamed of them and desire only that my connexion with them may seece on
payment. Sharper than the cerpent's tooth is n unsatisfactory ofspring, and I
trust that you will not mention my produkcions again – During my fflictions I
have been much chasend.

At the end of April the Burtons were ready for him. Burton was already doing quite well at the Wedgwood works, trying to rediscover the chemistry of some of the firm's earlier ceramic processes, and – though the point was never made explicitly – he and his wife seem to have taken up their old friend as an act of charity towards one who was sick and virtually penniless. For he was still very unwell. Exhausted on arrival, he relapsed with a fresh haemorrhage. He wrote to Morley Davies that "the hungry maw will presently engulf the Prophet of the Undelivered Spell and the unwarned world hurry on to Damnation".[15] It was all very well to feel a sense of mission, but what if fate decided that the world should go unwarned? "It is one of the most painful features of this form of human collapse", he sadly confessed to Elizabeth Healey on 1 May, "to feel continually power slipping away."[16]

The Burtons did their best by him, and enjoyed his high spirits, the way in which he would vividly mimic the life at Up Park, and even his habit of provoking arguments on any subject that came into his head. But they undoubtedly found him a trying guest. When the Burtons later criticised him for his behaviour, Wells honestly conceded that they in fact had had some reason. In September 1889 he recalled in a letter to Simmons:[17]

I was ill in a way that made me low-spirited & dull-witted & the amount of heavy sentiment in the atmosphere sometimes bored me beyond concealment into irony and argument . . . Burton used to get young men to his house and humbug them that Carlyle was a sort of Quaker, & read books to them till they were just hypnotised. Into which meetings I introduced controversy leading to scepticism. It made Burton dry up his monopoly & pass the cake around . . . Likewise I was very shabby which hurt Mrs B's feelings when a visitor came.

The change, however, was a stimulus. The Five Towns, with clusters of smoking pot-banks set in the rolling Staffordshire countryside, had a special and intense culture, and Wells was fascinated by the interweaving of town and country. In a letter to his father soon after his arrival he reported the powerful impression that the Potteries made on him, supplemented by a lot of detail about the local industry that he thought might be of interest to the old Master China Dealer. For the first time (and almost the only time in his life) he was in close contact with life in an industrial town and it stimulated him to write about this kind of community.

This work was to be "a vast melodrama . . . a sort of Staffordshire *Mysteries of Paris* . . . it was to be a grotesque with lovely and terrible passages". How much of the book he actually wrote is unknown, but Wells said that he had now reached the point where he knew what real writing was. It was "something I could read aloud to people I respected without immediate shame . . . good enough to alter and correct and write over again". One piece of that incomplete melodrama survived revision to appear as the short story called *The Cone*, in which the jealous manager of an ironworks leads his wife's lover to the top of a furnace and casts him in to his death. The menace builds up through the story, as the passion of jealousy is concealed beneath the apparent normality of a tour of the works – though Raut, the hapless philanderer, knows instinctively that the husband is leading him to his death. The theme of sexual competition, and the destructive jealousy which it produced, was one to which Wells often returned.

He was certainly thinking about love as a theme in his writing, if not his own life. On 19 June, shortly before he left the Burtons, he wrote to Elizabeth Healey:[18]

But don't you think there's a frightful lot of sentimental distortion of this important factor of human life called love? . . . For myself, who am a doubter and contemner of almost all the amenities of social intercourse, there is a simply frightful temptation to be glaringly improper in what I write – I am one of those beings who, with the simplest and purest of lives, have the most shocking scale of morals believable.

This letter had a more confident note. The complaints and self-pity of the Doomed Man had disappeared – possibly because Wells found his health at last improving and the role of the Doomed Man no longer satisfying. One afternoon he walked out in the woods and lay in the sun. He met a girl whose dress was caught by a bramble and chatted to her. "I have been dying for nearly two-thirds of a year", he said to himself, "and I have died enough." He found himself walking back to the Burtons with a buoyant stride, cheered by his discovery that Death was a Bore.

It was a moment of decision. He told Burton that he was leaving in two days. His only capital was a five-pound note – sent by Sarah in two halves in separate envelopes as a precaution against loss – and his new faith in himself. After eight months of depression, self-pity and illness, he decided to launch himself into the world again.

In the two days he remained with the Burtons Wells dashed off some letters to scholastic employment agencies. As soon as he arrived in London he followed them up by personal calls. There were no jobs, and all he had was the dwindling five pounds. Four shillings a week of this went on the rent of a bare cubby-hole partitioned off from an attic in a house in Theobalds Road on the edge of Bloomsbury. Wells had just enough money to last out a month if he ate less than he needed to maintain his precarious health. By the time he came to the end of his resources he had little that was even fit to be pawned. All he could muster was a cheap cane, worn underclothes and socks, two discoloured celluloid collars, an india-rubber and a halfpenny. The morning after he took this dismal inventory he was cheered to find that the coin was actually a blackened shilling, and he could now afford to buy breakfast. He had already written to his old friend A.V. Jennings to ask for help. The postcard was little more than a cartoon of Wells, carrying a pen and a bundle of manuscript, eyeing a placard with the slogan "Wanted. 1,000 men to carry advertisement boards". Above and below the sketch ran the message: "I am in London seeking work. But at present finding none. I am not in for the Intermediate or any such games. Yours in God. H.G.Wells".[19]

Jennings responded at once. He asked Wells to prepare some coloured wall-charts for him, to be copied from textbooks in the British Museum. This work, supplemented by some odds and ends of cramming, brought in a little money. It also left Wells time to scratch around in Grub Street for a few odd shillings. New penny weeklies were appearing to serve the semi-literate public created by elementary education – *Answers*, *Tit-Bits* and other papers "written by office-boys for office-boys". Wells discovered that he could get half-a-crown for inventing questions about science for such papers, and even more for writing the answers to his own questions. All through the autumn he picked up trifles in this way.

As soon as he began to earn something he went back to live with his aunt and cousin, who had left the house in Euston Road and were now living in rooms at 12 Fitzroy Road, close to Regent's Park. For more than a year he had apparently maintained only casual contact with Isabel. He said in his autobiography that when he was living in Theobalds Road "loneliness weighed upon me more and more. I began to wonder what my cousin Isabel was doing ... " Yet only two months earlier he had written to Elizabeth Healey from Basford, asking her as a kindness to call on Isabel at Fitzroy Road any Sunday afternoon.[20] He had, he wrote, been engaged to her ever since "I was an interesting and promising lad of eighteen. Living alone with her mother as she is, and seeing very few people, I have reason to believe I occupy a very considerable share in her thoughts." This is the only surviving reference to any such "engagement". In his autobiography Wells clearly implied that there had been some cooling of the relationship, if only because of distance and the fact that Isabel was not a great correspondent, but he offered no explanation why he let at least a month elapse after his return to London before getting in touch with her. It may simply have been a matter of pride. All Wells said of his return to the ménage is: "We resumed our old familiarity as though there had been no interval".

Wells went down to Up Park again for the Christmas holiday. The outlook was now much more promising, he wrote to his brother Fred in a letter that contains a satiric "picshua" of the dance in the Servants Hall.[21] He had given up working for Jennings and

... next January I begin as a non-resident assistant at a highly respectable school at Kilburn. I get £60 a year, partial board (dinner & tea five days in the week) and certain examination results. This is not very good though there are the advantages of living at home in comfort, and of having plenty of spare time, to set against the relatively low pay. And that's a consideration especially, since it will enable me to finish my degree of B.Sc. by next September, and so command a salary of 150 or 200. Isabel and myself are bringing the art of living on very little very happily to a high state of perfection. Since you were here we have set ourselves seriously to making our room look bright and cosy and I should really like you to see how jolly we are.

The last two sentences give an impression of domesticity, as if Isabel and her cousin had settled down to a platonic near-marriage. Half a century later Wells recalled that "I had indeed a gnawing desire to marry, and my life in close proximity to my cousin was distressing and humiliating me in a manner she could not possibly comprehend". Wells was now twenty-two, and had been accepted back on the understanding of an engagement of sorts rather than as a lodging relative. There was a curious gloss on his position in a letter Wells wrote to Elizabeth on 5 September 1889, when he was paying a brief visit to "that alcoholic savage, my father".[22] From experience, he wrote, "I object to engagements. They are a device of Mrs Grundy or the devil. You know, I think that I object to marriages as a general thing. The way in which two people after half a dozen weeks intercourse will bind themselves for the rest of their days is perfectly disgusting . . . ninety-nine per cent of marriages end in revolt or passive endurance."

Even if Wells found his domestic situation an emotional strain he was undoubtedly much happier. The new job was in an interesting school – yet another private academy. The owner struggled along with inadequate means. When Wells arrived he gave him a sovereign and told him to "get whatever apparatus you require for your science teaching". But he was neither a drinker nor a bully nor a fool. He was, on the contrary, an enlightened man whose ideas of teaching were far ahead of his day.

John Vine Milne managed to run his school in a pair of semi-detached villas, but the place was clean, the food was good, and he had an honest way of dealing with his assistants and pupils that gave Wells an idea of what a sensible education might be like.* Two years later he wrote to Milne, with whom he remained on friendly terms for many years.[23]

Long before I knew you I had my grudge against the particular variety of private school of which I honestly believe you live in ignorance. I have suffered badly as the son of not very well-to-do and rather illiterate parents at the hands of these scholastic pirates and I do not think I could refrain from the chance of sticking a knife under the ribs of this system of fraud if every friend I had stood on the opposite side.

Even in Milne's school, though the work gave Wells the chance to discover himself as a teacher, he became aware of the shortcomings of the kind of education that was being served up. The "subjects" were being taught, but why anything was being taught except to secure examination passes and earn grants was not explained. "We launched our boys", Wells said, "with, or more commonly without" matriculation certificates "as mere irresponsible adventurers into an uncharted scramble for life."

Something of the way Wells tried to teach may be glimpsed from a reference Milne wrote for him in January 1891:[24]

Mr Wells did his work here in a painstaking and thorough manner. I have particularly admired his teaching of science, where his extensive reading and his power of expression enabled him always to handle his subject in a manner at once exact and humorous ... The proof of his success was the enthusiasm aroused in his classes which was not dependent upon mere experiment.

In fact "mere experiment" had to be dispensed with because the previous master had blown up the apparatus and lost the weights of the balances!

The work at Kilburn was steady and pleasant. Wells, who was now twenty-three, began to settle his mind towards a teaching career. In May 1889 the household moved to larger premises at 46 Fitzroy Road, and in July he took the Intermediate examination for his BSc, passing with second-class honours in zoology. In August, after a brief family holiday at Whitstable, a cheap resort on the North Kent coast (and the first vacation Wells had had apart from visits to friends and relatives), he was planning his further studies. He told Simmons that he had selected zoology, geology

* He was the father of the popular writer A.A.Milne, who was a pupil under Wells. Milne's most notable pupil was Alfred Harmsworth, later Lord Northcliffe. About the age of twelve, with the aid of a jellygraph, Harmsworth started the *Henley House Magazine*, the first of the editorial projects that made his fortune. Wells "contributed largely" to the magazine, which was still flourishing though Harmsworth had left.

and mental and moral science – there being "so much humbug in mental and moral science that I believe it will be particularly easy for me".[25] The degree work, however, had to wait a little. Apart from the professional advantages of the teaching diploma, there were also money prizes for good performance, and he began to work hard for the examination which was to be held just after Christmas.

He described his situation in an unusually long and affectionate letter to his mother on 14 October, having omitted to write for her birthday four days earlier.[26]

I think it was mean of me to let the time slip by, only I have been very busy with different odd jobs in my spare time, doing some maps for Mr Milne, cramming for an exam at Christmas and so on; and one is not always in the mood to sit down and write a letter worth reading. Poor Little Mummy! I hope that before many of your birthdays go by, we may see you in a cosy little home of your own and shabby, scandal-loving Up Park left to congenial souls. What a tawdry mess of dull-brained, spiteful, useless people it is to be sure, that we four louts have left you among, to have all your finer feelings wounded everlastingly! Sometimes, dearest, dearest Mother, I think of you so dolefully and remorsefully that I have to fall to abusing the Governor to keep my spirits up. Well, well, there is a little vial of wrath for his portly indolence a-filling that will be administered if he is not careful. I wish I could write you a letter fuller of comfort than this . . .

Wells was acutely aware that the situation at Up Park was deteriorating, and this letter reflects his contrite inability to provide any practical help. "I often think", he went on,

how I have hurt you by hastiness and of the many brutal things I have done to you, cross letters written and feelings disregarded. Really I am very sorry for them. I agree about the cross letters I have too often written you perhaps more than you think. Sometimes it seems to me that I may have lost some of your affection by these things, and by what you have thought unsympathetic coldness – you know I never was given to demonstrations of affection. Do let me now assure you of my respect and tenderness for your dear devoted life, and do not forget if at any time you are in trouble. I know now far better than I ever did in the old days, how the sense of one being to whom our sorrow is sorrow helps us against the heavy trivialities that sometimes almost bear us down. So I want you to read this subscription to my letter not as the usual formality but as a truth.

Really believing me
Your most loving son

Bertie.

This was the kind of consolation that Sarah hoped for but seldom received from her sons. There are a good many entries in her diary which note that the post has brought nothing from Fred or Bertie: "My poor old birthday! Went to Harting. Not a word from my boys", or, "Frank came to tea. Cool as usual. Not a word that is kind. Bertie's cross letter. What a trouble they are to me, forgetting their duty to God".

The letter from Wells was the first sign that he might at last be "getting on". Of the twenty subjects he sat, he passed with honours in fifteen and secured all three prizes – ten pounds for education and five pounds apiece for mathematics and natural science. With these successes he persuaded Milne to raise his salary and allow him shorter hours (which would allow him both to spend more time studying for his BSc finals and take on extra coaching work). He broke the news to Simmons in a long bulletin.[27] This began:

Stock Exchange Intelligence

Great Boom in Wells's

We have to announce a surprising run upon the H.G. Wells
Limited Ordinary and Debenture A in consequence of the

Entirely Unexpected Improvement

in the prospects of that concern.

He added that he had received a "Mysterious Communication from a person of the name of Briggs requesting the honour of an interview at Cambridge and offering the Company His Fare there and back". It was followed by the offer of a job from William Briggs, the founder of the University Correspondence College, which gave postal tuition to students taking London University and other external qualifications. If Wells took over the correspondence work in biology he could have two pounds a week at once, and more if he passed his degree in the following October. If, moreover, he passed the degree with honours (this was important for the College prospectus) he could have a permanent post teaching thirty hours a week at a Tutorial College that Briggs had opened in an alley off the Strand – with a guaranteed income of four pounds a week or more.

Wells started his evening teaching right away, though he remained with Milne until the end of the summer term. He felt his luck had turned. "I *do* like being slapped on the back by my friends", he wrote to Simmons.[28] "It is just you and one or two others that made the great hard-up break bearable and now there are some inklings of success it is the thought of sharing the glee of it with you that makes it really worth having and persevering after. Plenty of work to do altogether – feel quite an active useful person." Yet he still had the sense that fate would catch up with him, for he added: "Pace too high though – life a bubble – smash at any moment." In the letter to Simmons of 9 February 1890 he went even further.[29] "I write with the weighty anticipation of some great calamity upon me. The good fortune that has come on lately cannot last – it cannot last. I know Providence too well."

For the present, luck seemed to hold. Wells passed his degree with first-class honours in zoology, and Briggs – whose establishment was about to expand into better and well-equipped premises in Red Lion Square – employed him for fifty hours a week. He was now earning at the rate of over three hundred pounds a year, a fair genteel income in those days, and five times the salary at which he had started with Milne. He was conscientious and untiringly helpful to his students. After Wells died, one of them described his memory of his teacher at the age of twenty-three.[30] He was

somewhat below average height, not very robust in health, with evident signs of poverty, or at least disregarding any outward appearance of affluence. In dress, speech and manner he was plain and unvarnished, abrupt and direct, with a somewhat cynical and outspoken scorn of the easy luxurious life of those who have obtained preferment and advantage by reason of social position or wealth . . . He lectured for an hour each morning, and this was followed by a period of two hours in a laboratory, when he came round to each student in turn to explain and correct his dissections . . . He was extremely painstaking and evidently anxious to help each student . . . He insisted that education consisted in the ability to differentiate between things of real importance and those of secondary or trivial import . . . There were a real kindliness and a very evident sympathy towards his pupils, many of whom were struggling against poverty and disadvantage, to obtain a university degree.

Wells later dismissed such cramming as "preposterous and necessary". The sudden expansion of education had produced a mass of private and public classes designed to cram students for a variety of examinations, especially those of London University which were open, externally, to all comers. "About a small and quite insufficient band of men who knew and wanted to teach, settled everywhere an earnest multitude of examinees", Wells said, and Briggs – who was an earnest man who took his responsibilities to his students seriously and gave good value – had developed what Wells called "an examiner-defeating mechanism". The system consisted in drilling students to write out model answers to the limited range of set questions that turned up over and over in the papers, and in compressing – so far as scientific subjects were concerned – the laboratory work into evening classes or a fortnight's hectic work in a student's vacation. It produced results "satisfying the biological requirements of the examiners . . . without incurring any serious knowledge of biology", so that Briggs prospered by serving a real need and his students flourished with their certificates and degrees.

Wells, who had early learned the trick of cramming, was a great asset to Briggs. His students did well, and he produced a biology textbook which, much revised by other hands, has remained in print through the years.* He also managed to pick up another qualification for himself along the way, after he had worked for Briggs for over a year, passing the Fellowship examination of the College of Preceptors and getting the Doreck prize of twenty pounds. He seemed to be comfortable in the routine, and set for the kind of career which he had first envisaged when Byatt had put him on the award-winning treadmill back in Midhurst.

He had become so much the professional teacher that even his talent for writing was pouring into that mould. He edited the house journal – the *University Correspondent* – that Briggs ran for his students. He wrote for other educational papers. With his friend Walter Low (another bright young man employed by Briggs) he worked out a profitable arrangement. Low was paid fifty pounds a year by the College of Preceptors to edit its paper, the *Educational Times*. He also had another fifty pounds to spend on contributions. It saved him a great deal of trouble when, rather than scout round for other authors, he simply commissioned Wells to write all the articles he needed. Much of what he wrote was reformist – attacks on bad teaching, on lack of commitment by the teacher and on the weaknesses of a curriculum that had no coherence and on examinations designed only to test factual knowledge.

During 1890, the strain of teaching, completing the cramming for his final degree examinations and trying to write in the remaining scraps of time proved too much for Wells. It intensified his dissatisfaction with his lot and led to another haemorrhage. Dr Collins interceded at Up Park and arranged for him to spend a month convalescing there after Christmas. Whenever a breakdown in health forced Wells into a period of rest and isolation he turned his pent-up energy in a new direction, as he had done at Up Park during the winter of 1887–8 and when he was staying with the Burtons. On this occasion he drafted an article called "The Rediscovery

---

* In 1893 he and Gregory collaborated on a textbook, *Honours Physiography*, for which they received ten pounds apiece.

of the Unique". Like another piece called "The Universe Rigid", written about this time, it was worked up from a paper originally given to the Debating Society at South Kensington. With some temerity he sent it off to the prestigious *Fortnightly Review*, and in February he was astonished to hear that it had been accepted. He was so excited that he sent the letter of acceptance on to Simmons with an ecstatic note scrawled on the back.[31] "Is this the dove with a sprig of bay? Is it poor Pilgrim's first glimpse of the white and shining city? Or a mirage?"

The article appeared in the July issue in 1891, along with a curious collection of contributions on such topics as "Foreign Pauper Immigration", "Card Sharping in Paris" and "With King Gungun Harna in Gazaland". Its originality caught the eye of Oscar Wilde, who spoke favourably of it to the editor – praise that led the editor to invite Wells to send a second article ("The Universe Rigid") and to call on him at his office. It was an intimidating encounter, for this editor was Frank Harris, already famous as a sensational journalist who had given the *Evening News* – from which he had just been dismissed – a reputation for scandal-mongering, though he was not yet known as a disreputable man of letters with a taste for high living, philandering, and a talent for eking out his writing with sponging and outright blackmail. Somehow Harris had talked the directors of the *Fortnightly* into appointing him as successor to the staid John Morley. He had an eye for talent, and he wanted to see what more this young man Wells might do. Like other editors of the crop of journals that sprang up to serve a new reading public in the last two decades of the century, he was hungry for copy and always on the lookout for new writers who might be trained up into successes. The man Wells faced across the editorial desk was neatly summed up by Grant Richards, a journalist and publisher who was his contemporary: "A little man, fierce of aspect and with a fierce moustache; his clothes were correct, but on the loud side; his nose was impertinent – but one forgot his inches and his appearance when he talked."[32] Harris himself left an account of his young visitor, equally small but as shabby as Harris was glossy. He had "a shapely head, thick chestnut hair, regular features; chin and brow both good; nothing arresting or peculiar in the face, save the eyes; eyes that grew on one. They were of ordinary size, greyish-blue in colour, but intent, shadowed, suggesting depths like water in a half-coloured spring; observant eyes too, that asked questions, but reflection, meditation, the note of them; eyes almost pathetic in the patience of their scrutiny."[33] When Harris read the manuscript of "The Universe Rigid" he could not make head or tail of it: "I can't understand six words of it. What do you *mean* by it? For Gahd's sake tell me what it is all *about*." Wells for once was inarticulate and embarrassed: "he was so effaced", Harris said, "so colourless, so withdrawn, that he wiped out the effect that his paper had made on me."

Wells poignantly explained in his autobiography what had gone wrong. He had been so nervous about the need to make an impression on Harris that he had been quite unable to explain what he meant by a four-dimensional universe; his mind, in fact, had been concentrated on his top hat. Dressed up for the great occasion by Aunt Mary and Isabel, a frock-coat seeming the appropriate costume, he had found his top hat in such a state of weariness that only assiduous sponging had given it the semblance of the proper shine. While he was trying to focus his thoughts on what Harris was saying, his eye had been caught by the nap drying into a tufty fuzz, and he "couldn't for a moment adopt the tone and style of a bright young man of science. There was my hat tacitly revealing the sort of chap I was."

When he got home Wells smashed that hat – the symbol of a failure which hurt him so much that he claimed he could not attempt another serious article for a year or more. Even his pleasure at actually seeing "The Rediscovery of the Unique" in print was not enough to stimulate him to try anything more in this line. Yet Harris had been right in picking out the first article and rejecting the second. "The Universe Rigid" was pretentious, and Wells did not really know what he was trying to say. He thought in later years that he had caught hold of the edge of ideas that were afterwards developed by Max Planck and Einstein, but, as Harris quickly discovered, he had to let go immediately he was challenged.

The significance of "The Rediscovery of the Unique" lies in the fact that Wells was challenging both the optimism and the assumptions of science. Did the growth of science promise an unlimited extension of knowledge about Nature and Man's place in it – or did it merely demonstrate that the more that was known, the more plain it became that there were further unknowable mysteries? And was not science based on the belief that all phenomena were consistent and continuous, and therefore could be classified? Certainly that belief had permitted science to make great practical gains, because it allowed experiments to be repeated and the theoretical advances of physics and chemistry to be practically applied. But what if all units of matter were unique, and if the deviations from standardised behaviour increased as the structures became more complicated, so that living organisms were more likely to behave in a unique fashion than aggregations of molecules in a chemical compound, and Nature – the ultimate in complexity – might be quivering with uncertainties at which men could only guess? This pastiche of an academic lecture ended with a brilliant concluding paragraph.

Science is a match that man has just got alight. He thought he was in a room – in moments of devotion, a temple – and that his light would be reflected from and display walls inscribed with wonderful secrets and pillars carved with philosophical systems wrought into harmony. It is a curious sensation, now that the preliminary splutter is over and the flame burns up clear, to see his hands lit and just a glimpse of himself and the patch he stands on visible, and around him, in place of all that human comfort and beauty he anticipated – darkness still.

Here Wells stated both the theme on which almost all his work was to be a series of variations and hit upon the best form in which to express it. What editors like Harris wanted were not high-flown abstractions but vivid metaphors which would illuminate for their readers the new and strange and even terrifying world into which science was carrying them.

6

ISABEL OR CATHERINE?

Isabel's terms for the marriage Wells ardently desired were simple: "I should first win my way to a fairly safe place and the status of a householder before my devotion was rewarded." By the middle of 1891 it seemed that Wells was set to satisfy both conditions. But there was a setback. The haemorrhage at the beginning of the year, and a second collapse after influenza in May meant that Wells was obliged to give up his classes for a time and pay someone else to do his work. "It is no good going into the details of the disaster", he wrote to his father on 15 June 1891. "It is a smash. Still living is not so impossible now as it would be if I had not a degree." And then there is a cryptic footnote: "Marriage postponed –forever?"[1]

It was not. By October Wells had taken a lease on 28 Haldon Road, Wandsworth, a solid eight-roomed corner house in a street of clerks and small businessmen. It rented at thirty pounds a year. They had measurably moved up in the world, and on 31 October 1891 he and Isabel were quietly married at Wandsworth Parish Church.

Materially, the marriage was a change for the better, with Wells in improving health, working steadily for Briggs, and playing the role of householder in Haldon Road. Isabel's style ran to the draped mirrors, heavy furniture and potted plants of the period. The rooms in Haldon Road were fussy rather than comfortable, and by the time that Aunt Mary's ornaments and knick-knacks had been accommodated there was enough in them to make Isabel house-proud and Wells irritated because there was nowhere he could sit easily. It was a convenient place to live, only a few minutes' walk from the Wandsworth shops and from East Putney station where Wells could catch a train to Charing Cross. From there he could stroll up to Red Lion Square in Holborn for his daily stint at the Briggs laboratory.

Wells had apparently given Isabel what she wanted. He soon discovered that he had not got what he expected. He said bluntly that "it was a secretly very embittered young husband who went on catching trains, correcting correspondence answer books, eviscerating rabbits and frogs and hurrying through the crowded business of every day." The fact of marriage had brought him down to earth and made him face the difference between his image of marriage with Isabel and the reality. When Wells had been a student, he had projected on to Isabel the half-formed dreams which he assumed she shared. "I had", he said, "laid hands on Isabel, so to speak, and I would not be denied. She was to be my woman whether she liked it or not. I tethered my sexual and romantic imagination to her." But behind the outward acquiescence she held out for her own simple view of things. "I was always wanting to board and storm and subjugate her imagination", Wells wrote, "so that it would come out at last of its own accord to meet mine. It never came out to meet me." He did not realise that the drive to subjugate Isabel crushed whatever chance there might have been that she could grow to meet him on more equal terms. It made nonsense of all the talk of them facing the world as "partners" when in effect what he was doing was playing Professor Higgins to her Eliza.

Isabel could not understand why Bertie remained restless and importunate, and could not settle for a cosy pattern of suburban domesticity. He no longer talked to her with the same eagerness. He began to keep his interests to himself, especially when he found that even conversation on petty topics died or escalated into irritable tiffs. Wells discovered that his ideal was an illusion, now that Isabel was his wife. When "what she said spoilt the picture I wanted to make of her in my imagination", Wells remarked, "I would become rude and over-bearing". The dream was also broken for Isabel. In her quiet way she hoped to convert Bertie into a reasonable breadwinner – a fantasy that was just as unrealistic as Wells's fancy of enlisting her as a fellow-rebel in the "marching column". When they had to live together as man and wife, their futile ambitions for each other turned the marriage into a mutual trap.

Like many marriages of their period, sexual ignorance and inexperience was the immediate problem. Wells claimed that he was a virgin until, just before he moved into Fitzroy Road, he "went furtively and discreetly with a prostitute", an experience that "deepened my wary apprehension that round about the hidden garden of desire was a jungle of very squalid and stupid lairs". Isabel had certainly resisted any serious love-making from her cousin, who conceded that he was "a very ignorant as well as an impatient lover", until after they were married. He then discovered that she was innocent and physically unresponsive, taking the conventional attitude that "lovemaking was nothing more than an outrage inflicted upon reluctant womankind".

Within a few weeks Wells found himself almost as frustrated as he had been during their long engagement. Before long, he seduced one of Isabel's friends, and in this casual encounter he discovered for the first time that sex could be enjoyable. The way in which, so soon after the wedding, he replaced "simple honesty of sexual purpose by duplicity", struck him later as "quite the most interesting fact about my early married life". This infidelity did not release Wells from his emotional attachment to Isabel. He continued to desire her, and he needed the bond of habit and affection that tied him to her. But once that bond had been formally tied he felt an inarticulate desire to cut it and set himself free. Just as, before marriage, she had been the focus of all his romantic aspiration, after marriage "she became the gently firm champion of all that I felt was suppressing me". Infidelity became a symbol of freedom.

Whenever Wells made a niche for himself it began to feel like a prison, and he felt that survival depended upon flight.[2] What his mother called "getting on", became for him "getting out". He had taken flight from Bromley, from Windsor, from Southsea, from Midhurst, from South Kensington, from Holt, Up Park, the Burtons' home, Milne's school – and now from marriage. What he saw as a series of "false starts" in life was actually a sequence of jumps from one bolt hole to the next. This process, which led him to catapult himself out of uncomfortable situations, had been transferred from the context of work into his emotional life. Though "my secret romanticism was still centred quite firmly in my cousin . . . I was presently letting my desires wander away from her and . . . was making love to other people". By way of explanation, he added, "I wanted to compensate myself for the humiliation she had so unwittingly put upon me."

During 1892, Wells had to take his mother's place at the head of the family. A brief entry in Sarah's diary for 24 August marks the beginning of her troubles: "Miss F. returned. Unpacked her boxes but not required to dress her. Felt my deafness very much but I must be thankful for good health."[3] It was not only Sarah's deafness that was at long last pushing her employer's patience to breaking point. Miss Fetherstonhaugh, herself getting on in years, was increasingly testy about the way Sarah used the house as a convalescent home for her sons, about her inability to keep the accounts

properly, and her failure to manage the staff. There was trouble with the
cook and a woman in the dairy. "What a miserable house this is", Sarah
complained on 31 August. "Felt unsettled, not knowing what to do for
the best", she added. On the following day she wrote: "That horrid
woman upset me again. Oh how hard to be obliged to stay in such a place."
On 17 September, the cook left, and Sarah seems to have realised that her
own tenure was coming to an end. "Queer how Miss F. has altered. It
must be my deafness", she noted, and the following entries contained a
number of references to "dullness" and assiduous churchgoing in search of
comfort.

On 29 November 1892, Miss Fetherstonhaugh drew on the London &
County Banking Company a draft for one hundred pounds in favour of
Mrs Sarah Wells.[4] She was not asked to leave forthwith. She stayed through
Christmas, and placed advertisements seeking another post. There were
no replies. She begged permission to stay a few days longer on 9 February
1893, but on 16 February – after "much unkindness" – she drove through
the rain to Petersfield Station and took the train to Clapham Junction
where Wells met her. She remained at Haldon Road for only a few days.
After years of separation it was arranged that she should rejoin her husband
at Nyewoods. Sarah's diary made no mention of this reunion. The entries
in March and April simply recorded her anxiety about finding another
post. "No bright news. What shall we do for a living? Please God to send
me some work to do", she wrote on one day. On another: "No news. Felt
dull. How cruel of that woman." And a day or so afterwards she wrote:
"Short walk. So unsettled. No money. All going." The first reference to
Joe was on 7 May, and it was characteristic. "J.W. went to C. match."
By mid-November Sarah was at last reconciled to her fate. "I fear I shall
never get a situation again", she wrote.

Sarah was not the only casualty in the first months of 1893. Fred had
been doing well in a draper's at Wokingham, but he was suddenly dismissed. His employer wanted to put his son in the job. Fred turned up at
Haldon Road, where he stayed while he sought unsuccessfully for another
post. Eventually he was offered a good post in South Africa. He remained
there for most of his life, building up a successful business and eventually
retiring back to England in 1923, settling in Bournemouth and surviving
both his brothers.

Money problems were so pressing at this time that Wells even arranged
to get some routine work for his parents from the Briggs organisation.
They were to copy out student work-sheets – a job they could do at home

on piece-rates. But it was not well-paid, and it did not last for long. The strain of keeping the family solvent was considerable – they needed about a third of his income. He opened a bank account in 1893, starting it with a cheque from Briggs for a little over fifty pounds. In the course of the year he earned £380.13s.7d. and had £25.15s.1d. left over as a balance. Apart from any earnings Isabel made from photographic retouching, they lived on about two hundred and fifty pounds that year, because the accounts show that one hundred and nine pounds had been paid out to various members of the Wells family as subsidies. The strain proved to be more than a financial one. Wells was heading for yet another breakdown.

When term began in the autumn of 1892 Wells found an attractive young woman among his new students. Miss Amy Catherine Robbins was a "fragile figure, with very delicate features, very fair hair, and very brown eyes", wearing black in mourning for her father. She was studying for a science degree with a view to teaching. Wells took to her at once. He found her intellectually lively, and he was soon much more at ease with her than he expected.

He had little experience of women with middle-class backgrounds who saw themselves as New Women, eager to be taken as equals, anxious to work hard for a career, and willing to talk outside the accepted conventions. But the type attracted him, and so did Miss Robbins. Before long Wells realised that he was fascinated by this girl, who was six years younger than himself. His abstract idea of the ideal woman, "Venus Urania", "had failed to embody herself in Isabel . . . My mind was seizing up on Amy Catherine Robbins to make her the triumphant rival of that elusive goddess . . . in her turn, I was trying to impose a role." Once again he found himself earnestly discussing socialism, atheism and women's rights – though this time the reaction was positive, rather than frigid or foolish. They met after hours in the newly-popular tea-shops, where men and women could now go without chaperoning. Since Miss Robbins also lived in Putney they often walked down to Charing Cross together and travelled home on the District Line. Higgins had found a new Eliza.

The relationship developed through the difficult spring of 1893, when Wells was coping with his family, turning out articles and working with Gregory on a physiography textbook. It was all too much. On the evening of 17 May, hurrying down to Charing Cross station, he found he was coughing into another haemorrhage. In the small hours the doctor was fetched, his chest was packed with ice-bags, and once again he found himself seriously ill. Once again he survived, and as he lay quietly it came to him he was done with the teaching classes for ever.

Five days later he wrote to "My Dear Miss Robbins":[5]

When we made our small jokes on Wednesday afternoon anent the possible courses a shy man desperate at the imminence of a party might adopt, we did not realize that the Great Arch Humorist also meant to have his joke in the matter. For my own part I was so disgusted, when I woke in the dismal time before dawn on Thursday morning, to find myself the butt of *His* witticism, that I almost left this earthly joking ground in a huff. However by midday on Thursday, what with ice and opium pills, and this soothing bitterness and that, my wife and the doctor calmed the internal eruption of the joker out-joked, and since that I have been lying on my back, moody but recovering. I *must* say this for chest diseases; they leave one remarkably cheerful, they do not hurt at all and they clear the mind like strong tea. My poor wife has had all the pain of this affair, bodily and mental, fatigue and fear. For my share I shall take all the sympathy and credit.

It was very kind of you to call this morning but my wife would have liked to have seen you. Next week – if I do not go to pieces again – I expect I shall be coming downstairs, and a visitor who would talk to me and take little in return, would be a charity. Will you thank Miss Roberts for the letter of con-dolence which – quite contrary, as she must be aware, to all etiquette, following your bad example – she wrote to my wife.

I guess class teaching is over for me for good, and that whether I like it or not, I must write for a living now.

With best wishes,
Yours very faithfully,
H.G.WELLS

This was followed four days later by another note, headed by a sketch of a disgruntled figure sitting up in bed.[6]

Your unworthy teacher of biology is still – poor fellow – keeping recumbent, though he knows his ceiling pretty well by this time, but no doubt he is a-healing and by Saturday he will be, he hopes, put out in the front parlour in the after-noon. But he will be an ill thing to see, lank and unshaven and with the cares of this world growing up to choke him as he sprouts out of his bed . . .

And, at the foot of the letter Isabel wrote a postscript: "I think he will not be fit to see you before Sunday but I will write you before then."

Other friends came to see Wells: it was almost certainly while he was ill that Elizabeth Healey met Miss Robbins at Haldon Road for the first time. "She wore a white blouse (muslin)", she wrote to Wells thirty years later, "and I thought her then one of the prettiest girls I had ever seen". As soon as Wells was fit to travel, he drew thirty pounds out of the bank and the whole family went off to the seaside at Eastbourne to recuperate.

They stayed in a cottage at the end of the town where the Downs rise up to Beachy Head. After they had been there eight days, Wells wrote a long letter to Miss Robbins reporting on the activities of "your humble servant" who had "been led out daily to an extremely stony beach and there spread out in the sun for three, four or five hours as it might be, and he has there inhaled sea air into such lung as Providence has spared him, sea air mingled with the taint of such crabs as have gone recently from here to that bourne from which no traveller returns". He was busy in the evenings marking examination papers, and spent his nights in "uneasy meditations on Death and the Future Life, and Hope and Indeterminate Equations". *

I am still in a hectic unstable condition. A more serious man than myself would be horribly miserable at his inability to play his part of man in all these troubles. Everything is pressing on my wife's shoulders now, and I dare not exert myself to help for fear I shall give her a greater trouble still.

I sincerely hope you are working hard for your examination. I shall take anything but a first class pass very much to heart, so that I hope you will out of consideration for a poor suffering soul who must not be depressed by any means, do your best. I am looking forward to visiting Red Lion Square next week and seeing you again and conversing diversely with you.

In a footnote Wells said a "dismal article full of jocularities" had seen the light in the *Globe*. He had also written a "feminine and acid" short story which had gone off to *Black and White*. "I think my mind stagnates. It is blocked up with a lot of things. I shall come and talk to you a long time I think and deliver myself."[9]

There is no means of dating the change in the relationship with Miss Robbins. Certainly, in August, he had no formed intention of leaving Isabel. They had moved out of London, to 4 Cumnor Place, one of a row of mock-Tudor houses within a few minutes of Sutton station in Surrey, where he believed that the fresh air of the North Downs would improve his health. He was also writing much more. In September he wrote to Fred in South Africa saying that he was barely covering expenses, but

* To Elizabeth Healey he wrote that he saw ahead "nothing but a long perspective of relapses to the inevitable end".[8]

that "does not really matter until I get a bit better. I am not fretting about it – I have been asked to write articles – which is very much better than writing them on spec. For *Knowledge*, the *Ed. Times*, *Science and Art*, and the *Correspondent*, and indeed I might be doing a lot more than I am."[10]

He had, in fact, at last hit on a way of finding a regular market, and he owed the idea to the chance reading of a novel by J.M.Barrie that he had picked up in the twopenny circulating library near the lodgings in East-bourne. In this book, *When a Man's Single*, one of the characters explains that saleable miscellanies were to be spun out of everyday things like pipes, umbrellas and flower-pots. Wells there and then scribbled the draft of an article, "On the Art of Staying at the Seaside", on the back of an envelope. He sent it off to Bertha Williams, his cousin from Wookey who did his typing in these early years. Then it went on to the *Pall Mall Gazette*. The editor printed it and asked for more. Wells had found the knack, at the moment when a whole new market was opening for just this kind of sketch. Even an incomplete list of his output in 1893 shows how quickly he learned to exploit the new situation.* At least thirty articles are traceable. Their titles range from "Out Banstead Way", "Angels", "The Coal Scuttle" and "Noises of Animals" to "The Art of Being Photographed" and "The Theory of the Perpetual Discomfort of Humanity".

The immediate market was the *Pall Mall Gazette*, one of the small evening papers that abounded in London, which had just been acquired by the American millionaire W.W.Astor. He wanted to work up its modest circulation of just over 12,000 by making it a prestigious paper. He had appointed as his editor a cultured young man named Harry Cust – a shot in the dark, since Cust had no journalistic experience, though he had very good social connections and was a friend of several well-known writers and critics. By encouraging Wells at a critical moment in his career Cust not only provided him with a reasonable income but also gave him the feeling that his work was worthwhile.

The launching of new papers, or the revamping of old ones, was a feature of the Nineties. Unknown adventurers like Newnes, Pearson and Harmsworth were making fortunes by exploiting the new market of the semi-literate. Astor and Cust had the wit to realise that the middle-class

* Two selections of these pieces can be found in *Select Conversations with an Uncle* (1895), the first book he published apart from his two scientific texts, and *Certain Personal Matters* (1897). They show how precisely he followed the model suggested by Barrie's character, whose comments he later said had been "precious words through which I found salvation".

market was changing too. What was wanted now were bright, controversial articles on politics, art, the theatre, travel and science, and this new public wanted good crisp criticism that might help form its still uncertain tastes. Other editors, such as W.T.Stead, W.E.Henley and Frank Harris, had come to the same conclusion, and quite suddenly the demand for good journalism of this kind was greater than the supply. Wells proved to be exactly the kind of journeyman who was needed, and before long Cust was permitting him to sign articles, was giving him books to review and introducing him to other editors who had shown an interest in his work. By November he was able to write to Fred,[11]

The stories I wrote do not seem to be a great success but I have found a good market for chatty articles, and I am doing more and more of these. I had a cheque for £14 13s. from the *Pall Mall Gazette* the day before yesterday for *one month's* contributions. Not bad is it? But that may be a lucky month. However I am not drawing upon my small savings, thank goodness, and I am keeping indoors, and I think pulling round steadily.

"I think now I am almost at the end of my news," he concluded. "It is not a very eventful record, but as someone has written, we are happiest when we have least history. Things have been going easily with us, and so I hope they may continue."

Was Wells simply making easy small talk about things "going easily" in his domestic affairs, or had the idea of breaking up his marriage not yet come to the point of action? On 15 December he was writing to his mother in much the same manner. That same afternoon, there was a curious development. He and Isabel left to spend the weekend with Miss Robbins and her mother in Putney. The meeting certainly precipitated a crisis. Wells was inclined to put it down to a "fit of claustrophobia", a feeling that he must get out of the marriage and that an elopement with Miss Robbins was the obvious line of escape. Possibly Isabel realised during the Putney visit how far things had gone between her husband and the innocent-seeming young girl, and on their return her jealousy had flared out and she had told him bluntly that he must choose between his marriage and the liaison that threatened it. That, at least, was the substance of the account she gave years later to his brother Fred, saying that the separation was on her initiative. *

* There are ten pages in *Tono-Bungay* which describe George Ponderevo's separation from his wife Marion which cannot be far from a direct account of the way Wells parted from Isabel. The events both come suddenly upon the revelation of an affair; in both cases an

Only a few days passed before Wells made his arrangements to leave. He sent for Gregory, who wrote to him many years later recalling the gloomy visit just after Christmas when "you asked me to come to 4 Cumnor Place to see you, and you told me in a walk towards Banstead what you intended to do. I remember very well seeing your trunk in the front room ready for you to take with you the following morning."[12]

On 27 December 1893 Wells gave a longer explanation in a letter to Morley Davies, who had written to say that he was about to be married.[13]

But I am very much afraid that I shall never be able to enter at all into your married life. I have been in very great trouble all of the past year – all the greater because it has been my own private affair. My own marriage has been a very great mistake. I love my wife very tenderly but not as a husband should love his wife, and – as quietly as possible – we are going to separate this New Year. This is putting a very great confidence into your hands. Our determination has been our absolute secret until now. I shall get this house off my hands, and we shall return to different parts of London before the end of January. We are parting not in anger but in sorrow because our tempers interests desires are altogether different. In the end I suppose the thing will be talked about and I want you to understand clearly, and when the time comes to say, that my wife has been noble, loving and faithful to me as few wives can be. It is I that am doing this, and I am doing it because I love another woman with all my being, and it seems a hideous thing for me to continue this comfortable life of legal adultery simply because I cannot have the woman I love.

It was only on 8 February 1894 that Wells wrote to his mother: "This trouble of ours is unavoidable, but I really do not care to go into details. Isabel and I have separated and she is at Hampstead." Joe was informed even later. On 10 August Wells wrote to his father. "I thought Frank who came up to see me a few weeks ago would have explained affairs to you", he said, and assured his father that "I shall be able to do my filial duty by mother and yourself all right."[14]

The elopement was not too easily accomplished. Mrs Robbins was a formidable lady, of genteel Low Church origins. Her husband's death in October 1892 had been a shock, as well as something of a mystery. He had been run over by a train on the up line at Putney station. The death

---

unspoken difference is brought into the open; there is an air of detachment in the way the two couples come to a decision; and both moved inexorably to a quick conclusion. "Our own resolve carried us on our predestined way", says George Ponderevo, adding that "we belonged to each other immensely" and that "there were moments when it needed but a cry, but one word to have united us again for all our lives."

certificate stated that there was not "sufficient evidence to show in what way he came upon the line". He had left her a modest capital. When Catherine ran off with Wells to lodgings in 7 Mornington Place, a barely respectable district between Euston and Camden Town, Mrs Robbins came up from Putney with tearful demands that she return home. Catherine refused. A number of male relatives were brought in to coerce the caddish seducer. He was unmoved. The Robbins family pointed out that both Catherine and Wells were consumptive and their financial prospects were flimsy (after Wells had provided for Isabel he had about one hundred pounds in the bank). The eloping couple chose to take their chances.

It was a strange elopement after all. There was no strong sexual passion driving them together. * Catherine proved as "innocent and ignorant of the material realities of love" as Isabel had been, and once again there were "immense secret disillusionments" though "not a soul in the world about us knew anything of that for some years". The difference was that Catherine fitted the role of understanding companion; she was quick, amusing, and more sophisticated. Her mind was able to move with his perturbations and her cool temperament did not react to his outbursts of irritation. But what, ultimately, held them together was Catherine's willingness to forge those links on the terms that suited Wells. She was willing and indeed eager to adapt herself to new circumstances, and she had a streak of rebellion that made her game for whatever larks and whims took her lover's fancy. Wells had abandoned a wife whom he had been unable to subjugate, and chosen a mistress who was willing to live her life through him and for him.

---

* The words Wells used were "there arose no such sexual fixation between us as still lingered in my mind towards my cousin".

PART TWO
A Man of Letters

7

WRITING AWAY FOR DEAR LIFE

"Queen Victoria", Wells once said, "was like a great paper-weight that for half a century sat upon men's minds, and when she was removed their ideas began to blow about all over the place haphazardly." Britain was approaching the end of a reign as well as the end of a century, and both dates exercised a curious fascination, as if 1900 might prove to be a crucial turning-point in human affairs.[1] The end of a century seems to produce a *fin de siècle* mood, and though the end of the nineteenth century was not marked by the outbreaks of religious millennialism that appeared towards the close of earlier centuries, there was still a widespread feeling that affairs were moving towards some vague reckoning. It might not be the Last Judgement, but a judgement of some kind appeared to be at hand. G. K. Chesterton ridiculed the magic of numbers. "Rationally speaking", he wrote, "there is no more reason for being sad towards the end of a hundred years than towards the end of a hundred fortnights." Yet he conceded that there was a climate of doubt and pessimism, and he attributed this to "a coincident collapse of both religious and political idealism". While there was "no arithmetical autumn . . . there was a spiritual one . . . the sense that man's two great inspirations had failed him altogether".[2]

The late Victorians themselves were very conscious of this sense of crisis. Words like "degeneration", "transition", "renovation" and "reconstruction" were in common use. *Degeneration*, in fact, was the title that Max Nordau gave to the influential book that he published in 1895. "The disposition of the times is curiously confused", he wrote, describing the intellectual mood as "a curious compound of feverish restlessness and blunted discouragement, of fearful presage and hang-dog renunciation."[3] A new order might be emerging, but its outlines shimmered with uncertainty.

In the heyday of Victorianism the key question had been "Is it right?"

After Darwin, Marx and Kelvin, Nietzsche and Schopenhauer, a much more common question was "Where will it all lead?" That anxiety lay behind the frenetic hedonism of the Nineties. They were, for some, a time of eating, drinking and being merry, of champagne suppers at the Café Royal and beer and winkles on Brighton beach, of the Gibson girls, the safety bicycle and the gas-lit stalls outside the music-hall. But what came to be called the "good old days" also produced the hysterical persecution of Oscar Wilde, a boom in beer-shops and pawn-broking, and a population so poorly nourished that half the men who volunteered to fight in the Boer War had to be rejected on medical grounds.

The rules of the Victorian order no longer bound social attitudes or personal taste and behaviour in an inflexible frame. The keyword of the age was "new". Art Nouveau was French; the new drama of Ibsen came from Norway; the new music of Wagner was German; England had the New Unionism and the New Woman, Scotland and Ireland had the new interest of the Celtic revival, and any page of advertisements in the Nineties reveals that the best adjective of commendation for any product was that it was "new". The new state of mind set painters such as William Rothenstein and Walter Sickert free from academic realism; William Morris and Cobden-Sanderson designed new fabrics and launched the Arts and Crafts movement which architects such as Charles Voysey carried through into house-building and furnishing. Bohemianism became acceptable, if not yet respectable. There was something more at work than a mere consciousness of change. There was a deliberate effort to break up the traditional pattern of life and, with defiant bravado, to use the search for novelty as a means of self-expression – shock whom it might. In 1891, in *The Quintessence of Ibsenism*, Shaw remarked that the implication of Ibsen's plays was that it might be morally right to do things one's predecessors had thought infamous – right, that is to say, in terms of self-realisation, because moral emancipation was paramount over moral duty. It was that single thought, more than any other, that energised the shift from Victorian to Edwardian values.[4]

New writers and new publishers seized their opportunity to serve the new literacy of the masses and the new curiosity of the classes. Newnes started *Tit-Bits* in 1891, Harmsworth's *Answers* appeared in 1888, his *Evening News* in 1894, and his *Daily Mail* in 1896 – the year that Pearson launched his *Weekly*. London in 1901 had nineteen morning and ten evening papers, and there were hundreds of weekly and monthly magazines. New publishers such as Heinemann, John Lane, Fisher Unwin, Dent and

Macmillan broke out of the staid conventions of the three-decker novel and the circulating libraries, and printed cheap books for clerks and commuters. Anyone with a spark of talent could get a cheque for five pounds for an article, and anyone with a flicker of reputation could find a publisher for a book. The man of letters was working in a seller's market. There were new novelists, realists such as George Moore and George Gissing, romancers such as Stevenson, Barrie, Rider Haggard, Conan Doyle, Anthony Hope, Marie Corelli and Hall Caine; Meredith, Hardy and James were in their prime, Conrad was beginning to write. But the Nineties were most distinguished by what Wells called an "outburst of short stories", they "broke out everywhere" and "no short story of the slightest distinction went for long unrecognised".[5] All the novelists wrote short stories as a matter of course, and they were joined by new writers who learned their trade and made their reputations in this genre – Kipling, Stephen Crane, Jerome K. Jerome, W.W. Jacobs, Edith Nesbit, Arthur Morrison, Kenneth Grahame and, after 1894, Wells himself.

"Earning a living by writing", Wells wrote in 1919 to his friend, E.S.P. Haynes, "is a frightful gamble. It depends neither on knowledge nor literary quality but upon secondary considerations of timeliness, mental fashion & so forth almost beyond control. I have been lucky but it took me eight years, while I was teaching & then doing anxious journalism, to get established upon a comfortably paying footing. That was in the giant & easy days of Cust."[6]

When Wells and Catherine arrived at their guinea-a-week pair of rooms near Euston early in 1894, they had, Wells said, "no suspicion how wise we had been in getting born exactly when we did. We did not realize we were like two respectable little new ordinary shares in a stock-exchange boom." His apprenticeship was now over. One of the factors in his decision to leave Isabel might have been the scent of success that he had caught in the last months of 1893, when he found that he could actually make a tolerable living from journalism. A letter to his mother, just before Christmas in 1894, summarised Wells's life during that first year with Catherine in a "picshua" of him scribbling away at his desk with the caption: "Little Bertie writing away for dear life to get little things for all his little People sends his love to Little Clock Man Little Daddy Little Mother."[7]

He liked this kind of whimsical intimacy in his close personal relations.

He and Isabel had used pet-names and joke-words, such as those in his letters to his family, to Simmons and Elizabeth Healey, and now he introduced the habit into his relationship with Catherine. As late as 1903 many of their letters were still couched in this style, and regularly signed "Bits" and "Bins". Neither of her given names appealed to him. Soon after she ceased to be Miss Robbins he was experimenting with new nicknames, and for a time they and their friends settled on "Euphemia" – a guise under which she appeared in several of his articles in 1894 and 1895. Eventually he hit upon "Jane", and it was by this name that she was known by intimates for the rest of her life, as he became generally addressed as "H.G.".

For the moment they had little social life. They found the sympathy and confidences of their landlady, Madame Reinach, so intrusive that in March they moved nearby to 12 Mornington Road, where a stoical Scots lady, Mrs Lewis, mothered them very agreeably. There they settled into a routine. Wells would work at a review or an article. Jane would make fair copies, or study for her science examinations – though she never completed her degree. Their afternoons were spent in what Wells called the "article hunt". He and Jane prowled London, from Highgate Cemetery to the Bond Street galleries, from the spreading woods of Epping to the animal cages of the Zoo, grubbing for saleable ideas.

All the time he was learning, both how to write effectively and sell his work at an economic rate, and one can see a relationship between this journalism and much of his later fiction which is not unlike that between *Sketches by Boz* and the Dickens novels. Anything was grist to his grinding mill – an account of his father as a veteran cricketer, an essay on swearing, "A Stray Thought in an Omnibus", or "My Abominable Cold". Squeezed in between these oddments were serious articles, such as "The Extinction of Man", "The Rate of Change in Species" and "The 'Cyclic' Delusion", as well as the first important short stories – "The Stolen Bacillus", "The Lord of the Dynamos", "In the Avu Observatory" and "The Flowering of the Strange Orchid". In the course of 1894 he sold at least seventy-five articles, five stories and one serial. The output was remarkable for a new and still inexperienced author.

For much of the year he continued to write for the educational press, but in a letter to his father in August he announced that he was dropping this work because it took too much effort for too little money. Later in the year he wrote to Simmons:[8]

Cash is an urgent necessity, of course, and if only I could get about 32 hours in the day it would be very well indeed with me. My short stories are going at last – *Truth* and *St James's*. I have the hope of making the best of my *P.M.G.* papers into a book. It makes my heart ache to see the educational papers so dull without me, and to be unable to get anything done for them.

The hope of the book came from discussions with John Lane, though the contract for *Select Conversations with an Uncle* (the character was based on Uncle Williams of the school at Wookey) was not finally signed until 12 March 1895, and even then Lane only undertook to print 650 copies.

Wells was at last "getting his name up". As well as buying his articles for the *Pall Mall Gazette*, Cust had also introduced him to Lewis Hind, then editing the *Pall Mall Budget*. Hind went into Cust's room one day to find Wells, a hunched little figure whose "face was like an electrified note of interrogation, questioning and absorbing everything". Hind commissioned a series of stories – "I touched the button only", he said – in which Wells was to draw upon his stock of scientific knowledge. Wells thought five guineas good pay for a short story with a scientific twist, and Hind soon had the manuscript of "The Stolen Bacillus" on his desk.[9] It was Hind, moreover, who passed Wells on to W.E.Henley, then editing the *National Observer*, which Hind later described as "the best-written paper of the day; it was anti-sentiment, anti-cant, anti-humbug". Though Henley was a high Tory, this posture appealed at once to Wells. In making friends with Henley he had made the contact that was to launch his career. The "rude, boisterous, windy, headstrong Henley", as Henry James described him, was a powerful and impressive man from the waist up and a cripple from the waist downwards – best remembered today as a writer of patriotic verse. As an editor, though given to grumpiness, he had an eye for new talent and collected round him a group of protégés, among them Barrie and Kipling.

When Wells went down to see Henley at Barnes they talked over possible subjects for the *National Observer*. Wells said, "I resolved to do my very best for him and I dug up my peculiar treasure, my old idea of 'time-travelling', from the *Science Schools Journal*." Since he left Holt he had made at least three attempts to improve "The Chronic Argonauts". Late in 1893, when Henley offered him space, Wells worked over the drafts for the fifth time, and produced seven articles which appeared in the *National Observer* between March and June, 1894. They were unsigned, were given different titles, and few readers would have noticed that they were more than a set of miscellanies on the theme of time-travelling.[10]

By the middle of the summer Wells felt his prospects were good enough to take the chance of spending a few months out of London. The local doctor thought that Jane, with tubercular tendencies, was even more poorly than Wells. Their decision to go down to Sevenoaks, where they took lodgings at Tusculum Villa, at 23 Eardley Road near the station, was reinforced by the need to accommodate Mrs Robbins, who had let her house in Putney, was herself unwell, and had sufficiently accepted her daughter's domestic situation to stay with the young couple. It was not a successful move. The landlady made trouble about their unmarried state. Both Wells and Jane felt harassed, and the situation became worse when the nosey landlady found a writ from the divorce court among their papers. Worse still, Wells had misjudged his market. Several magazines decided that they were overstocked with his unused contributions. The *National Observer* was sold over Henley's head and the new editor wanted no more curious peeps into the future. Marriott Watson, the literary editor of the *Pall Mall Gazette*, went off on holiday and his assistant cared less for what Wells was writing. Then Astor announced that he would shortly close the *Pall Mall Budget*, and Hind could buy no more of the scientific stories. Wells discovered he was spending more than he was earning, and he had virtually no reserves.

Henley, however, had not forgotten him. He wrote telling Wells that he was to start *The New Review* as a monthly in January 1895, and that he would like "The Time Traveller" as a serial, and would pay one hundred pounds for the rights. Even better, Henley secured a promise from William Heinemann to take the story in book form for an advance of fifty pounds on a first printing of 10,000 copies, and a royalty of fifteen per cent – a generous offer to an unknown author. Henley was confident that Wells could bring off something unusual. On 28 September 1894 he wrote to Wells:[11]

In your place I should go on! Rather! It may profit you little – though I am not so complacent, by a long way, about that as I was. But it is so full of invention, & the invention is so wonderful, so running over – as I have found – it must certainly make your reputation.

If you still doubt, go to Heinemann, & say I asked you to consult him as to the saleability of this thing in a finished state.

Wells began to work over the articles again. He knew that his "peculiar treasure" was well done, for he wrote that "it's my trump card and if it does not come off very much I shall know my place for the rest of my career".[12] Even when the manuscript was submitted, some important changes were made at Henley's suggestion. As late as 1 April 1895, when the serial was already running, Henley wrote asking Wells to expand the text.[13]

> It seems to me – at this point – with all time before you – you might very well give your fancy play, & at the same time, oblige your editor. The Traveller's stopping might, for instance, begin some periods earlier than they do, & he might even tell us about the last man & his female & the ultimate degeneracy of which they are the proof & the sign or – but you are a better hand at it than I!

Henley was convinced that the story "has gone some way towards placing its author as a man of letters". Henley's encouragement buoyed up Wells through the disagreeable autumn in Sevenoaks. For seven years he had toyed with the notion of time-travelling, and it had survived every distraction and setback. Now, with Henley's backing, the trump card on which he wagered his career as a writer was at last about to be played. Meanwhile, he had to wait, and to go on working.

When they left Sevenoaks Mrs Robbins went to stay with friends and Wells and Jane returned to the lodgings in Mornington Road. While he waited for *The New Review* to come out he went on "writing away for dear life". He pushed ahead with *The Wonderful Visit*, the satirical tale based on Ruskin's remark that if an angel were to appear on earth someone would be sure to shoot it. The first draft of *The Island of Dr Moreau*, the night-marish parody of evolutionary ideas, was already being sketched out.

Wells had touched the spring of creative energy which enabled him to produce new work in a flood in these months. He wrote almost as though he were in a trance, detaching himself from money troubles and shutting out the uneasy distraction of his domestic situation. He was in a state of repressed anger. The cool parting from Isabel had covered confused feelings of passion denied and resentment unexpressed. Just before Christmas he wrote to Elizabeth Healey, who had kept in touch with Isabel, now living in lodgings in Islington.[14]

> Is there anything I can do to help Isabel? I hope you'll go and see her if you possibly can and I'd be very glad to know about her. She writes to me but it's scarcely to be expected that she would tell me very much. It's a dismal tragedy and *it's entirely my doing*. Don't blame anyone else. I can't stop the law of Death. So far as I can see all that is possible for me is to go on with my own work and keep her at least from urgent material necessity and give

her the possibility of change and new interests. Beyond that the less I come into her life the better. She wants friends, sympathy, new interests. But *I* cannot go about finding friends and interests for her, can I? They must seem at least natural interests.

It was not merely guilt about Isabel that was upsetting Wells. He was sexually frustrated, depressed and full of unconscious hostility which broke through into the destructive and pessimistic imagery of his stories. At this point in his life, Wells was just another struggling young writer of talent, scribbling away to inch himself up from journalism into the profession of letters. But in the last months of 1894 and the early part of 1895, his emotional stresses so worked through his imagination that they carried him over the boundary between the superficial and the symbolic that separates the journeyman from the creative writer.

In the year after he left Isabel – their divorce came through in January 1895 – Wells made his mark as a journalist. Grant Richards, then working with W.T.Stead on the *Review of Reviews*, had been led to enthusiasm about this new writer and his stories in the *Pall Mall Budget*.[15] "Extraordinary stories they were – of their kind there have been none better; and apart from the matter, look at the manner, examine it closely, and then compare it with the manner of the other men who had short story reputations in those days." It was Richards, too, who drew Stead's attention to the "Time Traveller" instalments and evoked the first ecstatic compliment Wells ever received. In March 1895 the *Review of Reviews* stated flatly: "H.G.Wells is a man of genius."

Other editors began to take notice. One of them was Frank Harris, who remembered the young man who had written "The Rediscovery of the Unique" when he had been editing the *Fortnightly*. Frank Harris now edited the weekly *Saturday Review*. Once again he set about livening up what had been a dull journal, written by dons for clergymen.[16] Wells was summoned to the office, where he found Bohemia pushing its way up the stairs against the descending representatives of Academia who, dismissed, were on their way out. He was to review novels – armloads carried away to Mornington Road in a hansom cab. Kipling and Hardy had promised stories, Max Beerbohm was commissioned to draw the cartoons, while an Irish music critic and socialist stump speaker named Shaw was to be drama editor.

At the beginning of January 1895, Wells received another summons – a telegram from Cust, who had earlier promised him the chance of the

first vacancy for a regular job on the *P.M.G.* When he arrived, Cust put
two tickets into his hand and informed him that, from the following
night, he had become a theatre critic. Wells protested that his experience
was limited to Gilbert and Sullivan, the Crystal Palace annual pantomime
and two plays. "Exactly what I want", Cust drily replied. "You won't be
in the gang. You'll make a break." Wells had twenty-four hours in which
to get dress clothes made on credit before, on 3 January, he attended the
first night of Wilde's *An Ideal Husband*. Two nights later this new twist
in his career brought him into the company of two men whose lives
threaded significantly through his own a few years later. The play was
Guy Domville, a stilted melodrama that Henry James had persuaded
George Alexander to put on at the St James's Theatre. James badly
wanted a theatrical success, but his play was a humiliating disaster. Wells
watched while James allowed himself to be led out before the curtain. "I
have never heard any sound more devastating", Wells recalled, "than the
crescendo of booing that ensued." The weak plot and the desperate acting infuriated the audience. As Wells left the theatre – "fires and civil
commotions loosen tongues", he said – he struck up a conversation with
one of his colleagues from the *Saturday Review*, a young, bearded Irishman
who wrote articles on music and on the theatre. As they walked away
together, George Bernard Shaw gave Wells an impromptu lecture on the
fashionable three-act play.

Wells did his best to carry out Cust's assignment, but he never had much
sense of the theatre, nor did contemporary stage versions of his tales have
much success. Though he hugely enjoyed charades and amateur theatricals he could never catch the peculiar quality of illusion which must be
fused in a play. In any case, the strain of late nights and days of hard work
was telling on him, and his chest was again giving him trouble. Once more
he had to take the risk of moving back into the country and trying to make
a living from fiction rather than journalism. His financial position was
now reasonably comfortable. On 5 February 1895 he wrote to his parents
to say that he could afford to give them sixty pounds a year rather than
the forty they had asked for, and that it was "a dream of mine to get you
into rather a better house". He added affectionately: "Whatever success I
have, you are responsible for the beginnings of it. However hard up you
were when I was a youngster you let me have paper and pencils, books
from the Institute and so forth and if I haven't my mother to thank for my
imagination and my father for skill, where did I get these qualities?"[17]

In March he took a week's holiday at Sidmouth, in Devon, and then in

April he resigned his position on the *Pall Mall Gazette*, and he and Jane began to look about for a house outside London. He was not depressed, despite this new setback in his health. In May 1895 he wrote a cheerful letter to Simmons.[18]

I'm in a gorgeous state of cockiness just now, as Dent & Co have agreed to buy a book – a new one – of which there are missing the first sixty or seventy pages. It's bran new – not the beast people idea – but a thing about a vicar and an angel – grotesque and humorous. *The Island of Dr Moreau* is under offer with Methuens an American firm and from what Henley says it's going to go.

He went on to say that he had been day-dreaming about what fifteen per cent of various sales would bring in when Heinemann put "The Time Traveller" serial out as a book, and that he had been looking at a little house in Woking – to which they moved that summer.

Wells was relying very much on Henley's encouragement and advice. Yet, while Henley was coaching him, the experienced editor was honestly warning him as well. Later in the year, on 5 September, when *The Wonderful Visit* was published, Henley wrote saying how much the book had made him laugh and then offering a cautionary word.[19]

There is brains in the book; brains to any extent. Brains; & character; & humour . . . for heaven's sake, take care of yourself. You have a unique talent; and – you have produced three books, at least, within the year, & are up to the elbows in a fourth! It is magnificent, of course; but it can't be literature . . . I believe in your imagination; & I don't want to see it foundered. I believe in your future; & I don't want to see it commonplaced. And you really frighten me: you work so easily . . . but you could also do better – far better; & to begin with, you must begin by taking yourself more seriously.

Henley had seen what Wells was doing in an effort to establish himself quickly. Poor health and poor circumstances had combined to force on his native impatience, so that the very quickness and flexibility which enabled him to write so fluently were being used to put on a magnificent performance, "but it can't be literature". Wells himself knew the criticism was well-aimed, but he felt he could not afford to let it drive home. In a letter written only two years later, he looked back on this period and admitted that "for the last three years I have been banging away with the idea of keeping myself before the public. When *The Time Machine* came out (1895) I was a journalist living from hand to mouth & I thought it wiser to turn out a succession of striking if rather unfinished books & so

1 Sarah Wells

2 Joseph Wells

3 Bromley. Atlas House (No. 47) is on the left

4 H.G.Wells, aged 10
5 Dame School, South Street, Bromley
6 (*below*) Morley's Academy, the classroom built out at the rear

7 (*opposite*) Up Park. The Servants' Hall is at the extreme left, and the housekeeper's room occupied by Sarah Wells is at the right-hand corner of the basement
8 North Street, Midhurst. The Grammar School is at the far end of the street on the left
9 Normal School of Science, South Kensington

10 (*above left*) T.H.Huxley

11 H.G.Wells as a student. The skeleton is that used by T.H.Huxley for demonstrations in his lectures

12 Wells meditates on his future, summer 1886. "Picshua" in a letter to A.T.Simmons

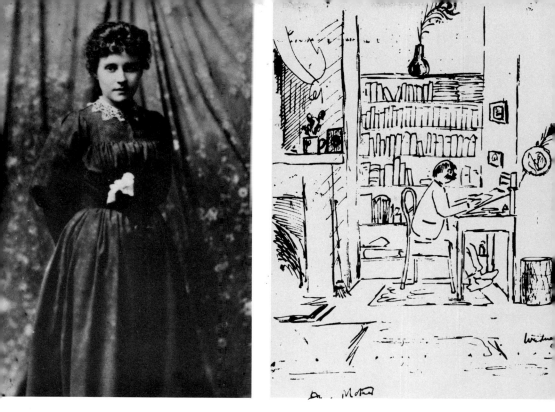

13 Isabel Wells
14 Wells at work. "Picshua" in a letter to Sarah Wells from Fitzroy Road, 21 September 1892

15 The invalid teacher. An early letter from Wells to Amy Catherine Robbins, 26 May 1893

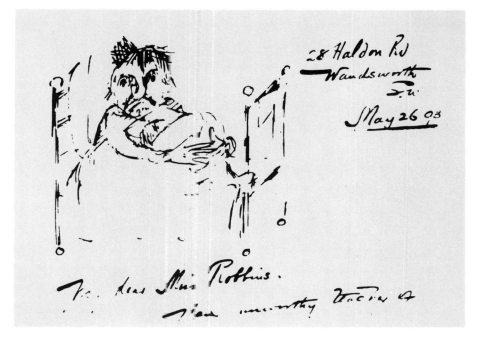

16 Tusculum Villa, Sevenoaks. The house in which Wells wrote *The Time Machine*
17 H.G. and Jane Wells. Cycling at Woking, 1895

18 H.G. and Jane Wells. Boating, 1895

19 Spade House
20 (*right*) Wells aged
thirty

21 Sandgate, Kent

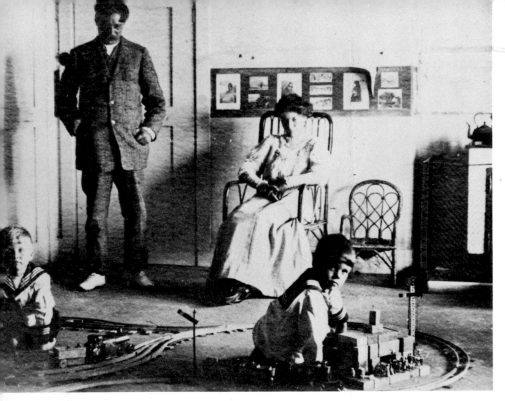

22 The nursery,
Spade House
23 Frank, Jane
and Gip Wells

escape from journalism than to let myself be forgotten again while I elaborated a masterpiece – saving my limitations."[20]

Meanwhile, it seemed that his effort to escape was succeeding. In 1893, when his income was made up of teaching fees and journalism, he earned £380.13s.7d. After he ran away with Jane, he raised the total to £583.17s.7d. in 1894. At the end of 1895 he had received £792.2s.5d., entirely from writing, and he was able to get his parents out of the Nyewoods cottage into a better house near Liss, where they went early in 1896.

The books provided only a fraction of that income in 1895. What mattered more was that they were on the market – *Select Conversations with an Uncle* in June, *The Time Machine* a day afterwards, *The Wonderful Visit* in September and *The Stolen Bacillus and other Incidents* in November. Though the first review, in the *Athenaeum*, declared that *Select Conversations* was "portentously foolish" and patronisingly observed that at least John Lane had provided it with "a very nice cover",[21] *The Time Machine* made a mark and *The Wonderful Visit* also received good notices, and both were selling well that autumn. By bringing out four books so close together, when his signature had already become known to the influential readership of the *P.M.G.*, the *Saturday Review* and *The New Review*, Wells made sure that the critics would discuss his work and that other publishers would seek him out.

In October Wells and Jane went back to their old lodging in Mornington Road for three weeks. They were married from this address on 27 October 1895. While they were staying there, Wells wrote to his mother in high spirits about *The Wonderful Visit*.[22]

My last book seems a hit – everyone has heard of it – and all kinds of people seem disposed to make much of me. I've told nobody scarcely that we were coming up and already I'm invited out to-night and every night next week except Monday and Friday. I've had letters too from four publishing firms asking for the offer of my next book but I shall, I think, stick to my first connexion. It's rather pleasant to find oneself something in the world after all the years of trying and disappointment.

Wells did not abide by his intention to "stick to my first connexion" in publishing. From late 1895 he began an extraordinary process of bargaining and badgering with publishers which lasted until his death.[23] It was not simply that Wells wanted money. He early formed the belief that if a publisher was forced to pay excessively favourable terms, he would then be driven to excessively energetic efforts to recoup his investment. He was also intensely suspicious, and one or two small instances of sharp practice confirmed his view that any unwatched publisher might well swindle him of his due. The result was that Wells was always in the market, and no publisher could ever be sure that he would have the next book, or on what terms he would get it; and even when a contract was signed he could expect a steady flow of criticism of his shortcomings and attempts to tell him how to run his business.

In Woking, Wells had found a house near the main-line railway to the South-West and close to open heathland. Lynton, in Maybury Road, was a semi-detached villa, which they furnished with a hundred pounds that Mrs Robbins raised by a mortgage on her Putney house. Wells had not yet been able to raise sufficient capital; though his income had begun to rise, he was paying Isabel alimony at the rate of one hundred pounds a year, and another sixty pounds were committed to his parents. It was pleasant to have a decent house and a garden of their own. A chirpy drawing by Wells in early September 1895 showed Jane and himself proudly walking up to the house carrying their first marrow.[24] Wells was more comfortable in Woking. There had been stresses in their social situation in London. Until they were married, it was not possible for them to go about together socially except to visit close friends, and when Wells accepted invitations Jane often had to stay behind. Even then he was uneasy in company, unsure of his manners and given to shyness. He knew he lacked polish. He had a very high-pitched voice, between a husky squeak and a falsetto, and something of a cockney accent. Though his appearance improved as he grew older and put on some weight and dressed better, he still gave an impression of being a counter-jumper.

In Woking they could make their own routine of work in the mornings and evenings, with the afternoons free for walks or bicycle rides through Surrey and Hampshire. Cycling had become a national craze. It was a cheap and healthy hobby, which spread through all classes with the coming of the safety bicycle. When men and women could take to the roads together, the last blow was struck at the declining habit of chaperonage. It was a mark of the New Freedom. Wells became an early enthusiast. Some of his letters at this time include amusing drawings of disasters that befell them on these trips. After one fall Wells jotted down a description of himself that he developed into the opening of *The Wheels of Chance*, the picaresque novel he wrote at Woking about the cycling holiday of Mr Hoopdriver, the draper's assistant. His enthusiasm for cycling was matched by an endurance that was remarkable for a small man in poor health. He and Jane took long rides, even holidays that took them as far as Devonshire. Wells also ordered a tandem of his own design from the Humber company – Jane perched on the front seat while Wells, behind her, held the special handlebars which guided the front wheel.[25]

Apart from a number of his best-known short stories, and *The Wheels of Chance*, Wells wrote *The Invisible Man* and *The War of the Worlds* at Woking. The cycling romance showed what he could do when he felt cheerful. It was a slight book of sentimental comedy which cashed in on the craze for cycling, with the charm and social sympathy which was the most attractive side of Wells's character and writing. The other two tales were in a different, more savage vein, with Wells revealing the gusto with which he could let his destructive feelings rip in a story. "I'm doing the dearest little serial for Pearson's new magazine", he wrote to Elizabeth Healey, describing how he cycled around to find the topographical detail for *The War of the Worlds*, "in which I completely wreck and sack Woking – killing my neighbours in painful and eccentric ways – then proceed via Kingston and Richmond to London, which I sack, selecting South Kensington for feats of peculiar atrocity."[26]

As Wells became a man of letters he acquired a man of business. The idea of a "literary agent" was a new one – it seems that the phrase was coined by the first of them, A. P. Watt, but soon after Watt a small lively Scotsman named James Brand Pinker set up in the same line. Pinker had worked his way up by journalism and had been appointed editor of the new *Pearson's* magazine. But he resigned before the first number appeared, establishing himself in an office just off the Strand with the intention of representing authors – for a former editor, a case of gamekeeper turning poacher. On 13 January 1896, just as he started his new venture, Pinker wrote to Wells saying "my friend, Marriott Watson, has written to you of my enterprise. He thought you might place your affairs in my hands."[27] Wells took the advice of the man who had done so much for him on the *P.M.G.* and became one of Pinker's first clients.

Pinker made a reputation as a successful agent as fast as some of the young men on his list made a name for themselves as authors – and for that reason. He had the knack of picking winners which made winners come to him. Oscar Wilde brought him *The Ballad of Reading Gaol*. Stephen Crane sought him out when he arrived in London. Through Wells he later added James and Bennett to his list, and it was his support that kept Conrad going in the years before his books began to yield a living income. Publishers knew him as a hard bargainer, as well as a man with flair. Some people liked him, but he was not generally popular and, some years later, D.H.Lawrence went so far as to call him "that little parvenu snob of a procureur of books".

He was indeed a parvenu. That was one of the things about him that appealed to Wells, who always felt easier with men who had risen from modest circumstances. Wells was not put off by Pinker's dash of *arriviste* flamboyance. What mattered to him was that Pinker seemed the man for the job. He knew the ropes. He stood up for his clients. He had good connections with publishers and editors in Europe and America. Not least, he was in with the "right" people, the *P.M.G.* crowd, several of whom lived near his Surrey home, Henley, Pett Ridge, Jerome K.Jerome, W.W.Jacobs, and Grant Allen.

Wells soon began to think of moving from Woking, because he needed more room to work (the books done at Woking were written on the dining-room table) and because Mrs Robbins now proposed to live with them. It was Pinker who helped him to find "Heatherlea" – "a picturesque and insanitary house in the early Victorian style", he wrote to Grant Allen, adding that Worcester Park "is inhabited by amateur poultry fanciers and dog lovers with occasional literary men".[28] It was a great improvement over the Woking villa, by the degree that half an acre of land is better than a garden near the railway tracks, and it marked the extraordinary success that Wells had enjoyed in the year after the publication of *The Time Machine*. His books were now widely noticed and discussed, and they were among the best-sellers for parts of that year. Translations were already in hand and where – a year previously – he had been glad to get an advance of fifty pounds from a publisher, Pinker was now talking in hundreds. H.G. had begun to form a widening circle of friends, who found him lively and amusing, and since his income now crossed the magic frontier of four figures for the first time, he at last had the means to entertain them in some style.

On the last day of 1896 he was able to write triumphantly to his brother Fred in South Africa:[29]

I have been still on the rise of fortune's wave this year, and it seems as though I must certainly go on to still larger successes and gains next for my name still spreads abroad, and people I have never seen, some from Chicago, one from Cape Town, and one from far up the Yung Tse Kiang in China, write and tell me they find my books pleasant. So far it has meant more fame than money to me, but I hope next year that the gilt edge will come to my successes – . . . I feel uncommonly cheerful and hopeful, not only for myself but for the whole blessed family of us.

All through 1894 and 1895 Wells had been writing away for dear life. By the end of 1896 he knew that the gamble had paid off. There was always the chance, he feared, that captious Providence might strike back at him again. His health was still precarious. Yet, whatever worries he had about his physical prospects, there was no longer any doubt of his prospects as a writer. On his thirtieth birthday he already felt the rise of fortune's wave that would carry him up into the new century as a prosperous and increasingly admired man of letters.

TALES OF SPACE AND TIME

Wells drudged for nearly ten years before he found a market as a writer. In three more years he achieved fame and put himself in the way of wealth. "It did not take us long", Ford Madox Ford* said, "to recognize that here was Genius. Authentic, real Genius. And delightful at that." What had caught public fancy, Ford added, was "Mr Wells's brand of Science . . . Fairy tales are a prime necessity of the world, and 'he and Science were going to provide us with a perfectly new brand'. And he did. And all Great London lay prostrate at his feet."[1]

Writing away for dear life, Wells produced *The Time Machine, The Wonderful Visit, The Wheels of Chance, The Island of Dr Moreau, The Invisible Man*, and *The War of the Worlds* in quick succession. They were all published before the end of 1897. In the same period he also wrote the majority of his short stories, which appeared individually and then in such short collections as *The Stolen Bacillus and Other Incidents* (1895), *The Plattner Story and Others* (1897), *Thirty Strange Stories* (1898) and *Tales of Space and Time* (1899). It was an astonishing burst of productivity for an inexperienced writer with indifferent health – an average of one book and thirty stories or articles every six months, and well over a million words in all.[2]

Ford was right to say that Wells took literary London by storm. Scarcely a week passed without a new piece over Wells's signature, or without some notice of his work which drew attention to the originality of his ideas, the compelling readability of his narratives and the freshness of his style. Wells was being talked up, and taken up.

It was clear at once that Wells had a great talent, if not the genius Ford acclaimed. It was not so evident at first – and his versatility made it more difficult to "place" him – what that talent was, or by what standards it

* Ford Madox Hueffer changed his surname to Ford during the First World War. For consistency of reference he is called Ford Madox Ford in all following pages.

should be judged. Was he a serious writer, an exponent of modern science, or simply a spinner of tales which gave a scientific twist to the popular vogue for the supernatural? Was he a man with a flair for the picaresque, or a critic of society who used satire in the manner of Swift and Defoe?

Wells himself, who was both experimenting in his work and anxious to sell whatever came freely from his pen, was partly responsible for this uncertainty. His apprenticeship as a journalist reinforced a natural gift for sensing the shifts in public taste, and throughout his career he was astonishingly successful at catching the wave of a new fashion as it began to break. The critics of the day were confused by the changes in literary style and tried to make sense of them by putting new writers into old categories. "Anybody fresh who turned up", Wells remarked, "was treated as an aspirant Dalai Lama is treated, and scrutinized for evidence of his predecessor's soul. So it came about that every one of us who started writing in the nineties was discovered to be a 'second' – somebody or other." Wells was successively labelled as a second Bulwer–Lytton, a second Dickens, a second Barrie, Kipling or Jules Verne. "A sheaf of second-hand tickets to literary distinction was thrust into our hands and hardly anyone could get a straight ticket on his own", Wells added. He was saved from being pinned down in any of these roles, he wrote, "by the perplexing variety of my early attributions".

The most obvious of all these comparisons was that between Wells and Verne. "There was a disposition on the part of literary journalists at one time to call me the English Jules Verne", Wells wrote in 1933.[3]

As a matter of fact there is no literary resemblance whatever between the anticipatory inventions of the great Frenchman and these fantasies. His work always dealt with the actual possibilities of invention and discovery, and he made some remarkable forecasts. The interest he invoked was a practical one; he wrote and believed that this or that thing could be done, which was not at that time done. It helped his readers to imagine it done and to realize what fun, excitement or mischief could ensue.

Verne took the same view. In an interview in 1903 he said of Wells that "I do not see the possibility of comparison between his work and mine . . . his stories do not repose on very scientific bases . . . I make use of physics. He invents."[4] The interesting comparison lies in the use each made of his talent for fusing science and adventure. Wells always wrote as a moralist, concerned with man's place among the mysteries of Nature, or the social implications of mastering them. Verne reflected mid-century optimism about progress, celebrated the advance of science, and conscientiously tried to work out what marvels might lie on the hidden agenda of the future. The similarity of their subject-matter obscured this contrast between the pessimist and the positivist.

What really distinguished Wells was the symbolic power of his stories. His tales whirled with images, theories and facts which were never brought into any systematic relation with each other. When Wells referred to the first drafts of *The Time Machine* as his "peculiar treasure" he had said more than he consciously intended. That book was only the first nugget in a vein that ran deep in him and, as he worked furiously to exploit it, yielded some of his richest work. The image of hidden treasure, or of a gold mine was apt, for it suggested that Wells had found a way of digging into himself to uncover buried feelings and even archetypal patterns of thought. His own account of the way he wrote at the beginning of his career described how his stories emerged from the twilight of consciousness.[5] He had found a knack of writing that was similar to the process of dreaming, in which powerful and primitive emotions were translated into visual images.

I found that, taking almost anything as a starting point and letting my thoughts play about with it, there would presently come out of the darkness, in a manner quite inexplicable, some absurd or vivid little nucleus. Little men in canoes upon sunlit oceans would come floating out of nothingness, incubating the eggs of prehistoric monsters unawares; violent conflicts would break out amidst the flower-beds of suburban gardens; I would discover I was peering into remote and mysterious worlds ruled by an order logical indeed but other than our common sanity.

By this means Wells produced stories which were rich in symbolism, and dreamlike in their structure. They had the same sudden shifts of locale and even viewpoint, the bizarre events erupting into the familiar, and even the inconsequential endings which are characteristic of dreams. Examples can be found in "Under the Knife", "The Remarkable Case of Davidson's Eyes", "Pollock and the Porroh Man", and at a more cosmic level, "The Last Trump" and "The Man Who Could Work Miracles". Several of the stories, moreover, used the theme of the *doppelganger* – the idea of double identity. In "The Late Mr Elvesham", "The Stolen Body" and "The Plattner Story" Wells revealed his fascination with the idea of dual personality which breaks out repeatedly in his later fiction.

It was this capacity to touch unconscious fears and fantasies, and set the archaic monsters produced by his imagination in a modern scientific context, that gave Wells the creative power which the serious critics were quick to notice. Yet this elemental level of writing lay beneath a veneer of the superficial, the sentimental and the sensational which Wells, in his haste for success, laid over it. He snatched quickly at any material that was at hand to furnish his stories. The demonic energy which powered his writing came from within him, but he cared little where he found the vehicles it drove.

Wells was not merely careless of the degree to which he allowed his own life to slide into his writing. He was equally free in his use of other sources. This does not mean that Wells plagiarised the work of other writers out of laziness or cupidity. It was simply that he thought no more about using a plot from Poe or Flammarion than he did about cannibalising his own newspaper articles, basing *Love and Mr Lewisham* on his student years at South Kensington, drawing upon his memories of Hyde's drapery store for *Kipps*, or describing his first marriage in *Tono-Bungay*. He candidly confessed that he had learned to write by imitation when he was at the Normal School, at Holt and Up Park, and when he began to compose at a great pace after 1894 there was no good reason for him to scrutinise what he wrote to assess his indebtedness to Poe, Maupassant, or contemporaries from whom he borrowed plots and ideas.[6]

The interest does not lie so much in the source of his stories as in what he made of the material he borrowed. Wells modified and improved, for example, a tale by Camille de Flammarion, the French writer of scientific and cosmic romances, who published *La Fin du Monde* in 1893. This story of a wandering comet on a collision course with earth was just another of the end-of-the-world fantasies which were popular towards the close of the century – along with tales of horror and the supernatural, romances of lost worlds and adventure books about ruined civilisations. Wells tried all these genres as a matter of course, but when he imitated he did so with a purpose. He selected models which matched his own psychic pre-occupations (such as the feeling of double identity or the alienation of the outsider) or his cosmic obsessions (such as the nature of man and the fate of his planet). "The Star", which Wells wrote four years after Flammarion's story appeared, illustrated the point. Flammarion had written a pot-boiler: Wells turned the crude little tale into an allegory. The Day of Terrors produced by the onrushing star became part of an apocalyptic design, intended to warn as well as shock, for the star was treated as a portent of the judgement which will precede the building of the New Jerusalem.

The sense of an impending apocalypse pervades all the scientific romances. Wells shared this sense with many of his contemporaries, but it was accentuated in his work by three important and equally gloomy influences upon the way he perceived the world and his own place in it.

The first was the brooding sense of impending collapse, both of the business and the family, which hung over Atlas House. This was intensified by his persistent ill-health and his fears of an early death. It was but a short step from his fears of his own extinction to a more generalised fear of the Extinction of Man. The second was the effect of his childhood religion, which made Wells peculiarly susceptible to any theory of biology or cosmogony which suggested that man's place in nature might be precarious, and that a way of avoiding the last of all judgements might lie – in Huxley's phrase – in his success in "checking the cosmic process at every step". And, thirdly, at South Kensington, Wells not only absorbed Huxley's pessimistic gloss on evolutionary theory, but he was also affected by the work of Kelvin and others who insisted that the law of entropy would eventually lead to a cooling of the sun and the reduction of the planets to a system of dead matter whirling in the nothingness of space.

Wells never clearly distinguished between the possible causes of the eventual fall of mankind. In some of his stories and prophetic writings he was obsessed with the idea of total extinction – of man, and of all living things. This, he suggested, might be the result of the law of entropy or of some cosmic disaster. In other books he was more concerned with the evolutionary process which, unchecked, might lead to the decline of the human race as the dominant species and its replacement by sinister successors lurking in the wings to take over. In a depressed mood he veered towards the prospects of extinction; and when he found that thought unbearable he swung back towards the hope that some means might be found to defy the laws of evolution so that mankind could become their master rather than their victim. The confusion between these two points of view ran right through his work, and it was compounded by the fact that he often ran one into the other in the same story or article. Their effect was similar, but their implications were different. In the first case there was very little man could do about his own destiny and that of his planet but accept it as stoically as possible. In the second, it was urgent for those who believed that salvation from evolutionary fate was possible to discover and preach the ways in which it might be achieved. The ambivalence shows how Wells always sought to reconcile the scientific concepts he had acquired at South Kensington with the doctrines of evangelical belief.

His uncertainty in this respect lasted through his life, but it was already evident when he was writing *The Time Machine* – a book whose main emphasis was on the running down first of the human race and then of the universe. For, simultaneously, he wrote a short but significant article for the *Pall Mall Gazette* on "The Extinction of Man". This stressed the hidden menace in Nature, and attacked the complacent assumption that having inherited the earth man could expect indefinitely to dominate it.[7]

Even now, for all we can tell, the coming terror may be crouching for its spring and the fall of humanity be at hand. In the case of every other predominant animal the world has ever seen . . . the hour of its complete ascendency has been the eve of its entire overthrow.

In this article Wells singled out the cephalopod and the ant as man's possible successors, and several of the short stories written at this time picked up the same idea. The cephalopods strike mysteriously in "The Sea Raiders", the ants take over in "The Empire of the Ants", great landcrabs appear in *The Time Machine*. Strange creatures rule the depths in "In the Abyss", come out of the darkness in "The Avu Observatory", descend from Mars in *The War of the Worlds* or inhabit the sub-lunar caverns in *The First Men in the Moon*. All of them are menacing, actual or symbolic adversaries to the human beings who, as Wells put it in the opening paragraph of *The War of the Worlds*, go "to and fro over this globe about their little affairs, serene in their assurance of their empire over matter".

A sense of time, as the dimension against which man's past and future might be measured, and his present complacency judged, was the most original contribution that Wells brought to English fiction. His feeling for the span of time was both biological and cosmic, and the device of timetravelling was only one of the means he employed to make this point.

Part of the appeal of *The Time Machine* was undoubtedly the contemporary concern with the problem of time. It was not merely the new biology that was evolutionary. Comte and Spencer had applied the idea to the growth of human society before Wallace and Darwin demonstrated its application in Nature. The new geology, the new astronomy, the new mathematics and the new physics were all sciences vitally concerned with time. From the middle of the century, in fact, science had been dramatically changing the dimensions of existence. Fundamentalists who clung to Archbishop Ussher's sacred date of 4004 B.C. for the Creation became as ridiculous as the flat-earthers. Within a couple of decades the chronologies of life and matter had been pushed back not by millions of years but by tens of millions. Ideas of the uniqueness of man and the special place of his planet in the scheme of things were undermined as astronomy enlarged the frontiers of the known universe to show that the solar system was dwarfed by an infinite series of galaxies, and that life might well exist on other possible worlds. The late Victorians, indeed, found new conceptions of time pressing upon them at every point. And this new view of the universe was matched by a new view of society as, under the impetus of population growth, urbanisation and the application of science and technology, the social system changed dramatically.[8]

For those who believed in progress, this feeling of movement could be inspiring. For those with doubts, it could be deeply depressing. Time's wingéd chariot might well be driving mankind and its habitat to a stop. "If you believe in improvement", Joseph Conrad wrote to Cunninghame-Graham in 1898, "you must weep, for the attained perfection must end in cold, darkness, and silence."[9] It was in this context that Wells and his contemporaries faced the vital question about the end of Victorian England. Was this confused twilight a dawn or a dusk? Was everything in every way getting better and better, or were all the signs of change simply harbingers of catastrophe?

The contrast between a smug faith in inevitable progress and the possibilities of degeneration was the main point that Wells was making when he launched his Time Traveller out of a cosy Richmond dinner-party into a series of increasingly frightening situations. This device of setting a "normal" individual in a strange or menacing environment was to be used repeatedly by Wells. It served his radical purpose of shocking bourgeois complacency. It also enabled him to make a more profound point than the mutability of the comfortable world of the late Victorian middle class. By setting the end of *The Time Machine* so far in the future, beyond the Golden Age in which the Time Traveller enters the world of the charming but decadent Eloi, beyond even the Sunset of Mankind, Wells converted Huxley's cosmic pessimism into a vision of the final nullity beyond all temporal ideas of good and evil.

The method whereby Wells arrived at this prophecy of extinction was itself significant. It was, to put it simply, the reversal of the Darwinian pattern of evolution – the process whereby man evolved was run backwards and, for the purposes of the story, the stages of the evolutionary process were telescoped.* In this way Wells explicitly rejected the idea of continuing linear progress, in which natural selection would lead to the evolution of ever higher forms of life and, picking up Huxley's belief that evolution was just as likely to result in regression as in progression, he turned post-Darwinian optimism into a cyclic theory. "The theory of evolution", Huxley had written, "encourages our intellectual anticipations. If, for millions of years, our globe has taken the upward road, yet, sometime, the summit will be reached and the downward route will be commenced."[10] When Wells let his imagination play on Huxley's phrase, the result was curiously close to much older religious concepts of Man placed at the centre of symmetrical chronology running from the Creation to the Last Judgement.

Throughout the narrative, moreover, Wells stressed the themes of degeneration and regression. The gentle Eloi are not the cultured people they seem at first. They are a decadent sub-species, farmed as cattle for the carnivorous Morlocks, the machine-minders who have retreated to a subterranean existence. Both the Eloi and the Morlocks have been produced by a genetic differentiation which stems from the earlier separation of the ruling class and the proletariat – and here Wells inverts the optimism of the Marxist theory of the class struggle as he had already inverted Darwin. His vision of the future becomes as shocking to the socialist or humanist as to the bourgeois reader. The imagery may also be read in religious terms. The Eloi are ethereal, wandering through what appears to be a new Eden, like pre-Raphaelite angels; the Morlocks are chthonic, children of darkness living in the pit from which they emerge as predators of the flesh and the spirit.† In visual terms, as well as conceptually, Wells thus conjures up the antithesis one sees in a triptych of the Last Judgement – with the difference that this vision leaves no place

* The way in which Wells changed the Darwinian seriation from a plus to a minus sign, so that the evolutionary mechanism unwinds before the reader, has been demonstrated by Darko Suvin, in an essay on *The Time Machine*. He shows how Wells makes the future a crude mirror-image of the past, so that the differentiation of Man into groups (Eloi and Morlocks) is followed first (in an earlier draft) by a marsupial phase, then by an age of land-crabs and primitive marine life – the "thing" from the sea – and finally by the last lichens on the shore of a cold dark sea. The succession, Suvin remarks, is more "a kind of folk biology" than a laboured effort to recapitulate each of the stages in the Darwinian series.[11]

† The image of the under-world is also an echo of the life of the "Downstairs Persons" at Up Park. The shafts above the tunnels leading to the lair of the Morlocks recall those which open into the Up Park drive.

for the hope of salvation. God has already gone from his world, and has been replaced by a remorseless decline towards the Absolute. Man, too, is about to disappear. The Eloi and the Morlocks live in the year 802701 (a numerical series that contains a further hint that the machine is running down), but the following episodes jump millions of years in a few pages, as if Wells was trying to shrink even further the brief ascendancy of the human species. The earth has stopped rotating, and one hemisphere constantly faces the dying sun in a black sky. The scene is painted in the cosmic colours of the final eclipse. Hope and fear have died together, and light and dark move towards their final merger. To the question, Is it Dawn or Dusk? Wells had answered that mankind was ultimately doomed, and that its prospect is not Salvation but Extinction. Despite all the hopes of Science the end must be "darkness still".

Superficially there appeared to be little in common between *The Time Machine* and *The Wonderful Visit*, but Wells had in fact inverted the story of the Time Traveller. In the first book an ordinary human being was transported into a future society very different from our own. In the second, the Angel plummets into the world of men, and the villagers persecute him in much the same way as the Morlocks pursued the Time Traveller. "The Angel of this story", Wells wrote, "is the Angel of Art", and his purpose is to suggest the narrowness and pettiness of ordinary life, especially the kind of positivist science he had disliked in his last years at South Kensington. The Vicar, who has shot down the Angel in the mistaken idea that he is a giant bird, is the only sympathetic character apart from the little parlourmaid who falls in love with the Angel. Dr Crump, the village savant, who is called upon to treat the Angel's gunshot wounds, mutters away about the Angel's deformities and his "degenerate" physique like a demonstrator in an anatomy class. Crump can only suggest one way of making the Angel more human, and that is to use manipulative surgery, the same technique that Dr Moreau employs to turn beasts into men. In *The Wonderful Visit* the Angel is a suffering and innocent victim of social Darwinism – the crude and competitive doctrine of the survival of the fittest.

"The strange thing", said the Angel, "is the readiness of you Human Beings – the zest with which you inflict pain ... Everyone seems to be busy giving pain ... " "Or avoiding it", said the Vicar ... "Yes, of course. It's fighting everywhere. The whole living world is a battlefield – the whole world. We are driven by Pain."

This Hobbesian image of life being nasty, mean and brutish was more fully developed in *The Island of Dr Moreau*, in which Wells described the agony of beasts made half-human by surgery. The idea which links the two books is that pain is the purgatory through which mankind must inevitably pass on its evolutionary pilgrimage. "Each time I dip a living creature into the bath of burning pain", Dr Moreau remarks, "I say, this time I will burn out all the animal, this time I will make a rational creature of my own." Much the same point had already been made by the Time Traveller. "We are kept keen", he said, "on the grindstone of pain and necessity. It is a law of nature that we overlook, that intellectual versatility is the compensation for change, danger and trouble." Wells had come to a grim conclusion that many critics found distasteful. The *Speaker* attacked the book for its "originality at the expense of decency . . . and common sense"; the *Athenaeum* asked "how far it is legitimate to create feelings of disgust in a work of art"; and *The Times* denounced it for a "perverse quest after anything in any shape that is freshly sensational". What really upset people, however, was what the *Spectator* called "a foul ambition to remake God's creatures".[12] The book seemed overtly blasphemous, as if Wells were implying that the Divine Purpose which had rough-hewn humanity from the instinctual animal had employed suffering for its instrument in the way that Moreau had used the scalpel. As *The Guardian* critic put it, Wells was apparently seeking "to parody the work of the Creator of the human race, and cast contempt upon the dealings of God with his creatures".[13] It would be more accurate to say that Wells believed that it was the evolutionary process itself which was both blind and cruel. The problem, as he saw it, was how to escape the laws of evolution so that mankind need no longer be their suffering victim.

Whether one regards Moreau as a parody of the Almighty, or Providence, or simply as a caricature of a scientist concerned with ends, rather than the ethics of means, the portrait is unrelentingly savage. "The study of Nature", Moreau says, "makes a man at last as remorseless as Nature", and there is nothing in the book to hold out much hope for man. He is still only half a human being, a creature torn between its mental aspirations and its instinctual drives, and thereby condemned to unending pain and torment. In case the analogy between Moreau's beasts and "normal" man had been missed, Wells underlined it. After the final horrors on the island after Moreau's death, the beast-men begin to regress. Prendrick, the scientist who has been cast away on the island, manages to escape, and he returns to London. There he looks at the "blank expressionless faces of people on trains and omnibuses". They frighten him, because "I could not persuade myself that the men and women I met were not also another, still passably human, Beast-People, animals half-wrought into the outward image of human souls." They too may regress. Prendrick fears that "they would presently begin to revert, to show first this bestial mark and then that". There is no evolutionary optimism here, no suggestion that progress will surely come from the working of the laws of Nature. On the contrary, it is fear and despair rather than hope that drive man to seek a way of escape from the evolutionary process that remorselessly carries his species towards extinction.

With *The Wheels of Chance* Wells gave himself and his readers an agreeable respite from monsters, but *The Invisible Man* soon picked up the argument where it had been left in *The Island of Dr Moreau*. Griffin, the mad scientist, is an atavistic figure who degenerates into a homicidal maniac. Like Moreau he is possessed by the illusion of omnipotence, and he is as murderous as the Martians in *The War of the Worlds* – and equally vulnerable, for all his science, to the laws of Nature. "It is killing we must do, Kemp", Griffin tells the "normal" and humane scientist whom Wells sets in contrast to him: "that Invisible Man, Kemp, must establish a Reign of Terror . . . He must take some town, and terrify and dominate it." Yet he is struck down by a labourer with a spade, killed like a dog with hydrophobia, just as the Martians are wiped out by earthly bacteria. Both stories are homilies on what Wells described as "the dangers of power without control, the development of the intelligence at the expense of human sympathy".[14]

They both also reveal Wells's continuing ambivalence about science and his fear of what, without control, scientists might become. Science is only admirable if it is used to master the brute in man: it is diabolical if it becomes the servant of the beast within. *The Invisible Man* was thus a telling exploration of the dualism in human nature, another sermon on a text by Huxley. Man needed, Huxley had said in "Evolution and Ethics", the qualities of the tiger and the ape to maintain his evolutionary ascendancy, but these were the very qualities which most threatened his precarious state of civilisation. By using the magical device of invisibility, Wells was able to demonstrate this paradox in the conflict between the "primitive" Griffin and the "civilised" villagers of Iping, who literally "see through" him.

It was a curious paradox, because Wells – the supposed protagonist of

science – made his scientist symbolise the beast in man, and it was the
rustic comics who represented order, reason and tradition, the qualities
on which civilisation depends. Yet Wells did not cast his characters perversely. The choice of the Sussex villagers may be explained by the
nostalgia that Wells often showed for pre-industrial England. The savage
absurdity of Griffin is enhanced by the fact that he is a scientist who has
lost his orientations. As the story proceeds, in fact, Griffin goes through
a series of regressions. At the outset he is a scientist who has betrayed his
vocation by preferring power to wisdom. He becomes in effect an
alchemist who has sold his soul to the devil. By the end he incarnates the
evil and insanity of Old Nick himself.

"With all his noble qualities", Charles Darwin wrote in *The Descent of
Man*, "with all these exalted powers, man still bears in his bodily frame
the indelible stamp of his lowly origin." In *The Invisible Man* Wells
transferred this "indelible stamp" of the brute from the body to the mind.
What makes men human, Wells was now asserting, is social morality. If
that is stripped off, like the clothing of the Invisible Man, there is nothing
left but the *bête humaine*. Man's progress, in short, has been achieved by
mental effort alone; the time since his appearance on earth has been too
short to permit any significant biological variation. "What we call
morality", he wrote in an article in the *Fortnightly Review* in October 1896,
called "Human Evolution – An Artificial Process", "becomes the padding
of suggested emotional habits necessary to keep the round paleolithic
savage in the square hole of the civilized state, and sin is the conflict of the
two factors."

So far as the plots of the scientific romances are concerned, Wells was
right in speaking of their "perplexing variety". Yet they are all variations
on a single theme – the nature of the evolutionary process and Man's
precarious place in the scheme of things. At the heart of each story Wells
states the same negative idea. It is a fallacy that evolution leads inevitably
to higher and better forms of life; man is only temporarily dominant on
a planet which itself is doomed. The Time Traveller makes the point
explicitly. Wells writes that he thought

... but cheerlessly of the Advancement of Mankind, and saw in the growing
pile of civilization only a foolish heaping that must inevitably fall back upon
and destroy its makers in the end. *If that is so, it remains for us to live as though
it were not so.* [Italics added]

There was, however, a shift in Wells's attitude in the course of the five romances. Though all of them dramatise his pessimistic view of man's nature and his prospects, he was beginning to seek for some way of escape from the gloomy implications of Kelvin and Huxley. The Time Traveller's reaction had been stoical: "it remains for us to live as though it were not so". But such stoicism did not offer Wells sufficient reassurance against the fears that he had expressed through these books. The relentless logic of evolution was as terrifying to him as the idea of his own death. He found both inescapable – yet unacceptable. If the laws of nature held out no hope, then hope must be found elsewhere, in some theory of change which offered a chance of defying and overcoming those laws. At this point in his life he had only a glimmering of an idea of what that super-natural hope might be that would enable man to transcend his fate. But it appeared for the first time in *The War of the Worlds,* in which he went back beyond Darwin to much older conceptions of the Great Change – to a theory of catastrophe much closer to Cuvier's doctrine of supernatural intervention in the Order of Nature and to even earlier millenarian visions of the Apocalypse.[15]

The invasion of the Martians is presented as a cosmic happening which reveals the pretentious frailty of human thought and behaviour. The monsters from space strike blindly and cruelly, rooting out the erring, the complacent and the fallible, and destroying the old society. "Cities, nations, civilization, progress – it's all over", says the Artilleryman whom the narrator meets on Putney Hill. All "those damn little clerks . . . the bar-loafers, and mashers and singers" are about to be turned into snacks for the voracious Martians, and "anything weak or silly" will be wiped out by their heat-rays as their tripods stalk on through the blackened ruins towards London.

The story is still deeply pessimistic. Catastrophe, for Wells at this time, is a judgement. It has not yet become – like Moreau's "bath of burning pain" – the purgative horror through which mankind must pass to reach the New Jerusalem of peace, brotherhood and wisdom. The Martians may symbolise an avenging God, but there is little in the story to suggest that they are – like the cosmic disasters in later stories – portents of the Second Coming.* The only hint of regeneration is to be found in the Artillery-

* In religious eschatology – predictions of the Last Days – there are many versions of the final catastrophe. It was a point of argument among seventeenth-century Puritans, for instance, whether the world would end with a cosmic collision, a blinding explosion, or the arrival of the host of angels to establish the Third Kingdom. Over the years Wells used all these forms

man's panegyric on the new breed of men who will form a resistance movement against the Martians – and it would be charitable to describe these as the forerunners of the Saints. They are the nastiest kind of Nietzschean supermen, and the Artilleryman's remarks read like a stump speech by a fascist yahoo. "There won't be any more blessed concerts for a million years or so; there won't be any Royal Academy of Arts, and no nice little feeds at restaurants", he gloats. Nobody but "able-bodied, clean-minded men" will survive, men who will obey orders, and ensure the future of an untainted race by mating with "able-bodied, clean-minded mothers and teachers". For the first time, Wells had hit on the idea that salvation would come at the hands of a superior élite. But he clearly found this particular prototype of the Samurai he eulogised in *A Modern Utopia* uncongenial and unconvincing. The Artilleryman has barely finished orating when a turn of the story shows him to be a worthless windbag.

The descent of the Martians is thus portrayed as a visitation, a warning of Old Testament severity that there is no hope for mankind unless it sees the error of its ways and repents. There was an obvious relationship between *The War of the Worlds* and the spate of books which appeared in the last decades of the century warning a decadent England of the dangers of invasion if nothing were done to regenerate the country. The distinction of Wells's romance lay partly in the power of the writing, but even more in the way he summoned the Apocalypse – a cosmic threat much more emotive than invading Frenchmen or Germans – to scare his countrymen into a mood of reform.

As he had written the romances, he had moved from feelings of utter despair, to which stoicism was the only response, through an attempt to offset gloomy Science by the hope of Art, to an insistence that a moral sense is the only means of controlling man's animal instincts. Finally, he had come to the idea of salvation. In looking for a way out of the evolutionary impasse he had released the latent messianism in his personality. By 1896, in fact, Wells had begun to secularise the Plan of Salvation which was central to the evangelical religion of his boyhood. What he had done was to equate man's animal inheritance with original sin. The Puritans had sought for a means of saving mankind from the curse of Adam: salvation now meant saving the human species from the evolutionary process which,

---

of the Apocalypse – the first in *In the Days of the Comet*, the second in *The World Set Free* and the third in *The Shape of Things to Come*. W.T. Stead, in *The Review of Reviews*, noted the "gloomy horror" of *The War of the Worlds*, which he described as "The Latest Apocalypse of the End of the World".

unchecked, damned it as surely as the Fall. But only the elect could hope for salvation, their righteousness triumphing over human fallibility and establishing the Rule of the Saints on earth. Wells, who now identified himself with the elect, had defined his mission. It was to struggle against the cosmic process as energetically as his Puritan predecessors had struggled against the primal curse. In both cases the price was profound anxiety and a repressed sexual guilt which broke out into demonology and the monstrous imageries of Judgement Day.[16]

The vein of "peculiar treasure" Wells had opened up for Henley had run out. The anti-evolutionary romances had made his name, brought him prosperity, and given him self-confidence as a writer. The frantic writing of the stories had proved therapeutically effective and enabled him to find the thread of purpose he teased out through life. At the end of 1897, when he was thirty-one, he moved to Worcester Park. He was ready to make another new start, in a new home, with new friends, and to advocate solutions to the human dilemma which could make the present bearable and the future less grim.

9

FRIENDSHIPS

On 20 November 1896 Wells went up to town for a dinner at Frascati's organised by the Omar Khayyam Club, a group of literary men who met from time to time for a convivial evening. He found himself sitting next to George Gissing, and took such a liking to him that he immediately wrote off what Gissing described as "the most amusing, the most enspiriting, and the most alluring invitation that I have received for a long time".[1] Gissing's warm reply encouraged Wells to repeat the invitation. "I want to see you now much more than I did . . . Take care of yourself, there's a good chap! because now I've written you so impudently . . . and you've answered so kindly, I've a sort of feeling that this should have happened before." Gissing had also taken to Wells. On 6 December he wrote to his Polish friend, Eduard Bertz:[2] "There is a new man called Wells whom I like very much. He has gone through great miseries, and declares that *New Grub Street* gives an absolute picture of his circumstances at one time." * He noted in his diary that Wells "seems the right sort of man". Wells was determined to pursue this new acquaintance, and on 6 December he wrote again to Gissing, suggesting that he come for a "real interminable gossip" four days later, and that he might then join H.G. and Jane at yet another literary dinner that evening.†

Gissing was nine years older than H.G. and already had seventeen books behind him. But he had made no profitable career as a writer, staggering from one crisis to the next. His whole life, indeed, had been painful and tortuous. His father, a pharmacist in Wakefield, died when he was thirteen, and he made his way by prodigious effort to a scholarship at Owen's College in Manchester. Once there, he insulated himself against loneliness

---

* This novel about the struggles of poor literary hacks, published in 1891, was based upon Gissing's own experiences.

† This was given by the New Vagabonds Club, with Wells as guest of honour. There is a "picshua" of this event in *Experiment in Autobiography*, with various literary lions bowing in homage. "Vain-glory is . . . offensively evident", Wells remarked.

by hard work and, like Wells at the Normal School, did well in his first year. In the spring of 1877, however, his troubles began. He stole money from the college cloakroom to give to a prostitute with whom he had fallen in love, and he was sentenced to a month's hard labour. In 1879 he married the girl but it was a disastrous liaison. Six years later she went back on the streets, dying of drink and poverty. At the beginning of the marriage Gissing wrote his first novel, *Workers of the Dawn*, but its social realism was unfashionable and it failed to sell. In 1891 he married again, this time to a servant girl given to fits of jealous rage. A child was born that year and another in 1896 but the children seemed to exacerbate their troubles. He could not, it seemed, cope with the world and he resigned himself to a philosophical pessimism. He was, as Wells wrote later in *Monthly Review*, "hidden from the light of himself".

It was a strange friendship that Wells was so keen to make, but it suited both of them. Wells could give Gissing comfort and affection, because he understood his difficulties. Gissing could share vicariously in Wells's success, and his support, as an older and more established writer, was greatly valued by Wells.*

Early in 1897, Gissing's domestic troubles and increasing ill-health had driven him to stay with Dr Henry Hick, an old schoolfriend from Wakefield, who was in practice at New Romney on the edge of the Kent coastal marshes. On 14 February Gissing wrote to Wells suggesting they meet for dinner as he had to run up to London to see "a scoundrelly specialist". The specialist urged him to move to a warmer climate and Gissing and his sister went down to Budleigh Salterton in Devon for a few months. On 16 April H.G., who felt in need of a vacation, wrote asking Gissing to book accommodation "not so genteel as to shame two dirty cyclists" and saying that he and Jane would set off for Devonshire two days later, taking about five days to make the journey. It was an enjoyable visit, though Wells found Gissing much changed. He was "a damaged and ailing man, full of ill-advised precautions against the imaginary illnesses that were his interpretations of a general *malaise*".[3] He spoke of returning to Italy "as one speaks of a lost paradise", and of making a new beginning there, and his enthusiasm sparked in H.G. and Jane the idea of making their first trip to the Continent. Their visit had certainly cheered him up, and on 22 May he wrote to Wells that it was "the kind of thing that sends a man back to work with exultant spirits". There had been a

* By 1896 Wells had earned over a thousand pounds: Gissing, with many more books published, had received less than three hundred.

favourable notice of *The Plattner Story and Others* in the *Daily Chronicle* and Gissing added admiringly: "With your gusto for work, your happiness, your capabilities, what may you not do!" The admiration was mutual. That August Wells wrote a critical review of Gissing's novels in the *Contemporary Review* and Gissing commented on it, "I believe you have seen justly and spoken as it behoved you to do". There was a characteristic misanthropic codicil. "I cannot hope with you that I shall make much more progress. I lack the vital energy that would justify such a hope; what I have is frittered away in mean squabbling and sordid cares."

Wells had ample energy, but he too had troubles to absorb it. "I've had a sort of nervous period since that article appeared", he wrote back, adding that "I have been very much worried by a commission for two short stories and an inability to get up to the mark with them – a consequent disorganization – nerves wrong – sleeplessness, swearing, weeping." Gissing wrote on 26 August to say that "I chanced to meet Pinker at Waterloo today, and he confirms my suspicion that you have been working too long and too hard." All through 1897, in fact, Wells had been in an irritable state about his work and his relations with publishers. On 25 March he had written an acid letter to W.M.Colles, the lawyer who launched the Author's Syndicate as a literary agency. It ended with a characteristic apology from Wells. "Of course we've quarrelled over *The War of the Worlds*", he wrote, "but that business is over, & in any such difference I think it preferable to be as unpleasant as possible at the time & to heal as quickly as possible – don't you?"[4] He was also involved in a running squabble with William Heinemann that lasted on and off for some years. On 7 August, while he was having a fight with another publisher, A.H.Bullen, about the design and price of *Certain Personal Matters*, he wrote to Heinemann:[5]

You not only bother an author to ask for what is due to him but you are uncivil over the payment. You say you overpaid me for Moreau (that agreement also covered The War of the Worlds). Do you really think you lose by me? If so I am prepared to do this in order that you may not complain to that effect further. *I will pay back every penny I have ever had from you for the book rights of Time Machine & Moreau, buy all stereo plates, copies ... at the valuation of any independent & competent person* on condition that all existing agreements between us are cancelled. I think that is a fairly generous offer of release to you. If you don't accept it, I hope you will at least have the grace to apologise for that "overpaid".

A year later, on 8 July 1898, he was still arguing with Heinemann about terms, saying that "I'm sick of seeing my good honest work fizzle in obscure corners", and telling Heinemann that unless he was prepared to print more than four thousand copies of *When the Sleeper Wakes* "it must pay me far better to print & bind myself & sell directly to the book-sellers". Authorship, H.G. tartly concluded in a deleted line, "is not solely for the support of the class of publishers".

That autumn Wells was driving himself on two new books. He and Jane were already planning to visit Gissing, who – after the final break-up of his second marriage – had returned to Italy, but he wrote to Gissing on New Year's Day 1898 that parts of *When the Sleeper Wakes* had been "reshaped, rewritten and retyped time after time. *Love and Mr Lewisham* too grows very slowly." It was still impossible to fix a definite date for the journey, even though "I am sick of this damned climate and of my perpetual catarrh." Gissing's letters from Italy had excited a romantic vision.

I mean to lead a great multitude of selected people out of this reek, sooner or later, artists and writers and decent souls and we will all settle in little houses along and up a slope of sunlight all set with olives and vines and honey mellowed marble ruins between the mountains and the sea. There we will sit in the evening of our days dressed in decent blouses talking talking of this and that.

Meanwhile, he and Jane borrowed an old Murray guide to Rome from the London Library and both of them were toiling at an introductory Italian grammar. The visit was settled for March. Gissing decided to stay with his visitors at the Alibert, where he had struck a good bargain. For seventeen lire (about fifteen shillings) a day, H.G. and Jane would have full pension with wine. "It is almost too good to be true", Gissing added on 18 February, "the thought of our having a second spring holiday all together. Well, well; fate is artful in withholding us from despair. Let us do our best not to quarrel. It would be a hateful thing to have disagreeable memories of Rome, due to such a cause."

On Monday 7 March H.G. and Jane left Worcester Park on their first foray into Europe, and they reached Rome late the following evening. Next morning Gissing took them on the first day of sightseeing – the Vatican, the Sistine Chapel and the Colosseum. While Gissing had been staying in Siena he had met Conan Doyle and his brother-in-law, E.W. Hornung, the creator of the gentleman-cracksman Raffles, and a young American, BrianBorú Dunne. All of them teamed up to make a congenial group that spent much of the next month together, walking, talking and dining. "There were", Wells wrote nostalgically six years later, "tramps in the Campagna, in the Alban Hills, along the Via Clodia, and so forth, merry meals with the good red wine of Velletri or Grotto Ferrata."[6] Rome filled with Easter visitors, and H.G. and Jane reluctantly left Gissing and went off to Naples, Capri and Pompeii, returning slowly by way of Florence, Bologna and Milan, through Lugano and Lucerne and arrived back at Worcester Park on 11 May.

Gissing too had gone back to England, where he met the woman who was to be the last of his emotional entanglements. Gabrielle Fleury, he wrote to H.G. on 30 July, "is the very best kind of Frenchwoman, uniting their fine intellectuality with the domestic sense". She had written to Gissing asking permission to translate *New Grub Street* into French. He asked Jane Wells to arrange for them to meet for luncheon at Worcester Park. H.G. found her "consciously refined", but Gissing was impressed and within a few days he asked her down to Dorking where they began work on the translation. At this time he made several visits to Worcester Park, and Wells made comic notes on his clumsy first attempts to master the knack of cycling. "It was curious to see this well-built Viking, blowing and funking as he hopped behind his machine ... He mounted, wabbled a few yards, and fell off shrieking with laughter."

Life at Heatherlea seemed to be settling into the routine of work and entertainment suitable for a rising young man of letters. Now Wells could afford it, he indulged his taste for social occasions, and Saturday afternoons in particular were devoted to literary parties. There is an extended account of one of these occasions, left by Dorothy Richardson, a schoolfriend of Jane's. It forms one chapter of her novel, *The Tunnel*, and Wells himself conceded that it "described our Worcester Park life with astonishing accuracy". The interesting point about her sketch is the way she sensed unconscious strains between "Hypo Wilson" and his wife "Alma", as if they were seeking to make an impression on each other as well as on their visitors. "To get on here, one would have to say clever things in a high bright voice", Miriam (the central character) muses. Hypo Wilson had "overwhelming charm" in the way he put things, "so that even while you hated what he was saying, and his way of stating things as if they were the final gospel and no one else in the world knew anything at all, you wanted him to go on". He made "little subdued snortings at the back of his nose in the pauses between his sentences as if he were afraid of being answered or interrupted before he developed the next thing". Alma, however, seemed to be unsure whether she was competing with him or needling him. She "told him nothing, or only things in the clever way he would admire". Dorothy Richardson's description of Alma has a hint of acid distaste. She "went on and on, sometimes uncomfortably failing, her thin voice sounding like a corkscrew in a cork without any bottle behind it, now and again provoking a response which made things worse because it brought to the table the shamed sense of trying to keep something going . . . Everything she said was an attempt to beat things up. Every time she spoke, Miriam was conscious of something in the room that would be there with them all if only Alma would leave off being funny." There was "a curious hard emptiness in their voices, like people rehearsing and secretly angry with each other". There were clearly unresolved difficulties between H.G. and Jane which reached a crisis at Worcester Park.

A symptom that H.G. was in trouble was an impulsive decision to see his first wife again. He cycled over to Twyford, near Reading, where Isabel was living, and they spent a pleasant day at Virginia Water. The overt reason for the encounter was financial. Isabel needed more money to extend her not-so-profitable chicken farm and Wells was never ungenerous in helping her. They spent "a day without tension, with an easy friendliness we had never known before", and Wells stayed overnight. "Suddenly", he recalled, "I found myself overcome by the sense of our separation. I wanted fantastically to recover her. I implored her for the last time in vain." Before dawn he decided to slip away, but Isabel heard him moving about and insisted on making him breakfast.

All our old mingling of intense attraction and baffling reservation was there unchanged. "But how can things like that be, now?" she asked. I gave way to a wild storm of weeping. I wept in her arms like a disappointed child, and then suddenly pulled myself together and went out into the summer dawn . . . into a sunlit intensity of perplexity and frustration, unable to understand the peculiar keenness of my unhappiness. I felt like an automaton, I felt as though all purpose had been drained out of me and nothing remained worth while. The world was dead and I was dead and I had only just discovered it.

It was a traumatic moment, and the vivid terms in which H.G. recalled it nearly forty years afterwards show the extent to which he had remained unconsciously involved with Isabel. The fantasies which he had woven around her during their long courtship had not been able to meet the test of reality during their marriage, but he had not released himself from them.

When he met her again, they overwhelmed him. Although nothing came of this encounter with Isabel, it was a symbolic occasion. It was an expression of Wells's life-long search for what he was later to call "lost orientations".

In late July 1898 H.G. was undoubtedly in a state of physical and emotional distress. He had been unwell all summer. As always when he was bothered, he felt a sense of claustrophobia and though he had only just returned from a long vacation he wanted to get away again from Heatherlea. He had already come to know Gissing's friend and doctor, Henry Hick, and he and Jane now planned a cycling holiday along the South Coast to include a visit to Hick. A trunk was sent off to Seaford, where they proposed to spend three weeks while the novel was finished, and they set off by bicycle on 29 July.

By the time Seaford was reached H.G. had a raging cold, a high temperature and severe kidney pains. A few days later he was so ill that a telegram was sent to Hick asking if he could take them in, and on 9 August – after an exhausting journey by local trains – Wells and his wife arrived at New Romney. He was dangerously ill with an abscess on the damaged kidney, and letters exchanged with Simmons, Gregory and his newer literary friends show their concern.[7] "Cheer up, old man", Gregory wrote on 18 August, "there are always two chaps who would willingly share your pains if they could, but here we are, helpless, and drinking whisky and soda, though it seems almost sinful to indulge in such luxuries while you are as you are." And on the following day Gregory wrote again to say he had hurried to King's College Hospital to see a specialist in the new technique of using Röntgen rays, only to learn that it would be a waste of time to use it to examine a damaged kidney. "How I wish I could come and sit by your bedside, and talk of follies to cheer you", Gissing wrote from Dorking on 15 August, and three days later he wrote to Jane: "I regard H.G. as the friend of a lifetime; I can't do without him; he *must* be his old self again. My debt to his kindness, his good humour, his wit, is infinite . . . In the last letter I had from him, H.G. spoke of you as the 'unfailing chum', and he could have no better nurse beside him." On 6 September Conrad sent a warm and encouraging letter:[8]

A few days ago I heard with great concern the news of your illness. It saddened me the more because for the last two years . . . I have lived on terms of close intimacy with you, referring to you many a page of my work, scrutinizing many sentences by the light of your criticism . . . I would like to hear how your recovery progresses and when you are *going back to work*. May it be soon! I – for one – cannot have enough of your work. *You* have done me good. You have been doing me good every day for many months past.

Wells was too sick to do any serious work, though he expressed his appreciation of the kindness of the Hick family by writing an illustrated story – *The Adventures of Tommy* – for the little daughter Marjorie. He feared, indeed, that he was "shattered" and that, as he wrote to J.V. Milne, "valetudinarianism is my game for the next year or so and the confounded world must manage itself, until I am better at least".[9] Hick insisted that he "must be on sand or gravel and high and sheltered", so as he convalesced he and Jane began to look for a new home. "Sandgate & Hythe & Rye present a certain suitableness of soil and aspect, but the houses!" H.G. told Milne. "Servant-murdering basements, sanitary insanities, and not a decent bathroom anywhere. I want a house with five sane rooms ... I'm ready to go to £80 and I can't get it."

At the beginning of September they spent a couple of weeks in a boarding-house and then moved to 2 Beach Cottages, Sandgate, a rented place right on the shore in this straggling coastal village three miles to the west of Folkestone. "I am giving up the Worcester Park house for some obscure geological reason", he told Elizabeth Healey, "and I have to live here ... We are in a furnished house with a back door slap upon the sea ... The shrimps will come in and whack about on the dining-room oil-cloth."[10] Gissing sent his approval of the move: "I think you have done very wisely", he wrote on 16 October, "you will be able to test the climate before committing yourself." As winter came on it was stormy, and from Wells's letters Gissing had a picture of the cottage "rocking in gales and lashed with furious rain".

Yet Wells felt better. "This place (plus Folkestone)", he wrote to Elizabeth Healey in December, "is the most habitable place I've ever been in. For an elderly invalid (as I am practically) it is incomparable." He was clearly well enough to finish *Love and Mr Lewisham*, though he was not satisfied with the result: in his own phrase, he had saved no more than one straight plank from the vast scaffold originally designed, though there is "really more work in that book than there is in many a first-class F.R.S. research, and stagnant days and desert journeys beyond describing".[11] And, with recovery, new ideas were beginning to well up. One of his "picshuas" shows that he first thought of Kipps soon after he moved to Beach Cottage, though the book did not appear for another seven years:

it shows Kipps hatching from an egg and has "5 October 1898" scribbled in a corner.[12]

Wells's worries had now focused on the problem of finding a permanent home, and he decided on the "desperate but I think unavoidable step" of buying a house, as he told Pinker in September.[13] "I am still so sorely ill that I cannot get away from this place to hunt around towns, to winter at Worcester Park would be suicide", and he thought he had found a pretty but dilapidated property that he could get for about eight hundred pounds. He then summarised the state of his finances to Pinker. He had £500 in hand, £180 due for stories in the *Strand Magazine*, £1150 coming from Heinemann for *The War of the Worlds* and *When the Sleeper Wakes*, £350 owing for the *Graphic*'s serialisation of *The Sleeper*, and some oddments that brought the total to £2,160. He therefore could count on about a thousand pounds which could be drawn on for house-purchase.

The deal fell through, however, and on 26 November H.G. sent Pinker "a howl of anguish. I am still a weedy creature and so damnably worried that I can barely get my wits together to write to you".[14] He now decided to build a house for himself, but the strain of getting the legal difficulties settled proved too much for him. "Really I am near the breaking point. If some sane man does not intervene I shall break down & start business as an unsuccessful literary man . . . The new novel which might be the finest thing I have done . . . is being fretted to rags. Morning after morning come letters to spoil my days work. Well, I'm doing this much in self abandonment – I'm going to ask charity". Pinker had to take over the negotiations with the architect and solicitor. H.G. told Pinker plainly how he felt.

Really I don't think things are going well. I see nothing before me but unrest, removals, worry interminable, hampering my work. I see no factors working together for any steady growth of reputation. I know I've done well & I shall come to my own someday, but the chances are more & more that I shall die miserably first. I am personally unimpressive, I do not excite loyalty, I am culpably careless over petty things that influence mens minds. My affairs drift beyond my control. I have watched my [illegible] work appear obscurely & slide towards oblivion & I have no confidence that any I may do in the future, whatever its qualities, will escape that fate. I cannot organize success & it is not being organized for me.

In December the "days of incapable rage" with "solicitors" & suchlike beasts" had passed, as he wrote to Elizabeth Healey: "at last I've cast these cares upon the good Pinker . . . & my mind is comparatively at peace again".[15] Before long he had found a neighbouring house which was more comfortable, and since it was unfurnished they could clear their things from Heatherlea and relinquish the lease. Arnold House (now 20 Castle Road) where they moved on 28 March 1899 was a solid semi-detached villa with a garden running down to the beach, and set in the curiously-sheltered Sandgate "riviera" where palmettos flourish and the sharp rise up the cliff to The Leas cuts off cold winds. "I rejoice to think of you as settling into a comfortable house", Gissing wrote. "Never mind about the building; it is a hideous business." The neighbours too were agreeable. Mr Popham, "that good man next door" Wells called him, had literary interests and, as Wells got stronger, taught him to swim and accompanied him on cycle rides.

Friendships, indeed, were the one compensation for the troubles that afflicted Wells all through the autumn of 1898 and the early months of 1899. While he was bed-ridden at New Romney, two distinguished visitors unexpectedly appeared to inquire about his health. Edmund Gosse was staying with Henry James at Rye about fifteen miles away when he heard that Wells was seriously ill. The pair of them set off on bicycles, ostensibly to pay a social call on the invalid. A few days later, J.M.Barrie turned up, and it was then – from his tactful discussion of the money problems of young writers – that H.G. realised that his visitors were discreetly sounding out his circumstances. (Gosse was at that time responsible for disbursements from the Royal Literary Fund set up to help needy writers.) He was touched by this kindness, not because he needed money but because he needed friends.

Another windfall was the arrival of Conrad in the area. On 11 September 1898 Conrad wrote "in a state of jubilation at the thought we are going to be nearer neighbours than I dared to hope a fortnight ago. We are coming to live in Pent Farm . . . on the 26th of this month and I shall wander out your way soon after that date".[16] Wells and Conrad had been in touch with each other for a couple of years already. Conrad, who had decided to settle down in England, published *Almayer's Folly* in 1895 and *An Outcast of the Islands* in March the following year. Wells reviewed both books enthusiastically in the *Saturday Review*, describing *An Outcast* as "perhaps the finest piece of fiction that has been published this year", though he thought it had "a glaring fault . . . Mr Conrad is wordy . . . He has still to learn the great half of his art, the art of leaving things unwritten . . . and he writes despicably. He writes so as to mask and dishonour the greatness that is in him". Conrad was intrigued by this anonymous review, and on 24 May wrote to his friend, Edward Garnett, who had encouraged Conrad to persevere with his fiction. "I was puzzled by it", Conrad said: "I wrote to the reviewer. I did! And he wrote to me. He did! . . . It is H.G.Wells. May I be cremated alive like a miserable moth if I suspected it! Anyway he descended from his 'Time Machine' to be as kind as he knew how."[17]

It was the start of a long and intimate association which flowered when the two men met. Two years later, after reading *The Invisible Man*, Conrad wrote: "I am always powerfully impressed by your work. Impressed is *the* word, O Realist of the Fantastic! . . . if you want to know what impresses me it is to see how you contrive to give over humanity to the clutches of the Impossible and yet manage to keep it down (or up) to its humanity, to its flesh, blood, sorrow, folly. *That* is the achievement!"[18] The friendship was mutually rewarding. Conrad needed the encouragement of Wells just as Wells wanted praise from writers he admired, and while Conrad was struggling against both a lack of money and a lack of command over the English language, he also needed someone as he told Pinker, "to whom I tell all my troubles". Though gradually the trials of the Conrad family – Mrs Conrad's heavy domesticity and Conrad's gruffness – came to irritate H.G., in the early years he made a generous confidant for a man who, like himself, was a restless outsider who was trying to realise himself as a writer.

Conrad's arrival at Pent Farm, less than half an hour by trap or bicycle from Sandgate, was the end of a chain of circumstances. This "mournful house under the bare Downs" belonged to Ford Madox Ford.[19] He and his wife, Elsie Martindale, lived there until March 1898 when they leased the farm to the socialist artist Walter Crane, and moved to Gracie's Cottage near Limpsfield, in Surrey. This was one of a pair of houses known as the Cearne, where Edward and Constance Garnett had settled in 1896, and the area had become the home of several "advanced" and literary personalities – Garnett called it "Dostoievsky Corner". One of the neighbours was Edward Pease, an earnest plodding man who was the first secretary of the Fabian Society, and there was a great deal of socialising among local radical writers and reformers. In his autobiography Ford made a jaundiced comment about "the troglodytic cottage on Limpsfield Chart where I lived severely browbeaten by Garnetts and the Good generally, though usually of a Fabian or Advanced Russian variety".[20]

Conrad had gone to stay with Garnett in September 1898, and had there met Ford. Ford's passionate concern was the technique of writing. He not only believed that the world was to be saved by Art, but insisted that the one responsibility of the creative artist was to think about the mental process whereby Art is produced. He fussed about the exact implication of every word, and Conrad sensed that in this concern for style lay the complement to his own talents. He was equally dedicated to his writing, but he was working in a language with whose nuances he was unfamiliar, and Ford could give him just the help he needed. Ford found something he lacked in Conrad. "Among the successful novelists of the late Nineties", he wrote after Conrad's death, "the conception of the novel as a work of Art was unthinkable . . . It was difficult in those days to strike out on that path alone. I owe a great deal to Conrad. But most of all I owe to him that strong faith – that . . . the writing of novels is the only pursuit worthwhile for a proper man."[21]

A decision to collaborate followed in a matter of days. Conrad was looking for somewhere to live. Pent Farm was vacant and Ford proposed that the Conrads should move in. On 15 October they took over the red brick farmhouse, isolated in the rolling countryside, and stayed there until 1907. Conrad was comfortable there: "On the brick path under the windows Conrad would pace for hours and hours, soothed by the lines of the country running away to great distances", Ford remembered. Ford himself soon settled nearby, in a farm labourer's cottage called Stocks Hill at Aldington. There was much coming and going as Conrad and Ford worked on their collaborative writing, or played chess and dominoes, or talked about literature. "It comes back as a time of great tranquillity", Ford recalled, "despite the agonies of Conrad's poverty, unsuccess, negotiations and misgivings."

Once at the Pent Conrad wasted no time in calling on Wells, but he was out. "I was glad to find you well enough to be out for an airing", he wrote afterwards, "though of course horribly sorry to miss you . . . I beg to be remembered to Mrs Wells. The first fine day (baby permitting) I shall bring my wife to be introduced to her."[22] He asked Wells to the Pent, offering to take care of all transport arrangements to ensure Wells was not overtired. Then he called again, after Ford's arrival, and once again Wells was out. While Conrad and Ford were at Sandgate Wells had gone over to the Pent. Conrad wrote ruefully: "Coming back we found your card. We haven't cards. We ain't civilized enough – not yet."[23] On learning of the proposed collaboration, which they had called to announce, H.G. cycled over to Aldington to discourage Ford, as it would spoil Conrad's "wonderful oriental style" which was "as delicate as clockwork and you will only ruin it by sticking your fingers in it". Ford insisted that Conrad wanted it, and told Wells he intended to go through with the arrangement: Wells rode away in a disconsolate huff.[24]

The triangle of friendship between Sandgate, Aldington and the Pent was the frame round which the social life of all three families was built in these first years. Ford liked Wells's "tough, as it were Cockney, gallantry of attack on anything", and found it an "unfailing delight to listen to Wells conducting a conversation. He monologued in a conversational tone until he had led the discussion into the strategic position he had chosen – and then defended it . . . He let his hearers say a word or two and then suppressed them either with superior knowledge or a quip that changed the course of discussion."[25]

Though Ford came to regard H.G. as an enemy in the world of art – "In the kingdom of letters Mr Wells and I have been leaders of opposing forces for nearly the whole of this century", he wrote in 1938 – Wells at first dazzled Ford. He was, Ford said, "the Dean of our Profession". It was an astonishing judgement about a man who had just burst into the literary set and was still terribly insecure and anxious about his reputation. Yet Wells clearly emerged as the catalytic agent among the heterogeneous literary group in his neighbourhood. "We regarded him", Ford said, "as having innumerable things, retainers, immense sales and influence, and the gift of leadership. So, in some mystic way, Mr Wells might have put Literature on the map. That was how it seemed."[26]

The differences between Wells, Ford and Conrad were concealed in the excitements of the first flush of friendship, when all questions were open as the three men explored ideas that had not yet hardened into convictions. The same was true of Wells and James. They were an incongruous pair. Wells was twenty-six years junior to James, with great charm but few of the graces to which James attached so much importance. Nearly half a century later, looking back on years of friendship with James, Wells still singled out his anxious manners: "He went", he wrote, "through a world haunted and mocked by the sense of this unseen standard of perfection . . . And it isn't there!"[27] Wells felt that "we were by nature and training profoundly unsympathetic", but they managed to maintain a close association for almost fifteen years.

It was partly that James saw at once that Wells, for all his gaucherie, had real talent and a genuine devotion to his craft as a writer. James's nervous concern for social niceties made him seem a snob, but there was no snobbery where writing was concerned – only a passion for professional standards and a generous desire to assist young writers who were sufficiently patient with his ponderous manner to profit from his counsel. James enjoyed talking to those who regarded themselves as his disciples, as Wells certainly did at the outset, and were able to listen to his periphrastic criticism of their work. As early as 20 November 1899 James was writing on the receipt of *Tales of Space and Time* that "you fill me with wonder and admiration ... Your spirit is huge, your fascination irresistible, your resources infinite."[28]

Wells, for his part, greatly needed the kind of recognition that James gave him. At the end of the century he aspired to be a great novelist, although his impatience for public notice, and a rising income, made him incapable of the artistic self-discipline which made Conrad and James willing to sacrifice popular acclaim for artistic satisfaction. On 16 January 1899 for instance, he wrote a letter to Pinker which reveals his state of mind.[29] We must, he wrote, "plant the pathway of the years with nice little bushy bargains to flower in due season. When we've got ten years ahead we'll come back & fill in between". But while he was busy in the market-place, he found it pleasant to be accepted at home as a genuine man of letters by men whose critical standards and professional integrity were unquestionable. The personal rewards of friendship apart, that was what he sought and received from his literary neighbours.

There was, for all their differences, something in common between them. Conrad, Ford, James and Wells were all, in their several ways, outsiders – as writers as well as in their backgrounds. None of them achieved a fraction of the sales that were reached by popular authors such as Hall Caine, Marie Corelli, or even Conan Doyle and Kipling, and all of them laboured to make a living at the edges of the literary scene – managing on hard-driven bargains with editors and publishers. They were outsiders too in another sense. Conrad was a Polish seafarer turned into an English novelist; Ford, who had a German father, had been brought up in the heart of bohemia; James was an American expatriate who had distanced himself from his family to achieve independence; and Wells was an *arriviste* from genteel squalor and Grub Street. Each, in his own way, was insecure. Each was trying to find, in literature, a means of relating his own special experience to the norms of society. They formed a strange, nervy little group, each of whom found in the company of the others some kind of reassurance that his efforts were meaningful.

In 1899 another outsider arrived and was immediately taken up. Stephen Crane had arrived in England two years before, encouraged by the success of *The Red Badge of Courage*. "With the *Red Badge* in the Nineties", Ford commented, "we were provided with a map showing us our own hearts."[30]

Stephen and Cora (she never married Crane because her second husband refused to divorce her) were an unconventional couple, and they had left the United States in 1897 because Cora was not socially acceptable: Crane had picked her up in Jacksonville in 1896, when he was on his way to Cuba as a war correspondent, and had patronised the Hotel de Dream which she managed. Cora was a courtesan, with wit, charm and intellectual curiosity, and genuine affection for Crane. He in turn was fascinated by this New Woman, who took pleasure in defying the conventions. Nothing could have been in greater contrast with his upbringing as the son of a Methodist minister. Crane's lapses from grace may have been a reaction from psalm-singing religiosity, but they left him with a deep sense of guilt and a melancholy which was accentuated by ill-health.

On their arrival in England the Cranes stayed with the Garnetts at Limpsfield, and then took a house nearby in Oxted. "I took him at once to be a god", Ford said, "an Apollo with starry eyes."[31] Conrad was equally impressed: "his thought is concise, connected, never very deep – yet often startling", he wrote to Garnett on 5 December 1897.[32] Yet he had doubts. Though "he ought to go very far . . . will he? I sometimes think he won't." The Cranes were quickly absorbed into the "advanced" set settled round the Cearne, and in 1899 – when they moved to Brede Place near Rye – they already knew the group of writers who lived in that area. Crane had written enthusiastically about Wells's work, especially his "genius for writing of underclass people". Wells thought highly of Crane too, though significantly he criticised him on the same grounds that he differed from Conrad, Ford and James. He wanted him "to deal with more passionate issues" of politics rather than devote his energies to the refinements of style and technique.

Brede Place was a weird house, and the Cranes lived weirdly in it.[33] It was a rambling, decaying property, over five hundred years old, which belonged to Garnett's friend, Moreton Frewin, and Garnett had persuaded Frewin to let the improvident Cranes have it for a nominal rent – rats, ghosts, draughts and all. The move, like most things in Crane's life, was a romantic gesture. He and Cora revelled in living in extravagant disarray, while Stephen wrote desperately to pay the mounting debts they incurred by their lavish entertainment of the writers, journalists and plain parasites who turned Brede place into a bedlam. "Baron Brede", as Ford called him, rode about the Sussex lanes on an enormous carriage horse, with "the air of a frail eagle astride a gaunt elephant".[34]

Neither Wells nor Crane stood on ceremony about entertaining, and the Cranes – with Stephen's niece, Helen, and their friend Edith Richie – were put up for the night in September, stopping at Sandgate before catching the Channel boat on their way to Switzerland. There was "music and fun after dinner. Jane accompanied Edith Richie at the piano; and then they all played animal grab, Stephen roaring like a lion, Wells barking like a dog, and Cora a twittering canary."[35]

Parties were quite the thing, but Crane's idea of a party was characteristically wilder than anyone's. He and Cora decided to mark the end of the century with a party which no one who attended it ever forgot. It was planned on a grand scale. There was to be a play, a ball, and a running house party for about fifty guests. The play was to be about the Brede ghost, and Crane invited "a distinguished rabble" to take a hand in writing it – A.E.W.Mason, Conrad, Rider Haggard, James, Gissing, Robert Barr and Wells. In the event, Crane wrote most of what the *Southeastern Advertiser* – after the astonishing single performance in the village hall at Brede – called "a combination of farce, comedy, opera and burlesque". Scenery was specially built for the play, an orchestra was hired for the ball, servants were brought from London, truckle-beds borrowed from the local hospital, and the blacksmith made dozens of iron brackets to hold the candles needed to light the place. The Cranes were determined that they would recapture the spirit of Merrie England. Most of the guests had to bring their own bedding and shake down in dormitories, but at least they arrived in style. The Cranes had ordered a handsome omnibus to be built to convey their visitors from Hastings station, and Lewis Hind afterwards recalled the agony of getting to Brede village. "It was a pouring wet night, with thunder and lightning . . . Again and again we had to alight and push, and each time we returned to our seats on top . . . I remarked to my neighbour, H.G.Wells, that Brede village is not a suitable place for dramatic performances."[36] The play was only a highlight in this revel, which Wells described as "an extraordinary lark" that ran to late nights and midday brunches of bacon-and-eggs for fifty. On the following night a tremendous fall of snow kept away many of the local people who had been invited. Perhaps it was just as well, Lewis Hind remarked, "for H.G.Wells . . . invented a game of racing on broomsticks over the polished floor, which I think would have staggered the local gentry if they had turned up". Pinker said he had heard it was "a Babylonian orgy".

It was also too much for Crane. Almost all the guests had retired after the ball when Crane, who was strumming a guitar to amuse the last of them as they sat by the fire, suddenly fainted. Cora woke Wells and he came down to find Crane with a tubercular haemorrhage. Borrowing a bicycle, he rode off through the drizzling dawn to fetch Dr Skinner from Rye. "I'll bet an even halo", he wrote afterwards to Crane, "that haemorrhages aren't the way you will take out of this terrestrial tumult."[37] But he was wrong. In May Cora took Stephen to the Black Forest where he died a month later.

Crane had passed through Sussex like a comet, blazed brightly in the last nights of the century, and gone in a dying fall. Those who had been swept up in his train went back to their normal occasions – and yet they returned to a different world. Chesterton's "arithmetical autumn" was over, and nothing symbolised its passing better than that final dramatic party at Brede. As it broke up, the mathematician Mark Barr was arguing pedantically that the new century would not begin for another year, but many of those who were there were about to shed the doubts and *fin-de-siècle* pessimism with which they had struggled through the Nineties. The Edwardian age had arrived and so had they, and – as Wells was now beginning to assert – the moment had come for the writers and reformers to make a new world.

TREASURE HOUSE
ON THE SEA SHORE

"Got there at last! No carpets no dining room table or chairs, little food but still – *there*!" Wells wrote to Arnold Bennett on 8 December 1900.[1] All that year H.G. had fussed about the new home that was being built on the hill above Arnold House. He had decided on the site early in 1899, but there had been protracted negotiations with the lawyers of the Earl of Sandwich (who owned the land), investigations about the suitability of the soil for a large house, and difficulties in settling upon a builder able to erect the unusual design on which Wells had set his heart. The first firm had withdrawn; and though a contract was finally signed with William Dunk, a Folkestone contractor, on 12 February 1900 for the sum of £1,760, Wells later estimated that before he was through he had spent close to three thousand pounds on Spade House.

He chose the name himself. His architect, C.F.A. Voysey, normally worked small hearts into the design of doors and windows as a trademark, but Wells inverted these into the shape of a spade. It was one of his smaller points of difference with his architect, a man of distinction but autocratic temperament who believed that his task was to design every-thing down to the last toothpick and considered that the only satisfactory client was one who went abroad whilst the house was building. Yet Charles Voysey, who was then building a series of houses which made his name as a pioneer of a new and simpler style, was just the man to translate Wells's advanced ideas into something very different from the normal late-Victorian villa.

The style was Voysey's – buttresses, rough-cast finish, a low-eaved roof of Westmorland tiles, iron casements and leaded lights, high-waisted interiors – but the conception was that of Wells, who wanted a house that was light and bright, fitted with the latest conveniences, as pleasant for its occupants to live in as it would be easy for servants to run – especially since, when he first planned it, he feared that ill-health would compel him to spend much of his time house-bound in a wheel-chair.

H.G. had met Voysey through Henry Hick, whose wife was Voysey's sister. Voysey was an eccentric after his own heart. He was the son of a clergyman who had broken away to found his own theistic congregation; and Voysey himself, breaking with Victorian orthodoxy, created his own variant of the Arts and Crafts movement. Wells at last had the money to pay for what he wanted, and Voysey gave him the home in which he spent his most productive years, entertained his friends and raised his sons.

The builders laboured all through 1900, watched and fidgeted by Wells, who had only to walk a hundred yards from Arnold House to see how they were getting on. He could scarcely conceal his irritation at the slow and clumsy manner in which they worked.

It has been my lot recently to follow in detail this process of building a private dwelling-house, and the solemn succession of deliberate, respectable, perfectly satisfied men, who have contributed each so many days of his life to this accumulation of weak compromises, has enormously intensified my constitutional amazement at my fellow-creatures. . . . It is a house built by hands – and some I saw were bleeding hands – just as in the days of the pyramids.[2]

Wells concluded that, in addition to the internal changes that would be needed in the house of the twentieth century (in 1900 he wrote an article for the *Strand* magazine declaring for electric central heating, air-conditioning, automatic sweepers, self-making beds and other labour-saving devices) the time had come to revolutionise building by prefabrication and the use of synthetic materials.

So H.G. and Jane watched and waited for what Henry James called their "treasure house on the sea shore" to be completed. In May 1900, once the builders had started work, they took off on a cycling tour in France with Frank Wells, and called on Gissing in Paris. "I have been prowling about the North of France on a bicycle and paying a visit to the Exposition and having influenza and so forth", Wells wrote to Elizabeth Healey on 24 May.[3] Having for the moment appeased his itch to move about, H.G. recognised that he was beginning to settle into a domestic routine. "Uneventful events constitute my days", he added. "I have got to the middle period of life, I think, the beginning of the middle at any rate, 'ammer, 'ammer, 'ammer, on the 'ard 'igh road, the first excitement of the start into 'literature' is over and I am working – I hope with an increasing strength and quality – at certain projected things." He felt the need to stress that he was settling down, for he went on: "The first excitement of the start is *quite* over. We never see a press cutting, insult interviewers, avoid literary dinners, pursuing our exalted way towards a goal of our own. Also we are building ourselves a home. Every symptom in fact of incipient Middle Age." And later that year, on 19 October, he wrote to Gissing in the same vein. "Our house is now very nearly done indeed . . . The plumber draws near the end of his labours, the last grate was being fixed today, every day I get paint on my clothes from some pleasingly unexpected quarter, there is glass in the verandah door and the scraper has come. Also there is a man a planting trees. Up and down the pergola . . . we have stuck 500 daffodils – or 800 – there is room for a dispute how many there were in a bag, but anyhow a marvellous number."[4]

The crisis in his health, and the move from Worcester Park to Sandgate, had indeed marked a change in his life – a change in outlook as well as circumstances. The burst of energy which carried H.G. through the rush of writing at Woking and Heatherlea had exhausted him. He was now having trouble writing the short stories he had promised for the *Strand* and even in thinking up magazine articles. Though he had begun the long travail with *Kipps,* he knew that would take time. Meanwhile, he had to live on the new editions and translations of work that was already published. He had made good bargains for his three latest books. For *When the Sleeper Wakes* he had £700 for the serial rights, and £500 on account from Harper for the English book edition; the American advance was another £300. The advances on *Mr Lewisham* came to another £1,200. *The First Men in the Moon,* for which the *Strand* paid over £800 and *Cosmopolitan* £300 for the serial versions, secured a further £1,000 for the London and New York book editions. Even with the expense of building Spade House, H.G. was comfortably solvent. Though *The First Men in the Moon* seemed likely to be commercially successful he no longer wished (nor felt able) to turn out that kind of story. With the end of the century, and possibly with rapidly improving health and the growing prospects of social and financial success, Wells began to see himself in a new role.

There are signs that this transition had begun in *The Sleeper,* a clumsy tale overtly modelled on Edward Bellamy's *Looking Backward* and using the same "time-travelling" device of a sleeper awakened in a different society two hundred years later. By comparison with the dramatic intensity of *The Time Machine* it is imaginatively weak, and a crude vehicle to carry predictions about the social life of the future. The attitude that Wells takes to this coming society is oddly ambiguous. This book, in which the boss Ostrog rules over a mass of routinised slave workers, prefigures George Orwell's *1984*. Yet Wells seems unsure whether to approve or disapprove of his projection, whether he is writing a utopia or an anti-utopia. The main interest, however, lies more in the shift from a projective technique based on science (and especially on evolutionary ideas) to one based on politics and sociology. In the process, H.G. also began to intrude his opinions at the expense of his art. *The Sleeper* smells of the lamp.

In writing *The First Men in the Moon*, Wells once more drew on earlier models, Cyrano de Bergerac, Poe and Verne among them. He also had some technical help from Gregory who, in June 1899, sent Wells a number of papers on lunar craters, and an article from *Nature* which was published in August 1900 in which a Professor Poynting gave an account of experiments made to determine whether any substance could screen off gravitation – the idea that Wells used under the name of "Cavorite" to carry Cavor's capsule between the earth and the moon.

The First Men in the Moon, written in the more relaxed conditions of Arnold House, is a much more attractive book than *The Sleeper*. Its strong narrative line and its sure-handed prose show that H.G. was recovering his touch. Some passages – notably the description of the plants growing rapidly in the lunar dawn, which T.S.Eliot years later recalled as "quite unforgettable" – are comparable to the best in the earlier romances. The idea was not very original, but the treatment is entertaining and the satire pointed. The ant-like Selenites live in sub-lunar caverns, like the Morlocks, and like the Morlocks they are machine-minders, among whom the division of labour has been carried to the point where the creatures are bred for specific tasks. Wells makes a contrast between Bedford, the imperialist adventurer who descends upon the moon rather in the manner of Dr Jameson's raid in furtherance of Cecil Rhodes's mining interests in South Africa, and Cavor, the scientist, who remains behind and radios descriptions of Selenite society which are deliberately used to comment satirically on human affairs. In *The War of the Worlds* Wells had made a comparison between the Martians' treatment of human beings and the slaughter of the Tasmanians by British settlers; in *The First Men in the Moon* the implicit reference is to the current mood of imperialism. The story, lacking the brooding obsession with fate of the earlier romances, clearly marks a transition in his writing.

Love and Mr Lewisham was also a transitional book. Wells now wanted to attempt a "real" novel, and planned this account of his rise from

Midhurst through South Kensington on a large scale. "It was", he wrote to Elizabeth Healey on 22 June 1900, "an altogether more serious undertaking than anything I have done before . . . I have torn up and shied away twice as much stuff as still stands in the story."[5] It was so close to his life that it convinced old friends such as Simmons and Gregory by its authenticity. "Many of his worldly experiences I knew by heart", Simmons wrote of George Lewisham on 15 June, "for haven't I lived them?" And Gregory told Wells that "I cannot get that poor devil Lewisham out of my head, and I wish he had an address, for I would go to him and rescue him from the miserable life in which you leave him." But, in using his own life as the model, Wells had run into the conflict which lay at the heart of all his serious fiction. The vein of pathos and aspiration which threaded through his early life appealed to the new reading public whose experience lay close to such struggles to achieve gentility, and the act of writing the novel undoubtedly helped him to discharge his own unhappy memories and frustrations. Yet several critics wondered, as the *Speaker* put it on 16 June 1900, whether there was "something radically wrong with the author's art . . . a disproportionate realism that almost amounted to vulgarity". Edward Garnett, writing on 21 June, noted that "the author *as artist* has not so completely absorbed & assimilated the author's philosophy" as to conquer "the rather hard prosaic exact creed of *explanation, analysis and demonstration*". Wells had been so involved in recording his personal life that he had failed to realise that "Life is so much greater than any possible *explanation* of it."[6]

The creed and the art, in short, were muddled, and because Wells had already discovered in the effort to bring off the book that he could not disentangle them he began to justify his inability to distinguish life and art into a principle. Henry James, as well as Garnett, had also perceived this tendency, and writing to Wells on 17 June he tempered his praise with a gentle note of caution.[7]

I have found in it a great charm, and a great deal of the real thing – that is of the note of life, if not all of it. . . . Why I haven't found "All" I will some day try and tell you. . . . Meanwhile be assured of my appreciation of your humour and your pathos – your homely truth and your unquenchable fancy. I am not quite sure that I see your *idea* – I mean your Subject, so to speak, as determined or constituted: but in short the thing is a bloody little chunk of life, of no small substance, and I wish it a great and continuous fortune.

Arnold Bennett wrote expressing his regret that Wells had abandoned imaginative romances. "Why the Hell have you joined the conspiracy to restrict me to one particular type of story?" Wells demanded on 15 June. "I want to write novels and before God I *will* write novels. They are the proper stuff for my everyday work, a methodical careful distillation of one's thoughts and sentiments and experiences and impressions." Bennett cited Balzac as the outstanding case of the writer who asserts the absolute values of literature. "No", Wells replied forcibly on 5 July, "it is *not* 'Balzac first and the rest nowhere' . . . For my own part I am a purblind laborious intelligence exploring that cell of Being called Wells and I resent your Balzac. But this sort of thing is more fitted for conversation than writing. I hope soon we may have some chance of an argey bargey."[8]

Bennett soon came down to go on with the argument, arriving on 18 August for a week-end visit – part of which was taken up with Wells's experiments in his new craze, photography. "What will you give us if we don't send you your photograph?" he wrote after Bennett had left: "We haven't printed it yet but the negative looks good for a fiver to me." He was on good terms with Bennett, whom he had known for the last three years and with whom he had formed a lively friendship.[9] It began on 30 September 1897 when Bennett had written to him, expressing appreciation of his work, asking how he had come to know about the Potteries (*The Cone*), and enclosing a review of *The Invisible Man* which Bennett had written for a penny magazine called *Woman* he was then editing. The two men were much of an age. Bennett's childhood and adolescence had been more comfortable – his father had worked himself up in the world as a solicitor – but he had known the struggle to keep up genteel standards and the agony of trying to establish himself as a writer. He was ambitious, like Wells, but where Wells had imagination to marry to his talent, Bennett had application. He had grown up in a hard family, full of repressed emotions, dominated by the father's authoritarian streak and lacking in maternal affection. Bennett had emerged as a stiff and unde-monstrative man, given to despondent moods, priggish in manner and anxious to observe the conventions of the society into which success carried him. Yet he had a laconic attitude towards H.G. which enabled him to take in his stride the irritations and embarrassments that flowed from any close relationship with Wells, and to appreciate his qualities. Above all, he found H.G. provocative and interesting, with an ebullience that complemented Bennett's own formal presence and a vitality he felt unable to express himself. Virginia Woolf was later to attack them both for disinterest in the mental and emotional life of their characters, and for the detailed realism of their novels. At the beginning of the century, it was that emphasis they found they had in common, and it bound them together as professionals as well as friends.

Wells certainly found Sandgate socially congenial, and as his health improved his spirits rose. He was beginning to look the part of the man of letters who had become the man of property. He was now fit enough to cycle over to Conrad at the Pent or on to Stocks Hill to see the Fords whenever he felt the claustrophobic need to dash out and see someone, and there was no lack of visitors to Sandgate. He was able to release the capacities for fun which made him an exhilarating, if somewhat exhausting, host. H.G. had already discovered a talent for inventing new games, or improving old ones, and he had no hesitation about enlisting any visitor into one of these larks. Charades, which became a regular feature of Spade hospitality, were much in vogue. Ford recalled one in which he was "the sole croupier at a green table in a marvellous Monte Carlo scene [in which] Jane was a gambling duchess of entirely reckless habits".[10] Jane, indeed, was the *patronne* of all the dramatic entertainments, and worked them up over the years into an elaborate ritual which her guests came to expect. Within three years their fortunes had changed dramatically. They had become wealthy enough to afford this new style of life, employing several servants and spending freely.

Occasionally Wells went over to Liss to see his parents and his mother paid at least one visit to Spade House before she died. Yet the contact with his family had become very slight. His brother Frank was still depressed by his failure to make anything of his life. "I'm stalemated", he wrote sadly to H.G. on one occasion. Instead "of coming up on the tide", he said, he was "water-logged and dead".[11] All the same, Frank carried the day-to-day problems of the ageing Joe and Sarah, and reassured H.G. who felt that, in success, he was doing too little to make his parents comfortable and, with characteristic generosity, wanted them to move at his expense, to a bigger house with a servant. That would be wrong, Frank told him, and an anxiety that was not wanted. "The GV would get all his old clothes in the best drawing-room, boots, etc . . . You see Mater will not have any help any suggestions are met with a blubbering let-out and she is as contrary on some things as a more juvenile woman. A larger house to rent you may take my word for it would be a big mistake. You know the Mater is not up to keeping a house thirty-five pounds a year tidy . . . she has not the strength and the old man has not the will."

Spade House was big enough for children as well as guests, and before the move took place Jane was pregnant. In the early summer of 1901 Wells wrote to Bennett that "visiting and receiving are alike 'off' for us just now for Mrs Wells and I have been collaborating (and publication is expected early in July) in the invention of a human being". He told Elizabeth Healey in July that "It makes me feel that youth is really over."[12] Before the child was born, however, he and Jane took a spring holiday in Italy and Switzerland, and called on Gissing in Paris on their way home. Gissing wrote to Bertz on 17 March saying that they had passed through a week before.[13] "Wells", he remarked, "is wonderfully prosperous. He has built himself a beautiful house on the cliff at Sandgate (near Folkestone) where, sitting at his ease, he communicates with London by telephone! That kind of thing will never fall to me."

Gissing was invited to pay a visit to the "beautiful house". Wells had been distressed by his condition, thin, ailing and almost unable to work. Gissing had gone through a form of marriage with Gabrielle Fleury in Rouen, and then settled with her and her mother in Paris, where they hectored and – in Wells's opinion – half-starved him. Wells thought a holiday at Sandgate might restore him but his French doctor wanted him to go to the Alps. Gabrielle, whose letters at this time show a fierce possessiveness and a fear that once in England the weak Gissing might again become the prey of his wife, strongly opposed the visit. It was only because Gissing had business in London that she relented. They arrived on 27 May, and Gabrielle went back four days later to care for her invalid mother. Gissing stayed on and saw Dr Hick, who did not consider he had tuberculosis, but a London specialist urged on him an "open-air and over-feeding" cure at a sanatorium in Suffolk. Before he left for Suffolk, Gissing spent several weeks at Sandgate, where Jane Wells did her best to fatten him.

During the visit H.G. took Gissing over to spend the night with James at Rye, and on 20 June, the day after the visit, James wrote to Wells: "I had much pleasure and interest in your having brought him over – for highly sympathetic he seemed to me. But, by the same token, worn almost to the bone (of sadness). Why *will* he do these things?"[14] Gabrielle continued to write hysterical letters to Jane about Gissing's continued stay, but they managed to get him off to the sanatorium for a few weeks before he went back to Paris.

Gissing stayed almost until the child was born on 17 July. The boy was called George Philip, though his name was soon shortened to "GP" and then to Gip. It seems not to have been an easy birth. Mrs Robbins, acknowledging a telegram and letter from H.G., commented that Jane "has had a hard time I can see, I feared it for her very much", and then wrote commiseratingly to her daughter. "I am so glad", she said, "so very very glad, so are you aren't you you poor little thing that it is over . . . Bertie says everything right, that is good to hear & you will be taken care of I know."[15]

While two doctors, a nurse and the servants coddled Jane through her recovery, H.G. reacted strangely. Soon after Gip was born he set off on an extended trip across the southern counties, visiting his parents at Liss and ending up in Ramsgate about the middle of September. Through the endearments and feyly-inaccurate spelling of the letters that Jane then wrote to H.G. ran a note of apologetic anxiety.[16] She begged H.G. to forgive her – apparently for making a fuss about his departure – and imploringly assured him of her affection. After something like three weeks had passed, when she had had some imperfectly audible telephone calls and H.G. had also written, she recovered her spirits and was writing a jokey letter about a planned reunion at the Torino restaurant in London.

It was a curious episode, part of the difficult readjustment of their marital relationship which had been going on for some time and may have been accelerated by Jane's pregnancy. H.G. was showing signs of the habit, which grew upon him, of going off impetuously. After 1900, he wrote many years later, a "compromise with Jane developed . . . the *modus vivendi* we contrived was sound enough to hold us together to the end, but it was by no means a perfect arrangement". Jane, he recalled, felt that he had been unlucky in mating himself "first to an unresponsive and then to a fragile companion . . . She suppressed any jealous impulse and gave me whatever freedom I desired . . . So long as we were in the opening phase of our struggle for a position and worldly freedom, this question was hardly a practical issue between us. There was neither time nor energy to indulge any form of wanderlust. But with the coming of success, increasing leisure and facility of movement, the rapid enlargement of our circle of acquaintance, and contact with unconventional and exciting people, there was no further necessity for the same rigid self-restraint".

Wells did not date this "compromise" more precisely. It is doubtful whether it was explicit before Gip was born and it may even have been as late as 1903 when the second child, Frank, arrived. It was a slow matter of half-truths and partial understandings, and episodes such as his "vacation" after the birth of Gip were the material from which it was painfully built. There can be no doubt of Jane's rather desperate attachment to H.G. It is clear from the remaining years of their marriage that he had a continuing dependence upon her unwavering support. But it is also clear that she was willing at all costs to conciliate him, even at the price of self-abnegation. There is a hint of fear, of a desire to appease his irritability as an apprehensive parent mollifies a self-indulgent child. It is as if, in mothering little Gip, she was discovering that she had to mother her husband as well.

PART THREE
Prophet and Politician

THE DISCOVERY OF THE FUTURE

When Wells moved into Spade House at the beginning of the new century he began a new career and a new way of life. As he recovered from his collapse at New Romney he had gone through a remarkable change. After his illness he no longer felt driven to write about terrifying monsters: he had discovered a sense of purpose. He now believed that mankind might be saved, and that he could play a significant part in that process of salvation. The clue to this shift of attitude can be found in a lecture which he gave at the Royal Institution with the significant title "The Discovery of the Future", which Gregory published in *Nature* on 6 February 1902. He recalled his old fear that the human race was doomed to perish, and that all life would become extinct in a dying world.

That of all such nightmares is the most consistently convincing. And yet one doesn't believe it. At least I do not. And I do not believe in those things because I have come to believe in certain other things, in the coherency and purpose in the world and in the greatness of human destiny. Worlds may freeze and suns may perish, but I believe there stirs something within us now that can never die again.

Wells was catching the more optimistic mood of the new reign, as much as he was projecting his own success and improving health into a cheerier view of the human prospect. But this new attitude gave him a fresh and different impetus. He now began to write as if "like that figure of Atlas which stood in my father's shop window – I sustained the whole world upon my shoulders".

The first result was what he later called "the keystone to the main arch of my work", the book called *Anticipations* which established him as a political prophet as quickly as *The Time Machine* had made his name as a dealer in horrors and spells. H.G. began work on a series of articles commissioned in 1900 by W.L.Courtney, who succeeded Frank Harris as editor of the *Fortnightly Review*, and they appeared in the course of 1901. They were, he told Elizabeth Healey on 2 July 1901, "designed to undermine and destroy the monarch monogamy and respectability – and the British Empire, all under the guise of a speculation about motor cars and electrical heating. One has to go quietly in the earlier papers, but the last will be a buster."[1] Towards the end of 1901 the articles came out as a book with the full title of *Anticipations of the Reaction of Mechanical and Scientific Progress Upon Human Life and Thought*.

The more Wells looked at what he had done, the better he was pleased with the new role in which he had cast himself. When the book came out he wrote to Gregory on 29 December 1901:[2]

We'll have a republic in ten years – or at any rate we may have if only everyone will buck up. The amount of latent treason that I am discovering is amazing. I shall talk treason at the R.I. I'm going to write, talk, preach revolution for the next five years. If I had enough mone behind me to keep me off the need of earning a living I would do the job myself.

To Bennett, who had written that H.G. either had the journalistic trick of seeming omniscient or was "one of the most remarkable men alive", he replied cockily on 25 November: "There is no illusion. I *am* great." And he added that reading the work in parts "gives you no inkling of the massive culminating effect of the book as a whole".[3]

Wells was in a euphoric mood. He had tried something new and pulled it off with *éclat* – the articles stirred up much discussion and Macmillan, after a pawky estimate of the book sales, had to reprint successive new editions as *Anticipations* sold as fast as a novel. It had been, as H.G. told Bennett, "a hell of a handful to manage", but he thought it would "do an infinite amount of good in the country". England was at the beginning of a new reign and a new century, and Wells had struck just the right note of prophecy in providing this "rough sketch of the coming time, a prospectus as it were, of the joint undertakings of mankind in facing these impending years".[4] The moment for gloomy cosmic predictions had passed. People wanted to know what was going to happen in their lifetimes.*

---

* Two years earlier, in an interview in *Cassell's Saturday Journal* on 26 April 1899, he had shown the way his ideas were developing. "I am strongly of the opinion that we ought to consider the possibilities of the future much more than we do. Why should four-fifths of the fiction of today be concerned with times that can never come up again, while the future is scarcely speculated upon? At present we are almost helpless in the grip of circumstances, and I think we ought to strive to shape our destinies."

Wells called *Anticipations* a "prospectus". That it undoubtedly was – of his opinions. The book was full of shrewd guesses, and some bad ones as well. H.G. clearly foresaw the Age of Motors, down to a detailed description of sweeping throughways, the congestion in city centres and the suburbanisation of the countryside. He was wrong about "the coming invention of flying": not, he said, from "disbelief in its final practicability" but because he did not see that "aeronautics will ever come into play as a serious modification of transport and communications".* He was equally doubtful about submarines. "I must confess that my imagination, in spite even of spurring, refuses to see any sort of submarine do anything but suffocate its crew and founder at sea." Yet he was brilliantly right about the tank, and its effect upon warfare: it was the only means he could see of breaking the inevitable stalemate that would develop when two great armies, equipped with automatic weapons, faced each other in a line of trenches from the Alps to the Channel.

Such technical forecasts, however, were merely attractive ground-bait to catch the public – as he told Elizabeth Healey. The real novelty of the book lay in its ambitious attempt to write the history of the future before it happened. The attempt was deliberate, as Wells made clear in his Royal Institution lecture. "It is our ignorance of the future and our persuasion that that ignorance is incurable", he then said, "that alone has given the past its enormous predominance in our thoughts." He believed that it was now possible "to attain to a knowledge of coming things as clear, as universally convincing, and infinitely more important to mankind than the clear vision of the past that geology has opened to us during the nineteenth century". Wells argued that this new kind of inductive history – what he later called Human Ecology, the working out of "biological, intellectual, economic consequences" – might be used both to chart the possibilities of the future and to provoke men into making sensible use of them. *Anticipations* was the first of many manifestos in which Wells developed that theme.

Wells was proposing a much broader vision of the future than might be obtained by making simple projections about the supply of coal or population trends, or by brilliant guesswork about technical inventions. By

* Only two years before the Wright brothers flew at Kitty Hawk he was obsessed with complex designs for airships, and the most he could say about heavier-than-air craft was that "long before the year AD 2000, and very probably before 1950, a successful aeroplane will have soared and come home safe and sound". This was still better than the *New York Times*, which had scarcely printed its prediction that it would take mathematicians and mechanics "from one to ten million years" to produce a real aircraft before the Wright Flyer was off the ground.

his method, as he tried to show in *Anticipations*, he considered it possible to synthesize human knowledge into a scenario of the years ahead, basing prophecy upon an analysis of social forces unleashed by modern technology and communications. He also presented the cast of characters who would act out the drama that he foresaw – the idle, functionless shareholders at one extreme, the increasingly "wretched multitudes of the Abyss" at the other, the fatuous, self-interested party politicians engaged in sham battles and, in marked contrast, the emerging élite whose destiny it was to save mankind and inherit the earth. There were obvious similarities between this interpretation of the future and the apocalyptic variant of Marxism which Lenin, living in London, was developing at much the same time. But, in trying to persuade his readers that there was a pattern to the future as well as to the past, Wells had not borrowed from Marx: he was tapping a much older tradition, reaching back to the millenarian doctrines of Cromwell's England for his vision of things to come. *Anticipations* was written in the language of sociology, but its plot was a morality play about the Last Judgement.

The analogy becomes much clearer as Wells warms to his argument. His "new mass of capable men", predominantly scientists and engineers, in fact are Puritans – men with "a strong imperative to duty" a will to subordinate their appetites to the service of the state. They will have no time for the antics of party politics, but will use the increasing influence which will flow from the key positions they occupy in modern society to impose "social order" on "the vast confusions of the coming time". Democracy will lead inevitably to catastrophe. In the short run politicians are concerned only "to keep appearances up and taxes down"; in the longer run, because democracy means inefficiency at home and competitive xenophobia abroad, they will blunder into a long and devastating war which will give the scientifically-educated élite in all countries the chance to see that they actually hold real power and can use it "in the cause of the higher sanity". The movement that will establish "a world state with a common language and a common rule" Wells calls "the New Republic". He makes it sound like a latter-day Roman Empire. "All over the world its roads, its standards, its laws and its apparatus of control will run", he wrote. Sometimes he seems to be arguing that the new order will emerge inevitably from the old, and that its coming will merely be hastened to the degree that the "naturally and informally organized, educated class" becomes conscious of its destiny. His New Republicans are described as "a sort of outspoken Secret Society . . . an informal and open freemasonry", whose common interests and attitudes will unavoidably lead to the creation of the new world state. Sometimes, however, he implies that this evolution is not inevitable, and that unless this class seizes its opportunity it will be impossible to save the human race from disaster. The ambiguity was always present, and it was the effort to resolve it that led Wells towards his utopias – a literary device that permitted him to write about a future state without having to explain how it might be reached or how human nature might be changed to make it possible.

His dilemma, in fact, was merely a variant on the old argument about determinism and free will, and he sought to deal with it much in the same way that Huxley had done. The laws of Nature (or God) may not be comprehensible or alterable, but in order to live within their framework mankind needs an ethical imperative. "If the universe is non-ethical by our present standards", he wrote, "we must reconsider those standards and reconstruct our ethics." Men must behave as though they have a choice between different values and actions, and this means that they must assume "personal moral responsibility" for their behaviour. By an extension of this reasoning, the chosen people will inherit the earth, if that is God's purpose, but in the meantime they must demonstrate their worthiness by striving for the new moral order. The language Wells uses is explicitly prophetic. There is no longer any need to fear "a mysteriously incompetent Deity exasperated by an unsatisfactory creation" and taking revenge on mankind's errors. In the new order, man's concern will not be "to work out a system of penalties for the sins of dead men, but to understand and participate in this new view of man's place in the scheme of time and space, a new illumination".

These are, of course, the words of the moralist rather than the humanist. The promises implicit in this revelation are reserved for the elect, rather than for the generality of undeserving mankind. When Wells comes to this point he writes in a manner which recalls the "superman" speech of the Artilleryman in *The War of the Worlds*:

... the ethical system of these men of the New Republic, the ethical system which will dominate the world state, will be shaped primarily to favour the procreation of what is fine and efficient and beautiful in humanity – beautiful and strong bodies, clear and powerful minds, and a growing body of knowledge – and to check the procreation of base and servile types, of fear-driven and cowardly souls, of all that is mean and ugly and bestial in the souls, bodies, or habits of men.

Wells, in fact, had decided that the best insurance against the kind of evolutionary regression which haunted his earlier writing is to secure the survival of the fittest by the elimination of the unfit. He applauds Malthus as well as the work of Alfred Russell, Wallace and Darwin which showed that "whole masses of the human population are . . . inferior in their claim upon the future . . . that they cannot be given opportunities or trusted with power . . . To give them equality is to sink to their level, to protect and cherish them is to be swamped in their fecundity." The alternative to the beautiful life is death, and the New Republicans will have "little pity and less benevolence" for "a multitude of contemptible and silly creatures, fear-driven and helpless and useless . . . feeble, inefficient, born of unrestrained lusts". They can only exist on sufferance, and the New Republicans will not "hesitate to kill when that sufferance is abused". There will be no place in the world for the "rough boys" of Bromley. This disagreeable diatribe against the unfit, the submerged mass that may otherwise become the Morlocks who will turn the scientific élite into helpless Eloi, was the product of fears of the underworld that Wells had in common with many of his readers. The way, indeed, that he touched on these fears was an important part of the powerful appeal of his anti-proletarian utopias. One of the strongest motives to social reform around the turn of the century, and one of the reasons why so much of the initiative for it lay with middle-class intellectuals given to élitist ideas, was this profound fear of the masses – dirty, ill-educated, and full of a dreadful potency. For Wells the new order should "tolerate no dark corners where the people of the Abyss may fester".

Naturally enough, this kind of reasoning led Wells to advocate birth-control and even sterilisation. Unlike many Victorian reformers, he did not object overtly to the sexuality of the masses. What bothered him was their propensity to breed useless, troublesome and miserable children. In the closing section of *Anticipations*, indeed, he argues forcefully for sexual freedom. Once one can separate procreation from sexual relations then the latter

become of no more importance than the morality of one's deportment at chess, or the general morality of outdoor games. Indeed, then the question of sexual relationships would be entirely on all fours with, and very probably analogous to, the question of golf . . . An able-bodied man continually addicted to love-making that had no result in offspring would be just as silly and morally objectionable as an able-bodied man who devoted his chief energies to hitting little balls over golf-links. But no more.

This excursion into matters of sexual morality, which took Wells as far as a cautious attack on monogamous marriage and a hint about endowed motherhood, did not attract much attention. Wells said so much else that was fresh and exciting. Yet it was significant. If *Anticipations* made his reputation as a reformer, in these few paragraphs about sex and the family it also contained the ideas that were later to bring that reputation to the brink of ruin.

"This happens to be my year", Wells wrote on 7 November 1901 to Sir Joseph Edwards, proposing himself for an entry in *The Year Book*, "and I should very much like to blow a little in your annual."[5] For once his anxiety about publicity was unnecessary. *Anticipations* was soaring without any need for Wells to puff it. It was a mark of Wells's ebullience at this time of success that he was unusually charitable about criticism. On 20 November he wrote generously to Pinker that Conrad "doesn't like it in a friendly & respectful way & would like very much to go for it in two or three articles".[6] Knowing that Conrad was short of money and in poor health, Wells asked Pinker to help in placing these articles which "could make instead of marring his reputation like this damn collaboration with F.M.Hueffer". Conrad's comments, in a letter to Wells, were certainly "friendly & respectful", yet they raised some fundamental objections to the argument of the book and to "what seems to me the opening of a campaign on your part".[7]

For this is what in the last and most general pronouncement the book amounts to. It is – and as a matter of fact the whole tone of it implies that – it is a *move*. Where the move to my apprehension seems unsound is in this, that it seems to presuppose . . . a sort of select circle to which you address yourself, leaving the rest of the world outside the pale. It seems as if they had to *come in* into a rigid system, whereas I submit that Wells should *go forth*, not dropping fishing lines for particular trout but casting a wide and generous net, where there would be room for everybody; where indeed every sort of fish would be welcome, appreciated and made use of . . . Generally the fault I find with you is that you do not take sufficient account of human imbecility which is cunning and perfidious.

Conrad had hit on the very point on which Wells was most vulnerable: his inability to see why rational men should not immediately accept his reasonably self-evident convictions – and his irritable, even contemptuous dismissal of the irrational in human nature.

When Wells sent a copy of "The Discovery of the Future" to Edmund Gosse, he replied: "I am sure the weak spot in all Utopias is the insufficient consideration of Man's intense instinctive determination to be happy. You prophets of the future are so occupied with the useful that you forget that it is only in individualism that we can be happy."[8] The weak spot in the case of Wells was that he feared irrational compulsions so much that he either attacked them, when he saw them as obstacles to his passionate desire to impose order on the disorderly human condition, or suppressed them, when they offered an almost insuperable objection to his argument. There is a direct analogy between the disaster which awaits those of his characters who surrender to "lower" impulses, and the catastrophe which confronts the human race if it does not master its brutish instincts. It was essentially this issue that led to the controversies with G.K.Chesterton and Hilaire Belloc and vitiated H.G.'s successive recipes for human salvation.

The criticism of *Anticipations* was trivial by comparison with the praise. At the age of thirty-four Wells suddenly found himself with a new public and an influence that surpassed anything that he had envisaged when he set out to write the series of articles for Courtney. Before he published *Anticipations* he had been an up-and-coming writer. Now he was a man of standing, sought after socially and courted politically. The success had a profound effect upon him. "Writing", Wells noted in 1909 in the preface to the first Russian edition of his work, "is a form of adventure . . . if your book has the least bit of luck . . . in England you become a prosperous man. Suddenly you are able to go where you like, meet whoever you like. All doors are open to you. You emerge from the closed circle in which you moved before."[9]

A door that opened immediately was that of the Fabian Society. The man who made the link between the Sandgate and Fabian sets was Graham Wallas, one of the founders of the Society along with Bernard Shaw and the Webbs. Shaw, in fact, asked Wallas to introduce him to Wells after reading *Anticipations*. Wells had come to know Wallas when he was living next door to the Pophams at Arnold House.* Popham and Wallas were married to two of the Radford girls, who came from a family of ten brothers and sisters, West Country nonconformists and business people with literary and artistic tastes. Wallas, the son of an evangelical clergyman, had been a classical scholar at Oxford but he was more

---

* The Pophams were connected by marriage as well as friendship to the Limpsfield set of Fabians and writers as well as to the Bloomsbury group. Their son, Hugh Popham, later married Brynhild Olivier, the daughter of Sydney and Margaret Olivier, who were neighbours of the Garnett family and of E.R.Pease, the secretary of the Fabians. Hugh Popham's daughter, Olivier Popham, then married Quentin Bell, the son of Vanessa and Clive Bell and the nephew of Virginia Woolf.

influenced by scientific thought than by the philosophical idealism of T.H.Green – which provided an alternative outlet for evangelical reformism.[10] He appealed to the puritanical side of Wells's nature, and especially to his interest in education. What Wallas later called the "Great Society" was a moral community which contrasted both with the bourgeois creed of complacent materialism and with what he saw as the sterile collectivism of the Webbs. Like Wells, he thought ordinary human nature was undynamic and incompetent, and needing leadership, and the means whereby men were to be changed was a massive campaign of popular education.

In all these respects, Wallas and Wells were working within a similar frame of reference. It was understandable that Wells should take a liking to him. He was, as Beatrice Webb said of him, full of "benevolence and kindliness and selflessness", though somewhat impractical and more of a teacher than a leader. Wells read and criticised manuscripts for Wallas, and the favour was reciprocated. In 1903 Wells and Wallas took a walking trip in the Alps. The idea of the two walkers who find themselves translated to a different society in *A Modern Utopia* came from that holiday. Years later Wells incorporated that autumn vacation in *The New Machiavelli*, in which his discussions with Wallas were recorded in the arguments between Remington and Willersley.

It was an important new relationship for Wells. Not only did Wallas have a brief, but significant influence upon his thinking. Wallas also provided him with the contacts and the intellectual cachet which he needed to enter the inner circle of the Fabians. On 8 December 1901, when Sidney Webb wrote a congratulatory letter about *Anticipations*, he introduced himself "as a friend of Graham Wallas & Bernard Shaw, whom you know".[11] While Webb admired the book, he felt that Wells had given too much weight to engineers, chemists and electricians as the coming men of power, and that he had undervalued the role of the professional administrator. He added that "all experience shows that men need organizing as much as machines, or rather, much more . . . It takes more imagination to organize men than machines – even more poetry!" It was flattering for Wells to be taken so seriously by the most influential socialist in the country. Sidney Webb and his wife, Beatrice, were then at the height of their reputation; with Bernard Shaw they dominated the Fabian Society and influenced key figures in the trade union leadership, the civil service, and the Liberal and Conservative parties. It was the heyday of the Fabian policy of "permeation", whereby like-minded men of intelligence and public spirit were to be persuaded to act in concert for the common weal. One can see why the Webbs were quickly attracted to the doctrine of the New Republic.

Before her husband wrote to Wells, Beatrice had already noticed this possible new recruit to the stage-army of the intelligent. She had a quick eye for those who might be taken up. *Anticipations*, she noted in December 1901, was the "most remarkable book of the year: a powerful imagination furnished with the data and methods of physical science, working on social problems. The weak part of Wells' outfit is his lack of any detailed knowledge of social organisations – and this, I think, vitiates his capacity for foreseeing the future machinery of government and the relation of classes. But his work is full of luminous hypotheses and worth careful study by those who are trying to look-forward."[12]

Wells was not a stranger to the Webbs, though they had not met. He had already been in touch with Edward Pease, the full-time secretary of the Fabians, who wrote to him on 10 January 1902 to ask "if you've yet met the Webbs: they are the pioneers of your New Republic. We have lived for years on Webb's new ideas of politics. We want someone else who also can think ahead, and that is why I welcome *Anticipations*."[13] H.G. wrote back to ask where Pease stood on the monarchy, the "centre of base & vulgar habits & ideas, the keystone of the real control of the country by fools, fanatics & society women". He was, he added, "going to have two whole days with Sidney Webb next week & I hope to thrash out all sorts of things. I've never met him and I'm tremendously expectant."[14]

The Webbs, after an exchange of correspondence, were invited to Sandgate. "The Webbs", Wells told Pease on 29 January, "are wonderful people & they leave me ashamed of my indolence & mental dissipation & awfully afraid of Mrs Webb."[15] Beatrice Webb recorded her impressions of their visit on 28 February 1902: "We have seen something lately of H.G.Wells and his wife", she noted in her diary.

Wells is an interesting though somewhat unattractive personality except for his agreeable disposition and intellectual vivacity . . . He is a good instrument for popularising ideas, and he gives as many ideas as he receives . . . Altogether it is refreshing to talk to a man who has shaken himself loose from so many of the current assumptions and is looking at life as an explorer of a new world.

Beatrice Webb was as careful, and as detached, in her judgement of Jane.

His wife is a pretty little person with a strong will, mediocre intelligence and somewhat small nature. She has carefully moulded herself in dress, manners and even accent to take her place in any society her husband's talents may lead them into. But it is all rather artificial, from the sweetness of her smile to her interest in public affairs. However, she provides him with a charming well-ordered home, though I should imagine her constant companionship was somewhat stifling. They are both of them well-bred in their pleasant tempers, careful consideration of the feelings of others, quick apprehension of new conventions and requirements, but they both of them lack ease and repose, and she has an ugly absence of spontaneity of thought and feeling.

It was understandable that Wells should seem to her a stimulating new recruit for socialism and "useful to gradgrinds like ourselves in supplying us with loose generalisations which we can use as instruments of research".[16]

Both she and Sidney lived a life of intellectual rigour and, supported by her private income, dedicated social enterprise. One of the famous Potter daughters, she had used her remarkable talents to become a specialist in social investigation. Apparently austere, and certainly so where personal indulgence was concerned, she was in fact more emotional and understanding than she seemed: those feelings she kept for her diary, and for the lifelong devotion she gave to her husband. He too gave the impression of a dry stick; small, bearded, pernickety, but immensely pertinacious, he was not only the public member of their partnership – engaged in such enterprises as the Fabian Society, the early work of the London County Council and the foundation of the London School of Economics – but was also the indispensable complement to his intuitive and handsome wife in their life of painstaking research and political contrivance.

After Beatrice Webb had coolly looked over H.G. and Jane she began to invite them to dinners and to introduce them about. Often it was only H.G. who went to social occasions. Jane was tied down with a small son at Sandgate, and H.G., who wanted to be easily available for meetings and other evening engagements, took a pied-à-terre at 6 Clements Inn. Towards the end of 1902 the Webbs gave a dinner for Wells to meet John Burns, the trade union leader, the Shaws, Herbert Asquith, the rising Liberal barrister who was to become prime minister, and Lady Elcho. H.G. was clearly a little overawed. Beatrice noted that he "was rather silent; when he spoke he tried hard to be clever – he never let himself go".[17] Lady Elcho, a notable hostess, was attractive and vivacious, married – in Beatrice's phrase – to a "card-playing and cynical aristocrat", and their home at Stanway in Gloucestershire was celebrated for weekend parties in the Edwardian years. The group which centred around the house was a smart social but intellectually able set known as "The Souls", though the Countess of Warwick observed that they were "perhaps more pagan than soulful". They were bright, and fast, and much involved with each other in their rejection of Victorian morality. The nickname was given to the group by Lord Charles Beresford at a dinner party of Lady Brownlow's in 1888: "You all sit and talk about each other's souls", he said, "I shall call you The Souls."

By the end of the century, they had made literature, art and ideas fashionable in Society at a time when Edward, first as Prince of Wales and then as King, was creating something of the style of a latter-day Regency. There were beautiful women, like Lady Desborough, Lady Ribblesdale and her sister, Margot Tennant, who collected round them a circle of clever and amusing men. They could talk well about science and politics when they met at Panshanger, Stanway, Ashridge, Wilton, Taplow and other country houses; and they had the habit of taking up talented new writers. At the time H.G. came into their orbit the dominant figure was Arthur Balfour who, Wells said, played the role of the receptive, inquiring intelligence; but there were other members of the ruling élite whom he already knew – such as Harry Cust, Lord Brownlow's heir, who had helped him in his early career. There were also clever Americans who were rich and wanted something more than the stuffy shooting-party at the end of the week; American heiresses and brides, like Winston Churchill's mother, who was one of the Jerome sisters; and men like W.W.Astor who financed the *Pall Mall* ventures. It was an alluring world. Wells felt immediately attracted and flattered by its patronage.

The draper's apprentice was now a familiar of a future premier, of cabinet ministers, dukes, earls and public servants. Their restless brilliance appealed to his own temperament; their apparent influence reinforced his dreams about beautiful New Republicans. Beatrice Webb, who knew them well, was less certain of their weight. In her diary in August 1892 she noted: "To me 'The Souls' will not bring 'the peace that passeth understanding', but a vain restlessness of tickled vanity. One would become quickly satiated."

As much as Lady Elcho Beatrice Webb had her *salon*, but she wanted it to be serious-minded and to exert a real and continuing influence on public affairs. Under the leadership of the Webbs, the Fabian Society was socialist but not committed to any party. The Webbs were as willing to work with like-minded Liberals or Tories as with cloth-capped union leaders. They found the politicians and public servants who ran the political system much more congenial than radical demagogues, and believed that they could work through them to achieve their ends. They were very doubtful whether "the people" would vote for collectivism. This conviction was the more plausible because party politics were in a state of flux. The Liberal Imperialists, who followed Joseph Chamberlain, and the Tory reformers, who had broken away with Lord Randolph Churchill, had much in common with each other, and with the municipal or "administrative" socialists like the Webbs – more than any of them had with the free-enterprisers of the plutocracy or the landed interest which still dominated the Tories. All of them were concerned with the Condition of the People at home and a strong forward policy abroad. It was a natural alliance, based upon élitism and a sense of national destiny, and very close to the set of ideas which Wells had canvassed in *Anticipations*. The "new men" in all parties were casting about for a policy, much as Wells had suggested when he talked about an "open freemasonry" to tackle the problems of the coming years. In November 1902, at a dinner party at the Webbs, on Millbank, Beatrice suggested something like a brains trust of a dozen men which might meet regularly for dinner to see what might be done, and the group convened for the first time at the house of Richard Burdon Haldane on 8 December.

Haldane himself was to be the reforming War Minister in the Liberal government after the 1906 landslide victory, the man who rebuilt the Army after the débâcles of the Boer War, and Lord Chancellor when war came in 1914. Sir Edward Grey, another of the group, was to become the Foreign Secretary who took Britain into that war. Leo Amery and Lord Milner were notable imperialists and Tory politicians; W.S.Hewins and the New Zealander, William Pember Reeves, were both Fabians, and the first and third Directors of the London School of Economics which the Webbs had founded. Sir Henry Newbolt also belonged and so, for a short time, did Bertrand Russell. Sidney Webb and Wells were members from the start.

The group met regularly in the winter season, at the Ship Tavern in Whitehall or the St Ermin's Hotel in Westminster, and they gave themselves the name of "The Co-efficients" to emphasise that they were there as experts interested above all in efficiency. Each in turn introduced a topic, and summary minutes were kept – for some time Wells was the recorder. On one occasion too few members turned up to justify a formal meeting and the brandy turned the evening into a jovial jest. Indeed, the group soon petered out, in Amery's phrase, "as a brains trust with definite political objectives" and became "a dining club for the informal discussion of serious topics" such as the powers of local government, the colour question, imperial defence and education policy.[18]

For Wells, however, his inclusion in this group was a reassuring sign that he was now regarded as a man of influence. The Webbs had asked him to join, Amery said, "nominally for literature", but he was wanted "for original thinking on all subjects". It was a heady experience for H.G. to find the eminent deferring to him; it naturally encouraged his belief that high-minded experts, who understood his message, were better levers for reform than democratic politicians who were driven to demagogy by the ignorant prejudice of the masses. Many people commented on the social versatility of Wells, which was aided by his charm and intelligence; it enabled him quickly to assume whatever role suited his immediate purpose. At the beginning of the century, he was already learning how to differentiate between his roles. He did not want merely to climb into conventional society. He wanted to get the best of all possible worlds, to indulge himself in whatever opportunity was to hand.

Intellectually, Wells gravitated towards the Webbs, Shaw and Balfour, just as his literary inclinations made him cling to Bennett, Conrad and James: but there was another part of his character that attracted him to the more eccentric and louche personalities who clustered round the fringes of the progressive movement – people who were vegetarians, spiritualists, believers in the New Life and sexual permissiveness. A common meeting place for these bohemians was Well Hall, the Eltham home of Hubert Bland and his wife, Edith Nesbit.[19] Bland, eleven years older than Wells, was a founder of the Fabian Society and one of the first group of Essayists.[20] He was one of the inner circle which was loosely called the "Old Gang". Bland was outwardly a Victorian gentleman, complete with high collar, ribboned monocle and frock-coat, and given to vigorous support of conventional morality. Brought up a Catholic, the son of impoverished gentry in the North of England, he had been swindled in his efforts to start a brush manufactory and had thereafter found it hard to make a living. When he first met Edith Nesbit, he was not only in financial straits but had embarked on the systematic philandering which contrasted so strikingly with his moral pretensions. Edith was equally unconventional; she was seven months pregnant when they married. It was only three years later that she discovered that Bland had never broken his engagement to a lady in Beckenham who was the mother of his illegitimate child. Bland had no hesitation about introducing Alice Hoatson into their home as housekeeper, on the excuse that as progressives they should help an unmarried mother, though she was carrying his child. Edith had even been persuaded to adopt the girl, Rosamund, before she discovered Bland was her father, and later, when she herself was in a pregnancy that ended in a still-birth, she condoned the birth of a son to Alice Hoatson and her husband.

Bland's interests were divided between his political activities, which he pursued lazily, and women – whom he pursued obsessively whilst, with equal obsession, he delivered himself of moral diatribes against sexual freedom. He once disarmingly explained to Wells that he needed the conventions because he found his pleasures in flouting them. It was more a case of perversity than conscious hypocrisy, and it is not surprising that this odd and undisciplined household was ravaged by secret storms. Visitors became accustomed to finding unattached young women and children of doubtful parentage about the place, and to hearing outbursts of argument or tearful complaints from Edith coming from behind closed doors. A talented and somewhat histrionic woman, she was given to scenes – she was noted for disrupting meetings with violent disagreements that often ended in fainting fits, but she was astonishingly loyal to Bland despite extreme provocation. Wells suggested that she "detested and mitigated and tolerated", her husband's amorous intrigues, and at the same time found them "exceedingly interesting". She provided the income which maintained their rambling and extravagant household, where the hospitality was generous but so ill-organised that H.G. described Well Hall as "a place to which one rushed down from town for the week-end to snatch one's bed before anyone else got it". Edith had become a very successful children's writer, and after *The Treasure Seekers* the Blands were able to afford the move to Well Hall in 1900. Wells believed that her success aggravated Bland's promiscuity as a compensation for "the wit and freaks and fantasies" of his wife, whose talents and earning power were so much greater than his own.

In 1903 Wells was week-ending fairly regularly, from the country houses of the smart set at one end of the social spectrum to the jolly irregularities of Well Hall at the other. The Blands also had a seaside house at Dymchurch, only a few miles west along the coast from Sandgate. More and more of his new friends were linked in some way with the Fabians. Among the inner group were another couple who, like the

Blands, were to play major roles in the drama which followed Wells's entry into Fabian affairs – William Pember Reeves and his wife Magdalen (Maud). The Bland household was disorderly, despite Bland's public genuflections to morality. By contrast, Reeves and his wife were fundamentally conformist, though all the talk in the family was about advanced ideas.[21]

Reeves had come to England in 1896 as the agent-general for New Zealand, which had recently elected the first Labour government in the world, and was experimenting with such progressive measures as votes for women and the nationalisation of the railways. He had been a member of that government, and as a man with long-standing Fabian sympathies he had been welcomed by the Webbs and worked up into a public figure. Even before he became High Commissioner in 1905 he was a familiar speaker on social problems to luncheon and dinner meetings, and though his official position precluded him from taking an active part in the Society, his book *State Experiments in Australia and New Zealand* became a text of practical Fabianism. His wife, Maud, however soon made a position for herself in the Society; she was energetic and handsome, and saw herself as a protagonist of the New Woman. She had played an important part behind the scenes in promoting the vote for women in New Zealand, and on arriving in London she soon found herself active in the suffrage movement and in other organisations concerned with women's rights, such as the National Anti-Sweating League. Her enthusiasm for such causes was communicated to her daughters, especially to Amber, one of the first girls to make her mark at Newnham College and get a double-first in her Cambridge examinations.

Wells got on famously with Edith Nesbit and Maud Reeves, both dominant and successful women who indulged and flattered him, but there was no spark of sympathy between him and their husbands. Bland hid his insecurity behind a haughty and quarrelsome personality; Reeves was by nature bitter and self-pitying, caustic with others and supercilious in his manner. Both were suspicious of Wells, and when trouble came it was they who proved his enemies.

For the present, however, H.G. was comfortable with these ambivalences. The antitheses of personality in these two families epitomised the dualism in the Fabian frame of mind. Its public image of high-mindedness and order masked the permissive attitudes and behaviour of many of the members, especially the younger ones. The dialectic of order and disorder was one which Wells had known from childhood, and in the

Society he found a congenial setting in which it was accepted. The Fabians curiously combined moral earnestness in public matters with at least verbal tolerance of private peccadilloes.

As H.G. began to win an audience as a prophet, and a place for himself in radical politics, his convictions and his art came into conflict. There were small indications of this antagonism cropping up in his daily life. There was, for instance, the confrontation between Shaw and Conrad, when G.B.S. went down to Spade House in the spring of 1902 and was taken over to the Pent. Nothing went right. Jessie Conrad, who was a notable cook, was put out because both Wells and Shaw were on peculiar diets. Conrad himself could not understand Shaw's blunt irony, or perceive when he was being teased. In a letter to Edward Garnett in August he recalled that "four or five months ago G.B.S. towed by Wells came to see me reluctantly and I nearly bit him".[22]

Ford, too had little use for moralising social reformers, or for the statistical collectivism of the Fabians. He disliked the style of his progressive acquaintances.[23] It was, he said, a "curious thing, made up of socialism, free thought, the profession of free love going hand in hand with an intense sexual continence that to all intents and purposes ended in emasculation, and going along, also, hand in hand with lime-washed bedroom walls and other aesthetic paraphernalia. It . . . really frightened me out of my life." James was also having doubts about Wells's new aspirations and friends. "You'd say that he had everything", Ford recalled him saying. "His . . . gift, his . . . popularity . . . his stately treasure house on the sea shore, richly endowed with the splendid gift of youth . . . You don't suppose . . . it has been whispered to me . . . you know swift madness *does* at times attend on the too fortunate, the too richly endowed, the too altogether and overwhelmingly splendid. You don't suppose then . . . I mean to you too has it been whispered? . . . that . . . well, in short . . . that he-is-thinking-of-taking-to-politics?"[24]

Throughout 1902, though Wells was enjoying considerable social success, he was still deeply concerned about his literary prospects. He was badgering his new publisher, Macmillan, to get more "woosh" behind his books. In *Anticipations* he had once again paraded his distrust of publishers, who "stand a little lower than ordinary tradesmen in not caring at all whether the goods they sell are good or bad . . ." Now he was equally severe with Pinker: "I can see it all now. The little flicker of interest, the little splutter of advertisement, the slump, the slump." So far as Pinker's attempts to find him a market across the Atlantic were concerned he was equally scathing. "Instead of trying to impress these blasted Americans with the idea that I'm something smart & snappy", he wrote, "why don't you insist upon my literary position . . . The Americans don't buy Tolstoy by the bale because he's a real life second Kipling or anything of that sort . . . You have got to make the American who doesn't know all about me feel like an ignorant ass."[25]

Bennett's efforts on his behalf were more satisfying – though Pinker had had a hand in persuading *Cosmopolitan* magazine to commission Bennett to write a long article appraising Wells as a serious writer. Bennett was making amends for the omission of Wells from his book on contemporary writers, *Fame and Fiction*, in the previous year – an omission which, on 19 August 1901, drew from Wells an angry letter headed "PRIVATE AND ABUSIVE". Claiming that he was "an absolutely unique figure", Wells listed the prices his stories then commanded and complained that "I am doomed to write 'scientific' romances and short stories for you creatures of the mob, and my novels must be my private dissipation. 'Damn this Bennett!' I say, with all my heart." Bennett consolingly answered that he had left out Wells because he "felt incompetent" to assess him: "I kept saying to myself: 'Now will the incurable and amazing modesty of this great man prevent him from guessing the true reason why I have left him out of this my book?' . . . You will have to see a doctor about that modesty of yours." The laudatory article appeared in August 1902, and H.G. was "enormously satisfied" because "it takes me as being really good". When it was being drafted Wells had only refrained with difficulty from telling Bennett what he wanted said; as it was, in counselling Bennett against "stupid praise" he still asked to be noted as "a First Class Man", hoped Bennett would stress his "new system of ideas", and asked that "in a corner" Bennett would make it clear to the "damned ignorant snobbish public" that he had scientific qualifications and a string of foreign translations to his credit.[26] Bennett indeed dealt fairly with him.

The current Wells novel, in fact, was a poor piece of work. *The Sea Lady* was hurriedly written, and neither the style nor the satire had much edge. The story used the same device as *The Wonderful Visit* – on this occasion it was a mermaid, rather than an angel, who served as the foil for conventional English life. The family into whose life she swam was clearly based on that of the Pophams, who lived next door to Arnold House, and whose home provided the locale. The comedy was not strong enough to carry the serious point Wells introduced. Adeline Glendower, the ambitious bluestocking whose engagement to the aspirant politician Chatteris is threatened by the sensuous mermaid, is just a first sketch of a character that Wells worked up into Helen Walsingham in *Kipps*, and all the other members of the seaside party are thin and dreary. The book only comes alive when Chatteris has to choose between duty and beauty: "We have desires, only to deny them", he cries, "senses that we all must starve." Yet the sole way he can escape from the entangling mesh of arid conventions is to go with the mermaid, to foreswear ambition for desire, even if the price is death. Once again, as in *Mr Lewisham*, the Wells hero is faced with a conflict between spontaneous feelings and the demands of a career, and H.G. was honest enough in later years to recognise that he was articulating his own ambivalence. *The Sea Lady*, he recalled in his autobiography, reflected his "craving for some lovelier experience than life had yet given me", but this "sensuous demand" was seen as something disruptive rather than as a means to happiness, for "love, instead of leading to any settling down, breaks things up".

The demands which the new style of social life and his work made on Wells began to show in restlessness, poor health and problems with his writing. Apart from the spells he spent in London, and his jaunts to country-houses, he had fallen into the habit of regular trips abroad. In 1902 he and Jane spent June in Switzerland, and – after an August trip to Paris with his brother Frank – H.G. went back to Locarno in September. In 1903, since Jane was expecting their second child in the autumn, they spent June in Italy. In August H.G. was ill again with kidney trouble, and in September he went off to recuperate on the Swiss walking holiday with Graham Wallas. Though this began pleasantly, Wells managed to fall out with Wallas, possibly because his moral-minded friend disapproved of his flirtatious habits, and Jane wrote to commiserate with his disappointment about the trip.

Not long after Wells returned to England, his second son, Frank Richard, was born, on 31 October 1903. "How full your life must be of work and pleasure", Gissing commented in a note of congratulation.[27] Work was going ahead, though less easily and satisfactorily than Gissing, far away in France, enviously assumed. *The Food of the Gods* was running as a serial, and *Mankind in the Making*, the successor to *Anticipations*, had been appearing in the *Fortnightly Review* through the summer and also in the New York *Cosmopolitan*. *Mankind in the Making* was published in September. It was another tract on education, housing, morality and politics. It became, Wells said thirty years later, "the most completely forgotten of my books . . . the text degenerates into mere scolding . . . it is revivalism, field preaching", and he thought parts of it were "my style at its worst and my matter at its thinnest". Bennett complained that it was turgid, full of bad grammar and sloppy thinking – "a fundamental inability to grasp what art is, really". H.G. took the criticism in good part: "I have known most of what you say", he replied.[28] He was nevertheless glad enough to get more favourable comments from Ford and from James, who wrote over-generously that "the humanity and lucidity and ingenuity, the pluck and perception and patience and humour of the whole thing place you before me as, simply, one of the benefactors of our race".[29] Conrad was more reserved.[30] "What surprises me", he wrote, "is to find you so strangely conservative at bottom . . . The divergencies which arise from the dissimilar sides of our natures become more definite." He was beginning to wonder whether Wells might not be giving prodigally to mankind what ought to be reserved for his novels; in his judgements on what Wells was doing he often went against the drift of popular opinion. He praised *Twelve Stories and a Dream* which came out at that time and had only a lukewarm reception. "Your power of realization", he told Wells "is astounding . . . There is a cold jocular ferocity about the handling of that mankind in which you believe, that gives me the shudders sometimes. However, as you do believe in them, it is right and proper and excellent that you should get some fun in making their bones rattle."

The compliments came the better from Conrad because he was going through a miserable phase.[31] "Things are bad with me", he told H.G. frankly on 30 November, "there's no disguising the fact. Not only is the scribbling awfully in arrears but there's no 'spring' in me to grapple with it effectually." His wife, Jessie, had just aggravated an old knee injury and become partially crippled; and his bankers, Watson and Company, had collapsed and he had lost his limited savings. Typically of Wells, whose sharp tongue so often belied his generous spirit, he wrote unsympathetically to Bennett that "the Conrads are under an upset hay cart as usual, and God knows what is to be done. J.C. ought to be administered by trustees" – and at the same time he sent Conrad a cheque for twenty-five pounds.[32]

Wells was always responsive to a claim on his sympathy. With Conrad it was simply a case of tiding him over a misfortune; with another close friend, Gissing, the situation was far worse. Just before Christmas 1903

Gissing took a turn for the worse, and Gabrielle sent telegrams to H.G. and another friend, Morley Roberts. When Wells discovered that Roberts was himself too unwell to leave at once for France, he set off alone on Christmas Eve for St Jean Pied de Port near the Spanish frontier, where Gissing had settled for his health.

In the afternoon of Christmas Day Wells arrived at the chalet. Gissing, he discovered, had caught a cold which had turned into double pneumonia. He was delirious, and H.G. was not permitted to see him until the following day – when Gissing, in a moment of clarity, pathetically begged to be taken back to England. That was impossible, but Wells believed that his friend's situation was being exacerbated by the way Gabrielle was nursing him. They had already fought one battle over Gissing's treatment and now the struggle started again. Wells believed that he was being starved by a light diet, and during the night he fed Gissing beef tea, wine, coffee and milk, to build up his strength. The result was a sharp rise in temperature, and an attack of hysteria from Gabrielle, who – backed by the local French doctor – insisted that Wells was killing the patient.

The deathbed drama intensified. Wells acted as nurse. He sponged Gissing's fevered body with alcohol – when that gave out he used methylated spirits. The only towel became sodden. Wells asked for handkerchiefs, but Gabrielle refused to provide them – according to Wells – because of the laundry bills. The two days Wells spent at the chalet were a nightmare which left a profound effect on him. He left on the evening of 27 December and Gissing died the next day, as sordidly and tragically as he had lived. He was, James wrote to Sir Sidney Colvin, marked out "for what is called in his and my profession an unhappy ending". But, he went on, "what a brick is Wells to go to his aid. I doubt if he has another creature to look to – in the way, at any rate, of a sane and sturdy man".[33]

Wells came back deeply distressed. It was his first experience of death. In the next few days, he became even more concerned. Edmund Gosse, as adviser to the Royal Literary Fund, was trying to persuade Balfour – then Prime Minister and the ultimate arbiter of such patronage – to authorise a grant for the support of Gissing's sons. He wrote confidentially to Wells asking for details of Gissing's irregular private life: he needed, he said, to know the worst so that Balfour would not take him by surprise.[34] On 4 January 1904 Wells summarised the whole dreary story. As he did so, he apparently became alarmed: what could be decently glossed over when a man was alive might emerge, as the intimate details of his life were exposed, to sully his reputation after death.

The point struck him forcefully because at this time he had just learned that his cousin Isabel had married again – though she had concealed the fact for almost a year, partly from fear of angering him and partly because she seems to have needed the alimony. The divorce settlement had been so loosely drawn that the alimony did not automatically cease on her remarriage. Her letter referred to her financial problems, but the tone was friendly: "You will wonder perhaps at hearing from me in this informal way after so long but time heals many sores and we are first cousins."[35] Wells was furious – he was jealous of the ineffectual Mr Fowler-Smith whom Isabel had married, angry with Isabel, cross about the financial arrangements.

Gissing's death and Isabel's marriage thus made Wells reflect on his own past, and particularly on those parts of it he did not then wish to be remembered. He burned many private papers, some of them letters and other documents concerning Isabel.* He then wrote to the intimate friends of the South Kensington days. "I am rather anxious about one little matter", he told Elizabeth Healey on 18 June 1904. "I have recently been seeing very much of poor Gissing's affairs . . . & I am very much impressed by the ghoulish side of my fellow men. Frankly, have you any old letters of mine? I know they are safe in your hands, but one never quite knows how these scraps of paper may not presently fly about. Do you mind making a little holocaust of anything you have, if so be you *have* kept anything. It might save my widow someday something highly disagreeable."[36]

Elizabeth Healey returned the letters she had carefully treasured, but Wells afterwards sent them back to her. Years later, when her husband's fatal illness left her short of money, he gladly gave her permission to put them on the market for collectors if she was in need. It is impossible to say what he may have censored. Certainly he destroyed a few of the letters that Simmons sent him in answer to a similar request: on 22 January he told Simmons that "I burned one or two that most wounded my vanity."[37]

The attempts to obliterate the past had been an act of panic. Yet it was also symbolic. Wells now saw himself as an established public figure, and from this moment onwards he considered that it was his public acts and his published ideas that were relevant to his reputation. He began to insist that they bore no necessary relation to his private affairs, and that any

---

* He afterwards regretted what he had done. Before long he had forgiven Isabel and was again on friendly terms with her. When he came to write his autobiography he was no longer anxious to conceal the details of his first marriage.

attempt to demonstrate links between what he wrote and his own life was as wrong-headed as it was intrusive. It is significant that his autobiography, which deals fully and frankly with his life up to 1904, virtually terminates at that date, the last chapters being mainly a restatement of his political opinions. Isabel's second marriage seems to have punctuated his life, putting a period to his past. "I was at least half-way through life", he wrote when he was nearing seventy, "before my emotional release from that original matrix (of family emotions) was completed." The future now took the place of the past as his point of reference, but fulfilment in the present still eluded him.

FAULTS OF THE FABIAN

In February 1903 Wells joined the Fabian Society. More precisely, he became a Fabian because, as he remarked three years later, admission took "as much fuss and trouble as one takes to make a member of a London social club".[1] A new recruit was sponsored by two members – in the case of H.G. these were Graham Wallas and Bernard Shaw – and a single blackball on the executive could exclude him. Even when he was admitted there was still a probationary period before his membership was confirmed. It is not surprising, therefore, that twenty years after the Society was formed in 1884 there were only seven hundred members, and among these there were less than a hundred who formed a core of active Fabians who gave the lectures, wrote its tracts or attended the regular discussion meetings in Clifford's Inn.

It was more like an extended family than a political organisation – a group of like-minded middle-class reformers who had clustered round the Old Gang which still effectively ran the Society. Their contacts with the trade union movement, and even with other socialist bodies, were limited to speaking engagements and to personal acquaintances among the leaders; and Fabian influence upon the working-class was indirect.[2] The Fabians were the most genteel of all revolutionists, seeking to achieve a socialist society without abrogating any of the social conventions: the New Jerusalem was close at hand, in the form of the Hampstead Garden Suburb. Influenced by the utilitarian tradition, and by the evangelical idealism of T.H.Green, they substituted the State for God as the means by which they were to live, move and have their being.

By the early years of the century, however, the Fabians were losing ground. They appeared to be isolated, a prestigious but self-centred group. They had broken with the Liberals in the Nineties, and had a minor role in the foundation of the Labour Party. They were divided on the issue of starting a new socialist party. And they had also split over their attitude to the Boer War. Their main influence on the course of events came through the eminent politicians and influential public servants who attended Beatrice Webb's dinner parties at Millbank. Even the leadership was wondering whether the time had come either to wind up the Society or to withdraw and let a new generation see what it could make of things. Yet the Webbs and Shaw were reluctant to relinquish their guardianship. They had invested too much in Fabianism simply to let the Society collapse. Since they had created a state of mind rather than an effective political organisation, there would in fact be very little to hand over if they pulled out.

In this situation Wells appeared as a most welcome newcomer. In *Anticipations* and *Mankind in the Making* he had shown both his skill as a propagandist for new ideas and an affinity for just the kind of efficient, middle-class socialism which appealed to the Webbs. Wells was needed, and, for his part, was eager to be accepted. The Fabians came closest to the intellectual élite which he first called the New Republicans and then, in *A Modern Utopia*, the Samurai; and their method of working, through the association of educated persons irrespective of party allegiance, was very like the "open freemasonry" he had advocated as the alternative to the sham battles of parliamentary democracy. Given his distrust of the masses (he always insisted that the aim of socialism was to abolish the working-class as he knew it, not to give it power), his distaste for trade unionism, and his ignorance of the realities of industrial life, the Fabian Society was the only agency he could use to further his role as a political prophet. Though it might seem a weak lever with which to move the world, it was the only lever to hand.

His first lecture, given a month after he joined, had the appropriately Fabian title *The Question of Scientific Administrative Areas in Relation to Municipal Undertakings*. It was a development of his argument in *Anticipations* about the effect of faster communications: he now moved out over national boundaries and concluded that the World State was the necessary unit of government. H.G. was never a good speaker. He described himself at Fabian meetings as "speaking haltingly on the verge of the inaudible, addressing my tie through a cascade moustache that was no help at all, correcting myself as though I were a manuscript under treatment". Neither subject nor delivery gave any idea of the power he was later to acquire in the Society. For more than two years he simply coasted, appearing seldom at meetings, and making little effort to influence policy.

In 1904 he suddenly offered his resignation, having objected to a tract drafted by Shaw on *Fabianism and the Fiscal Question*. His friend Graham Wallas, who resigned from the Society on this issue of tariff reform versus free trade, set him against the tract, which – Wallas told Pease on 21 January – he thought "insincere and mischievous as a whole". "Were I able to attend the meetings with any regularity", H.G. wrote to Pease on 17 March, "I would do my poor best to establish my views . . . against the prevailing influences, in spite of my distinguished ineptitude in debate. As things are, however, I do not see what service I can do the Society by remaining in it." Edward Pease sent Wells a mollifying reply on 29 March, observing gently that in democratic organisations it was unusual to resign simply because one was in the minority on a particular matter.[3] Wells had had no experience of belonging to anything except dining clubs since his departure from the South Kensington Debating Society almost twenty years before.

Bernard Shaw also took it upon himself to read H.G. the first of many lectures on tactics.[4] On 26 March he wrote to Wells asking why, when "every idiot had his little go" at improving the draft, Wells had done nothing to help and then resigned in pique because "the job is not exquisitely to your liking".

I dont believe you have any views on Free Trade or any other subject. I believe you are so spoiled by living in a world of your own invention, peopled by your own puppets, that you have become incapable of tolerating the activity or opinions or even the phrases of independent individuals. Since you have had live infants to play with you have become worse than ever. Jane is greatly to blame. She spoils you in a perfectly disgusting manner . . . you live in a Pearson's Paradise . . . discharging your Fabian gardeners because they have sent you crumpled rose leaves . . . Give my love to Jane. Observe, *my love*. I will not have her affections starved in Sandgate with nobody but you to cherish her.

The Webbs, too, were drawn in to soothe H.G. Two weeks later, when Jane came back from a holiday in Paris, they were down in Sandgate for a couple of days, and on 8 April Wells withdrew his resignation though, he wrote to Pease, "I highly disapprove of the Fabian Society". H.G. and Jane returned to London with the Webbs as guests for a special dinner with the Shaws, Arthur Balfour and the Bishop of Stepney. "We like him much", Beatrice noted on 19 April, "he is absolutely genuine and full of inventiveness . . . somewhat of a gambler but perfectly aware that his hypotheses are not verified. In one sense he is a romancer spoilt by romancing – but in the present stage of sociology he is useful."

From the middle of 1903 to 1905 Wells was in an unsettled state. He felt that he should be capitalising on the success of *Anticipations*, and yet he could not see how to maintain the momentum that it had given him. He had had a tiresome and unsatisfying struggle to finish the book that became *Kipps*. Almost as soon as that was finished in May 1904 he was ill for two months. In the final phases of the work, moreover, he had been upset by Gissing's death and Isabel's second marriage. He was still clearing up the unfinished business of his old life, both in fiction and in fact, and uncertain how to direct his ambitions and his talents in the next phase of his career.

The irritation came out clearly in his relations with his agents and publishers. Trying to drum up interest with a New York firm, he wrote a long letter on 9 October 1903 insisting on his merits as a "unique" author, with a "new & interesting personal attitude towards life". In spite of "my comparative failure with America so far", he declared, "due to my bad management & Pinkers bad management & a general conspiracy of adverse accidents, I am certain that if I am properly done, I have all the makings of a big thing in America".[5] Nine months later, in June 1904, he was harping on the same point to Brisben Walker of *Cosmopolitan*, complaining that "in the past I have been crudely victimized by both editors and publishers."[6] On 29 September 1904 Pinker was told that he was not "likely to do anything effectual . . . In the last three or four years you have not relieved me of anxiety or saved me from several losses."[7] At the time when H.G. became ill in May, in fact, he had already told Pinker that "my nerves will not stand this drift. Nothing happens unless I do it myself." For this reason, he had taken on all the negotiations with Frederick Macmillan, whom he was trying to persuade to make a package deal to publish all his books and to buy the rights to his previous works so that all his titles could appear under a single imprint.[8]

In the summer of 1904 Macmillan was already learning that, in addition to demanding large advances, H.G. expected to be involved in all decisions about promotion, and was liable to arrive in the office without warning with a new idea. When Macmillan was publishing *Kipps*, he was tormented by unorthodox ideas from Wells, who wanted to send sandwich men parading the West End with billboards and put up posters outside Portsmouth station saying "Kipps Worked Here". Macmillan's reluctance to adopt such methods drew a threat from Wells to withdraw from his agreement. "You are sceptical about me", he told Macmillan in a mid-August letter, "as you would have been sceptical about Coleridge, if you had been his contemporary . . . and you force me to unbecoming lengths of self-assertion." Wells was arguing two different but related points – first, that he was not being sufficiently remunerated and, secondly, that his talent was inadequately recognised. Both complaints were repeated to Bennett during a long ramble at Sandgate in July 1904. "We talked shop and women most of the day", Bennett noted in his journal.[9] Wells was cross that Halkett, the editor of the *Pall Mall Magazine*, was reluctant to serialise *Kipps* because "the range of the story was rather narrow". Even more, H.G. wanted money. "He talked seriously of gambling with six months of his time in order to try to do a couple or so of plays that would possibly bring in a fortune", Bennett added. "He said he wanted £20,000 as a capital basis." Wells put the same idea to Shaw, who sent a painstaking reply on 29 September 1904 pointing out that success in the theatre demanded patience and hard work.[10] Characteristically, H.G. wanted a quick success. Shaw modestly observed that in ten years he himself had earned only five thousand pounds and that "if you are going to write plays, the 20,000 pounder will only be one of them". The letter was intended "to knock the thing straight in your head, as the career of a dramatist is not to be entered on without careful consideration, and the great game in it cannot be won without an apparently reckless preliminary expenditure of genius on all sorts of side shows".

As Wells struggled to finish *Kipps*, he was far from sure what he should do next. It seemed unlikely that *The Food of the Gods* would do much better than its advances. Though it was serialised simultaneously in London and New York, and foreign translations appeared concurrently with the English edition, it was a run-of-the-mill book. Though some of the critics liked it, the fantasy was hard to place. The story of a race of giants raised on the magic "Boomfood", who were stronger and wiser than ordinary mortals, had some things in common with the earlier romances but the satire was used to make the kind of social criticism that Wells had been advancing in *Anticipations* and *Mankind in the Making*. The book was an allegory which reflected Wells's growing obsession with bigness. It was, as G.K. Chesterton neatly remarked, the tale of Jack the Giant Killer told from the point of view of the giant.[11] Wells insisted that the supermen were unjustly feared, since they were in fact a beneficent ruling élite. But how could one accelerate the evolution of the human race from its present ignorance and stupidity into the utopian state? In *The Food of the Gods* the lame answer was Boomfood. "One cannot go very far towards the reform of humanity", a reviewer caustically noted in the *Manchester Guardian*, on 3 October 1904, "with an equipment of contempt and a new drug."

Wells immediately went on to another and more ambitious statement of his opinions. He had been reading widely in the classical utopian writers – Campanella, Cabet, Howells, Bellamy, Morris and Hertzka – but according to Ford it was More's *Utopia* that had most caught his imagination. "You know", H.G. exclaimed one day as he was walking along The Leas at Folkestone with Ford, "if I had the education of this country in my hands I could make something of it yet."[12] *A Modern Utopia* was the result of his reflections. In *Anticipations* he had tried the technique of extrapolation; he had produced a tract in *Mankind in the Making* and a fable in *The Food of the Gods*. He now turned to the explicitly utopian device of switching two men on a Swiss walking tour into another society whose morals and behaviour could be contrasted with those of Edwardian England. It was, of course, a familiar technique for Wells. He now used it cleverly to translate the narrator and his sceptical friend into a parallel planet to earth, where everything is astonishingly duplicated – down to counterparts of the two travellers – yet is significantly different. The Utopians have adopted the policies Wells is urging on his fellow men. All that seems to be required on earth is "an act of imagination" to enable mankind to change course. Wells asserts that "Will is stronger than Fact, it can mould and overcome Fact."

Men can learn to will the good life, Wells was saying, but this can happen only if inspiring examples of the shape of things to come – such as *A Modern Utopia* – are set before them to emulate. Each generation in its turn will produce new dreams, "until at last from dreams Utopias will have come to be working drawings" which can be implemented. Once again H.G. had gone to biblical models, and specifically the Book of Revelations, to show that what was needed was an act of conversion. In the last pages of the book, when the travellers find themselves back in Trafalgar Square, beset by tramps and whores and confronted by newspaper placards shrieking details of human violence and idiocy, the narrator has a final apocalyptic vision of an angel above the Haymarket, "a towering figure of flame and colour, standing between earth and sky, with a trumpet in his hands". When the trump sounds, all the elect "will know themselves". But then he reflects that "God is not theatrical, the summons comes to each man in its due time for him . . . single men and then groups of men will fall into line." Wells, in effect, was bearing witness rather than arguing a political case.

Providence may be working through the elect, that band of "voluntary noblemen" that Wells now christens the Samurai, "who have taken the world in hand" and created "a sane order". Though the laws of evolution still apply, natural selection is no longer the nightmare of "futile struggling, pain and discomfort" that Wells had taken over from T.H.Huxley. The State can now control selection, and eliminate the unfit – and who knows what the fit may not achieve when freed from this incubus? The control of procreation thus becomes the central argument of the book. Though Wells rehearses some of his favourite notions about public ownership of energy sources and the land, the modernisation of transport and the provision of social security for the unemployed, the ill and the aged, all these are really subordinate to the real function of the ruling caste. Its benevolent dictatorship, which works through a World State and maintains a central index system in Paris which keeps track of every person in the world, is directed primarily towards the improvement of the race. Wells admiringly describes the Code of the Samurai, whose concept of sex is "a straight and clean desire for a clean and straight fellow-creature" rather than the "uxorious inseparableness" which leads to "sexual excess" and the collapse of society through uncontrolled fecundity.

The Samurai have been able to release themselves from the laws of Nature by rejecting the idea of Original Sin and thus rising above the frailty of ordinary men. For the concept of the Fall they have substituted that of the Rise of Man. Where the Christian tradition had taught, as Chesterton noted, that mankind had misused an essentially good world, Wells was now insisting that the world was naturally evil and that superior men could only escape from the primal curse by rising above it. It is significant that the Samurai, like the New Republicans, live by self-denial. They use no tobacco or alcohol, they keep no servants, forswear trade, abjure the stage, and neither play nor watch games. Ordinary Utopians, ruled by these latter-day Puritans, are less constrained – on condition that they breed only according to the rules. Women are given economic equality, for motherhood is "a service to the State and a legitimate claim to a living", but since the parentage of children must be known, the wife who is unfaithful is immediately divorced and treated like a public offender. "A reciprocal restraint on the part of the husband", Wells adds in a new gloss on the double standard, "is clearly of no importance whatever" except as an "emotional offence to the wife . . . if she does not mind, nobody minds, and if her self-respect does not suffer nothing . . . is lost."

Wells had already made it clear in *Anticipations* that he considered sexual relations as a private matter unless they had issue in children. In *A Modern Utopia* he spelt out in detail the attitude towards marriage which figures largely in the books written from 1904 onwards. Marriage should be a binding contract only for those who voluntarily – since birth control was available – become parents. All other relationships should be a matter of choice and a matter of indifference to the State. Since Wells had no sacramental view of marriage, he scarcely paused to consider the religious argument at all. To his younger readers, searching for ways to emancipate themselves from Victorian morality, this type of marital relationship made Wells appear a prophet of the New Freedom. But to the crusaders for public purity, who began about this time to mount a counter-attack on "demoralising" writers, his views on marriage were to occasion far more offence than his radical social ideas.

Most comment on the Utopia was enthusiastic, of the kind which Richard Gregory expressed in a congratulatory letter to Wells on 8 May 1905. Thoughtful critics rightly appreciated the book, he wrote, but "its greatness will not be adequately understood by this flag-waving, Empire-booming, fiscal-fencing generation . . . You have painted an ideal world and I am going to live in it, in my thoughts at any rate."[13] Similar private praise came from William James, the novelist's philosopher brother whom Wells had met in Rye and by whose pragmatism he had been greatly influenced.[14] "Your virtues are unparalleled and transcendant", William James wrote in a shipboard letter from the *Cedric* on 6 June: "in fact you are a triumph and a jewel, and for human perception you beat Kipling and for hitting off a thing with the right words you are unique . . . You are now an eccentric; perhaps 50 years hence you will figure as a classic." Beatrice Webb, too, reacted warmly. On 17 April 1905 after an overnight visit from Wells, she noted in her diary: " 'The chapters on the Samurai will pander to all your worst instincts', he laughingly remarked when I congratulated him. He is full of intellectual courage and initiative." A month later, after she and Sidney had been to Sandgate, she reported that his mind was still running on the theme of adult freedom.

Two articles of our social faith are really repulsive to him: the collective provision of anything bordering on religious or emotional training and the collective regulation of the behaviour of the adult . . . he is obdurate as to education: no form of training must be provided out of common funds that he personally objects to . . . "I don't believe in tolerance, you have got to fight against anything being taught anybody which seems to you harmful, you have got to struggle to get your own creed taught." We all got hot and exaggerated in our arguments and were no nearer agreement when we parted.

Wells was now on the upswing of his cycle of euphoria and depression, since *A Modern Utopia* had been a success, and his political reputation continued to grow. Sydney Olivier, on his return from service in Jamaica, wrote to H.G. proposing himself as a friend, "I recognise your trumpeting Angel of the Samurai as my desire for the League of Sane Men."[15] Praise of this kind made Wells feel that he should play a more active political role, and that the moment had come to assert himself in the Fabian Society. All through 1905 he was becoming more involved in its affairs. And there was a crisis brewing in the Society which H.G. sensed might be his opportunity.

Kipps was published in the autumn of 1905. The travail of its last chapters reflects Wells's conflict between his desire to be a serious artist and the allurements of public life. He had been working on *Kipps* for seven years. The first draft of what was then *The Wealth of Mr Waddy* had been done at Arnold House and sent to Pinker in January 1899.[16] It was incomplete, but the manuscript of it which was found in his papers and subsequently published runs to a completed section of thirty-five thousand words, plus another fifteen thousand which are merely outlines for the unfinished last twenty chapters. What, from April 1900, became *Kipps*, was developed from the later part of *Mr Waddy* which, he said, had been planned on "too colossal a scale". Wells changed his mind about the book as his health and spirits improved – shifting the emphasis from the irascible man of property in a wheel chair to the fortunes and misfortunes of the draper's apprentice who inherits his wealth. By the time the book was done, he wrote to Pinker, it had become "the complete study of a life in relation to England's social condition".[17]

The book was certainly the best attempt Wells had made to fuse his own experience into a more general statement about the condition of the genteel poor and their agonising efforts to find a place for themselves in Edwardian England. It had humour, pathos and a cutting edge to its social criticism. He was once again describing himself as he might have been if he had not escaped the entanglement of poverty. "The country ought to be ashamed of me", remarked Mr Hoopdriver, the draper's assistant who had been "caught" in the trade: "I'm done for. I've woke up too late." Mr Lewisham was also "done for". Like Hoopdriver he was permitted a glimpse of another life, but failed to attain it. "We're in a blessed drain-pipe", said one of Kipps's fellows at Shalford's emporium, "and we've got to crawl along it till we die." Kipps himself would never have escaped but for the magical trick of the legacy which translated him temporarily and anxiously into a "gentleman". The moral in all three stories was deterministic. In each there was an attempt at self-improvement, to "wake up", which fails. Hoopdriver, Lewisham and Kipps all fall back in the end into their original reality when their dreams prove illusory. The "little men", to whom Wells gave his best writing as a novelist, stoically come to terms with life when they learn that they are not fated to escape into their wish-fulfilments. They are nostalgic figures and, unlike their author, they are not permitted to cross the frontier of success. They are not fit to be supermen.

The struggle that Wells went through to finish *Kipps* during the years in which his own position and point of view were changing shows the degree to which there was growing conflict between his opinions and his art. He felt more and more compelled to talk at his readers through his characters, rather than to allow them the room they needed to emerge as personalities. When he began *Kipps* he let his comic genius have free play, and the first two of its three parts show a sureness of touch he never surpassed. They brilliantly describe the origins of Artie Kipps, the servitude of his apprenticeship and his schooling in gentility. The third part, pieced together with difficulty, was written when Wells had already opted for a new career as a prophet, and it is patchy and uncertain as if he did not know how to hold the book together and bring it off to a coherent end. Manuscript materials found in his papers reveal that he tried to convert the final section of the book into overt socialist propaganda – and found he could not do so without wrecking what had already been done.[18] In the middle of the book, he introduced the character of Masterman, the consumptive socialist whose manner of life and tragic death were closely modelled on George Gissing. Masterman was already a late thought, dovetailed into the design after Gissing's death and after Wells had begun to take himself seriously as a socialist. In *Kipps* as it was published, Masterman is permitted one tirade against the wastes and miseries of the system. But Wells had originally developed Masterman into a major character in the last third of the book, and the passages which he cut out were intended to form the centrepiece of the concluding section.

Wells made at least two unsuccessful attempts to work out the effect of socialism on Artie Kipps. One showed Kipps converted by Masterman's vision, and concluding that his son must be educated to be one of the new men; the other fuzzily dismisses everything that Masterman has said because "it was 'is 'ealth being out of order made everything seem wrong to 'im". Finally, in desperation, H.G. cut Masterman out of the last part of the book completely. He had failed in his effort to find a compromise between his politics and the tragi-comedy of his narrative, and even the effort had flawed what might have been the most "complete study" of the many "lives" that Wells wrote. Enough remained of his original integrity as an artist to make him throw away the unsatisfactory transition to the ideological novel, but too little to sustain him in finishing it in the spirit in which it had been started. He had now chosen to be an ideologist, and to turn his literary talents to that end. One reason that *Kipps*, in his phrase, had been "scamped", perhaps, was that he was now eager to get on with *A Modern Utopia* where he could escape the constraints of literature.

Bennett was quick to take that point. *Kipps*, he wrote to Wells on 9 November 1905, was "distinctly a fighting, '*tendencioux*' book" with "immense animus . . . ferocious hostility to about five sixths of the characters", and this did not make for "righteousness of any kind, and certainly not for artistic righteousness". If H.G. had "any larger aim, any aim of showing how and why one class of persons generally is superior or inferior to another", then he had not succeeded.[19] James, just back from a year in the United States, was less cautious and more generous.[20] *A Modern Utopia* and *Kipps*, which he had read together on his return, had, he wrote on 19 November "left me prostrate with admiration . . . I am lost in amazement at the diversity of your genius . . . what am I to say about Kipps, but that . . . He is not so much a masterpiece as a mere born gem – you having, I know not how, taken a header straight down into mysterious depths and observation and knowledge . . . it is of such a brilliancy of *true* truth." James, who was out of touch with Wells in this critical period, had obviously not perceived the extent to which *Kipps* was a carry-over rather than, as he hoped from H.G., a sign of a new commitment to his art.

By the middle of 1905 the Fabian Society was ripe for an argument about its future. New members were coming in who wanted a more active policy which would reflect the leftward swing of opinion in the country. Bernard Shaw sensed this change of temper. On 5 June 1905 he wrote to Edward Pease suggesting that at the next meeting of the executive there should be a discussion of his motion for an inquiry into the effectiveness of the Society's work.[21] He wanted a report which would show if the results up to date had been satisfactory. If they had not, "the sooner we have a definite eye-opener on the subject, the better". Wells was the obvious leader for any reform movement. He alone had the kind of prestige which could match that of the Webbs and Shaw. He was also temperamentally disposed to make a bid for leadership. In the summer of 1905 he had made his intentions clear to Ford.[22] "Fordie", Wells suddenly declared, "I'm going to turn the Fabian Society inside out and then throw it into the dustbin." Something had clearly been in the wind before Shaw made his proposal for an inquiry. One of the radical Fabians, a writer who became both a doctor and a Labour member of Parliament, played an important part in goading Wells to an intrigue.[23] This was Leslie Haden Guest, who wrote to him on 11 June 1905. "We must get our attack on the Fabian definitely into focus", Guest urged: "We ought to have it out in a meeting in July. My own attitude is that we should be content to be satisfied with nothing less than the most brilliantly inspired City of the Sun." The reference to Campanella's utopia came from *A Modern Utopia*, and it shows how the dreams of Wells for a revolutionary transformation of society were being picked up by younger Fabians.

At this stage the leadership had no serious objection to attempts to rejuvenate the Society. On the contrary, on 4 July 1905 Shaw wrote to Edward Pease suggesting that the demands of Wells and his allies for a new policy should be fairly handled.[24]

The proper thing would be two reports, pro & con. If you and Webb were to make out the best case you could for the old policy & the old gang, and Wells, Guest & Chesterton [Cecil, the brother of G.K.] were to do all they could to explode us, we should get something that would really give us an overhauling. Our methods are substantially what they were fifteen years ago; and they and we must be getting rather stale. .... All I want is a stir up and a stock taking to make Fabianism interesting again.

By the end of the year Wells was gaining ground. His complaints that the Society was in the doldrums and that something vigorous should be done about it were reinforced by the marked movement to the left in British politics. Quite apart from the growth of other socialist groups, such as the Independent Labour Party, the Labour Representation Committee was winning a great deal of trade union support and, in the election in January 1906, which produced a staggering landslide victory for the Liberals, it won twenty-nine seats in Parliament, establishing itself at once as a significant new force in politics. Wells wrote to "dear ill-treated

Guest" on 12 December 1905 saying that he would be "having a go at the Fabians" on 12 January,[25] and added that it was his intention "to make things hum in a business-like way". The Society, he insisted, "ought to have 7,000 members instead of 700 and everything else to scale". Wells's first attempt to translate this mood of rebellion into tactics was to propose a new method of electing the Fabian Executive to ensure that he and his associates had more influence upon it. When that move failed for procedural reasons, he increased his pressure on the Old Gang. On 12 January 1906 he delivered a memorable tract to a Society meeting. *This Misery of Boots*, which brilliantly satirised England from the bottom up – the soles of pedestrians passing over the basement grating at Atlas House was turned into an ironic social paradigm – exemplified the kind of propaganda that H.G. wanted. It also ridiculed those "calling themselves Socialists, ... who will assure you that some odd little jobbing about municipal gas and water is Socialism, and backstairs intervention between Conservative and Liberal is the way to the millennium". This direct jibe at the Webbs ended with the contemptuous metaphor: "You might as well call a gas jet in the lobby of a meeting-house the glory of God in heaven."

H.G. was now pressed for time as he had decided to go off on an American tour at the end of March, and he wanted to see his campaign well launched before he left. On 9 February he delivered his manifesto *The Faults of the Fabian*. It began with the argument that the Society was too small to rise to its opportunities. It had done well in the past in working out practical socialist policies, though it had achieved less than it might in socialist propaganda: "it strikes an observer as being still half a drawing-room society", and "its hands are tied by poverty". Most of the work would go on just as well if the Society ceased to exist, and so far as the organisation was concerned it was marked by "wasted good intentions, and wasted time and energy. . . . It is almost as if we were being amused to keep us out of mischief . . . playing at politico-sociological research." Wells wanted more "woosh" from the Fabians, just as he wanted it from his publishers. Urging its members to compare their "little dribble of activities" with the vigour and strength of "the world whose very foundations you are attempting to change", he accused them of being "unbusinesslike, unadaptable and uninventive" and crying socialism as the reduced gentlewoman cries oranges, discreetly in the hope that no one hears. The Basis, a statement of principles to which all applicants had to subscribe, was "ill-written and old-fashioned, harsh and bad in tone, assertive and unwise, and . . . likely to deter all sorts of wavering people".

It should be replaced by a definition of socialism "in compact, persuasive and untechnical phrases".

So far Wells had been presenting a case which could command a great deal of support. It was H.G. in his most convincing style. Suddenly, however, the animus broke through. Wells, the outsider, was offended by the habit of family jokes: "A little giggling excitement runs through all our meetings . . . It flows over and obscures all sorts of grave issues." Disclaiming any suggestion that he was aiming at Mr Shaw's "natural inclination to paradox", H.G. denounced the imitators of Shaw who were turning "this grave high business of socialism" into "an idiotic middle-class joke". They infuriated him as much as those who believed that "the world may be manœuvred into socialism without knowing it". The tone of exasperated ridicule was rising. Fabius Cunctator, the Roman general from whose patient tactics against Hannibal the Society had taken its name, had begun by being discreet and ended in impotence. It was the energetic Scipio who had taken the war to the enemy and destroyed Carthage. The Society must do the same. It must raise more money, rent new offices, appoint more staff, admit new members freely; it should commission attractive tracts and undertake a large-scale propaganda campaign. If H.G. was to give himself to the Society, in effect the Society must give itself to him.

That meeting, at least, did so. It instructed the executive to set up a committee to review the Society's organisation, finances and activities, and to postpone the annual meeting and elections until it had reported. The Webbs, Shaw and Bland decided that H.G. should be given his head, and his chance. It was, indeed, his moment of triumph. There was a delay, caused in part by the aftermath of the general election and in part by the reluctance of the executive to let any of its members sit on a committee which was to judge them all. Wells complained that the executive was trying to dodge. "I strongly urge you to assume that the Exec. is friendly", S.G. Hobson assured him on 14 February.[26] Even Pease was beginning to come round because he had visions of a vast organisation, "and that warms the cockles of his heart". The next day Pease himself wrote to ask Wells to meet the executive on 23 February, so that all the arrangements might be tied up before H.G. left for his American lecture tour. "Although your plans have evoked considerable heat", he remarked, "I confidently hope that it may turn to light, & may result, as we all wish, in extending the influence of the Society."

More advice came from Shaw. A postcard on 14 February told Wells that he could call on anyone he wished to give evidence: "examine me, Webb & Bland *separately* and compare our stories & views". That would "provide all the levity you want".[27] On 17 February in a long letter, Shaw tried to explain why it was unwise for a minority of the executive to join the Wells committee, and once again reminded Wells that there was no desire to oppose sensible proposals for change.[28]

We cannot afford to quarrel with you because we want to get tracts out of you; and in any case you will see that we are not hostile as we let you have an absolutely free run at the meeting. Your paper was full of small misapprehensions which could easily have been seized on to secure an easy debating triumph; but we felt that they really didnt matter, whereas the general drift of the thing was to the good. But the affair, however friendly, must be in clear form. You must not go about amiably disclaiming any intention of attacking us. . . . You can be of no use unless you attack us and meet our defence. The Society will say "If you are not attacking the old gang, then what the devil are you wasting our time for, and where does our fun come in?" On the other hand when we treat your onslaught *as* an onslaught, and hold the fort against you, don't suppose we are in a huff. It is only by placing ideas in clear opposition that any issue can be created. It is our business & yours to create an issue; and if you consider your feelings or ours in the matter you are simply unfit for public life and will be crushed like a trodden daisy.

Wells was in a powerful position, with a good deal of backing in the Society, and he received many letters supporting him. "Socialism is very real to us", wrote the secretary of a Socialist League branch in a Yorkshire mill town, "we daily risk our employment in an anxiety to make converts. . . . We look up to such as you to convert the professional and middle classes to socialism. . . . Your audience is assured already, let the prophet appear."[29] Shaw recognised the influence of Wells, and he and Charlotte were quite willing for the reform movement to succeed as long as it really was a movement and not a disruptive lark. Wells was even allowed to get his way about the committee membership. Four members of the executive were appointed, all of them broadly sympathetic to his point of view: these were Sydney Olivier, who was to be chairman, Charlotte Shaw, G.R.S. Taylor and Stewart Headlam. Jane Wells was to be secretary. Wells himself, Maude Reeves, Haden Guest and two other supporters of the reform group made up the total of ten members. But Shaw was still worried, sensing that Wells had let his emotions get the worse of him. The question was quite simple. Was Wells serious or not? Shaw's doubts would have been strengthened if he had seen the letter that Wells wrote to the essayist E.V.Lucas on 22 February. "I have been up to my ears lately", he cynically remarked, "in 'straordinary intrigues to upset the Fabian Society by making buttered slides for an old lady. Most amusing."[30]

The Old Gang temporarily checked the momentum of the Wells campaign. He had gone too far, too fast, and been rude to everyone as well. He tried to push through a quick draft, based largely on *The Faults of the Fabian*, and to get the executive to sanction its publication before his departure on 27 March. The Old Gang refused to be stampeded. Wells put it about that they had endorsed his proposals, but in fact the most they would accept was that a summary of the special committee's activities to date should appear in *Fabian News*.

It was to this episode that Beatrice Webb was referring when she noted in her diary on 1 March 1906 that H.G. had "broken out in a quite unexpectedly unpleasant manner". The remainder of the entry shows how the lines had begun to form for the battle that was to be fought out when Wells returned from America.

I doubt whether he has the skill and the persistence and the real desire to carry a new departure. But what is interesting is that he has shown in his dealings with the executive – and with his close personal friends on it – Shaw, Bland and Webb – an odd mixture of underhand manoeuvres and insolent bluster, when his manoeuvres were not successful. The explanation is, I think, that this is absolutely the first time he has tried to co-operate with his fellow men – and he has neither tradition nor training to fit him to do it. It is a case of "Kipps" in matters more important than table manners. It is strange for so frank a man that his dealings have been far from straight – a series of naive little lies which were bound to be found out – when at last he forced the executive to oppose him he became a bully and remained so until he found they were big enough to knock him down.

Beatrice Webb was already wondering whether the organ-grinder could be persuaded to go away from under the window. G.B.S., however, was determined to make him play a more attractive tune. For years he had produced his fellow-Fabians as if they were actors, and he now decided to groom Wells for a leading part in the performance. It was to be done by a mixture of teasing, admonition and sensible advice. If Wells was willing to be directed, Shaw would guarantee him the star role. If he wanted to take over the show himself, discharge all the old actors with ignominy, and run the risk of bankrupting the company with unsound schemes for expansion, then Shaw was in a position to turn him out on the streets.

In a letter which G.B.S. sent to Wells on 24 March he agreed that the new Basis which Wells had drafted was certainly superior to the old one, but "anybody who was the least bit of a literary workman could have produced a better basis any time these 20 years".[31] That was beside the point. The old Basis was the result of compromises. "To get anything through a corporate body, you must say the same thing over again in different ways." It was foolish of Wells to amuse himself "by treating us to several pages of cheek to the effect that the imperfections of the basis are the result of our own folly and literary clumsiness". He went on to read Wells a lesson.

> You may say you are making superhuman efforts to be amiable. No doubt you are; but you are not amiable enough, in spite of your efforts. And you are too reckless of etiquette ... You had no more right to report that debate than you had to write our cheques; and that is just one of the things that the human animal will not stand ... Even if your report had been approximately accurate instead of a blaze of wanton mendacity from beginning to end ... *any* human committee – would have jibbed at having its account of its own action dictated to it. You must study people's corns when you go clog dancing.

> Generally speaking, you must identify yourself frankly with us, and not play the critical outsider and the satirist. We are all very clever; and long ago we have come to understand that we must not play our cleverness off against one another for the mere fun of it ... Our experience has humbled us until we are morbidly afraid of playing off our experience against you, and willing to allow you to teach your grandmother to milk ducks to any extent on the chance of getting a workable idea here & there, and, at all events, a fresh impulse. But there are limits to our powers of enduring humiliations that are totally undeserved ... You havnt discovered the real difficulties of democratic work; and you assume that our own folly and ill will accounts for their results.

Wells had been put in his place, though Shaw – determined to keep personal relations going – relented into a friendly jest at the end: "Give my love to Jane, that well behaved woman. Why she married you (I being single at the time) the Life Force only knows." H.G. sent a testy answer. "You leave my committee alone while I'm in America", he wrote on 26 March: "If I'm to identify myself with 'us'; who's 'us'? I'm not going to identify myself with your damned executive, nohow!"[32]

13

STORM IN A FABIAN TEACUP

The *Carmania* sailed for New York on 27 March. Wells set off to write what he described to Henry James as "loose large articles mingled with impressions of *The Future in America* (no less)". He wrote to James two months before his departure to ask for introductions "to any typical people" who might be useful to him, even offering to brave the long journey on to Salt Lake City if James could suggest anyone who might give him an insight into the social life of the polygamous Mormons, especially their divorce laws.[1]

H.G. went off to the United States optimistically. He hoped that the visit would help to establish him in the American market. A change of scene also had its attractions. His mood in the winter of 1905–06 was edgy and cantankerous. The plan for putting more "woosh" into the Fabians had proved more complicated than he had anticipated. There were also difficulties in his personal life. Behind the jolly façade of life at Sandgate there was increasing strain. As early as 1903 his frequent absences had led Jane to write to him that "Gip has three theories about you. 'Dadda coming' 'Dadda gone away' 'Dadda aseep'!", and by early 1906 Jane was well aware that home had become a place where H.G. retired to write, and to receive friends at weekends.[2] They talked of giving up the house at Sandgate.

Jane missed him when he was away, but she usually concealed her depression and loneliness. One of the letters she sent off to reach H.G. at Chicago, written on 26 April, contained a rare glimpse of her self-deprecating unhappiness.[3]

I feel tonight *so* tired of playing wiv making the home comfy & as if there was only one dear rest place in the world, & that were in the arms & heart of you.
There is the only place I shall ever find in the world where one has sometimes peace from the silly wasteful muddle of one's life – think: I am thinking

continually of the disappointing mess of it the high bright ambitions one begins with, the dismal concessions – the growth, like a clogging hard crust over one of home & furniture & a lot of clothes & books & gardens & a load dragging me down. If I set out to make a comfortable home for you & do work in, I merely succeed in contriving a place where you are bored to death. I make love to you and have you for my friend to the exclusion of plenty of people who would be infinitely more satisfying to you. Well dear, I don't think I ought to send you such a lekker, it's only a mood you know but there's no time to write another and I have been letting myself go in a foolish fashion. It's all right you know really only you see I've had so much of my own society now & I am very naturally getting sick of such a person as I am. How you can *ever* stand it! Well!

Your very loving Bits.

While Jane moped at Sandgate, H.G. was hectically busy and stimulated. For two months he toured – New York, Boston, Chicago and Washington, giving occasional lectures at universities and being thoroughly lionised. While he was there Maxim Gorki arrived to raise funds for the victims of the 1905 revolution in Russia and was held by the immigration officials at Ellis Island on grounds of moral turpitude because he was not married to his common-law wife. H.G. was enraged by the case. America, he wrote to Jane on 6 May from Chicago, "can't stand Gorki's morals" yet it tolerated open prostitution under powerful political protection, as Lincoln Steffens and the other "muckrakers" were now demonstrating to the shame of one city after another. Doc Green, the boss of the Republican machine in "the wards of dubious reputation", took him on a tour of the Chicago honky-tonks.[4] Late to bed and up early, H.G. spent the next morning at Hull House with Jane Addams and some of her staff of social workers talking about the Fabians.

In Washington, he had a long talk with Theodore Roosevelt, "the most vigorous brain in a conspicuously responsible position in the world in 1906". The President fitted his idea of a New Republican: "I know of no other a tithe so representative of the creative purpose, the *goodwill* in men as he." All the pieces of his pragmatic view of life seemed to fall together as he walked in the garden of the White House with a man who apparently shared his own view of life.[5] The President conceded that the pessimism of *The Time Machine* might be justified; he said that he had no way of disproving the idea that mankind generally, in America in particular, might have reached its apogee and be on the decline. Yet, like the Time Traveller, he chose "to live as if this were not so". Wells described him vividly, one knee on a chair, a clenched hand outstretched, "the friendly peering snarl of his face, like a man with the sun in his eyes".

'Suppose, after all', he said slowly, 'that should prove to be right, and it all ends in your butterflies and morlocks. *That doesn't matter now.* The effort's real. It's worth going on with. It's worth it – even so. . . .'

It was the style that attracted Wells rather than the policies ("all that was needed to keep the world going was strenuous 'go' "), and he thought little of the President's individualism, his ideas of conservation and trust-busting. Still, Roosevelt was about the best omen H.G. could find. His report, *The Future in America*, appealed to his friend William James, who described it as "*the* medicinal book about America. And what good humour. And what tact."[6] The praise from Lamb House at Rye was even warmer. "I have done nothing today but thrill and squirm with it and vibrate to it almost feverishly and weep over it almost profusely . . . for intensity of mere emotion and interest", Henry James wrote on 8 November.[7]

James's comments were particularly apt since he had himself recently been in America and was then writing *The American Scene.* He had seen "absolutely *no* profit in scanning or attempting to sound the future", he wrote to Wells, "yet here you come and throw yourself *all* on the future, and leave out almost altogether the America of my old knowledge; leave out all sorts of things, and I am gripped and captured and overwhelmingly beguiled". But amidst the warmth and enthusiasm there was, as usual, a nugget of criticism. "I think you, frankly – or think the whole thing – too *loud*, as if the country shouted at you, hurrying past, every hint it had to give and you yelled back your comment on it", he remarked: "but also, frankly, I think the right and the only way to utter many of the things you are delivered of *is* to yell them – it's a yelling country, and the voice must pierce or dominate; and *my* semitones . . . will never be heard."

H.G. arrived back on the *Cambria* on 27 May. He had enjoyed the United States. The pace and scale of American life suited his temperament and made him feel even more dissatisfied with the constraints of English society. In this respect, as so often in his career, he was reflecting a shift of popular attitude. The pessimistic uncertainty of the Nineties had given way to a different mood. From the middle of Edward's reign it was clear that the old order had broken up. The future still seemed uncertain, but at least it appeared to be full of opportunities. It was at last possible to challenge the conventions, to propose reforms and launch new ventures with some hope of success. The great Liberal landslide of 1906 was only one sign that this was a time of criticism and of causes. Wells was just the man to ride this wave of insurgency.

While his writings articulated what many radicals were feeling, and helped to focus their ideas, his actions were concentrated on the campaign he had laid aside for the past two months. The special committee had to be reactivated, new drafts of its report discussed, and his supporters rallied for the battle. The habit of long summer holidays, in which the Shaws went off to Charlotte's house in Ireland and other Fabian notables retired to rented houses in the country, meant that nothing much would happen until early autumn. "Enthusiasm always does wane at this season of the year", Wells wrote to Haden Guest on 1 June, telling him that "next autumn is the time . . . Keep your pecker up. We'll have a big rush next September to make a good fight, but it's no use doing much now."[8] Wells, meanwhile, was finding a good deal of backing among rank-and-file Fabians, and also from socialists outside the Society who saw him as a champion for their attacks on the cautious reformism of the Webbs and the moderate trade union leaders whom they influenced. He put out feelers to some leading socialists whom, he thought, might be induced to join the Fabians and assist him in his efforts to regenerate the Society. Most of them replied by urging him to abandon this lost cause and to join them instead. On 13 June, for instance, H.G. received a letter from Keir Hardie, the Scots miner who had founded the Independent Labour Party in the Nineties and become the nearest the Left then had to a national leader.[9]

I think it is more or less a waste of time and effort and not quite fair to endeavour to convert the staid and steady-going Fabian Society into a semi-revolutionary organisation. I say this in all seriousness and believe that all your efforts in that direction could only end in disappointment and lead to a good deal of friction in the Society itself. Why not leave it to pursue its own way by its own methods and come in and take your part in the political side of the movement as represented by the I.L.P.? The Fabians have done good and useful work along their own lines and I have no doubt will continue to do so and any attempt to interfere with this would only unsettle the existing foundations of the organisation. The time has come when men like yourself should be available to become Socialist candidates under our auspices.

Hardie offered sensible advice, but H.G. had no intention of disentangling himself from the Fabian intrigue and taking the stump round the mining and textile areas of Britain on behalf of candidates with slender chances of success. He had little in common with the left-wing socialists of the ILP and the dogmatists of the SDF. What Wells wrote in *Anticipations*, *A Modern Utopia* and *This Misery of Boots* made converts to socialism and won support for him personally but he was quite incapable of turning that capital into the small change of political action. He wished, on the contrary, to use it for his take-over bid for the Fabians – to acquire the prestigious family business which much more nearly accorded to his own idea of a collectivist élite which would benevolently abolish the distasteful working classes.

There was also an element of impatience in all he did, the same desire for some stroke of magic which – like the transformation scenes whereby utopias were achieved in his books – would make all the tedium of reform or the grind of political action superfluous. Beatrice Webb had just spent a day at Sandgate and had sensed something of this irresponsible posture, and on 15 July 1906 commented at length in her diary on "the strain of a certain disillusionment" between the Webbs and Wells.

He is, we think, grown in self-confidence, if not conceit as to his capacity to settle all social and economic questions in general, and to run the Fabian Society in particular, with a corresponding contempt for us poor drudgers, who go on plodding painfully at administration on the one hand and investigation on the other, without, as he thinks, producing any betterment. He dreams of a great movement of opinion which would render all this detailed work unnecessary – which would jump all obstacles whether brought about by man's selfishness or by his ignorance. He distrusts the devious and narrow ways whereby we reach one position after another – minute steps in advance – when, as he thinks, the position could be rushed at one sweep . . . there is little room for friendly and hopeful discussion. And the difference of opinion is heightened by his desire to discredit the old methods of the Fabian and supersede them by methods of his own. About these methods he will say, at present, nothing: all we can extract from him is an animus against Pease and a desire to oust him from the secretaryship.

The Webbs listened patiently while H.G. told them that Sidney and G.B.S. would have to fall in with his schemes or retire. Beatrice simply noted privately that they "would gladly give up the leadership of the Fabians to younger hands – they are so full of work that they would be relieved if someone else would take it over and push ahead on other lines". But H.G. gave them no specific idea of what he wanted. "He proposes no new departures that he himself is willing to try out." It was now clear to Beatrice at least, that trouble was coming, and that the Old Gang had best prepare to ride out the storm.[10] "I incline to the prophecy that five years will see H.G.Wells out of the Society", she wrote. "He has neither the patience nor the good manners needed for co-operative effort – and just at present his conceit is positively disabling. A little failure . . . and failure I think will be his fate . . . may sober him . . . or it may embitter him. . . . He is in a state of unstable equilibrium."

Beatrice spoke coolly of "disillusionment". That may have been true of the Webbs, but her comments show quite clearly that by the early part of 1906 H.G. was seething with frustration and hostility to a degree that made reasonable argument impossible. His irrational hostility to the Old Gang was undoubtedly intensified by the galling discovery, early in 1906, that all the praise for his talents as a prophet and propagandist was not to be translated immediately and uncritically into acceptance of his grandiose plans for transforming the Society. Many years later he came to regret his behaviour – "no part of my career rankles so acutely in my memory with the conviction of bad judgment, gusty impulse and real inexcusable vanity, as that storm in the Fabian tea-cup". Even then he still qualified the apology believing that "from the first my motives were misunderstood . . . I was fundamentally right".

The most charitable explanation of the way H.G. now flung himself about is that social success and the discovery that he actually had political influence had gone to his head. For once in his life he found himself in a position where his early fantasies of omnipotence could be acted out: like the hero in his story "The Man Who Could Work Miracles", his wish became the father to his actions and he felt powerful enough – to wave away all objections to his ambitions.

The troubles in the Fabian Society had already taken on the characteristics of a family row, and H.G. now widened the issue into a row about the Family. His attack on conventional marriage in *A Modern Utopia* had been masked by other matters, but when *In the Days of the Comet* appeared that summer, it was clear that Wells was advocating the Great Change as much for sexual freedom as for socialism.

This romance describes England, before the coming of the comet, gripped by industrial disorder and preparations for a coming war with Germany. The narrator, Leadford, is an angry, jealous man, left desolate by the loss of his mother. "So long as my mother had lived", Leadford says, "she had in a measure held my heart, given me a food these emotions could live upon, and mitigated that emptiness of spirit; but now that one possible comfort had left me." His passion for Nettie is unrequited: when she marries his rival, Verrall, Leadford pursues them in a rage in order to shoot them both. The comet passes, and the mysterious gas it leaves in its train magically transforms England into a land of peace and fellowship, in which new and nobler forms of love are possible. Leadford marries Anna Reeves and tries to forget his desire for Nettie. In the new conditions which had "brought the lord of life, Eros, to his own", Leadford again meets Nettie and Verrall. All jealousy has now gone. The cure for it is "unstinted" love. The kind of group marriage which Wells had hinted at in *A Modern Utopia* is now possible. In an epilogue that was taken as advocating promiscuity, Leadford recalls, "We four from that time were very close, you understand, we were friends, helpers, personal lovers in a world of lovers."

H.G. made little effort to disguise the resemblances between this fantasy and his complex emotional experiences. Those who knew him intimately would have caught the references to the death of Sarah Wells, who had died on 12 June 1905 while the book was being drafted, and to his old friend Richard Gregory, who appears as Parload the astronomer. They may well have noticed that Leadford's attachment to Nettie was very like that of H.G. to his cousin, Isabel, and that Leadford's fit of jealousy on her marriage to Verrall echoed what Wells felt when Isabel married for the second time. Yet even those who had been close to him for years, and were accustomed to the frank way in which H.G. talked of his personal affairs, may have found it difficult to appreciate the degree to which this book reflected his sexual wish-fulfilments.

In letting his obsession with polygamous relationships erupt openly into his fiction, however, H.G. was running a considerable risk. The philandering that was accepted in literary circles, or in the "fast" social set H.G. was now meeting at country-house weekends, was still not tolerated by publishers, critics, and much of the reading public. It was not merely a legal matter. A host of religious and welfare organisations could be mobilised against "demoralising" books. Wells may not have cared personally about the opinions of the YWCA, the Salvation Army, temperance enthusiasts and campaigners against vice and white slavery, but they could be potent enemies, as he discovered when he shifted sex from the relatively safe context of sociology to the more vulnerable one of fiction.

The campaign against him began moderately. *The Times Literary Supplement* on 14 September 1906 picked up the association between his attack on private property and his denunciation of "proprietary" love. "Socialistic men's wives, we gather", it remarked in a phrase that was to torment Wells for the next few years, "are, no less than their goods, to be held in common. Free love, according to Mr Wells, is to be of the essence of the new social contract. One wonders how far he will insist in the tracts which he is understood to desire to write for the Fabian Society, and what the other Fabians will say." A month later H.G. made it plain that he was going to insist on his views within the Fabian Society, regardless of what the other Fabians said. On 12 October he delivered a lecture on "Socialism and the Middle Classes" to one of the largest Fabian meetings ever held. It contained another attack on the "unimaginative" Webbs, whose "philanthropic and administrative attitude to socialism was that of 'district visitors' without any warmth to qualify their arrogant manners". Such people, he said, could never win the young to a great campaign of constructive science and education. He then repeated his opinions on "private ownership" in marriage. For Wells, economic exploitation and sexual exploitation were two sides of the same coin, and freedom from one implied freedom from the other. Already the "strike against parentage" showed the decline of the "once-ascendant male". Educated women resented the loss of their independence in marriage, and "were it not for the economic disadvantages that make intelligent women dread a solitary old age in bitter poverty, vast numbers of women who are married today would remain single . . . This discontent of women is a huge available source for socialism." Wells concluded by repeating the argument from *A Modern Utopia* that endowed motherhood would strengthen the position of women, and that freedom outside marriage was complementary to stricter marital ties when children were involved.

By attacking private property as the source of inequality in marriage, Wells isolated himself from the moderate movement for women's suffrage, which was demanding the vote as a means to sexual equality – and, being largely middle-class in character, made much more fuss about the vote than about the conditions of millions of working women. At the same time, by insisting that discrimination stemmed from economic factors, he lost the support of militant feminists who believed that women were the victims of male sexual chauvinism. He could not even count on the backing of his fellow Fabians, some of whom insisted that sexual matters had nothing to do with politics, while others considered, as a question of tactics, that it was embarrassing to create the impression that socialists were sexual anarchists. Hubert Bland felt very strongly on this point. He wrote to Pease on 14 October after Wells had given his lecture (without any indication of the irony of such strictures coming from his pen) that "I am inclined to think one might do worse than force this 'sex and child' question to an issue as amongst Fabians. We had to do that with the Anarchists and we may have to do that with the Free Lovers."[11] A week later Pease refused to print as a Fabian tract the article on "Socialism and the Family", which Wells had written for the *Independent Review*.

The struggle between Wells and the Old Gang was not simply about the way the Society should be organised and the kind of propaganda it should conduct – or even a compulsive bid for power on the part of Wells. It was equally, though less obviously, a dispute about sexual attitudes and behaviour, in which H.G. was repudiating the morals of the Fabian family at the same moment that he was trying to take it over. It was this aspect of the affair which gave it a hidden agenda.

Beatrice Webb had already begun to sense that the two issues were interwoven before H.G. gave his Fabian lecture. On 1 October she wrote in her diary that she and Sidney had "called on H.G. Wells and his wife at Sandgate – deliberately to relieve the strain caused by the Wells revolt . . . We found him in depressed and rather angered state. His own affairs had not been going well". *In The Days of the Comet* had fallen flat. "Another failure and I should have to go back to journalism for a maintenance", H.G. told her. He was, she reported, furious because the committee had cut his report. It had removed "all the little clever malicious things he had put in about the Executive and watered down his grand schemes". She thought that his anger at the Old Gang was ambivalent. On the one hand he feared they might defeat him. On the other hand he suspected that if he won, "they might retire from it and leave him all the bother – the unremunerative bother of 'running it' without them". What he really wanted, Beatrice concluded, was a victory for his ideas which would commit the old leadership to carry them out. "Just at present", she reflected, "in the reaction from exaggerated self-complacency, he is anxious to 'gore' everything and everybody – the executive of the Fabian society, the family, the Anglican clergymen, the non-conformist conscience, the anti-puritan and the believer in regulation. But in the place of these worn-out institutions and new-fangled frauds he has nothing to suggest but a nebulous utopia by H.G. Wells."[12]

H.G. was now under severe attack from press and pulpit, and the criticism gathered strength all through the autumn. Between the lines of criticism there were already hints that Wells was rationalising from his private life. H.G. went off to Venice in November for a holiday, hoping to get away from the campaign against him. Before he left England, its viciousness inspired John Galsworthy – stimulated, perhaps, by his own recent experience of ostracism after eloping with his cousin's wife – to write a friendly letter, saying that he was unhappy to see the dogs barking around Wells and adding that, if it was any comfort, this was but one more example of the trials that the man of advanced ideas must expect from the conventionally-minded who could not understand him.[13] Beatrice Webb, writing on 18 October, confirmed that Wells was being pilloried.

H.G.Wells is, I believe, merely gambling with the idea of free love – throwing it out to see what sort of reception it gets – without responsibility for its effect on the character of hearers. It is this recklessness that makes Sidney dislike him. I think it is important *not* to dislike him: he is going through an ugly time, and we must stand by him for his own sake and for the good of the cause of collectivism. If he will let us – that is to say.

All through the early autumn of 1906, H.G. was working off his depression at the unfavourable reception of *In the Days of the Comet* in a frenzy of activity. Apart from his social and political commitments, he was hard at work drafting *Tono-Bungay*. It was, however, the attempt to force the special committee to condemn the Old Gang that preoccupied him. He was driving them so hard that on 4 September Charlotte Shaw protested that, contrary to his promise to be constructive, he had turned it into nothing but "a Committee of Public Safety to try the Executive"; with the foregone conclusion that they were all to be condemned. "I have been very anxious, all through our sittings, to keep friendly to your Committee, & I feel quite friendly still", she told Wells. "But I dont agree with you & I wont sign your Report. I know what happens at & about the Executive & you dont; & what you have put in the Report about it is not what I know but what you dont know."[14] To her complaint that "you have let me in in the most abominable manner, you treacherous man", Wells replied on 6 September: "No! dear lady, you have betrayed me. You want everything better and everything just the same & it can't be done."[15]

The pressure on Wells to be reasonable was increasing. Pease was refusing to publish *This Misery of Boots* as a Fabian tract unless H.G. removed "sneers" at Shaw and Webb. More significantly, Sidney Webb sent a careful letter on 3 September explaining why, despite the fact that the Wells report "contains much that is very interesting, and well put", he could not "believe that the Society will accept your proposals". There was no chance of raising the money to set up new offices, start a weekly paper and engage a larger staff, and it was equally unlikely that any senior members of the Society could be found to serve on the three triumvirates that H.G. suggested should be made responsible for running the day-to-day work of the Society.[16]

Shaw joined in on 11 September.[17] He told Wells bluntly that, as a matter of "intellectual loyalty", the offending passages must be removed. He reminded H.G. that he had "chucklingly gloried" in these "deliberate gibes" when they had talked at Spade House, and that Wells had then promised that he would delete them from the printed version. In a footnote, G.B.S. gave his first reaction to the report. It was "Webbism gone mad". He also told Wells to take care over his tactics and conciliate the committee members, "or there will be ructions". Shaw was trying to take control of a wrangle that was threatening to get out of hand. Without his intervention, he believed, both Bland and Webb would force Wells into a corner from which he could not escape. On 14 September he wrote again, in an apparently jocular letter which began with an elaborate jest that Wells, Jane, Charlotte and himself should set up a *ménage à quatre* like the characters in the *Comet*.[18] Then he noted "the moroseness and discontent" which Wells had been displaying of late, and warned him that the energy wasted on senseless quarrelling would reform the world three times over if it were concentrated on achieving socialism. "The whole thing is so ridiculous", he wrote, "that if you once let your mind turn from your political object to criticism of the conduct and personality of the men round you, you are lost. Instantly you find them insufferable; they find you the same; and the problem of how to get rid of one another supersedes Socialism, to the great advantage of the capitalist."

G.B.S. then went on to make the offer which attempted to call H.G.'s bluff. He reminded Wells that "I have had 22 years of the Fabian".

There must be an end to it someday. There are not wanting those who say that it has done its work. It hasnt; but *I* have done *my* turn. Webb has done his turn. The old gang has done its turn. Pease has burnt his boats and must stick to the ship because he cannot afford to drop his £150 a year; but you have no idea how strong the temptation is for the rest of us to unload on you. We have done enough for honor: why not let you walk over? If you really mean business; if you will steer that crazy little craft for five years to come, making the best of it no matter how ridiculously it may disappoint you, I will abdicate and the others will do the same. That is the real and hideous danger that confronts you.

Shaw again proceeded to coach H.G. in politics – how to work in a committee, how to run meetings and conduct propaganda. "You cannot go on spinning comets out of your head for ever", he told Wells, "if you . . . are ever to be anything more than a novelist bombinating in vacuo except for a touch of reality gained in your early life. We have all been throug[h] the Dickens blacking factory; and we are all socialists by reaction against that; but the world wants from men of genius what they have divined as well as what they have gone through. You must end either in being nothing, or in being something more than a man with a grievance, which is what your Comet chap is."

The tone of the letter was sufficiently friendly to conciliate Wells. "You are wonderful", he replied to Shaw on 18 September: "The amazing thing is that just at one point your wonderfulness stops short. Why don't you see how entirely I am expressing you in all these things? Don't you see that to abolish that fourteen-in-hand, the executive, has been the vague passion of your life? Fall in with my triumvirate. (They'll never elect me.) . . . For God's sake say it plainly next time & let it be soon. Then we can eliminate our last trivial differences."[19]

Shaw, busy finishing a play in Ireland, had to write back plainly on 22 September to say that Wells had still failed to grasp the point. Step by step he explained the situation.[20] It was very difficult to find new leaders.

We want a new set to unload on, and have wanted it for a long time past; but we automatically repel the capable, because the capable will not take up a burden which is being carried by somebody else in a manner which, on close examination, proves to be as efficient as is possible under the circumstances. If you came on the executive – which is a thing much to be desired by us – you would retire at the end of two years at the very outside unless you personally enjoyed it, or unless you could develop & lead a new policy (and we have tried all the new policies years ago).

Despite his liking for Wells, and his recognition that H.G was a gifted propagandist, Shaw could not bring himself to believe that Wells was really prepared to come down to earth and abandon his elevation as a prophet. H.G. was already contemplating another socialist book, which eventually appeared in 1908 as *New Worlds for Old*. From Venice, on 11 November, he wrote to S.McClure in New York about a series of articles which might be worked up into a volume.[21] "I hate this class war idea", he said, "I would suggest that I drop socialism out of the title." Socialism was "no piece of political strategy, no economic opposition of class to class; it is a plan for the reconstruction of human life, for the replacement of a disorder by order". The difference between himself and almost all other contemporary socialists, he told McClure, was that he stressed "the need for self-discipline & moral training in relation to the new institutions".

It was ironic for H.G. to use the phrase "self-discipline" when he was running amok among the Fabians, and Shaw was doing all he could to restrain him before he created a disastrous split in the Society. Apart from the letters he was writing to H.G., he was also trying to make the Old Gang realise what was at stake. On 29 September, still in Ireland and trying to stage-manage the deteriorating situation by correspondence, Shaw wrote to Sidney Webb to say that "H.G.W. has cheered up & is now as friendly as ever with me". G.B.S. was relieved that he had averted a "personal quarrel with so considerable a man". He went on to advise Webb that it would be unwise to play Wells off the stage: "on the contrary, I want to star him for all he is worth as an addition to the strength of the company". What would please the rank and file "is to have such a swell as Wells taking the juvenile lead". To achieve this, it would be desirable to accept several proposals from the Wells committee, particularly the new Basis and the idea of group organisation, while opposing the change of name to British Socialist Society, the concept of the triumvirates, and the commercial utopia of a big publishing business. Some other matters, such as the size of the executive, the amount of the subscription and the running of Fabian candidates at elections could be left as open questions.[22]

In a later letter, on 25 November, as the crisis came to a climax, Shaw repeated to Webb what he had previously told Wells.[23] The Old Gang, he said, could not make a "mere habit" of the Society, "knowing all the time that we shall have to drop it within, at the utmost, 5 years from now, & that it will then perish miserably & abortively unless we make the end of it the beginning of something else". Shaw thought that this new beginning might take the form of a socialist parliamentary party with much more middle-class support than the Labour Party, especially speaking for the trade union interest, could hope to rally. Such a move would dish the Fabian radicals, such as Haden Guest, S.G. Hobson and G.R.S. Taylor who were backing Wells's campaign. It was "eminently probable", when it came to the point, that Wells would jib at such a scheme. But, Shaw added: "Do not underrate Wells. What you said the other day about his article in the Independent Review being a mere piece of journalism suggested to me that you did not appreciate the effect his writing produces on the imagination of the movement."

Shaw was well aware that the Wells agitation was arousing a new interest in the Society's affairs. The membership had begun to increase significantly and most of these recruits were attracted by the growing influence of Wells in the country. Within five years, his literary and his propagandist work had made him a charismatic figure. The rhetoric and ambiguities of his political tracts were an advantage. They reflected the sweeping but confused enthusiasms of the day far better than the precision of the Fabians or the dogmatism of the other socialist sects. Shaw was in fact warning Webb that, in Wells, they were not dealing with a useful missionary for the ideas of the Fabians but a prophet with a mission of his own.

A year had passed since Wells had been given his special committee, and the Society was at last to have its say on the matter. At the end of November, two reports were sent out to the membership with a notice of a meeting at Essex Hall on 7 December to discuss them.[24] Both were long. The reform manifesto was largely the work of Wells, toned down by his colleagues; the executive's reply presented the ideas of Webb, toned up by Shaw. Neither said anything that was not already familiar to active Fabians.

The special committee's report followed the broad outlines of *The Faults of the Fabian*. The Society was too small. It needed to improve its propaganda. Its organisation could be improved by setting up local groups.* The day-to-day control of the Society should be vested in three new committees, each of three members, who would be responsible for propaganda, publications and general purposes, and report to an enlarged general council of twenty-five. The Basis would be rewritten, and the conditions of membership relaxed to attract recruits. The Society should be renamed the "British Socialist Society"; it should abandon its policy of permeation; and it should join with like-minded bodies to run socialist candidates for Parliament. Finally, in order to accommodate its new activities, it should move to larger premises.

* Like every reformist group for a century, it was borrowing from the pattern of "connectionism" established by Wesleyan Methodists. In advocating this model of local organisation Wells was again showing how his mind ran in the mould of his evangelical upbringing. One member, F.A.Underwood, noted this similarity in a letter to Pease on 10 December. The Wells report should be called "An Americanised Evangelical Attempt to Bring About the Revival of the Fittest".[25]

The executive's reply began disarmingly, taking the same line that Shaw had adopted in his private letters to H.G. Criticism was welcome; "the more impatient the better, perhaps even the more unreasonable the better". Some of the proposals for reform were admirable, as "pious aspirations", but no one had shown how sufficient money was to be raised to implement them. The executive had no objection to enlarging itself under the new name of a general council: this expansion would simply permit it to absorb the opposition without losing any of its present members. It also accepted the idea of three standing committees. It simply felt that a slightly smaller executive of twenty-one was desirable, and that the three committees should have seven members apiece instead of three.

Thus far, the differences between the reformers and the executive were not insuperable. It was more difficult to agree to a change in the Basis, not least because the necessary debate would consume much time and the new draft proposed by Wells seemed superior only in its "comparative literary smoothness". The conversion of *Fabian News* into a weekly was a pipe-dream, though – anticipating the decision that the Webbs and Shaw took in 1913 to found *The New Statesman* – it was conceded that someday there would be "a Socialist *Spectator*". All the talented writers preferred to write for more reasonable fees and a larger public. Why should their best work be hidden away in a Fabian flysheet? Local groups were another matter. Provided that this was not simply a device to allow the Fabians to be captured by ILP branches all over the country, the executive gave the plan its blessing. It even looked forward, on certain conditions, to the creation of a new socialist party, though the document contained a defence of the policy of permeation and argued forcibly against a "breathless" attempt to rush into such a venture. It had taken long enough to persuade the trade unions to go in for independent parliamentary action, and the next task of getting "the unpropertied middle, upper and intellectual classes similarly organised" had to be tackled cautiously and thoroughly.

Looked at dispassionately, the two reports did not represent two irreconcilable positions. They were part of a serious and intelligent debate about socialist tactics at a time when it was generally agreed that politics were in flux. The day before the first meeting Graham Wallas wrote H.G. a thoughtful letter saying he thought some such crisis in the affairs of the Society was inevitable "after the rise of a strong Labour

Party in Parliament and the way in which Cecil Chesterton and Bland had in effect imposed their policy in religious matters on the Society". If Wells managed to win on the following evening, he felt, "the reason for the existence of a Fabian Society separate from the Labour Party will disappear".[26]

Yet the excitement that had been aroused was confusing the issue. It was not now a question whether one set of constitutional proposals was superior to the other but whether Wells would trounce the Old Gang. It seemed likely that he would. Several of those present at the crowded meeting in the Essex Hall, to which over one-third of the entire membership came, later recalled that Wells could well have carried a majority with him – provided he was prepared to play the game according to Fabian rules. Wells himself, as Shaw had noted, was influential, and he had a number of well-known supporters who encouraged the impression that for once the members were being offered a real alternative to the staid policies of the Old Gang. He had successfully maintained his offensive throughout the year, and won a number of tactical victories.[27] Holbrook Jackson, writing to Pease on the eve of the meeting, expressed his anxiety: "Like a good many Fabians I am concerned as to the way the vote will go next Friday, because I believe there is a strong feeling in favour of the Wells amendment, especially among the numerous new members."[28] The one weakness in Wells's position was his insistence on the "confidence" amendment at the expense of his arguments of substance.

The meeting opened quietly, under a chairman with the curiously inappropriate name for a Fabian of H.Bond Holding. Shaw, who had persuaded the executive to let him deal with Wells, moved the first clause of a long resolution based on the executive report. H.G., who should have left this task to Sydney Olivier, the chairman of his committee, took it upon himself to propose an amendment endorsing "the spirit and purport" of his report, and calling for the election of a new executive which would implement it. He spoke for well over an hour, rehearsing the arguments that had already been circulated, chiding the Old Gang and slowly losing his audience as he directed his piping voice down to his manuscript or up to the roof. His platform manner, Shaw once said unkindly, was that of a shop assistant addressing a customer.

Only two speeches of importance followed. Sidney Webb told the members that they had to choose between the old policy and the new, and that he thought they would be ill-advised to turn out an executive that had so long enjoyed their confidence. Sydney Olivier, supporting Wells, said no one wanted wholesale dismissals, but the Society was "becoming a small, hidebound, learned body": the reforms were worth attempting. Nothing was to be settled at that late hour, and the members were sent away to mull the matter over for a week.

Shaw was worried in case the second meeting should prove an anticlimax. There was a danger, after Wells had made a mess of his speech, that members who supported the Old Gang might not bother to turn up in the belief that there was now no risk that Wells would carry his amendment. To make sure that there was an overwhelming victory for the executive, on 11 December Shaw circulated a printed postcard to the Fabian membership which made it quite clear that he and his colleagues would resign if Wells secured a majority, with "the most serious consequences to the Society".[29]

The meeting on Friday 14 December was even larger and more excited than the one held the previous week. G.B.S. had already decided on his tactics.[30] He told Bland to keep out of the debate and not to allow himself to be provoked by Wells. Shaw believed that Wells knew himself to be beaten. "He came here on Saturday morning quite blithe and affectionate", Shaw wrote to Bland on 10 December. "He said 'Shaw: I apologise. NOW!' I tried to explain that this would not get him out of his corner . . . all I gathered was that he expected defeat, but thought it so near a thing that I might compromise." It was this approach by Wells that had prompted Shaw to send off his urgent whip to the membership, and to decide "to take the weight of the debate on myself . . . I am the only one whose mind has been really laid to the job . . . I have all the points of detail noted, and can smash him to atoms on every one of them." But there was a word of warning to Bland, who was burning with personal animosity towards Wells. The Old Gang, Shaw said, "must be careful not to compromise our moral superiority by saying anything unkind. His speech was AWFUL – SHOCKING."

When the meeting began, there were some routine exchanges, Maud Reeves appealed for peace and unity. Bland, ignoring Shaw's plea, at least kept himself under control, and pointed out that the "flamboyant self-constituted championship of youth had come not from the young but the elderly and middle-aged members of the special committee". Clifford Sharp and S.G.Hobson, both of whom had shown sympathy for Wells earlier in the year, plumped for the executive. For them, as for many others in the hall, the attacks that Wells made on the Old Gang were a personal outrage that vitiated his political criticisms.

By nine o'clock, when Shaw rose to reply, it was clear that whatever support Wells may have won for his ideas, a majority of those present were not prepared to follow him if it meant driving the Old Gang into the wilderness. Like Charlotte Shaw, they did not feel that they could thus summarily repudiate all that the Society had so far represented; Wells had worked himself into the impossible position of asking them to pass judgement on themselves. That was what Shaw had predicted earlier in the year, and why he had repeatedly urged H.G. to moderate his language and seek a compromise. His advice spurned, he could now do nothing but mercilessly (albeit good-humouredly) squash the rebellion.

He began with a neat tactical trap. If H.G. would withdraw his amendment, the substantive proposals of the executive could be debated. In that case, no item would be made a question of confidence on which the executive would feel obliged to resign. The amendment itself, however, specifically called for a new election to replace them, and if it was passed none of the present members would stand again. Wells and his supporters, Shaw added, made it equally clear that unless the amendment was carried they would give up their efforts to regenerate the Society.

Shaw's reduction of the issue to a choice between two threats of resignation created a commotion. Wells then walked into the trap. As soon as he could make himself heard, he indignantly assured Shaw that he had no intention of resigning. "That is a great relief to me", said Shaw, "I can now pitch into Mr Wells without fear of consequences." He went on wittily to review the whole course of the dispute, excoriating Wells for misrepresentation, for inventing grievances, and for blocking serious discussion with an amendment that amounted to "dismissal with dishonour" for the Old Gang. The speech was Shaw in a mood of cordial but effective malice, teasing Wells to distraction.

With the audience won as only Shaw knew how to win it, he was able to close the trap. "There is nothing for it now but annihilation of the present executive or unconditional surrender by Mr Wells", he said. Most of his colleagues wanted to press the matter to a vote, but that would have put such members of the special committee as Sydney Olivier and Maud Reeves in an ignominious position. H.G., faced by an audience he had lost completely, had no option but to rise and – with the best grace he could muster – withdraw his amendment. The cheers and applause that greeted this belated gesture of unity were no compensation for such a humiliating defeat.

H.G. had been fairly caught. Even his supporters conceded as much, though, like G.R.S.Taylor (who withdrew from the executive on the point), they felt that the Old Gang had neatly managed to avoid any discussion of substance by putting up Shaw to defend their honour. As Beatrice Webb noted the day after the meeting, it was Wells who had made that manoeuvre inevitable. "The odd thing", she wrote, "is that if he had pushed his own fervid policy or rather enthusiasm for vague and big ideas, without making a personal attack on the old gang, he would have succeeded ... Wells has just now a great glamour for the young folk with his idealism for the future and clever biting criticism of the present ... But his accusations were so preposterous – his innuendos so unsavoury and his little fibs so transparent that even his own followers refused to support him." She thought his mauling by Shaw an "altogether horrid business". Wells had fine qualities of heart and intellect, "but he has no manners in the broadest meaning of the word".[31]

Shaw was still determined to make it possible for H.G. to play a constructive role in the Society. On 17 December he sent a hurried letter to Wells, making no apologies for crushing him three days earlier but explaining precisely what had to be done next.[32] Wells should wait for the executive elections in the spring; "you can easily retrieve the situation if you will study your game carefully, or else do exactly what I tell you". In the early part of 1907 there were to be more meetings to discuss the remainder of the executive proposals left undiscussed during the two evenings devoted to the Wells–Shaw debate. Wells and his supporters should use these occasions for making their case and winning votes, and they might even carry some of their arguments: "I always make a point", Shaw assured him, "of accepting what I can". Yet Wells had to accept two facts of political life: "First, that the moral superiority tack is an impossible one as against such strong and straight players as we are, and second, that you must carefully study the etiquette of public routine." H.G. had "outrageously disregarded" the feelings of his own friends, and his reckless tactics had embarrassed them. The justice of Shaw's remarks was soon underlined for H.G. when even Haden Guest, the most militant of his supporters who had urged him to drive out the Old Gang, insisted after the meeting that Wells must take more account of his colleagues in the reform movement and – as H.G. himself put it in a letter to *Fabian News* – take up "a secondary position for a time". Angry at his defeat, Wells was now behaving towards his allies with the same self-righteous irritation that Beatrice Webb had noted in his attitude towards the Old Gang. "We've got to co-operate", Guest wrote to him on 6

February, "& you will make it easier by endeavouring to imagine the possibility that your views & judgments may occasionally be wrong. My fear is that your mental peculiarities may – despite the great value of your ideas & your writings – isolate you from the socialist movement & render any attempt to realize good ideas very difficult."[33]

"At this point", Shaw recalled in an article more than two years afterwards, "any other man would have been hurled out of the Society by bodily violence with heated objurgation." But Wells was permitted to continue "unhindered, unchecked, unpunished, apparently even undisliked". He had all the sins he ascribed to his colleagues – touchiness, dogmatism, irresponsibility; to these must be added "every other petulance of which a spoiled child" is capable. Multiply these to the millionth power "and you will still fall short of the truth about Wells. Yet the worse he behaved the more he was indulged, and the more he was indulged the worse he behaved."[34]

TAKING LIBERTIES

Wells was never able to adjust himself to the tempo of Fabian affairs. When he moved into public life he was impatient to translate his enthusiasms into actions, as if his imagination flooded into everyday life in the same way as his experience poured into his books. Of course he intended to behave in a more orderly fashion. That much is clear from his reiterated emphasis on the word "order" in his utopias and on "morality" in his schemas for social reconstruction. That theme was present in his letters as a student and it persisted in his writings until his death. But it remained an unattainable ideal in his personal behaviour – a paradox which distorted both his life and his art, for his inability to distance one from the other led to inextricable confusion between them. It was a weakness that he recognized in his calmer moments. On 30 March 1907, for instance, he made a significant confession in a letter to Maurice Browne.[1]

Well firstly I'm a thoroughly immoral person – not "non-moral" or anything like that – but just discursive, experimental & fluctuating & I have no organizing energy & very little organizing capacity. I am interested in discipline, I try out all sorts of things, I have presented this idea of the Samurai & I shall probably return to it & kindred problems again. But I couldn't create any "order". I think an "order" could be created by a man or group of men of the right sort now upon the lines of my Samurai, but I am the last man to do it.

While the Fabian affair was consuming his time and more energy, and he was toiling hard on the draft of *Tono-Bungay*, H.G. wrote on 16 January 1907 to C.F.Cazenove, who ran the Literary Agency, with an idea for a new story. The "socialism papers" which were to make up the influential *New Worlds for Old* were "running off the loom now at a great rate". If someone would put up at least £1,200 the book he now proposed could be done between March and September. "I've had my vision", Wells wrote. It was "a vivid eventful story of about 50–70,000 words describing a campaign, a sort of aerial Battle of Dorking".[2] The vision had been prompted by talk with "a man from Aldershot about the flying machine work that is going on". In the middle of the Fabian uproar H.G. had been cultivating his friendship with the inventor, J.W.Dunne, who later turned his interests to dreams and precognition and after World War I wrote *An Experiment with Time*.[3] They had kept in touch over the years. Dunne, indeed, served as the model for the aviators in several Wells stories, and Wells himself had been much involved with him in patent discussions and in trying to enlist the backing of the armament manufacturer Sir Hiram Maxim. It was also Dunne who gave H.G. the essential idea of the tank which was worked up into *The Land Ironclads* – "big fat pedrail machines" he called them in a letter which gives a brilliant sketch of armoured vehicles and aircraft combining in the highly mobile warfare of the future. Ideas he picked up from Dunne could be woven into a new and potentially profitable novelette that would combine the current interest in aircraft with popular fears of a war with Germany.

The War in the Air, which appeared in 1908, was an extraordinary concoction – as if H.G. had shaken up *Kipps* and *The War of the Worlds* and poured out a new story that would appeal both to those who liked his social comedies and those who had been impressed by his early fantasies of terror. The story of Bert Smallways, the Cockney cycle-repairer who is carried off by a drifting balloon and caught up in a surprise German air-attack on New York City, was also – as Wells had said – "a vision". As the war widens into a world disorder, it brings the "collapse of the civilization that had trusted to machines, and the instrument of its destruction was machines". Smallways is the common man faced by the ghastly reality of doomsday, brought about because mankind "had not the will to avert it", and he survives to see that "every organised government in the world was as shattered and broken as a heap of china beaten with a stick". Men survive the panic and the pestilence, but only as beggared peasants creeping hungrily through the ruins. The story is an object lesson. This, Wells was saying, even more explicitly than in the comparable passages in *The War of the Worlds*, is what will come if mankind is not aroused from complacency to understand that national passions, imperialism and secret armamemts will bring utter ruin.

"Will you interrupt your labours for a moment", Shaw wrote to H.G. on 16 January 1907, "to send a note to Pease ... withdrawing that long letter you wanted put in *Fabian News*." G.B.S. wanted to stop the squabbling, now that Wells had been patently beaten, and to ensure that

the remaining discussions about the future of the Society were constructive.[4] At the same time Shaw wished to prevent Wells pushing the
argument to the point where H.G. and his associates would be unable to
win places on the executive at the coming elections.* The cue for Wells,
Shaw suggested, was "to come up smiling", but once again H.G. refused
to take a hint on tactics from Shaw, and he insisted that the Society
publish his letter complaining that he had been the victim of an "entirely
personal attack". The executive then felt obliged to add a footnote
saying that this letter gave "some idea of . . . his incurable delusion that
the ordinary procedure at public meetings is chicanery, and that the
executive committee is a conspiracy of rogues to thwart and annoy
him". H.G. however, was bent on vindicating himself. In addition to an
effort to find a slate of reform candidates to run for the executive, he was
trying to drum up support outside the Society and to bring in other
eminent socialists to support him. J.Ramsay Macdonald, the future
Labour premier, wrote on 29 January to refuse. He had been a Fabian and
had left after a dispute with the Webbs about the Boer War, feeling
disgusted with the Old Gang.[6] "Personally, I don't like the men", he
told Wells, "and I hold them neither in honour nor respect." A refusal on
different grounds came from John Galsworthy, who wrote on 7 March
to say that theoretical socialism of the kind Wells was advocating did not
suit the English character, and that Wells was squandering his time by
his entanglement in politics. The business of writers, Galsworthy argued,
was to set down the truth, and they should have no other link with
politics than the chance of temperament that impelled them to set down
truth as they saw it.[7]

Despite the confusion that Wells had created, he was still popular in
the Society. At the elections for the executive he came fourth from the
top, running closely behind Webb, Pease and Shaw. But by the time the
result was known in April, nobody could make out what he wanted. Was
he still making a bid to oust the Old Gang and control the rump of the
Society? Had he some secret plan to link the Society to the Independent

* Shaw had another reason for trying to calm matters down. Years before a wealthy Fabian
named Hutchinson had left the Society £10,000 to support its propaganda. Sidney Webb had
persuaded his fellow trustees to accept what Shaw called a "free construction" of the legacy,
and some of the money was used to found the London School of Economics. Shaw feared that
Wells would ask awkward questions, for it would be difficult to sustain the case that the
Society was too poor to support the Wells reforms if Wells could claim that there were hidden
reserves or, alternatively, that Webb had abused the trust. In fact, it was only on 30 April
1908 that H.G. asked about the Hutchinson bequest, and his enquiry was then brushed aside by
Pease who coolly told him that the trust was wound up.[5]

Labour Party? Or was he arguing that it ought to maintain its traditional policy as a forum for socialist discussion and keep clear of any direct association with party politics? In this period he seemed to be advocating all these positions, sometimes simultaneously or according to the company in which he found himself. The most definite statement of his views appeared in a memorandum which he circulated widely in May, receiving seventy-two replies but only twenty-seven signatures in support – among them G.M.Trevelyan, Philip Snowden and Joseph Fels. This called for "party-neutrality" on the part of the Society, and a continuing "development of socialist theory . . . propaganda and education". But even some close supporters, such as F.W.Galton, refused to endorse this circular, not least – as he told Wells on 22 May – because the document contained yet another threat of resignation, which created "an air of petulance".

The streak of consistency that ran through Wells's agitation was his belief that there was a strong tide of opinion setting towards socialism and that the Society was failing to take advantage of it: he was especially suspicious of proposals, which he suspected were supported by Shaw, to form a new middle-class socialist party. This, he felt, was bound to be limited in appeal and unable to offer a "means of reconciliation and concerted action" for socialists of every type and party. But he could not bring himself to work consistently within the formal framework of the Society. Anything that was to be done had to be done as the result of his initiative, or he would have no part in it. He responded grudgingly to his new role on the executive and to its decisions to launch a wide-ranging discussion of the Society's future and to set up, in June, a political committee to consider its relationship to party politics. Even those who knew him well were utterly confused about his intentions. When Harley Granville-Barker, the actor-manager who had done so much for Shaw at the Court Theatre, received the memorandum he was nonplussed. "I have lost the thread of you over this political business", he wrote to H.G. on 23 May 1907. "Have you ceased to be angry with us because we are not pledged body and soul to the ILP? Or do you now think that as we are not we should never move politically at all?"[8] Sidney Webb was also uncertain what Wells wanted. "I resisted you when you wanted to submerge the FS in the ILP or the Labour Party", he wrote on 12 June, "whichever it was you meant in the report of the Special Committee. Equally do I resist the proposal that the FS should create a party of its own. And equally do I object to your last proposal that the FS should give up political action."[9]

The confusion, which was to persist through the next year in a long wrangle about the drafting of a new Basis for the Society, was understandable. Wells, who was always prone to see a special magic in words, was really more interested in stimulating arguments than in the more tedious task of converting ideas into coherent actions. Socialism, for him, was essentially a state of mind rather than a set of practical policies, and he was liable to sponsor whatever policy seemed best to reflect his immediate impulse without any regard to consistency. He was already coming to see all forms of socialism as merely partial and inadequate attempts to move towards his own grandiose conception of a regenerated society. In June 1907, when he wrote an article for the *New Age*, he made that unmistakably clear. The task of all brands of socialism then current, he insisted, was to give birth to "a complex systematic idea" of a higher civilisation.[10] By such superior standards, the bickering at committee meetings and the small change of debate were bound to seem little more than a storm in a Fabian teacup.

Shaw and Beatrice Webb had shrewdly guessed that if H.G. did not quickly get his way in the Society he would lose interest in it. By the summer of 1907 there were already some signs that he was beginning to drift away from the centre of Fabian affairs. Though he was quite active in addressing meetings, he missed several sessions of the executive. Sidney Webb complained in June that life would be easier for everyone if H.G. would attend to discuss policy documents rather than write long comments on them afterwards. And H.G. and Jane declined a cordial invitation from Charlotte Shaw to spend a few days with the Shaws at the house they had rented in North Wales for the Fabian Summer School at Harlech.

H.G. was finding his socialist and his social compensations elsewhere. He was seeing much more of the bohemian set around the Fabian Arts Group, whom he found more congenial than the serious-minded executive members. On 12 February 1907, he sent a note to the flirtatious young writer Violet Hunt, the daughter of the well-known pre-Raphaelite painter Alfred Hunt, asking her to lunch at the Torino to "be nice to a very melancholy man ... I'm rather down, cross, feeble." He had, he added pointedly, "no afternoon appointments". Less than a month later, on 9 March 1907, he wrote again to Violet Hunt about Rosamund Bland, the daughter of Hubert. "I have a pure flame for Rosamund", he wrote, "who is the Most – Quite!" It was this scarcely pure flame which had brought Hubert's temper close to boiling point during the Fabian row.[11]

Rosamund Bland was one of the group of younger Fabians who had formed the "Fabian Nursery" in 1906, and given H.G. flattering support during his struggle with their parents and elders. Apart from Rosamund Bland, who was its secretary, and Clifford Sharp, who acted as treasurer, there were other young people in the group whose politics were radical and whose behaviour was uninhibited. Beatrice Webb watched their relaxed attitude with some apprehension.[12] At the Harlech summer school in 1908, she observed that "the young folk live the most unconventional life . . . stealing out on moor and sand, in stable or under hayricks, without always the requisite chaperonne to make it look as wholly innocent as it really is . . . conversation is most surprisingly open. 'Is dancing sexual', I found 3 pretty Cambridge girl graduates discussing with half a dozen men. But mostly they talk economics and political science."

Another active member of the Nursery was young Amber Reeves, the daughter of William and Maud Pember Reeves, a student who had founded the Fabian group at Cambridge. On 8 November 1906 her father wrote to Wells that "Amber has just made her first speech – to express sympathy with the Russian bomb-throwers and bank-robbers!"[13] Amber had become one of H.G.'s protégées, and a guest for holidays at Sandgate. She could, Maud Reeves wrote to H.G. in March 1907, be "very sweet and coaxing. Mrs Webb might laugh at the possibility of this but I find her so. And when she wants the moon I have a tough time of it."[14] All these young people were lively and iconoclastic. They found Wells a much more appealing symbol of personal and social freedom than the austere members of the Old Gang. They could make his revolt against their parents and elders their own, while their support convinced him that the younger generation could be won for his ideas. He became, in effect, a permissive father-figure for them, exciting them with his sweeping ideas of reconstructing the world and his arguments for a new morality. It was at their invitation that Wells gave the three lectures in the autumn of 1907 which were subsequently worked up into *First and Last Things* – what H.G. called "A Confession of Faith and A Rule of Life". When, that autumn, he again came under fierce public attack as an advocate of free love, they treated him as a martyr while their parents regarded him with embarrassment.

The campaign against Wells which began in 1906 with *In the Days of the Comet* and "Socialism and the Family" had simmered down. When it first started H.G. had defended himself vigorously. He wrote, for instance, in the *Manchester Dispatch* on 10 October 1906 that he hoped that he had nailed the "whacking lie" that he advocated "something nasty called free love . . . a sort of utopia of salacious freedoms . . . the absolute antithesis of that regulated parentage at which socialists aim". Yet the charge that socialism meant promiscuity was electorally too valuable to neglect, and it was revived during a by-election at Altrincham in October 1907. *The Times Literary Supplement* had said in a review of the *Comet* that "Socialistic men's wives, we gather, are, no less than their goods, to be held in common". This phrase was picked up by the Tory candidate, Joynson-Hicks, who later became a notoriously moral Home Secretary, and assiduously circulated by Horatio Bottomley, then at the beginning of his career as a fraudulent demagogue. Wells, threatening a libel action, demanded that Joynson-Hicks withdraw the implication that he was "a nasty-minded advocate of promiscuous copulation", and sought to counter Bottomley's press campaign by sending a standard hand-out to every paper in which Bottomley's agents had managed to plant the "forgery" which H.G. described as part of "an organized campaign of filth-throwing."[15] It was, however, the attack in the *Spectator* on 19 October 1907 which was the most wounding. St Loe Strachey was an influential moralist, and when his weekly journal claimed that Wells made "Free Love the dominant principle for the regulation of sexual ties in his regenerated State" and accused him of advocating both polyandry and polygamy, Wells was put on the defensive. Whatever he said in an effort to rebut the charge – and his letter of reply was curiously lame – he knew that in the relatively small circle of London journalism there was already gossip about him, and that behind the *Spectator*'s criticism of his opinions there lay a strong hint of reproach about his personal life. Some of his acquaintances, indeed, thought it disingenuous of him vociferously to deny in public the very beliefs he advocated in private. When Bertrand Russell put that point to him, H.G. replied that he had not yet saved enough money to live on the interest and that he did not propose to espouse free love openly until he could afford to do so.[16]

There was, as yet, no great scandal about his affairs, though there was a good deal of gossip. H.G., in Beatrice Webb's phrase, was "dining with duchesses and lunching with countesses" as he kept up with the social set that revolved around Lady Desborough and Lady Elcho. He was also on intimate terms with leading politicians, writers and theatre people, such as Harley Granville-Barker and his actress wife Lillah McCarthy. When H.G. was fraternising with the young Fabians, he could combine his rebellious idealism and his louche social behaviour without exciting more comment than was inevitable when an eminent middle-aged man showed a penchant for the company of clever and pretty girls. But the discrepancy between his radical politics and his style of life was beginning to attract criticism. In February 1908 H.G. found it necessary to defend himself in a letter to the editor of the *Labour Leader*. Wells conceded that he said, arguing that in time, energy and damaged sales of his books, this luxuries, and took holidays abroad. "But my chief luxury is Socialism", he said, arguing that in time, energy, damaged sales for his books, this had cost him at least £2,000 in the last four years, "and that is only the beginning of the damage it will do to the solid world of success I have within my grasp." He saw no sense "in making myself uncomfortable & inefficient", he added, "& cutting myself off from association with any but the working class & risking the lives & education of my children by going to live in some infernal slum or other at a pound a week or so. I don't believe in anyone living like that. Why should I set a bad example? . . . I am ready to go on working for [Socialism] . . . in the meantime having just as good a time and just as many pleasant things as I can." He was in London a good deal, sometimes away at country houses for the weekend, and even when he was back at Sandgate the house was usually full of visitors. His invitations were indiscriminate. Liberal politicians were expected to rub shoulders with bohemian writers and actors, or smart friends who had dropped over while staying at the Sassoons nearby, journalists and young members of the Fabian set.

There was nothing H.G. enjoyed more than a party, and few things he did better than acting the host – lively, generous and full of ideas for strange romps. Anyone was welcome who was not a bore, and proved willing to be carried along by the seemingly tireless host. There were many hilarious afternoons on the lawn at Spade House. Lucy Masterman, whose husband C.F.G.Masterman was then a rising star in Liberal politics, remembered a holiday at Sandgate through "the haze of time" as an "impression of perpetual sunshine, health and ease".[17]

No one stood on ceremony at Spade House. Jessie the cook told a newcomer to the household not to be "surprised if you see Mr Wells walking barefoot about the place. As a matter of fact, most people who come here have something odd about them and behave in a strange way."[18] Many of the visitors were attractive young women. Nell de Boer (nicknamed "Bokes") was the separated wife of Sidney Bowkett, the boyhood friend of Wells at Bromley. Dorothy Richardson, Jane's schoolmate, had been a regular visitor since the Worcester Park days. There were the Radford girls, Rosamund Bland and others whom Wells had met on visits to Well Hall, or at Fabian meetings and London parties. One of them was Violet Hunt, whom Grant Richards described as "one of the cleverest, best-looking and kindest people of this period". She was just beginning to make a name for herself as a writer, and she had a driving force of ambition which led her to flout social conventions and made her the centre of a bohemian literary set. In her diary she recalled the Sandgate flirtations, and noted how she teased H.G.

I hardly see H.G. alone. He sometimes wiles me into a tool shed which he calls his study, a place with bare boards and all window and a trestle table with a typewriter on it. . . . I am demure the moment I go into the house. . . . I am such a devil I am only nice to him *outside*.

But in the garden the bushes did not provide enough cover for H.G., who was "in continued terror of Dorothy's sharp eyes". Dorothy Richardson, Violet Hunt observed, was hotly pursuing Wells at this time and showed her jealousy whenever he dallied with other lady visitors.[19] Wells, Dorothy Richardson recalled late in life, had "a fascination that could not be defined; that drove its way through all the evidence against it. . . . Married. Yet always seeming nearer and more sympathetic than other men."

In the Edwardian years, H.G. was in his prime, sturdy and vigorous. Though he was never handsome and his high-pitched Cockney voice was unattractive, he had immense charm, humour and a never-failing capacity for lively talk, and almost everyone who met him was struck by the pene-trating power of his limpid blue eyes. He had a seductive personality, and was willing in his turn to be seduced. And the more his reputation grew as a man who was successful with women the easier he found it to make new conquests. It was not, however, simply a matter of physical attrac-tion. Wells had charisma, and the women who were drawn to him were all of a romantic, independent and rebellious temperament. His icono-clastic enthusiasm fed their dreams: he encouraged them to believe that they were not only right to defy society but that it was this very defiance which was the key to changing the world. Young women, scarcely grown out of the vanities and fantasies of adolescence, were swept up by the euphoria of his large and exciting ideas.

Wells had learned how to exploit his attractiveness and surround him-self with young women who flattered him. It was not surprising that, at some of the Spade House parties, Jane showed signs of strain. She "does look overworked", Violet Hunt said, "and she is no longer so pretty, for to save trouble she does her hair in a knot on the top of her head which doesn't suit her". She cattily told Jane so, and got a chilly reply. "I don't think she likes me", she said casually; "I don't see, all things considered, why she should." All things considered, indeed, Jane was leading a difficult life, trying to keep up with the varied demands that H.G. made upon her. She had been pushed forward when he needed her on the Fabian committee. She had to cope with his literary business, bear with his outbursts of irritation and depression, act as a very efficient housekeeper and hostess, and bring up her two sons.

In the autumn of 1908 Jane decided to engage a Swiss governess for the boys. The applicant, the advertisement stated, "must be a good disciplinarian". Mathilde Meyer, whom she interviewed at the Lyceum Club, remembered her first impression of Jane as "a little lady, as delicate as Dresden china, very simply dressed in brown, and wearing no ornaments whatsoever. She had an abundance of beautiful fair hair, lovely, soulful brown eyes, a soft voice and great charm." Yet she "thought there was a certain wistful melancholy about her". Fraulein Meyer developed a great sympathy for her mistress and a lifelong affection for her charges. When she arrived, Jessie the cook told her that Mrs Wells was "very nice and understanding. Mind you, she knows what she wants, and she tells you so straight. She's businesslike, you know, and commands respect." The demure Swiss girl found it harder to come to terms with H.G. Jessie had been quite frank about his shortcomings. "I keep out of his way whenever I'm able to do so", she told the governess. "You see, he can be pretty prickly at times, and most exasperating and impatient. It all depends on his mood. There are days when he goes skylarking about the house and garden like a schoolboy home for the holidays, and the next day everybody seems to get in his way and annoy him. So beware . . . " When Fraulein Meyer first met him he was just over forty, "a young-looking man of medium height, slight, with a large forehead, a heavy moustache, bushy eyebrows and small hands and feet. He was wearing a soft collared shirt, a dark blue bow-tie with white spots, a dark blue flannel blazer, grey trousers and black shoes." What she admired most about him was the enthusiasm he threw into his role as a father. His eyes twinkled with boyish gaiety when he talked to Gip and Frank: "They assailed him with endless questions and how interesting were the answers which the learned man was ever ready to give them." Whenever he was home, bedtime was a ritual. H.G. would sit between the boys inventing stories and drawing endless "picshuas" to illustrate them.

H.G. himself so enjoyed boyish games that his two sons gave him a marvellous chance to indulge himself – the two books he wrote for them, *Little Wars* and *Floor Games* remain in print – and many visitors remembered being drawn into these elaborate operations. Charles Masterman left a vivid description of them.[20]

It is not only the attraction of the man himself, with brain crammed with ideas – fantasies, new original plans of scientific and mechanical development, just pure nonsense, or, if you wish it, the preaching of his ideals for the healing of the hurt of the world. Nor the hospitality of the gracious lady who is his wife; nor the two jolly boys. . . . It is the general air of intimacy and fun, of the days being a lark, and the joy to be gained over simple things. I remember . . . the invention of the War Game, in which I claim to have some part of authorship. The floor . . . was converted by toy bricks and impedimenta into a wild and rocky scene . . . The instruments were the ordinary large tin soldiers and some extraordinary accurately shooting little brass cannon. . . . Its charm lay in the combination of actual skill in shooting, with the planning of cunning device in strategy and tactic. Moves were limited by time on each side and everything depended on rapidity. So that I have seen harmless guests, entering for tea, greeted ferociously with the injunction: "Sit down and keep your mouth shut" . . . a game which began at ten and only ended at 7.30, in which Wells had illegitimately pressed non-combatants into his army – firemen, cooks, shopkeepers and the like – and in which a magnificent shot from the other end of the floor destroyed a missionary fleeing on a dromedary – the last representative of the nation which had marched so gaily into battle so many hours before.

The boyhood imagination was still active: H.G. liked nothing better than fantasies in which his enemies were routed.

It was not so easy, however, to win victories in real life. Wells could play the part of Scipio on the nursery floor, but the tactics of Fabius were slowly wearing him down. A letter from G.B.S. on 22 March 1908 complained that H.G. had left out women's suffrage and other democratic implications of socialism in his new Basis for the Society. He went on to scold him.[21] "You are forgetting your committee manners", Shaw said tartly, "if a man can be said to forget what he never knew." H.G. had ignored one draft written by Webb and Shaw for a year, and then come up with a new version of his own which he wanted adopted immediately.

Now I dont mind this. But if I were an opponent desiring to thwart you, and at all hostile to you personally, I might seize the opportunity to take serious offence, and put you hopelessly in the wrong before the society ... you musnt do these things. You can treat me privately without the least ceremony; and though you annoy Webb extremely by your unruliness and by your occasionally *cold* incivilities, he has to put up with you. But ... I cant get up at Fabian meetings & put the matter to them as a series of private larks between us. ... There is an art of public life which you have not mastered, expert as you are in the art of private life. The fine art of private life consists almost wholly in taking liberties: the art of public life consists fundamentally in respecting political rights. Intimate as I am with Webb, I should no more dream of treating him as you have treated him than of walking into the House of Lords & pulling the Lord Chancellor's nose.

Wells tried to answer in the same tone of bantering abuse.[22] "If you were modest and respectful", he wrote to G.B.S., "instead of being resentful, suspicious, greedy and ... habitually red-haired, you might supplement my obvious, beautiful, gigantic and attractive defects ... You are obsessed more and more by the craving to be disrespectful to me, to be impertinently familiar ... You invent explanations of me and subtle unnecessary detractions." The joking was all very well, but the edge to it was growing sharper. Though H.G. did well in the Fabian executive elections that spring, again coming fourth and pulling in several of his supporters – Jane among them – he had almost reached breaking-point.

Trouble came on an apparently minor issue. Winston Churchill was running as a Liberal in a by-election in North-West Manchester. One of his opponents was a scarcely impressive socialist named Dan Irving; the other was Joynson-Hicks, the Tory whose allegations of free love had caused H.G. such distress the previous autumn. H.G. sent off a letter to the press saying that, as a socialist, he thought that Irving stood no chance at all and that socialists should support Churchill whose "active and still rapidly developing and broadening mind" showed that he was "entirely in accordance with the spirit of our movement". Churchill was slightly surprised, but politely grateful. Arthur Fifield, the publisher who had put out "Socialism and the Family", thought it "jolly good sense, & wonderful magnanimity ... to recommend a good Liberal instead of a bad socialist". But many socialists bitterly attacked H.G. for his treachery to "the glorious principles of Socialism".[23] Wells was no doubt motivated by a desire for revenge against Joynson-Hicks. He also liked Churchill, and disliked the idea of supporting socialist candidates where they were doomed to defeat. But his intervention was significantly tactless. Apparently, he no longer greatly cared what the Fabians thought of him. The matter came up at the annual meeting on 22 April.[24] Sidney Webb skilfully defended H.G. against his critics. The executive was not a Cabinet bound by collective responsibility, he said, adding a mild note of reproof that it would nevertheless have been better for Wells to have told the other members what he proposed to do. At this point Wells rose, and ostentatiously left the platform. Webb shrugged his shoulders and remarked: "We all know our Wells." It was not, all the same, just another of the little scenes with which the members were now familiar. The next day H.G. wrote to *Fabian News* saying that "I am prepared to resign my position on the executive and to become a subscriber instead of a member of the Society . . . the prospect of it sinking to the position of one among many competing political socialist bodies" was intolerable.[25] No one answered the letter. The Old Gang and Wells were getting a little tired of each other, and, though all the excitement had attracted a surge of new members, H.G. had shot his bolt.

That summer the Webbs were busy drafting the famous Minority Report of the Commission on the Reform of the Poor Law – the document which provided the basis for a generation of reform in social welfare. Shaw was busy writing plays. H.G. spent a great deal of time at Sandgate. There was no occasion for them to meet socially, and the correspondence dwindled. H.G. had taken no more than a perfunctory interest in the Fabian Society after he walked out of the annual meeting, and the letter he wrote to Pease on 16 September 1908 to offer his resignation was offhand by comparison with earlier complaints. Ten days later the executive met. Even Shaw now realised that there was no chance of taming Wells into a Fabian asset, and that it was best to let him go his own way. The other members were clearly pleased that all the fuss was over. Pease was directed to send a letter which barely concealed a sense of relief behind the formal regrets.[26] Jane Wells decided for the present to remain on the executive. It was, perhaps, a face-saver for them all.

Though Wells had dropped, or been dropped by, the Old Gang, he kept up his contacts with the younger Fabians. In May 1908, he was making a visit to Cambridge to see Amber Reeves. Sydney Olivier, home from Jamaica on leave, went up to give a talk to the university Fabians – to whom his daughter Margery, along with Amber Reeves, belonged. They all went on to a party. Rupert Brooke wrote to his mother on 11 May

1908: "Yesterday there was a dinner in Keeling's rooms – in honour, more or less, of Sir Sydney Olivier. Wells also was there, Lady Olivier, and the two youngest Olivier girls. . . . Amber Reeves (your friend!) and Wells were perched up behind on a window-sill. They came in late and couldn't find a seat . . . we all assaulted Wells (you'll be sorry to hear) about his Manchester letter. He argued in his little thin voice for a long time, in a very delightful manner."[27]

All through that summer Wells was seeing a good deal of Amber Reeves, and Beatrice Webb suspected that there was something between them. On 15 September, after a party at her house, she noted in her diary:

I also had the brilliant Amber Reeves, the double first Moral Science Tripos, an amazingly vital person and I suppose very clever, but a terrible little pagan – vain, egotistical, and careless of other people's happiness. This may be a phase, for she is a mere precocious child, but the phase is unpleasant and not promising for really sound work. However, the little person can work and can work easily and play at the same time. A somewhat dangerous friendship is springing up between her and H. G. Wells. I think they are both too soundly self-interested to do more than cause poor Jane Wells some fearful feelings – but if Amber were my child I should be anxious.

Wells had told the Fabians that he wished to return to writing novels. That was more than an excuse. He had been casting round for some time for a new project. In May 1907 he had written to Frederick Macmillan suggesting a volume of short stories as a stop-gap.[28] Once *Tono-Bungay* was finished, he said, "I've got nothing arranged for book publication except a little volume on Socialism . . . I am doubtful whether in these feverish times it's well to lie quiet so long and then to intensify my association with the idea of Socialism." Almost a year later, Arnold Bennett took his wife Marguerite down to Sandgate to be introduced to H. G. and Jane. On 5 March 1908 he noted in his journal that Wells "seemed discontented about money, while admitting that he was making three thousand pounds out of *War in the Air*, which he wrote easily in four months". By 14 May 1908, Wells had settled with Macmillan for an advance of £1,500 on *Tono-Bungay*, after another threat to change publishers, and he was thinking about plans for serialisation.

He was also speculating about another money-maker. On 18 May he tried out on Cazenove the idea of "a big popular serial" which "might be a sort of caricature of myself as a prophetic journalist . . . full of a dream of seeing the world five hundred years ahead". It sounded very similar to *When the Sleeper Wakes*: the narrator would be put into suspended animation by "a fall into a cold storage vault". On being resuscitated, he would find civilisation "not developed but in an immense phase of decay". The proposal came to nothing, possibly because H.G. wanted a guarantee of two thousand five hundred pounds before he would start work; the only trace of it was the revised version of *The Sleeper* which appeared in 1910.[29] Yet the suggestion reveals the way his mind was running at this time. Once again it was pessimistic: the London of the future was no utopia but the parish of barbarians. And, as in other Wells stories, one of the main characters – who dreams of a great regeneration – "falls violently in love with a beautiful girl and throws everything to the winds". During the summer of 1908 as he dropped out of Fabian affairs, he was in fact getting on with the novel to be called *Ann Veronica*. On 15 September, the day before he sent his letter of resignation to Pease, he wrote to Macmillan to say that *Ann Veronica* was "under revision" and that it was "the best love story I have ever done".

Wells had clearly revoked his political ambitions, and turned his attention back to his career as a writer. But there was a significant change of emphasis. His frustration at his failure to defeat the Old Gang and his irritation at their prurient attitude to his views on sexual freedom had to find an outlet. He turned his anger against himself. The clue lies in the letter to Cazenove. He now saw himself as the man of promise who "throws everything to the winds" for passion.

PART FOUR
Passions and Passades

15

LOST ORIENTATIONS

For ten years, H.G. had been riding "fortune's wave" that had lifted him out of Grub Street and carried him to Spade House and the Reform Club.* As he approached forty, it seemed that he had at last found a sense of direction. He had moved away from the scientific romances and short stories which had made his reputation. He had established himself as a novelist, as a serious writer on social problems, and as a significant figure in socialist politics. He was financially successful and lionised in society. There was, superficially, no reason why his career should not continue comfortably in the same course, without further crises of the kind which had punctuated his rise to fame. Yet he was not done with false starts. Fame simply changed the circumstances in which they occurred. In his own life he managed to break through the constraints that had proved too much for Lewisham and Kipps, but that triumph had brought no relief from the feeling that the world conspired against him – that, as he had told Elizabeth Healey years before, a malign Providence was always ready to strike back. His childhood and adolescence had been full of genuine frustrations, and he had developed his sense of identity by struggling against them and releasing his underlying anxiety by displays of aggressive mastery. But as the years passed the pattern became ingrained, and he came to thrive on frustration as if he could experience the world only when he was in conflict with it.

The heroes of the earlier novels were little men crushed by life. After Wells had proved to himself that success was possible, his spokesmen became more masterful characters whose aim was to bring order to a world full of waste and chaos and whose lives followed a similar trajectory to his own. Yet they remained driven creatures, as restless as their author, equally at odds with a social system that brought them material rewards

* In March 1905 Wells had been elected to the Reform Club, a centre for the liberal and literary Establishments.

239

but eventually disillusioned and destroyed them. "All my life", George Ponderevo remarks in *Tono-Bungay*, "has been at bottom *seeking*, disbelieving always, dissatisfied always with the thing seen and the thing believed, seeking something in toil, in force, in danger . . . something I have ever failed to find." They were obsessed, like Wells, with the hope that the next turn of events would reveal the secret of happiness, and like Wells they were constantly disappointed.

Arthur Salter, who saw a good deal of him during this Fabian period, believed that there was "a recurrent cycle" in "his questing mind".[1]

The first phase would be one of ardent hope and he would idealise like an ardent lover; in the second he would discover how far short the object of his desires and devotion fell short of his romantic picture; in the third he would turn with all the fury of the disillusioned lover and attack what he had idealised. Nothing was so fatal in the end to an institution or a person as to be at first too generously assessed and praised.

Soon after the Fabian dispute reached its climax H.G. began to display all the characteristics of the last phase of this cycle. He was about to invent a new plot, and during the winter of 1907–08 he was casting round for a set of characters to support him in his new role. Unlike G.B.S., who behaved towards his associates as if he were a producer rehearsing them in parts he had already written, H.G. had to play the lead himself in a drama he made up as the action proceeded. Everyone was expected to improvise, and to run the risk of a scolding if their lines and actions did not fit. Wells played at life, indeed, in the same way as he played the games he invented for his guests.

As H.G. moved away from the Fabians, his first impulse was to pick up the literary associations that he had neglected for his political enthusiasms. In the summer of 1908, a visit by William James to Rye provided an excuse for social calls to Lamb House. Wells wrote a jocular letter to greet him, and to say that the portly G.K.Chesterton was spending a holiday there: the profile of Rye seen through a telescope "seems to distend post-prandially". William James had not yet met G.K.C. though, he replied on 17 July, "I shall myself admire to see him (as we say in New England) if the chance be allotted."[2] The trouble was that Henry James had not yet been introduced to his temporary neighbour. When Wells arrived at Lamb House, he found a disconsolate William who had been reproved by his brother for using the gardener's ladder to peek over the wall to catch a glimpse of Chesterton. Taking William and his daughter back to Spade House, H.G. ran across Chesterton and made the necessary formal introduction. James wrote to Jane Wells on 28 July explaining that "the American season" so harassed him with visitors that he could not get over to Sandgate.[3] He added that she was to tell H.G. that "I really love him, and am subject to his potent spell, none the less".

Conrad left the Pent in the previous year, but just before he moved away he had written to H.G. asking for permission to dedicate *The Secret Agent* to him: "pray observe that in this definition I have stated what the perfect novelist should be – chronicler, biographer and historian". Yet he no longer had the same hopes of Wells as an artist that had been aroused by his earlier work. "The difference between us", he told H.G. later, "is fundamental. You don't care for humanity but think they are to be improved. I love humanity but know they are not."[4]

Conrad and Wells, however, were associated with Garnett and Ford Madox Ford in the summer of 1908 in the plan to launch the *English Review* which Ford declared was "to give imaginative literature a chance in England". The men of letters who had been struggling for recognition in the early years of the century were about to come into their own – to be seen as a movement as recognisable in literary affairs as the Vorticists, Cubists and Futurists were in the world of art.[5] Wells was much involved, from the early discussions in January 1908 through all the preliminaries to the appearance of the journal a year later, helping to plan it, to drum up contributors and subscribers and, in effect, to finance it. For the original agreement with Ford had been that H.G. would act as joint editor and bear half the cost. When Wells decided to back out of this understanding he was still willing to let Ford have the serial rights to *Tono-Bungay* in exchange for one-fifth of the profits. By the end of 1908 Wells had come to regret even this bargain. Ford was a talented but notoriously incompetent editor, as capable of losing manuscripts as he was incapable of organising his time. Douglas Goldring, who was his assistant editor, recalled that the only way he could disentangle Ford from his social commitments was to put him in a hansom cab and take him off to a music-hall, where Ford would do his business during the duller acts.[6] What was worse, Ford had no sense of money, was unable to keep proper accounts, and stayed abreast of his creditors by borrowing from rich friends and relations.

To Wells, who had the rectitude and skills of a book-keeper in such matters, this irresponsibility was intolerable – though he gave Ford much more rope than some of his hard-headed colleagues. It was some relief when Ford managed to draw in Arthur Marwood as a partner, for Marwood then undertook to carry half the cost of the journal. Yet Wells was still not out of the wood. He had hoped to make as much as six hundred pounds for each part of *Tono-Bungay*, on the original assumption that the review would sell about 5,000 copies and secure a reasonable advertisement revenue. From the outset, however, it was clear that Ford was going to lose money. After the first four issues, in fact, he had already lost something over one thousand six hundred pounds. There was no prospect that H.G. would make anything at all from his share of the profits.

In January 1909, Wells wrote a tart letter to Ford, stating plainly his dissatisfaction. Ford then sent back a defensive letter to Jane, rehearsing all the grievances against H.G. that he had accumulated over the past twelve months. "Wells is quite aware that as far as I am concerned", Ford wrote on 29 January, "he is at liberty to swindle or rob me or to do anything that he likes with my property" but he must not damage the *Review*. . . . "Wells, as you must know, has behaved again & again most treacherously to me. I have always ignored the treacheries on account of his art which I admire sincerely." Ford, who thought he had done well in launching a journal with such distinguished contributors as Tolstoy, Conrad, James, Hardy, W.H.Hudson and Wells, felt betrayed by sordid commercialism. In his exasperation, and allowing his self-pity to colour his judgement, he was unable to see that Wells really had a case – and that Wells was justifiably worried when he heard a rumour that Ford intended to remainder unsold issues even before *Tono-Bungay* appeared as a book. Ford, indeed, was so afraid that publication of the book version of *Tono-Bungay* would make the *Review* unsaleable, and so worried about its financial difficulties generally, that he continued to insist that H.G. had reneged on his bargain. The fight became so tiresome that, when it was all over, on 28 October 1910, Ford wrote to Edgar Jepson that H.G. would end either in a country house with a Tory seat in Parliament or in "the chains and straw of Bedlam. At one time I thought very strongly it would be the former, now I would put one hundred to thirty-three up on the latter."[7]

All that Ford had got out of this association with Wells, apart from the distinction of launching the *Review* with one of the best books H.G. ever wrote, was the long affair with Violet Hunt. Wells was in the habit of sounding out publishers on behalf of his protégées. (In 1908 he was trying to find one for Amber Reeves.) Impressed by the stories of Violet Hunt, which were not at all the nice-minded fiction then expected from literary ladies, H.G. sent her along to see Ford at the *Review* offices above a fishmonger's shop in Holland Park. Ford was equally impressed by the stories, and by their author, whom he adopted as his mistress and manuscript reader.

With *Tono-Bungay* Wells reached the peak of his career as a novelist. All the earlier books led up to it and the later ones away from it. He made his customary denials that any autobiographical significance could be read into it. When a proof reached the *Glasgow Herald* as part of the initial publicity for the *English Review* a columnist suggested it was drawn from life, and H.G. scribbled furiously on the press clipping he sent to Ford that he must "trace the *Fool* who started this to his lair and cut his obscene throat".[8] Yet, of all his novels, it was the epitome of Wells. *Tono-Bungay*, a critic remarked in the *Observer*, "is not only Mr Wells but it is all the Mr Wellses".[9] In his social comedies, the heroes were H.G. as he might have been, making their exit at the point where Wells himself had gone onwards and upwards. In *Tono-Bungay*, however, the trajectory is continued. George Ponderevo rises as Wells had done, through "an old and de-generating system, tired and strained by new inventions and new ideas". His picaresque adventures, as the patent medicine invented by his uncle Edward rushes them up through the commercial world like a bubble, are deliberately episodic – a means whereby Wells could "sprawl and flounder, comment and theorize" as he tried to present an "extensive cross-section of the British social organism". George Ponderevo was used to re-flect on what was wrong with England and what might be done about it.[10]

It is not the condition of George Ponderevo that the reader is invited to consider. There is no pretence that this is in any sense a novel of character, and the most memorable sketches in it are caricatures rather than portraits. The subject of the book was the Condition of England. Soon after it appeared Charles Masterman published a book of social criticism with that very title in which he openly acknowledged his debt to *Tono-Bungay*. Wells had at last done what he had long wanted to do – to make a work of fiction serve as "a powerful instrument of moral sug-gestion". When he was drafting *Tono-Bungay*, he was absorbed in social and political matters and buoyed up by success. With its virtues, as well as its faults, it was a demonstration of his theory of the novel.[11] Wells, who was still defending his position in 1933, argued that the conventions

243

of the English novel had been established in a period of social stability. This provided a frame within which characters could develop and interact. These conventions, he claimed, were no longer relevant when, "through a new instability, the splintering frame began to get into the picture". Wells, indeed, had gone even further. The frame had come to matter more to him than the narrative and the characters. The real task was to describe just how and why the frame was splintering.

In *Tono-Bungay* this is brilliantly done by using the stable virtues of the Bladesover country-house system as the scene into which the subsequent disorder intrudes – the "spectacle of forces running to waste, of people who use and do not replace, the story of a country hectic with a wasting, aimless fever of trade and money-making and pleasure-seeking". These virtues, moreover, are expressed topographically. They are seen to derive from an ordered environment, just as the images of disorder all stem from the central theme of a disintegrating social fabric. Wells never used his talent for description better than in the sustained metaphor of the Bladesover estate, which symbolises the golden age (or paradise lost) that balances the hope of paradise to be regained in some future order like that which H.G. was advocating in his utopian writings.

George Ponderevo is scarcely a candidate for the Samurai. He is simply a chronicler of his uncle's fraudulent career, in which he has been a fascinated and corrupted partner. The best he can do, after recounting the rise and fall of the patent-medicine empire, is to hint that beyond the confusion "something drives, something that is at once human achievement and the most inhuman of all existing things. . . . Sometimes I call this reality Science, sometimes I call it Truth." This final nod towards some vague scientific order does little to offset the cumulative effect of all the epithets of chaos and decline: the novel echoes with such negative words as disease, decay and dissolution. "It may be", George Ponderevo says significantly, "I see decay all about me because I am, in a sense, decay." He is as haunted by pessimism as Wells had been when he wrote his scientific romances, and the decay which George sees behind the hedonistic façade of Edwardian England frightens him just as much as the bourgeois complacency which Wells had attacked symbolically in *The Time Machine* and *The War of the Worlds*.

The sense of an apocalypse, so strong in the books written in the late Nineties, had been attenuated by the passage of the years but it had not been forgotten. Even the humour of the book is used ironically to heighten the overall effect of stupidity and ensuing chaos. The indictment is relentless, and no one is permitted to say anything positive or do anything that is useful.

Wells made a point of sending each of his books to a long list of acquaintances, and when *Tono-Bungay* was sent around he received the usual tribute of thanks. One letter jarred on him. Beatrice Webb was tired, and she had read the book casually. Writing to Wells on 10 February 1909 she compared it unfavourably to *The War in the Air*. H.G. was furious, and sent back an outraged letter which Beatrice considered a "real gem" of bad temper.[12] He was, she observed, "at his worst in anything that concerns the Shaws or us or the Fabian Society – conceit, bitterness, and an element of treachery to past intimacies". For all that, she regretted their differences. "It will be sad if he turns completely sour", she reflected, and added a compassionate comment. "I suspect that man is going through an ugly trouble, and I would like to help him through it, instead of serving as a source of bitterness and antagonism."

Beatrice was not explicit about the cause of this trouble. On 24 February she sent off a friendly letter to Wells in an effort to maintain agreeable relations. She told him that she was delighted to hear from Amber Reeves that he was now "at work on a novel which is to combine all the great qualities of *Tono-Bungay* with a study of the more ideal elements of human character". H.G., however, was not to be appeased by soft words. He wrote back accusing Beatrice of being "wilfully unsympathetic". He insisted that "you & Sidney have the knack of estranging people & I think you have to count me among the estranged . . . I've never had a generous moment from Webb. He's been the ready ally of Bland or anyone to minimise my influence."[13] Beatrice could bear no more.[14] "It is strange", she concluded, "that he seems obsessed with the notion that we have some scheme to undo his influence. Bless the man; we never think of him, now he has resigned from the Fabian Society."

While he was there we *had* to think of him, because he spent his whole energy attacking us . . . We wanted to keep him as an asset to the cause; but we could not let him simply smash the thing up without having the least intention of working out a new plan of campaign.

The evidence supports Beatrice's claim. Wells cast himself in the role of the victim, not the cause, of the trouble. Nothing would persuade him that he was not the object of a conspiracy in which Shaw's part was to mock him and the aim of the Webbs was to minimise him.

His hostility towards the Old Gang was so intense that it surely stemmed from powerful unconscious motives – among them a strong feeling of guilt. The more Shaw and the Webbs tried to mollify him, the more he became convinced that they were playing a double game – that, not content with driving him out of the Fabian Society, they were bent on using the disorder of his personal life to ruin him socially. He suspected that Hubert Bland, in particular, was feeding gossip about him to the clubs and the press, thus providing ammunition for the campaign against his unorthodox views on sex and marriage. His aggressive reaction to Beatrice's mild criticism of *Tono-Bungay* was only one of the symptoms of an uneasy conscience.

At the same time that he was engaged in political intrigues against the Fabian Old Gang, he was involved in an emotional intrigue in the Fabian Nursery. The Edwardian smart set in which H.G. moved socially had notoriously lax morals, as did many of his bohemian friends. Of his reputation in such circles Beatrice Webb noted, on 22 August 1909, that "I imagine he let himself go, pretty considerably, with women." During his Fabian phase, however, he transferred his attentions to impressionable young people who were more vulnerable and more likely to become emotionally entangled with him, and he increasingly sought refuge in their flattery from the humiliating defeats he received at the hands of their elders.

Rosamund Bland was an obvious target. Berta Ruck, who knew the Blands well, recalled Rosamund as "a beautiful girl, with brown eyes and brown hair. She was plump, with a natural complexion that needed no make-up, and she enjoyed the admiration of the men she attracted." One of her admirers was Cecil Chesterton, and jealousy may have been one of the reasons why he turned against Wells in the Fabian row.[15] Coming from the Bland household it was understandable that she should lend herself to the attentions of Wells. In fact, what angered Hubert most about the relationship between Wells and his daughter was that, as part of his seductive ploy, H.G. told Rosamund the details of her father's sex life. Wells had known Rosamund for years, since the two families had long been on visiting terms, but it was only in the course of the Fabian row that he became closely involved with her. She obviously encouraged him in her turn, and something of the power of his influence comes through from a letter she wrote to him ten years later. She had been ill and had taken the opportunity of reading some books by Wells.[16]

I think there is some deep place in me that is still my H. G. . . . I found then that what I had, for years, thought of as "Rosamund" was simply something made up of bits of H.G. Wells. It was a shock to find that there was no "I" at all, that thoughts and feelings I had supposed to be all my own were all to be found in you. . . . I don't exist except simply as a thread on which all sorts of odds & ends are strung together.

The liaison was broken off before it came to anything substantial. Hubert Bland intervened at a crucial moment: the story ran that he had intercepted H.G. and Rosamund at Paddington station and read Wells a public lecture on his behaviour. Bland certainly made it clear to H.G. that he would have no compunction about exposing him if matters went too far. But a good deal of damage had already been done, as Wells revealed in a letter to Shaw.[17]

I think you do me an injustice – I don't mean in your general estimate of my character – but in the Bland business. However you take your line. It's possible you don't know the whole situation.

While I had some handsome ambitions last twelvemonth & they've come to nothing – nothing measured by what I wanted – and your friendship & the Webbs among other assets have gone for my grass of green spectacles. Because it's all nonsense to keep up sham amiabilities. I've said and written things that change relationships and the old attitudes are over for ever. On the whole I don't retract the things I've said & done – bad & good together it's me. I'm damnably sorry. We're all made so.

And damn the Blands! All through it's been that infernal [illegible] of lies that has tainted this affair & put me off my game. You don't for a moment begin to understand. You've judged me in this matter & there you are.

Shaw had done his best to prevent a scandal, just as he had tried to contain Wells politically in the interest of Fabian unity. He was not much more successful with one than he had been with the other. In another letter H.G. made it plain that Shaw's attempt to play the peacemaker was unwelcome.[18]

What an unmitigated moral Victorian ass you are. You play about with ideas like a daring garrulous maiden aunt but when it comes to an affair like the Bland affair you show the instincts of conscious gentility and the judgment of a hen. You write of Bland in a strain of sentimental exaltation, you explain his beautiful romantic character to me – as though I didn't know the man to his bones. You might be dear Mrs Bland herself in a paroxysm of romantic invention. And all this twaddle about "the innocent little person". If she is innocent it isn't her parents' fault anyhow . . . You don't know, as I do, in blood &

substance, lust, failure, shame, hate, love & creative passion. You don't understand & you can't understand the rights & wrongs of the case into which you stick your maiden judgment any more than you can understand the aims in the Fabian Society that your vanity has wrecked. Now go on being amusing.

H.G. was bitter, and frustrated. He was now writing openly to Shaw about the issue that had been hidden behind the public debates on Fabian policy and soured his relationship with the Old Gang.

It was a curious and common feature of all H.G.'s emotional entanglements that he managed to assume the posture of the innocent pursued, holding out against blandishments to which he ultimately succumbed. That posture, which put the onus of seduction on the woman, was the most shocking thing to many people about the novel which reflected Wells's association with the young people in the Fabian Nursery. The heroine in *Ann Veronica* defied convention by proposing to her college teacher that she should become his mistress. To young people struggling to emancipate themselves from the stifling limitations of Victorian family life, this gesture expressed their mood of rebellion: Wells had portrayed the generation gap between Ann Veronica and her parents from the standpoint of the young, not the middle-aged. It was this defiance of morality that made the story seem so daring that many of those who then read it still recall *Ann Veronica* as the Wells book that made most impact upon them.

It was written during the first part of 1908, and the manuscript was sent off to Frederick Macmillan at the end of September.[19] Macmillan realised at once that there might be a scandal about the novel. On 16 October he took the serious step of refusing to publish it, though he recognised that this meant the end of his contract with Wells. He justified his decision on the grounds that the plot "would be exceedingly distasteful to the public which buys books published by our firm". H.G., however, already had another arrangement in mind. Stanley Unwin, who had just joined the publishing firm of his uncle T. Fisher Unwin, persuaded his uncle to let him circularise a number of eminent authors who might have uncommitted work. One of them was Wells who, to Unwin's surprise, wrote back proposing *Ann Veronica* for "a firm offer of £1,500". The deal was clinched, and the book was put in hand to appear in the autumn of 1909.[20]

Ann Veronica was a tract masquerading as a piece of romantic fiction. Had the plot not been blatantly immoral by the standards of the day it would have been dismissed as banal, humourless and sentimental. Being "in love" turns out to be some kind of intellectualised attraction between two "partners" challenging the world together. When Capes, the science tutor, leaves his wife and runs away with his student Ann Veronica Stanley, he describes it as "a great lark" which "turns life into a glorious adventure". It is the escapist's daydream fulfilled. The married man runs away with the beautiful and intelligent girl to live happily ever after, and even her parents are ultimately reconciled to the elopement. "Life is rebellion or nothing", said Capes. "That's really our choice now, defy – or futility." The words which Wells wrote for Capes described his own feelings. The book, indeed, was another instalment of autobiography in which H.G. rewrote the past to make it fit his current concerns. When he was writing it he was already toying with the idea of running away and making a new start, as he had done when he left Isabel for his student, Jane. In the first part of the novel he went back and described, specifically, the circumstances of that elopement. Then, as he wrote himself into the story, he was clearly dealing with a different and contemporary situation, in which a new "Venus Urania" had been found to take the part that Jane had played fifteen years earlier.

16

JANE OR AMBER?

Amber Reeves was now the focus for Wells's dreams and desires. Pretty and forceful, she was ready to take the place that Jane had occupied in 1893 and to join H.G. in a rebellious escapade. She had made her mark at Cambridge as a brilliant student, and her emancipated attitude had been indulged by her parents. Wells, for his part, saw in Amber an escape from the increasing frustrations of his life.

There was, first, his relationship with Jane, which was breaking down in much the same way as his marriage to Isabel. He continually hoped that he would be able to satisfy his emotional needs with an ideal woman, and each time the ideal proved to be unattainable. For in a marital situation H.G. was torn by the conflict between his sexual instincts and his desire to be "saved" from them by some moral and domestic order. When he was married to Isabel, he thought he had found his ideal type in Jane. Once he was married to Jane, he again began to feel stifled, and his infidelities became more frequent and blatant. By 1907 the unconscious pressure to escape had again built up. Rosamund Bland and the other young ladies with whom he dallied were more the object rather than the cause of his distracted behaviour. Secondly, what he had described to Shaw as his "handsome ambitions" in politics had come to nothing. The Old Gang had called his bluff, discovering that his criticisms were no more than a substitute for taking real responsibility. In the process they had become authority-figures who were feared and had to be fought. Amber was a pawn to be captured in that battle. Thirdly, H.G. was now at an age when he could either come to terms with the fact of middle age or defy it by embracing the fantasy of youth. All through his writings he had revealed a profound anxiety about decay and death, and now – in the magic of his relationship with Amber – he hoped to find a means of cheating fate. If Wells had been a young man, another elopement would have been easy. But the situation in 1908 was not the same as it had been in

1893. Apart from his domestic ties he was a public man with both political and literary reputations, and he could not take risks as impulsively as he had done when he was an insignificant young journalist earning a living in Grub Street.

For a time H.G. tried to avoid a choice. He wanted to get the best of both worlds and Jane did nothing to prevent him. Amber was often invited down to Spade House as a family guest, and H.G. met her openly in London and Cambridge. Their relationship was brazenly indiscreet. But there was only one way in which H.G. could get the best of both worlds. That was to set up a polygamous relationship which offered both the security of home and an escape into adventure. This was obvious to Beatrice Webb, looking back on the past year in August 1909.

... he dropped completely out of our set and preserved an attitude of contemptuous hostility towards us and our work. Meanwhile he and Amber were becoming intellectual comrades and he was evidently considering the advantages to their respective development of a polygamous relationship. His wife had no hold on him. What he desired to do, and what he evidently thought he could do, was to lead a double life – on the one hand to be the respectable family man and famous litterateur to the world at large, and on the other, to be the Goethe-like libertine in selected circles. Now he is raging because he is found out and his card castles are tumbling down round about him.

The idea of polygamy had been implicit in his writings since *In the Days of the Comet* in 1906. Even in *Ann Veronica*, which ostensibly opted for elopement as the solution to an unsatisfactory marriage, Richard Gregory had noticed it. "The worst of reading a book like this", he wrote to H.G. when the book appeared, "is the desire to experience a woman like V. It was the same with Beatrice in *Tono-Bungay* and others back to Weena in *The Time Machine*. In spirit I am a polygamist with the lot."[1] So, too, was Wells. Both Jane and Amber accepted the situation. When, in the first flush of passion, Wells had talked of "throwing everything to the winds" and marrying Amber, she had refused and preferred to become his mistress.[2] That was how matters stood all through 1908 and the early months of 1909. They might have so continued. But in April 1909 there was a dramatic change. Amber was pregnant.

H.G. could no longer let things drift without making up his mind what he really wanted. A decision of some kind was forced upon him. His impulsive reaction was to run away with Amber. They eloped to France, where he rented a house at Le Touquet. Once there, he talked of making a definite break with his old life, and he actually wrote from France what Beatrice Webb called "an impudent letter" to Amber's father saying that this was his intention – adding that Maud Reeves had already condoned his intimacy with Amber.[3] At the same time he decided to sell Spade House. On 24 May he wrote to the playwright Henry Arthur Jones to ask whether he would buy it.[4] While he put it about in Folkestone that the reason for the move was the inadequacy of the train service to London, he was more honest with Jones. "I want very much to leave the place and live in London soon", he wrote, "by reason of a web of almost impalpable reasons that affect people of our temperament, and the house is therefore in danger of going very cheap." He was willing to take £3,200 for a quick sale, though it had cost almost that sum to build ten years before.

Previous crises in his career had been punctuated by what H.G. called "domestic claustrophobia, the fear of being caught in a household", and eased by a sudden removal. The life that had been woven around Sandgate had now become a bondage, and H.G. had a similar impulsive desire to get away from the house which he and Jane had constructed as a monument to his success: "otherwise it would become the final setting of my life". He proposed to buy a house for Jane, leaving himself uncommitted. The new place, at 17 Church Row, Hampstead, was taken in her name. The move was quickly accomplished. One day, without warning to the boys, who found the departure from the house in which they had grown up inexplicable, they were dressed and whisked off to London without even the preparation of packing.

Even before the move took place, however, H.G. was finding it difficult to settle down in Le Touquet with Amber. They had run away together, but they had not gone far and they had not gone finally. H.G., Amber recalled, could not bring himself to cut his ties to England, to face the fact that if the liaison continued he would be forced to drop out of society and accept social ruin. Beatrice Webb had realised that such a prospect would make him "*supremely and permanently* wretched. I doubt whether he will keep his health – and he may lose his talent. It will be the tragedy of a lost soul."[5] Amber recognised that he was anxious about the situation.[6] "It was not successful", she said. "I could not cope, because I was pregnant. H.G. got more and more restless and kept going back to England. He kept hankering to go back whenever he got invitations from Lady Desborough or anyone."

There was another reason for stress at Le Touquet. Though Amber was ready to live with H.G., she refused to let him divorce Jane and marry her.[7] "I didn't think it right to break up a marriage when there were children", she said many years later: "I did not wish to marry him, though I did want to have his child." H.G. now found himself in a situation where there was no chance for the happy ending that he had provided for Capes and Ann Veronica. The coming of the child made it impossible to carry on the relationship simply as an affair, and he could not just abandon Amber and return to Jane.

Before long they were back in England. They both went to Jane, compounding her earlier connivance by going to her for comfort in a situation that had become unbearably stressful for them both. Amber eventually persuaded H.G. to accept her solution. She chose to engage herself to an old friend who had previously proposed to her and now repeated his offer in full knowledge of the circumstances.[8] By the summer a marriage had been arranged, though – as Wells told Bennett – there appears to have been some doubt concerning the husband's position. H.G., who provided a cottage at Woldingham in Surrey for the young couple, wished to continue what Beatrice icily called "business relations" with Amber, "a sort of *Days of the Comet* affair".[9] Among intimates he made no secret of the fact. He wrote to Sydney Olivier about the arrangement, saying (Beatrice reported) "that he thought we were much too timid about these things".

He had, in fact, made a brief effort, with Amber's marriage, to give her up, but as he wrote to Bennett in July 1909 they had "under estimated the web of affections and memories that held them together".[10] To put convention before feelings outraged Wells's view of life and he was determined that he and Amber should go on seeing each other. There was a note of cockiness in his letter to Bennett: "And by the bye, it may interest you to know that that affair of philoprogenitive passion isn't over." Despite "violent emotional storms", he added, "I am extremely happy and I have never worked so well". The tension of the situation, it seemed, had stimulated him. He was working on *Mr Polly* and *The New Machiavelli* was in hand. But to onlookers like Beatrice Webb and Shaw it appeared that he and Amber were carrying on with little regard for the feelings of relatives and friends and courting trouble with bravado.

Beatrice Webb thought H.G. should make a complete break with Amber and leave England for a year, saving his talent at the expense of his reputation.[11] From the middle of August, with the child expected at the end of the year, more and more pressure was put on Wells to do what Beatrice suggested. He was well aware what people were saying, and this gossip intensified the anxiety caused by the harassment of the moralists who took their cue from the *Spectator*. "I can't stand this persecution", he told Amber in desperation.[12]

Shaw again became a go-between, showing sympathy to Wells, who responded with an unusually appreciative letter.[13] "Occasionally", Wells wrote on 24 August, "you don't simply rise to a difficult situation but soar above it & I withdraw anything you would like withdrawn from our correspondence in the last two years or so. . . . Matters are very much as you surmise. We should all be very happy & proud of ourselves if we hadn't the feeling of being horribly barked at by dogs". He told G.B.S. that he continued to visit Amber at Woldingham, and her husband also "gets down there in his leisure time. I like him & am unblushingly fond of her & I go down there quite often – the Reeves's don't know how often & the heavens will fall if Reeves does. My children are staying there now while Jane moves to London. It could be very nice & amusing if you ran down to Blythe one day with Mrs Shaw." The Webbs were right in suspecting that the affair had by no means ended with Amber's marriage, and that H.G. was somehow hoping to brazen out the situation which now almost exactly corresponded with that which he had fantasied at the end of *In the Days of the Comet*.

By September the inner group of Fabians was agog with the affair. The gossip filtered through to the clubs and dinner parties. Some details of H.G.'s goings-on with Rosamund Bland were so mixed up with the scandal about Amber Reeves that ever since the two episodes have been confused and entangled. Wells himself attributed a lot of the trouble to the malice of Bland, when he wrote to Beatrice Webb early in September protesting that she and Sydney were circulating untrue gossip about him and Amber.[14] He threatened her with "a public smash to clear up this untraceable soaking nastiness about us". Beatrice was not, however, a woman to be put off by bravado and she now knew the facts of the case from Shaw. By 11 September she had decided to intervene herself.[15] H.G. showed no signs of withdrawing from the ambiguous situation at Woldingham, so Beatrice wrote to Amber expressing regard for the "courage and faith" of her husband, but coming frankly to the point. Whether or not the marriage was sustained was a personal matter between Amber and her husband, and on that "I do not propose to utter another word". Beatrice undertook to try to stop the gossip, but she added firmly that "there can be only one end to the continuance of your friendship with H.G.Wells" – the break-up of the marriage. Should Amber wish to talk matters over, she would be glad to visit her, because of affection for her parents, "a *real* liking for you" and respect for her husband. "I have", she added charitably, "even a quite genuine desire to see H.G.W. saved from a big smash." Shaw was equally anxious to prevent a public scandal. When he wrote to Beatrice on 30 September he confessed that he saw no purpose in striking a moral attitude, or even in trying to sort out the rights and wrongs of the case. He was convinced that Wells would eventually break off the affair and go back to Jane, and in the meantime H.G. had to be saved from his own recklessness whether he liked it or not.[16] If there was a smash, it would damage the reputation of other people more than it would harm Wells, and so everything possible must be done to avert it.

At the beginning of October, Beatrice travelled down to Woldingham to see what she might contribute to a settlement.[17] Amber was in a "restrained state of mind" and had "lost the deceit and the artificiality of former days". She "was absorbed in her care for H.G.W. and her affection for his and her coming child". Yet Beatrice was still unable to prevail on her to repudiate Wells. Since Amber's father was now insensate with rage against "the blackguard Wells and his paramour", and was refusing to see his daughter, it might be better if lawyers were called in. Beatrice thought that Amber and H.G. were "so far cleverer and more unscrupulous than the others that they may remain as they are at present, masters of the situation in the sense that they are living the life they please in spite of the misery they are inflicting on all others concerned".

Through the autumn of 1909 H.G. continued to insist that he was happy and that the relationship with Amber was vital to him. He explained his feelings frankly to his old friend Violet Paget, who wrote under the pen name of Vernon Lee.[18] "I can't talk about things now", he told her towards the end of September. "It's vital to us all that we should be left alone to straighten out our affair in our own way – & thought of & dealt with generously. . . . Will you, if you can, silence talkers & hasty judges." Two months later, he insisted that the "facts of the scandal are perfectly plain & simple, but unfortunately they can't be published broadcast in their simplicity". The facts were that "I was & am in love with a girl half my age, we have a quite peculiar & intense mental intimacy, which is the finest & best thing we have had or can have in our lives again – & we have loved one another physically & she is going to bear me a child. We had made the most careful & elaborate plans to save this from scandalizing our friends & the public & all that was wrecked by the violence of her father." Amber had married a man who was devoted to her, and who had agreed that the relationship could continue "on an understanding of course that we rigidly respected: that we should cease to be in common parlance 'lovers'. . . . We are fighting to keep in touch with each other, which is a matter of quite vital importance to both of us. . . . The parents clamour for our divorces & that we should marry or have an absolute separation. . . . I won't leave my wife, whose life is built up on mine or my sons who have a need of me, I won't give up my thinking with & working with my lover, I mean somehow to see my friend & my child & I mean to protect her to the best of my powers."

It was not merely private gossip that now threatened him. In October 1909, *Ann Veronica* appeared. Vernon Lee urged him, to keep his own affairs out of his writing: "you *must not* give us who are faithful to you the misery of the discussions that will ensue if at this moment you write more things that can be connected with your own personality." These words were written at the height of a campaign against Wells which made the earlier criticism of *In the Days of the Comet* seem feeble. *Ann Veronica* had appeared just as a national crusade for moral purity was reaching a peak. Frederick Macmillan had judged correctly that the book would be offensive to many people, even though it might be commercially successful. It provided just the excuse that the moralists needed for a counter-attack on Edwardian permissiveness.

The attack was led by St Loe Strachey's *Spectator*, though he dragged a trail of other critics behind him – some of them recognised reviewers, some public figures such as the presidents of the Girls' Friendly Society and the YWCA.[19] There was a hue-and-cry for censorship, and the pressure persuaded the circulating libraries to set up a watch committee to prevent "literary filth . . . polluting the moral atmosphere of our home life". The *Spectator*, denouncing the "pernicious teaching" of this "poisonous book", spared few epithets. It would undermine "that sense of continence and self-control . . . which is essential in a sound and healthy State", teach "that there is no such thing as woman's honour", and suggest that if "an animal yearning or lust is only sufficiently absorbing, it is to be obeyed". The "muddy world of Mr Wells's imaginings . . . is a community of scuffling stoats and ferrets, unenlightened by a ray of duty or abnegation". So far as Ann Veronica was concerned, in Dr Johnson's phrase "the woman's a whore, and there's an end on't". The ferocity of the language, directed not merely at the book but also at H.G. personally, was savage. As the weeks went on, the outcry increased, stimulated by successive issues of the

Spectator and reinforced by anyone who wanted to denounce immorality in general or Wells in particular. For once he could do little to defend himself, and for once there was virtually no one else to defend him. His close friends were embarrassed by his domestic difficulties, which could easily become public knowledge if he moved towards a divorce or even committed some new indiscretion.

Some people were becoming reluctant about mixing socially with Wells, though outwardly life went on in Church Row much as it had in Sandgate. When Bennett went to lunch on 23 December he found a cheerful pre-Christmas party which included Robert Ross, Constance Garnett, the Sidney Lows and "the young Nesbit girl who was mad on the stage".[20] The crisis which loomed over Wells was disregarded except when "he and I talked his scandal from 12.15 to lunch-time". But Wells had by now given in under pressure, and offered an undertaking that he would stay away from Amber for at least a couple of years. "He was frightened into better behaviour", Beatrice Webb noted frigidly, "by the way in which one friend after another was sheering off and by the damning review of his book in the *Spectator*."[21]

The day of the lunch-party, in fact, Wells received a considered and considerate letter from Vernon Lee.[22] She was a woman of high literary standards and personal principle, though as a lesbian she was not indifferent to the vagaries of sexual behaviour. Though she had found his story "easy to understand, easy to sympathise with, even easy to excuse", it jarred "with some of the notions deepest engrained in me".

My experience as a woman and as a friend of women persuades me that a girl, however much she may have read and thought and talked, however willing she may think herself to assume certain responsibilities, cannot know what she is about as a married or older woman would, and that the unwritten code is right when it considers that an experienced man owes her protection from himself – from herself.

What also upset Vernon Lee was not "that those who have eaten the cake and drunk the wine should pay the price of it, but that part of the price should be paid by others who have not had their share . . . In all this story the really interesting person seems to me to be your wife, and it is *her* future, her happiness for which I am concerned." On New Year's Eve 1909, H.G wrote back to Vernon Lee to tell her that a daughter had been born to Amber that morning.[23] "I don't think that there is any faultless apology possible for Amber & me", he confessed. "We've been merry &

passionate – there's no excuse except that we loved very greatly & were both inordinately greedy of life. Anyhow now we've got to stand a very great deal – of which the worst is separation & we're doing it chiefly for love of my wife & boys."

The crisis had now reached breaking-point. At the moment when his popular influence was at its peak, as his books caught the sense of excitement which stirred all those who felt that the time had come to claim their rights, his attempt to practise what he preached had brought him close to ruin. It was not simply that H.G. had quarrelled with influential friends and become a somewhat scandalous author, who was a risky bet for respectable publishers and a liability in the circulating libraries. The real danger came from the scandal about his private life, which had begun to jeopardise his social position and make him think seriously of running away to make a new start abroad. Even in the more tolerant moral climate of Edwardian England there were limits to what was acceptable in polite society. Early in 1910, indeed, Beatrice Webb thought that H.G. and Jane would be "permanently dropped", because "he is too old to live it down". Jane, who had now been asked to resign from the Fabian executive, seemed as blameworthy as H.G., though Beatrice felt sorry for her.[24] Jane had "pandered to him and deceived friends like the Reeves", and Beatrice wished bitterly that "we had never known them".

H.G. was undoubtedly under a great deal of pressure. To Mary Barrie, who was breaking up her marriage with James Barrie, he wrote sympathetically early in 1910 to say that he too had been going through a "rather bad time. . . . Amber & I are being forced never to see or write to each other. I suppose it's the same thing in the long run – except that I rather hanker after bolting – but it hurts horribly & leaves one the prey to all sorts of moods."[25] Wells tried to put a brave face on things, taking comfort from friends who did not drop him, and he defended himself vigorously. "I have done nothing I am ashamed of", he told Vernon Lee.[26] To his old friend Elizabeth Healey he wrote with resigned honesty, soon after his daughter was born:[27] "I'm awful druv! All the rumours are true & false in various measure. . . . I'm afraid I've behaved rather scandalous but nohow mean in the past year. Believe everything scandalous & nothing mean about me & you'll be fairly right."

H.G. saw himself a man as much sinned against as sinning, and his mind turned much more upon the sins of his critics than on his own. He wrote for instance to his friend and lawyer E.S.P. Haynes explaining why he had left the Savile Club.[28]

I left the club a year before there was any scandal with the Reeves family. I did so because I knew a scandal might arise & as Reeves introduced me to the Savile & as club life seemed to be of some importance to him I thought it kindlier to anticipate trouble & leave him in possession. It was a stupid thing to do, the club was turned into a barroom of rant & lies about me, & I had lost the right to go in & face the fuss as I should have liked to do. Throughout this business I have had every reason to regret any generosity I have ever shown Mr or Mrs Reeves. I have never told my story but they have campaigned against me and still I meet fresh misrepresentations of this or that phase of Amber's affair.

By thus projecting his own hostility on to his critics he insulated himself from their criticism. If he was at odds with the world, it was the world that must change before things could be comfortable again. Even when his pride, professional position and his passion had all been touched by the attacks on *Ann Veronica* and on the related affair with Amber Reeves, he took comfort in his martyrdom. Looking back on the troubles of 1909 and 1910, he wrote in April 1911 that "incapacities, illnesses, enemies all turn to good fortune with me". The attempt of "a group of eminent and influential persons . . . to obliterate me", he remarked, had entailed its own failure: "an enormous, unpremeditated popularity has come to my work". He had "become a symbol against the authoritative, the dull, the presumptuously established, against all that is hateful and hostile to youth and to-morrow". In a revealing aside he added that "it will brace me to feel the existence of that hostile group . . . the certitude of abuse and unfair treatment releases me from my easy disposition to be propitiatory and accommodating".[29]

Although the affair with Amber was finished, it was a turning-point. From this time on his will took increasing hold over his personality and flourished at the expense of his imagination.

A TANGLE OF MOODS
AND IMPULSES

The affair with Amber Reeves was over by the spring of 1910, but H.G. had come to the end of the career which had opened so promisingly at Sandgate. Some assets remained, not least his growing public reputation and his increasing sales, but much else had been recklessly hazarded and once again he was faced by the prospect of a fresh start. He could not go back, dismissing the affair as an aberration, for it had meant too much to him and too many people knew of its consequences. In any case, the pressures of personality that had driven him into it were still at work. Yet he had no idea what he wanted to do next, after his attempt to run away had been thwarted.

The first necessity was to make a new accommodation with Jane. He now had to find some way of living with her which was privately tolerable and publicly enabled them to face down the gossip about them. Jane was willing to resume the role she had played so well for years before the crisis over Amber Reeves had faced her with the bleak prospect of a permanent separation from H.G. During those months of stress she had borne the uncertainties and the gossip, and when the affair was over she behaved as though nothing had happened. She had a remarkable capacity for suppressing her feelings, and few of her many friends were permitted a glimpse of what lay beyond the vivacious sociability which she displayed in public.

All her energy went in being wife, mother, typist, sometimes literary agent and sometimes income-tax expert to H.G., patiently picking up the loose ends that trailed behind him as he bustled through life. When these chores were done, she was expected to cater for the stream of visitors that H.G. needed to stimulate him when he was at home and wanted distraction from his writing. It was, in fact, as a hostess that she most impressed people. William Rothenstein, the artist, was one of the Hampstead neighbours who often dropped in at the house in Church Row.[1] They were, he said, "as hospitable to people as they were to ideas. Room was always found at their table for visitors, and table-talk was free, adventurous and gay; indeed Wells was the jolliest host imaginable." Jane, who actually arranged the details of all the entertainment, from generous meals to the provision of costumes for charades, allowed H.G. to have the limelight but it was she who made certain that the show went on without a hitch. Her role, as ever, was self-effacing.

Only a few close friends could see how much strain entertaining imposed on her. Frank Swinnerton, the critic and novelist who saw a great deal of Jane and H.G. after 1912, gave a vivid sketch of her at this time.[2]

She was not much above five feet, a tiny woman with fair hair and a timid manner, rather pale, pretty, an amusing mixture of terror and confidence. . . . Her voice was small and insignificant; she had no manner; and her conversation was merely that of one who – sometimes desperately – introduced topics for others to embroider. . . . She never seemed quite free from painful concern lest some hitch, some argument, some breakdown in conviviality should occur, and for this reason I feel sure that while she enjoyed these large parties as much as anybody else did, the confrontation of so many people at mealtimes, when . . . they were stationary and thus liable at any moment to think of something terrible and disturbing to say, were occasions of great strain. She would look anxious, almost frightened. But let the company once be dispersed without mishap, and she would escape from constraint and become as loquacious as a child. . . . To myself without question, she was ever warm-hearted and affectionate to an almost maternal degree.

Most of the clever and distinguished guests for whom Jane catered never saw through that mask of appearances. After her death H.G. said that "she had been ready and willing to wear for everyday use and our common purpose a congenial presentation of herself that we had christened 'Jane'. To most of our friends and acquaintances she was Jane and nothing else. They hardly caught a glimpse of Catherine."[3]

In that dual personality lies a clue to the strange relationship between Jane and H.G. His behaviour towards her was wildly inconsiderate by the normal canons of marriage. He made little effort to conceal his amours from his intimates and was quite open about them with his wife. Bennett recalled that he kept photographs of his women friends in his room, and Jane met them socially. He came and went from home as the whim took him. He shrugged off on Jane all the petty inconveniences of household and domestic affairs which tried his patience. Yet in one respect he acknowledged the self-denying loyalty which for the most part he selfishly exploited. He never spoke ill of Jane to others, and when he disclosed something of their relationship after her death he was restrained and respectful. Though he always related to her as "Jane", he was aware that there was a secret "Catherine" whom he had failed to reach.

Nor did she offer that aspect of herself to him. There is no evidence that she asserted herself emotionally – to give or to demand. "Jane" complaisantly accepted the role in which H.G. had cast her, while "Catherine" protected herself from the world with dreams. Wells himself said that she was inaccessible in her reverie. Most of what is known of that inner person must be inferred from what H.G. wrote in his memoir of her, and from the group of her stories that he printed with it.[4]

What comes out of these stories is a feeling of loneliness and longing, of the kind of fantasies that are characteristic of adolescence. Some of them, such as *In a Walled Garden* and *May Afternoon*, describe young and virtuous wives who are neglected by their husbands and are painfully aware that their marriages have been mistakes. They read like fairy stories in which a sleeping princess is awakened by a Prince Charming. Yet the idyllic loves cannot be consummated. The lovers have to be denied. "All this life I have led so long has come to fit me like my skin", says the heroine of *May Afternoon*: "If it was torn off me I should bleed to death. There's my children. In the long run my children and their happiness mean far more to me than you do." In *The Draught of Oblivion* the beautiful woman seeks a potion to attract the man she loves from another woman, but even the draught the apothecary provides cannot efface the memory of the lost mistress.

Like H.G. himself, Jane was profoundly ambivalent – her stories reveal both a desire to become a woman in the fullest sense and a simultaneous fear of such potency. H.G., indeed, came close to perceiving this duality in her nature. "Desire is there", he wrote of the stories, "but it is not active aggressive desire. It is a desire for beauty and sweet companionship. . . . Frustration haunts the desire. And also fear is never far away, an elvish fear like the fear of a child's dream." This was one of the most perceptive comments H.G. ever made about his wife. The first years of their marriage, he wrote, had been "a slow discovery of the profoundest temperamental differences between us and of the problems these differences created for us". He and Jane had "strained against each other" to find a viable way of life, without much insight into the real source of their difficulties. "We had", H.G. said, "to work out our common problem by the light nature had given us." Yet the evidence suggests that the tragedy of their estrangement lay less in the differences which he stressed than in the likenesses he overlooked. Wells was never able to understand why they had been driven to seek separate solutions to the problem of their marriage, always avoiding rather than facing the confrontation of feeling that might have finally divided them or enabled them to come to terms with each other. Their life together was a succession of accommodations and compromises held together by their mutual dependence.

Looking back on their marriage after Jane died, H.G. remorsefully saw only his faults and her virtues. In the most moving and direct account he ever gave of their relationship, he insisted that it was Jane's quality of self-denial that enabled it somehow to survive all the crises through which he dragged it.[5]

I am appalled to reflect how much of the patience, courage and sacrifice of our compromises came from her. . . . We had two important things in our favour, first that we had a common detestation not only of falsehood but of falsity, and secondly, that we had the sincerest affection and respect for each other. There again the feat was hers. It was an easy thing for me to keep my faith in her sense of fair play and her perfect generosity. She never told a lie. To the end I would have taken her word against all the other witnesses in the world. But she managed to sustain her belief that I was worth living for, and that was a harder task, while I made my way through a tangle of moods and impulses that were quite outside her instinctive sympathy. She stuck to me so sturdily that in the end I stuck to myself. I do not know what I should have been without her. She stabilized my life. She gave me a home and dignity. She preserved its continuity.

This confession contains much that is revealing about H.G., about Jane, and about the tie that held them together. When it came to the point, whatever the temptation, he could never formally desert her. The emphasis on the need for "a home and dignity" in his memoir is significant, for that she unfailingly provided. So, too, is the stress on "perfect generosity". Wells, who always expected too much from people and felt betrayed when they disappointed him, was never "let down" by Jane. She accepted as much of his life as he was willing to give her, and acquiesced in the fact that the rest of it – including his passions – lay outside the scope of their marriage. She was thus able to tolerate a situation that most women would have found intolerable. There is no hint that she ever proposed separation, let alone divorce, though the grounds on which she might have done so were embarrassingly public. She was willing to make any concession to avoid a final breach, and as the years passed H.G. steadily pushed those concessions from tacit connivance at his infidelities to practical participation. At the height of the crisis with Amber, "when everyone was rushing to lawyers", Lucy Masterman recalled, "Jane did the practical thing and went out and bought the baby clothes."[6]

Wells described but made no attempt to explain how this had come about. To him it was simply a *modus vivendi* which had slowly been established by trials and errors and proved more comfortable than any other arrangement either of them could conceive. Yet its survival for more than twenty years suggests that it was much more than a conventional marriage of convenience. There was some bond between them which was unconscious but unbreakable. It seems as if H.G. could only indulge his fantasies of freedom outside marriage, and needed to retain the formal tie of marriage as an assurance of order and continuity. A complaisant wife was thus essential for him. That role seems to have been an equal necessity for Jane. The closest anyone came to an explanation was a comment that Beatrice Webb made in her diary in August 1909 when she was musing on Wells and Amber Reeves. She thought that "probably the only person of his own ménage who will suffer is his patient and all-enduring little wife, who, having entered into that position illicitly herself at the cost of another woman, cannot complain". Beatrice Webb's belief that Jane's self-denial stemmed from guilt about her earlier elopement with H.G. is perhaps too simple, but it is significant that several contemporaries came to much the same conclusion. If Jane unconsciously felt that she had no right to H.G. as a husband, it would be more understandable that she should adopt a passive attitude towards his mistresses. Indeed, if that were the case, the fact that he found satisfaction with another woman could well alleviate her sense of guilt and lead her masochistically to condone, even encourage, his infidelity. Despite her self-effacement, Jane was a potent factor in the emotional dramas of H.G.'s life.

It would, of course, have been much easier for H.G. and Jane to resume the old pattern of life if they had not left Sandgate. In Hampstead, they were continually in the public eye, and closer to the gossip of the clubs and dinner-parties. H.G., who had never intended to establish himself in a town house, was distinctly uncomfortable in 17 Church Row. When he had acquired it, he had had it in mind to go away with Amber. When he had to live in this pleasant Georgian terrace, he found himself saddled with a house which was much less spacious, more difficult to run, and unsuitable for the kind of entertaining he enjoyed.

He certainly liked the fact that he could stroll out on to Hampstead

Heath, or go for longer walks into the country with Haynes and other friends who shared his taste for a good tramp. It was agreeable to have old friends living near by. The Radfords had moved to Hampstead. So had the Garnetts, who had taken a house in Downshire Hill, and the Rothensteins were round the corner in Oak Hill Park. And Hampstead was near enough to town for people to come out for lunch or dinner, or to parties where the customary games and charades were carried on as energetically as ever. David Garnett recalled how, as a young man, he went to Church Row expecting a formal occasion and found that within a few minutes H.G. had all the guests chasing round the room and knocking over the furniture. Yet H.G. found himself cramped in the place, and before long he was looking for a means of getting the family out of London and thus reconstructing the arrangement that had suited him so well in the Sandgate years. As early as January 1911 he told his friend Robert Ross that he wanted to move.[7] Writing from Wengen, where he had taken Jane and the boys for a winter sports holiday, he told Ross that Jane had been ill and had gone back to England. He had caught a severe influenza and was depressed at the thought of returning to Hampstead. Fraulein Meyer recalled that he was more crotchety than usual. "We'll have to get out of Church Row", he wrote to Ross, ". . . to a larger airier, warmer house with a garden for the children and more space. . . . Have you found a house *we* might like, – a warm house where you can feel well when you're ill."

Every move that Wells had made in his life was associated with some change in his fortunes. Atlas House, as his detailed account of it in his autobiography makes clear, represented everything from which he spent the rest of his days trying to escape. The succession of homes that followed each had a similar symbolic significance for him. He projected the phases of his life into the places where he lived, and when he was done with one he was ready to be done with the other. This preoccupation with houses, and the belief that the conditions under which people live are a clue to their personalities, also breaks out in his books. *Kipps* carries the description of building Spade House to the point of boring the reader with detail. *Tono-Bungay* is dominated by the fact and the imagery of Bladesover. *Anticipations* and *A Modern Utopia* contain long digressions on domestic architecture. Even the later novels, such as *Mr Britling Sees It Through*, *The World of William Clissold* and *Apropos of Dolores*, make the same connection between a style of life and a state of mind. It was a particular application of the general way in which he used topographical details to make a psychological point.

The departure from Sandgate marked the end of one era. His dissatisfaction with his uncongenial perch in Church Row was one indicator that H.G. was profoundly uncertain how to begin the next.

The two novels which appeared in 1910 were both symbolic in this sense. They were planned when he had escape in mind, and each was the story of an escape. *The History of Mr Polly* describes how the little shopkeeper burns down his house to liberate himself from an unsatisfactory marriage, runs away from the "Beastly Silly Wheeze of a hole", and finds contentment in the riverside idyll of the Potwell Inn. *The New Machiavelli*, begun when the affair with Amber had reached the point of crisis, is about a flight from responsibility. Remington, the successful politician, is also fleeing from a claustrophobic marriage. The stuffy household which his wife Margaret has furnished as the set on which they play out their parts as public characters becomes intolerable to him. His solution is to destroy his old life quite as thoroughly as Polly had done and to seek a new life.

Superficially, *Mr Polly* and *The New Machiavelli* are very different books. The picaresque history of Polly is perhaps closer to that of Joe Wells than to that of his son. Joe, who died soon after the book was published, had never gone so far as to burn down Atlas House and take to the roads as a cheerful vagabond. But the first part of the book has a close resemblance to the miserable years Joe spent with Sarah in Bromley, and the change in Polly's personality when he is set free reflects the change Wells saw in his own father after the Bromley household broke up. Frank, the eldest son, did run away from the drapery trade and became an itinerant before he joined his father in the dishevelled cottage at Nyewoods. H.G. in fact dredged up this story from his childhood memories at the moment when he was proposing to seek, and justify, a comparable liberation for himself. The book is a comic masterpiece, and Polly is obviously a member of the same family as Hoopdriver, Lewisham and Kipps. Remington, who tells his own story in a rambling narrative which reeks of bitterness and self-pity, is another and less attractive version of George Ponderevo. His career, essentially, is that of Wells himself, following the same trajectory of success and frustration, as he forswears his attempt to set the world to rights for the sake of love. Polly and Remington are variants on the same type – the maladjusted man who, unable to make the objective world conform to his subjective desires, runs away into the comfort of his fantasies. The difference is that Polly is realised with fun and warmth, while Remington is consumed by self-pity.

In both books Wells was in fact exploring the results of a surrender to impulse and a defiance of convention. Tedium and taboo have driven Polly to the edge of suicide before he realises that there is within him what he calls a "Joy de Vive" – a sense that "over and above things that are jolly and 'bits of all right', there was beauty, there was delight". At the last moment he "understood that there was no inevitable any more, and escaped his former despair". He has been saved by erotic impulse. Remington likewise abandons himself to passion. He accepts the ruin of his political ambitions with little more remorse than Polly surveys the smouldering embers of his shop. What links them together is their belief that freedom is to be achieved by an act of impulse – and that freedom is fundamentally libidinous.

Some critics, relieved that Wells had again produced a low-class comedy, were glad to welcome Polly as a dyspeptic figure of fun, whose appearance suggested that Wells might be losing his distasteful concern with socialism and sex. A few of them noticed that *Mr Polly* was yet another expression of the moral relativism which underlies everything that H.G. wrote in these years. It was difficult for them to make this case, not least because Wells always flew into a rage when anyone suggested that his books were in any way immoral. He seems to have had no more insight into the implications of his books than of his own behaviour. When he wanted to sue a critic who alleged that *Mr Polly* was erotic, E.S.P. Haynes had to give him a tactful reminder that his case might not be so strong as he believed.[9] On 27 May 1910 he wrote to H.G.

It is very difficult for any man to realize exactly his own position in the world and not to exaggerate the importance of the hostile criticism which he may receive. You will remember that the more famous Lord Tennyson became, the more sensitive he became to criticism and this was doubtless because the small criticism which he got bulked larger in his mind as the praise became greater. You are now an author of world-wide reputation, and such hostility as you have had to encounter has been confined to what is really a very small circle which might almost be called a "clique". I am, therefore, inclined to advise you to accept an apology if we are offered one, and to hesitate considerably before going further if we do not get one.

All through the spring and summer of 1910 Wells was in a combative mood and, for obvious reasons, extremely touchy about suggestions that his writings were immoral. The struggle to find a publisher for *The New Machiavelli* made matters worse. He offered the book to Sir Frederick

Macmillan in October 1909, saying that it was a "large and outspoken" novel about politics. Macmillan wanted to get Wells back on his list, even though H.G. now wished to drive a more profitable bargain than Macmillan had given him for *Tono-Bungay*. After some haggling, the contract was signed. Jane Wells sent the first copy to Macmillan in February 1910 saying that the instalments would start in the *English Review* in May and that Macmillan could bring out the book any time after the end of September. As the manuscript came in, Macmillan apparently did not bother to read any of it until the proofs were back in his office late in May.[9]

On 21 June, shocked by what he had bought unseen, Macmillan wrote to Wells complaining that he had been misled. The novel was only incidentally political: "in its essence" it dealt "with social questions, and particularly with the question of sex". There was "twice as much reason" for rejecting it as there had been for objecting to *Ann Veronica*. There could, he concluded, be no question of any breach of contract on his part, since Wells had ignored the proviso that the book would eschew any improper matter. Wells immediately denied that there had been any agreement for "such exclusion of sexual interest as you now suggest. Every novel *must* have a sexual interest." After some negotiation, H.G. attempted to revise the book to placate Macmillan, and offered the assurance that the "next book I'm planning won't cause any of this trouble – I'm passing out of a necessary phase in handling my medium. Sex *must* be handled, and few writers escape the gawky phase." Macmillan was still dubious. The revised proofs were sent in on 7 July and Wells insisted that after "a very thorough revision . . . I do not really think there is much left of your objection." Macmillan stood firm. The best he could offer was the hope that Heinemann might take over the book.

Neither Heinemann nor Chapman and Hall were willing to take the book as it stood, but Wells – who by the end of the summer was becoming worried about the book's prospects, not least because he had been spending heavily and needed a substantial advance – took the matter up directly with William Heinemann. On 20 September Heinemann told him that though it was "certainly one of the most brilliant books I have read for years and one which has given me the greatest possible pleasure in reading" he could not take the risk of handling a novel "so charged with a dangerous (and perhaps libellous) atmosphere".

The grounds of objection had now changed.[10] Heinemann was generally worried about the recognisable sketches of such public figures as Arthur Balfour, the members of the Co-efficients dining club, and, above all,

Beatrice and Sidney Webb who were pilloried with no more disguise than the change of surname from Webb to Bailey. He particularly disliked the way in which Wells had laid the blame for the scandal that destroys Remington on the couple who were patently identifiable as the Webbs. "It seems to me", he wrote on 29 September, "very unnecessary and, in this case, I think perhaps a little malicious. . . . The knowledge of its origin does not help at all." And since he was willing to take a risk on the novel, he thought that Wells was being unduly demanding about terms. The important thing, he added, "is that one should feel that one trusts and is trusted by an author and that one works with him in perfect harmony. We cannot somehow feel now that this is likely to be the case between us, and it is better, therefore, for us not to go on."

Financial matters apart, it was the clear identification of Remington's mistress Isabel with Amber Reeves that had become the main concern with Macmillan, Heinemann and other publishers who were well aware of the gossip in the London literary set. Wells took some time to grasp this point, as he complained to Macmillan in an undated letter some time in September. "I wish extraordinarily you could have put the real objection to me in June", he wrote.[11] This, apparently, was the "enormous campaign of scandal going on about the character Isabel, who is supposed to be the portrait of a particular friend of mine". Disingenuously, H.G. insisted that Amber and her husband had read the proofs: "they not only don't object to the work but they don't see where they come in". The bother was caused by the "scarcely sane accusations of a near relative of the lady who seems almost as anxious to ruin her as he is to ruin me". The relative was Amber's father, who was nearly frantic with rage and shame, and made no secret of his animus to Wells, whom he denounced as a blackguardly seducer. The only way that H.G. could counter the campaign was to threaten to fight a legal action which would make "an open and public row". Wells made a last attempt to "settle the business in a thoroughly amiable way" with Macmillan. But to no avail. After months of searching, Macmillan had found a publisher who was willing to risk the book. This was John Lane, who had made his mark by publishing *The Yellow Book* in the Nineties, and whose imprint still carried a slight taint of bohemianism. Wells was not happy to be thus farmed out, although he wrote to Sir Frederick to say that he closed the incident "with my liking for and confidence in Messrs Macmillan very considerably enhanced".[12]

There were no libel actions in the event, though Wells circulated with the book an arranged interview with Ralph Straus in which he again insisted that no one in the book was identifiable and that he was the victim of malicious gossip. Beatrice Webb noted that she had read the caricatures "with much interest and amusement", considering them "really very clever in a malicious way".[13] She thought the book "lays bare the tragedy of H.G.'s life – his aptitude for 'fine thinking' and even 'good feeling' and yet his total incapacity for decent conduct . . . What annoyed him was our puritan view of life and our insistence on the fulfilment of obligations . . . he passed back again to . . . sexual dissipation and vehemently objected to and disliked what he knew would be our judgment of it." She recognised that the whole book was in fact shot through with bitterness and a desire for revenge, but though she and Sidney had been so viciously lampooned she was still capable of a cool comment. The hostility of Wells, she considered, was a guilty reaction to the "baseness" of his deception of the Reeves family, the Webbs and other friends. But "the idealisation of the whole proceeding in *The New Machiavelli* is a pretty bit of work and will probably enable him to struggle back into distinguished society; I find myself feeling that, after all, there is a statute of limitations and that I shall take no steps to prevent this so long as no one expects us to meet him on terms of friendship".

Since the instalments in the *English Review* aroused a good deal of interest, and the book began to sell steadily when it appeared in January 1911, Wells was now free of immediate anxiety about it. He was relieved when the adverse public reaction that the publishers had feared turned out to be no more than its banning by a few public libraries and booksellers. He was even able to take the private criticism of old friends without reacting waspishly. Jane wrote to ask Vernon Lee to visit them in Normandy in the summer of 1911. In her reply she apologised for her long silence by explaining that she did not know what to say about *The New Machiavelli*.[14] "I feel awfully out of sympathy with Mr Wells's present attitude", she wrote, "an attitude which I cannot but attribute to exasperation at the unjust criticism he has had to suffer from. I don't believe that under other circumstances the writer of *Anticipations*, *Lewisham* & *Tono-Bungay* would rail and scold at the world's imperfections as if he carried the remedy in his own small pocket." What she disliked was the "sort of bravado . . . the perpetual reiteration of the words sex and sexual were – forgive me saying so – mere inverted Puritanism". Yet, she concluded gently, "all this is a moment of strain, and we have taken different sides . . . surely the atmosphere will clear and we shall find each other again".

Henry James, writing from Boston on 3 March, took an equally critical but sympathetic line. Though he was generous about the book, he disliked the "terrible fluidity of self-revelation" of books written in the first person. In what proved to be almost the last of his efforts to convey to Wells his conception of the novelist's craft he remonstrated verbosely but effectively against this defect in *The New Machiavelli*.

There is, to my vision, no authentic, and no really interesting and no *beautiful*, report of things on the novelist's, the painter's part unless a particular detachment has operated, unless the great stewpot or crucible of the imagination, of the observant and recording and interpreting mind in short, has intervened and played its part – and this detachment, this chemical transmutation for the aesthetic, the representational, end is terribly wanting in autobiography brought, as the horrible phrase is, up to date.

Wells responded with humility to what he called "the most illuminating of comments. So far as it is loving chastisement I think I wholly agree and kiss the rod. . . . God helping me, this shall be the last of my gushing Hari-Karis. But the guts and guts and guts and guts I've poured out all over the blessed libraries and J.A.Spender and everybody! . . . I wish you were over here. I rarely go to the Reform without a strange wild hope of seeing you."[15]

H.G. managed to swallow his pride when he replied to James, but the humiliations of the past year had left him hurt and bitter. William Rothenstein observed that "he had something on his mind that made him resentful, and he complained of old friends who had turned against him".[16] He was, therefore, glad to snatch at any praise that offered some compensation for the real and imagined injuries. When he had been crushed by the Old Gang at the end of the Fabian row he consoled himself with Amber Reeves. When that led to ostracism and to the trouble about *The New Machiavelli* he struck up another consolatory friendship – this time with the well-known writer, Elizabeth von Arnim.

She was a romantic figure, small, exquisitely made, with charming irregular features that made her notably attractive. Her original name was Mary Annette Beauchamp, and she was born in the same year as Wells.[17] Her cousin Katherine Mansfield described her as "such a little bundle of artificialities", but she had a saleable sentimental talent. She had grown up in Australia, come to Europe, married a German count and gone to live on his bleak estate in Pomerania. There she had brought up her three daughters and her son – for a time E.M.Forster and then Hugh Walpole were employed as tutors at Nassenheide – and shown a talent for gardening which led to her book, *Elizabeth and Her German Garden*, which had a runaway success in Edwardian England. She spent much time travelling abroad. When her play *Priscilla Runs Away* enjoyed a long run in London, she used the proceeds to build the Chalet Soleil at Randogne, near Montana-sur-Sierre in Switzerland, where she gathered amusing people about her and entertained agreeably. She had tried to arrange a meeting with H.G. in 1907 but nothing had come of it, but after *The New Machiavelli* she sent him a letter that bubbled with seductive enthusiasm. "You must forgive me for bothering you with my extreme joy over your wonderful *Machiavelli*", she wrote in November 1910: "never did a man understand things as you do – the others are all guess and theorize – you *know* – & the poetry of it, and the aching, desolating truth – what one longs to read, written by you, is the story of the afterwards – what happened to them as the dreadful ordinary years passed."[18] Later that month, when Elizabeth was on one of her visits to London, she followed up her letter with a call at Church Row. Jane, who was away at the time, had a note from H.G. saying that "work & the gravity of life much alleviated yesterday by the sudden eruption of the bright little Countess von Arnim at 1 with a cheerful proposal to lunch with me & go for a walk. . . . She talks very well, she knows *The New Machiavelli* by heart, & I think she's a nice little friend to have." The note to Jane concluded a little oddly with the reassurance that "her conversation is free but her morals are strict (sad experience has taught her that if she so much as *thinks* of anything she has a baby)".[19]

The morals of the countess were not so strict as H.G. suggested. She was a woman who, behind a kittenish and teasing manner, was powerful and possessive: one of her contemporaries acidly described her as a "devouring" personality. It was a type that appealed to H.G., and he was soon pursuing Elizabeth. She refused a proposal that they should go away to Ireland together, and played him off against the last of her children's tutors. This provoked H.G. into a jealous spate of letters and telegrams, which culminated in his importunate arrival at her home in Switzerland. The liaison followed an erratic course through 1911 and 1912. In the early part of 1913 H.G. spent several weeks at the Chalet Soleil, writing *The World Set Free* – the novel in which, after a devastating war, the leaders of the world meet in Switzerland to work out a peaceful dispensation for mankind. But though Elizabeth thought him the most intelligent of her friends, she also found him a trying and tiring suitor, and during a holiday together in Italy she came to the conclusion that a pleasant friendship was preferable to a closer relationship. H.G. too, by that point, had transferred his amorous enthusiasm elsewhere. Yet the friendship was maintained. After the war, when she had a flat above H.G. in Whitehall Court, and then in the middle Twenties, when she was a near neighbour in Provence, she saw a good deal of Wells in a casual fashion and he treated her as a confidante in his personal life – in which for two years she had played a minor role.

In the early part of 1911 Wells was casting about in the hope of catching some new interest. It was a mark of his isolation from affairs – as well as a sign that he was uncertain about his future as a writer – that he toyed with the idea of making a world tour. London was gripped by the crisis over the reform of the House of Lords, as well as by the growing excitements of the suffrage movement. There was widespread labour unrest, and the socialist propagandists were at last beginning to get significant support in the country. Yet H.G. fidgeted on the margins of these events, spending a good deal of effort on his plan to go off through the Middle East to Asia, then on to the United States, Mexico and the Caribbean, taking almost a year on the trip. The desire to get away from the troubles of the previous year was strong, even though this tour meant that he would have to put aside serious writing and concentrate on journalism to pay his way. The idea came to nothing. Wells wanted a guarantee of two thousand pounds for his articles, in addition to all expenses, and he could not find a newspaper to back him on such a scale.

At the same time he was looking for a new house. One weekend he went down to stay with his friend R.D. Blumenfeld, the editor of the *Daily Express*, at his Essex home, Hill Farm at Great Easton, near Dunmow. It was in a part of Essex that, only forty miles from London, had escaped the suburban sprawl. Wells was immediately attracted by the untidy and gently rolling country, dotted with pretty half-timbered and white-plastered houses. When he told Blumenfeld that he would like to take a house in the district, "Blum" got in touch with Frances, Lady Warwick, who owned much of the local property, and discovered that she was willing to rent the Old Rectory at Little Easton to Wells.

Before the negotiations could go much further, the Wells family went off to Normandy for the summer. They had taken a house on the Seine near Pont de l'Arche, near Rouen, and in their usual style Jane and H.G. set about filling it with guests. Bennett, who left some pleasant sketches of the place as souvenirs, was there: so were the scientist Ray Lankester, the Rothensteins, Maurice Baring and other friends. Wells began to relax with the picnics, the bathing and rowing in the sunshine, which recalled the jolly house-parties at Sandgate. When he returned to England he was all the more determined to get out of Church Row and find a suitable country home where this way of life could be resumed.

The Rectory at Little Easton seemed just right. It was an elegant four-square Georgian house in red brick, surrounded by wide lawns, and looking across the sloping cornfields towards the village. It stood between the Manor, a lovely Tudor house, and Easton Lodge, a much more imposing mansion set in its own park. Though it was secluded, it was easily accessible to London; there was a good train service, and visitors could come to the private station built at the entrance to the Easton estate.[20] The offer attracted Wells. Lady Warwick herself was a draw. She was a beautiful and eccentric great lady, who had been a notable heiress in her youth and for many years the lover of the Prince of Wales. At the end of the century she was converted to socialism, and made her home a centre for writers, artists and radical politicians; she installed progressively-minded clergymen in her livings, promoted education for her tenants, and encouraged journalists and intellectuals to settle in the neighbour-hood. Though "Daisy" Warwick's ménage was run very differently from Up Park, there was something about it which made H.G. feel comfortable. It seemed as though at last he could again live under the shadow of a "Bladesover". Lady Warwick was delighted that H.G.Wells might occupy the Rectory. She offered to let him have it on a short lease at one hundred pounds a year. On 31 August 1911 she wrote to Jane to say that "my spirits run so high at the thought of you and Mr Wells & your boys becoming our nearest neighbours that I become reckless & apolo-gise" for writing without a formal introduction.[21] The details were soon settled, and it was arranged that the move should take place early in 1912. Church Row was kept as a base in London until it was sold two years later when Wells took a flat in town.

For the first time since the affair with Amber Reeves had disrupted his life it seemed that H.G. might be able to make yet another fresh start. The scandals were subsiding. He had a new novel, *Marriage*, about to appear. He had made an effort to rebuild a more normal domestic life and to concern himself with the interests and education of his sons. It had been an impulsive decision to leave Sandgate, and for two years he had been miserably unsettled. The return to the country might enable him to recreate in Essex the pattern of living that had served so well for a decade at Spade House. He was forty-five, and with characteristic ebullience he had set about rehabilitating himself after the crisis which had brought him to the brink of ruin.

THE FRAME AND THE PICTURE

"I find before me a considerable accumulation of material", Wells wrote in his autobiography, "first assembled together in a folder labelled 'Whether I am a Novelist'. . . . It refuses to be simplified. It is like a mental shunting yard in which several trains of thought have come into collision." H.G. always disliked the idea of being "typed" as a writer. He had a versatile talent, he wanted to be free to experiment with style and subject matter, and in deciding what he wanted to do next he was always guided by his mood and by his search for a profitable market. André Gide, indeed, considered that the failure of Wells as a novelist did not lie – as Conrad and James had argued – in his refusal to regard the novel as a form of art but in his disregard of unity in his audience. Each time he shifted his interest he had to build a new relationship with a new set of readers; and this instability of purpose was emphasised by the cavalier manner in which he rang the changes on his agents and publishers. He did not shirk hard work, but he did not understand the meaning of professional dis-cipline, of the rigour that was necessary to distance life from art in the sense that James had written to him after the publication of *The New Machiavelli*. In the years when H.G. was close to Conrad, Ford and James he valued their good opinion, and did his best to assure them that he really sought to be a serious novelist. Yet even then, while he nodded agreement with their criticisms, he had found it impossible to control his didactic and journalistic impulses.

The New Machiavelli showed both the virtues and faults of Wells at their extremes. The potential that his contemporaries so much admired still showed in flashes of brilliance, but he had permitted his life to sprawl into the novel so carelessly that self-indulgence had ruined it as a work of art. Wells, of course, did not concede that point. By 1911 he had come to realise that he was incapable of writing fiction that was comparable to the work of James and Conrad, or even Bennett and Galsworthy, and that he was perpetually at a disadvantage if he allowed himself to be measured by their standards. It was necessary for him to make up his own rules and thus free himself of the nagging complaints that he failed as an artist. If he was to be attacked for allowing the frame to get into the picture, he would at least offer some justification for his fascination with the frame.

The opportunity came when he was asked to deliver a lecture in May 1911 to *The Times* Book Club on "The Scope of the Novel".[1] It was a sustained attack on those who thought fiction should be trivially entertaining or, conversely, be subject to "fierce pedantries" of technique. It called for "a laxer, more spacious form of novel-writing" which should be "irresponsible and free" and "aggressive", and insisted that the author should be allowed to "discuss, point out, plead and display" and to intervene personally in his work whenever he considers that this would help to make his readers think about his ideas. The novel, H.G. argued, "is the only medium through which we can discuss the great majority of the problems which are being raised in such bristling multitude by our contemporary social development ... in this tremendous work of human reconciliation and elucidation, it seems to me it is the novel that must attempt most and achieve most". And "before we are done", H.G. concluded ambitiously, "we will have all life within the scope of the novel".

Wells could not have stated more sharply the grounds of his difference with James, nor put more clearly his future intentions. His attitudes had hardened during the crises of the past few years, when he had been cold-shouldered by old friends, mauled in the press, and painfully reminded that his foothold in established society was precariously dependent upon grace and favour. He became increasingly touchy, finding trouble where none was intended. "Life is too short to bother about little rubs like that", E.S.P. Haynes wrote to him in July 1912, when he flew into a rage about some trifling errors in an article that Orage had printed in *The New Age*.[2] It was silly to threaten an action that he might lose, and, Haynes added, "you have hit others quite as hard in your own writings".

He reinforced his new posture in March 1912, by further widening the gulf that had opened between him and his old literary friends. On the initiative of Edmund Gosse and James he was invited to become a member of the Academic Committee of the Royal Society of Literature, a distinguished group which included Conrad, Barrie, Hardy, Yeats and Shaw besides Gosse and James. With the approval of Bennett, who told him that he disliked this "grotesque institution", H.G. wrote back declining the proposal.[3] Gosse then persuaded James to write to Wells. On 20 March James sent H.G. a flattering letter asking him to reconsider his "unsociable attitude", and urging him not to "make too much of rigours and indifferences, of consistencies and vows". James added persuasively that "I have no greater affinity with associations and academies than you – *a priori*; and yet I find myself glad to have done the simple, civil, social *easiest* thing in accepting my election – touched by the amenity and geniality of the thought."[4]

Five days later H.G. replied with warmth and revealing honesty, expressing regret because "I like to be about with you and in the same boat with you". But, he explained, "I have an insurmountable objection to Literary or Artistic Academies as such, to any hierarchies, any suggestion of controls or fixed standards in these things. . . . This world of ours, I mean the world of creative and representative work we do, is I am convinced best anarchic. Better the wild rush of Boomster and the Quack than the cold politeness of the established thing. . . . So far as that body does have a use and exert a good influence it will do it the better without my turbulent indiscretion."

James was not content to let the matter rest, and he replied at length on the same day, sympathising with the fact that Wells was indifferent to public bodies, "caring as I do for nothing in the world but lonely patient virtue, which doesn't seek that company". Yet he wished Wells had given his friends the benefit of the doubt "for the sake of the good-nature". The claim that art must be anarchic, he gently chided, was "essentially wrong. . . . There's no representation, no picture (which is your form), that isn't by its very nature preservation, association, and of a positive associational *appeal* – that is the very grammar of it; none that isn't thereby some sort of interesting or curious *order*." Whether Wells liked it or not "you are *in* our circle". Sadly, James said, "I prolong the sigh as I think how much you might have done for *our* freedom – and how little we could do against yours!"

This was precisely the kind of recognition that Wells had once craved, and it was reasonable for James to assume that only encouragement was needed to overcome his objections. But James did not know how much H.G. had changed. It was a shock for him next day to meet Wells in the Reform Club and to discover, as he wrote to Gosse, that H.G. was "absolutely immovable".[5] Moreover, he now appreciated that Wells was determined to cut himself off from the world of letters that had previously meant so much to him. The lecture to *The Times* Book Club had been no casual discourse, tossed together for the occasion, but a deliberate act of separation from his old associates. As they talked, James came to the conclusion that "he is right about himself and that he wouldn't at all do among us ... our whole literary side – or indeed any literary side any-where – is a matter of such indifference to him as I felt it to be today – to an extent I hadn't been aware of. He has cut loose from literature clearly – practically altogether; he will still do a lot of writing probably – but it won't be *that*. ... He *had* decently to decline, and I think it decent of him to have felt that."

James had seen the significance of this refusal to accept a well-inten-tioned honour. It had come too late. Something decisive had happened to Wells, at which James merely hinted in writing to Gosse that "my impression of him today cleared up many things". Only three years later, when the American critic Van Wyck Brooks was making the first real appraisal of Wells as a writer, he noted what James had perhaps glimpsed that day over lunch in the Reform Club.[6] Writing of *The New Machiavelli* he said that with this book Wells seemed to have lost "some secret virtue". Since then "his ideas have hardly been more than a perfunctory repetition and his experience more and more remote and unreal; and looking back one seems to discover something highly symbolic in the tragical conquest of ideas by passion with which *The New Machiavelli* concludes".

That book, in fact, had proved to be an end and a beginning – it was the last attempt that Wells made to write a classical novel and, at the same time, it was the first of his cold and humourless "prig" novels in which exposition dominates character, and the pages are stuffed with what he later conceded frankly were "impossibly explicit monologues and duo-logues". He had now determined that all his books must serve what had become his overriding purpose, the presentation of his notions of re-constructing the world. That had become the urgent task, and the drive to teach and preach grew stronger every year. His fiction became simply a vehicle for his evangelism, and his imagination began to wither in the pulpit.

The New Machiavelli indeed marked a change. For more than ten years Wells had struggled to be a serious novelist, but none of his major novels had been fully realised. When he spoke of "scamping" the end of *Love and Mr Lewisham*, and when *Kipps* was finally pulled out of the design for *Mr Waddy* and patched up to an ending, H.G. conceded that both these books were remnants which had fallen short of his original ambitious intentions. With all his talent and application he seemed unable to get far beyond what James regarded as his obsession with himself as hero. The autobiographical theme was used as a substitute for self-revelation, rather than as a means to it. Wells indulged himself in his past, relying on his power of vivid description and good story-telling to obscure the fact that he was unable to use his experience at the emotional level required to transmute life into art. He drew upon his own life for plot and detail like a reporter rather than a novelist, setting the scene brilliantly but failing to people it with characters that were anything more than comic caricatures, puppets for his ideas, or projections of himself. At each point where his larger designs required him to transcend the obvious, to explore behind the self-image of which he made such free use in his fiction, some emotional inhibition frustrated him.

He was, moreover, continually distracted. He genuinely aspired to be a writer of distinction, but he was pulled away by other and powerful drives. While he was finishing *Love and Mr Lewisham* he was forming up the ideas which broke out into *Anticipations*: he was so anxious to get on with *A Modern Utopia* that he grudged the time needed to get *Kipps* into publishable form. He could never dedicate himself single-mindedly to his fiction. He had always been haunted by his sense of mission, and with the collapse of his literary aspirations he fell back into the abiding concern of his life – the salvation of mankind. Artie Kipps had been abandoned for *Homo sapiens*. In 1912 he had begun to work again on the book that appeared four years later as *Boon*. In the section he called "The Wild Asses of the Devil" (written at this time) he reveals that his fears had styled his imagination and that he had again been caught by the undertow of apocalyptic anxiety. The destiny of literature, he insisted, was "to assume the great task of becoming the thought and expressed intention of the race, the task of taming violence, organising the aimless, destroying error, the task of waylaying the Wild Asses of the Devil and sending them back to Hell . . . we have to do it because we know, in spite of the darkness, the wickedness, the haste and hate, we know in our hearts, though no momentary trumpeting has shown it to us, that judgment is all about us and God stands close at hand".

Wells had fallen into the habit of using his novels as a manoeuvre in his own life, and *Marriage* – written in the bad period after *The New Machiavelli* – reflected his intention to make a new start. Bertrand Russell suggested that H.G. had composed the book to rebut the charges of immorality that had been made against its predecessors, because the novel was concerned with a failing marital relationship that was finally restored by joint hardship in the wilderness of Labrador. Certainly, that was how Sir Frederick Macmillan took it, telling Wells that he was "delighted" with the book, and grateful to him "for sticking to us after the bothers we had".[7] He thought it "not only very clever, but admirably suited to the large novel-reading public". No doubt he was also relieved, since H.G. had not yet earned back the advances on earlier books and *Marriage* might help to wipe out the deficit.

Once again, Wells rehearsed his own problem – the story of a successful man who reaches middle age and, in his disillusionment, thinks of throwing up a marriage that has become restrictive and unsatisfying. This time, however, the fantasy of escape is not built round the dream of elopement with a younger mistress. Trafford, the physicist, feels that his integrity has been lost in the search for wealth, and that his love for his extravagant wife Marjorie has been dissipated by their sybaritic existence. "My life's no good to me any more", Trafford says, "I've spent myself." The wastes of Labrador, which Trafford and his wife choose as a retreat where they may go through a perilous *rite de passage* which restores both their love and his faith in himself, might seem a bizarre locale for self-discovery. Yet, symbolically, the frozen wilderness was the image that H.G. needed to make his point. Trafford has become one of the Samurai of *A Modern Utopia*, and in that book Wells had described the austere code of the order which required its members to withdraw to a lonely place to rededicate themselves to their life of high-minded service. "I've always believed in salvation", Trafford remarks at the end of their testing adventure, "I want to go back and watch and think and write." Trafford, Wells conceded, was "not so much a solid man as a scientific intelligence caught in the meshes of love", and it was his mental turmoil that interested H.G. – "the interior situation, this controversial matter stewing and fermenting in all our brains, and its ventilation in action". The novel had been turned into a means of arguing at the reader, for presenting the idealist notion of superior mentality which Wells had always opposed to instinctual man. It was a view of human nature quite as utopian as the utopian societies which Wells believed such New Aristocrats alone could create.

The reaction to *Marriage* was an anti-climax after the fuss that had been aroused by *Ann Veronica* and *The New Machiavelli*. Though it was not immediately apparent that Wells had crossed the watershed of his literary career, and that his fiction would henceforth substitute argument for feeling, a few critics noticed signs of change. Edmund Gosse, writing to James on 9 October 1912, thought the book "too hard, metallic, rhetorical", and said that he had plucked up his courage and warned Wells "against the growing *hardness* of his books".[8] Nine days later, James himself sent H.G. a long comment in which he admitted that, in dealing with Wells, he had to put aside the critical principles which he applied to the work of other authors.[9] About this time James wrote to Mrs Humphry Ward of his concern at the direction Wells was taking in his work, of "the co-existence of so much talent with so little art, so much life with (so to speak) so little living! But of him there is much to say, for I really think him more interesting by his faults than he will probably ever manage to be in any other way." He was more guarded in what he said to H.G. himself, assuring him that his fiction was "more convulsed with life and more brimming with blood than any it is given me nowadays to meet". James no longer reproved H.G. for intruding his own life into his fiction, but accepted that this intrusion had become the main source of interest. "I live with you and in you and (almost cannibal-like) *on* you", he wrote, "on you H.G.W., to the sacrifice of your Marjories and your Traffords, and whoever may be of their company ... the ground of the drama is somehow most of all in the adventure for *you*." The characters in the book might "people the scene and lead on the attention" but "you beat them on their own ground ... your 'story', through the five hundred pages, says more to me than theirs". H.G. sent a friendly reply next day, saying that he was destined to get worse before he got better, that the next book was "scandalously" bad in form, and that he hoped he was suffering from "a prolonged acute disease rather than a chronic decay". Thereafter, he told James hopefully, "I will seek earnestly to make my pen lead a decent life, pull myself together, think of Form."[10]

Trafford's search for his identity was the central theme of *Marriage*. Yet, in order to show that "love and fine thinking" must go together for a man to accomplish the change from corrupt human nature to the more noble code of the Samurai, Wells had to complement Trafford's conversion by a similar sea-change on the part of his wife. She, too, has to abjure the worldly possessions which are merely the corrupting accessories of life. The conventional existence of middle-class women, "half-savages, half-pets, unemployed things of greed and desire", in which marriage brings only "dresses and carpets and hangings and pretty arrangements", is rejected in favour of an intellectual euphoria which Wells calls love.

Though Wells was writing at the peak of the suffrage agitation, and though *Marriage* gives a vivid impression of the frustrations of women who longed to be something more than decorative housekeepers, he gave the conception of the New Woman a personal and characteristic twist. The ordeal in Labrador turns Marjorie into a suitable mate for a Samurai, not into a woman with rights of her own and independence of thought and action. This was, of course, another variant on the Pygmalion theme, which Wells wove all through his fiction and into his own relationships with women. The New Women are called to life by the needs of the New Men, forming partnerships from which the New Race will eventually emerge to safeguard the future of the species. Love, in this context, is the instrument of natural selection, the pairing of the Fit for survival; and the question of female emancipation becomes a matter of making such relationships possible rather than a search for formal equality between women and men. H.G., indeed, was at best a fellow-traveller of the feminists, and in *Marriage* he explicitly attacked the "Gawdsakers" of the suffrage movement who "burke the proper discussion of woman's future". He had always been more concerned with the economics and eugenics of motherhood than with the education and employment of women, and the issue of political rights was to him merely one means of ensuring the kind of citizenship for women which he had discussed in *Anticipations* and *A Modern Utopia*.

He had made his position clear a year earlier, in an article published on 7 December 1911 in the feminist paper, *The Freewoman*.

I want to see women have the vote because I believe the vote may be a useful educational symbol (even if it has to be a temporary political nuisance) in the necessary work of establishing the citizenship of women. . . . At present women are not regarded as citizens; they do not regard themselves as citizens, they behave accordingly and most of the troubles of life ensue. Apart from a natural opposition of sex, I believe there is very little difference between men and women that is not imposed on them through the sex-mania of our social system. Humanity is obsessed by sex. I have always been disposed to take sex rather lightly and to think that we make a quite unnecessary amount of fuss about it. . . . I do my best to avoid the present suffrage agitation because it over-accentuates all those sexual differences I want to minimise and shakes my faith in the common humanity of women.

One of the regular contributors to *The Freewoman* hit back at him in a review of *Marriage* on 19 September 1912. In a clever polemical review, Rebecca West tore apart the "worthlessness" of Marjorie and the spurious means whereby Wells had emancipated her. "The mind reels", she wrote with a glancing reference at the Wellsian scheme of endowed mother-hood, "at the thought of the community being taxed to allow Marjorie, who would steal her lover's money and barter the brightness of his soul for brass-footed workboxes, to perpetuate her cow-like kind." Wells had simply produced another version of subsidised domesticity whose fatuity could be exposed by asking what would happen to Marjorie if she had to fend for herself.

Rebecca West was then only nineteen, but she had already revealed the talent which made her a writer of note while she was still a young woman. Her reviews in *The Freewoman* and her political articles in the socialist weekly *Clarion* revealed that she had something fresh to say and could say it with a combination of wit and plain-speaking. She was an ardent suffragist and a political radical, and her pseudonym – taken from the "advanced" young woman in Ibsen's *Rosmersholm* – reflected her opi-nions.[11] Her real name was Cicily Fairfield, and her childhood had been overshadowed by the early death of her father, a restless Anglo-Irishman who had tried a dozen occupations across the globe. Mrs Fairfield, who was Scottish, brought up her three daughters in Edinburgh on limited means, but with an appreciation of music – she was a trained pianist – and literature. While Cicily was still at school, her performance in a play attracted the notice of Rosina Filippi, a well-known teacher at the Royal Academy of Dramatic Art in London, who encouraged her to apply for a place. But when she arrived at RADA a year later, Miss Filippi had quarrelled with the Administrator, Kenneth Barnes, and left. Cicily suf-fered in consequence, Barnes and some of his colleagues making it clear that they had no intention of encouraging a protégée of Miss Filippi. When she failed to get promoted to the final term, she left the Academy and went off to look unsuccessfully for theatrical parts.

Chance diverted her to a different career when she sent an article to *The Freewoman*, a new militant feminist weekly. It was so well received that she became a regular writer for the paper. From the first her work was notable for outspoken attacks on the conventions and the conventional, and she soon made interesting and influential friends, among them the group round Ford Madox Ford and the *English Review*. Violet Hunt described Rebecca's first visit to Ford and herself.[12] Rebecca West (for she was soon generally called by her professional name) "had a pink dress on and a large wide-brimmed, country-girlish straw hat that hid her splendid liquid eyes . . . she was sweet and reasonable, but not to be kidded. . . . And quite superiorly ostentatiously young – the ineffable schoolgirl! . . . She *must* count; once she is in a room you cannot imagine it without her. . . . If she wants to hurt you she will; if she wants to be kind to you, well and very good!"

H.G. had not met her before she reviewed *Marriage*, but the review caught his eye. Whatever he thought of suffragettes as a group, he was prepared to take up a lively and attractive young girl making a literary reputation and with the kind of personality which fitted his notion of the New Woman. She was immediately invited down to Little Easton for lunch, and Fraulein Meyer noted in her diary on 27 September 1912 that "Miss Rebecca West arrived today. She looks about 22 years of age, and is very vivacious."[13]

Though patronage of the promising young by the eminent was common in this period, it is a little surprising that H.G. – who was normally sensitive about trenchant criticism – should have responded so eagerly to a review which certainly did not mince words about the weaknesses of *Marriage*. Yet what Rebecca West had written was acceptable to him because it was based on the same assumptions as his own about the novel and society. James was concerned with the artistic integrity of a work of fiction, and judged characters and relationships solely in terms of the author's success in realising them convincingly. Rebecca West, however, had shown that, like H.G., she believed words were weapons, and that fiction could be criticised – as well as written – from a political standpoint. When she delivered a vigorous onslaught on the "cow-like" personality of Marjorie, she appealed at once to Wells as a woman after his own heart, someone who despised the boring responsibilities of marriage and prized her independence. Even before they met, she had touched H.G. where he was most vulnerable to dalliance, and when she arrived at Little Easton the combination of wit, intelligence and directness with real style and beauty had an immediate and overwhelming impact on him. Once again, he had met a young woman who fitted the ideal type of his fantasies.

The attraction was mutual. Even though H.G. was not physically handsome, he had a fine head on his neat, plump body, and his exuberant charm in a good mood more than compensated for his lack of presence. Frank Swinnerton gave a vivid impression of H.G. at a Hampstead dinner-party, sitting at the far end of the table. He was, Swinnerton wrote:

In a mood to justify Bennett's gloomy "He *talks*, you know". He talked and talked, brimming with destructively ridiculing anecdote, full of ideas and inventions and raillery and nonsense. . . . His blue eyes dart and mischievously roll as he keeps command of every face before him . . . it is as pleasant and amusing to see him listen as it is to hear him improvise. He nods sharply, his eyes shine, he laughs, and then he impulsively takes up the thread of what his companion has been saying and gives it his own twist of fun.[14]

That lively, outgoing side of H.G. was immensely seductive, and it was as a benevolent and avuncular personality that he struck Rebbeca West.[15] Some years later, she wrote of Shaw, Galsworthy, Bennett and Wells that they "hung about the houses of our minds like uncles – the generosity, the charm, the loquacity of visiting uncles. Uncle Wells arrived always a little out of breath, with his arms full of parcels, sometimes rather carelessly tied, but always bursting with all manner of attractive gifts that ranged from the little pot of sweet jelly that is *Mr Polly* to the complete Meccano set for the mind that is in *The First Men in the Moon*." There must have been a sharp visual memory behind the metaphor, because the image captures so precisely the impression H.G. made on many people at this period in his life.

Before Wells met Rebecca West he had been making an effort to get his life in some manageable order again. The move to the Rectory at Little Easton had been a relief. "We're rooting here firmly", H.G. wrote to Bennett in September 1912.[16] His social life was improving, too, as the Reeves scandal was forgotten. There were dinners at Church Row, and a memorable fancy dress party, though when the house was given up in May 1913 and the London base transferred to a flat at St James's Court the focus of entertaining shifted to the country weekends. Frank Swinnerton caught the scene after an evening supper party when, "up in the drawing-room, quite unexpectedly either Wells or Mrs Wells sat down at a piano or pianola and began to play the Brahms waltzes; and the whole party at once joined in a rushing dance about the room. Nobody waltzed; everybody . . . danced and pranced in a merry fandango. The music, not as Brahms, perhaps, intended, was recklessly played, with spirit and pace and great infectiousness." One guest, the playwright Henry Arthur Jones, arriving late, "swathed himself in a curtain of crimson velvet, with an upturned brass flower pot on his head and a poker in his hand, rendering a Roman speech in the manner, not of a dramatist and castigator of society . . . but of a mime, a droll, a dignified clown".[17] There was always a mood of manic enthusiasm when H.G. threw himself into a lark with friends. One escapade in these pre-war years was the zany film got up by Harley Granville-Barker and James Barrie. "A few piratical spirits and a cinemato-graph", ran Granville-Barker's invitation, proposed to spend a weekend in Hertfordshire making a movie for their own amusement.[18] In addition to Wells he had enlisted Shaw, Chesterton, William Archer and Maurice Baring. It was a piece of inconsequential nonsense in which the eminent authors find themselves romping through the countryside in fancy dress. H.G. was game for any adventure, whether it was a juvenile lark or a more challenging test of nerve. He had kept up his association with J.W.Dunne, and often visited him at Farnborough to see how Dunne's experimental aircraft were progressing. He had a fascination with mechanical devices that led him into friendships with inventors and industrialists, such as the marine designer Thornycroft whose novel torpedo-boat served as a model for the craft on which George Ponderevo slips out to sea at the end of *Tono-Bungay*. But it was not Dunne but Grahame-White, the pioneer aviator, who took H.G. for his first flight, taking off from Eastbourne in a Farman seaplane on 5 August 1912. Wells, who had imagined so much flying in his stories, was entranced and acquired a taste for air-travel which he never lost.

Some of these activities gave H.G. copy for articles which filled the gap left by the decline in his creative work after *Marriage*. He was also a ready contributor to radical papers like the *New Age* and the *New Witness*, as well as to the more lucrative popular press. He was becoming a pundit, who was expected to have views on any topic of current interest. Success-ful writers at this time were "stars", as much in the public eye as film stars and then television personalities became in later years. They made news, and they commented on news, and they were printed whether their opinions were trivial or portentous. Arnold Bennett, indeed, remarked that an eminent novelist should take care that some newspaper mentioned him every day.

The appearance of a series of articles by Wells in the *Daily Mail* in the middle of May 1912 was one indication of his changing status. He was now sought after as a commentator on social problems and great events. By 1914 he was able to publish a collection of his pronouncements under the title *An Englishman Looks at the World*. In the following years he threw himself into such work, until it came to provide a significant part of his growing income.

The *Mail* articles were on "The Labour Unrest", and Northcliffe asked him to write them because of the wave of strikes then sweeping the country. They contained few facts, but they were packed with the rhetorical generalisations which H.G. employed whenever he wrote on politics. The strikers, he said, had "put the whole social system on trial" and the problem for the governing class was how "to lay hold of this drifting, sullen and suspicious multitude, which is the working body of the country". The answer was better housing as well as higher wages, more education as well as improved social security. All this, he urged, could only be secured by "a National Plan". In his view clergymen and classicists crippled the growth of science and made the better schools "the last preserves of an elderly orthodoxy and the last repository of a decaying gift of superseded tongues". These reactionaries, supported by an unrepresentative Parliament and an irrelevant party system, were responsible for the decline of England by obstructing "the great task of social reconstruction which lies before us all".

In the following year, on 24 April 1913, H.G. published an article in the *New Witness* regretting that he had not been invited to take part in a quite different journalistic venture. Sidney and Beatrice Webb had long considered launching what they called a "socialist version of the *Spectator*". With Shaw's early co-operation, with the backing of some wealthy Fabians, and with Clifford Sharp as editor, they finally started *The New Statesman* in 1913. Wells, piqued because he was not asked to contribute, could not resist the chance to pick at old scars. Complaining that the Webbs had neglected "their graceful duty" by ignoring him after all he had done to liven up the Fabians, he grouched at the new weekly for its "old Fabian deadnesses" – for publishing dreary articles on municipal reform and for allowing Mrs Webb, "who is about as mystical as a railway whistle", to write "mystically about the soul of Japan". The paper as a whole, he added, "is as dull as a privet hedge in Leeds. . . . I will trouble myself about these old Fabians no more . . . This last resuscitation is not journalism but printed mumbling."

In the early summer of 1913 H.G. attacked yet another old associate. In articles published in *The Author* in May and June, he announced that he was being plagued by literary agents who wanted to handle his business. Pinker believed that H.G. had been unfair to him personally, and to agents generally, and he was delighted when Bennett came to his defence.[19] "I am glad to think that I have never written to him in the way he speaks of", Pinker wrote to Bennett on 6 June, "but I do think he is most misleading for the ignorant authors in his spitefulness. . . . I only wish that it were possible for me to make public the history of our connection, with Wells's letters to back me up." Bennett wrote in the July issue of *The Author* that it was H.G. who originally sent him to Pinker, and "if I had not followed his advice I should be very decidedly worse off than I am. Bennett shrewdly observed to F.S.A.Lowndes of *The Times*, "Wells on agents is a chump. I have often told him so. He is down on agents *because* he . . . dropped a lot of money by trying to manage his affairs himself."

Wells was bothered about money, and his irritation with agents was a sign of it. Though he earned well, and his backlist brought in good royalties from new editions and foreign rights, he had heavy outgoings – a house in London and another in the country, a growing family, the new relationship with Rebecca West, a taste for entertaining at home, dining out in good restaurants, and staying in expensive hotels when he travelled. He was no penny-pincher, but he liked to feel he was assured of a substantial sum from the next book and he had become accustomed to sizeable advances. By 1913, the prospects were less bright – partly because of the confusion he had created with agents and publishers, partly because he kept switching styles and markets, but mainly because he seemed unable to get back into the swing of writing books of the kind that had made his reputation.

Emancipated women fascinated H.G., and during 1913 and 1914 he was in close touch with the feminist movement through Rebecca. He approved of the claim of the feminists to be treated as human beings with whom a man could form a real intellectual partnership. That had always been implicit in his conception of the ideal type, but he had been unable to find such a "mate" in either of his two marriages. As each of them proved to be a disillusionment he had at first assumed that the fault lay in personal incompatibility and that he had chosen unwisely. But he had gradually come to believe that the fault actually lay in the institution of marriage itself. Marriage was a denial of freedom, destroying love, and putting possessiveness and jealousy in its place. He had arrived at the same conclusion as the extreme wing of the women's movement. As early as 1906, with "Socialism and the Family" and *In the Days of the Comet*, he had begun to explore alternatives to conventional marriage and to show his concern with the theme of jealousy. He had then been bitterly attacked for suggesting that marriage was really a form of private property and that a free relationship was only possible when women had the security of their own income. Once he became involved with Rebecca, and stimulated by the excitement of the women's revolt, his opposition to marriage again spilled out into his fiction.

Both *The Passionate Friends* and *The Wife of Sir Isaac Harman* were un-happy books about women imprisoned by marriage whose hearts were "black with rebellion", as Mary Justin puts it in *The Passionate Friends*. She has refused to marry her lover precisely because he is her lover and she wishes to preserve him as an ideal. "If I were to come away with you and marry you", she tells Stephen Stratton, "in just a little time I should cease to be your lover, I should be your squaw. I should have to share your worries and make your coffee – and disappoint you, disappoint you and fail you in a hundred ways. . . . I don't want to be your servant and your possession." She marries a man she does not love, and when her husband discovers that she has secretly met Stephen and threatens to divorce her she commits suicide. To have left Justin to marry Stephen would have been to exchange one living death for another, and the ultimate gesture of independence was self-destruction. In the following year Wells produced his counterpart of *The Doll's House*. Lady Harman, like Ibsen's Nora, is the plaything of a dominating husband who makes her feel like a child. "To be a married woman", she feels, "is to be outside justice. It is autocracy." She achieves some degree of freedom with suffragette friends and in building hostels for working girls. When her husband dies she is glad because she has then achieved real freedom, and she asserts this by refus-ing to marry her Wells-like friend, Mr Brumley. What comes out of both books is a sense of bitterness, frustration and despair. Through the women who suffer in marriage Wells expressed his own claustrophobic feelings. In both cases death provides the only means of release. Happiness is to be found only outside marriage, where the emotions are free from the con-straints of mutual responsibility and a bargain can be struck between two people who confront each other without obligations.

When Henry James received *The Passionate Friends* he was clearly at a loss what to say, and the effusive compliments with which he larded his letter to Wells on 21 September merely avoided repetition of his earlier comments on H.G. as a novelist. H.G. immediately replied that he was "the soul of generosity. That book is *gawky*. . . . It has been thrust into the world too soon." Once again, assuring James that he really wanted to be an artist, he put the blame for his failure in this respect on his "unworthi-ness and rawness".[20] The letters were still cordial, and Wells wrote warmly to James when he was sent a copy of the autobiographical *A Small Boy and Others*. Occasionally James was invited to dine, or he and Wells met casually in the Reform Club. Yet the old friendship had cooled, and Wells began to suspect James of gossiping about him and of setting the literary establishment against him. His suspicions increased when in March and April 1914 James published two articles in *The Times Literary Supplement* on "The Younger Generation". In these two pieces James summed up his views on Wells, Bennett, Conrad, Walpole and Compton Mackenzie. The burden of his criticism was that they all, and Bennett especially, saturated the reader with material. He described their work as "the squeezing of a plump and juicy orange", full of formless energy, lacking discipline and emotional depth. Though James made no direct reference to the lecture on the novel which Wells had given to *The Times* Book Club, his whole thesis was an implicit rebuke to the claims that Wells had made in it.

H.G. made no direct reply, though James had now said gently in public what he had been telling Wells privately for years. He was, however, already working on what became the most formless of all his books, in which he was to vent all the accumulated irritation that had built up against the literary set.

Boon was published in 1915, but parts of it had been drafted in 1905, other sections in the aftermath of the Reeves scandal, and the remainder in tormented moods around the outbreak of the 1914 war. The book is a rag-bag of pieces supposedly written by the popular novelist George Boon who is forced to write successful romances while he secretly yearns for literary success. Into these fragments H.G. inserted a bitter satire on James, portraying him as a portentous mandarin who pontificated on art and who denigrated those who wished to use literature as a means of saving the world from ruin. The selection which James thought essential to the novel was, for Wells, "just omission and nothing more . . . For example, he omits opinions. . . . All that much of humanity he clears out before he begins his story. It's like cleaning rabbits for the table." For H.G., who had now abandoned the posture of the acolyte to the Master, the Jamesian novel was stuffy and sterile.

It is like a church lit but without a congregation to distract you, with every light and line focused on the high altar. And on the altar, very reverently placed, intensely there, is a dead kitten, an egg-shell, a bit of string. . . . And the elaborate copious emptiness of the whole Henry James exploit is only redeemed and made endurable by the elaborate, copious wit. . . . He spares no resource in the telling of his dead inventions. . . . He splits his infinitives and fills them up with adverbial stuffing. His vast paragraphs sweat and struggle. . . . And all for tales of nothingness. . . . It is a magnificent but painful hippopotamus resolved at any cost, even at the cost of its dignity, upon picking up a pea which has got into the corner of its den.

He eked out his bitter attack with a parody of a James novel that mocked as well as wounded. Late in 1917, writing to Hugh Walpole to complain that the adverse reaction to *Boon* "was a little unjust", H.G. defended his unkindness to the ageing and ailing James.[21]

> The old man was a little treacherous to me in a very natural sort of way and the James cult has been overdone. Anyhow nothing I've ever written or said or anything anyone has ever written or said about James can balance the extravagant dirtiness of Lubbock and his friends in boycotting Rebecca West's book on him in *The Times Literary Supplement*. My blood still boils at the thought of those pretentious academic greasers conspiring to down a friendless girl (who can write any of them out of sight) in the name of loyalty to literature. It makes the name of James stink in my memory.

The extravagant language of this letter, written three years after the event when James had been dead for more than a year, shows how the episode still rankled and gives some indication of the vindictive temper in which Wells had finished *Boon* in the dark winter of 1914. It was the work of a disappointed man, uncertain and depressed about his role in life, and jealously envying James even while he was deriding him.

The whole book, indeed, was an attempt by Wells to explore his own ambivalence, and the tirade against James was only a particular expression of his uneasiness. The fragments were linked together by a continuing dialogue between Wells in two guises – as Boon, the idealist with intellectual aspirations who wants to educate The Mind of the Race into the Age of Reason, and as Wilkins, who sardonically insists that history is the record of inconsequential idiocy. The only resolution of that internal debate was the belief that the Word (or, as Boon put it, Literature) was the means to "illumination, the salvation of ourselves".

The spring of Wells's anger against James, therefore, lay in James's denial of the world-saving power of the Word and his insistence that art must serve its own ends and not those of human redemption. For fifteen years, in what Wells called his "phase of social acquiescence", he had tried to run his literary ambitions and his messianic beliefs in double harness and to ignore the fact that they were pulling in opposite directions. When he came to the crisis of 1910 he had been forced reluctantly to choose between art and evangelism. It was James who had to bear the brunt of his anguish.

The agony of this only half-conscious choice may account for the fact that H.G. personally delivered a copy of *Boon* for James at his club. On 6 July James sent Wells a kind reply saying that comment was difficult when

H.G. had found him "extraordinarily futile and void".[22] They had known each other so long that there had "grown up the habit of taking some common meeting-ground between them for granted, and the falling away of this is like the collapse of a bridge which made communication possible". There was no complaint in the letter, only a note of regret and a firm restatement of the position which James had spelt out so often and at such length in their long friendship. Two days later H.G. wrote to explain that "my sparring and punching at you is very much due to the feeling that you were 'coming over' me, and that if I was not very careful I should find myself giving way altogether to respect. There is of course a real and very fundamental difference in our innate and developed attitudes towards life and literature. To you literature like painting is an end, to me literature like architecture is a means, it has a use. . . . I had rather be called a journalist than an artist, that is the essence of it, and there was no other antagonist possible than yourself." There was a last but formal effort at an apology from H.G., who called himself a "warm if rebellious and resentful admirer". He was sorry that he had not expressed "our profound and incurable difference and contrast with a better grace".

James, whose eyesight was now failing, dictated his final and still dignified letter on 10 July. "I am bound to tell you that I don't think your letter makes out any sort of case for the bad manners of *Boon*, so far as your indulgence in them at the expense of your poor old H.J. is concerned." Wells had sought to minimise the sting of his book by dismissing it as "just a waste-paper basket". That, James replied, "strikes me as the reverse of felicitous, for what one throws into that receptacle is exactly what one *doesn't* commit to publicity". He was equally severe on the distinction that Wells had made between painting and architecture. "It is art that *makes* life, makes interest, makes importance, for our consideration and application of these things, and I know of no substitute whatever for the force and beauty of its process. If I were Boon I should say that any pretence of such a substitute is helpless and hopeless humbug; but I wouldn't be Boon for the world, and am only yours faithfully, Henry James."

The last word, which came from Wells three days afterwards, accepted the inevitable. "I don't clearly understand your concluding phrases", he wrote, "which shews no doubt how completely they define our difference." This was in fact a confrontation between two views of culture and its significance for progress. For James, the task of the artist was to achieve insight into the human condition by exploring the relationships which expressed it. In this way, slowly and painfully, one might hope to raise the level of social consciousness. There were no short cuts. Wells, however, was in revolt against the human condition, and was impatient with the relationships and conventions that flowed from it. Consciousness could only be changed by conversion, which could be achieved quickly and dramatically, and the artist must use his art deliberately as a means to this end. To James it seemed that H.G. was betraying his talent for meretricious purposes, while to Wells it appeared that James was betraying the human race in the name of artistic purity. That issue had always been there between them. But as the friendship withered, and Wells began to assert his messianic feelings more forcibly, the dialogue fell away. James died in February of the following year.

PART FIVE
A Man of Destiny

19

THE WAR THAT WILL END WAR

The summer of 1914 laid a golden spell over the countryside. Monday 4 August was a Bank Holiday, and Lady Warwick's grounds at Easton Lodge were open as usual for the annual fête and flower show which attracted crowds from the local villages and distinguished visitors from London. In the meadow between the Lodge and the Rectory there were four great marquees containing the flowers and fruit ripened by the remarkably hot weather, and beside them a motley collection of steam roundabouts and sideshows erected by Greenaways and Thurstons – the travelling showmen who came to Easton every year for this holiday. It was the Edwardian idyll of a peaceful and contented England, and it was almost over. For the past two days German troops had been pouring into Belgium.

The Wells family walked up to the fair with the week-end guests, all of them arguing about the crisis. No one knew what Britain would do, and there was only rumour to feed the speculation. War had come so suddenly that no one had yet adjusted to the idea. The young son of R.D. Blumenfeld of the *Daily Express* went along with his father, and remembered a heated discussion between Shaw and Wells. "G.B.S. said that it served us right. We could have seen it coming if we hadn't been black-mailed by Edward Carson over Ulster. H.G. got excited. 'Never mind about that now!' he cried in the high-pitched voice which he could never control when he felt deeply. 'The Germans are frightfully efficient and will invade us too. We must have a *levée en masse*. We must get out our shot guns and man the hedges and ditches, but it will be the end of civilisation'."[1] For years Wells had both dreaded and prophesied the coming of a catastrophe, and now the theme which had run through his works of fantasy had dramatically erupted into real life. To Wells the impact of war was "like the shock of an unsuspected big gun fired suddenly within a hundred yards".[2]

"I will confess", Wells wrote years later, "I was taken by surprise by the Great War. Yet I saw long ahead how it would happen, and wove fantastic stories about it. I let my imagination play about it, but at the bottom of my heart I could not feel and believe it would really be let happen."[3]

He felt somehow responsible for letting it happen, as if he were answerable for the whole world – as if, in the thoughts that two years later he put into the mind of his auto-character Mr Britling, the world was his egg, and he had a delusion that he had both laid it and let it addle. There was only one way to make that dreadful reality bearable. If he had been right in foreseeing the collapse of civilisation, then he felt he must also have been right in predicting that this judgement on mankind must be made the prelude to its salvation – the war must be made the means to establishing the everlasting peace. On the evening of 4 August, in an apocalyptic mood, H.G. sat down to write the article which quickly – and in the end, ironically – became the national slogan. It was, he wrote as a title, "The War That Will End War".

Wells rightly claimed that he had foreseen the conflict which burst on the world in 1914. His books had also suggested that it would be the harbinger of a new and better world order – though this would come about through some utopian transformation scene in which, almost in the twinkling of an eye, the minds and hearts of men would be changed to make the new world possible. *In the Days of the Comet* had described a situation very like that of August 1914, but in that story the mobilising armies had been halted by the cosmic miracle of the wandering comet whose trailing gas had converted mankind to peace and fraternity.

In the summer of 1913 H.G. came back to a similar idea in *The World Set Free*, the most curiously prophetic of all his books, in which he swept ahead to a mid-century conflict between the Free Nations and the Central Powers. The device he used to accomplish the transition to his utopia must then have seemed quite as miraculous and cosmic as the comet. It was the invention of an atomic bomb, which laid the world waste so fearfully that mankind experienced a lasting revulsion against warfare. He was writing twenty years before the Joliot-Curies demonstrated that artificial radioactivity was possible, but had so anticipated the concept of a devastating release of nuclear energy that Leo Szilard – one of the scientists whose work lay behind the Hiroshima bomb – said that when the idea of chain reaction first occurred to him in 1934 he was influenced by *The World Set*

Free which he had read the previous year. "Knowing what this would mean – and I knew it because I had read H.G.Wells", he wrote, "I did not want this patent to become public."[4]

The idea of a nuclear bomb provided Wells with a perfect means to make his point that if human beings cannot be persuaded rationally to create a new world order, they must be scared into the task by the threat of extinction. In *The World Set Free* Wells described how, after a ruinous war has wrecked all the old social systems, the survivors set out to construct his ideal World State, unhampered by national boundaries and rivalries. They are a new kind of ruler, much like the Samurai – and also like the airmen who, in the later *Shape of Things to Come*, emerge from their retreat to impose order on a world devastated by war and pestilence. The apocalypse has been followed by the Rule of the Saints, which begins in the high places of the Himalayas and spreads over the globe. It is these superior beings who have enabled humanity to escape the fate facing all those who surrender to atavistic instincts. Under their enlightened control mankind can at last realise "the great conceptions of universal rule", and then begin to reach out hopefully into the vast darkness of the heavens.

This was, of course, a restatement of the position that H.G. had taken consistently for some years, with the difference that the threat to the survival of the species was now man-made and immediate rather than the result of the long-term working of the laws of evolution. Since he produced the earlier romances, Wells had shortened his time-scale, and had come to believe that the race between education and catastrophe would be run very nearly within the span of his own life. This change not only gave a new note of urgency to his prophecies. It also explains why the outbreak of a world war both frightened and elated him, so that from the first days he began to write at a pitch of hysteria. The war could be the beginning of the end: it might also herald a new beginning. It had, therefore, to become a crusade, in which the crushing of German militarism was merely the first step towards the smashing of all the nationalisms which prevented men from seeing the need for a new world order and working constructively to establish it.

At the age of forty-eight Wells was too old to fight, but he wrote with the frenzy of a man who believed that words are also weapons. "I shouted various newspaper articles of an extremely belligerent type", he confessed later, and already by September 1914 he had collected some of these "shrill jets of journalism" into a shilling pamphlet which took its title from the leading article "The War that Will End War". They were full of bellicose phrases. "Never has any state in the world so clamoured for punishment . . . Every sword that is drawn against Germany now is a sword drawn for peace . . . By means of a propaganda of books, newspaper articles, leaflets . . . we have to spread this idea, repeat this idea, and *impose upon this war* the idea that this war must end war."[5] Through the maudlin self-righteousness, so characteristic of the jingoism that swept England in the first weeks of war, Wells was still insisting on the message which provides the one thread of consistency in his wartime writings. The war was destroying all that had been stable and familiar, and thereby offering an unprecedented chance for will and ideas – "the two sorts of rebel that ordinary times suppress" – to assert themselves. How, asked Wells, "are we to gather together the wills and understanding of men for the tremendous necessities and opportunities of the time? . . . This monstrous conflict . . . is all of it real only in the darkness of the mind. At the coming of understanding it will vanish as dreams vanish at awakening . . ." Even while he drummed up support for the war his sense of what might lie beyond its end made him unusual among the energetic patriots. He was already canvassing ideas of general disarmament and international control.

This concern with war aims, however, was not enough to appease many of his old friends, some of whom were opposed to the war as simply a conflict of rival imperialisms, some of whom were pacifists, and some merely level-headed people who were nauseated by jingoism. His belligerent attitude, for example, finally broke the long friendship with Vernon Lee which had already been severely strained during the crisis about Amber Reeves. When Wells published an appeal to the American people to impose a virtual blockade of Germany, Vernon Lee wrote sarcastically to the New York *Nation* about the "self-righteousness" with which H.G. would "deprive Germany of food for the speedier coming of the kingdom of peace and good will upon earth". She never forgave him for the way in which he "enlisted at once for the Fleet Street Front and bid us unsheath the Sword of Peace for the final extermination of Militarism".[6]

At the same time Wells found himself again at odds with Shaw, who had raised a storm of public protest by publishing an article called "Common Sense About the War" in *The New Statesman*, ridiculing the moral pretensions of the Allies. Wells, then writing a series of violent articles in the *Daily Chronicle*, could not refrain from attacking G.B.S. and raking up old grievances from the Fabian row. H.G. was particularly angry when Shaw called Tsarist Russia a "tyranny". In January 1914, Wells had made a brief trip to Russia with Maurice Baring. He had been charmed by the liberal aristocrats who had entertained him and fascinated by long talks with Maxim Gorki – with whom he felt he had a great deal in common. He was also impressed by the fact that the first collected edition of his work had appeared in Russia where he had been translated from the beginning of his career. For Shaw to denounce this ally, as if the Russian government were "a thing of insatiable ambition and incredible cunning and wickedness", was an act of "senile make-believe". All through the war Wells concluded, "we shall have this Shavian accompaniment going on, like an idiot child screaming in a hospital, distorting, discrediting, confusing . . . '. By contrast, Wells saw himself in the midst of the hurly-burly, "resolved to wring some good out of this great agony of mankind".[7] Anyone who opted out was guilty of treachery, not so much to the English war effort as to the far greater cause of mankind. In a somewhat similar onslaught on Romain Rolland, to whom he wrote after the publication of Rolland's book, *Above the Battle*, Wells was scathingly indignant.[8] "A great number of those who toil & attempt down below 'in the battle' ", he said, "who are convinced that only by sweat & agony & blundering & sacrifice can any solution of our catastrophic problems be hammered out, do find your attitude, up there above the clouds in Switzerland, irritatingly self-important & irritatingly unhelpful."

The attacks on Shaw, Rolland and others were typical of the outbursts which estranged Wells from old literary acquaintances, some of whom were conscientious objectors and even more of whom were distressed by the brutal hypocrisies of the war. The Bloomsbury group, which had never greatly cared for H.G., was outraged by his vulgar ferocity. Clive Bell, for instance, was so antagonised that he could not bear to meet H.G. for years afterwards, and both Lytton Strachey and Bertrand Russell were as waspishly vindictive about him in private conversation as Wells was about their "shirking and screaming". Writing in 1917, after he had been on a tour of the battlefields, Wells denounced the anti-war radicals for a "scream of extreme individualism, a monotonous repetition of incoherent discontent with authority, with direction, with union, with the European effort . . . The very ideal of the world going right does not exist in their minds."[9] Though H.G. continued to insist that he was seeking "to impose on this war" a nobler purpose, most of the popular articles he poured out in the first years of the conflict simply primed the pump of war hysteria. While they estranged old friends, they were winning him a new reputation among the general public.

The strain of the war undoubtedly exacerbated the capacity for intemperate polemic which H.G. displayed all through his life. When it was over he regretted much that he had written. Yet there was a reason other than patriotic passion for the tension which found release in this spate of bigoted rhetoric. Once more he was overwrought by a personal crisis.

On the day that war broke out, while Wells was entertaining his friends at the Easton flower show, Rebecca West was giving birth to their son Anthony. For the past two years there had been no secret about their relationship. But the situation had changed when H.G. returned from his Russian journey early in 1914 and learned that Rebecca was pregnant. He again became edgy and restless, and his uncertainty characteristically revealed itself in the idea of moving house once again. The initial lease on the Rectory at Little Easton had been a short one, and in April H.G. was making inquiries about other properties.

While this new affair caused nothing like the fuss created by the Reeves scandal, there was gossip and there were practical problems to be faced. In the affair with Amber, H.G. had struck at the heart of the Fabian family and run into trouble with the influential Fabian elders and their friends. The situation was different with Rebecca.[10] She had already established herself as a proudly independent woman, earning her own living and enjoying a fast-growing reputation. She moved in a set much less censorious than the priggish Fabians, and more ready to accept free relationships, but when Anthony was born things were not so easy or pleasant. She was in a more invidious position. She began to experience unpleasant fusses with domestics and neighbours, and to receive disagreeable letters and threats of blackmail. Her professional career, which she valued highly, suffered. She had not only dropped out of the swim of things in London. She also found that social ostracism extended to editors and publishers who had previously encouraged her work.

There was no serious suggestion, however, that she and H.G. should marry. When Amber had become pregnant, the news jolted Wells into a panic. He had not known what he wanted, or what to do next, and there had been weeks of drama, confusion and tears. With Rebecca there was no question of an impulsive elopement. They had already established a domestic arrangement which H.G. saw no reason to alter merely because Rebecca was having a child. In 1909 his nerve had failed him, but in 1914 he carried off the consequent emotional and practical difficulties with bravado. Since he found marriage claustrophobic there was no question of leaving Jane to marry his lover. As he saw it, that would destroy everything that he found in his relationship with Rebecca. He was forced to pursue a double life. One woman served his social needs, the other gave him intellectual and emotional satisfaction.

There were, of course, problems, but as he admitted in a letter to E.S.P. Haynes, he cockily believed that he could surmount them. "Of course Jane knows", he wrote. "And don't you go . . . calling me a Chadband because I pulled your leg at lunch. It's nothing to what I *will* do. Also you mustn't begin to criticize your friend in a crisis. This *is* a crisis – though I appear to be enjoying it. I *do* enjoy it but there are considerable precipices & I look to you not to start pushing & relapsing towards Xtian morality."[11]

Jane did know. What puzzled people like Haynes was that she tolerated what was going on. It seems that she protected herself by freezing the wounds to her pride and her position as a wife, so that she condoned H.G.'s emotional rejection of her. "Jane" could cope because "Catherine" was not touched. At this level she was disingenuous about the way H.G. behaved, retreating into her role as his "White Goddess". If H.G. had hardened over the past few years, so had she. Since she made no emotional demands for herself, and had no intention of divorcing him, she was left with no alternative but to accept his mistresses. She had weathered the crisis with Amber by being coolly practical and motherly. She had tolerated Elizabeth von Arnim. There seemed to be no serious threat in that relationship, and Jane even enjoyed visits to her chalet in Switzerland. But Rebecca was a different matter. For the first time Jane was faced by a rival ménage with a prospect of some permanency. There were at last grounds for the kind of jealousy which H.G. so feared in marriage. Jane, however, was toughly determined to make her own terms which would firmly establish her position at Easton.

She made it clear that *she* was Mrs H.G. Wells, the wife of the public man, and that she expected him to provide an appropriate style of life at Little Easton and to co-operate in making a success of it. The sign that this was settled in the spring of 1914 was the decision not to give up the Rectory but to take it on a long lease, commissioning expensive alterations to the house. She was never able to complain that Wells was parsimonious in such matters. There was always plenty of money for her to spend as freely as she wished. Her complaint, especially in the initial period of uncertainty about the time that Anthony was born, was that H.G. seemed unable to settle comfortably to the new arrangement. The stress of his personal life made him restless and difficult company, and he was continually away or obviously eager to get away when he was at home.

When Jane protested, H.G. sent an outspoken reply.

My abundant absence just at present is due to my need here not to any hostility to my home.

My irritability at home is due to the unsettled feeling due to rebuilding. I do not think you understand what a *torment* it is to an impatient man to feel the phantom future home failing to realize itself. I *hate* things unfinished & out of place. I want things *settled* I want a home to live in & have people into – people one can talk with. At present home is a noisy, unsympathetic, uninteresting muddle. I want to get at it. I want to see it changing. I feel like *Removals*. When we get it all cleared up perhaps it will be possible to get human beings interested in things that matter about us again. Anyhow we must try. Whatever else is done, it is impossible for the Rectory to go on as it is going now, so that I cannot bring a visitor down or get to feel that my work is anything but an income-getting toil.

While there had been fidgety irritations when H.G. and Jane were building Spade House, that had been a joint endeavour. This letter now implied that the upheaval was her responsibility, and that he was entitled to opt out of all the nuisances with builders until she had done her housekeeperly duty and put the place in proper order. That, however, was only one reason for staying away. H.G. went on to give another.

And also when I have been at the Rectory for a few days I get into a state of irritability because of sexual exasperation. Later on I shall be able to get pacified in London – For that business I still fail to see any perfect solution . . . the present situation is particularly calculated to make a peaceful sojourn at L. Easton impossible. Later in every respect I think it will be better. The brute fact is that I am not & never have been – if there is such a thing – a passionate lover. I am affectionate & tremendously interested in things & bodily vigorous & I want a healthy woman handy to steady my nerves & leave my mind free for real things. I love you very warmly, you are in so many things, bone of my bone, & flesh of my flesh & my making. I must keep you. I like your company & I doubt about never spending that holiday together again & so on. But the other thing is a physical necessity. That's the real hitch.

This letter was a statement of the terms on which he proposed henceforth to base his behaviour.[12] He was no longer in a marriage punctuated by infidelities: he was beginning a double life, in which he switched moods as quickly as he doffed his role as husband and host at Easton and, at the other end of a train journey, appeared at Rebecca's house in the part of a lover. The magic transformations which had characterised the *doppelganger* figures in his stories had now become habitual in his own life. And when he was not at Easton, or at Hunstanton, Hatch End or Leigh-on-Sea, where Rebecca lived at different times in the war, he was squeezing in patches of social life and business in London at the flat he took at 52 St James's Court in Westminster in 1913.

With the coming of the war, in fact, H.G. went through a phase of settlements and new beginnings. In early September 1914 he sent Robert Ross a letter asking him to act as his literary executor as he was making a new will. In the same month both Gip and Frank were placed in a boarding school at Oundle. After a long search H.G. had found in F.W.Sanderson – "a great modernist with a fruity sense of humour" Bennett said[13] – a headmaster whose view on education came close to his own.

Once the builders were out of the house, now renamed Easton Glebe, H.G. was able to throw himself into the weekend partnership with Jane. It is in the memories of those who were their guests at the Glebe that they are most frequently and cheerfully remembered. Apart from friends in the neighbourhood, who came to the Glebe as informally as Wells dropped in on them for a good chat, there were usually visitors staying in the house – which now had twelve bedrooms and six bathrooms. Bennett thought that it was "fairly comfortable and very bright; but some of it is badly planned and arranged". He felt it was "like a large cottage made comfortable by people rich but capricious".[14] It had a pleasant stone-flagged entrance hall. To the right were a morning-room and a big dining-room, to which H.G. and Jane had added a large bow-window with a view across the valley. On the left was a study, and beyond it a long drawing-room lined with bookcases. They had also added a bow-window to this room, which looked out through the blue cedars to the lawn which was used for hockey and other games. Upstairs H.G. had a small suite, with a study in which he worked in the early mornings, a bathroom and a bedroom. At the west side of the house, near the stables, was the timber barn which was converted into a playroom. Between the house and the Lodge there was a tennis court. In front of the house, to the south, the land sloped away through the woods to the four large lakes which separated the house from the Manor.

Jane took a good deal of trouble with the garden. She laid out a sunken garden, planted rose-bushes and worked closely with Grout, the gardener. Her passion for tidiness extended even to the lawn. One visitor remembered receiving a reprimand for cutting the grass: Jane darted out of the house crying out agitatedly "I do hope you aren't spoiling the rows", and adding ruefully that "it's so nice when the rows are perfectly straight, isn't it?" Host and hostess had complementary talents for entertaining. Jane saw to it that the house was well run, as the setting in which H.G. could indulge his passion for playing. She enjoyed organising house-parties, which provided an outlet for her capacity for orderly planning, and gave H.G. stimulating company when he was not working. Even the restrictions of wartime imposed only marginal constraints. "Under the present regulations", Jane wrote to the historian Philip Guedalla, "week-enders bring 2 oz of sugar (not more) ½ oz butter (it must not melt on the way) & a contribution of one or two sausages – or a rasher!"[15]

Lady Warwick often came over, bringing some of her own mixed bag of guests which ranged from members of the Edwardian smart set to literary adventurers such as Frank Harris and trade union leaders and Labour politicians. Within a mile or so there were other friends, R.D. Blumenfeld of the *Express* brought over Fleet Street colleagues. There was S.L.Bensusan, who wrote witty pieces about rural men and manners in Essex. J.Robertson Scott, who edited *The Countryman*, lived just down the road. So did the popular novelist H.de Vere Stacpoole. To redress the political balance there was H.A.Gwynne, who edited the *Morning Post*, and the Cranmer-Byng brothers made up the local clique of writers. Conrad Noel, the "Red Parson", settled in the nearby living of Thaxted by Lady Warwick, was less congenial to Wells, who had fallen out with him over his contribution to the symposium of socialist essays called *The Great State*, which H.G. had unwisely undertaken to edit jointly with Lady Warwick not long before the war. All this group were at least as socially involved with each other as Wells had been with Conrad, Ford and James at Sandgate, and once again it was Wells – with some help and rivalry from Lady Warwick – who played the role of *animateur*. He seemed to need some such cast as a repertory company into which, each weekend, he could draft his distinguished guests from London to play the leading parts.

No one who visited Easton Glebe was permitted to remain inactive. Cabinet ministers, playwrights, critics, scientists, publishers and novelists, whatever their age or dignity, were driven on by the relentless energy of Wells and the stage-management of Jane. The weekends, recalled Frank

Swinnerton, who had become a close friend and frequent visitor, were "whirls of unceasing activity".[16]

They began, sedately enough, with partial unpacking and tea; but by Sunday night the entire house would be strewn with dozens of pairs of white shoes which had been used from store in every kind of outdoor game, with discarded costumes hunted out of great chests and closets for the exacter verisimilitude of charades, and with the general litter of a tempestuous assembly. No late nights were kept; but from nine o'clock in the morning until ten or eleven in the evening ... the pace was terrific. And through it all was Mr Wells, leader in every activity from lawn tennis, hockey, quoits, and dancing to bridge and a frightful pastime known as Demon Patience; Mr Wells, full of hospitality and the high spirits always engendered in him by the society of young, active, laughing people; Mr Wells, above all, the animated, unexhausted, and inexhaustible talker, who to the last moment of the day would receive with every word dropped by another person, and every small incident that occurred or was described, fresh inspiration ...

The barn was used for the most confusing and demanding of all these sports – the Ball Game which Wells himself invented and at which, since no one else seemed ever to grasp the rules or understand the scoring, his side inevitably won. And the great tithe barn, which Lady Warwick had converted into a theatre in 1913, served for the more organised amateur theatricals in which Jane took a prominent part.

Wells had not yet brought the war into his fiction. *Bealby*, which appeared in 1915, was a light-hearted story in the vein of *Mr Polly*, describing the adventures of a small boy unwillingly put into service in a country house like Up Park who then runs away in search of freedom. Yet in *The Research Magnificent*, which came out late in 1915 and was set wholly in the pre-war years, H.G. had already begun to express a mood of bewilderment and to show signs that he was searching for a new mission. It is a laboured book, put by and taken up again in the first months of the war, and written in a melodramatic and sentimental style. Benham, its hero, is a rich young prig with a possessive mother, who slowly discovers from an odyssey of world travel that his destiny is to transcend the constraints of fear and pain and preach the necessity of the World State. Though Wells clearly intended this to be an exemplary tale, Benham turns out to be a failure in every respect. He runs away from his love-match with the beautiful Amanda, believing that the suffocation of sex will stifle his ambition to be "king of the world". Wells used the story to try out the first version of his new doctrine of the Invisible King. Benham felt the need for God, who alone can provide the courage to sustain the loneliness of such a New Aristocrat as himself, and elevates Him into the unseen presence who will be the leader of all those who are seeking to build the world republic.

While H.G. was writing of a new world order, the old order was dying in the mud and misery of Flanders. In the summer of 1916, the British army had launched its Somme offensive; by early autumn nearly half a million men had been killed and wounded, and nothing had been done to break the stalemate of trench warfare that Wells had foreseen more then ten years earlier. Even though his notion of "Land Ironclads" was tried in September, the advantages of tank attack were wasted by ignorance and prejudice. The French army was also bleeding away at Verdun, while shipping losses and a growing scandal about munitions were beginning to shake the Asquith government. The war that would end war was neither being won nor showing any signs of turning into a crusade for a world state.

Northcliffe, who was close to Lloyd George and increasingly influential, went on a visit to France and came back with demands for more effective leadership. H.G., increasingly impatient and anxious about the way things were going, wrote in April 1916 to congratulate him on "playing a supremely useful part in goading on our remarkable government", but added that he was now convinced that salvation could come only by "a *revolution* . . . And there is nobody in the country with the imagination, the instruments, and the prestige for revolution except yourself. The war has brought you into open and active conflict with the system as it is."[17] It was an odd illusion to see the press lord as a revolutionary. Though he was, like Wells, a successful outsider with no commitments to the old ruling class, his passion was power rather than progress. But H.G. took comfort from the radical phrases that Northcliffe used to cover his intrigue to bring down the Asquith government, and he was delighted when Northcliffe wrote back on 22 April in words that seemed to confirm his hopes.[18] "I wish even now that you would go and look at the little part of the war in France and Flanders . . . I am very much with you as to the future, though I see it probably not as clearly as you do. It is not unlikely that the war itself may produce within the next few years something approaching a revolution."

That summer H.G. in fact accepted an invitation to tour the battlefields. It was government policy to despatch influential writers on brief visits to the front, and both Shaw and Bennett were among those who crossed the Channel. When H.G. left in August the bloodletting had already begun on the Somme, and he reached France after the battle of attrition had been going on for over a month. Another disastrous push was being planned for mid-September.

For a man who had written so ferociously, and was normally given to excitable reactions, he made a curiously flat response to the experience. When he got back to the Hotel Continentale in Paris he wrote a numb letter to Jane.[19] "Dear Mummy", he began, describing the sector near Soissons, and adding that he had seen nothing that he could not have seen in *The Illustrated London News*. He was unimpressed by the French generals he met. "I doubt if they will affect history very profoundly. They are all so sure . . . that it will be over in six or eight months. . . . It's an imbecile expedition." The letter was signed "Poor bored Daddy". The trip seems to have been planned to avoid, rather than confront, the nightmare in which a whole generation of his countrymen was perishing. He had not intended to visit the British sector at all. The object of his visit was the relatively quiet front in the Italian Alps, and he had only whisked up for a brief visit to the French front when he had found his onward journey from Paris had been delayed. His account of his trip in *The War and the Future* contained as much hysterical rhetoric as description, as if the reality of the grim situation were unbearable.* "This war is *queer*", he wrote, and "like a dream". He could offer only a dream-like solution to it. The means to human happiness and security was to accept God as the Invisible King of the World State.

As the war ground on, H.G. was in a dreadfully muddled and unhappy state. "My mind", he remembered, "did not get an effective consistent grip upon the war until 1916." He was turning out articles for the *Daily Chronicle*, the *Daily Mail*, the *Daily News* and other popular newspapers on such topical matters as the role of aviation, the scandal of private profit in the armaments industry, the role of women in the war effort and the idea of a customs union among the Allies. He was also showing increasing frustration, feeling that his opinions were being ignored and resenting the failure of the government to make use of his inventive talent. He was jealous at the influence of such acquaintances as Max Beaverbrook and Northcliffe, and – just as he bombarded *The Times*, the *Manchester Guardian*

---

* The gusto in some of its war descriptions, Wells said later, showed that the "mighty statesman-strategist, that embryo Hitler-Cromwell" who fought the fantasy battles in the Bromley fields, "was by no means dead in me, even in 1916".

and the *Morning Post* with letters proposing new ways to win the war and build the peace – he pestered his friends in high places with demands for a job commensurate with his abilities. Believing that he had, in fact, invented the tank, he found it "absurd that my imagination was not mobilized in scheming the structure and use of these contrivances", and on his return from the front in 1916 he thought up a better means of conveying supplies to the trenches than humping them up through the mud on the shoulders of weary men stumbling under shellfire. This was a simple telepherage system, rather like a collapsible ski-lift, which could be raised quickly under cover of darkness. Though he enlisted the help of Winston Churchill, the project was starved of resources, and it was developed on too meagre a scale and too late to be used to any effect. This experience merely intensified the dislike Wells had already developed against conservative soldiers and apathetic politicians.

By 1916 Wells had come to regret his early and uncritical jingoism and he turned resentfully on a system which had been unable to prevent the conflict or wage it efficiently. This "war to end war" had become "no better than a consoling fantasy". Dying for King and Country, he said, was much the same thing as dying for Kaiser and Fatherland "so far as the World State is concerned". His old radicalism asserted itself in attacks on generals, politicians, war profiteers and the public school system which had produced such an incompetent ruling élite. At the same time, and appealing to the hopes of a people that was already becoming war-weary, his utopianism began to fasten on a dream of a lasting peace. The fusion of anger with aspiration caught precisely the public mood, and accounts for the immediate success of the novel in which he chronicled his feelings about the war.

Mr Britling Sees It Through was the first book since *The New Machiavelli* in which H.G. had plainly built his story around his own life – and he was even less inhibited than he had been in the earlier novels about introducing real persons and events. Mr Britling, the famous author, is Wells himself, changed in nothing but name, as Mrs Britling is un-mistakably Jane. The background to his story is Easton, drawn in detail down to portraits of Lady Warwick, the station-master, and other recognisable neighbours, to accounts of life at the Glebe and even the difficulty that Wells had in driving his car in a reasonably safe fashion. The disguises are so transparent that there is no better account of the way H.G. lived and what he thought through the first years of the war than he himself provided in this book. He made few changes for the sake of plot. The only one of importance was the death of Britling's son at the front, and this was so convincing in the context of the book that Wells actually received many letters of condolence for his loss. He had touched the public nerve so exactly that, in addition to the commercial success counted in thirteen editions of the book before Christmas 1916 and American royalties of over £20,000, it won praise from many who had been alienated by Wells in the preceding years. Mrs Humphry Ward, for instance, had dismissed him as writing "for a world of enemies or fools, whom he wishes to instruct or show up", but she remarked that there were "no more brilliant pages of their kind in modern literature than the pages describing Mr Britling's motor drive on the night of the declaration of war".[20] Galsworthy thought it a "fine, generous, big-hearted book",[21] and in Russia, as soon as a copy reached him, Gorki began to translate what he called "the best, boldest, veracious and human book written in Europe in this accursed war!"[22]

Mr Britling, fresh from the flower-show in his village of Matching's Easy, reacts to the outbreak of war in an article as hysterical as that which H.G. had written on that August night. But as, every day, "some new detail of evil beat into his mind", he becomes despondent, then despairing, and then gradually begins to take hope from a new scheme of things in which the League of Free Nations will order the world aright. But Mr Britling no longer has any faith that any good can be done by corrupt and footling politicians. If the individual is to be subordinated to the well-being of the species, the courage needed to bear the trials of the universe can come from nowhere but from belief in "the Master, the Captain of Mankind". This emotional climax was the more telling in its impact on the public because it came from the pen of Wells, the notable agnostic.

Wells had finished *Mr Britling* before his visit to the battlefields, and its success was something to cheer him up as the war news worsened in the autumn of 1916. It tellingly caught the mood of its time, its conclusion an expression of faith at a moment when the British armies were bogged down and the government was on its last legs, about to be brought down by a mixture of its incompetence and Lloyd George's intrigues with the press lords. Wells seemed to be less concerned with strategy and politics than with his own search, in those dreadful months of successive disasters, for a religious faith which could make all the anguish bearable. In *Mr Britling* he announced that he had found it. *God the Invisible King*, published in March 1917, made it clear that he proposed to take charge of it, and act as the self-appointed spokesman for the Captain of Mankind.

The apparent conversion of Wells in *Mr Britling* was a great subject for wartime sermons, but when he came to spell out his new theology it proved to be a conglomeration of old Christian heresies, with the now-familiar Wellsian recipe for saving mankind. Some people thought that he had gone out of his mind. Others, among whom H.G. later counted himself, considered that this was a temporary aberration, induced by the stresses of war and the need for a positive belief to offset despair. Yet the book cannot be dismissed as a maundering deviation. Wells released into it much that, for most of his life, he expressed in secular language that concealed the religious framework of his thought.

The book attacked the concept of the Trinity, replacing it by the idea of a single finite God; in short, God as a person. Christianity, with the doctrine of the Holy Ghost, had attempted to reconcile two different notions of God – one, God as Nature, the Outward God, standing aloof from the men he has created, as the symbol of the Absolute; the other, God as Redeemer, is an Inward God who rules the human heart. God the Father H.G. rejected because he was the Avenging God of his childhood, a figure of fear and retribution and punishment. In the atmosphere of gloomy evangelical conviction Wells had been terrified by the image of the Almighty presented daily by his mother. "He and his Hell were the nightmare of my childhood; I hated him while I still believed in him, and who could help but hate? I thought of him as a fantastic monster, perpetually spying, perpetually listening, perpetually waiting to condemn and to 'strike me dead'; his flames as ready as a grill-room fire." Joe Wells, often absent, and given to outbursts of rage when he was at home, must have done little to mitigate the anxiety aroused in little Bertie when his mother conjured up the fear of the Lord to keep him in the path of righteousness. In that trinity, there was no one to provide the abiding love of strength and forgiveness.

It was understandable that, with such an emotional background, of all the Trinity only God the Son was acceptable. The Redeemer was a finite conception, the "undying human memory, the increasing human will" embodied in the anthropomorphic figure of the Captain of Mankind who will lead all men with austere but brotherly love. The idea of the Superman, first declaimed by the Artilleryman in *The War of the Worlds*, and elaborated in successive novels and tracts, had now been developed into the ultimate metaphor. Wells had never yet spelt out the authoritarian implications of his beliefs so clearly. The new conception, he wrote, does "not tolerate either kings or aristocrats or democracies. Its implicit command to all its adherents is to make plain the way to the world theocracy. Its rule of life is the discovery and service of the will of God . . . and the performance of that will, not only in the private life of the believer but in the acts and order of the state and nation of which he is a part". The individual has no rights against God, whose task as "the invisible King of the whole world" was to impose on mankind the Wellsian version of the New Jerusalem. Later in life H.G. conceded that "by a sort of *coup d'état* I turned my New Republic for a time into a divine monarchy". In the mood of religious search created by the stress of mass slaughter few of his contemporaries noted the messianic overtones of his book. They were either shocked by his seeming conversion, like his old friend William Archer who challenged him in the pamphlet *God and Mr Wells*, or caught up in argument about his doctrinal errors.

This "conversion" broke out again in *The Soul of a Bishop*, which appeared in September 1917. It was an attempt to present his new ideas in fictional form, taking a side-swipe at the established Church in the process. Scrope, Bishop of Princhester, is passing through a spiritual crisis, having lost faith in the Trinity and come to the conclusion that the Church had failed to meet the challenge of the war. After being given a tonic for his depression, he experiences a state of ecstasy in which he receives a new illumination – "the salvation of one human brotherhood under the rule of one Righteousness; the Divine Will". When H.G. was later trying to minimise this theocratic phase, he wrote deprecatingly to a correspondent that "I wilfully tweaked the noses, and pulled the ears and generally insulted 'Christians' in order to wake them up to an examination of their religion. I'm not founding a 'New Religion' or looking for adherents."[23] Yet these books, far from being irrelevant to the main thrust of his ideas, lie very close to it. There was little difference between God the Invisible King and the Mind of the Race which had appeared in *Boon*. One was the overtly theological version of the other.

In 1916 H.G. was writing to Northcliffe about the need for a revolution to come out of the war. In March 1917 it happened, and Wells was among the first to welcome the overthrow of the Tsarist régime. In May he sent Maxim Gorki a letter which reads more like a manifesto, welcoming the revolution as a step in "this struggle to liberate mankind, the German people included, from the net of aggressive monarchy and to establish international goodwill on the basis of international justice and respect".[24]

The declarations of Kerensky and other Russian leaders, who proclaimed their intention to continue the war against German militarism while freeing their people from an autocratic monarchy, were just what Wells wanted to hear. It was proof to him that the time had come to repeat his call for a New Republic. On 21 April, in fact, he had written a letter to *The Times* proposing the formation of a Republican Society "to give some definite expression to the great volume of Republican feeling that has always existed in the British community".

The timing of the letter was provocative – apart from the feeling aroused by the Russian revolution, there were mutinies in the French army and even among the British troops there were clear signs of growing war-weariness. Not long after H.G. wrote this letter, soldiers ran riot in a base camp at Etaples shouting republican slogans. And the immediate reaction to what Wells had suggested was so strong that within two days he felt compelled to disclaim any attack on British royalty. Though "it has been assumed there is some movement afoot for the setting up of Republican institutions here. . . . No such profound changes as these have been advocated. . . . We do not wish to discuss the British monarchy at all." Wells was close enough to the centre of things to know what was going on, and yet he was unable to find any satisfying way of translating the ideas that buzzed in his head into any useful activity. He was more than usually irascible and unsettled. A few days after he had written to *The Times* Bennett ran into him in the Reform, and commented in his journal: "Wells was talking about the after-war exacerbationary reaction on nerves, which would cause rows, quarrels, etc., unless it was consciously kept well in hand."[25] A few months later, Bennett recorded a similar encounter, when "Wells came in, and slanged the Webbs as usual, and incidentally said: 'My boom is over. I've had my boom. I'm yesterday.' " He told Bennett that he was afraid of going to pieces, and that he had been through several air-raids at Leigh-on-Sea, where Rebecca was now living. When the Gotha bombers came over, he stood out on the balcony to conquer his fear. "I get huffy and cross", he said, "just as if . . ." – but Bennett forgot what comparison he had made.[26] H.G. himself said afterwards that at this time he was "baffled and worried beyond measure . . . and my nerves were so fatigued that I was presently afflicted with *allopecia areata*" – a condition related to anxiety which made his hair fall out and left patches of shiny baldness.

All through 1917 Wells was harping on the idea of a League of Free Nations, which might emerge from the war and settle the peace. He had canvassed such an idea in general terms early in the war, and by 1917 a number of public figures were taking the same line. Leonard Woolf and other members of the Bloomsbury group formed a League of Nations Society in 1915, and H.N.Brailsford, the socialist journalist, was also doing much to popularise the idea. Wells certainly claimed no copyright in the idea or the phrase, but by 1917 he was energetically campaigning for it, and in the course of the summer he began to write a series of articles which appeared in the *Daily Chronicle*, the *Daily Mail* and the *Daily News* and were published in the following spring as a book called *In the Fourth Year*. "There is ... no alternative", he wrote in one of these pieces, "if we are to have a satisfactory permanent pacification of the world, but local self-development in these regions under honestly conceived international control of police and transit and trade ... *there is no other way of peace.*"[27]

For Wells, however, the problem was how to find some more effective means of pursuing this objective than merely publishing articles in the newspapers. He was, for a time, active on the "Research Committee" of the League of Free Nations Association, with Gilbert Murray, Wickham Steed, Leonard Woolf, J.A.Spender, J.L.Garvin and others, and he was involved with a Labour Party group working on a policy statement on war aims. But he wanted, above all, a position from which he could exert a direct influence on government.

At the end of 1917, both the political and the military situation had forced Lloyd George to take steps to improve public morale, and among other changes he brought the press lords into his government. In November 1917 Lord Rothermere was made the first Minister of Air; on 10 February 1918 Max Beaverbrook became Minister of Information; and he in turn prevailed on Northcliffe to take on the post of Director of Enemy Propaganda. In May Northcliffe asked Wells to visit him in his office at Crewe House, and invited him to take charge of the Committee for Propaganda in Enemy Country. H.G. began to rehearse his familiar argument that the war must be made the occasion for great changes, "You want a social revolution", Northcliffe replied. "Isn't our sitting here social revolution enough for you?"

It was not. As soon as Wells took on the job he discovered that he was expected to concentrate on propaganda warfare directed at the German army and the civilian population. But he thought this useless unless the Allies clearly stated their aims for the peace – and unless Allied governments were also willing to educate their own peoples in the need for a

constructive settlement. He had already, in November 1917 sent a letter
to this effect to the American diplomat Bainbridge Colby for onward
transmission to President Woodrow Wilson.[28] And though no direct link
can be established between this letter and Wilson's famous "Fourteen
Points" (of which Wells later said he thought "very poorly"), the central
idea of both was similar.

Wells therefore set to work, with a distinguished advisory committee,
to draft a memorandum from Crewe House to the Foreign Office to
advance this argument. It showed astonishing prescience, not only about
the League of Nations that eventually emerged but even, in some respects,
about the United Nations which came out of a similar situation in the
Second World War. Among other ideas it contained proposals for a
trustee system for developing nations and a security council of five or
six great powers who would serve as the custodians of world peace. But
in his enthusiasm, H.G. was naive about the realities of power politics.
He had no knowledge of the secret agreements which Britain had made
during the course of the war, and even less appreciation of the fact that he
and his colleagues were being cynically used as decoys by a government
which had no intention of turning fine phrases into deeds. The memorandum never progressed beyond an evasive discussion with a senior
official at the Foreign Office.

Within a matter of weeks, indeed, H.G. was beginning to feel frustrated,
and on 27 June he wrote directly to Northcliffe to complain of "great
disorganisation, waste and internecine conflict" in the work of Crewe
House.[29] With typical asperity he exhorted Northcliffe to "suppress,
slay, stop, any official obstruction, General Headquarters arrangements,
or freak journalism" which would thwart the plans he had dreamed
up. Crewe House was plainly no place for his idealism, and his irritation
increased as Northcliffe's *Evening News* backed the xenophobic attacks
on the German people launched by a body called the War Aims Committee. "Cannot we get to some better understanding in this matter with
your newspapers", he wrote with irritation to the man who, with one
hand, was supposedly sponsoring an attempt to define reasonable terms
of peace and, with the other, was encouraging his editors in fervent
demagogy to exactly the opposite effect. "Lord Northcliffe of Crewe
House has sent Mr Balfour a very remarkable document indeed, em-
bodying his conception of the Allied war aims. Will he not now induce
Lord Northcliffe of Printing House Square and Carmelite Street to insist
upon that document becoming the guiding memorandum upon foreign

affairs of *The Times*, the *Daily Mail* and the *Evening News*? . . . Under the influence of the War Aims Committee, which does nothing but rant at the Germans and holds out no sort of hope of a happy world after victory, and your penny papers, the country is getting nervy, hopeless, irritable and altogether rotten. We are not developing a victory psychology. We are developing an incoherent pogrom spirit."

Northcliffe refused to rise to the charge that he was two-faced.[30] "Let me say at once", he replied, "that I entirely agree with the policy adopted by my newspapers, which I do not propose to discuss with anyone. I have not wandered about Prussia for two years without learning something, and if you will wait you will find that I will unearth much sinister and active Prussianism in England." Wells, who was quick to pounce on inconsistency in an opponent, was not prepared to let him get away with such duplicity. "I am sorry that you insist upon being two people when God has only made you one", H.G. wrote back: "I cannot, for my own part, separate the *Evening News* from Crewe House while you remain one person." The disillusionment had as usual been quick, and when a young man of German descent was forced to leave the staff of Crewe House, Wells treated this as the excuse to resign himself.

Wells took nothing away from his brief spell of government service but a sense of futility, and his mood of frustration found expression in *Joan and Peter*, published in the autumn of 1918. It was an unpleasant book, turgid, didactic and cantankerous: one critic called it a "hymn of hate". It covered the years from 1893 to 1918, and though it was notionally the story of the education of Joan and Peter the book was dominated by the sour-tempered diatribes of Oswald, the scientist, empire-builder and educator. Oswald is a disappointed man, who vents his spleen on everything and everyone – the monarchy, the army, the churches, pacifists and schoolteachers, on "that fool" Sir Edward Carson and that "bumptious little Welsh solicitor" Lloyd George, on Gothic architecture, Home Rule and the party system. H.G. had been living through a world disaster, and after four years his accumulated resentment at the "uneducated block-heads" who had caused it – and who still refused to heed his warnings – poured out in a torrent of recrimination.

The word "uneducated" was significant. Wells had now come to the conclusion that "the war was an educational breakdown . . . and in education lay whatever hope there was for mankind". He had tried politics; he had tried to reach men's minds through the metaphors of fiction; he had sought to sway public opinion by journalism. The last hope lay in what had been the first of his occupations. He must again become a teacher, but a teacher-at-large to the human race, driven by the immensity and urgency of his new task. "We've got to live like fanatics", said Peter. "If a lot of us don't live like fanatics, this staggering old world of ours won't recover. It will stagger and then go flop." H.G.'s sense of impending disaster had not been purged by the experience of living through one. "Everything is going to rack and ruin", Peter says, "driving straight to an absolute and final smash . . . It's the appalling waste, the waste in *us*, the waste of everything."

SALVATION BY HISTORY

"I think for a time I must give up all League of Nations work", Wells wrote to Gilbert Murray in the spring of 1919. "Not for pique, but because I feel physically unable to go on with it. This Committee work fills me with a horror of great darkness. I scarcely slept at all last night & I can do no work today."[1] At the same time he wrote a rather less guarded note to Philip Guedalla. "I'm ill and oh! how the L of N gatherings bore me ... I wish I could kill Bryce; he's the damndest old fool alive – except Asquith."[2]

It was not merely the tedium of sitting through long meetings that was irritating H.G., nor even the fussy wrangles with Lord Bryce and other scholars about points of detail. To Wells, these were pedantic quibblers, holding up the grand design for world organisation that he had hoped would come out of the war. His impatience stemmed from a combination of nervous tension and growing awareness that the victorious Allies had no intention of sacrificing their national interests in a magnanimous and imaginative peace. He was almost as disillusioned with his fellow-members of the League of Nations Association as he was with the cynical statesmen who were beginning to draft the treaty at Versailles. His colleagues, he felt, were too eager to snatch at the shadow of a League and ignore the fact that its substance was a swindle.

The decision to break with this group was only an outward sign of an inner decision that had been maturing during the last year of the war. The attempt to work through the politicians and the professors to build a new world order was ineffective and frustrating. H.G. had come to the conclusion that he must use his talents as a writer to reach past them to the public, taking upon himself almost single-handed the task of bringing the world to its senses. "I'm naturally a solitary worker", his letter to Gilbert Murray continued. "Team work for me is like using a razor to carve marble. It's really the best use I can make of myself now to get out of all the . . . acutely disappointing distressing stuff & go on with individual work again. For some time I've thought of writing an Outline of History as a sort of experiment . . . I believe the *History of Man* can be taught as easily as the *History of England* & that a world educated in [illegible] history will be a different & better world altogether."

The idea of "salvation by history" had already been put forward explicitly in the last novel H.G. had written during the war – the modern-dress version of the Book of Job which he called *The Undying Fire* and published in 1919. It was a forceful "dialogue" book, in which Job's modern counterpart, Jacob Huss, triumphs over his tribulations to discover that the "substance of all real education is to teach men and women the Battle of God . . . to show them how man has arisen through the long ages from amidst the beasts". The Captain of Mankind has been replaced by the Great Teacher. The sole hope for the survival of the species lies in knowledge, and the means to that knowledge is education.

He had always felt the need to tell that message, and the "general account of man's story in the universe" that he now proposed to write was merely the most systematic and ambitious of his attempts to satisfy it. He had first discussed the theme in his talk to the Debating Society at South Kensington on the "Past and Present of the Human Race", set in its evolutionary context. *The Time Machine* had been a first imaginative attempt to produce a comprehensive outline of man's place in the world. As far back as November 1901, after the success of *Anticipations*, H.G. had written to Simmons to say that he thought "there are people in the world who would stand a whole book of me, pungent, detailed, elaborated & complete, on education . . . It would be a year of pretty steady work for me . . . the devil is to make it pay. I will *not* do work for nothing if I can help it."[3]

By 1918 H.G. felt confident enough, emotionally compelled, and sufficiently prosperous to realise this lifelong dream. The capital of £20,000 with which he had started the war had been depleted by investment losses and heavy spending, but *Mr Britling* had amply replenished it. There was no financial reason why he should not risk a year's work on a project that seemed unlikely to pay its way. Only a writer who was "by nature and choice as remote from academic respect as he is from a duke-dom", Wells wrote of himself in *The New Teaching of History*, "a literary Bedouin, whose home is the great outside", would be so presumptuous as to take on such an immense task. It is a mark of his emotional commitment that H.G. was willing to face both the labour involved and the risk that he would be torn to pieces by his critics. When he began, H.G. already knew that the design was secure, because it had been shaped in his mind for nearly thirty years, and the essential arguments had been rehearsed repeatedly in his fiction and his journalism. His only concern was whether he had the energy to assimilate the mass of detail needed to support the arguments, and to form it into a manageable and readable text. Though he had a quick mind and a retentive memory, he recognised that the project was beyond his unaided capacity.

By the autumn of 1918 he had worked out his plan for the project. An outline went off to Macmillan's in New York on 20 October, and H.G. had already set about enlisting associates who would give him both reassurance and some practical assistance. Though he was feeling frustrated by the "Research Committee", he asked such colleagues as Ernest Barker and Gilbert Murray for help, and he also recruited the scientist Sir Ray Lankester, the former colonial civil servant Sir Harry Johnstone, and the historical biographer Philip Guedalla. In a letter on 5 June 1919 he was quite frank with Murray about what he wanted. It was "checking back and support", and Murray was to provide this for the classical period.[4]

What I want you to do is to blue pencil howlers and to note serious . . . omissions in your own regions of special interest . . . This book will rouse everybody in the history textbook & history teaching line to blind fury. It is a serious raid into various departments of special knowledge (and my God! how badly they do it!) . . . There will be a sustained attempt to represent me as an ignorant interloper & dispose of me in that way. Well, what I want is to be able to name some indisputable names on the title page . . . It will be a new sort of history that will twist the minds of its readers round towards a new set of values. There's really nothing more to be done with our present public until its ideas about history are changed.

Murray and the others who agreed to come in on the scheme soon found themselves hard driven by Wells. Most of the work was done initially by himself and Jane, often working long hours at a stretch, pillaging references and blending them up into a smooth mixture – the principal ingredient being the *Encyclopaedia Britannica*, with large gobbets drawn from Winwood Reade's old classic, *The Martyrdom of Man*, Robinson's *Mediaeval and Modern Times*, Fairfield Osborne's book on primitive man, Holt's *World History* and Church's *Botanical Memoirs*.

Frank Horrabin, who had been enlisted as illustrator, map-maker and general factotum, spent several days at a time down at Easton Glebe.[5] H.G. would work furiously until lunch, when he would relax, and then take a chatty stroll across Lady Warwick's grounds. After tea, there would be joint work until dinner, and H.G. would afterwards play cards or turn out some tunes on the pianola before going off to bed with several books tucked under his arm. On one occasion, Horrabin recalled, H.G. finished a spell of writing and came out of his study chanting "Here we come over the High Pamirs – and mix with the Aryan peoples".

The jingle was a neat summary of the book, as H.G. plotted the great movements of races and religions, the fusion and the fall of cultures, and the futility of great men. When the book was done he put its central theme succinctly in an article in the monthly magazine of the League of Nations Union.[6]

No one has ever attempted to teach our children the history of man as Man, with all his early struggles and triumphs . . . his specialization in tribes and nations, his conquests of Nature, his creations of Art, his building up of Science . . . an enormous amount of work has to be done if we are to teach the peoples of the world what is the truth, viz., that they are all engaged in a common work, that they have sprung from common origins, and are all contributing some special service to the general end.

What H.G. originally planned as an essay on the concept of European unity now stretched out in all directions, becoming a scheme as vast in its way as the *Cosmology* of Humboldt which had so influenced him as a child. The associates received drafts, sent back comments, received new versions, and then page proofs.

Ernest Barker recognised that Wells had no training as a historian, and felt that he had no inner sympathy with other times and ideas, and no scholarly passion for the truth. All the same, Barker and the other helpers were carried along by the sweep and vigour of the work which, when it was completed, Arnold Toynbee called "a magnificent intellectual achievement".[7] Though there were many willing to point out the errors H.G. had made when, as Toynbee put it, "in his long journey through Time and Space" he happened "to traverse their tiny allotments", they seemed not to realise that "in re-living the entire life of Mankind as a single emotional experience, Mr Wells was achieving something which they themselves would hardly have dared to attempt".

The enthusiasm of Toynbee, which was matched by the admiration of such distinguished historians as H.A.L.Fisher, Carl Becker and Carlton J.H.Hayes,[8] was understandable, for the underlying argument of *The Outline* was very close to that which Toynbee later advanced in his own *A Study of History*. H.G. insisted that there was a rhythm in the historical process – nations rise and fall much as species become dominant and decline in biological evolution. But the rise of a nation is due to the presence of a creative ruling élite – predecessors, so to speak, of his New Republicans and Samurai – which is capable of making an imaginative response to the challenge of its times. Then bureaucratic castes take over: the "community of will" which has inspired progress becomes a "community of faith and obedience" which enslaves and exploits the masses, and degeneration begins. The society is then threatened by barbarians, and because it has lost the will to save itself it disintegrates or succumbs to its conquerors.

The parallel between this cycle and contemporary events was not lost on Wells. It might, indeed, be truer to say that he had projected back into history his reading of the history of his own times – a reading which had provided the background to all his books. The industrial and scientific revolution of the previous century, brought about by men of spirit and vision, had failed to fulfil its promise because it had occurred in a world that was divided into competing nation states ruled by narrow-minded oligarchs. The phase of degeneration had begun, the barbarians were at the gates, and the human race was now threatened with the choice between disaster – all the more terrible because the engines of destruction were now world-wide in their effects – and the adaptation which could be achieved only by the emergence of a new educated and creative élite.

Wells had thus summoned up the whole human past as an argument for his vision of the future, forging the link by an interpretation of history which accorded precisely with his own dualism – and with the dialectic of ethics and evolution (or ideas and instincts) which he had taken over from T.H. Huxley. The drive to adaptation and survival found expression in the constructive civilising process, in the emergence of a world consciousness and the world state which alone held out a hope of salvation for the species. The atavistic drive to destruction, reflected in national rivalries and racial passions, would, unchecked, obliterate mankind and turn the earth into a dying wilderness. In this struggle between the life-force and the death-wish, H.G. had come forward as the prophet of righteousness, and *The Outline* was his testament. When the book finally appeared that point was immediately taken by Sidney Dark.[9] Wells, he suggested, had felt an unconscious need to provide an alternative to the Bible, retelling the story of mankind in secular terms. Now he satisfied that need with an epic that began with the Creation and ended with a vision of the New Jerusalem.

The completion of *The Outline*, H.G. told Bennett in November 1919, had taken "more than a year of fanatical toil". That was merely to produce the part-work version that appeared in twenty-five instalments, and beyond that he had the task of producing the book and then the popular summary, *A Short History of the World*, which was published in 1920. One way and another, he was at it for three years, and at the end had written more than 750,000 words. "How the fellow did the book in the time fair passes me", Bennett wrote to Jane Wells on 22 January 1920: "I cannot get over it. It's a life work." It was not merely the physical effort that impressed Bennett. In this same letter he declared that *The Outline* "was the most useful thing of the kind ever done, and it is jolly well done".[10] There could be no doubt that Wells had found a new market, and one that was far larger than anything that he had expected when he planned *The Outline*. The parts were selling steadily at a 100,000 print, and bringing in much money. Early in April 1920, when Bennett lunched with Swinnerton and Wells, he told H.G. jocularly that he ought to spend some of the proceeds on a new suit. H.G. replied that the profits were ruining him with income tax.

As soon as the book came out it was clear that the new venture was going to be an immense money-spinner, and in the next few years it ran to over two million copies in America and England alone, apart from numerous and continuing foreign translations. It was making Wells far more wealthy than he had ever been before. His fear that, by devoting himself to this work, he would "risk dropping below the novel-reader's horizon – for good", proved to be irrelevant. He could now afford to write whatever he pleased without worrying about the financial return. There were, inevitably, specialists who drew attention to mistakes and omissions, and H.G. was quick to note where changes were required for later editions. There were some, like Hilaire Belloc, who thought the book superficial and prejudiced, especially in its attacks on the Catholic Church. But on the whole H.G. got off lightly, and the criticism was trivial by comparison with the praise. The prophet was no longer without honour in his own country, and his charismatic appeal had begun to spread throughout the world.

The growing influence of Wells was a particular annoyance to one old friend, the playwright Henry Arthur Jones, to whom in 1909 he had offered to sell Spade House. In September 1920 Jones had read an article in the *Daily Mail* which observed that "Wells today is thinking for half

Europe" and he dashed off a hysterical letter to H.G. complaining that his influence was dangerous because he had good words to say for the "junta of desperadoes" who ruled Bolshevik Russia. Jones, like Wells, had begun life as a draper's apprentice, and during the pre-war years they had got on pleasantly together – though Jones was drifting towards a peppery conservatism. During the war, Jones had become a super-patriot and conducted a long vendetta against Shaw's sceptical view of the Allied cause. When the war was over he turned on Wells in a book called *Patriotism and Popular Education* which denounced H.G. for "mischievous fallacies" and schemes which threatened to undermine the British Empire. When he found Wells cautiously sympathetic to the Soviet régime, he started a new diatribe which lasted for more than a year, exacerbated by the fact that Wells had decided to pay a brief visit to Russia to see the state of affairs for himself.

H.G. had consistently argued after 1917 that the Allies would be wise to take a reasonable line towards the Bolsheviks, and that military intervention and a blockade were folly. He had kept in touch with Maxim Gorki, who had written several times to assure Wells that much that was said about the Bolsheviks was untrue.[11] "I do not close my eyes", Gorki had said in one letter, "to the negative results of war and revolution – but I see on the other side how awakens in the Russian masses the creative power, how the people gradually becomes an active force." Gorki assured H.G. that Lenin was utterly unlike the stories printed about him in western newspapers. "Lenin is free from any intoxication with his power. By nature he is a Puritan, lives in the Kremlin just as simply and quietly as he did in Paris when an emigrant. He is a great man, and an honest man, as much as a politician can be honest. In Russia he has played the part of the colossal plough which indefatigably ploughs a soil polluted, sterile." In another letter Gorki had asked Wells to organise a supply of fats and sugar for Russian scientists who were starving through the winter of 1919–20. "Of course", he said, "it is necessary to spare the feelings of pride and dignity of these splendid men. They must not know that I have asked you to help them."

Gorki had suggested that the "best thing would be if some Englishman would bring them himself – grease and sweet things above everything", and it may have been these words that had sparked off the idea of a visit by Wells himself. The visit was planned for the latter part of September, and H.G. proposed to take his elder son, Gip, with him. He had already decided that it was preferable for his sons to learn Russian rather than classics, and during the preceding year Gip had been given special coaching by "Kot" – the emigré S.S.Kotelianski, who, as a publisher, later persuaded H.G. to write his autobiography.

When H.G. and Gip arrived in Petrograd, their main contact was Gorki, though they also met Pavlov, Chaliapin, the Bolshevik leaders Zinoviev, Chicherin and Lenin himself, and Wells was paid the unusual compliment of an invitation to address the Petrograd Soviet. Much of the time was spent in wandering about the city, faded and grey with poverty compared to the St Petersburg Wells remembered from his visit in 1914, and – as he described it in the articles he later published as the book *Russia in the Shadows* – profoundly depressing. Their guide was an old acquaintance, the young Marie von Benckendorff whom Wells had met in 1914, a handsome, intelligent girl, whose husband had been shot in the course of the revolution. She herself had become involved with Robert Bruce-Lockhart, whose activities in the Soviet capital are described in the famous *Memoirs of a British Agent*, in which she appears as "Moura". She had been arrested and imprisoned in the Kremlin for her part in the so-called "Lockhart plot" to overthrow the Bolshevik régime. On her release, she had found a job with Gorki as his secretary and adviser in translations.

The focus of the visit, however, was the journey to Moscow to meet Lenin. No verbatim account of this interview was ever published, and the only two sources are the versions given by Wells and by Leon Trotsky, who was not present but who later published a vituperative attack on the article Wells called "The Dreamer in the Kremlin". It was clearly an unsatisfying exchange on both sides, Wells remarking afterwards that he had found it "a very uphill argument" and that "our multifarious argumentation ended indecisively". Lenin talked about the hopelessness of trying to reform the capitalist system, and about his dream of modernising Russia by a vast scheme of electrification. H.G. apparently took it upon himself to expound his own conception of evolutionary collectivism, and his belief that a huge educational campaign was an essential condition for any reconstruction of the old order. Trotsky's long polemic added very little to the facts, beyond the claim that Lenin's summary of the conversation afterwards was "Ugh! What a narrow petty bourgeois! Ugh! What a Philistine!"[12]* Even the praise which Wells gave to Lenin, for "his frank

* After his return, Wells busied himself with a scheme whereby the Royal Society and the British Academy were to send scientific books to help their Russian colleagues, cut off by years of war and blockade.

admission of the immensity and complication of the project of Communism and his simple concentration upon its realization", was twisted by Trotsky into an example of bourgeois condescension.

Trotsky's attack on Wells was just as hysterical and unfair as the outburst from Henry Arthur Jones which Wells had to face on his return home. He had sought to occupy some reasonable ground between the Bolsheviks and the frenetic anti-Communism of the English and American press. He wrote to Gorki from Easton Glebe on 21 December 1920:

I have done all I can to make our people here realize that the Soviet government is a government of human beings and not a peculiar emanation from the Nether World, and I think I have done a good deal in one way and another to make civilized relations between the two sides of Europe more possible. I am having the book sent to you. You will see that I have not flattered the Bolsheviks. To have done so would have absolutely defeated the purpose of the book.

But this commonsense position satisfied neither Soviet apologists nor those concerned only to overthrow Lenin's régime. The Communists disliked his revelation that the Soviet system was on the verge of collapse, and his critics detested the fact that he had seen signs of hope, not least in the powerful personality of Lenin. Even Shaw thought that H.G. had decided that Lenin was really a New Republican and that he might eventually establish something like a Wellsian utopia.

It was Jones, however, who really harassed H.G.[13] by sending a stream of frenzied letters. "A special thud in the mornings", H.G. said, "always represented another bomb from Jones." He also wrote to the *New York Times* and the *Morning Post*, accusing Wells of whitewashing the Bolsheviks. The fuss Jones raised drew a more substantial opponent into the controversy. Though Wells had no use for what he called the "poor muddled and I fear afflicted mind" of Jones, the comments of Winston Churchill were a different matter.

In December 1920 Churchill opened his attack on Wells in an article in the *Daily Express*. He had been one of the most vigorous promoters of the anti-Bolshevik campaign, and since he was well aware that Wells had acquired a substantial influence on public opinion he had no intention of allowing H.G. to arouse sympathy for Lenin and his system. "When one has written a history of the world from nebula to the Third International and of the human race from protoplasm to Lord Birkenhead in about a twelve month", Churchill sarcastically observed, "there ought to be no difficulty in becoming an expert on the internal conditions of Russia after a visit of fourteen days." H.G. came back at once, to say that to Churchill it must have seemed "an act of insolence that a common man like myself should form judgments upon matters of statecraft ... But Mr Churchill not only poses as a statesman; he is accepted as such. He is the running sore of waste in our Government ... He has smeared his vision with human blood and we are implicated in the things he abets."

The exchange with Churchill, unfortunately for Wells, goaded Jones to even greater excitement, sending one letter in the course of which he sustained a joint attack on Shaw and Wells for a single sentence which ran for three pages. His inability to get any reaction from either of them drove Jones to collect his tirades into a fatuous book entitled *My Dear Wells*. He had got hold of a letter H.G. had written to Sinclair Lewis, saying "don't write me down a Bolshevik. I'm a Wilsonite ... For the first time in my life there is a man in the world that I am content to follow." H.G. had then gone on to say that "Lenin, I can assure you, is a little beast ... just a Russian Sidney Webb, a rotten little incessant egotistical intriguer ..." Jones quoted this as proof that Wells had become disillusioned with Lenin, but when H.G. replied in the *Morning Post* he pointed out that the reference to Lenin and Webb had been in a letter written to Lewis some considerable time before his visit to Russia, and that he had since formed "a better estimate" of Lenin.

Wells was more embarrassed by the publication of his spiteful remarks about Sidney Webb, and he was reduced to the unconvincing excuse – at least to those who knew the inner history of his feud with the Webbs – that in "private discussions, in letters and little caricatures, it has been my habit to guy him and abuse him grotesquely ... Will you permit me here to tell Mr Sidney Webb that . . . I have the utmost respect and admiration for the great mass of fine work he and Mrs Webb have done ... and for the lives of sustained and unselfish toil they have lived for the community."

H.G. was all the more sensitive about the raking up of the old quarrel since he had recently taken steps to bury it. On 29 November 1920 Beatrice Webb had noted in her diary: "We are reconciled to H.G. Wells. He sent me his *History* with an inscription; I wrote a friendly acknowledgement; which he bettered in reply." An invitation to dinner followed, and she had found him "fat and prosperous and immensely self-congratulatory; towards us he was affable; but suspicion lurked in his eye and I doubt whether he is really friendly". Nor did Beatrice "desire any renewal of friendship. But", she added, "I am too near to the end of life to care to keep up a vendetta with any human being. Also I have never ceased to respect his work, and his *History* is a gallant achievement."

Wells had been driving himself hard all through 1920. Apart from the continuing work on the history, and the Russian trip, he had started to write *The Secret Places of the Heart* and he was working on a series of lectures that he proposed to deliver in the course of an American tour in December and January. These drafts, eventually published in *The Salvaging of Civilization*, went over familiar ground once again, advancing the case for a world state and for ambitious educational schemes. Two of the chapters, however, were devoted to a new proposal – what Wells called "The Bible of Civilization". It was a restatement of the great plan of Johan Comenius, the Czech contemporary of John Milton, who had put forward the idea of a "common book, a book of history, science and wisdom, which should form the basis and framework for the thoughts and imaginations of every citizen of the world".

To H.G. this seemed the next logical step from his *Outline*, and it was a notion which he revived at intervals throughout the remainder of his life. He did not propose to compile it himself. Most of it, indeed, was to consist of extracts from the great works of religion and literature, to which modern savants would add the latest advances of human knowledge. This project has sometimes been cited as proof that Wells saw himself as a *philosophe*, a system-maker who would animate a contemporary version of the work of Diderot and the Encyclopaedists. There is, of course, a good deal to the comparison, but the scheme that Wells drafted shows that the model in his mind was more the Bible itself.[14] It was "to begin with the Historical Books, and to move through the Books of Conduct and Wisdom and the Anthologies of Poetry and Literature to the last significant section, the Book of Forecasts, taking the place of Prophets and Revelations".

The grandiose plan was there, but H.G. did not have the energy to push it. He could not even go to the United States to canvass it publicly, for in December 1920 a cold developed into congestion of the lungs and the lecture tour was cancelled. H.G. was thought to be too poorly to face the English winter, and he was sent off to the sunshine in Italy. On 21 January he scribbled a note to Bennett from Paris, on his way to Amalfi with "a warm-hearted secretary" who "will look after me night and day", saying that he was taking a rest for two months.[15]

H.G. came back to Easton early in March, bringing with him the manuscript of *The New Teaching of History*, the pamphlet in which he replied to some critics of *The Outline*, and the plan for *A Short History of the World* which was to be done that summer. But these were merely a carry-over of the momentum of the last two years. Once again physical illness was linked to a sustained period of overwork and to a psychic crisis. When H.G. returned to England, he was in better health but he was like a machine without oil, driven compulsively to work yet unable to work except in short bursts, and grinding himself to death in the process.

The metaphor was his own, though he applied it to Sir Richmond Hardy, the main character in *The Secret Places of the Heart*, who turns to the psychiatrist Dr Martineau for help because his life has become meaningless. This novel reveals that by the end of 1920, and despite his recent success and increasing wealth and prestige, H.G. was in a desperate state of mind – as restless and uncertain of himself as he had been during earlier crises in his career. Hardy, like Wells himself, wants to impose order on a chaotic world, and is deeply frustrated because he cannot get others to co-operate with him in preventing "the break-up of the entire system". He is disillusioned, and personally unhappy, not least because he cannot solve his own sexual problems. Hardy dreams of "some extravagantly beautiful inspiration called love", but something always goes wrong. He sees women as a vital source of energy, and says that "often I cared nothing for the woman I made love to. I cared for the thing she seemed to be hiding from me." His affairs, he tells Martineau, "are at once unsatisfying and vitally necessary". He no longer finds his current mistress satisfying, and when Martineau takes him off on holiday he seizes the occasion to pick up a young American girl – and then finds himself torn between this new infatuation and feelings of guilt about his obligations to his mistress. Though he decides to return to the mistress, this provides no relief from his gnawing death-wish, and he dies soon afterwards.

Wells, like Richmond Hardy, saw women as a vital source of energy and turned to them for stimulation when he was in trouble. Whenever the frustrations of his life became unbearable, increasing his forebodings of death, he sought renewal in relationships with younger women who seemed to have the elusive secret of life. This is what lay behind his impulsive responses to the fascination of women – and even when he was involved in a serious emotional relationship an attack of depression could push him towards what Hardy called an "unsatisfying but vitally necessary" *passade*. There had been many episodes of this kind in his life, as he admitted in his autobiography when he wrote of them as "frequent escapades of a Don Juan among the intelligentsia". Only a few of these developed into significant affairs: some were the most casual flirtations. The difficulty about them all, Wells conceded, was that there was no way of knowing where any beginning might lead. "The casual lover", he wrote, "loves always on a slippery slope." By the time he reached middle life the habit of flirtation had become ingrained, and his reputation for it undoubtedly enhanced his attraction for some women and made it easier for him to look for this kind of relief when he was troubled. He seems to have been unaware, on some occasions, whether he was merely teasing a new acquaintance or taking the first steps on "a slippery slope".

In the summer of 1920 he had discovered a close affinity with an American woman, Margaret Sanger, then in her middle thirties, who had already made a reputation as a feminist and campaigner for birth control. A contemporary described her as "very beautiful, with wide-apart grey eyes and a crown of auburn hair, combining a radiant feminist appeal with an impression of serenity, calm and graciousness", but with this charm went a romantic, rebellious and assertive personality. She looked, talked and behaved like a Wells heroine, and he was immediately attracted.[16] In 1912, chafing at the mediocrity of her marriage, she had moved into the radical bohemia of New York, becoming a close friend of Emma Goldman, Mabel Dodge, John Reed and Eugene Debs, and had started her own paper, the *Woman Rebel*. She had been imprisoned for challenging the "Comstock" law preventing the advocacy of birth control. By 1920 her marriage had ended in divorce, and she made a brief trip to England to renew her contacts with the birth-control movement. When H.G. was planning to visit New York at Christmas-time that year he wrote to propose a rendezvous with her in New York, saying "I'll want sadly to bolt from the crowd", but when his illness forced him to cancel his lecture tour he told her that "our hopes evaporate" and that he looked forward to a later arrival.[17]

This was to come in the following year, when H.G. was commissioned by the *New York World* and the *Daily Mail* to cover the Washington Conference on disarmament. But in the intervening months Wells was distracted and unwell, and no more able to settle his work and his personal affairs than he had been in the previous years. There was no great change in the routines of life, and he was enjoying the social rewards of success, yet he was drifting, still lacking a purpose which could absorb him and increasingly uneasy about the way his life was organised. In 1921, moreover, his old friend Tommy Simmons died. H.G.'s immediate, and characteristically generous, reaction was to send the widow six hundred pounds to tide her over her immediate difficulties. He had never been slow to help an acquaintance, and as he grew wealthier there were increasing calls on his purse. In 1921 he wrote to E.S.P.Haynes saying that he would rather be left out of some charitable effort if Haynes could raise the money elsewhere as "I'm being pressed on various sides for similar efforts". His former wife Isabel, whom he had continued to assist financially – even after her death he gave money to her second husband – wanted something over a thousand pounds as capital to start a laundry. There were, he told Haynes, school bills and other expenses to pay for Amber's daughter, and an "old fellow-student who runs a motor factory is in difficulties. All these transactions mean a fearful lot of looking into & bother . . . & the prospect of selling out securities & going into these various difficult & unfamiliar investments just gives me a hot head. Can't you manage?"[18]

By the autumn of 1921 H.G. was glad to get away to the United States for two months. His extensive reports on the conference in Washington were made the vehicle for another series of essays on the need for an effective world organisation of peace, but he was so outraged by the intransigence of the French that his articles became increasingly distasteful to Northcliffe, then supporting the hard line taken by France. Wells soon discovered that on Northcliffe's instructions the *Daily Mail* was censoring his despatches, first omitting paragraphs and then a complete article. He not only sent irate cables back to London, but induced the *New York World* to take issue with the *Mail* for attempting to dictate what he should say. Before the conference was over, Max Beaverbrook – recalling that the reports Wells had written on Russia had sent up the circulation of the *Sunday Express* by more than 80,000 – intervened and bought Wells away from the *Mail*.

The row had made H.G. anxious to get away for some relaxation, and on 7 December he wrote to Margaret Sanger from Washington that "my plans in New York are ruled entirely by the wish to be with you as much as possible – *& as much as possible without other people about*. I don't mind paying thousands of dollars if I can get that – I'm really quite well off you know . . . If I take that apartment could you come to me there abundantly? . . . You know how things are in N.Y. & the risks & dangers that are about you. It's much better that you arrange than that I do . . . I just want to sit about with you in the costume of a tropical island more than anything else in the world . . . everything else is secondary to that." After

H.G. left for Spain, where he met Rebecca for a long winter vacation in the sun, he continued to correspond with Margaret Sanger. In 1922 she was back in England and Wells invited her down to Easton. Cornelia Otis Skinner found "Mrs Birth Control Sanger" as one of the house-party which she described in *Our Hearts Were Young and Gay*, giving one of the wittiest of all accounts of the way H.G. and Jane still entertained their guests at the Glebe.

In November of that year, Margaret Sanger secretly married an oil tycoon named J.Noah H.Slee who was twenty years older than herself. It was a bizarre marital arrangement whereby Mr Slee would keep both her and her movement in funds, yet leave her free to have her own domicile and social arrangements, and even to retain her own now celebrated name. It was not unlike the situation that H.G. had created for himself. Over the years she became a close and good friend to H.G. He found enormous pleasure in her company. "Wonderful! Unforgettable" was how he described one meeting.

Since the Fabian fiasco before the war, Wells had taken no direct part in politics, though many of his friends were closely involved in the Labour movement and, down at Easton Lodge, Lady Warwick was making her home a centre for Labour Party and trade union meetings. Yet H.G.'s advocacy of the League of Nations, and his sympathy towards the Russian revolution, had gradually restored some of the links with the Left which had been broken by his intemperate chauvinism in the early years of the war. As the Labour Party began to gain ground and prove itself "fit to rule", Wells came to see it as something more than a creature of the trade unions. It seemed to him the only party which offered a positive remedy for "this progressive break-up of civilized organization that is going on". Early in 1922 he became a member of the party, and in May he agreed to run as Labour candidate for Lord Rector of Glasgow University – a contest in which he ran third to Lord Birkenhead and Sir John Simon. The decision shows that, temporarily at least, he was looking for some means of exerting a direct influence on politics, and for a while he talked of dropping his other work in order to write propaganda for the Labour Party. In November 1921, indeed, he was persuaded to run as the Labour candidate for the parliamentary seat of London University, endorsed by a cluster of socialist notabilities such as Harold Laski, Eileen Power, and both Beatrice and Sidney Webb. He came bottom of the poll, but the Tory government soon fell and at the next general election which came a year later, giving Labour enough seats to form its first minority government, H.G. again stood unsuccessfully in the Labour interest.

The *Daily News* invited Hilaire Belloc and G.K.Chesterton to comment on Wells as a candidate. "In morals, temperament, instruction and type of oratory", Belloc remarked ironically, "I know him to be admirably suited for the House of Commons." Chesterton made much the same point. "The question is not whether Wells is fit for Parliament", he said, "but whether Parliament is fit for Wells. I don't think it is. If he had a good idea, the last place in the world he would be allowed to talk is the House of Commons." But Wells had waged his campaign solely for propaganda purposes, and once Labour had taken office he felt that he had done enough. In any case, he had now become as disillusioned with the Labour Party as he had been with his previous ventures in organised politics. None of them had proved amenable to his will, or been willing to serve as the instrument for his plans for reconstructing the world on a grand scale, and nothing less than that was acceptable to him.

He had, in any case, been diverted into another task. In the summer of 1922, H.G. was presiding at a public lecture given by his friend F.W. Sanderson, the headmaster of Oundle School whose educational views he greatly admired, when Sanderson suddenly dropped dead on the platform. H.G. agreed to compile a memoir of Sanderson, both from affection and because it offered him a chance to restate his own views on education. But he ran into difficulties with Sanderson's widow, who objected that his draft failed to do justice to her husband's scholarship.[19] After a troublesome correspondence he made a number of amendments which left him so dissatisfied with the project that he went over the ground again and brought out a less constrained biography which he called *The Story of a Great Schoolmaster*.

The effort that Wells devoted to the Sanderson memoir, at a time when he was also writing *Men Like Gods*, shows that he was still capable of consistent work, and outwardly life went on much as before. He had signed a lucrative contract with the McClure syndicate for a weekly column, the collected articles being published later as *A Year of Prophesying*, and he was much in demand as a guest for luncheons, dinners, and country weekends. He was still on good terms with Lady Elcho, now Lady Wemyss. He was an old friend of Sybil, Lady Colefax, who with Lady Cunard and Ottoline Morrell, was one of the leading hostesses of the Twenties. Leonard Woolf called Sybil Colefax an "unabashed hunter of lions", and H.G. was among those she liked to entertain at Argyll House.[20]

Yet there was no cohesion in his life, or in his work. The articles he wrote were stale with repetition of familiar arguments, and he was beginning to discover that his impact on public opinion was declining in inverse proportion to his output and his income. This state of affairs, Rebecca West believed, "was inevitable in view of the life we were living".[21] His usual programme, she said, "was a feverish week-end at Easton, from Monday to Tuesday in the London flat, two days with me, two days at London again, back to Easton. He was then very chesty and in poor condition, and often in a pitiful state of overwork and exhaustion. Of course it was death to his writing. And in the end it made him quarrelsome, not just with me but with such people as tollkeepers and ticket-collectors, and very vain, ridiculously so at times."

The strain and the vanity had become obvious to others besides Rebecca. In July 1923 when Sidney and Beatrice Webb were down at Easton Lodge for a social week-end arranged by Lady Warwick for the newly elevated Labour leaders and their wives, they stayed at the Glebe. Beatrice saw little apparent difference in H.G., though she had remarked after a visit in April that he had "coarsened". She noted in her diary that Jane "had won through a terrible ordeal and come out the mistress of her circumstances."[22]

He is the same brilliant talker and pleasant companion – except that he orates more than he used to do and listens less intelligently. . . . He is far too conscious of literary success, measured in great prices for books and articles – he has become a sort of "little God" demanding payment in flattery as well as in gold, for his very marketable goods and he has grown contemptuous of his customers. Moreover, he has another and even more damaging consciousness – he feels himself to be a chartered libertine. Everyone knows he is a polygamist and everyone puts up with it. He is aware of this acquiescence in his sins – an acquiescence accompanied with contempt. And this contemptuous acquiescence on the part of friends and acquaintances results in Wells having a contempt for all of us, because we disapprove, and yet associate with him. In short, he feels he has *imposed himself – sins and all – on the world by the sheer force of his knowledge and marketable genius.*

The malaise that was repressed, or at least concealed, during the jovial week-ends at the Glebe, was gaining ground. As he neared sixty, he was still unfulfilled for all his triumphs. "I was", he wrote of himself at this period, "oppressed by a sense of encumbrance in my surroundings and of misapplied energy and time running to waste."

BEGINNING AGAIN

Wells knew his own moods well enough to recognise the symptoms of the claustrophobia which enveloped him when he came to a crisis in his life. They began with a feeling of discontent, followed by a restlessness which drove him in a near-panic to seek refuge in flight into a new dream-world. He was quite explicit about this, noting that it had happened when he fled from Hyde's Emporium, when he ran away from Isabel, at the time of his intended elopement with Amber, and again in the early Twenties. "At phase after phase", he noted, "I find myself saying in effect: 'I must get out of this. I must get clear. I must get away from all this and think and then begin again. These daily routines are wrapping about me, embedding me in a mass of trite and habitual responses. I must have the refreshment of new sights, sounds, colours or I shall die away.'" H.G. had struggled against this fugitive impulse for more than two years, but the strain was becoming unbearable. It had already broken through into his fiction in *The Secret Places of the Heart,* and the novels which succeeded it were clearly the work of a man who was, in his own phrase, "in grave mental distress". *Men Like Gods, The Dream* and *Christina Alberta's Father* were poor fiction but they show that once again H.G. was obsessed with the fantasy of escape.

Mr Barnstaple, in *Men Like Gods,* is a journalist suffering from overwork and unrelieved worries about the condition of the world. He is "ceasing to secrete hope". Sent off on a holiday, he runs into a magical ambush, and finds that he has been carried off to Utopia, in company with Arthur Balfour, Winston Churchill and Edward Marsh, all thinly disguised under pseudonyms. The Utopians' philosophy turns out to be the Wellsian belief that there is a choice between controlling the universe and, as mortals have done, leaving everything to the evil laws of nature. The earthlings are expelled from this paradise because the Utopians fear their contamination, but Barnstaple is consoled by the thought that he can serve Utopia best by becoming a missionary for its ideals. In *Men Like Gods*, Barnstaple is an ordinary man living in the Age of Confusion who is permitted a glimpse of a happier future. In *The Dream*, Sarnac is a man of the future who dreams of his earlier incarnation as Harry Mortimer Smith, unhappily born in the Age of Confusion. By giving Smith a childhood very similar to his own, H.G. juxtaposed the heaven of the future and the hell of the past.

In *Tono-Bungay* and *The New Machiavelli* his recollections had begun with adolescence. In *The Dream* he went back further. The first memory that he gives Smith is of lying on a sofa screaming wildly at his angry father. He, too, had a childhood in the gloomy basement of a shop, "a world of suppression and evasion . . . a fear-haunted world" where in the name of religion it was "dinned into the minds of young people . . . that mankind was worthless and hopeless, the helpless plaything of a moody, impulsive, vain and irresistible Being". Smith's father was feckless and irritable, his mother's "moral harshness had overshadowed and embittered" his adolescence. Smith himself, after spells of apprenticeship with a draper and a chemist, becomes a journalist. He marries and divorces his first sweetheart, Hettie, but still hankers after her and is eventually shot by her worthless second husband. When, as Sarnac, he wakes again in the future, he finds Hettie – now called Sunray – reunited with him.

In *Christina Alberta's Father* Wells dealt explicitly with the theme of insanity for the first time. Sir Richmond Hardy had suffered from a severe neurosis, but Mr Preemby appears to be the victim of a more serious psychotic condition. "He's always half lived in a dream", Christina Alberta says of her father, and after a spiritualist has told Mr Preemby that he is Sargon the First, King of Kings, he completely assumes this second personality. * "I can't get him back", Christina Alberta tells a friend. "It's a reverie no longer. . . . He's walking about in a dream of glory." In this new incarnation Preemby is obsessed by much the same vision that Wells had described in *God the Invisible King*. He feels himself to be the lord and protector of the whole world whose mission it is to preach peace to mankind. In fact the shadow of mental illness lay across the four novels written between 1921 and 1924, as if Wells were trying to clear his mind of its troublesome fantasies by transferring them to paper. He had used this

* This Sumerian king, of whom Wells wrote approvingly in *The Outline*, was illegitimate and brought up as a gardener. Wells suggested that the finding of Sargon in the rushes was the origin of the story of Moses. It was a significant identification for Preemby – and for Wells.

auto-analytic technique in much of his earlier writing, but the current crisis was more severe than any which had preceded it, and its torments were reflected in both the structure and the symbolism of these novels. Even the dreams and hallucinations which run through them are not enough to relieve the death-wish of their main characters. Three of them, Sir Richmond Hardy, Harry Smith and Mr Preemby actually do die at the end of their stories; and Mr Barnstaple, in returning to earth from Utopia, suffers a pseudo-death. Many of the books in which Wells explored his own life concluded with a dying fall, but the obsession with death had never been so explicit as it became in the group of books written after 1921.

Wells knew something of psychology – he had read the work of his friend William James, and later some work by Freud and Jung. But there is nothing to suggest that he had much insight into the role that auto-analysis played in his life and fiction, ensuring that his books were dominated by projections of his own personality and preventing him from giving depth to the characters which peopled them. He merely felt compelled to write about himself. Yet the remedy was no more than a palliative. However effective writing may be as a means of self-diagnosis, and even as a passing release from tension, in the long run it has great limitations as a form of therapy. As its effects wear off, the symptoms come back more insistently than ever, because nothing has been done to remove their cause.

Whenever H.G. had found himself in this situation in the past, he had sought escape from the impasse by turning the fantasy back into life and seeking to act it out, as if he were a character in one of his own novels, commuting across the frontier between illusion and reality. Now, in the early Twenties, the solutions conjured up in fantasy were more frightening and depressing than ever before. From the evidence of the novels it is clear that, if he could find no means of escape in real life, H.G. felt himself to be threatened by insanity and death.

Wells spoke of himself at this time as "a creature trying to find its way out of a prison into which it has fallen", of using his books and articles as a means "to get my soul and something of my body out of the customs, outlook, boredoms and contaminations of the current phase of life".[1] It was a general disorder of temperament that affected him. Overwork was a contributory factor, though that in itself was only an expression of his search for some way out of the cage he had built for himself. "He went round and round like a rat in a maze", Rebecca West recalled when she described the last year of their relationship.[2]

What made him so desperate was the fact that this relationship and his domestic situation at Easton were no longer compatible. His emotional balance had depended upon an implicit collusion between his wife and his mistress, and when that was threatened his whole dualistic life was in danger of falling apart. He was, in fact, being pressed to face the implications of his life – and that was something which he desperately sought to avoid. The equilibrium had changed because Rebecca was finding her situation increasingly unsatisfactory. Intellectually, she and H.G. were as compatible as they had ever been. They were happy in each other's company, enjoying talk and looking at things together. They were generally free of the friction and rows which blighted some of H.G.'s friendships. It was in the practical implications of their relationship that the difficulty lay. This was something which H.G. did not wish to face. To make a commitment to Rebecca – or to Jane – would mean making a decision and facing a loss. For H.G. this seemed so unbearable that he had continued so to contrive his life as to avoid it. It led him to keep love cocooned in a dream world. Rebecca, however, was pressing to be released from the dream. She was growing older and wanted to make a more satisfactory life for herself. She was now thirty, with a growing son, and her position became less tolerable every year. Anthony was suffering from his unsettled background, with his father appearing only at intervals. Rebecca herself was now a noted literary critic and had recently published two novels. She was anxious to make headway with her career without being hampered by the impossible conditions of her home life with H.G. Her increasing confidence in herself led her to make stronger demands for a more realistic settlement of their affairs. At the same time she grew less tolerant of H.G.'s shortcomings – his selfishness, his vanity, his disregard of her work. "He never read more than a page or two of any of my books", she recalled. The more she pressed him to come to a decision the more he evaded the issue and the more frustrated she became.

The tension inherent in this situation reached breaking-point in 1922 when H.G. and Rebecca were holidaying in Spain. He had sailed directly from New York in January to meet her at Gibraltar, and to go on to Algeciras. "When he landed", Rebecca remembered, "he was desperately tired and practically off his head; enormously vain, irascible, and in a fantasy world." She found his behaviour "intolerable, then and for a long time afterwards. . . . His temporary deterioration was appalling." His distressed condition dragged on into 1923. Throughout that time he and Rebecca were caught in a tangle of grievances. She later recalled the stress in their relationship.

He would go away after a happy time and have to stay away and I would get furious letters alluding to imaginary misfortunes and failures on my part, and this would go on for ten days or so, to my great distress, and then he would come back and there would be complete pleasantness. Or there would be some trouble with the servants and he would then tell me that I was causing all such difficulties by my incompetence and would accuse me of dwelling on these difficulties, if not actually causing them in order that he should leave Jane and marry me.

She complained about him; he complained about her. Rebecca struggled to find a way out of the entanglement. She had realised that, whatever happened, H.G. would never leave Jane. "If Jane divorced him and I married H.G. we would have had a ghastly life. H.G.'s sense of guilt would have thrown him off balance. He could not have survived." If the uncertainty of it all was becoming impossible for Rebecca, there was only one solution left. By the beginning of 1923 the question was not whether the liaison between Rebecca and H.G. would end but merely of how and when it would break up. The initiative finally came from Rebecca, who felt that he had become careless both of her feelings and her reputation. A strange incident brought matters to a climax.

A woman who had done some professional work for H.G. turned up at his flat one day in a distressed state. Not knowing how he could help her with her personal problems, he sent her with a letter of introduction to Rebecca who was equally at a loss and somewhat resentful at being so put upon. The lady, now more desperate than ever, returned to Wells's flat at Whitehall Court, where she half-heartedly attempted suicide. She was found there by Jane, who impulsively telephoned for the police and an ambulance. Reporters got hold of the story and Rebecca found herself hounded by journalists. H.G., ill, overwrought and exhausted as he was, now grew frightened and anxious. But he seemed incapable of action and Rebecca was again manoeuvred into a position of responsibility. She succeeded, by interceding with influential friends, in keeping the drama out of the papers but H.G. showed no appreciation. It was her final grievance. She had had enough of her half-life with H.G. and she sent him an ultimatum. She said he must choose. He could leave Jane and marry her; go on living with her with a guarantee of £3,000 a year; or say goodbye. She knew that the last was the only possible choice. Still H.G. havered.

Rebecca was adamant. He continued to procrastinate. Finally she put an end to it all by sailing for America in October 1923. Their ten-year love-affair was over.

The stresses of the past two years and the strain of a second election campaign in the summer of 1923 brought H.G. once again to the point of collapse. He had worked hard and what he once called "the stupefaction of fatigue" had provided an anaesthetic for the powerful feelings aroused by the impending break with Rebecca. An attack of bronchitis added to his troubles and by the end of November he was so unwell that Bennett wrote him a commiserating letter suggesting where he might be comfortably cosseted in the sun of Portugal.

There was no question of Jane accompanying him. It was now accepted that she had her own life in which, outside the visits to Easton, he took little part. She had her sons as a focus for her emotions, she lived very comfortably, she was admired as a hostess, she went to the theatre and the ballet as often as she wished with her own friends, and she took frequent holidays in Switzerland. She had been out to Zermatt that summer with Gip; as soon as Christmas was over she went back to the snow in Switzerland and H.G. went off to nurse himself at the Estoril. He stayed until March, working hard on *Christina Alberta's Father* and the prefaces for the collected Atlantic edition of his books. Though his physical health improved, he was still deeply depressed. When he went up to join Jane in Paris on 25 March, he was turning over in his mind a plan for an extended world tour – the same notion that had appealed to him when he was trying to recover from the enforced separation from Amber a decade earlier. But this was much more an expression of his state of mind rather than of any positive sense of direction. G.K.Chesterton once said that "whenever I met H.G. he always seemed to be coming from somewhere rather than going anywhere".[3] The epigram was truer than it had ever been. He had again become an emotional wanderer. He passed an uneasy summer in England, dividing his time between Whitehall Court and Easton Glebe. He spent a stimulating evening with C.G.Jung, who had come to England to give a lecture, and found that Jung's idea of the collective unconscious was encouragingly similar to his own concept of the Mind of the Race. He met Rebecca again, and he was cheered up by the return of Margaret Sanger for a visit. There were the usual Easton week-ends to distract him. Yet he was still bent on going away. There was nothing to keep him in England.

He was persuaded, on what was intended to be the first stage of his world tour, to go to Geneva to see the League of Nations Assembly at work and to make a speech. He had also made a rendezvous there with an ardent admirer.

Her name was Odette Keun. She was thirty-six and H.G. was fifty-eight, at the height of his reputation. Odette belonged to the generation that was enchanted by his ideas of free love, of uninhibited radicalism and of the creation of new worlds for old. Odette said later: "We had an adoration for him. He was a super-star."[4] It was this hero-worship that made her send him her book, *Sous Lenin*, which described her adventures in Soviet Russia, and after Wells had written a favourable notice of it they began a correspondence. This became more frequent, more intimate, and on her part more ardent. She concluded by a declaration of love and by telling H.G. of her desire to meet him.

So he arranged a rendezvous in Geneva. Odette travelled up from Magagnosc, near Grasse in the South of France, where she was then living, and waited for him to turn up. When he eventually went to her hotel, she turned out the light before she opened the door, and without either seeing the other they went to bed. "I did not know whether he was a giant or a gnome", she recalled, "but it did not matter." The attraction was mutual. H.G., who was "sinking in boredom" and desperately needing a new liaison, was in just the mood to be swept away. Odette, dark-haired, bright-eyed, and gaminesque, was an attractive and assertive admirer. Late in life she recalled herself at that time as "gay, social, quarrelsome, warm-hearted and given to scandalise people by my language". Her rebellious sentiment matched that of Wells, and her romantic past gave her an added appeal. She had been born in Constantinople, the daughter of a Dutch diplomatist and an Italian mother. By her own account she had been "a wild and maladjusted child", given to lonely horseback rides through the woods of Asia Minor. At the age of eighteen she had gone to university in Holland, had become converted to Roman Catholicism and became a nun in a Dominican convent. But her vocation broke down after three years and she returned to Constantinople. From there she went to Paris, where she wrote articles for *La Revue de Paris* and published three novels. There she acquired a lover, a professor of law at the Sorbonne, with whom she travelled in North Africa. After the war she went from Algeria to Georgia in the Caucasus, where the Menshevik government was holding out against the Bolsheviks, and wrote articles for the French press. When the Georgian regime was overthrown she again went back to Constantinople. "I quarrelled with all the European missions there", she said afterwards. She was arrested by the British military authorities and deported to the Crimea; after a series of adventures she reached Moscow and was then allowed to leave for Paris. There she wrote and published the book that H.G. had admired.

H.G. did not need long in Geneva to intensify his disillusionment with the League, which he saw as a sham Parliament of Man serving merely as a stage for demagogic politicians and their hangers-on. He wanted to get away – to find the kind of retreat that he had once advocated for his Samurai. Odette provided the means of escape that he needed. They met on 4 September. Within two weeks they had gone back together to Grasse, where they rented a farmhouse called Lou Bastidon in the grounds of the Chateau de Malbosc with a view down the long wide valley to the Mediterranean at Cannes. They had found the house through Félicie Goletto, the housekeeper to the previous occupant, and she became their cook and her husband Maurice was hired as chauffeur. Years later H.G. recognised that he had made the move that he had dreamed about in an earlier period of despair. "If I did not get to writing in Italy in the pose of the New Machiavelli", he wrote, "I got to the South of France. It was much the same thing. It was the partial realization of my own fantasy after twelve years." Odette had acted out her fantasy too. She found H.G. irresistible, a wonderful talker and an erotic lover. She had no ties. On the contrary, she had been unsettled and hard-up, and H.G. had come suddenly into her life as a Prince Charming.

The arrangement whereby H.G. now "began a life in duplicate" suited everyone. Since there were complications which prevented Odette from securing a visa to England, there was no likelihood that she would accompany him there; she did not wish to marry him, and she was satisfied with a relationship which depended upon his grace and favour. Jane, for her part, was relieved that H.G. had transferred his polygamous proclivities away from Rebecca and out of the country. She had had enough of his stormy affairs on her own doorstep. "What I did", H.G. recalled, "I did with the connivance and help of my wife, who perceived that I was in grave mental distress and understood how things were with me."

H.G. was so satisfied with the turn of events that there was no more talk of the intended world tour. Before long he was inviting Margaret Sanger to visit Grasse. He had dashed back to England at Christmas and from there wrote to Margaret to say that he was living with "a very amusing & interesting Levantine writer Odette Keun (who adores me, is very observant & a little disposed to be jealous). She knows your work & would love to meet you. Would you care to come over & have lunch in our primitive MAS one day in the early new year?"[5]

The change in his life was sufficiently stimulating for him to launch a new book to record it, and he was soon hard at work on the first volume of *The World of William Clissold*. He had found that he could not get on with it at Easton, where he had returned at Easter, and on 25 May Jane wrote to Frank Swinnerton to say that there were too many distractions for H.G. when he was at the Glebe. "It is just all that incessant claim upon one's time that has sent H.G. away at last out of the country, where he can't be got at even by telegrams since I censor all his post and where there is nothing in the whole day long but his book."[6] Jane, as usual, was putting the best face on things, for it was not merely pressure of work that kept H.G. away. He had transferred the emotional core of his life to France, leaving only the husk of his business affairs with Jane in England. He stayed away most of the year, taking Odette with him to Brittany in September, and returning to Lou Bastidon in November for another long spell that lasted, with only a brief visit to England, until May 1926. Apart from occasional visitors, and calls on friends staying on the Côte d'Azur, he lived quietly, working hard at his novel and continuing to turn out his weekly article for the McClure syndicate, which brought him in thirty thousand dollars a year as a bonus on top of the very large royalties from *The Outline*. Money had ceased to matter, and he could afford to let all his substantial commitments run on in England while he lived casually in Provence.

The World of William Clissold was a description of Wells's world. Before it was published he sent his agent A.S. Watt, who feared a libel case, a long and forceful denial that the book was a *roman à clef* and the first volume was prefaced by a tortuous disclaimer to the same effect.[7] Yet as H.G. conceded later in his autobiography the book was self-dramatisation under a thin veneer of fiction. Clissold, a self-made industrial tycoon, has retreated to Provence to reflect on his life and to think through the state of the world. After a series of distressing and sometimes squalid love affairs, he has fled from the last of them to exorcise its memory in company with Clementina, a lively young woman of mixed ancestry and rebellious temperament whom he had picked up in the street in Paris. Though H.G. dedicated the book to Odette, she was hurt by the implication that she was a woman of easy virtue like Clementina. By presenting her in this light, H.G. unconsciously revealed a profound truth about his attitude towards the women he desired sexually: that the search for passion in successive infidelities led him to devalue, and then discard, the women he possessed.

Although the novel was widely reviewed in England and America, the reviewers were critical. Some suggested that Wells was disingenuous in his disclaimer that it was not autobiographical, and that his preoccupation with his own opinions prevented him from creating real characters or taking an interest in the views of other people. D.H.Lawrence described the book as a mouse's nest, and Shaw, who wrote to Wells about it at length, said that it was a hotch-potch of history and sociology which barely contained a trace of fiction, as if Wells had forgotten that he was a novelist and gone back to writing *The Outline of History* all over again.[8] The obsession with the evolution of his own soul, Shaw remarked, was as bad as Mr Dick's fixation – in *David Copperfield* – on the head of Charles I. But it is not merely the obsession that Shaw had noted that intrudes throughout the book. It runs the whole gamut of Wellsian notions. Shaw, indeed, observed that in the course of the novel Wells had gradually ascended from the real world into a state of olympian detachment very similar to the godlike superiority which H.G. had previously attributed to his utopian spokesmen.

Clissold was making a new start for himself, and also proposing one for the world. It was a fresh version of the freemasonry of the elect that Wells had proposed as early as *Anticipations* – in calling it the "Open Conspiracy" H.G. had picked up the phrase he had used in the preface to the 1914 edition. Shaw, indeed, may have remembered the context when he made reference to Mr Dick, for H.G. had then written: "That conception of an open conspiracy of intellectuals and wilful people is always with me; it is my King Charles's head . . . It is my faith." The membership, however, had now changed. The model for the Open Conspirator is not so much the scientist but the great industrialist, banker or trustbuilder, men like Brunner and Mond whose vast and ramifying investments transcended national frontiers and, H.G. now believed, gave them a vested interest in efficiency, stability and peace. Wiser and more powerful than politicians, they would create the economic world-state. They would, of course, stand no nonsense about democracy. "Realization of a new stage of society", Clissold insists, will "be effected without the support of the crowd and possibly in spite of its dissent."

Wells had now stated the programme to which the remaining years of his life were to be devoted. In the quietness of Provence he had recovered his confidence, as if the lively relationship with Odette had rejuvenated him.

In the South of France H.G. discovered that he could successfully insulate himself from ordinary life, and within two years he decided to secure this discovery by building a more permanent and comfortable home for himself and Odette. To the south of Lou Bastidon there was an old Provençale farmhouse belonging to Félicie Goletto. At the end of 1926 H.G. had arranged to buy the property, which was on a sloping piece of land with a brook running across the bottom. Though Grasse was within easy walking distance, and H.G. liked to stroll up to take lunch there, the town was hidden from the house by a fold in the hills which were covered with olive trees and vineyards. On this site H.G. began to build the home which he called Lou Pidou, the contraction of *Le Petit Dieu* which Odette used as his pet-name. When it was finished, H.G. had inscribed above the fireplace the legend "Two Lovers Built This House". *

The house gives the impression of an attempt to recreate Spade in a local idiom, and – although it was simply furnished – its six bedrooms and six bathrooms made the kind of provision for entertaining that Wells always enjoyed. Félicie and Maurice coped with the house, and with H.G.'s erratic use of his Voisin car, with the help of a *femme de ménage* and several part-time gardeners. When Lou Pidou was being built, in February 1927, Arnold and Dorothy Cheston Bennett turned up in Grasse for a visit.[10] At Lou Bastidon, Bennett noted, Odette "enveloped us in welcome. The 'feminine touch' all over the place. Excellent lunch, Provençale, with appreciable garlic in it . . . We went over to see the new house in process of construction . . . H.G. designed it himself and got an architect to 'redraw the plans'. What he would call a jolly little house. But it wouldn't suit me. Rooms too small and windows too large, and no tradition behind the design. Still the open-air rooms will be very 'jolly' for eating and sitting about in. Much charm in the situation." The care that H.G. took in planning the house and laying out the grounds made it plain that he envisaged it as a home for years to come. He had

* According to Chaplin, who noticed the inscription on a visit, H.G. said that "We've had it put on and taken off a number of times. Whenever we quarrel, I instruct the mason to take it off and when we make up she instructs the mason to put it back. It had been put on and taken off so many times that the mason finally ignored us and left it there." Despite the jocular hyperbole, the remark was a summary of domestic life at Lou Pidou.[9]

become a popular figure in the locality. Long afterwards Félicie recalled his charm, his generosity and his genuine friendliness to the ordinary people in the neighbourhood. For the first few years, indeed, Lou Pidou was his real home and there was very little to attract him back to England for more than visits. He showed how settled he was in a letter to an influential friend in Paris asking for help in securing French citizenship for Odette.[11]

She was a very wild, indiscreet, ready-tongued & adventurous young woman, but I know her well enough to be assured that she has always been too honest, impulsive & headlong ... for any sort of political mischief makers ... I make this appeal less for her than for myself. I want to do a few years of good work yet before I die and it happens that through odd compatibilities of taste & temperament that she can give me a happiness and a serene friendly contentment down there in Provence that no other person in the world will ever be able to give.

H.G. certainly found the life more agreeable than it was in England. The Labour government had collapsed while he was living in Provence, and the government of Stanley Baldwin was grinding its way towards the confrontation with the trade unions that ended in the General Strike of May 1926. He went back to London in March and April of that year, but he had already returned to Grasse to superintend his building operations when the strike started. For him, that dramatic event was something that he saw as through a telescope. He could not however miss the chance to launch a diatribe against the class-war produced by Winston Churchill's obduracy and the fatuity of the trade unions: an account of the strike was inserted as a series of letters in *Meanwhile*, a novel about a group of people on the Riviera.

Early in 1926, indeed, H.G. was much more concerned with history than with current events, having been drawn into a dispute about his *Outline* with Hilaire Belloc which dragged on all year. They were old antagonists, neither of them given to sparing epithets in a quarrel, and they had fought a series of exhibition bouts over the years in the columns of the radical press, with Shaw and G.K.Chesterton coming in as sparring partners. But where Shaw and Chesterton were controlled, using their wit lightly and never allowing controversy to make malice between friends, Belloc was even more hot-headed than Wells and seemed to need a row to stimulate him. Most of these rows stemmed from his passionate Catholicism and his intellectual snobbery.[12] He shared with Chesterton a vision of England as a jolly medieval fair which had been put out of business by Protestants and capitalists – a state of mind which kept them both on the fringes of the socialist movement but in a continuing posture of disagreement with it. Between them they had hammered at Shaw and Wells before the war, and Chesterton had occasionally restrained Belloc when he had been carried away by polemical enthusiasm. During the war, however, Wells had been continuously irritated by the way he was attacked in the *New Witness*, the review which Belloc had founded with Chesterton's brother Cecil. That animus was a contributory factor in the growing antipathy which H.G. displayed against Roman Catholicism, just as his personal morals and his open advocacy of birth control made him a natural target for Belloc's pugnacious intemperance.

The latest occasion for a row was *The Outline*, which Belloc attacked when it first came out, writing an article in the *London Mercury* to which H.G. replied, along with answers to other Catholic apologists, in his pamphlet, *The New Teaching of History*. But that was only the warm-up for the main encounter, which began at the end of 1925 when H.G. published a revised and illustrated version of *The Outline* in fortnightly parts. Belloc, who had been accumulating his ammunition, began by firing off a series of articles in the Catholic weekly *Universe*. H.G. struck back, when Belloc had spread himself over twenty-four articles, with a series of six which he hawked about Fleet Street without success. Failing to interest anyone in the issue, H.G. offered his articles to the *Universe* without payment. After a month's delay, the editor merely offered to correct any demonstrable mis-statement of fact. Enraged, H.G. turned his reply into a vituperous book, *Mr Belloc Objects*, provoking the further reply *Mr Belloc Still Objects*. The controversy aroused a certain interest. Though other historians had picked up Wells on points of detail and interpretation in *The Outline*, Belloc was the only popular writer to denounce him with bell, book and candle. Both of them banged away, Wells deriding Belloc's arrogance as "the self-protection of a fundamentally fearful man. He is a stout fellow in a funk", and Belloc jeered at H.G. for considering himself an expert on Catholicism "because he now winters on the Riviera . . ." Wells, no doubt, felt obliged to defend his faith as energetically as Belloc championed his Church, but it is doubtful whether either of them carried conviction beyond those who were already committed one way or the other.[13]

Wells stood by his work vigorously. He was very anxious that the reputation he had gained with *The Outline* should not be whittled away, and that he should be seen as the protagonist of rationalism and science.

He had come to hope for some public recognition of his work, and what he wanted most of all was election as a Fellow of the Royal Society. Late in 1926, his old friend Richard Gregory, whose position as editor of *Nature* ensured that he had influential contacts in the scientific world, wrote to H.G. saying that the only possibility was through a special rule which permitted the choice every two years of two persons who "either have rendered conspicuous service to the cause of science, or are such that their election would be of signal benefit to the Society".[14] Gregory sadly noted that H.G. might have dished himself by a recent slighting to the Prince of Wales. He could have added that the scandals which clung about the name of Wells would have been a further problem. But he was not deterred from trying to help, and one thing he could do was to ensure that H.G. got significant notice in the columns of *Nature*. He had already commissioned a long and favourable review of *William Clissold*, and he now rallied *Nature* behind Wells in the row with Belloc.

As H.G. emerged from the long haul to complete *William Clissold*, his thoughts were again turning towards following *The Outline* with the second of the three books which were to make up the "New Bible" he had first conceived at the end of the war. They were to be his special contribution to the educational work of the Open Conspiracy, and it had always been in his mind to produce a series of books as the basis for "a modern ideology, historical, biological and economic". When he went back to England in the summer of 1926, he had finalised his plans for the *Science of Life* with his son Gip, now a zoologist at University College, London. A second collaborator, Julian Huxley, who had already made his mark as a young don at Oxford, had recently been elected to the professorship of zoology at King's College, London; he had the additional merit, in the eyes of H.G., of being the grandson of his old and revered teacher, T.H.Huxley.[15]

H.G. proposed to plan the work as a whole, to take responsibility for welding together the parts written by his two younger collaborators, and to write some sections himself. He had already made a satisfactory financial arrangement for the book: with the success of *The Outline* behind him he had no difficulty in securing terms that enabled him to promise each of his helpers ten thousand pounds for their share in the enterprise. But he intended to get value for his money, and to push the task through as expeditiously as possible. Julian Huxley soon found that he would have to resign his professorship, and that even with the help of two secretaries he was going to be hardpressed. "H.G. demanded every ounce of my knowledge", he wrote, "and called upon a gift I had never fully exerted before – that of synthesizing a multitude of facts into a manageable whole, aware of the trees yet seeing the pattern of the forest, and drawing conclusions which gave the whole work vitality. This, I may add, did not come easily." The correspondence that followed, as well as the verbal exhortations that H.G. heaped upon his young collaborators, show the pressure which Huxley quickly felt. After some months of planning, for instance, during which H.G. became irritated because Huxley seemed to be slow in disembarrassing himself of other obligations, a firm letter arrived from H.G. in July 1927. "Let us go right on with it", H.G. wrote: "Time slips by and the mass of the work ought to exist by the beginning of December next . . . You do not know, as I do, how these things crumple up at the end if the bulk of the work is not done swiftly and furiously *soon* . . ." H.G. was a hard taskmaster, and only four weeks later he was threatening to cancel the project. "I can't cluck after you and Gip like an old hen after ducklings", he wrote to Huxley . . . "holidays, research, the Leeds gathering, a summer holiday, any little thing of that sort, is sufficient to put off work on the *Science of Life*. Well, that means scrapping it and the sooner it is scrapped the less it will cost us to get out of it."

In March 1927 H.G. was asked to give a lecture at the Sorbonne, and Jane crossed to join him in Paris for the occasion. The talk, "Democracy Under Revision", was a summary of the view he had expressed so often: the spiritual initiative needed to establish the world state could come only from a creative élite which was akin to a religious order in its fanatical dedication to the salvation of mankind. It seems to have been a pleasant event and Wells was glad Jane was present when he received this academic recognition. Soon afterwards he was back in England for another ceremony. His son Gip was marrying Marjorie Craig, who had lately been H.G.'s most efficient secretary. But on 21 April, the day after the wedding, he went back to Lou Pidou.

On 2 May Jane wrote to Kotelianski to say that H.G. had "gone off again to get a quiet spell of writing" and she added that "I am rather tired out & out of sorts after a busy time". After the wedding, and only a day or so after H.G. went off to France, she consulted a surgeon about a mild and progressive abdominal pain. After taking X-rays the doctor sought a second opinion, and further examination revealed that she was in an advanced state of cancer.

Her son, Frank, on hearing the news, wrote immediately to H.G. who received the letter on 10 May. Jane had apparently given him no inkling of her condition when he was home, and he wrote back at once.[16]

Dearest Mother, my dear, dear wife

I have had Frank's letter today and for the first time I learned how seriously ill you have been & that you may still be very ill. My dear, I love you much more than I have loved anyone else in the world & I am coming back to you to take care of you & to do all I can to make you happy . . . There are one or two things I want to settle here before I leave so that everything here will be able to look after itself for just as long as you need me. My dear, my dear, my dearest heart is yours. Your loving Bins.

He knew at once that Jane was doomed. Before he left Lou Pidou, he wrote on 13 May to Margaret Sanger explaining that he was unable to attend the World Population Conference at Geneva as he had intended, because "my little wife has to die of cancer & I want to spend what time remains of her life with her . . . My wife's illness came upon us all very suddenly. She was ski-ing this winter, & I left her in London not three weeks ago, smiling & alert, but looking a little tired".[17]

The close friends who had known Jane for so many years were shocked at the news. On 30 May Charlotte Shaw wrote to say: "It is one of the most tragic things that has come into my life, for, as you say, she is *valiant* & has been the gayest & pluckiest person I have ever known, I think". Shaw himself, who had strange views on the causes of illness and a lifelong antipathy towards doctors, reacted perversely, suggesting that Jane's cancer was due to the fact that she had poor thoughts, and that these created the poorer tissue of the cancer. The only possible cure, he proposed, was homeopathic treatment.[18] His insensitivity greatly upset H.G., who had already told Margaret Sanger that although he would welcome any sensible advice, "the world is full of cancer quacks who prey upon desperate hopes". A week later, Bennett went down to Little Easton.[19] "Jane was lying on a broad sofa in the drawing room", he noted in his journal: "she looked ill, but not so ill as I had expected. Enlarged eyes. A sort of exhausted but determined wild cheerfulness in her. H.G. kept going in and out." At the end of June he found that she was up and about, but H.G. told him privately that she was no better. She was actually getting worse, and when Bennett visited on 27 July he noted that she was carried downstairs and wheeled everywhere, though she continued to supervise all the domestic arrangements and to cope with a stream of callers during the afternoon. He found that H.G., anxiously watching the advance of her disease, was now searching for unconventional remedies, and Bennett agreed to act as an intermediary with a man called Raphael Roche, who claimed that his "Science of Curative Medicine" could at least prolong the life of cancer patients.[20] Shaw, too, was pressing his point, though his comments were tactlessly unhelpful. On 4 August he wrote from Stresa, where he and Charlotte were holidaying. In the course of a long and rambling attack on "Harley-streetism" he recommended nature cures or at least a first-class young physician. The contempt he had shown for "assassins" like Cutler Walpole and Sir Patrick Cullen in *The Doctor's Dilemma* now made him feel anxious lest Jane should fall into the hands of their contemporary counterparts. But Charlotte, who realised how the letter would distress H.G., sent a hurried note apologising and begging H.G. to bear with him. Wells sent back a reassuring note.[21]

He was doing what he could to keep up a normal life at the Glebe. "In a sort of way we are happy together here", he wrote on 21 July to a correspondent in Geneva: "we are both stoics, & we have music, roses, books & many things like that to give us bright days – but I wish we had more sun. Write her a letter about things in general to amuse her – *not* what she calls an Obituary Notice."[22] Every month H.G. crossed the Channel to spend two days in France with Odette and he went up to London for occasional dinners and business engagements. But for the most part he stayed at the Glebe. He kept himself busy with the *Science of Life*, and both Gip and Julian Huxley were brought down for week-ends to go over their drafts. "H.G. demanded an impossible rate of progress", Huxley recalled, and "the atmosphere was apt to become stormy ... Supercharged, and as if indestructible, H.G. worked, talked and played with a sort of fury."[23] When the day's work was done, however, he was still driving all the guests out to ball games, or promoting a wild game of bridge.

"Slowly, day by day, Jane loses strength", H.G. wrote to his brother Frank on 21 September.[24] "There is no cure for these cases of widely diffused cancer. She has no pain we cannot control with morphia ... but that won't turn back the clock." One of her wishes was to survive long enough for the marriage between her son Frank and Peggy Gibbons, a local girl whom he had known for years, and the wedding was fixed for 7 October. The Bennetts went down for what proved to be their last visit on Sunday 25 September. All the family were there, but Jane was too ill to come downstairs or see anyone. "I think", Bennett observed,

"H.G. likes a lot of people to distract him." He clearly took the chance to talk to Bennett about his plans for the funeral, for Bennett undertook to ask T.E.Page, a notable orator, to deliver the address that H.G. was already drafting.[25] "We came home very depressed", Bennett wrote to his nephew the next day.[26]

Jane Wells died at 6.30 in the evening of Thursday, 6 October, and on the following day H.G. wrote a sad note to his brother. "Jane died last night quite painlessly", he said. "She will be cremated at Golders Green at 2.30 on Monday. She wanted to have Frank married before she died. We had everything arranged for that to take place today and so we decided to have the ceremony carried out in the morning very quietly."[27]

There were lots of people at the funeral, Bennett recorded in his journal, but very few from the great world. "Shaw", he noted, "had an amber handkerchief and no overcoat." Charlotte Shaw found it an embarrassing occasion, as she wrote to T.E.Lawrence.[28]

It was dreadful – dreadful – *dreadful!* I haven't been so upset . . . for a long time . . . the organ began a terrible dirge. We all stood up – and stood for what seemed hours and hours . . . while that organ played on our nerves and senses and knocked them to pieces. H.G. began to cry like a child – tried to hide it at first and then let go. After centuries of torment the organist stopped (if he hadn't I'm sure in two more minutes G.B.S. would have gone up to the organ loft and killed him) and we all sat down and pseudo-Balfour [T.E.Page] began to read a paper, written, as he told us, by Wells. It was terrible beyond anything words can describe; a soul in torment – self torture. He drowned us in a sea of misery and as we were gasping began a panegyric of Jane which made her appear as a delicate, flower-like, gentle being, surrounding itself with beauty, and philanthropy and love. Now Jane was one of the strongest characters I ever met. She managed H.G. and her good curious sons and her circle generally according to her own very definite and very original theories – with almost unbroken success – *from the point of view of her theories.* Then there came a place where the address said "she never resented a slight; she never gave voice to a harsh judgment". At that point the audience, all more or less acquainted with many details of H.G.'s private life, thrilled, like corn under a wet north wind – and H.G. – H.G. positively howled. You are no doubt aware that he was not a conventionally perfect husband . . . O it was hideous – terrible and frightful. I am an old woman and there is one thing I seem, at least, to have learned. The way of transgressors is hard . . .

A few days later H.G. left for Paris, and by November he had again established himself at Lou Pidou.

VEXATIOUS LITIGATION

As soon as H.G. was back in France he began to write a memoir of Jane, which he published privately as *The Book of Catherine Wells*. The use of "Catherine" in the title deliberately emphasised that part of her personality which she had hidden behind the persona of "Jane" so effectively that even H.G. had seldom done more than glimpse the unattainable ideal which had first attracted him to her more than thirty years before. Their marriage had failed long ago, in the conventional sense. And yet, in a different sense, it had succeeded, and had survived to the end. They had, in fact, played complementary roles in life, in which each provided the kind of security the other needed without touching the deeper issue of true emotional satisfaction. It was an unconscious collusion which permitted them both to shut out their inner passions from their marriage. H.G. lived out his ambivalence, releasing his romantic dreams into relationships with other women. Jane repressed her other self, so that she gave the impression of being a "Snow Queen". Their implicit agreement to sustain this distance enabled their marriage to survive, but it was also its tragedy.

Despite the stress of his bereavement, H.G. was sufficiently comfortable at Lou Pidou to get on with his work. *Mr Blettsworthy on Rampole Island* was ready for the publisher that autumn, and so was *The Open Conspiracy*. *Mr Blettsworthy* was a more ingenious and less laboured book than *Men Like Gods* or *The Dream*, but it relied on a similar dualist device to make its allegorical point. Arnold Blettsworthy, a young man with a weak and divided personality, is shipwrecked among a group of cannibalistic savages whose beliefs and rituals parody those of modern society. His position is somewhat like that of the Time Traveller if he had found himself on the island of Dr Moreau. But he then awakens to find it has all been a delusion. He had, in fact, been picked up insane, and brought back in the care of a psychiatrist in New York, where he has been living a double life for the past five years. Within his body, Dr Minchett explains, there are two beings with a common head, and he has simply translated events around him into the fantasy life on Rampole Island. When Blettsworthy recovers, he understands the symbolism of his experience and realises that there must be a Winding-up of the Past which will enable mankind to make a new start.

The idea that somehow the human race was groping in the dark for a new sense of direction (as if, in Jungian terms, the collective unconscious was seeking a faith by which mankind might survive) was set out at length in *The Open Conspiracy*, which was a formal manifesto of the beliefs sketched out in *William Clissold*. H.G. now presented a grandiose seven-point programme for the building of "the new human community", which repeated his case for a world directorate "serving the common ends of the race". But the argument was developed in a fizz of rhetoric whose impact was further diminished by the manner in which, after piling up the imperatives for urgent action, H.G. weakly argued that the Open Conspiracy was "a system of purposes" rather than a plan for any definite action by anybody. On 29 May 1928, when Shaw read the book, he wrote at once to Wells telling him that he must stop using the style of a leader-writer, which was neither clear nor intellectually honest, and he went on to read Wells a lesson in the economics of capitalism and the theory of Marx, suggesting that Wells misunderstood capitalism and under-estimated Marx.[1] But his strongest complaint was the old one that Wells was habitually splenetic, and that this innate quarrelsomeness damaged good causes they both had at heart. During the spring of 1928 H.G. was away a good deal from Lou Pidou, making at least two trips to England, since he was moving to a new flat at St Ermin's. From this new address he replied to Shaw on 9 June. "I'm setting up a flat in Paris", he told him, "so as to lead a quadrilateral life, – here, Paris, Grasse, & Easton (where God & my careless offspring are making me a grand-father). Your criticisms are very wise & valuable & also you are, as ever, quite wrong headed. But you are always sound hearted & I am always, through all our disputes & slanging matches, yours most affectionately, H.G."[2] He would not be drawn into the oretical argument with Shaw about Marx.

The Paris apartment, at 124 Quai d'Auteil (now Quai Bleriot), was in a modern block looking upstream across the Seine to the Eiffel Tower. The decision to add yet another residence to the list, coming so soon after Jane's death, was due in part to Odette's complaint that she was bored at Lou Pidou, especially when he was away, and her desire to have a base in

Paris where she could be near friends and relatives. It was also a sign that, far from settling down in Provence with Odette, H.G. was now as restless as ever. He led a peripatetic existence, commuting between his four homes with side-trips in Europe and to America. "In a sort of way my life finished last year", he wrote to his brother Frank from Paris on the first anniversary of Jane's death, "& I try to live a fresh sort of existence here with the fag end of it. I keep on Easton exactly as it was & mean it to be a home for my grandchildren ... I can't live much in England. My heart has gone out of it."[3]

The main focus for his urgent energies, however, was in the drive to complete the *Science of Life* and, at the same time, launch the parallel and equally demanding project which was provisionally entitled *The Science of Work and Wealth*. All through 1928 and into 1929 he was, as he told Enid Bagnold, "frightfully driven" ... Explaining why he was unable to visit her and her husband, Sir Roderick Jones, he added: "I hate to think I can't scrap everything & come & see you, but I must get Julian & Gip through with the *Science of Life* & the only thing to do that is to sit over them & work away with them the whole time."[4]

During his row with Henry Arthur Jones, H.G. had been irritated by the way letters from Jones thumped through his letter-box. Julian Huxley had much the same feeling as Wells feverishly drove him on with what Huxley called "strong blasts".[5] In March 1928 H.G. sent a stern reproof, complaining that Huxley was wasting time on "side-shows" and reminding him that originally he had "proposed to break the back of the work before Xmas 1927. And here we are!" By the autumn Wells was insisting that he wanted the book finished by February, and that though Huxley was producing "an excess almost of written matter" it was so poorly organised that he was "putting no end of thought and toil upon Gip and myself in recasting it". In his letter of 3 October H.G. spelt out exactly how he expected his collaborator to plan his work, provoking a long and reasonable apology from Huxley which was not enough to assuage H.G.'s thirst for copy. On 29 October he came back with more complaints that Huxley was serving up too much undigested material. "I can't do any other work", he concluded, "I might just as well be writing the whole bloody thing with Gip myself ... Look at this letter! If it was an article I could get 1500 dollars for it. Look at the waste of time and attention, Oh my collaborator!"

As Huxley began to get his work into shape, the pressure from H.G. subsided into more general admonitions about the project. His sense of what was needed to get the task completed, and of what the intelligent but insufficiently-educated reader required, was the gift which enabled H.G. to create the best popular introduction to the biological sciences. While his collaborators brought modern knowledge and accuracy to the work, it was his conception, and he gave it the form which ensured it a wide readership, which he described as "the intelligent lower middle classes", not "idiots, half-wits . . . greenhorns, religious fanatics . . . smart women or men who know all that there is to be known".[6] He would have no kind of "namby-pamby, 'make-it-all-so-clear-to-the-dear-children' illustration which will drive away twenty modern readers for the purpose of attracting some old lady who may or may not buy the work for her grandchildren". By August 1929 the book was completed. The influence of T.H.Huxley had now come full circle, not merely in the book in which Wells had at last paid the debt he had owed since his days in South Kensington, but also in the person of Julian Huxley who now in turn owed much to his association with H.G. In his subsequent career as a populariser of science, and in the role he played in the establishment of UNESCO after the Second World War, he became the very model of an Open Conspirator.

The intensity with which H.G. toiled at the *Science of Life* while planning its successor in the social sciences did not inhibit either his journalism or his fiction. In 1928 he brought out a collection of articles with the title *The Way the World is Going*, and in 1929 he published the address he had given to a conference in the Reichstag in Berlin in April as *The Common Sense of World Peace*. But, though his name was constantly in the press and his reputation as a prophet and educator continued to grow, he was now dropping below the novel-reader's horizon – as he had feared when he first decided to concentrate on more didactic tasks.

The Autocracy of Mr Parham, written in 1929, demonstrated clearly what happened when H.G. tried to do several things at the same time. The story of Mr Parham, an Oxford don with dreams of glory was intended as a satire. Parham attaches himself to a powerful tycoon – Sir Bussy Woodcock was a neat caricature of Max Beaverbrook that was made explicit by the David Low cartoons that illustrated the book – and with a group of Woodcock's friends he sets out on a round of spiritualist seances. In one of these Mr Parham is possessed by the spirit of a Martian War lord, and so becomes the leader of a fascist movement of national regeneration which attempts to rally European reaction for a holy war against Bolshevism. He produces nothing but disasters. His arrogant fumbling gives Wells an opportunity to make another attack on the Great Man theory of history. Parham, now Lord Paramount, is opposed by a group of enlightened businessmen. The opposition to him is led, so to speak, by the Clissolds of Britain, who have secretly manufactured a gas which he thinks will give him world mastery. But the gas turns out to be a new version of the "peace" gas which had swept over the world in *In the Days of the Comet*, and these courageous members of the Open Conspiracy propose to use it to "clean the mind of man as it has never been cleaned before", sweeping away nationalism and war and creating a new world of brotherhood. At this point Parham wakes up from what has merely been a dream at the seance. Sir Bussy, who seems to have had a similar vision, realises the danger of power-seeking demagogues with fantasies like those of Mr Parham and decides that his power must be used to get rid of the "bloodstained clutter" they create, "damn soon. Before another smash." H.G. had dug up several devices he had used before – the spiritualist seance, the idea of possession, the apocalyptic war from which a new scientifically-minded élite rescues mankind by some kind of magic, and the dream which continues to work on the minds of men after they waken. As an attempt to present his ideas in popular form it was neither funny nor convincing and as a novel it was boring and silly.

Wells was trying to find a means of putting over his theories to a wide audience, and he came to the conclusion that he should perhaps try a different medium. He therefore turned to the cinema, at the moment when that industry was about to be transformed by the invention of sound films. Several of his tales were made into movies during the Twenties – *The Wheels of Chance, The First Men in the Moon, Kipps* and *The Passionate Friends* – though none with much distinction or success. In 1928, he wrote three short comedies, *Bluebottles, The Tonic* and *Daydreams*, which his son Frank adapted for Ivor Montagu to direct. And, in the same year, he worked up a scenario which had been conceived three years earlier when he first went to Lou Bastidon. "The Peace of the World", which was intended to use the film as propaganda for the world state, was never made, and so H.G. converted it into a curious and flat novel which had the form of a film script. *The King Who Was A King* shows how right Shaw had been when, many years ago, he had doubted whether H.G. had it in him to write a money-spinning play.

The language of exposition is very different from the language of literature, and H.G. had settled for the former – as he reminded James Joyce in a letter from Lou Pidou on 23 November 1928.[7] H.G. had once recognised Joyce's original talent, but he had now lost touch with *avant-garde* writing for reasons that he explained. "The frame of my mind", he wrote, "is a world wherein a big unifying & concentrating process is possible, (increase of power and range by economy & concentration of effort), a progress not inevitable . . . but possible. That game attracted & holds me. For it, I want language & statement to be as simple & clear as possible." With unconscious irony, Wells then told Joyce that "your mental existence is obsessed by a monstrous system of contradictions . . . you were brought up under the delusion of political suppression, I was brought up under the delusion of political responsibility. It seems a fine thing for you to defy & break up. To me not in the least." He then read Joyce a lesson from the stance of a reasonable constructive man, concerned above all with the welfare of the race rather than the expression of individual consciousness.

When H.G. was explaining to Joyce his idea of plain writing for plain men he was not only driving on his son Gip and Julian Huxley with the *Science of Life*, but he was also trying to launch the third volume of his trilogy. It was proving difficult to bring "the contemporary economic life of man" into the same sharp focus as history and biology, and for some years H.G. "had cast about in vain how to produce the work". He knew he would need collaborators, but he found it hard to select them. There were no such obvious candidates as his own son and Huxley, and in any case for this task he did not want equals so much as "intelligent, industrious, and interested fags".[8]

It was difficult for him to bring social institutions into the same evolutionary pattern that had served to organise his views of history and biology. Though he felt that society was subject to the same laws, he found the material to hand was intractable and diffuse, and he struggled hard to make it conform to his scheme of things. At last by the middle of 1928 he had drawn up a first prospectus of what he wanted, and he had enlisted two helpers, a writer on industrial problems named Edward Cressy, recommended to him by Richard Gregory, and an old acquaintance called Hugh P. Vowles. He led them to believe that they would each earn a minimum of six thousand pounds, and set them to work. Cressy turned out to be a satisfactory choice, and H.G. made no complaints against him. But he had gravely misjudged his man when he chose

Vowles, a mechanical engineer and free-lance writer whom he had known since 1912. In an early letter to Wells Vowles described himself as introspective, impressionable, volatile and rather weak-willed, but H.G. seems to have forgotten this warning and rashly to have employed a man whom he now described as "a curiously cantankerous character; he was quite extraordinarily self-important and 'touchy', weaknesses of which I had no previous intimations".[9]

Before the first year of work was done, H.G. was becoming uneasy about the plan for the book, and was thinking of dropping it, and his doubts were intensified when he found that Vowles was trying to control the work, that he was quarrelling with Cressy, and that the material he produced was poor in quality. H.G., still deeply involved with the *Science of Life* had undoubtedly taken on too much; the attempt to run the new book in parallel with much less suitable collaborators was a failure. After some preliminary work, he sent Cressy and Vowles a memorandum complaining of their "irritability and recrimination. . . . I shall not go on if there are any signs of mutual sabotage."[10] The job, Wells said afterwards, "collapsed on me . . . I fell into a state of neurasthenia . . . I felt horribly old and done-for just then. I was failing to carry out an integral part of my scheme of activities."[11] He therefore told Cressy and Vowles that the project was indefinitely postponed. Cressy accepted the settlement he proposed, and H.G. thought that he had behaved decently to Vowles by proposing that he should keep the eight hundred pounds already advanced and, in addition, have the right to publish the material he had prepared. But Vowles insisted that H.G. was committed to him, and that he would be ruined if the project were to be abandoned. Thus, in the summer of 1929, began what Wells later described in a privately-printed pamphlet as *The Problem of the Troublesome Collaborator*.

H.G. went back to France for a holiday in July and August, to recover his spirits and his temper. He decided to make a new start on *The Science of Wealth* and to find some face-saving role for Vowles in the work. But in his absence abroad Vowles had already gone to the Society of Authors to complain of mistreatment. He persuaded G. Herbert Thring, the secretary of the Society for almost forty years, that he had a legitimate grievance and – without informing Wells, though H.G. was a prominent member of the Society – Thring took counsel's opinion and advised the Committee of Management that Vowles was entitled to substantial damages for breach of contract. On 8 November 1929 Thring wrote to Wells asking for his defence to the charges made by Vowles. In a long letter H.G. set out his arrangements with Cressy and Vowles asking what contract was supposed to have been broken. He also wrote to Vowles saying "my understanding is that we agreed to abandon" the book, but "if you do not agree, then I suppose it must go on . . ." On the same day, 20 November, H.G. also wrote to Thring insisting that there was no binding contract, and he followed this up with another letter on 24 November saying that he would go on with the book, because "it is a necessary part of my career", and that he therefore considered the difference with Vowles as settled, at least so far as the Society of Authors was concerned.

H.G., however, let his irritation with Thring carry him too far and he incautiously made a personal attack on him. "You can congratulate yourself", he told Thring, "upon having caught me in a phase of neurasthenic breakdown and to have used your opportunity to insult and trouble me." Instead of trying to seek an amicable settlement between two members of the Society, H.G. wrote, "you sat in your office and dictated the sort of letter a blackmailing solicitor might have written to a wealthy personal enemy. . . . Nothing seems to have mattered but the opportunity of annoying and bleeding me while I was ill and depressed." Whether or not he had incurred a legal liability to Vowles, H.G. had now certainly put himself at the risk of a libel action from Thring, and he was caught up in a train of troubles that ran on all through the winter. Thring's first reply was to say that he had put the whole matter before the Committee of Management, and a few days later he reported to Wells that the Vowles affair would be dropped if he could agree a new contract for Vowles with the Society's solicitors, Field, Roscoe. The matter became even more complex, and after a fierce and protracted correspondence through December and January, H.G. found that on 14 February 1930 Vowles had finally instructed the solicitors to issue a writ for breach of contract.

All three principals in the dispute had behaved so foolishly that a reasonable agreement had become impossible. It is doubtful whether Vowles had a strong case. H.G. had paid him generously for the work done, and offered to take him back. His claim for the full six thousand pounds seems to have been as much a matter of injured pride as professional loss: an arbitrator eventually awarded him another seven hundred pounds. Thring had made no allowance for the intemperate manner in which H.G. was liable to conduct any controversy, and had so clearly sided with Vowles that H.G. could reasonably feel that his position in the Society of Authors had been prejudiced by the way Thring had prejudged the matter. And H.G., with some provocation, had lost all sense of proportion. He became so obsessed by his grievance against Thring that the affair rapidly degenerated into a vendetta that alienated even those who thought H.G. had some reason for irritation.

The first pamphlet was sent to all members of the Society of Authors early in 1930 after an irritable tussle in which H.G. had to employ his solicitors to extract the membership list from Thring. At this point Thring went privately to Shaw, asking him to use his good offices with Wells. In February, Shaw wrote to Wells at Lou Pidou saying that he agreed that Thring was not the best of employees, but he had been an underpaid and devoted secretary to the Society and he could not be cast aside simply because he was liable to bite both parties to a dispute. In any case, Shaw added consolingly, Wells was too successful and eminent to hit a subordinate when he was down.[12]

Shaw knew that Wells was bent on ruining Thring, who was then on the verge of retirement and that he was trying to get Barrie, Galsworthy and others to bring pressure to bear on Lord Gorell, the chairman of the Society, and the Committee of Management, to repudiate Thring's actions. When H.G. continued intransigent, Shaw wrote again on 12 March warning Wells against an undignified campaign against the Committee, and urging him to let them make the running.[13] Repeating the advice he had given Wells during the Fabian row more than twenty years before he insisted that it was sound tactics in a campaign to leave one's opponent an easy line of retreat. Wells still would not listen and Shaw sent a third letter a few days later.[14] Wells must be content with a bloodless victory and avoid the temptation of being vindictive. He conceded that the Committee of Management had a weak case in the way it had handled the dispute, but he urged Wells not to go to extremes and make a violent attack on the Committee, and to avoid impugning Thring's character. If H.G. let himself be carried away by a thirst for vengeance, then he would forfeit the sympathy of everyone on the Committee, including Shaw.

Wells went on expostulating, trying to mobilise all his friends against Gorell and Thring. He had, for instance, pressed Galsworthy so hard that Galsworthy had finally been driven to tell him flatly that he refused to be involved in the matter. Arnold Bennett, who thought H.G.'s pamphlet "a rather sad exposé . . . of his violent demeanour in writing business letters when he gets cross, ill or worried",[15] nevertheless did intervene on behalf of his old friend, writing to Lord Gorell on 10 March to say that he thought the Society had behaved rashly and rather unfairly to H.G.

On 17 March Shaw made a last attempt to bring H.G. to his senses, explicitly reminding him how he had ruined his case with the Fabians by overplaying his hand.[16] The last letter he received from Wells, he wrote, could only be described as a wilful attempt to destroy himself. It was like old times. Years ago H.G. had alienated his supporters in the Fabian Society by forcing them to choose between throwing over the Webbs and abandoning him – and had ended by failing to get a single vote in a meeting full of his sympathisers. He was about to repeat that astonishing feat.

The pressure from Shaw gradually had some effect, and on 8 April Wells sent Thring a letter of apology which ought to have settled the matter, regretting "that ill-advised campaign which has wasted so much of my time and disarranged my work for the past six months . . . I withdraw unreservedly anything I may have said or done that might shake . . . your credit in the world of affairs." But Thring was not to be appeased. On 10 April he informed H.G. that he was consulting his solicitors with a view to a libel action; two days later, on their advice, he sent Wells a model letter of apology which H.G. refused to sign. At the same time on 11 April Thring wrote to Shaw to explain his obduracy. "I am not going to refuse the olive branch," he said, "but I am going to have a proper apology from Wells." On 23 April Wells offered a different, less formal and more defensive draft, and suggested that the whole correspondence should be published in The Author. The next day, Thring accepted. At that point H.G. introduced a new issue. He had finally agreed to arbitrate the dispute with Vowles, but he demanded that the Society should bear all the legal costs he had incurred because of its campaign against him. There had also been delays in producing the promised pamphlet containing the correspondence, which was called Settlement of the Trouble Between Mr Thring and Mr Wells, and arranging for it to be circulated to all those who had received the first blast from Wells. Before the matter was settled Thring again threatened legal action; Shaw in fact had sent a further letter in March warning H.G. that he should at all costs avoid the temptation of carrying the matter into the courts.[17]

There was a good and immediate reason why Wells should take Shaw's advice about the troubles of litigation. For more than five years he had been bothered by a lawsuit which was about to come to trial, and the wearisome preliminaries were a continuing harassment to him – especially since the case was being heard in Toronto and everything had to be handled by intermediaries and by correspondence.

He was being accused of literary piracy, and the Macmillan company in

Canada – which had published *The Outline of History* there – was named as accessory before the fact and co-conspirator. The plaintiff was a Miss Florence Deeks, a Canadian feminist who had drafted a large book on the role of women through the ages called *The Web of History* which, she claimed, H.G. had substantially plagiarised in writing *The Outline*. She issued a writ in 1925. Her case was rejected in the Supreme Court of Ontario, and she then carried it before Mr Justice Raney in the Appelate Court in Toronto, whose judgement was delivered in September 1930.

There is no doubt that Miss Deeks genuinely believed that she had been wronged, and as she tried to establish her case she became so consumed by a sense of injustice that she devoted herself to it entirely and eventually became that pathetic figure, a vexatious litigant. "She was", Wells wrote later to Mr Justice Maugham, "a silly woman who acted in good faith." She had apparently written her book between 1914 and 1918, when she submitted the manuscript to Macmillan's Toronto office, which retained it for about six months, during the period when Wells was at work on *The Outline*. She was convinced that during that time the manuscript some-how reached Wells in England and that while it was in his hands he copied large parts of it – an allegation, as the judge commented, that H.G. was guilty of plagiarism, of receiving stolen goods, and, jointly with Macmillan's, of criminal conspiracy.

H.G. sought to defend himself at first by trying to prove that he had been planning to write *The Outline* for some time before Miss Deeks had sent her book to Macmillan's. He dismissed as mere coincidence the fact that he had actually begun to write his book two months after Macmillan first received the manuscript from Miss Deeks. Her case rested on two arguments. One was that Wells could not possibly have written so long a book in so short a time without the aid of her draft; and the other was the similarities between the two works. The court proceedings were thus mainly given over to evidence from academic specialists who supported her case by textual comparisons between her manuscripts and *The Outline*. Both covered the span of history from the formation of the solar system to modern times, and both depended upon the outmoded La Place theory of its origin; both gave the same relative emphasis to western civilisation; both contained very similar sub-headings, though Wells usually put the word "man" into such phrases as "Man Discovers Agriculture" while Miss Deeks put "Woman Discovers Agriculture" – her book having been written as a feminist interpretation of human evolution.

Her witnesses certainly worked hard for Miss Deeks, confirming her feeling that she was entitled to very large damages. One of them, William A. Irwin of Toronto University, seems to have been carried away by his discovery of similar facts and mistakes. Justice Raney remarked that "so strong was Professor Irwin's self-persuasion that he could visualise Mr Wells sitting at his desk writing the manuscript of his book with the *Encylopaedia Britannica* at his right hand, Robinson's *Mediaeval and Modern Times* at his left, and Miss Deeks's manuscript in front of him". Irwin could not believe that Wells could otherwise have produced so vast a work, written in longhand, in less than a year, and he insisted that the work had been essentially one of copying, padded out by Wells with "old hobbies and half-baked opinions of his own" and rushed on frantically because of his anxiety "to forestall the publication of *Web*". If that case were proved, Justice Raney observed, the only issue before him would have been the legal question of whether there could be piracy of a non-copyrighted manuscript. But he found that Irwin's memorandum was "just solemn nonsense", and added that "his comparisons are without significance, and his argument and conclusions are alike puerile". All that had been demonstrated was that both authors had drawn heavily, and often without explicit acknowledgement, upon the same sources. Justice Raney dismissed the action, and insisted that it should never have been brought. Miss Deeks, he said, "was not in a condition of mind to judge fairly of the very serious charge she was bringing against a reputable publishing house and an eminent and respectable author".

Yet Miss Deeks was neither discouraged nor finished. Even though costs were given against her, she continued to press her case. She had no money of her own, except a small allowance made by her brother, and H.G. became convinced that she was being supported by undisclosed backers – possibly some wealthy person who was bent on using her to ruin his reputation, or someone who was willing to pay her expenses in the hope of securing a large share of any damages she recovered. He considered employing private detectives to ferret out the facts, and all through the case he vehemently complained that he was being forced to meet heavy legal fees (which in the end came to over three thousand pounds) which he could never get back by forcing Miss Deeks into bankruptcy for nonpayment of costs. Wells had always been afraid of libel actions based on the resemblance of some of his characters to living persons, believing that the law of libel exposed novelists and publishers to the risks of extravagant and impudent claims, and he thought that the Deeks case was an attempt to use a misguided woman as a blackmailing venture to wring money out of him. He became more than ever convinced of this when Miss Deeks managed to carry the case to the Privy Council in London, then the final court of appeal for Canadian litigation. Though this appeal was based on legal issues, all the evidence was now submitted again at length and eventually published in a Privy Council report in 1932.[18] The report itself gave a simple reason for finding against Miss Deeks. Even if her book had been published, there would have been insufficient evidence to support an action for infringement of copyright: as it had never been printed, there were no legal grounds at all for the action.

There, legally, the case ended. But it had now become an obsession with Miss Deeks who, like the wretched Miss Flite in *Bleak House*, hung around London courts as a persistent complainant, irritating Wells so much that he sought legal advice to see whether she could be silenced or deported, or some means found to cut off the unidentified source of money on which she relied for legal and living expenses. In December 1932 she took the last step possible under English law, the extraordinary action of petitioning the King to review the judgement of the Privy Council. Her request was refused, and she returned to Canada, leaving Wells to pay his bills. The experience was enough to make him feel that there should be a quicker and cheaper way of dealing with allegations of this kind, and on 23 November 1932 he sat down and drafted a letter to *The Times* to this effect. "I have a cockney cheerfulness that has sustained me against her imputations", he wrote, . . . "but for a more sensitive and less lucky writer, this persistent persecution might have meant irritation and distress of an altogether unendurable sort."

During the winter of 1929 H.G. had come to the conclusion that the attempt to maintain four homes was impossible. His first move was to give up his apartment at St Ermin's and to take a modern flat in Chiltern Court, a new block over Baker Street station into which Arnold Bennett was also moving. More dramatic was his decision to give up Easton Glebe. He had not used it much since Jane died, and found little pleasure in going down there. The relationship with Lady Warwick, moreover, had become tiresome. She was getting old and crotchety, and even before Jane had died there had been a series of rows. She had let Easton Lodge run down, as her money dwindled away, but she kept its grounds as a kind of nature reserve where animals roamed freely, and she continually complained that the Wells family and their guests used her drives as short cuts to the station, letting the cattle escape because they could not be bothered to

Photographs taken by Wells at Sandgate
24 (*above*) Joseph Conrad
25 (*below*) Bernard Shaw

26 (*above*) Arnold Bennett

27 (*below*) George Gissing

28 Violet Hunt
29 (*above*) Ford Madox Ford
30 (*below left*) Henry James

31 (*opposite*) The Reeves family. Amber, Beryl,
Maude, William Pember and Fabian Reeves
32 Hubert Bland
33 Edith Nesbit

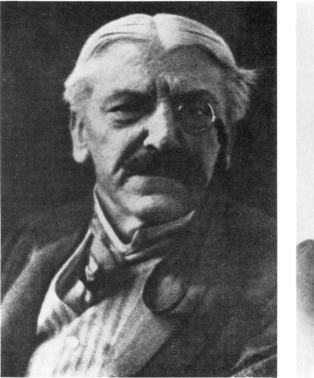

34 (*above left*) Church Row,
Hampstead
35 (*above*) Rebecca West in
1912
36 (*left*) Beatrice and Sidney
Webb

37 (*opposite*) Warwick Castle
party. Mrs S.L.Bensusan,
(not known), H.G.Wells,
R.D.Blumenfeld, Frank
Wells, Lady Warwick, Jane
Wells (*standing*), Mercy
Greville, G.P.Wells, Hugh
Cranmer-Byng and S.L.
Bensusan
38 Hockey at Little Easton.
H.G.Wells is in the centre
39 Easton Glebe

40 H.G.Wells, Maxim
Gorki and Moura
Budberg. This
photograph was taken
in Petrograd in 1920
41 Margaret Sanger

42 (*opposite*) Lou Pidou,
Grasse
43 The terrace, Lou
Pidou. Anthony West,
visitor, Odette Keun
and H.G.Wells

44 The drawing-room, Hanover Terrace

45 (*right*) Wells at war. A cartoon sent by David Low in reply to an irate letter from Wells

46 The study, Hanover Terrace

H. G. DRIVE · PRESSURE INCREASING

STRONGHOLDS STORMED | HEAVY SLAUGHTER
BATTALIONS WIPED OUT | RIVERS CROSSED ETC. ETC.

close the gates. In August 1930 H.G. decided to move away. Lady Warwick died in reduced circumstances not long afterwards.

During the latter part of 1930 H.G. was in London a good deal, settling into his new flat and finishing off what had now become *The Work, Wealth and Happiness of Mankind*, which was to be published the following year in the depths of an economic depression which made the title seem sadly ill-chosen. Charlie Chaplin, on a visit to London for the opening of *City Lights*, called at Chiltern Court where H.G. was working with "four lady secretaries inundated in books of reference, checking and making notes from encyclopedias, technical books, documents and papers".[19] Though the book was turning out a good deal better than H.G. had feared earlier, and he had taken much more of the work on himself than he had originally planned, by comparison with *The Science of Life* it was a flop. His attempt to treat economic affairs as a special branch of human ecology was neither well understood nor, with the world economy convulsed by the crisis, well received by a public whose thoughts were directed to more immediate and dramatic palliatives than to a wide-ranging review of social policies. Intended to round off the new Bible of Civilization commenced over ten years previously, the book was the last attempt Wells made to produce a massive "popular educator" of the kind that had so impressed him as a young man. He no longer possessed the energy to carry through such undertakings almost single-handed.

In the course of 1930, in fact, he was clearly tiring. Apart from completing the big volume on the social sciences, he produced only the pot-boiling political book, *The Way to World Peace*, and another instalment of his campaign for the Open Conspiracy, which appeared the following year under the title *What Are We To Do With Our Lives?* – a book which set out his current plan for the salvation of mankind and revealed his feelings of irritation and impotence at his failure to influence the course of events.

Much of his time was spent on social engagements with the eminent and influential, and on most week-days he could be seen lunching at the Reform Club with literary friends. In October 1930, he went back for a brief visit to the South of France, where Odette was becoming vocally remonstrative about his long absence and the useless boredom of her life when he was away. He promised to return at the end of the year. But before he left England, he had been seeing the former Marie von Benckendorff, now Baroness Budberg, who had looked after him during his visit to Russia in 1920. They had kept up a desultory correspondence during the years when she had been living in Italy with Maxim Gorki, and when she visited England briefly in 1927 she went down to Easton to visit H.G. and Jane shortly before Jane's death. At the same time, Gorki returned to Russia for a trial visit, and eventually he decided to settle in his own country. Moura had decided not to follow him there, fearing that it would be an embarrassment to him, and she began to make visits to England with a view of settling permanently in London. In October 1930 when Gorki was making one of his trips to Moscow, Moura came to London to see her children and friends, and H.G. was among them.

In November, when H.G. was back in England, he renewed another old relationship. His daughter, born at the end of 1909, was approaching her twenty-first birthday, and he wrote to Enid Bagnold asking her to join him "at a rather difficult little dinner". He was going to entertain Amber Reeves and her husband – "we have a common interest in their eldest daughter" – and "after years of estrangement . . . a cheerfully irrelevant guest will help the little party extremely."[20]

Soon afterwards H.G. went back to Lou Pidou for the winter, and when he had finished *What Are We To Do With Our Lives?* he began *The Bulpington of Blup*, subtitled "Adventures, Poses, Stresses, Conflicts, and Disaster In A Contemporary Brain" but in fact a barely-disguised satire on Ford Madox Ford. He had had little to do with Ford after their old intimacy had broken up in the row about *Tono-Bungay* and the *English Review*, but they had kept in touch through the vagaries of Ford's life and loves, and in 1929 when Ford lost all his savings in the Wall Street crash he successfully appealed to Wells for financial help.[21] It was a better novel than its predecessors, and it effectively made fun of Bulpington, revealing him as a fantasist with no real sense of identity. Yet, in gibing at this dual personality, H.G. had found yet another vehicle for his own dualism. Theodore Bulpington, a commonplace youth who becomes so imprisoned in his fantasy of self-importance that he is driven to act it out in a series of increasingly pathetic poses, belongs as a character with Mr Blettsworthy, Mr Preemby, Mr Barnstaple, and the other divided selves through whom Wells projected his own difficulty in distinguishing between reality and illusion. In basing his character on Ford, H.G. was paying off old scores, not least the unflattering portrait that Ford had drawn of him in *The New Humpty-Dumpty*, a satire on the pre-war literary world in which he hit Wells hard.

Wells returned to England from Lou Pidou on 25 March 1931. Two days later he was shaken by the loss of Arnold Bennett, who had contracted typhoid in France and died on his return to England. It had been a long intimacy. "You are the best friend I've ever had",[22] H.G. had written to Bennett the previous October, and Bennett had indeed stood by him stoutly through every crisis in his life, receiving his confidences and defending him against his critics. It had been a remarkable relationship for over thirty years, marked by uncompetitive professional respect and genuine affection. Bennett was one of the few close literary associates with whom H.G. never quarrelled, and from whom he could receive home-truths and advice without rancour. The explanation for this unusual achievement lies largely in Bennett's ability to see himself and his friends with the same honest detachment he displayed towards the characters in his books. He was a realist and he never allowed his relationship with H.G. to be soured by emotional judgements. It was, Wells wrote to Enid Bagnold two days afterwards, "such an *unnecessary death*. I'll miss him right enough."[23]

H.G. was now sixty-four, and he had money, reputation and immeasurable influence. But for all his success his life was unsettled and unsatisfying. The long and increasingly difficult involvement with Odette held out no prospect of an easeful and peaceful retirement. Having given up Easton Glebe, and changed his London flat, he now suddenly decided to give up his Paris apartment. It was not merely that the attempt to lead "a quadrilateral life" had proved too complicated and unsatisfying: the shuffling of his residences was the usual sign of an impending change in his domestic arrangements.

Another death came in September, when his first wife and cousin Isabel died suddenly. For some years she had been suffering from diabetes, an illness which H.G. himself had recently developed in a mild and controllable form. H.G. had long since resumed friendly relations, providing her with an income and with additional monies for her business ventures, and entertaining her at Easton for a period of convalescence after an operation. Yet her death broke a spell that had lasted for almost fifty years. While she lived, his feelings about her had broken through into several of the novels which had dealt with love and marriage. With her death, he seems to have been set free to let his memories play more easily over the years of youth.

The process had already started after Jane died. He had previously taken umbrage at several books of memoirs which contained gossip about him, as well as at works of fiction in which he appeared in thin disguise, but his attitude changed when Jane was dead. On 30 April 1930, for instance, he wrote to the publishing firm of Jonathan Cape to say that he did not care if it now issued a book by Edwin Pugh, the minor writer who had known him back in the Worcester Park days, which he had previously found offensive.[24] He had not wanted it to appear while Jane lived "because she liked me to be dignified – *and* I kept dignified to the best of my ability. But now she is dead and it doesn't matter a damn if I'm figured as a little Cockney cad." He was surprisingly receptive to a proposal that a young man named Geoffrey Wells should write his biography. H.G. suggested that a pen name would be helpful. Unwittingly he chose the pseudonym of Geoffrey "West".[25] H.G. not only talked to West of his own memories: he gave him every encouragement to dig into the facts, and to consult relatives and old friends. "He is the only person ever likely to get names & dates etc. right about me", H.G. wrote to Elizabeth Healey in November 1929 "so I let him nose about where he likes . . . He is the soul of discretion & exact & trustworthy in every way."[26] It was Geoffrey West's energetic research that turned up many letters and forgotten events that might otherwise have been lost.

As H.G. read through the material, which touched so directly on the spring of autobiography which had driven him as a writer throughout his life, he was undoubtedly moved to think of going over the same ground again in his own way. Geoffrey West had given him the stimulus he needed, at the moment in his life when he had been released to write *en clair* of the feelings and experience which had hitherto gone into his fiction. In January 1933 the project was well advanced: he wrote to Kotelianski that he was dealing only with his life up to 1900, since the story beyond that year would involve persons who were still living.[27] The renewed concern with his past was significant. At each previous crisis in his life, he had found it necessary to work through his feelings by producing an autobiographical novel which paralleled his experience and canvassed a fantasy solution to his difficulties. The task of producing the autobiography served much the same purpose. It was a form of psychic book-keeping which enabled him to close old accounts and strike a balance in his affairs. As the work progressed, it became increasingly clear that the French phase in his life was over and that it must be wound up before he could begin another of the new starts that had so regularly punctuated his career.

The signs of change had been there for some time, and they had been increasing since the middle of 1931. On 7 October of that year, H.G.

sailed on the *Aquitania* for a brief visit to New York, where Margaret Sanger had invited him to be the guest of honour at a Waldorf-Astoria dinner in support of her campaign for a federal law on birth-control. He caught a heavy cold and returned feeling poorly on the *Vulcania* on 13 November, going straight back to Lou Pidou for the winter and staying there until late March. By now he had become involved in the social life of the Riviera smart set, and spent much of his time entertaining or being entertained. There were Somerset Maugham, the Aga Khan, Lord Beaverbrook, Winston Churchill and other politicians, industrialists, writers, and socialites of the day, as well as old friends, such as Elizabeth von Arnim, who lived nearby. Though he continued to write articles on the state of the world, they became more and more abstract, as if made up by fusing information picked up at dinner parties with his own general theories. His journalism, though still immensely remunerative, conveyed boredom as well as distaste at the way the world was going. Compulsive repetition revealed his mental sterility.

When he felt frustrated, H.G. was liable to pick petty quarrels with his critics, and in the spring of 1932 he had such an exchange with Leonard Woolf, who had unwisely quoted a quip from an unnamed Oxford don to the effect that Wells was "a thinker who cannot think". Wells immediately seized on what he called "a pseudo-quotation" which "looks as though you wanted the thing said and hadn't the guts to say it on your own". Through the whole of March, H.G. chased the matter, and secured a disclaimer from the alleged author. "This puts you in a very queer position indeed", he wrote to Leonard Woolf: "Here you are launching a statement that the brightest and best of the sons of the morning are throwing me aside – and it isn't true." Then, back in England, he suddenly called the whole thing off and sent an amiable letter to Woolf saying that "we are too much in the same camp to knock the paint off each other in the sight of our enemies".[28]

It was a characteristic fit of pique, of a kind that was to recur increasingly throughout the Thirties, as H.G. felt that his reputation was slipping and that he was being written off as a survival from the past who had nothing to say to the present. He was, after all, getting on for seventy, and he disliked any evidence that he was ageing. He was beginning to feel, Odette Keun recalled of him at this time, a decline in his physical powers which worried him, and this intensified his resentment against anyone who in any way implied that he was no longer the man he once was.[29] Sex had always given him a quick if temporary release from anxiety, and all through his writing life there seems to have been a hidden link between his need to prove his potency in fact and his drive to assert himself publicly and in print. A critic who challenged his capacities as a writer was likely unwittingly to touch a deeper spring of pride and to incur a scathing attack that was usually disproportionate to the offence.

From the last years at Lou Pidou, Odette remembered "outbursts of passionate hostility" which contrasted strikingly with the gay façade of the *bon viveur* which H.G. displayed towards the Riviera smart set. "When he was irritated he could be *ferocious*", she said, describing the manner in which he dredged up a lifelong hatred of the upper classes with whom he now mingled so freely and fastened it on a casual victim. In such a mood he could be "quite demonic". Despite all the compensations of his life, she wrote later, he was unable to forgive "wounds inflicted so early by a social system that did not single him out for sacrifice" but rather "gave him the means to strike and at last opulently repaired the damage it had wrought . . . There is a morbid principle in tissues that cannot heal after such numerous and exceptional remedies have been applied. . . . He was never sane enough to forget – much less to throw off – his personal bitterness."

H.G. seemed increasingly unable to keep a grip on himself. Odette dated the deterioration in their relationship from the period after Jane died. Her death was not only a terrible blow to H.G.: it also removed one side of the triangular frame which contained his emotions. Odette, who had been a symbol of love and freedom, now, without her counterpoise, became a tiresomely demanding companion. Their affair had degenerated into an aimless, time-consuming obligation: the dream was over. For her part she had become disillusioned, not merely because she felt neglected in his long absences and unhappy in his presence, but also because Wells's towering self-pity and abrasive pettiness had gradually eroded the idol she had worshipped. The destructive impulse was reciprocal. Odette increasingly became the scapegoat for his fears and anger, which were always near the surface: though, in public, these broke through in attacks on critics and denunciations of the state of the world, in private H.G. released them in fierce quarrels with Odette. Passionate hate had taken the place of passionate love, and its impetus was becoming strong enough to carry him away from Odette for good.

By 1932 the situation was becoming intolerable, and during that winter H.G. found little peace at Lou Pidou. He was irritated by the way Odette would interrupt his work for trivialities, and the mannerisms that he had once found so attractive were beginning to pall. Jealousy, too, had begun to embitter their relationship. H.G had seen Moura Budberg again in London in October 1931, and kept up a correspondence with her thereafter. Odette was convinced that there was more to their friendship than the revival of an old acquaintanceship, and when she came across some letters from the Baroness there was an ugly ill-tempered quarrel. Odette was not calmed by H.G.'s assurances that her suspicions were groundless, and by the spring of 1933 things had reached breaking-point. H.G. had made an arrangement to meet Moura Budberg at the coming conference of the PEN Club in Ragusa (Dubrovnik), and to spend a holiday with her in Austria. The result, Odette said subsequently, was "a diabolically bitter row" which meant that the coming separation would be irrevocable.

H.G., characteristically seeing himself as the injured party, put the blame for "the débâcle at Lou Pidou" on Odette. Writing to Félicie afterwards he said flatly, "It is madame who caused it. It was impossible for me to live in a perpetual storm. . . . You know that I did my best to assure the success of this life, but it is the temperament of madame to spoil everything". He was still hoping to recover the house from Odette – who had been given the usufruct in the original deed – or at least to persuade her to let him have the use of it for some weeks in the year. But the effort failed, and he had to tell Félicie that "the separation between Madame Keun and myself is definite and final and for some years, perhaps, we shan't meet."[30]

It had been a hard decision to leave the house he had built for himself. But on 22 May H.G. walked through his olive grove for the last time and went down to Cannes to catch the train for Trieste. "It needed an effort", he wrote a year later, "but once more the liberating influence was the stronger."

THE BURDEN OF ATLAS

"I am very much in the 'take it or leave it' mood", H.G. wrote to C.E.M.
Joad on 14 October 1932: "I can't be Aaron to my own Moses. I can't be
a whole damn party by myself."[1] For more than thirty years Wells had
exerted enormous political influence through his writings, but his personal interventions in politics had been trivial, argumentative and
ineffective. He had always seen himself primarily as an ideologist rather
than as an organiser, and much though he wished to see his ideas taken
up he believed it was for others to apply them in practice. The correspondence with Joad was a case in point, for it related to a new scheme in which
Wells was to use his immense prestige to try and establish some common
ground among left-wing movements throughout the world. In November
he wrote the "creed" as a private memorandum, circulated in the first
instance to a number of friends in England, Europe and America. It
rehearsed familiar arguments – for the replacement of private profit by
public ownership, for the creation of a world monetary system, for
treaties to control armaments, for a vast educational programme, and for
the rights of free speech, publication and movement. He had gone over
this ground earlier in 1932, in the address to the Liberal Summer School
in Oxford which was published in *After Democracy*, and had then come to
the conclusion that the time was ripe to seek a wider audience for these
ideas. Though wealth and comfortable isolation in Provence had insulated
him from the impact of the depression, he was well aware that the slump
had broken up the pattern of politics that had seemed so secure in the
Twenties. A manifesto of this kind seemed the only means whereby he
could hope to affect the course of events.

The document was not particularly original or compelling in its prose.
Without the magic of the name of Wells it would have passed unnoticed.
Yet, in England, where left-wing intellectuals were casting around for
some new rallying-point after the disillusioning collapse of Ramsay
Macdonald's second Labour government, it did evoke a limited response

– mainly due to the efforts of Joad, then a young writer of popular books on philosophy whose views of life had been modelled on those of Wells. He helped to form a group of progressives into what looked like a local branch of the Open Conspiracy. The Federation of Progressive Societies and Individuals, whose title was more impressive than its membership list, never came to much, but it started with a fine flourish of sponsors who included Julian and Aldous Huxley, Rebecca West, Harold Laski, Bertrand Russell, Leonard Woolf, Harold Nicolson and Kingsley Martin. It did not impress H.G. for very long. Its notepaper was scarcely printed before he dismissed the lot of them as a miscellany of dilettantes. These publicists and professors were old friends, whose attitudes were close to his own, but they were nothing like the great industrialists, financiers and other men of power whom he had seen as potential recruits for the Open Conspiracy. Such men, he had believed in the Twenties, were groping their way towards the form of supra-national organisation which he had long advocated, and they controlled the means whereby it might be achieved – whereas radical propagandists were two-a-penny. The trouble was that his hopes had been shattered by the Great Crash. The world of the Clissolds was in ruins, and for the moment there were no obvious candidates to take the place of the bankrupt tycoons. As the depression swung politics to the left, the manifesto was simply an attempt to put out feelers again to the left-wing movement in which H.G. had shown very little interest for many years.

It is too simple to say that Wells himself moved left, though his political associations in England for the remainder of his life were almost wholly with left-wing causes and organisations – most of them on the eccentric fringes of the Labour movement. He had a distinctive position in politics which could not be neatly classified in contemporary terms as "right" or "left", and anyone who tried to locate him along that spectrum found puzzling contradictions. Cartels and trusts were generally anathema to socialists, but H.G. supported them because he believed that they were harbingers of a new world order. He hobnobbed with potentates and capitalists, yet he called himself a revolutionary and openly condemned the execution of the anarchists Sacco and Vanzetti. Because he admired large-scale planning, he approved of the Soviet Union – and simultaneously denounced Marxism as nonsense and Stalinism as a tyranny.

H.G. never saw politics in conventional terms. His apocalyptic beliefs had given him the notion of an élite whose mission it was to save mankind and, after an inevitable catastrophe, establish the New Jerusalem.

From that had stemmed the idea of the New Republicans, the Samurai and the Open Conspirators. The teaching of T.H.Huxley, which reinforced this Puritan inheritance, had led him to see society in a biological perspective, in which the survival of mankind depended upon the evolution of superior forms of social organisation. These concepts provided him with the ruling ideas of his life, and every political argument he advanced was some kind of permutation upon them. From *A Modern Utopia* onwards, he set up an antithesis between order and chaos, between the positive values of science and the negative values of a society which neglected it. These views cut right across normal political categories. For Wells, the cleavage did not lie between parties, or between nations. It was at work within them, and the dividing line separated the Open Conspirators – whatever their nominal beliefs or allegiances – from the rest.

Wells, as he told Joad, was a Moses and not an Aaron, and he felt he had fulfilled his prophetic role when he brought down the tablets of the law. He did not feel that it was incumbent upon him to interpret them, or to diminish their significance by becoming a follower of some other – and, in his eyes, lesser – ideology. It was this, quite as much as any distaste for the doctrines of the Communists and the Nazis, which kept him out of the totalitarian movements of the Thirties which appealed to so many intellectuals of his generation – and, indeed, to thousands of young people who read his books and had been influenced by his dreams. Ideologically, and emotionally, he had an affinity with them: they spoke the same millenarian rhetoric, they shared a contempt for bourgeois democracy and touched a similar streak of destructive fantasy. Yet, by his standards, the Nazis and Communists were primitives, nothing but crude and early approximations to the new social forms which he had already conceived, and tried to describe in his visions of utopia. There was no more question of his becoming one of them than there could be of man choosing to climb back down his family tree and become an ape. In his mind, Wells had already charted the next stages in the evolution of humanity.

The Shape of Things to Come, completed as H.G. began to work seriously upon his autobiography, was not irrelevant to the crisis of the early Thirties. That, in fact, was its starting-point. But it was deliberately designed as a work of prophecy rather than as political argument from which anyone might draw practical conclusions. After attempting, in

Clissold and the books which immediately succeeded it, to persuade his readers to improve the world, Wells concluded that fear was a more potent incentive – a decision which was much more in line with the grim mood of the times.* "Only through personal disaster", he wrote, "or the manifest threat of personal disaster can normal human beings be sufficiently stirred to attempt a revolutionary change of their conditions."[2] To bring this lesson home H.G. proceeded to cast a frightening horoscope for the next century and a half. This scenario of the future used a dream device like that which Wells had employed in earlier utopias. Referring specifically to the "time" theory of his old friend, J.W.Dunne, H.G. pretended that an eminent official of the League of Nations had been able to read a textbook written a hundred and fifty years hence. But, within this frame, the style of the book was that of *The Short History of the World*. To intensify the illusion that he was writing of actual events, H.G. devoted the first quarter of the book to his version of the years between the world war and the depression, and then wrote on in the same style to describe the years ahead. The next conflict breaks out in 1939, over a dispute between Germany and Poland about Danzig, and a devastating war gradually reduces the world to ruins, populated by sick and hungry people with scarcely a vestige of civilisation. It is essentially the story that H.G. had told before the First World War in fictional form in *The War in the Air*. From this doomsday only one group emerges with any cohesion and sense of purpose. The airmen who have made the slaughter now become the instruments of salvation, banding themselves together in an élite which begins to impose order on mankind. They are internationalists, dedicated to the world state, and because they control the airways and the sources of energy they can begin the building of the new world.

The Rule of the Saints has begun. In his previous apocalypses Wells had implicitly expressed that chiliastic vision, but in speaking of the dictatorship of the airmen he used the phrase explicitly. It is a "Puritan Tyranny", controlled by men whose moral standards are those of the Samurai in *A Modern Utopia*. They are bent on remaking human nature, because civilisation "is made against man's natural instincts". Because there is "one sole right way of doing things" their Act of Uniformity stamps out "every facile system of errors" suppressing the old religions and rooting out the cultural differences of the past. And they are as joyless as they are dedicated. They permit no card-playing, gambling or

---

* Reflecting at this time on the First World War he wrote: "I remain persuaded that there will have to be a last conflict to inaugurate the peace of mankind."

sport. They have a fear of leisure, but like all Puritans they make a fetish of work and productivity – believing that it is "morally necessary to keep going and to keep everybody else going" because it is too risky to permit a rush back to prosperity until mankind has shed the last vestiges of its acquisitive and competitive instincts.

It is the story of *Dr Moreau* all over again, though manipulative psychology has taken the place of manipulative surgery as a means of turning beasts into men, and war has replaced the operating table as "the bath of pain" through which they must pass to become free of their evolutionary heritage. That is the significance of the purgative years of the Puritan Tyranny in *The Shape of Things to Come*. It is not utopia itself, but its anteroom, and gradually – much as the Marxian apocalypse foresees the withering away of the state – life becomes rich, beautiful and congenial. Because men now share a common stock of knowledge and a single unifying purpose there is no more need for coercion, and they can bend their energies to the task of remaking the world as their garden. As the book ends they have mastered the secrets of genetics, producing new forms of life for their use and pleasure, and with their new-found powers they are beginning to raise mountains at will, control the rainfall and direct the winds. The myth of the Second Coming has been fulfilled, and the mind of the race is at one with the universe.

Thirty years before, in the address to the Royal Institution, Wells had talked of *The Discovery of the Future*, and in that speech he had declared that he had nothing to set against cosmic pessimism but a faith "in the greatness of human destiny . . . there stirs something within us now that can never die again . . . that gives the lie to our despair". Over three decades he had rung the changes on his metaphors, but he had not altered his view of man's place in the world or his conviction that the only hope of ultimate survival lay in finding a means of escape from the laws of evolution. One day a new race would "stand upon this earth as one stands upon a footstool . . . and reach out their hands amid the stars". With *The Shape of Things to Come* he recapitulated that prophetic message for the last time, completing, as he said, "the main arch of my work" which was intended to build a bridge into the darkness.

Wells knew that he had taken the world upon his shoulders. In the early Thirties he wrote that he had begun by carrying the burden of Atlas House and ended by carrying the burden of Atlas. In the spring of 1934 he took it into his head to descend upon Roosevelt and Stalin to judge how far "these two brains" were working towards the "socialist world-state that I believe to be the only hopeful destiny for mankind".

H.G. had been interested in the first stages of the New Deal, and he had already had some correspondence with F D.R. before he went to Washington early in May 1934. He took an immediate liking to the White House "Brains Trust". Such men as Raymond Moley, Felix Frankfurter and Rex Tugwell were the kind of dedicated experts he had always hoped to see take control of affairs. The fact that they were intelligent outsiders, called in when the professional politicians and public servants had failed, appeared to confirm his theory of the way the new ruling élite would emerge. Such persons would make the "Competent Receivers" he had always sought. Within a few days he had come to the conclusion that the President was surrounded by Open Conspirators and that if Roosevelt himself was not consciously attempting to create the Open Conspiracy, "he represents the way thither". It was an encouraging thought for Wells. "I do not say that the President has these revolutionary ideas in so elaborated and comprehensive a form as they have come to me", H.G. wrote patronisingly, but he considered that "these ideas are sitting all round him now, and unless I misjudge him, they will presently possess him altogether." He had found his ideal politician at last. Roosevelt, he declared after he left the United States, was "the most effective transmitting instrument possible for the coming of the new world order. . . . He is continuously revolutionary in the new way without ever provoking a stark revolutionary crisis."

Only six months before the visit to Washington, H.G. had written an article in *Liberty Magazine* predicting the failure of the New Deal, but after he had met Roosevelt he changed his opinion. The next question was whether Stalin would make a similarly favourable impression. "I confess that I approached Stalin with a certain amount of suspicion and prejudice", Wells wrote. "A picture had been built up in my mind of a very reserved and self-centred fanatic, a despot without vices, a jealous monopolizer of power." Seven weeks after he returned from America, on 21 July, H.G. flew off to Moscow. Despite his reservations about Stalin, he was ready to give "this lonely overbearing man" the benefit of some doubt, since he had heard good things of the progress of the first Five Year Plan. He was also ready to give Stalin a piece of his mind, if Stalin would listen, because he proposed to read the Russian leader a lecture on the world-state and, if opportunity served, to act as a *postillon d'amour* between the White House and the Kremlin.

The interview with Stalin was very like that with Lenin some fourteen years before, though on this occasion there was a transcript to record what was said during the three-hour meeting.[3] Wells sought to convince Stalin that large-scale planning was the inevitable result of modern methods of production and communication, and that it was bound to occur whether the system was socialist or capitalist. The corollary was co-operation between the great industrial powers for constructive purposes – what, in more recent terms, would be called "peaceful co-existence". This argument, spiced with a dash of Wellsian polemic against old-fashioned ideas of the class war, made no impact at all on Stalin, who proceeded to take Wells through a pedantic lesson in revolutionary history to prove that a propertied class yields power only to force. When Wells insisted that the new revolution was in fact to be made by the technical intelligentsia, Stalin came back with the complaint that in Russia this group had opposed and sabotaged the Soviet system: it was not a real class at all, being merely the servant of whichever class – capitalists or proletarians – held political power. "You, Mr Wells", said Stalin, "evidently start out with the assumption that all men are good. I, however, do not forget there are many wicked men. I do not believe in the goodness of the bourgeoisie." Confronted by this crude assertion of Marxist morality, Wells was at a loss. It was clearly impossible for him to make Stalin understand that he did not believe all men were good – that, indeed, he divided the educated élite as clearly from the remainder of mankind as decisively as Stalin distinguished between the proletariat and the bourgeoisie. What H.G. was trying to do was to persuade Stalin that all his Marxist imagery was little more than verbal camouflage on a system that was essentially state-capitalist, and that the Soviet and American economies were moving towards rather than away from each other. This was not a line of reasoning so fashionable as it became.

Though Wells's description of the managerial revolution was closer to the realities of Stalin's Russia than he could have realised, Stalin refused to shift an inch from his dogmatic repetition of the party line. It is difficult to understand why, except for the formal civilities of the discussion, H.G. came away feeling that he had "never met a man more candid, fair and honest" and that it was to these qualities "and to nothing occult and sinister" that Stalin owed his power. It was an extraordinary judgement in the circumstances, for Stalin at that moment was planning the purges which liquidated the old leadership of his party, decimated its membership, and finally established his undisputed and arbitrary control of the Soviet Union.

Stalin had made an agreeable personal impression on Wells, but the overall effect of this interview was in marked contrast to the sense of hope with which H.G. had come away from Washington. And, as Wells went on a round of conducted visits to schools and public works, he became increasingly depressed. The inefficiency of the Soviet régime irritated him; so did the complacency and self-satisfaction of its officials, continually harping on the uniqueness of an achievement that did not seem to him so very splendid. But the most deadening experience was a visit to Maxim Gorki whom he had once admired as a lively and critical spirit and who, to the distress of Wells, had now lapsed into unqualified apologetics for Stalinism.

Not long before, H.G. had become international president of the organisation of PEN clubs, which John Galsworthy had built up as a means of promoting friendly contacts among writers in different countries. At the time that Wells succeeded Galsworthy, the organisation was being drawn into the problems raised by the persecution of Jewish and radical writers in Germany and other fascist countries, and H.G. was taking the lead in an effort to preserve some freedom for men of letters in a darkening world. When he met Gorki and some other Soviet writers, he made the unpropitious suggestion that they should form a free PEN club in Moscow, and seek to liberate themselves from state control. It distressed him to find Gorki, once a proud rebel, basking "half-deified" in Stalin's approval and lending himself to the suppression of literary freedom. Even worse, he found Gorki "devising shrewd questions to reveal the spidery 'capitalist' entanglement he suspected me of spinning". H.G., who had spent his life in passionate controversy, had never wavered in his conviction that free speech was vital to human dignity, and he was appalled to find that all his arguments were reduced to the simple proposition that he wanted exiled White Russian writers to return to Moscow to conduct propaganda against Communism. It was the last straw to discover that Gorki's Soviet patriotism now led him to reject another nostrum that he once shared with Wells – the belief that birth control was essential to a planned world.

"I had expected", Wells said, "to find a new Russia stirring in its sleep and ready to awaken to Cosmopolis, and I found it sinking deeper into the dope-dream of Sovietic self-sufficiency." The visit left H.G. "acutely frustrated and disappointed". His sense that "Russia had let me down" forced upon him the sobering conclusion that "there is no short cut to be found to the Open Conspiracy". It was this despairing thought which pressed upon Wells as he left Russia. He went directly to join Moura Budberg in Esthonia to rest, and set down his impressions of his Soviet visit and write the final pages of his autobiography. Nothing, he wrote, now stood between the human race and universal freedom and abundance but "mental tangles, egocentric preoccupations, obsessions . . . bad habits of thought, subconscious fears and dreads and plain dishonesty". But it had proved beyond his capacity to change human nature: it remained as intractable as ever. "Though most of the people in the world in key positions are more or less accessible to me", he wrote in a sad footnote to all his endeavours, "I lack the solvent power to bring them into unison. I can talk to them and even unsettle them but I cannot compel their brains to see."

On his return to England H.G. was given another tiresome reminder that his powers of persuasion were limited. He had offered Kingsley Martin, then still in his first years of editing *The New Statesman*, a valuable scoop by allowing him to publish the Stalin interview. Martin then asked Shaw to comment on the discussion, and printed a teasing letter in which Shaw insisted that Wells had behaved boorishly by preaching at Stalin and refusing to listen to Stalin's sound sense. Shaw, at this time, had seen Stalin himself and shared the discovery of Sidney and Beatrice Webb that Stalin's Russia was remarkably like an idealised version of a Fabian state.

The row was like old times.[4] The vision of Wells, said Shaw, "is so wide and assured that the slightest contradiction throws him into a blind fury of contemptuous and eloquently vituperative impatience". Wells replied that Shaw's "touchily defensive egotism and his disposition to dramatise, make so brilliant a clamour that he is practically stone deaf". Despite more sober interventions in the debate by Maynard Keynes and others who tried to make it a serious discussion about the prospects of socialism and capitalism, Shaw and Wells could not be distracted from their knock-about turn. Shaw said that Wells "trots into the Kremlin and tells Stalin that his head is over-stuffed with some absurd nonsense called class warfare". Wells, referring to the interview which Shaw and Lady Astor had recently been given by Stalin, gibed back that Shaw "can have all the glory of saying that I 'trotted' into the Kremlin while, by implication, he and Lady Astor, with the utmost grace, strode, swam, stalked, danced, slid, skated or loped in, and conversed in some superior imperial fashion of which no record survives". Shaw refused to withdraw the word "trotted". A man's mood, he said, "is always reflected in his locomotion.

Wells did not strut; that would have been vulgar; and Wells is not vulgar. He did not stalk nor prance in the Shavian manner. He did not merely walk; he is too important for that. Having eliminated all possible alternatives, I conclude that he trotted. If not, what *did* he do?"

It was splendid copy and Kingsley Martin decided to publish the correspondence as a pamphlet. He telephoned H.G. to ask his permission. "Of course", Wells said: "Shaw has behaved like a cad and ought to be exposed." Martin then spoke to Shaw, who refused his consent. "Certainly not," he told Kingsley Martin: "I have a great respect for my old friend, H.G. He's made a perfect ass of himself and I wouldn't want it put on permanent record." Martin persevered, and Shaw said that he would reluctantly concur if Wells and Keynes "want to exhibit themselves at their worst".[5] Apart from the letters and telephone calls that passed through Martin's office in Great Turnstile, there was a parallel correspondence going on between Chiltern Court, where H.G. sat in a dudgeon, and Whitehall Court, where Shaw was in bed feeling poorly, with Charlotte endeavouring to act as peacemaker.[6] In her view, Martin was playing them off against each other, and she wrote to H.G. on 27 November to say that she and G.B.S. thought the whole thing should be dropped. Wells, however, would not be appeased, insisting that the proposed pamphlet would square the account, because Shaw's "wicked little onslaught on me (which really hurt me very much) has been quoted all over the USA, Russia and the Communist press". At the same time he wrote to Martin to say that "the Shaws want the pamphlet suppressed, but I want it published . . . G.B.S. made a rotten attack on me and he ought to take his dose like a man."[7]

Even in the middle of the row – so like others Shaw and H.G. had fought in the past about Fabian politics, the jingoism of Wells in 1914, about Lenin, Darwinism, Samuel Butler, vivisection, Pavlov's psychology and the Life Force – H.G. wrote regretfully of the waste of effort. "Here are Shaw and I nearing the end of our lives", he said, "and we can do nothing better with each other than this personal bally-ragging. It is ridiculous to be competitive and personally comparative after 65."

The pair of them had formed a lifelong habit of barbed banter which fused rivalry and friendship. "What have I done to God that he should plague me with you in this fashion?" Shaw wrote to H.G. only a few weeks later, on the appearance of the second volume of his autobiography.[8] "I seem to spend my life rescuing the victims of your outrageous assaults and seeming to remonstrate with you and make fun of you whilst I have to boost you subtly all the time." In a long letter which explained his attitude towards the *Experiment in Autobiography*, G.B.S. retold the story of the Fabian row to show why Wells had misunderstood what happened. "You think that when you came along you antagonized me, but you are wildly wrong", Shaw wrote.

. . . I did my best to keep you in the Society. My nearest to a real quarrel with the Webbs was when I forced them to recognize that Ann Veronica and you had the upper hand of them because they could not expose you without discrediting the London School of Economics by a sexual scandal. Bland was savagely furious with you because you tried to shake the resistance of Rosamund by citing the example of her parents. A debate between you and Bland would have been a butchery: one with Webb would have been very painful. I was the obvious alternative; but they mistrusted me deeply (and quite rightly) because they knew that I was a Wellsite as far as it was possible for anyone to be a Wellsite in the face of your wild behavior. There was no fear of not defeating you; you were sure to defeat yourself hopelessly every time you opened your mouth or put pen to paper.

. . . However, I would not have you other than you are. All the idols are the better for having an occasional brick shied at them . . .

The publication of the autobiography was the occasion for many people to reflect on H.G. Wells. There was a rewarding letter from F.D.R. to say that "*Experiment in Autobiography* was for me an experiment in staying awake instead of putting the light out. How do you manage to retain such vivid pictures of events and such extraordinarily clear impressions and judgements . . . I believe our biggest success is in making people think during these past two years. They may not think straight but they are thinking in the right direction – and your direction and mine are not so far apart."[9]

Among letters from H.G.'s old friends, there came a warm note from Richard Gregory to appreciate the affection Wells had shown to the South Kensington crowd, in which he made the interesting comment that "no one analyses women better than you do or expresses more candidly the feeling of normal men towards them. That is why so many women are attracted to you."[10]

H.G. had been writing much of his life in fictional guise off and on for more than thirty years and still, now he came to put down the true plot that lay behind all the transparencies, he found something fresh to say. It fascinated Beatrice Webb, who had grown more charitable towards him as they both aged.[11] She thought that he emerged from his self-portrait as "a splendidly vital man: an explorer of man's mind, a critic, artist, derider and visionary all in one. In spite of deplorable literary manners, and mean sexual morals, H.G. is to me a likeable and valuable man. He has been on the side of the angels; he has wanted to make life better for the masses of men and he has subordinated his art to that purpose."

Conventional Christianity, of rather low calibre, resulted in a violent reaction towards a derisive atheism . . . There was no code of conduct and no rational outlook as to the relation of man to man, or of man to the universe. . . . Except for his admiration of Huxley, Wells grew up with a contempt for his fellow human beings, notably for the existing governing class, on the one hand, and for the multitude of manual workers on the other. His swift rise through his rare gift for imaginative journalism – to wealth and social position – increased his self conceit and stabilised his bad manners . . . But unfortunately Wells has not been satisfied to be a delightful romancer – he has thought of himself as a great thinker – as a shaper of the world to come . . . that is to redeem the lot of the human race . . . this grandiose aim needs some knowledge of social institutions – and H.G.Wells is as innocent of this specialised knowledge as I am of the mysteries of mathematics . he did not want to examine the origin, growth, disease and death of social institutions; he wanted to judge them . . .

Beatrice Webb, like Shaw, had no illusions about H.G.'s claims to save the world, and both of them could write plainly and unemotionally about him. In this respect, as Beatrice noted in her diary, they differed from Odette, "the discarded loved one of the last ten years", who had known him intimately and had become bitterly disillusioned. She used the opportunity of reviewing the autobiography to write three long articles, published in *Time and Tide* during October 1934, which were an astonishing public analysis of her former lover's character.[12]

Odette Keun had begun as a disciple of this "gigantic personality" who "imposed his dream on all of us", and she now attempted to define the flaw in his genius. This "noisy, rude, selfish, sulky, ungrateful, vulgar, and entirely insuppressible" little boy had been miraculously "over-sensitized". H.G. had no moral discipline Huxley's rationalism had destroyed his religious sense, and his behaviour depended wholly upon the impulsive likes and dislikes of an "outraged ego". He had no humility, and for him life was a game rather than a vocation. Though he won an enormous following, he was a player rather than a true leader, and he would never take responsibility for the role in which he had cast himself.

"His unparalleled capacity for shifting and changing", Odette wrote, was "shattering for the men and women who aspired to be disciples." His forays into the Fabian Society, the League of Nations and the Labour Party were no more serious than the floor games he had invented for his sons. "I cannot remember a single instance", Odette wrote in a glancing reference to the symbolism of his removal from one home to another, one woman to another, and one political loyalty to another, "when he remained with perseverance inside a house he had chosen."

Even then Odette was not done. Wells was flawed by his "brutality . . . He turned intellectual debate into a private quarrel . . . He ridiculed his adversaries. He blinded his audience to the nature of his play . . . This idol of course . . . is cruel. He had no conviction of reality about either humanity or the individual. The game was the thing." The bitterness was more than the malice of a rejected woman. It was a curse on the fallen idol. "I have heard that voice before" was H.G.'s scornful comment.[13]

The autobiography received good notices, though H.G. was irritated by the failure of reviewers to take the second volume – which summarised his ideas – as seriously as his account of his childhood and his struggle to become a writer. He was annoyed with his publisher, "the dodgy Gollancz who has published two complete books" when the work had been intended as a unity.[14] H.G. was making the kind of complaint with which his publishers had long been familiar. Gollancz was not doing enough to promote the book. There was trouble with booksellers because Wells had allowed cheap editions of his work to be issued by the *Daily Mail* and Odhams Press, as part of the promotion schemes newspapers were then using in a circulation war. Booksellers who thought this unfair competition were refusing to display *Experiment in Autobiography*, and selling it only on special order. If Gollancz refused to do anything about this boycott, H.G. told him, "I suppose I must find other channels of distribution." He was thinking of selling his work directly in cinema foyers and similar places: "I prefer to exert myself to test that and other possibilities before I go under."[15]

The idea that H.G. might "go under" was ridiculous. His taxable income in America alone was $21,000 in 1933, $45,000 in 1934, and $29,000 in 1935, despite the depression. But he never lost the anxiety he had shown in his earliest days as a writer that his publishers might fail to push his work sufficiently, and he was always attracted by the idea of large cheap editions which would get his books into the hands of a huge readership. For both these reasons he quarrelled with publishers, changed them frequently, and continually irritated the bookselling trade. On 4 June 1934 he frankly explained his motives to a member of Gollancz's staff. "I *always* ask for as big a cheque as possible", he wrote, "because from my point of view it will guarantee that the publisher will go all out for the book in question. It is his role, not mine, to take risks on the book and lose if the book fails."[16] This attitude accounts for the fact that in the late Thirties at least nineteen London publishers were carrying books by Wells in print. *The Bookseller* noted after his death that this "bee-like promiscuousness was one of the reasons why – reckoning purely by book-trade measurements – Wells never became the solid institution that one would expect from an author of his stature".[17]

This lack of consistency cannot be explained on financial grounds. Wells in fact lost more than he gained by such restlessness. It was a matter of personality, the search for the fresh stimulus which always came as the rebound from the disappointments of a previous and exaggerated hope. What was true of publishers was true of ideas, organisations and personal relationships. "Every so often", Odette Keun recalled, "he became intolerably bored and stale, immeasurably fed-up and wearied by circumstances which kept going wrong, and he desperately craved for renewal."[18] One way to find renewal was with a new woman. "A novel emotional experience", Odette added, "could change his state of mind, release cooped-up energies, give him freshness and vigour, a surge of intellectual curiosity and power, and the hope that at least, after a lot of travelling, he had reached an enchanting oasis." But when the oasis proved to be arid and the flowers were replaced by weeds, he sooner or later "embarked on another expedition. There was always an abundance of women who were very eager indeed to participate in his voyage." Somerset Maugham, who saw a good deal of H.G. in the South of France, had the same impression. "If his companion was not intelligent", he said of Wells, "he soon grew bored with her, and if she was her intelligence sooner or later palled on him. He did not like his cake unsweetened and if it was sweet it cloyed." Wells, as Maugham noted, had strong sexual instincts, "and he said to me more than once that the need to satisfy these instincts had nothing to do with love. It was a purely physiological matter." It was actually more than that: Wells found sex a vital anodyne for despair. When he was depressed by overwork, he would break down – sometimes with rage, sometimes to the point of tears – and then the release of emotion would pass into love-making, followed by a sound sleep from which he would wake early in the morning and resume writing with fresh enthusiasm. Charlie Chaplin remembered an illuminating remark by H.G. at Lou Pidou. "There comes a moment in the day", Wells said, "when you have written your pages in the morning, attended to your correspondence in the afternoon, and have nothing further to do. Then comes that hour when you are bored; that's the time for sex."[19]

The separation from Odette was not followed by the simple substitution of one domestic relationship for another. At the end of October 1934 Beatrice Webb noted in her diary that G.B.S. had told her that H.G. was "ill and worried . . . he has fallen to the charm of 'Moura' . . . 'She will stay with me, eat with me, sleep with me', whined the love-sick H.G. to G.B.S. 'But she will not marry me' . . . H.G. aware of old age, wants to buy a 'sexual annuity' by marriage: 'Moura', looking back at his past adventures, refuses to give her independence and her title away. And no wonder!"

The association was taken for granted, even though H.G. and Moura maintained separate homes, after she finally settled in London in 1935. Moura herself was explicit on the point, telling Enid Bagnold much the same as Shaw had told the Webbs. "I'm not going to marry", she remarked. "He only *thinks* I am. I'm not such a fool."[20] There was, nevertheless, a kind of symbolic wedding – a large dinner party at the Quo Vadis restaurant in Soho. Apart from H.G.'s sons and their wives, the guests included the cartoonist David Low and his wife, Violet Hunt, Max Beerbohm, Maurice Baring, Harold Nicolson, Juliette Huxley, Lady Cunard, Lady Lavery, Enid Bagnold and other old friends. It was Enid Bagnold who lent H.G. and Moura the house in Rottingdean, on the Sussex coast, which had once belonged to Rudyard Kipling, for what she called their "honeymoon".[21] While they were there, H.G. remarked to her that "you only look a fool if you fall in love with a *young* woman", a sober thought that he repeated in a letter of explanation to his old friend Elizabeth Healey on 29 October 1934. "I'll let Moura know of your good wishes", he wrote. "We live in open sin & you must meet her some day. But for two grandparents with lives of their own there is neither marrying nor giving in marriage."[22]

Though, by mutual consent, H.G. was to live alone, looked after by his domestic staff, and with all his professional arrangements in the capable hands of Marjorie Wells, the new liaison was marked by the inevitable change of residence. The flat at Chiltern Court was luxurious but without any character: H.G. had a poor sense of style. The apartment, one visitor said, "might have been furnished by any large furnishing firm. There was absolutely no sign of personal taste, or personal life about it. It might have been a suite in a hotel."[23] Once the relationship with Moura was settled, H.G. decided to take a house at 13 Hanover Terrace, one of the splendid Regency groups built by Nash within and overlooking Regent's Park. It had been the home of Alfred Noyes, the poet, and when H.G. was negotiating with Noyes to take over the lease he made the sardonic remark that he was "looking for a house to die in".[24] His behaviour at the time, however, gave no indication of failing energies. Noyes gave a wryly comical account of the way Wells descended upon him in the Isle of Wight by plane to discuss the details and made a terrible scene on his arrival because his bag – supposedly containing the manuscript of *The Shape of Things to Come* – had been lost. H.G. immediately began to write letters organising a search, starting with the Associated Press, Lord Beaverbrook and Scotland Yard! Noyes simply got to work on the telephone and traced the bag to the airport at Newcastle. When it was found and opened, there was no manuscript, and Noyes apprehensively informed H.G. that this was the case. To his astonishment Wells simply dropped the matter and began to complain about the pyjamas and the razor that Noyes had lent him. Soon afterwards an extending fire-escape fell on him at Hanover Terrace and bloodied his nose: within an hour or so H.G. had a report and a photograph of himself in bandages in the London papers – the stories giving the impression that Noyes had somehow tapped him in the face. Thereafter, Wells refused to forward letters that came to Noyes at Hanover Terrace. Noyes had the impression that Wells at this time was in a highly nervous state.

When H.G. moved into Hanover Terrace he asked his old friend Sybil, Lady Colefax, to "do" the house. While the house was being readied he spent a long holiday with Moura in the South of France, to get away from the English winter, and in March 1935 he went off for a month's visit to the US to update himself on Roosevelt's activities and write the articles which were made up into *The New America: The New World*.

Throughout 1934 H.G. had driven himself hard. Apart from the readjustment in his personal life, and the tiring journeys to Washington and Moscow, he had thrown himself with his usual energy into the film version of *Things to Come*. For the first time he had an opportunity to devise a movie version of his prophecies. He had met the young Hungarian film producer Alexander Korda, who had recently come from France with his

brother Vincent, and was about to play a significant role in the expansion
of the British film industry. Korda had already produced the film version
of *The Man Who Could Work Miracles* as a low-budget picture in the
primitive Isleworth studio, and Frank Wells had then worked as an
assistant on the set designs.

Soon afterwards Korda persuaded H.G. to produce a new scenario,
based on the latter part of the book *Things to Come*, and by the summer of
1934 the work had begun. It was an ambitious undertaking, which raised
many problems.[25] Moura was used as an interpreter, the two Korda
brothers speaking French and H.G. English. There were technical
hazards, too. Sound recording was still a new technique and the fine new
studios that Korda was building at Denham were not yet completed. Part
of the film had to be made at the old studio at Isleworth, part out at
Elstree, part on a huge outdoor set. A combination of enthusiasm and
inexperience led the Korda brothers into recruiting a distinguished team
which proved incapable of translating what they and Wells wanted into
film. They brought over the architects Le Corbusier and Gropius to design
sets, and sent them away again. Vincent Korda imported the French
painter Fernand Léger to design costumes, and four weeks were wasted
before his "functionalist" ideas were rejected and the job handed over to
the young English painter John Armstrong. Vincent also brought over
the Hungarian artist Moholy Nagy to design back-projections for the
sequences showing the rebuilding of the world after the catastrophic war.

This miscellany of talents created a situation in which H.G. was
alternately enthused and frustrated. Korda gave him a free hand. It was
H.G.'s idea, for instance, to enlist Arthur Bliss to write the score.[26] "I
continue to be confident and delighted", he wrote to Bliss on 29 June
1934. "But I am not so sure of the Finale. Perhaps I dream of something
superhuman, but I do not feel that what you have done so far, fully
renders all that you can do in the way of human exaltation. It's good dash
– nothing you do can fail to be good – but it is not yet the exaltant shout
of human resolution that there might be – not the marching song of a new
world of conquest among the atoms and stars." While H.G. was coaching
Bliss, however, he was having a struggle with Korda, who wanted to add
the music after the film was finished and edited. "I say Balls!" H.G. wrote
to Bliss on 16 October. "I say 'A film is a composition and the musical
composer is an integral part of the design, I want Bliss to be in touch
throughout.' I don't think Korda has much of an ear, but I want the
audience at the end not to sever what it sees from what it hears. I want to

end on a complete sensuous and emotional synthesis." * Wells got his way: much of the music was actually recorded before the scenes were shot, and the long sequence where automatic machines rebuild the ruined world was filmed and cut to Bliss's music rather than to scripted dialogue.

For two years, Wells, the Korda brothers and a talented group of actors and technical people struggled to bring this ambitious film into a manageable – and marketable – form. It had no strong story-line to hold it together. Wells tried to pack a simplified version of mankind's progress through a devastating war, the coming of the dictatorship of the airmen and the reconstruction of the world state, to the final escape into space from the soulless and hygienic utopia constructed by the scientific élite. And, though the film had some striking visual effects, Vincent Korda later conceded that it lacked rigour and that it had been planned on an impossibly ambitious scale. Bliss sensed that, as it was assembled, Wells was becoming more disillusioned with it. "My film is a mess of a film & Korda ought to be more ashamed of it than I am", H.G. wrote to the Webbs on 29 October 1936, when it was finished [27] He had hoped to use the film as an object lesson on the dangers of war and the need for scientific planning to create a new world of peace and leisure. But it became a crude morality play, in which Wells appeared to be trying to frighten the wits out of the public and then offering them an inhuman future dominated by autocratic technicians. This was the reaction of Beatrice and Sidney Webb when, in November 1936, "out of friendly curiosity" they went over to Farnham to see the film. Beatrice thought the destruction of civilisation by war was "vividly impressive; without H.G.'s expansive imagination and artistic talent it could not have been conceived". But she found the new social order "the epitome of meaningless mechanisation".

The human home of future ages is to be without an outlook on the beauties of nature . . . Within masses of moving machinery, multitudes of men and women and children scurrying about like ants in a broken open ant hill: they seem moved by herd impulse not by individual minds. Restless, intolerably restless, is this new society of men: ugly and depressing in its sum total . . . As an attempt to depict *a new civilisation* the film is a disastrous failure.

Wells himself had a flicker of doubt about the denial of art and feeling in the future utopia; in the book he had briefly described a revolt by the artists against the Puritan Tyranny. But in the film this became no more than a piece of hurried melodrama which implies that the world is again about to regress and that the future of the superior breed of man lies in flight to the stars. H.G. had always made this one concession to the idea of beauty. As early as *The Wonderful Visit* he had set up the Angel of Art as against positivist science, and all through his utopias there ran a hint that the New Jerusalem of the scientists might prove to be a pretty inhuman place. But *Things to Come* seemed to confirm the popular impression of his writings that he welcomed, as well as predicted, the triumph of technology as the means to the survival of the race against the evolutionary odds. The future of man demands that he use the earth as a footstool to the stars.

The effect was to numb, rather than to inspire. Years before, when Ford Madox Ford found himself in the front line during the First World War, he noted that he had been so conditioned to modern warfare by reading the novels of Wells that when he actually experienced it he felt apathetic and resigned. Something of the same sort seems to have happened with *Things to Come*. The scenes of the sudden air attack on London in 1940, shown in a film that was widely distributed in the late Thirties, had an undoubted effect on public opinion, giving the cinema public a most vivid anticipation of what war might suddenly bring to England. What was intended, both by Korda and Wells, as an anti-war tract seems to have been one of the factors which created public support for the policy of appeasement.

H.G. had been caught up by the excitements of the film world. He had made many new friends among the actors and directors, and he was talking of going on with movie-making instead of writing books. While his enthusiasm had been directed to the studio, he had virtually dropped his journalism and there was no substantial book in preparation. It was these new connections that gave him the idea of a trip to Hollywood, planned for the autumn of 1935, while the technical work was being done on *Things to Come*. He arrived in California on 26 November after an arduous cross-country flight. He was staying with Charlie Chaplin and Paulette Goddard, and he wrote to Sinclair Lewis to say that he found Chaplin "more sympathetic than ever. He is struggling here with parallel difficulties to mine at Isleworth. The film industry is still the old silent industry & C.C. has the enduring amateurishness & freshness & enterprise of the really great. He will come out of the silent film in his own way but he will be a tired man by the time he does it."[28] Hugh Walpole, then living in Hollywood, noted that H.G. was lionised by the film community and enjoyed it hugely, being "delighted with the pretty women".[29] Cecil

B.de Mille gave a party for him at his ranch, and the Chaplins took him to visit Hearst at the fantastic castle at San Simeon. There, according to Walpole, H.G. delivered a long and tactless speech after dinner, "saying in his whispering squeaky voice that the past hundred years in American history were nothing for Americans to be proud of, and that since 1920 Americans had behaved like idiots. They had the chance to rule the world, but because of greed and pusillanimity had lost all their chances. The Americans at table looked blue and were very polite." But he was even more disparaging about Russia. Chaplin, who had long been a Soviet sympathiser, took him to task for judging the Soviet régime too soon. "If you, a socialist believe that capitalism is doomed", Chaplin said, "what hope is there for the world if socialism fails in Russia?" Wells replied that "Socialism won't fail in Russia, or anywhere else, but this particular development of it has grown into a dictatorship."[30]

When Wells got back to London in mid-January, he found waiting for him the huge book that Sidney and Beatrice Webb had written on their Russian visit. *Soviet Communism: A New Civilisation?* had been written as meticulously and extensively as every study that the Webbs had produced, but it described Stalin's Russia in the way it was supposed to work rather than in the way it actually was working on the eve of the great purges, and lent the prestige of the Webbs to the campaign that Soviet apologists were then beginning to mount around the "democratic" nature of the Stalin Constitution. H.G. sent off a quick note of appreciation.[31] "It's a great piece of work", he wrote. "I think the design and handling couldn't be better . . . You keep your feet on the ground & yet you seem to have everything within your reach . . . You're great people. Sometimes in the past, in the heat of our mutual education, I may have seemed a trifle 'detractive' of you. I'm glad to have this occasion to render you a phrase or so of unqualified respect." He put his finger, however, on the main weakness of the work. "I would like to take up the issue of free discussion with you. There I think you are a little disposed to take Soviet assurances for facts." Over a year later, on 27 July 1937 H.G. wrote a postscript to the same effect, when he had thought a good deal more about the Webbs' enthusiasm for the Soviet Union: "you underestimate", he wrote, "the stress of personal autocracy & I think that also you ignore the real deterioration of the 'controlled' intellectual and that makes us question your optimism quantitatively. But we agree substantially. It is a new civilization."[32]

Though H.G. had not changed his views about the Communist Party, which he thought a "mischievous" collection of pseudo-revolutionaries, several close associates were members of the party, or fellow-travellers and, in the political climate of the mid-Thirties, H.G. was influenced by the Popular Front campaign. His concern for literary freedom, and the role he was playing in the PEN Club in helping refugee writers, led him to take a strong stand against European fascism. The outbreak of the Spanish War was one of the factors in arousing his latent anti-Catholicism, and he began to see the hand of the Vatican behind the policies of the British Foreign Office. And, for all his disillusionment after his own visit to Stalin, he was always impressed by any evidence that the Soviet Union might eventually emerge as the prototype of a planned socialist society. Politically, as he wrote to the left-wing Labour politician George Mitchison on 12 September 1934, he was now describing himself as "an ultra-left revolutionary. I want to see socialism everywhere in the world."[33] He lent his name to the notepaper of good causes. In July 1936 for example, he became vice-president of the Abortion Law Reform Societ And he began to give donations to a number of left-wing organisations – a little later he was one of the backers of the Unity Theatre promoted by the Communist Party. Yet, as he neared seventy, he was content to see himself as a journalist and pamphleteer, and to keep his distance from active politicians.

On 1 June 1936 when H.G. was spending the week-end in South Wales as the guest of Lord Tredegar, a rich coalowner, he wrote to Shaw thanking him for a new volume of plays which he had read "with the same mixture of irritation & admiration that has been my normal response to you for years".[34] He had always teased G.B.S. for his abstemious habits, and now he wrote: "How you go on! God grant me in spite of my drinking & meat-eating & whoring the same vitality. You go on, less & less propitiatory to the public & more & more yourself. Bless you".

H.G. was himself feeling under the weather. In September 1935 the ladder which fell on him at Hanover Terrace had set off an attack of neuritis which plagued him for two or three years, becoming severe in the course of 1937. The condition was bad enough at times to make writing and normal social life difficult, and to intensify his propensity to irritability. It required little provocation to start a row, and H.G. does not seem to have minded whether this happened in public or private. On several occasions he made a scene in a restaurant, ending a loud quarrel by stumping out in a rage – an episode almost always followed by a dis-arming apology in person or by letter. Lance Sieveking, then a young BBC producer, recalled a ferocious argument in which Wells was so rude that Sieveking assumed that they would never again be on speaking terms. A little later, Wells spotted him at a party and came across the room to say, with a good-natured grin: "What! Still alive! I thought I'd left you for dead on the battlefield".[35] With some people such aggressive behaviour led to a complete rupture and a continuing dislike for him. When he was on the rampage he was impossible, and once he was launched into a full-scale row – as he had been with the wretched Thring, for example – he would harry a man down to the last comma. But most of those who knew Wells in all his moods had long ago come to take his tantrums for granted. At his best he was so genuinely likeable, such excellent company and so transparently well-intentioned that he was always indulged when he behaved like a spoilt child.

Ever eager for recognition, he positively glowed when it was given to him. "I cannot tell you how much I enjoy being praised and in having my importance so generously and so delightfully exaggerated", he told the large gathering of distinguished friends who assembled to honour him at the seventieth birthday dinner organised by the PEN Club, held in the Savoy Hotel on 13 October 1936. After J.B.Priestley and others had paid their tributes, H.G. rose to say that he felt like "a little boy at a lovely party, who has been given quite a lot of jolly toys and who has spread his play about on the floor. Then comes his Nurse. 'Now Master Bertie', she says, 'it's getting late. Time you began to put away your toys.' " Several of those present long remembered the poignancy with which H.G. said those words, and added: "I hate the thought of leaving . . . Few of my games are nearly finished and some I feel have hardly begun."[36]

It was a long and regretful speech. H.G. spoke of his plan for a new encyclopaedia, for making another film, for writing a few more novels, and of his work for the PEN Club, for "freedom of expression, the *utmost freedom* of expression and criticism, and a frank and friendly brother-hood and *mutual patience* among all honest writers, thinkers and creators". Mankind was adjusting itself painfully and confusedly to unprecedented changes: "the world will be worse before it is better . . . The rational life becomes a struggle against hysteria . . . Only a great *free* intellectual and moral drive – an educational encyclopaedism – can restore the shattered morals of our race and give a definite direction to its disordered will."

The message, that evening, was the old one – a mood of despair tempered by the hope that the freemasonry of science and art could somehow work its way through to the "intellectual and aesthetic world republic".

PART SIX
The Darkling Wood

EDUCATION OR CATASTROPHE

"You have romped through the world", Beatrice Webb wrote to Wells a week after the birthday celebration, "living the life you liked, and doing the work you intended to do, amid a multitudinous applause." Why, then, did H.G. feel so baulked and dissatisfied that he now produced a book with the revealing title *The Anatomy of Frustration*? "I don't complain of being frustrated personally. I've had a wonderful time", he wrote to Beatrice on 29 October. "But Man is being most damnably frustrated & I've tried to diagnose *why*".[1] Beatrice Webb thought that H.G. in fact expected too much from his fellow men, and that he therefore felt misunderstood, misrepresented and disappointed. A letter H.G. sent to Frank Swinnerton a few months later, on 2 March 1937, contained an indication of this state of mind. He objected that the main interest of his life, "the forecasting & preparing for a new world that may or may not emerge from the bloody disorders of the present" was treated as though it was "a dull attempt to blight & enslave mankind". "Swinny", he complained, was accepting what had become the common verdict of the critics. "Practically what all you chaps say is, 'Wells is a darling. Get his autograph but for God's sake dont read him. Or you'll be sorry.' "[2]

At the end of the nineteenth century, Wells had worked out his pessimistic plot for the cosmic drama and man's role in it. His journalistic flair for topicality had enabled him to revise the script and bring on his characters in a succession of contemporary costumes, but the play remained essentially the same. After such a long run, the audience was thinning at last and the critics were openly complaining that he had nothing to say and that his writing had become boring and repetitious.

Wells and Bernard Shaw were commonly rated as the most influential writers of the first thirty years of the century. H.G. had taken up new ideas and so popularised them that, by the time he reached middle age, they had come to seem platitudes. He had been one of the first to write about the crisis of world civilisation, long before its first calamitous break-down in 1914, and among the first to discuss the need for an international organisation. He had been a spokesman for the creative possibilities of science and for a rational conservation of world resources, a champion of a reformed and mass educational system, and a protagonist of a more per-missive morality. In all these respects his impact had been immense, and world-wide, to the degree that there was some justice in calling him "The Man Who Invented Tomorrow". Yet the old evangelist was convinced that mankind had remained blind to his original vision and that the task of conversion was as urgent in 1936 as it had been half a century earlier when, with *The Science Schools Journal*, he had first felt compelled to set it down on paper. Writing a commemorative article to celebrate the jubilee of that venture, he explained how that vision "has clung to me ever since, it has ridden me like the old man of the sea."[3]

It was this fixation upon a set of ideas formed at South Kensington, or even earlier, that made Wells seem increasingly old-fashioned despite his contemporary journalism and his pronouncements on public affairs. In the Thirties there were other and more potent prophets of the apocalypse loose in the world. The Communists and the Nazis had produced ideolo-gies which both influenced the minds of men – as Wells had done – and, as he had been unable to do, moved them to fight for the success of their conspiracies. Before the first world war, a generation of English socialists had grown up on books like *A Modern Utopia*, *Kipps* and *New Worlds for Old*. By the early Thirties, their successors did not turn to *The Open Conspiracy* but to John Strachey's popular Marxist tracts such as *The Coming Struggle for Power* and *The Theory and Practice of Socialism*. To them, as the Marxist Christopher Caudwell wrote in *Studies in a Dying Culture*, Wells was a petty-bourgeois humbug who preached a doctrine of "humanity" in an age when the class struggle was sharpening and im-perialist war loomed on the horizon. Even literary London, which treated him indulgently as an old trouper, had lost interest. It read *A Room of One's Own* rather than *Ann Veronica*, Aldous Huxley rather than the disciple of T.H.Huxley, and took its notions of sexual freedom from Joyce and Lawrence rather than Wells. Publishers who had once bid against each other for a Wells book now found a manuscript from him an embarrassment. There was pathos in the way that H.G. persevered, with books that bore the marks of hurried or slipshod writing. The novels were tedious and argumentative, the more serious books too pretentious for the general reader and lacking the cutting edge that would have made them acceptable to intellectuals. But he continued to write compulsively, as if by one last effort he would discover the secret that had so far eluded him and find the magical words whereby the world might yet be saved. H.G. often said that he had been born ahead of his time. Now he had begun to outlive it.

The Anatomy of Frustration was a case in point. When Beatrice Webb received her customary complimentary copy – for Wells still kept a long list of friends to whom every book was sent on publication – she thought it full of "his self-conceit". Writing a diary entry on 2 November 1936 she remarked: "As is usual with his later philosophical essays, he asserts that he knows the way out of the tragic world situation, that he could save the world from the coming disasters if he were dictator. But his vision of the future turns out to be a series of bombastic sentences, big emotional phrases, without intellectual content."

H.G. adopted the same device that he had used before, in *Boon* and even in that first adolescent book, *The Desert Daisy*. The work was presented as the papers of a friend which had been collected and published by Wells – the friend in this case being a William Burroughs Steele who, though dismayed and neurasthenic, "never ceases to be combative", and presents "an aggressive diagnosis of the disorders of life". His *Anatomy* is nothing less than a prescription whereby the human race might avoid the ultimate frustration of mortality. Man is unique, says H.G. through the pen of Steele, in having foreknowledge of death and all his drives are to overcome "this primary frustration". The "immortality of the soul, the oversoul, the overman, the superman, the mind of the species", all of which were concepts with which Wells had played for forty years, and "undying fame, progress, service, loyalties, are all expressions ... of the same essential resolve: not to live so as to die". Wells had now made explicit the implicit philosophy of the Time Traveller.

Given that there can be no hope of personal immortality, the chance of survival lies in what Steele is made to call "merger-immortality", and to achieve this mankind must devote itself to the Next Beginning – the creation of the World Peace, which will require a much greater effort of the collective will than slothful acquiescence in nationalism and war. "Either we take hold of our destiny or, failing that, we are driven towards our fate." Scattered through the short essays are some old themes, and some new glosses on them. There is, for instance, a disquisition on love and marriage, with a revealing note about his own relationship with women. "He expected too much, he promised too much; he bilked and was bilked", he wrote. "None of these chosen ladies could altogether resist his storm of worship and expectation . . . he began, usually through some accidental shock to 'find them out'. Then came reaction, recrimination, a phase of vindictiveness passing into indifference." What he had always wanted, he conceded, was a "mother-mate, not mistress. With some mistress thrown in".

He also included a long discussion of his attitude towards the Jews – an answer to accusations that he was anti-semitic. He was at pains to make it clear that although he abhorred the Nazi persecution of the Jews he did not consider this sufficient reason to abstain from criticising Zionism. Disliking all nationalisms, he regarded Zionism – which made the Jew "an alien with an alien mentality" within any national community – as a particularly pernicious form of separatism which prevented the assimilation of Jews into a wider and supra-national community. If the Jews suffered, it was because they regarded themselves as a chosen people and thereby made themselves the victims of the paranoia of others. Nazism, indeed, was simply "inverted Judaism", the effect upon the Germans of centuries of teaching from the Old Testament. H.G. was not deterred by the criticisms of Jewish and liberal-minded friends who thought such comments tactless, giving aid and comfort to the fascists. He again made his position clear in a letter on 11 November 1933, in which he declined to join a committee against anti-semitism – a state of mind which he thought "a natural reaction to the intense nationalism of the Jews and to the very distinctive role they play in the world of art and business . . . A careful study of anti-semitic prejudice and accusations might be of very great value to many Jews who do not adequately realize the irritations they inflict."[4] In *The Anatomy of Frustration*, the Jews are singled out as a special example of obstructive nationalism, but the lashing they received was in essence no different from that which H.G. was to mete out to Catholics, monarchists, imperialists and all who appeared to be frustrating the Wellsian plan of salvation.

In *The Anatomy of Frustration*, as in his speech at the birthday dinner, H.G. had come back to his old conception of a world compendium of knowledge – a repository for the mind and knowledge of the race. He had been thinking about it all through 1936. "The idea", he wrote to his agent Watt on 18 May, "is to fuse a number of books, like *The Outline of History*, *The Science of Life*, *The Work, Wealth and Happiness of Mankind*, a biographical dictionary, a gazetteer, some group of natural histories and some modern mathematical and scientific treatises and to produce a new encyclopaedia, for which I think the time is ripe. Personally, I would like to do the plan and prefaces for such an enterprise."[5] Encyclopaedism had replaced the Open Conspiracy as the "hope of our species meeting the serried challenges of destiny that advance upon us".[6]

Part of the renewed impetus came from Sir Richard Gregory, who was now playing a leading role in the British Association for the Advancement of Science. Gregory, trying to get the Association to promote science as a means of regenerating the world, invited H.G. to the annual meeting at Blackpool in September 1936, and Wells used the opportunity to canvass his encyclopaedic project with a number of scientists. Gregory then arranged a lecture by H.G. at the Royal Institution to rally public support. His speech, delivered on 20 November, was a great success according to Gregory, who wrote to him two days later that "the vast audience showed what a large number of people look to you for inspiration and guidance".[7] Gregory also devoted a special supplement of *Nature* to it the following week.

The speech itself, however, was more of a polemic than a proposal. After Wells had delivered his usual reprimands upon the shortcomings of his fellow-men in general and the supposedly educated part of them in particular – "in this vein", one of his friends remarked, "he always sounded like a disgruntled inspector-general of the universe" – he confessed his disappointment with the *men of science* who were failing to live up to the responsibilities of the *science* "we want to enlighten and animate our politics and rule the world". Science, when Wells employed it in this manner, was a term as all-embracing as education, and virtually its equivalent as a metaphysical abstraction. It was to be expressed through the world knowledge bank, "a world brain: no less', and H.G. suggested that a promotion committee should immediately be set up to launch the scheme, create suitable editorial boards, and get the first publications under way. Then, allowing his imagination to leap over all the practical difficulties, he already saw the World Encyclopaedia as "a world monopoly", acquiring an income vast enough to finance its activities, and becoming the instrument for manipulating "everyone who controls administrations, makes wars, directs mass behaviour, feeds, moves and starves populations . . . It would have a terrible and ultimately destructive aloofness." H.G. insisted that it would be "a better investment for for the time and energy of intelligent men and women than any definite revolutionary movement, Socialism, Communism, Fascism, Imperialism, Pacifism or any other of the current *isms* . . ." He assured his audience that unless it was successful, as a means "to hold men's minds together in something like a common interpretation of reality, there is no hope whatever of anything but an accidental and transitory alleviation of any of our world troubles. As mankind is, so it will remain, until it pulls its mind together. And if it does not pull its mind together then I do not see how it can help but decline."

Though H.G. was now over seventy, and suffering severely from neuritis, he seized on this new variation on his lifelong mission with the same energetic enthusiasm with which he had embarked on earlier versions. His state of mind came out clearly in a letter he sent to Margaret Sanger on 4 November 1937, regretting that he had missed her during a quick visit to New York.[8]

Last spring I had neuritis very badly & had my doubts whether the fag end of life was worth living. But people like you & I have so many people getting a sort of courage to live out of us, weak as we may be in reality, that we cannot afford to do anything but live with the utmost apparent stoutness to the end. I can tell you now that I have loved you very dearly ever since I met you first and I always shall.

In 1937 Gregory arranged for H.G. to deliver the presidential address to the education section of the British Association meeting in Nottingham. It was a long speech on "The Informative Content of Education" in which he produced a plan for educational reform which was the school counterpart of his encyclopaedia: Schools, he insisted, were simply producing "hordes of fundamentally ignorant, unbalanced, uncritical minds, at once suspicious and credulous . . . Mere cannon-fodder and stuff for massacres and stampedes". At the same time H.G. decided to stir up the academics with *The Camford Visitation*, a short book gibing at the cloistered dons whose dry scholarship prevents them making a "stir to save knowledge and thought before undisciplined ignorance destroys itself with its own machines". The device H.G. employed to project his own arguments into a common-room not unlike that of All Souls, Oxford, was that of a utopian ventriloquist, the voice of the Visitant from space who insists that Camford stands both at the head of education and in its way. "Your littleness here has blocked the education of the English and blighted the educational development of the rest of the world through a century of opportunity, and still your predominance is unchallenged."

H.G., writing in 1937, was saying in effect that the education system in Britain was as inadequate to the demands on it by the modern world as the system in which he had been educated had been to the needs of late Victorian England. He was making almost the same case that his old master T.H.Huxley had argued in his campaign to create a decent elementary and scientific education in the Sixties and Seventies. Without educational reform, national decline was inevitable, Huxley had said. Enlarging the argument on to a world scale, H.G. was insisting that life had become a race between education and catastrophe. On 20 August 1937 he went over to Paris to deliver a speech to a world congress of bibliographers, greeting them as "the beginning of a world brain . . . a memory and a perception of current reality for the entire human race"; and in October and November he was in the US on a lecture tour as part of the same campaign for a New Encyclopaedia. On his return, he was busy circulating a memorandum to influential friends, explaining that he had no intention of imposing his own beliefs on the project. Methuens, the publishers, expressed interest, but the idea made slow progress, not least because H.G. never managed to make it clear to potential collaborators whether he sought to act as an animateur for a practicable undertaking, a rival to the *Encyclopaedia Britannica*, or whether this proposal was merely the stalking-horse for the much more ambitious political crusade that he was advocating in his books.

In the three years before war broke out, H.G. produced a series of novels as a counterpoint to his public activities. *The Croquet Player*, which appeared in 1936, was a short allegory written under the stimulus of the Spanish War. The croquet player is the narrator who describes the nervous breakdown of Dr Finchatton, who has fled in panic from his home at Cainsmarsh where he has become frightened by evil and horrendous dreams. The local vicar, a bigoted Puritan, dismisses the evil as a manifestation of original sin, "the doom of Cain", which is responsible for "the unhappy, wicked spirit which creeps into us all". Seeking comfort from the Anglo-Catholic priest in a neighbouring parish, Finchatton encounters an equal fanaticism in which everything that is wrong in the world is blamed on the Reformation. Both men, Finchatton concludes, had "high and noble convictions . . . But what they really wanted to do was fight . . . It wasn't their beliefs that stirred them but their fears". His panic intensified by this discovery that he is caught between two mutually destructive powers, Finchatton seeks help from the local man of science, the museum curator. This savant asserts that "the cave-man, the ancestral ape . . . have returned", and that "the past, the long black past of fear and hate that our grandfathers never knew of, never suspected, is pouring back upon us. And the future opens like a gulf to swallow us up." (It seems, indeed, that Cainsmarsh is not very different from the island of Dr Moreau.) Finchatton then turns to Norbett, a Harley Street psychiatrist, who tells him that he has created all these menacing fantasies in his mind because he is unable to cope with the monstrous realities of the world.

This story, written as Europe drifted towards the Second World War, is a curious echo of that part of *Boon* which H.G. had called "The Wild Asses of the Devil", and had drafted before war broke out in 1914. Both dealt symbolically with the eruption of profound unconscious drives towards destruction. The difference lies in the vigour with which Wells had insisted that the devil's asses must be driven back to Hell, because "judgment is all about us, and God stands close at hand", and the note of resignation which he struck in *The Croquet Player*. Though Norbert gives Finchatton the stoical advice "Face the facts. Go through with it", and suggests that "we have to bind a harder, stronger civilization like steel about the world", the book is a counsel of despair. The human race has failed to heed his warnings, and it must take the consequences if, like the croquet player, it insists on playing futile games as if it were deaf to the growing drone of the bombers.

In the following year, when H.G. wrote *Star Begotten*, his mood changed again, and he reverted to his old theme of a secret élite which will save the world. The story of Joseph Davis and his wife Mary, who give birth to a miraculous child, is used to explain how the superior Martians have found a means of using cosmic rays to achieve a saving mutation of the human race, creating an exceptional breed of men who will come to replace ignorant, bellicose *Homo sapiens*. This is yet another means to the Wellsian utopia. What would happen, Wells asks, if the world were to become sane? It would "make the whole course of history up to the present day seem like a crazy, incredible nightmare before the dawn". The superman fantasy has returned. Once Joseph Davis has realised that he, his family, and others like them are the new chosen people, he becomes as arrogant as the Artilleryman in *The War of the Worlds*. Their triumph, he concludes, will mean the end of common humanity. "This oafish crowd . . . gaping, stinking, bombing, shooting, throat-slitting, cringing brawl of gawky under-nourished riff-raff. Clear the earth of them."

In all the novels written in these years H.G. gives the impression of a man rummaging in the attic of his memory, taking out old ideas and plots and dusting them off for the last time. *The Croquet Player* is a reminder of *Boon, Star-Begotten* of *The War of the Worlds,* and *Brynhild* – which also appeared in 1937 – harks back to *Marriage*. Brynhild's marriage to Rowland Palace is breaking down, and Wells used this situation to revive his discussion of the conflict of morality and passion. The emancipation of women has done nothing more than stimulate a spirit of rebellion. In this mood Brynhild meets the writer Alfred Bunter, a man with a feverish imagination who has made almost as many escapes from his past as Wells himself. "Life is a flight", says Bunter: "the past haunts me . . . What is human life? . . . Fear – incessant fear . . . A mind perpetually thinking of mistakes and dangers." The one saving idea, which H.G. picks up again from the theme of *Star-Begotten*, is that of "being born again . . . Wherever you are in life, you are only starting. Against nature, you say? This whole world of nature may be a scheme of fate and damnation. Then we have to fight the whole scheme of nature."

As H.G. became less active, spending more of his time in Hanover Terrace writing, or receiving friends, or strolling down for lunch at the Savile Club, he seems to have been reflecting on the loose ends of his life. *Apropos of Dolores*, published in 1938, was a savage recapitulation of his life with Odette Keun, in which he paid off an old score. H.G., however, was as obdurate as he had been about *Clissold*, or *The New Machiavelli*, that there was no connection between any living person and his characters. He became angrily insistent on the point when publishers proved reluctant to handle the book for fear of libel. On 23 June 1938 he wrote to Mr Dakers at Macmillan that "if some damn fool can be found to take his oath that he *recognizes* Dolores as Madame Keun, what can be done about it . . . To be on the safe side I should advise you to stop publishing novels altogether . . . if this book is to be twisted into an 'attack' on that vociferous lady at Grasse, and the book is to be buried in tittle-tattle, I suppose it had better be withdrawn." The book, he added, "amused me to write, and I wrote it without malice".[9] His agent received a similar letter on 14 July because Methuen had raised the same problem. "But it is quite clear", H.G. wrote, "that some silly influence is at work in the firm of Methuen trying to suggest an identification of Dolores with Madame Odette Keun . . . it is impossible for me to entrust my book to a publishing firm which is subject to such influence."[10] Eventually Cape agreed to publish the book, and there was no libel action.

Wells admitted that there was a "community of temperament" between

Dolores, the hysterical wife of the writer Stephen Wilbeck, and Odette. Dolores is described as "a born murderee . . . a human being stripped down to its bare egotism . . . the most completely, exclusively and harshly assembled individuality I ever encountered". But the physical description, "costume, scent, accent, mannerisms, dogs and decoration", was also made to match as was their harassing life in the Paris apartment, their tiresome expedition to Brittany, and the temperamental involvement which made it impossible either to agree or to separate. The novel, in one sense, is a case study of frustration and exasperation which degenerates into the administration of an overdose of drugs to Dolores as if she were a troublesome pet that had to be put down.

The novel, however, served a larger purpose. Wilbeck sees himself as a superior mutant, a "New Adam, *Homo rampant* . . . a longer-lived and mentally more consistent and substantial creature". Such supermen need not even concern themselves any longer with saving civilization. "It is not worth salvaging", Wilbeck concludes. "There were some pretty things about it but its patterns are played out. It comes to an end – it tears and rends into warfare by a senile enlargement of its own traditions . . . we are only preparing for something, something altogether new. Escaping from the ruins is quite a different business from bolstering them up." As against this paragon there stands the figure of Dolores, full of "storming lust, limitless self-glorification and fantastic malice". She is made to be as symbolic as her condemning husband. Human beings are divided into the Dolores type and the Wilbeck type. "Its idea of the future is not, as mine is", Wilbeck says, "a magnificent progressive achievement continually opening out, forgiving everyone, comprehending everyone, but a judgment day, a day of bitter reckoning." Dolores is thus seen as "all the obdurate, grievance-cherishing, triumph-seeking people in the world. She becomes everything that stands in the way of a World Pax and a universal system of mutual service. I see her down the corridors of time, the unyielding guardian of her own ways, refusing to adapt, refusing to tolerate, confronting her enemies, pursing her malice, unable to forget her old world, unable to learn a new one."

The remarkable feature of this outburst is the way in which it reveals how, through his life, H.G. had avoided the implications of his own dualism. The psychological mechanism was simply one of projecting all that he was unable to accept in his own nature and behaviour on to other people or other groups. The antagonism that he describes in this novel is only superficially an antithesis between Dolores and Wilbeck. It is, in fact, his own ambivalence and his own conflicted view of human nature. Dolores, the instinctual animal, the victim of unconscious fears and impulses, is damned and she may damn the whole world with her. Wilbeck, intellectual, the calculating élitist, is the man born out of his time, the Samurai in a lounge suit and panama hat, waiting impatiently to be born again when *Homo sapiens* has had his judgement day. At each successive crisis in his life, H.G. was possessed by the emotional conflicts of his childhood, but he could find no way to release himself from this obsession with his past. He merely transferred it into his books, so that they became a long chronicle of these seizures. *Apropos of Dolores* was merely the latest of the series, and *The Brothers*, which followed in a few weeks, was yet another metaphor of his own dualism, which revealed how his lifelong insistence on imposing a régime of order and brotherhood upon the world – the World Pax which would make humanity at one with itself – expressed a psychic longing for the unity which alone could still the antagonisms that he had internalised long ago in Atlas House.

His awareness of that conflict, and his angry impatience at its persistence in spite of all his efforts, accounts for the irritation with which H.G. regarded party politics, and what he considered to be a destructive confrontation between the "defensive hate systems" of Left and Right. In this case the antagonism has been dramatised by two brothers, Bolaris and Ratzel, separated in early childhood, who find themselves leaders on the opposite sides in a war. When Bolaris captures Ratzel they find that, behind their rival rhetorics, they have much in common, and that the only way to peace lies in an attempt to build a new civilisation: "What business have we either on the left hand or the right hand of the Common Fool?"

H.G. was now writing constantly about approaching war, and at the time of the Munich crisis he became marginally involved in one of the more mysterious attempts to avert it. A mixed group of journalists and other public figures, several of whom later played important parts in wartime intelligence and propaganda against the Nazis, had been keeping in touch with a loose network of highly-placed anti-Nazis in Germany. H.G. became associated with this clandestine link through his friend Ritchie Calder, then science correspondent of the *Daily Herald*, who was in contact with a German visitor to England who represented a mysterious doctor – "the man whose name is never mentioned" as Calder described him to Wells.[11]

The man of mystery was, in fact, Dr Goerdeler, who remained a focus of opposition to Hitler and was eventually executed in 1944 for his part in the

20 July conspiracy. Goerdeler was feeding information to his English counterparts about German rearmament and the resistance to Hitler in the leadership of the German army. He hoped that this intelligence, which revealed that top-ranking German soldiers, public servants and industrialists were ready to move against Hitler to prevent war, would persuade the British government to stand firm against Hitler's blackmailing demands over Czechoslovakia. Wells was one of those who were apprised of this information, and he was told that he could use it with discretion in trying to get influential friends to put pressure upon Neville Chamberlain. Chamberlain's refusal to credit Goerdeler's reports helped to convince H.G. that the British establishment had no intention of checking Hitler, or Mussolini, and that the Foreign Office was so permeated by Roman Catholic sympathisers of the Axis powers that the danger of outright capitulation was even greater than the risk of war. He had been able to glimpse some of the complex intrigues that lay behind the Munich betrayal, and the experience did much to shape his political attitude when war actually broke out – especially his increasingly violent hostility to the Vatican, which he saw as the centre of a world-wide conspiracy against freedom and rationality.

The emotional shock of Munich sprang equally from a rising wave of fear and the bitter reaction of shame and relief which followed the betrayal of the Czechs. The world had come to the edge of war: the shelter trenches were dug in the London parks, the children were prepared for evacuation from the cities, windows were criss-crossed with sticky tape against blast, and the first primitive black-outs improvised in every home. All Europe waited, and the rest of the world watched, through two weeks of tension which might at any moment have been ended by the wail of sirens and the whine of falling bombs.

It was in the immediate aftermath of this crisis, when sudden catastrophe had become credible, that an extraordinary event happened in the United States.

On the evening of 30 October 1938 listeners to the radio network of the Columbia Broadcasting System heard a series of announcements describing the arrival of Martians in New Jersey, and their rapid advance on New York. Within a few minutes, a wave of panic rippled across the United States. The situation which Wells had fantasied forty years before, in his account of London's panic in *The War of the Worlds*, was now occurring in towns and villages across America: life was imitating art.

As a Halloween jape, Orson Welles had decided to present the Wells story transposed from Victorian Surrey to contemporary New Jersey. It was tellingly realistic – using the real names of places, introducing commentators, professors, policemen and even a Secretary of State to add conviction. The effect of this, coming over a radio network on whose authenticity the public relied, was far more immediate and convincing than anything that Wells himself had been able to achieve with a book – or even with such a film as *Things to Come*. Those who missed the first announcement that this was a play, or tuned in late, were understandably persuaded that some real disaster had suddenly struck. The Gallup poll estimate was that as many as twelve million people listened to the CBS stations that evening, and the lowest audience figure was at least six million. Of these, up to a quarter thought the broadcast was genuine, and the majority of these people were frightened – possibly over a million people. A team of psychologists, led by Hadley Cantril, collected case studies which showed how people reacted – the religious who thought that the end of the world had come, the Jews who believed that this was a sudden Nazi attack, families that made frantic efforts to get in touch with each other to face doomsday together.[12]

Wells himself was furious at this unexpected demonstration of the capacity of his work to terrify people, and threatened an action for damage to his reputation. But the episode in fact provided unique evidence about the way that Wells touched upon latent apocalyptic fears, and about the personality factors which made people respond to doomsday fantasies. A majority of listeners were well aware that they were listening to a play, even if they had tuned-in late. The interest lies in the psychology of those who panicked, and the characteristics which predispose such people to be susceptible to suggestion in the face of apparent danger.

The first of these was a deep sense of insecurity, a fear of unemployment, a sense of being inadequately educated, of having some defect of appearance, or belonging to a minority religious or ethnic group. The second was a tendency to be phobic, fearing the dark, or loneliness, or high places or crowds. Many of those interviewed, moreover, tended to be fatalistic, and to lack a critical faculty, and with this went a kind of religiosity – a feeling of guilt, a belief that anything might happen at any time, either to punish an individual or even the whole human race. For some the thrill of disaster actually brought a sense of relief, discharging their anxieties by irrational and excited actions. The account of such people recalls what has been inferred about the personality of those who supported millenarian movements in the past, such as the Anabaptist utopians of Munster and similar chiliastic sects in Cromwell's England, and what later research has revealed about supporters of totalitarian groups in contemporary society. Such people provide the membership for organisations like the Nazi Party, the Ku Klux Klan, and societies obsessed with unidentified flying objects and other supernatural and occult fears.

One reason for the panic created by the broadcast might have been that there was nothing practical those who were frightened by it could do to relieve their anxiety: their only recourse was collapse into fear or flight. The prophecies of doom that Wells wrote undoubtedly raised the general level of anxiety and intensified the sense of frustration among his readers. Unlike Fascist and Communist propagandists, he did not take the next step in the process and create a movement aimed at winning power. On the contrary, he was desperate to "save" himself, and mankind, from the folly of such a destructive solution. That is why he was so fiercely critical of the Nazis, Communists and the Catholic Church. In the conditions of the Thirties, as the conflict between these mass movements intensified, Wells was unable to offer a realistic alternative to them. The more that he was pressed to give a lead, the more general and rhetorical his answers became. This was inevitable. He feared the consequences of real totalitarian power, but he had no faith in the capacity of democracy to create the kind of society that he had always advocated. For forty years he had been a herald of doomsday and had proposed a series of world-saving devices to avert it. The nearer it came in fact the less convincing his proposals appeared. To tell a man that he should join the Open Conspiracy or support a campaign for a World Encyclopaedia does not offer much relief from anxiety when he has been led to believe that Judgement Day is close at hand.

In his writings Wells had bridged the gap between catastrophe and the utopia that might follow it by magical transformation scenes. What Anthony West called "the internal struggle with his demon" could thus be resolved in works of the imagination. But when this internal struggle was projected into public life it became clear that Wells had little to say that was practically relevant. His gift for anticipating the future was indisputable. So was his capacity for cataloguing the ills of the world in passionate invective. The combination of these two talents was the source of his influence, and his inability to find a way of linking one to the other in a programme of action was the source of his ineffectiveness when he turned from prophecy to politics. Though he powerfully expressed the underlying anxiety of his times he offered no acceptable means of discharging it, and he became increasingly isolated and frustrated. Behind the rhetoric of his repeated appeals for the salvation of mankind there wa a cry for help, for personal salvation from a nightmare of extinction. But from that fate no one could save him, any more than he could save the human race from its evolutionary destiny. He had taken on the burden of Atlas to save himself from his fear.

To Wilson Harris, the editor of the *Spectator* and a frequent luncheon companion at The Table in the Reform Club with J.A.Hobson, Frank Swinnerton, A.G.Gardiner and other journalists and politicians, H.G. wrote in 1938 that "I am tired, I am old, I am ILL I have no gang, I have no party. My epitaph will be 'He was clever, but not clever enough. . . .' I write books, and it is like throwing gold bricks into mud. I write books because I have a habit of writing, but I do not care how soon now I go to bed for good and all." Such moods of depression had become more frequent, despite the cheerful face Wells could still put on things at a party or a public appearance. C.P.Snow recalled meeting him at the British Association meeting in Cambridge in the autumn of 1938, where he had given an impression of urgent vigour. They were sitting together over a nightcap of whisky, and the conversation languished. Suddenly Wells looked up and said: "Ever thought of suicide, Snow?"[13]

The fantasy of an invasion from Mars created a panic in the United States, but in Europe the invaders flew Heinkel bombers and arrived in tanks. All through the Thirties refugees had been reaching Britain, though only in a miserable trickle as the Chamberlain government sought to keep their numbers down. For those, like H.G., who were concerned to bring out as many writers and intellectuals as possible from the countries falling under fascist control, each visa meant a battle with officials under instructions only to admit those who were in danger, who could be sure of financial support, and from whom there was least risk of political subversion. H.G., who was now earning much less and whose income was both heavily taxed and carelessly spent, was often asked to give money.* To one appeal he replied that he was "nearly broke", though this was a considerable exaggeration, and that "to pull the blanket" over one needy case meant pulling it off another.[14] He was also involved, as a leading figure

---

* He was generous about money, and gave away large sums in the course of his life. When he died he left £59,811. He had received more from *The Outline* than from all his other books combined, but most of that money had been spent or given away in the Twenties and early Thirties when, Rebecca West said, "he lived like minor royalty".

in the PEN Club, in writing testimonials and otherwise trying to help refugee writers. In this task he was never less than generous, though he often found himself antagonised personally by some of the new arrivals – especially if they began to argue with him about Zionism. After the Munich Agreement, when the Czech leader Eduard Beneš fled to London, it was Wells who took the initiative in organising a letter to *The Times* paying tribute to Beneš and complaining at the Chamberlain government's betrayal of Czech democracy. By the end of 1938 there was no doubt that war was coming. The atmosphere was very like that in the opening sequences of the film of *Things to Come*, which had shown a complacent London celebrating Christmas 1940 while enemy bombers droned towards the capital. Hopelessly, with increasing desperation, H.G. found an outlet for his anxious energy in insisting that somehow education must change the mind of mankind.

It was in this mood that, in the summer of 1938, H.G. agreed to go out to Australia to address the Australian and New Zealand Association for the Advancement of Science (ANZAAS). "I was", he said afterwards, "becoming more and more impatient with the failure of the new encyclopaedia idea to secure any energetic support, and also I was growing more and more impatient with my own personal ineffectiveness in the matter."[15] He sailed for Australia, by way of Bombay and Colombo, in December. The long voyage out East, on what H.G. called a "pukka sahib" ship, intensified his hostility to complacent and narrow-minded empire builders. But he had hopes for the Australians. The lectures would give him the chance to make his case clearly to a new audience, and he took a good deal of trouble in preparing them. The first, delivered in both Sydney and Canberra, was devoted to "The Role of English in the Development of the World Mind". "If the human race is not to go on slipping down towards a bottomless pit of wars, conquests and exterminations", H.G. insisted, "it must be through the rapid and zealous expansion of the intellectual organizations of the English-speaking communities." The second, given to the Education Section of ANZAAS, was a repeat of the lecture "On the Poison Called History" which he had prepared for a League of Nations Union meeting for teachers in London. It rehearsed the familiar Wellsian argument against national histories and competing mythologies, with a particular attack upon the falsities of the Judaeo-Christian religion. This speech had been a flop in London, and H.G. hoped it would evoke a better response in the Antipodes.

As provocative entertainments, both lectures were a success. They were also a bitter disappointment to H.G. After he had been applauded and congratulated, he was naively astonished that "everything went on just as it had been going on before". The most ironic moment for him came in Sydney, when he delivered himself of "all the reasons for believing that the human species was already staggering past the zenith of its ascendancy and on its way through a succession of disasters to extinction". When he finished this prophetic exordium, the chairman – the veteran Australian statesman William Hughes – led the singing of the national anthem. Then, said Wells, "we shook off the disagreeable vision, and lifted up our voices in simple loyalty to things as they are."

By this time H.G. was tired, irritated and unwell, and he reacted by lambasting his Australian hosts from whom he had expected better things. Anticipating the crisis of 1942, when, after the fall of Singapore, the Australians found that their sea defence depended on the American rather than the British navy, he reprimanded them for their easy-going indifference. Though they might hope to be left alone, that the world crisis would pass them by, for them too Wells thought the day of reckoning was almost at hand.

Wells had gone to Australia in the hope of finding a society which was isolated from the fears and futility of Europe. But behind its apparent indifference he discovered the same repressed panic, the same tendency to see the world in extremes, which characterised the Thirties everywhere. The hysteria which broke through his own writing was universal, and there was no prospect of relief from the tensions which were driving the world to war. The journey, begun with hope, had merely intensified his own confusion, depression and anger.

While he was in Australia, H.G. was sending back articles to the *News Chronicle*, and in one of these – published on 23 January 1939 – he wrote sourly about the similarity between Australia and Britain in the way the ruling group "mysteriously stifled and frustrated . . . the same living spirit of freedom", and found himself in hot water with Lyons, the federal premier, for attacking Hitler – "a friendly Head of State" – as a "certifiable lunatic". As he flew back, by way of Java, Burma and India, he discovered that his articles had been causing offence elsewhere. One, sent to the *News Chronicle* on the eve of a Royal visit to Washington, was a repetition of his denunciations of the British monarchy for cultural sterility and dubious interventions in politics. Wells was in Bali when he learned that this "insult" to the King and Queen had raised an outcry in London, and he was made desperate by his efforts to persuade a Balinese cable operator to transmit his defence to London. The article, eventually sent from Singapore, was not printed by the *News Chronicle*. Wells said it had been suppressed because the King and Queen were due to visit the chocolate factory owned by the family which held a controlling interest in the newspaper. H.G. was in trouble in America too, about an article published in *Liberty* just before he sailed to Australia, in which he made another onslaught on Zionism. It not only got a bad press, but it also drew protests from many prominent Americans, including Eleanor Roosevelt. H.G. insisted that she could not have read the article, and was simply reacting to hearsay complaints that he had proposed a world pogrom of Jews.[16]

Wells was depressed rather than stimulated by his journey, convinced that the human race was now in the position of the man who sat drinking in the bar of the sinking *Titanic* and was heard to say: "Well, anyhow, the damn thing hasn't gone down *yet*." He did not know what to do next, or what more might be done, and he confessed that while the approaching "catastrophe is well on its way . . . education seems still unable to get started, has indeed not even readjusted itself to start. The race may, after all, prove a walk-over for disaster."[17]

The more that Wells despaired for the future of the species, the more insistently he asked why human beings seemed so bent on self-destruction. The common man, he told the readers of the *News Chronicle* on 13 March, "knows that a varied and abundant life is now a physical possibility for every soul alive, but he finds himself menaced unaccountably and impeded and frustrated at every turn, in his will to live happily". This paradox had puzzled H.G. all his life, and almost all his books had been attempts to come to grips with it. "Even my novels are studies in frustration", he wrote, "from Kipps the under-educated to Dolores the uncontrollable egotist and Rud Whitlow, the man who was so terrified by life that he could not feel safe until he was the dictator of all mankind."[18]

H.G. had written the story of Rud Whitlow in *The Holy Terror* before he left for Australia. When the novel appeared, shortly before he returned to London, it was assumed that Wells had been so impressed by the rise of the dictators that he was now, in the phrase of *The Times Literary Supplement*, a "Fabian-Fascist". Beatrice Webb thought it "one long screed of abuse of existing men and women and of all present day manners, customs and creeds" in which a dictator – "a queer type of mental defective, with a mystical strain of self-deification and a superb energy and cunning"[19] – makes himself the ruler of the world state.

The interest of the novel lies in Wells's attempt to explore the pathology of a man who dreams of a new world order, proceeds to create it, and then seems driven to destroy it. Rud Whitlow, an aggressive and rebellious child, spoilt by his mother and terrified of his father, kicks and screams against any effort to control him. As an adolescent he spins fantasies of victory over imaginary enemies, and identifies himself with the great men of history. Clever enough to win a university scholarship, he feels an un-focused sense of destiny, and casts around for a cause which will absorb his unconscious desire for omnipotence. Rud discovers that he has a charismatic appeal, and he and a group of followers seize control of a party which is simply a caricature of Sir Oswald Mosley's Blackshirt movement. At first, as one of his associates remarks, Rud has "a plague of Manx cats on the brain", too many ideas with no conclusions to them, but he soon begins to deliver speeches which read like extracts from everything that Wells had been writing since *Anticipations*. The old world is "rotten". The political parties, trade unions, parliament, the City, and the news-papers are all hindrances to the aspirations of the common man: they will deliver him into a new world war, cheating him of his rights and hopes on the way. By the time that war breaks out, Rud is already leader of an international movement – the Party of the Common Man – which is pledged to a programme indistinguishable from that which H.G. had proposed for the Open Conspiracy. At the end of the war, control of the world has passed into the hands of the airmen, who support Rud's scheme of a World Pax. These new revolutionaries then impose order on a ruined civilisation and begin the great work of reconstruction.

Thus far *The Holy Terror* follows the usual Wellsian scenario. Though Rud Whitlow is an unpleasing character, incapable of close relationships – his aunt suggests that he has a powerful oedipal complex – and obsessed by his messianic vision of world salvation, neither his triumph nor the conditions in which it occurs differ significantly from similar situations in the earlier apocalyptic books. Had Wells finished the novel at that point, when Rud has became World Director, Rud would have seemed no more sinister – though personally nastier – than the leader of the League of Airmen at the moment when in *Things to Come* the Puritan Tyranny was set up to establish the scientific world state. The difference between Rud and the world-saviours in the previous books begins at this point. At the moment of victory he changes from a demagogic liberator into a tyrant, his propagandists begin a nauseating cult of personality, his secret police begin to chase dissenters and spy on his closest associates, and all the achievements of the revolution are threatened. Having begun by identifying himself with mankind, Rud now identifies mankind with himself. He has become the God he repressed when, in adolescence, he turned atheist. "Who wants Providence when they can have me?" Rud asks, and complains that he has become "Prometheus-Atlas" with the whole world upon his shoulders. He has made himself master of all men because he has always been driven by a frantic fear of power – in the hands of anyone but himself. He has "a profound maybe innate dread of the closest of all forms of domination – love . . . His capacity for love atrophied", one of his associates observes. "It has vanished and then returned in a vague, cloudy desire to be appreciated, admired, obeyed – loved by the whole world. Without any return." Once Rud has become Master World Director, he finds himself more frightened than ever. He can find relief from his paranoia only by beginning to destroy the new world he has made and by killing the men who took his vision seriously.

Rud, in short, is a paradox. When H.G. indicted Rud, whom he had endowed with much of his own childhood and many of his own ideas, he struck at his own messianic fantasies and suggested an answer to his own question why the prophet is doomed to frustration. Behind the grandiose pretensions of Rud Whitlow, Wells insisted, there shivered a terrified child, a rebel whose promises of salvation concealed a death-wish against himself and his fellow-creatures. Wells had already made a similar connection in the passage in his autobiography which compared his adolescent fantasies in Bromley with those of the contemporary dictators. "In fact Adolf Hitler", he wrote, "is nothing more than one of my thirteen year old reveries come real." Wells believed that he had long ago grown out of what he called "my Hitler phase". He seemed to be unaware that, in telling the story of Rud, he was demonstrating the link between the unconscious fears and aggressions which were so marked in his youth and the plans for the saving of the world which ran through his adult writing. Insight stopped short at that point. For, at the age of seventy-three, H.G. was still torn by the conflict between his fantasies and his reason – the tension which had provided the mainspring of his life and his fiction. When he dramatised that divided self in the person of Rud, he came closer to understanding the paradox, but he had still not resolved it.

That failure was revealed by the final chapters of the novel, in which H.G. relapsed into his customary solution. Rud has been presented as a double personality, part angel, part devil: he is a "*holy* terror". H.G. clearly felt that there was nothing wrong with the ideas for which he had made

Rud his spokesman; the source of Rud's destructiveness lay in his instinctual drives, the part of him that was "merely animal". When, therefore, Rud has been killed, the scientific élite is able to inherit the revolution he has made and go on to create utopia just as the elect had always done in Wells's prophetic books. The apocalyptic formula had worked after all. Wells had merely adapted it to take account of the contemporary dictators, whom he now saw as the makers of the coming doomsday. Rud had been the fallen angel, and with his destruction Paradise had been regained.

When Wells arrived back in London from Australia, he found nothing to raise his spirits. "All the dreary old cants are crawling about damaged but mischievous, like lions that have been peppered but not put out of action", he wrote in the *News Chronicle* on 6 March just before the Nazis completed their occupation of Czechoslovakia. "I have never met so many bad-tempered people." A few days later Beatrice Webb lunched with him in "his attractive and luxuriously fitted house', and gave a sad description of him.[20]

He was at work summing up the human race - as a species of animal, living on this planet. Would it survive and progress, or would it die out like other species had done, because it could not adapt itself to changing environment; or control its own development? I found him a physical wreck. He had flown to Australia and back via Rangoon and had picked up some poison. He was obsessed with his own vague vision of a world order; with a search for a "competent receiver" of the power to organise mankind. The mass electorate and its representatives were totally unfit for the job. But he utterly failed to make me understand what sort of social institution he had in mind. He rejected all those existing; he insisted that his organ of government must represent and govern the world at large; he ignored the problem of race and religion, of rights and sexual habits and above all how the production, distribution and exchange of commodities and services should be carried on. But of industry and agriculture, commerce and finance, he knows nothing. Poor old Wells – I was sorry for him. I doubt whether we shall meet again – we are too old and tired.

Beatrice Webb had called when H.G. was working on *The Fate of Homo Sapiens*, intended to be his unhappy valediction to the human race, and a demonstration of the fact that he had always had great hopes of its potential and grave doubts about its prospects – the theme he had stated as long ago as 1887 in "The Extinction of Man". To those who felt that he had lost his faith in progress, he retorted that he had always been pessimistic but, like the Time Traveller, had tried "to live as though it were not so".

On 26 June 1939 for example, he wrote a letter to the *British Weekly*. "What have my books been from *The Time Machine* to *World Brain* and my *Fate of Homo Sapiens* (now in the press)", he asked, "but the clearest insistence on the insecurity of progress and the possibility of human degeneration and extinction? I think the odds are against man but it is still worth fighting against them."

Sir Ernest Barker recalled seeing Wells slumped in a chair at a reception, and he asked him how he was.[21] " 'Poorly, Barker, poorly', he said. I asked him what he was doing. 'Writing my epitaph.' I asked him what it was. 'Quite short', he said, 'just this – God damn you all: I told you so.' "

HAMMERING AWAY

When the Nazi tanks began to roll into Poland, Wells was in Stockholm, where he had planned to deliver a speech to the PEN Club congress. Though this meeting had been cancelled as the crisis developed, H.G. still went in the hope of making useful contacts with other writers. Twenty-five years lay between the day when he had gone home to write "The War That Will End War", and the moment in Stockholm when he had to abandon his address on "The Honour and Dignity of the Human Mind" because the war had dispersed his audience. Yet, despite the differences between his patriotic outburst and his plea that the community of science and letters should "stand for something greater than any government or nation on earth", they contained a similar message. War will smash the old system of power politics, and mankind must take that opportunity to make a new beginning. "The whole intellectual life of man", H.G. wrote in the closing paragraph of the undelivered speech, "revolts against this intolerable, suffocating, murderous nuisance, the obsolescent national State. A world revolution to a higher social order, a world order, or utter downfall lies before us all."[1]

He had been back in England for only three weeks when his eye was caught by a correspondence in *The Times* on "War Aims", and he was at once reminded of his attempt – during his brief spell at Crewe House in 1918 – to persuade the Lloyd George government to say precisely what it would do when the war was over. This time H.G. proposed to start that argument at the beginning of the war. "The thing I am most terrified by today", he wrote to *The Times*, "is the manifest threat of a new weak put-off of our aspirations for a new world . . . If we are to go on with this present régime of vague insincerities, mutual sabotage and distrust, I for one can see no hope for mankind."[2] When this letter evoked encouraging comments, he followed it with another on 23 October, announcing that with a few friends he had drafted "a trial statement of the rights of man brought up to date". The letter included this draft, which declared that all men were entitled to sufficient welfare and education, to the protection of their persons and property, to reasonable employment, to free movement throughout the world, to speedy public trial on arrest, and protection against secret evidence.

Ritchie Calder, then the science correspondent of the *Daily Herald*, persuaded his editor to offer a whole page every day for a month for a "Great Debate" on the manifesto.[3] He proposed that Wells should act as chairman both of the discussion in the columns of the *Herald* and of a drafting committee of distinguished men and women who would endeavour to bring the debate to the issue of a new and more comprehensive Declaration of Human Rights. The plan appealed to H.G. It was just what he wanted, especially since the war had clearly put an end to his campaign for the World Encyclopaedia, and another campaign, this time to promote the Declaration, was just the thing to put in its place. Calder's plan was also timely, in that winter of the "phoney war", when most people were not even sure whether the war would go on and, if it did, what would come of it. The uncertainty was such that Bernard Shaw even proposed that the war should be wound up at once, before it had really started.

Shaw, writing under the same title "Common Sense about the War" which he had given to the article which caused such an outcry in 1914, published an equally provocative piece in *The New Statesman* on 7 October 1939. Attacking "fools who come to the top in wartime by their self-satisfied folly though nobody would trust them to walk a puppy in peace time", Shaw asked: "What in the devil's name is it all about now we have let Poland go?" Taking a very similar line to that which Wells was arguing, Shaw insisted that "if we won, it would be Versailles all over again, only worse, with another war less than twenty years off" and he proposed immediate peace negotiations with Hitler "instead of making more mischief and ruining our people in the process". He sympathised with that "unhappy outcast" H.G. Wells, though he disagreed with his letter to *The Times* on one point. Wells had said that the whole human race was at risk. "Dear H.G.", Shaw apostrophised him, "let us not flatter ourselves. The utmost we can do is to kill, say, twenty-five millions of one another, and make the ruins of all our great cities show places for Maori tourists."

The first winter of the war was miserable. The front in France was quiescent, and the Chamberlain government seemed to be more concerned about the Finnish war with the Russians and with petty infringements of free speech than it was with its plans to fight Hitler. Morale was at a low ebb, and H.G. became more than ever anxious about the purposes and the possible outcome of the war. With Calder's help, the campaign for the Rights of Man was pushed on, and a committee set up consisting of Sir Richard Gregory, that faithful friend, Lord Horder, the eminent physician, the Labour politician Margaret Bondfield, the economist Barbara Wootton, Sir John Boyd Orr, the nutritionist, Sir Norman Angell, Lord Lytton, Ritchie Calder, his editor Francis Williams, and the former Lord Chancellor, Lord Sankey. Before it could get started on its work, however, there was a characteristic fuss. On 5 February 1940 in the first of his "chairman's" articles in the *Herald*, H.G. launched an attack on Chamberlain and on his Foreign Secretary, Lord Halifax. Lord Lytton immediately resigned from the committee; even though he shared Wells's distrust of these two "Men of Munich" he felt that H.G. had reduced the campaign to "merely a left-wing political debate". Lord Sankey also resigned, because he thought Wells had prejudiced an impartial discussion. It was left to Calder to patch the matter up as best he could. Calder immediately went to Sankey and asked him to withdraw his resignation and replace H.G. as chairman. To Sankey's astonishment, Calder persuaded Wells to accept the implicit reprimand and allow Sankey to take his place.

While the discussion continued in the *Herald*, the committee worked on a comprehensive draft. When, after many meetings in which, according to Francis Williams, H.G. was like a suppressed dynamo that might blow up at any moment, the Declaration was completed, it burgeoned with Wellsian concepts and phrases. H.G. had been able to sweep his colleagues along by his insistent enthusiasm. The only significant modification was the inclusion of the right to democratic government – a right which H.G. had left out of his original list in *The Times* and which he again omitted when four years later ,in *'42 to '44*, he published a rewritten version of the Rights. *The Rights of Man* and *The Common Sense of War and Peace*, both published by Penguin, were reminiscent of the pamphlets and articles which H.G. had turned out during the First World War. Kingsley Martin said that he thought Wells the greatest journalist of his lifetime, and even when he was old H.G. had lost none of his facility for reacting quickly to each turn of events. One of the chapters in *The Rights of Man*, headed "What is the German Answer?", made it clear that H.G. had reverted to essentially the same position he had taken up after 1916. The first objective was to smash German militarism – "let the Germans have their medicine now", Wells cried, though this was not the most convincing slogan to advance at a time when the remnants of the British army were being snatched off the beaches of Dunkirk. The second was the "dissolution of the French and British imperial systems". The war, Wells was insisting, must be turned into a revolution. He had already suggested in the speech he had drafted for Stockholm that the immense effort of war would impose "collectivism" on the combatants, and he now saw the Rights of Man as a means of ensuring that "free criticism, universal instruction, free publication, free discussion" would convert that inevitable collectivism into the foundations of the new world order.

Everything that H.G. wrote in the ensuing years of war was based on these propositions. The Declaration, in various forms, cropped up in his writings with the same persistent regularity that had once been true of the Open Conspiracy and then of the World Encyclopaedia. All three themes reappeared in *Phoenix: A Summary of the Inescapable Conditions of World Reorganisation*, and again in *The Outlook for Homo Sapiens*, both of which were published in 1942, and finally in *'42 to '44: A Contemporary Memoir*. To promote the Declaration, H.G. spent himself during 1940 on a transcontinental tour of the US, delivering the lecture "Two Hemispheres or One World", which may have prepared the way for Wendell Willkie's best-selling book *One World*. Part of the time in America Wells spent chafing in California, while the presidential campaign distracted public attention. When Somerset Maugham met H.G. in New York on the way home, he noted: "He was looking old, tired and shrivelled. He was as perky as he has always been, but with something of an effort. His lectures were a failure. People couldn't hear what he said and didn't want to listen to what they could hear . . . He was hurt and disappointed. He couldn't understand why they were impatient with him for saying much the same thing as he had been saying for the last thirty years. The river has flowed on and left him high and dry on the bank".[4] Despite this setback, H.G. was undeterred. As soon as he was back in England he began an extensive correspondence, with the humble as well as the eminent, trying to whip up support for the Declaration and to arrange for its translation into as many languages as possible, including Basic English.

It is difficult to assess the impact of this campaign because it merged into so many similar initiatives prompted by wartime idealism. Harold Laski, the professor of politics at the London School of Economics who had become the Labour Party's most articulate ideologist, was arguing for a "revolution by consent" which would convert the war into a social revolution, though his emphasis was more on domestic change than on world organisation.[5] Clarence Streit's Federal Union movement, which greatly irritated Wells because he believed that this "Federationism" was a pseudo-solution like the League of Nations, was winning a good deal of support for the idea of supra-national government. And there was the groundswell of opinion which led to the Atlantic Charter of 1941, to Franklin Roosevelt's declaration of the Four Freedoms, and eventually to the United Nations. Wells was certainly not swimming against the tide; and yet his personal influence declined sharply in the first years of the war. His ideas, in a generalised sense, were popular, but they were at a level of polemic which stopped short of practicable proposals. When H.G. did take up a specific issue, such as the activities of the Polish government-in-exile, or the role of de Gaulle, or the question whether Rome should be bombed, he did so in a manner which often alienated people and gave him the reputation of a querulous critic who thought everyone was out of step but himself. His decline may also be explained by over-exposure. He repeated himself interminably, without adding anything new except topical references to his well-worn arguments.

One of the writers to whom he had written soliciting support was the novelist Martha Gellhorn, who wrote from Cuba to say why she found the Declaration "unsatisfying". It was "because it made no shock of recognition, joy, excitement, etc. in my mind . . . You ought to be able to make words that burn and have light . . . unforgettable to the ear, the heart and the mind. You have to remember how little time people have, after they have done their daily necessary living, for thought . . . you have to speak in a good ringing voice, like the angels, but not for more than five minutes: and your words have to be like that stuff that was written in fire on a wall somewhere or other."[6] That, of course, was what H.G. wished to do, but his prophetic talent had always run best in the vein of warnings that unless mankind adopted his ideas it would face disaster. And the nadir of British fortunes in the war was no time to win adherents by frightening people. What the public wanted, as it came out of the air-raids of the winter of 1940–41, and as the military situation deteriorated, was hope, not fear. But H.G. had very little hope to offer to his readers.

This continuing emphasis on anxiety, rather than inspiration, as the means to change was expressed in a lecture which H.G. gave at the Royal Institution on 27 September 1941.[7] "If you will not share in this dreaming", he said, "if you will not, in the dwindling time that remains to us, do your utmost to realise this dreaming, then, instead of going out to make a dream come real, fresh nightmares will overtake you, you and yours and all you care for ... the trend of things is still, I think, towards disaster and extinction." The "dream" that he then summarised was the same programme. Man must adapt or perish, and the test of his capacity to adapt is whether he accepts international control of the air, the conservation of world resources, the Declaration, a universal language, and the World Encyclopaedia. Nothing else would do. And because nothing else would do, H.G. was bound to find himself perpetually frustrated and his audience drifting away to other causes.

Wells sensed that he was ceasing to command attention, and the discovery intensified his depression. The war, as well as his advancing years, made it difficult to keep up the social life on which he had depended for stimulation, and he spent more time at Hanover Terrace, writing with a mixture of exhaustion and urgency on the worsening state of mankind. The publisher of *Phoenix* had asked him to end the book with suggestions for practical activities which would ensure "its maximum effectiveness as a revolutionary instrument". All H.G. could propose was that his readers should read it again, and then talk about its ideas, "organise groups ... write to newspapers, heckle politicians", and help to translate it into foreign languages. The campaign for the Open Conspiracy had been reduced, in the end, to the politics of the parish pump. The world was in flames, and H.G. was trying to beat them out with a Fabian tract.

In a curious short allegory, published in 1940, H.G. used a different metaphor – the Flood. *All Aboard for Ararat* was the story of Noah in modern dress, in which God – who appears to have escaped from a lunatic asylum – presents himself to Mr Noah Lammock and tells him he has been chosen to save mankind from final catastrophe by building an ark which will save the seeds of civilisation for a new sowing. The ark is to be a cache which preserves the best of the human inheritance, like the museum in *The Time Machine*, or the World Encyclopaedia, containing all history and knowledge on microfilm. The Flood will achieve, as fire had been used in previous utopias, "a purification, a cleansing of minds, a will unified and reborn ... something quintessential for the élite and something very strong and clear and simple for the masses of mankind". It is Noah's task to create a new religion: "one opinion and one only can be the nearest to truth, and the rest are wrong and have to be rejected". For his crew, after considering the weaknesses of most human types and the shortcomings of all current political parties, Noah is to choose men who resemble the enlightened eighteenth-century gentlemen – the paragon

Wells had described, on the model of Sir Mathew Fetherstonhaugh, in the opening pages of *Tono-Bungay*.

The book contained some witty dialogue between Noah and God, but it was fundamentally a depressing tract. If the colleagues of Wells on the Sankey committee had read it carefully, they would have found it difficult to reconcile the contradiction between its insistence on "one opinion and one only" and Wells's earnest advocacy of free speech. But few of his contemporaries seem to have noticed that paradox, though it had run through his writings from *A Modern Utopia* onwards. The failure to perceive it, or to take it seriously enough to cast a shadow on the generally "progressive" image of Wells, was perhaps a comment on radical politics in the totalitarian century. Shaw and the Webbs, for example, were other notable instances of the same paradox which enabled them to remain, so to speak, within the body of the church of progressivism – and even to be regarded as sincere defenders of liberty – at the same time as they became apologists for Stalinism. But it was also a comment on the utopian devices that H.G. employed to carry his message. It was too easily assumed that what he wrote was one thing, a set of metaphors which were to be taken in a literary rather than a literal sense, and that what he "actually" believed was something else. This inability on the part of his public to realise that H.G. did believe in his "utopian" ideas was one of the sources of his frustration, and one of the reasons why he alternated between fictional and factual books, seeking to make one reinforce the arguments of the other. Even if other people did not take his allegories seriously, he certainly did.

That point comes out quite clearly when the ideology of Wells's fiction is compared with that of his social writings and his journalism, and it is underlined by the fusion between the two styles that produced the "discussion" novels that he had been writing on and off since *The New Machiavelli*. The last of these, *Babes in the Darkling Wood*, published in 1940, was, Wells said, "the most comprehensive and ambitious dialogue novel I have ever attempted". Stella and Gemini are two students who are trying to shake themselves free of traditional morals and stuffy scholarship, and to get on "with the understanding and promotion of that World Revolution" which is "the real business of the Queen and King of Prigs". Stella's uncle, Robert Kentlake, is a tedious know-all who serves as her guru, and when Gemini has a nervous breakdown it is Uncle Robert who takes over where the psychoanalyst fails. He points out that "the mind is not something that can be taken to pieces but something that is being put together". There is no "concrete thing in a human being called the mind, the psyche or the soul". Uncle Robert patches up the love-affair, Stella becomes a nurse and Gemini goes off to serve on a minesweeper. They have discovered that their troubles are merely stresses as the mind of the race seeks to escape from the animal frame and become more purely cerebral.

Wells was to write one more novel, *You Can't be too Careful*, which appeared in 1941. *Ararat* had been the last utopia, *Babes* the last of the "prig" books, and *You Can't be too Careful* was the last of the novels which H.G. built around his own upbringing. Albert Tewler, whose father – employed in a china and glass business – dies when he is a boy and leaves him to be brought up by a pious mother, is another Wellsian it-might-have-been-me little man, full of prejudices, chauvinistic, devoid of insight or feeling. He speaks in the clipped Cockney of Kipps and his fellow-apprentices, and like Kipps he receives an unexpected legacy. He is inveigled into marriage with a girl remarkably like Miss Walsingham, but divorces her and settles down with a motherly managing woman who brings up his child of the first marriage. Tewler is full of resentment against a world that he cannot understand. He is dominated by the feeling that "you can't be too careful" because life is full of snares and delusions. He is *Homo Tewler*, and his time on earth is nearly up. He is fit for nothing except to be a victim, because he has no will to change the world. The only hint of hope lies in his son, who turns out to be a rebel who rejects his father and catches a glimpse of "a fundamental law for a united and recivilized world." Young Tewler may be one of the handful of "desperate men" who are "bored to fury by the vista of aimless, incessant and finally suicidal bloodshed ahead of them". There is no reason why, Wells says with equal desperation, they "should not put a new face upon reality very rapidly indeed . . . quite a small number of men in earnest and in unison could wrench the whole world into acquiescence."

Their immediate target, the novel implies, must be the Catholic Church, "the most evil thing in the whole world . . . Wherever the Catholic priest prevails, among the decadent pious [French] generals of the surrender, in Croatia, in Japan, in Spain, in that spite-slum Eire, in Italy, in South America, in Australia, there you will find malicious mischief afoot against the enlightenment of mankind." This outburst against Catholicism has nothing to do with the substance of the story, but a great deal to do with the eruption of militant anti-Catholicism in Wells in the first years of the war. It is matched in the book by a comparable attack on

Communism as "the identical twin of Catholicism ... psychologically the same". Practically all "the educational machinery on earth", Wells says, "is still in the hands of God-selling or Marx-selling combines ... selling mankind to destruction". The novel began reasonably by exploring the crippling emotional conditions which H.G. still bitterly remembered from his own childhood, but degenerated into a demonstration of their consequences – not so much for Tewler, as for Wells himself.

With a good deal of time on his hands, and with much pent-up frustration which could not be adequately released into his books, H.G. continually entangled himself in irritating disputes. Some of these were occasioned by the unfavourable reviews of his books. He was particularly annoyed by Kingsley Martin's habit of passing his books to C.E.M.Joad, who had been a Wellsian acolyte in the early Thirties but was now asking the pertinent question how anything practical could be done about the hammering sermons that Wells kept delivering to his readers.[8] On 26 December 1939 Wells wrote a letter to Martin headed "SOS", informing him that *The New World Order* was to be published the following week. "Will you for once save a bit of my work from the hands of that philosophical defective, Joad", he asked. "Book after book of mine he fumbles, misrepresents & mauls. Just for once give me a holiday from him." The request did not persuade Martin to drop Joad as a regular commentator on Wells. On 17 August 1940 *The New Statesman* permitted Joad to return to the attack with "An Open Letter to H.G.Wells", in the course of which Joad reminded H.G. that it was little use proposing to get rid of the politicians if he could not suggest any better instruments for saving the world. Wells replied a week later that *Ararat* had shown how an élite could be got together for the purpose. The duel with Joad went on intermittently. In January 1942, Wells met Kingsley Martin at a party and had an amiable chat with him. Two days later, when *The New Statesman* appeared, H.G. found another critical review and wrote to Martin accusing him of duplicity in displaying friendship when "you had that stinker up your sleeve when you greeted me so warmly". Martin wrote back an admonishing letter in the manner of Shaw.

With your note in front of me it takes some effort to recall that you are not really the vain and abusive little man that its petulance would suggest. .... I know well that by some inner compulsion you must work off your anger when anyone is in the least critical of you, but being a scientist and therefore interested in facts, you will realise after a minute's thought that on this occasion you have been more than usually hot-tempered.

Martin went on to explain that when they met he was not even aware that the book had been sent for review, but that was beside the point. "Do you mean to suggest", he asked H.G., "that because a reviewer had written something unfavourable to you that I should therefore cut you when I met you? Or that I should be in tears or blushing from shame? Or what *do* you suggest?" H.G. was determined to have the last word. A card came to Martin by return of post. "Now you are pretending you don't edit your own paper!" H.G. exclaimed. A few days later relations were back to normal.

H.G. usually recovered his temper after a row, but sometimes the outcome was less happy as in his clash with George Orwell.[9] Though Orwell owed a great deal to Wells, stylistically as well as in the conception of his anti-utopias,* they had never met until the spring of 1941 when H.G. invited "this Trotskyist with big feet" to dinner in Hanover Terrace, and they got on well enough. Later that year, Eileen Orwell invited Wells to dinner, but before he arrived Cyril Connolly's literary review *Horizon* had published Orwell's article, "Wells, Hitler and the World State".[10]

Orwell paid tribute to the influence of Wells, saying that "I doubt whether anyone who was writing books between 1900 and 1920, at any rate in the English language, influenced the young so much. The minds of us all, and therefore the physical world, would be perceptibly different if Wells had never existed." But he was, Orwell said, no longer a true prophet, and he had "squandered his talents in slaying paper dragons". While this might well have been said of what Orwell called "the usual rigmarole about the World State", his insistence that Wells was unaware of the coming of a new Dark Age was as inaccurate as his belief that Wells was an uncritical apostle of scientific progress and that the Wellsian utopias were merely paradises of technology. When they met at Orwell's flat they indulged in an inconclusive argument about whether Wells had under-estimated Hitler. A few weeks afterwards, H.G. strolled down the garden to call on Inez Holden, who was living in the mews flat behind Hanover Terrace, and finding that Orwell was visiting her he had a polite though somewhat strained conversation with him. What led later to the breach was a talk that Orwell gave in March 1942 on the Indian service of the BBC that was afterwards reprinted in the *Listener*. When H.G. saw that Orwell was repeating the claim that Wells believed that "science can solve all the ills that man is heir to", he wrote Orwell an angry note

* Orwell's novel *Coming Up for Air* was an ingenious parody of *Men Like Gods*.

insisting that "I don't say that at all. Read my early works, you shit." In an ensuing correspondence in the *Listener*, he objected to Orwell's argument that he "belonged to a despicable generation of parochially-minded writers who believed that the world could be saved from its gathering distresses by science", and claimed that from his earliest works he had been trying to say the exact contrary.[1] Orwell had undoubtedly misrepresented him at a time when he was unwell, and more than usually sensitive to suggestions that his ideas were out-moded, wrong-headed and inconsistent.

If Orwell had seen some of the letters that Wells was writing in the course of 1941 he could scarcely have argued that H.G. then felt complacent about the prospects for mankind or even, in the short run, the prospects for effectively winning the war. On 22 April 1941, for instance, H.G. wrote to Shaw reproving him for "assuming that man is a rational being, whereas he is nothing of the sort".[12]

At present the whole species is mad, that is to say mentally out of adjustment to its environment. We are as a people, a collection of unteachable dullards at war with an infectious lunatic & his victims. . . . I dont care if all the treasures of art in the world are ground to powder. (This is between ourselves.) I want to see humanity de-cultivated and making a fresh start. Culture is merely the ownership of stale piddle. Mantagna, Brahms my Tang Horse, St. Paul's Cathedral, I rank a little higher than the lavender smelling correspondence of my nicer great-aunts. I would like to keep them out not if they lead to idolatry.

This outburst was occasioned by Shaw's attempt to get H.G. and Gilbert Murray to join him in saying something cool about a possible settlement, with a hope of reducing the bombing. But Wells was not intimidated about bombing. He had calmly sat out the London blitz, taking his turn at fire-watching – as if "there was some magical quality, some gift to account for my immunity".[13] But when the issue of whether Rome should be spared as an open city was being debated H.G. called for fire from heaven to descend on that centre of the Catholic conspiracy against peace, the Vatican.*

When, two days before the Nazi attack on the Soviet Union on 22

---

* "Why don't we bomb Rome?" was the title of what the *Sunday Dispatch* in 1941 called "the most provocative article" ever written by Wells, who mplied that the Holy City was being protected by Catholics in the Foreign Office. Two years later, writing to Margaret Sanger on 7 July 1943, he was still asking the same question. 'People are waking up to the Roman Catholic mischief here", he wrote. "The test issue is: 'When do we bomb Rome?' "

June 1941, David Low published a cartoon criticising Wells in the *Evening Standard* H.G. let fly at his old friend.[14]

Your poor wits have given way under the war strain and you have become a Gawd-saker. What the hell do you think will keep people fighting Nazism if the outlook our own side offers is equally ambiguous and unattractive. Give me Goebbels any time if the choice is between his promise of a new world and the "new world" of the Emperor Otto, Otto Strasser, Franco, the old English school-tie lot and a gang of syphilitic Poles which your heart seems to desire – with Hess thrown in. Who has got *hold* of you, David? Who is pumping stuff into your brain arteries?

Sorry to lose you, Low. Regretfully, H.G.

Low reacted with good humour. Like many friends, he knew that the best way to deal with Wells was to avoid being drawn into an argument, and so he sent another cartoon as his reply – this one showing Wells as a tank rolling over a motley collection of his enemies. On 29 July H.G. sent an engaging withdrawal of the kind that made his friends forgive him. "I quarrelled seriously with you some fortnight or three weeks ago, I excommunicated you, and now I've forgotten what it was all about (but you must have been very wrong and annoying). The excommunication is now cancelled but be very careful not to do it again, and believe me to be as ever, your most faithful admirer." There was a cheeky PS: "Halo in asbestos box by next delivery."

The tank was not, perhaps, the most tactful image to use at this time, because H.G. had become involved in a libel action which arose from his conviction that he had originated the idea of armoured vehicles. On 15 February 1940, Major-General Sir Ernest Swinton had made a BBC broadcast claiming that he had invented the tank during the First World War after looking at a caterpillar tractor working in a field. Wells wrote to the *Listener* disputing this claim and insisting that the notion had in fact been first put forward in his *Strand* magazine story of 1903, "The Land Ironclads". "I lost my temper in proving this", Wells said in a long memorandum circulated privately,[15] and Swinton sued successfully for libel. But the main issue had been lost in a maze of irrelevancies. Swinton's damages were for the defamation of his character, not for proving that he had invented the tank. And Wells was more concerned about the way the BBC had behaved, trying to get him to apologise and to avoid an expensive court action, than with the injustice he believed that Swinton had done him. The last straw was that the BBC proposed a settlement whereby Wells paid £500 and the Corporation only £100.

The case, Wells said in the memorandum, "is merely one sample of the BBC behaviour, and if the same negligence, evasiveness and timidity on the part of its officials that has let me down in this affair and wasted my time and some of my money, passes without enquiry, it may manifest itself again tomorrow upon some fresh and immediately disastrous occasion".

Wells had never been able to persuade the authorities to take his inventive talents seriously – apart from the inadequate experiments with the telepherage system in the First World War – but this did not deter his enthusiasm for promoting new ways of waging war. His encounters with the Admiralty in 1941 and 1942 read like the efforts of the pertinacious Daniel Doyce to deal with the Circumlocution Office in Dickens's *Little Dorrit*.[16] His attempts to make the naval authorities take up a number of supposedly war-winning ideas provided him with a motif that he proceeded to embroider with sundry allegations of official incompetence, going back to the Spanish Armada, the Bourbons, Napoleon, the battle of Jutland and the British generals in the First World War, and winding up with the heavy losses caused in the current war by "the British obsession . . . of the invincible might of the British Navy". All this proved that "not only is *Homo sapiens* a fool to make war, but in the way he sets about it, he is a dazzlingly silly fool".

Nor did the Left escape his strictures. H.G. had been engaged on and off for years in a controversy with Shaw about Marx, for Shaw had never been able to persuade him to moderate the violence of his attacks on Marx. As late as 7 December 1939 Shaw sent him a long letter saying Wells's habit of disparaging Marx "as a shallow third rate Jew" was bound to shake his readers' confidence in his judgement and temper. Wells, Shaw declared, could easily ignore Marx in his propaganda, but if he was going to drag him in the references should at least be good-natured and attempt to do Marx justice.[17] And in 1941 Shaw reminded H.G. that Marx "lifted the golden lid off hell" when Europe was in the heyday of its prosperity, and that such an achievement was more than the work of "a lousy Jew".[18] But H.G. continued to denounce Marx generally, Communism more specifically and the Communist Party in Britain in particular, all the time insisting that the Soviet revolution had been "a mighty step in the march of mankind towards an equalitarian federated world socialism". The trouble was that the revolutionary movement had fallen into the hands of half-witted fanatics. "It is difficult", Wells wrote in 1942, "to over-estimate the harm the dogmatism of the Communist Party has done to human emancipation . . . enormous mischief in discrediting genuine radical and revolutionary thought."

These sentiments did not commend themselves to R.Palme Dutt, the chief Communist theoretician and editor of the *Labour Monthly*, who on 3 October 1942 asked H.G. to contribute to a symposium on the 25th anniversary of the Russian Revolution. Dutt refused to publish the article Wells wrote, saying that it was an attempt to blacken the occasion with malicious factional squabbling and telling Wells to take it off to some right-wing periodical.[19] Wells insisted that the article be printed, putting Dutt in an awkward position because H.G. was an important potential ally whom the CP wished to capture if it could.* Wells had already shown some support for the party line by speaking out against the suppression of the *Daily Worker*, and he had sent money to the *Daily Worker*'s Defence League just as Dutt was trying to squash his article. Dutt therefore gave way and in the December issue of the *Labour Monthly* he printed what was probably the harshest criticism of the Communist Party which had ever appeared in its press. He added a tortuous defence which led H.G. to repeat that the "Roman Catholic Church is my *bête noire* and the Communist Party my *bête rouge*", both of which "fight mental liberation tooth and nail". As a clinching example, H.G. produced the foolish attempt of Ivan Maisky, the Soviet ambassador in London, to prevent the performance in England of Gorki's play *Lower Depths* although it was currently being performed in Moscow. Maisky's argument was that to present "a corner of old Russia" at a time when the Red Army was the ally of Britain "would introduce confusion into the public mind" and prevent understanding between Britain and the USSR. H.G., for whom the moral of the situation was that "we shall march towards separate disasters if we do not get together in a common vision of the future", thought this episode revealed that the Communist machine was just as much an obstacle to such an understanding as anti-Communism in the US or the "malignant" Roman Catholic Church.[20]

H.G. had now reached the point where every organisation was out of

* Though Wells openly attacked the Communist Party for years, ridiculed Marx, and thought the Soviet regime had betrayed the revolution, he gave money to Communist causes and had many close associates who were party members. Just before the 1945 general election he wrote a letter to the *Daily Worker* to say that "I am an active supporter of the reconstituted Communist Party. I want to vote to that effect", and complaining that there was no Communist candidate in his constituency in which the Labour Party seemed concerned only with whist-drives to raise funds. He said that left-wing unity was needed to prevent "the next war", which would be an Anglo-American campaign against the USSR.

step. He could not stomach the dogmatism of the Communist Party. He thought the Labour Party silly, narrow-minded, and dominated by the trade union mentality. And he was severely critical of other radical groups even when they professed to support his ideas and sought to enlist his co-operation. A case in point was his objection to Sir Richard Acland, a former Liberal who had been trying to rally an independent movement of the Left against appeasement and for a broadly socialist policy. Wells had kept up a correspondence with him since 1937, but he distrusted Acland's ambition for leadership and his tendency to flirt with progressive Christian opinion. When, in May 1940, Acland proposed some kind of link-up between the Rights of Man group, the Federal Union movement, and the group of radicals he had attracted round him after publishing the Penguin *Unser Kampf*, he received a brusque repudiation from Wells of this "incoherent combination of progressives, in a movement going nowhere in particular under some foggy 'leadership' of your own". A little later, after J.B.Priestley had revived a mood of radicalism in Britain by a series of influential broadcasts on the BBC, a new group called the "1941 Committee" was formed, which included Priestley, Acland, Tom Wintringham (the former commander of the British volunteers in Spain) and Wells. Meeting at the house of Edward Hulton, the owner of *Picture Post*, which was contributing to a leftward swing of opinion in the country, the committee debated at length, Wells objecting to Acland's attempts to rally liberal opinion in the Churches.[21] Out of this committee there emerged the Common Wealth movement, which took advantage of the political truce in which the main parties in the wartime coalition refrained from fighting by-elections, and successfully contested a number of constituencies. These victories, straws in the wind which revealed that public opinion was drifting towards the Labour landslide in 1945, were dismissed by Wells as "the flights and plunges of the Acland kite". He would have nothing further to do with this movement, though it contained many people who had learnt their politics and taken their inspiration from Wells himself.

Apart from the personal and political controversies in which H.G. found an outlet for his antipathies, he continued – even when his health was poor – to keep up a running fire of articles in the press, almost all of them devoted to exposing some inadequacy in the war effort or attacking monarchists, politicians and Catholics. His disposition to harry the Pope and his flock was a cause of difficulty with editors. It was certainly one of the reasons why his income from journalism declined sharply in the war years, and he began to worry about money. When he was in New York in 1940 H.G. made an arrangement with the C.R.Miller company to cable a weekly article for syndication in American papers, and he wrote the first of these early in 1941. There followed a correspondence with Rube Wardell, the executive responsible, telling Wells with embarrassment that the sales prospects were poor. The replies from several papers revealed that the trouble was not merely that the articles were too expensive, or that they contained too much general Wellsian propaganda: the editors wanted H.G. to "lay off" the Pope. H.G., unusually compliant, offered to trim his articles to suit the market, but by early March it was clear that Wardell wanted to get out of the arrangement.[22] The day when H.G. could command top prices was over. Yet he continued to work as hard as ever, "writing away for dear life" as he had done half a century earlier as if he were trying to make his career rather than bring it to a close. H.G. found it impossible to accept a leisurely retirement. Though he spent a good deal of his time with Moura Budberg, going out to lunches and dinners, or to the ballet, he could not relax. Ideas kept buzzing in his head, and when something new occurred to him he was impatient to do something about it. "Where can I get hold of you in a hurry?" he asked Frank Horrabin in a note on 5 October 1942.[23] "I have a scheme which I hope I'll be able to mature in a week or so which is in effect a world atlas of . . . the substances that are *essential* to modern warfare." He thought that if all the key resources in the world could be charted it would be easier to set up international commissions after the war to control these crucial substances against "the private enterprise of warmongers and against every sort of imperialism, nationalism, gangsterism etc, etc".

In the course of 1942, H.G. decided to improve his academic qualifications by seeking a doctorate at London University, under the regulation which permitted the award of a DSc to a graduate on the basis mainly of published work, though Wells also had to prepare a thesis. There was a strong motivation for taking on this additional and intellectually demanding work. The one honour that H.G. had always coveted was election to the Royal Society. At intervals he had raised this with Gregory, and had repeatedly been gently assured that he did not fit the technical requirements. While he claimed to be a social scientist, he had to face the fact, as Gregory told him on 29 June 1942 that "there is no hope of the Royal Society extending its field to include the social sciences or to increase its numbers to include representatives of them".[24] H.G. believed that if he could secure an advanced degree in his original subject of zoology, he might thus enhance his chances of being elected, and he sat down to write a thesis entitled "On the Quality of Illusion in the Continuity of the Individual Life in the Higher Metazoa, with Particular Reference to the Species *Homo sapiens*".[25] The short point of the thesis was the view that Kentlake had stated in *Babes in the Darkling Wood* – that man does not possess an original mental unity, and that the idea of an integrated personality was "a biologically convenient delusion" which held together "a multitude of loosely linked behaviour systems which take control of the body and participate in a common delusion of being one single self".

This argument, supported by selective quotations from psychologists and anthropologists, contained an important clue to the attitudes and behaviour which H.G. had displayed throughout his whole life. There was not *one* John Smith, he claimed, but *many* John Smiths within the single organism, and there was no necessary reason why they should be in harmony with each other. They might well respond differently to different stimuli. Wells, in fact, was seeking to offer a scientific explanation of inconsistency, both in himself and others, and to spell out his feeling that "practical life" was essentially an illusion. Each individual's belief that he was an independent personality, he suggested, was nothing more than a hallucination, which caused "most of the foolish dogmatisms and ultimate 'explanations' of life, the priestcrafts, presumptuous teachings, fears, arbitrary intolerances, tyrannies and mental muddles, that have embittered human relationships hitherto". The only reality lay in the collective existence of the species, and the only hope for human advancement lay with "some sort of super-individual, a brave new *persona*" who, realising that world unity and a common law will create "the great impersonal society of the days to come", will live "a life of superb completeness of co-operation with his fellow élite".

The thesis was a summation of the Wellsian view of human nature, and to support it H.G. also submitted *The Outline of History, The Science of Life, The Work, Wealth and Happiness of Mankind* and *Phoenix*, explaining that all these works were a contribution "to the ecology of *Homo sapiens*".[26] Six months later, on 13 July 1943 H.G. was able to write to Gregory saying that he had been awarded the degree. The next step was to secure publication of the thesis in the *Philosophical Transactions*, but for that it must be sponsored by a FRS who need not be in agreement with the document but who considers it of sufficient interest and value to merit publication . . . Will you do this for me?"[27]

Gregory, to his sorrow, was still unable to help his dearest friend to what he most desired. In the end, the thesis appeared on '42 to '44, and the Royal Society never gave Wells the recognition he had always wanted as a serious man of science.

The disappointment was bitter. And it came at a time when H.G. was still recovering from the illness which affected him through much of 1942. But he was well enough by the autumn to pick up controversies which had languished during his illness. On 19 September 1942 hearing that he had been sick, Margaret Sanger sent him the first of several letters urging him to abandon wartime London and to convalesce at her home.[28] "Arizona is a wonderful state", she said, "and a lovely extra guest-room is awaiting you. Why not come there and get the sunshine and the vitamins from the wonderful fruits? Charming company, both male and female, will also await you." But H.G. could not bring himself to quit Hanover Terrace. He had at last done with travelling, and in the following years he kept more and more to the house and to a small circle of friends. Some of his oldest associates were now slipping away, to inaccessible retirement and to death. In April 1943 Beatrice Webb died, unhappy only that she was leaving Sidney alone and incapacitated by an earlier stroke, and writing her diary to the last days. "I cannot tell you how distressed I am to hear of your loss", H.G. wrote to Sidney on 30 April.[29] "My one consolation is that long ago all our ancient bickerings died out & my relations with you both was one of the warmest friendship & admiration." In the summer, G.B.S. was very poorly, and on 8 August H.G. wrote with characteristic concern to Dr Robin Lawrence, his own physician for whom he had a great liking and respect, saying that he had persuaded Shaw to consult Lawrence despite his lifelong antagonism to doctors.[30] Just a month later, on 12 September, Shaw wrote sadly to H.G. to say that Charlotte had died early that morning.[31] It was about this time, prompted by such reminders of age and mortality, that H.G. privately arranged an annuity for his old friend Elizabeth Healey, now a widow in reduced circumstances. With Gregory, she was the last of the old friends from South Kensington with whom he remained in close touch.

26

THE LAST JUDGEMENT

At the end of 1942 Wells published his last comprehensive statement of his ideas. *The Outlook for Homo Sapiens* was not in fact a new book but a combination of *The Fate of Homo Sapiens*, published in 1939, and *The New World Order*, which had appeared the following year. His decision to reissue these works, however, showed that the war had not changed his diagnosis of the world situation. It had only increased his desperation to the point where he declared that "there is no creed, no way of living left in the world at all, that really meets the needs of the time", repeating his conviction that *Homo sapiens* was on the verge of decline, that "the universe is bored with him" and he is being carried "along the stream of fate to degradation, suffering and death". Without a wilful and strenuous effort to adapt forthwith, mankind will blunder "down the slopes of failure in the wake of all the monster reptiles . . to his ultimate extinction".

Wells then rehearsed the obstacles to the adaptation in man that he had so often demanded, singling out the Catholic Church as the most dangerous of all enemies of progress. H.G. had been indoctrinated against Catholicism at an early age. As an apprentice in Southsea he had read anti-Catholic propaganda in the rationalist paper, *The Freethinker*. In those same years he had once wandered into the Catholic cathedral in Portsmouth and been dismayed and frightened by a threatening sermon. It had revived his "old childish nightmare of God . . . the sort of thing to scare ten year olds". It was at this moment, he declared later, that he realised that this revolt against religion was not merely "again t the God of Hell in his most Protestant form" but also against this "parallel attack upon my integrity, the Catholic Church, a mass attack, the attack of a great organization". He suddenly glimpsed the moving power of an apocalyptic preacher, claiming a single truth and seeking to impose it by putting "hell and fear and submission into people's minds". Wells never saw that what he was describing was the mirror image of his own gospel of salvation – that though

439

he believed that he had rejected the Church he had unconsciously identified with its claims and methods, and that all his life he had been struggling to develop a rival theology and to create, in the notion of the Open Conspiracy, an organisation which could compete with it. This theme cropped up insistently in almost everything H.G. had written since the outbreak of war, and the degree of his intolerance towards Catholics had been increasing each year. Wells had made much of his campaign for human rights and free speech, but Roman Catholics seemed to be excluded from his dispensation. In *Phoenix* he had actually suggested that it would be desirable to go back to the Test Acts, abolished in England in 1829, which were a device to prevent Catholics from holding public office. At the minimum he wanted to have them excluded from the Foreign Office, the War Office, the diplomatic service and key positions in education. As he later put it in an interview with the editor of the American *Freethinker*, he wished to "fight intolerance with intolerance".[1] He also opposed mixed marriages, and suggested a boycott of Roman Catholic bookshops.

After his illness in 1942, Wells concentrated his attack upon the Catholics in a book which Penguin published in 1943 with the title of *Crux Ansata*. It was a blast against the Vatican for its contemporary entanglement in international politics – Wells feared that it was seeking to re-establish the Holy Roman Empire – and against the record of the Catholic Church in history. It made no pretence to be anything more than a polemical outburst. A long account of the massacre of Protestants in Ireland in the reign of Charles I, for instance, said nothing about Cromwell or the fate of the Catholic population of Drogheda. And much of it was little more than repetition of arguments from militant Protestant and freethinking propaganda sheets. Wells had harked back to the oldest enemy of the millenarian Puritan, the Scarlet Woman of Rome, the Anti-Christ in the Vatican. The fact that none of the main papers reviewed the book only confirmed Wells's conviction that there was a conspiracy to suppress anything that might annoy the Catholics. He found further evidence of this in his failure to interest any American publisher in *Crux Ansata*. One American who was sympathetic, however, was Margaret Sanger, and for the next few years she conducted an active correspondence with H.G. on the issue.[2] She had come from a Catholic family herself, and her initial interest in birth control stemmed from her reaction against the price women had to pay for uncontrolled pregnancies. Along with the food parcels she occasionally despatched to Hanover Terrace she sent packages of anti-Catholic material. Wells in return sent *Crux Ansata*, and when it still failed to find a publisher in the US he assigned all American rights in it to her. Even though she arranged for the book to be handled by what the *New Republic* described as an "underground" publishing firm, accustomed to put out anti-Catholic publications, the difficulties were not yet over.[3] When it was printed, Catholics in the bindery went on strike rather than work on it. And when it was published, it went unnoticed by almost every American paper except those with a bias against Catholicism.

In the succeeding months, Margaret Sanger kept Wells posted on her efforts to promote the book, and when he was seriously unwell again in early 1944 she repeated her invitation for him to go out to recuperate in Arizona. In the summer of 1944, there was an additional reason why she urged H.G. to leave for the sunshine of Tucson: the V-weapon bombardment of London had started. But these robot bombs, H.G. wrote to her in July 1944, "break a lot of windows and so forth but are quite ineffective from a military point of view, and they are nothing to those of us who went through the hard times of 1941". In any case, "just now I have to stick to London. If this religious war grows, they must not be able to say I beat a retreat to a place of security and sniped at the Church from there".[4]

H.G. had no intention of moving. On 4 July he wrote to Elizabeth Healey complaining of rumours spread about the V-bombs by "panic-stricken bores, who when they get to the country lie & exaggerate to justify their own disgraceful cowardice. Here I am in the middle of it all & only one window cracked by the concussion of an AA gun on Primrose Hill. Do show people this letter & shut up the pro-German panic-mongers. We stood up so well to the Blitzkrieg at the beginning of the war & now this silly behaviour is disgracing the country in the eyes of the world."[5] Though Wells was now in indifferent health, and tired easily, he had not lost his capacity for controversy. While he was battling against the Catholic antagonist, he still had the energy for a campaign of his own in Hanover Terrace where he was irritated by the effect on property values of the conversion of one of the houses into a club for servicemen. While he did not object to the club, he thought the vulgar signs on it would help some speculators who dreamed of "acquiring the terrace in the post-war scramble so many shady people are preparing for". The target for his attack, which included side-swipes at Tories and Roman Catholics, was Sir Thomas Moore, the Conservative MP who normally occupied the house. In a ferocious letter to Moore, accusing him of having "studied controversial method at the feet of the editor of the *Catholic Herald*",

Wells insisted that he would go on fighting "against the Roman Catholic cancer in the world's affairs" and "the strenuous efforts of the Catholic right wing to frustrate the efforts of the scientific intelligence to bring about a final rational phase in the world of mankind".[6] Mr Wells, he announced, "is pugnacious in the service of truth and he hopes to die fighting".

He had, in fact, begun to think about his death. In March 1944 he brought out an expensive and limited edition of '42 to '44, which was a miscellany made up of newspaper articles and unpublished jottings of the kind that might well have been kept to a commonplace book. He later regretted that he had "flung together in needless haste" a book which had been inspired by the thought that it might be his last, and he had no desire to see it remain in print when he recovered.[7] It had been rushed out at a time when he was housebound and suffering from a combination of diabetes, a weak heart, catarrh and various complications, and he feared that he might be dying. He had begun to compose what he called "hemlock letters" to friends, explaining that he must leave sooner than he expected and hoping that they would see "the rebirth of that greater new world of which I had dreamt".[8] But none of them was sent. The doctors refused to set a definite term on his life. "I found it exasperating beyond measure", H.G. wrote, "to have them all humming and hawing ... to avoid giving me a plain answer." But he was touched by the affectionate response that so many friends had made when he was ill. He valued the stimulus of friendship, and no public man of his generation had been more gregarious. As he recovered, he had little strength to go about. He would walk the few hundred yards across Regent's Park to the Zoo or the rose garden, and sometimes go down to the Savile for lunch. Though he was often drowsy, and his conversation, always so energetic, became more spasmodic, as if he were trying hard to keep or find a train of thought that was eluding him, he was still able to concentrate sufficiently to write articles or draft passages for possible books. It was a slow physical decline, punctuated by periods of apparent improvement. He had always believed that he would die suddenly, victim to the fatty degeneration of the heart to which his brother Frank and other male members of his family succumbed, but it was neither his heart nor his diabetes that was gradually killing him. He had trouble with his liver, which in the final stages developed into cancer.

In February 1945 he wrote to Elizabeth Healey that "I am keeping remarkably fit, but public affairs irritate & disgust me. I mend clocks &

fuss about the decorations of the house to keep my mind off the follies of mankind. Bombs come & go . . . but they never hit me." And in July he wrote again to say that he could send the cheerful news that he was able to come downstairs and that he was enjoying "short relapses into health": he added, "I wish I could send you a big chunk of today's mood."[9]

It had been in one of these more cheerful moods that H.G. wrote *The Happy Turning*. He had begun it early in 1943, but finished it in the course of 1944 during a spell of writing which produced about fifteen newspaper articles and a good deal of unpublished manuscript which he was collecting for a book with the provisional title of *Exasperations*.[10] A large part of *The Happy Turning* came out in *The Leader* in October 1944, and all of it as a slim volume of fifty pages early in 1945. He described it as an account of "the more adult and modern and civilized part of my being" which now expressed itself in dreams. Wells recalled the nightmares of his childhood, and the anxiety dreams which had broken his sleep when he was overstrained with worry. At the end of his life, he declared, he had found peace and fulfilment down what he called " the happy turning". In this recurrent dream, which recalled the transformation scenes whereby he had so often translated his characters into utopia, he found himself taking an unexpected route on his daily walk which led him into a "delightful land of my lifelong suppressions, in which my desires and unsatisfied fancies, hopes, memories and imaginations have accumulated inexhaustible treasure". He felt like a child again, reborn into a paradise without anger, despair and frustration, without war, and without death to carry off old friends. He had at last entered into his promised land, in such contrast to his waking life, which was "now one of very fierce and definite antagonisms". His most congenial companion in this Beyond was Jesus, in whom he recognised a fellow martyr, disappointed in his mission by the stupidity and indifference of mankind. But he also found himself in the company of great artists and poets – something like a seminar of cultural Samurai – who agreed that "the human mind may be in a phase of transition to a new, fearless, clear-headed way of living". It was the old dream, at last consciously recognised as a dream, which had run through all his writings as the counterpoint to the nagging fears of disaster and extinction.

Yet the fear that the human race would fail to rise to the challenge of that dream remained, and grew more insistent in the early months of 1944, when H.G. worked hard at a much grimmer manuscript than *The Happy Turning*. He began to see signs "manifest in the Heavens above and on the earth below" that *Homo sapiens* was "at the close of his specific existence", and produced a completed (but still unpublished) book of thirty thousand words describing the impending fate of mankind. It was the matching panel to *The Happy Turning* in the triptych of the Last Judgement, with the ominous title of *Mind at the End of its Tether*.

That autumn Wells was in a state of deep pessimism. It was as if he had once again carried himself forward to the ultimate dark prospect of *The Time Machine* in which all life, not only that of the human species, tends to darkness and extinction. But there remained a flicker of hope, the last expression of the optimistic belief that there must be some way out of the impasse into which man seemed to be carried by the laws of entropy and evolution. He could not make up his mind, still, how to resolve that dualistic paradox, with which he had wrestled throughout his career as a writer. Towards the end of the year, when he produced a new summary of organic evolution as the conclusion for the revised edition of *A Short History of the World*, he again left himself a loophole of escape – the faint possibility that future evolution might produce a superior breed of men capable of the adaptation needed for survival.

He was now too old, and too tired, to make a choice between these two visions of things to come that had been intertwined in his earliest work and never clearly disentangled in his prophecies. Jettisoning the long draft of *Mind at the End of its Tether*, in December 1944 he produced a much shorter version which was an amalgam of its first three chapters and the evolutionary essay from *A Short History*. The result, as his son Gip pointed out in his introduction to *The Last Books of H.G.Wells*, was a contradiction. On the opening page H.G. declared apocalyptically that "within a period to be estimated by weeks and months rather than by aeons, there has been a fundamental change in the conditions under which life, not simply human life but all self-conscious existence, has been going on since its beginning . . . this world is at the end of its tether . . . the end of everything we call life is close at hand and cannot be evaded". For Wells as an individual that was now true. In some way he felt that his own life had epitomised the rise and fall of life on earth, a parabola from protoplasm through the zenith of ascendancy and down to nothingness, and that shape had provided, in his own relevant phrase, the "arch" of his main work. Now, he concluded, Nature – or what he called "the unknown implacable" – had turned against life on earth. "Mind near exhaustion still makes its final futile movement towards that 'way out or round or through the impasse' . . . this, its last expiring thrust, is to demonstrate that the door

closes upon us for evermore. There is no way out or round or through . . .
Our universe is not merely bankrupt; there remains no dividend at all; it
has not simply liquidated; it is going clean out of existence, leaving not a
wrack behind."

In these gloomy phrases Wells was expressing emotions and fears which
reached back to his childhood and haunted his life. But the will and the
intellectual beliefs that had fused in his buoyant conviction that one must
"live as though it were not so", and seek to the very end a Plan of Salvation, produced one last assertion that man might yet triumph over fate.
Though the "stars in their courses have turned against" man, there remains
the hope that he will "give place to some other animal better adapted to
face the fate that closes in more and more swiftly upon mankind", and that
this new species "may arise as a new modification of the *hominidae*. . . . We
want to be in at the death of Man and to have a voice in his final replacement by the next Lord of Creation." It is, after all, "ordinary man" who
is damned to perish. The hope of salvation lies with a new race who will
cease to be men as we now know them, and this means that only "a small,
highly adaptable minority of the species can possibly survive". Once again,
and to the very end, Wells had found his way to the Rule of the Saints who
will inherit the new heaven and the new earth. The coming of this millennium will not be part of the natural order of things. It will be the result of a
victory over them, by the defeat of the Antagonist who has captured the
soul of Man the Animal. To Wells, in the shadow of his own extinction,
that possible new birth seemed at last only the most slender of hopes, as
he asserted his faith "in that small minority which will succeed in seeing
life out to its inevitable end".

During the last year of his life, H.G. painted a revealing mural on a wall
behind his house in Hanover Terrace. It was a set of panels depicting the
story of evolution, and this Darwinian gloss on the Last Judgement
ended with the appearance of the horned devils that Sarah Wells had concealed from him as a child by covering them with stamp paper. Beneath the
figure of Man he wrote the words "Time to Go".

The dropping of the atomic bomb on Hiroshima in August 1945 roused
Wells to make his last appeal. He began to work upon the scenario of a
new film for Alexander Korda.[11] H.G. said that it was to be *Things to Come*
brought up to date with the reality of nuclear weapons. In a statement
protecting his copyright in the scenario, he wrote:

The human situation is grave and tragic, a thing he has been writing and saying for the past half-century; it is and has been obvious to the clear-sighted for all that time, but that is all the more reason why man should face his culminating destiny with dignity and mutual aid and charity, without hysteria, meanness and idiotic misrepresentation. . . .

It was the same message as the end of *Mind at the End of its Tether*. There was, in the prospect before mankind in the nuclear age, no more ethical imperative than there had been in Huxley's evolutionary doctrine. Man might well be "cruel or mean or cowardly". But just as Huxley had insisted that man must still strive to be good and noble, so Wells insisted that the fight for life must go on to the end however threatening the odds might be. He had changed nothing and withdrawn nothing since he wrote *The Time Machine* and "The Extinction of Man" fifty years before.

During the last months, though H.G. was weak and ailing, he could still husband his energies, "surfacing", as Anthony West recalled of his visits at this time, "only occasionally when he wished to give his full attention to something or somebody".[12] He had not lost the thread of life. Two months before he died, Compton Mackenzie called on him. H.G. was "sitting with his coat and waistcoat off, thus displaying a remarkable pair of braces decorated with nymphs and lilied pools. He looked much less ill than I had expected to see, and for a man not three months away from his eightieth birthday wonderfully young." While they were having tea, the maid brought in the evening paper. H.G. looked at it and tossed it aside. "I have just read an article I wrote fifty years ago and if it was reprinted today I should not have to change one word of it", he said.[13]

From the beginning of August H.G. kept to his room, but he seemed better and his family expected him to rally. The end was quite sudden and peaceful. On the afternoon of Thursday 13 August 1946 he told his nurse that he would take his customary nap, and sent her away. A few minutes later, at 4.15, he died.

H.G. Wells was cremated three days afterwards at Golders Green. In a short address J.B. Priestley bade farewell to "the great prophet of our time". Wells, he said, had "worked with passionate loyalty for the whole toiling, contriving, endlessly hopeful family of Mankind", and spoken for "the ordinary little citizen" who, baffled but touchingly gallant, was swept along by forces he could not understand "into a world of gigantic conflict and sinister chances". For Priestley, as for so many others who had enjoyed all that was best in H.G., there was also a warmer memory of the man who could write *Kipps* and *Mr Polly* and *Tono-Bungay*, the man who could enrich his letters with droll little drawings, who could invent uproarious family games, whose blue eyes twinkled with mischief and whose famous voice, which never lost a kind of reedy Cockney impudence, rose higher and higher in friendly mischief; who was not only a tremendous character but also a most lovable man. . . . When he was angry, it was because he knew, far better than we did, that life need not be a sordid greedy scramble; and when he was impatient it was because he knew there were glorious gifts of body, mind and spirit only just beyond our present reach.[14]

Priestley, indeed, had spoken for the generation who felt that Wells had been their spokesman, giving himself to a great vision and martyring himself in its service. It was by that dream that he had lived, and was remembered, rather than by the shadow which had haunted and distorted his real life. No other man, spanning the years between *The Origin of the Species* and the Hiroshima bomb, had so faithfully mirrored the dualism of his own kind or demonstrated better the conflict of the divided self that could not accept the human condition.

Gip Wells and Anthony West took the ashes of their father down to the Isle of Wight and scattered them over the sea. The journey of the Time Traveller was over.

REFERENCES

The main collection of Wells material is in the Rare Book Room, University of Illinois, Champaign-Urbana. This is referred to below as the Wells Archive. It includes correspondence to and from Wells, original manuscripts of his writings, personal documents and press cuttings. The Archive also holds a large number of books by and about Wells, as well as a substantial part of his personal library. No place and dates are given below for books written by Wells, as these are listed separately in the Bibliography. All references in the text to writings by Wells which are not otherwise attributed in these notes come from *Experiment in Autobiography*, the main, though by no means the only, source for Wells's own autobiographical statements. Where quotations from other sources are clearly identified in the text of this book, no additional reference has been given. It should be noted that Wells often omitted dates from his letters.

Chapter 1

1 The diary of Sarah Wells is in the Wells Archive
2 Meade-Fetherstonhaugh, Margaret, *Uppark and its People* (London 1964)
3 Wells Archive
4 The account books are in the Warwick county archive
5 Entries in the diary of Sarah Wells
6 Appleman, P., Madden, W.A. and Wolff, M. (Eds), 1859: *Entering on an Age of Crisis* (Bloomington 1959); Houghton, Walter E., *The Victorian Frame of Mind* (New Haven 1957); Young, G.M., *Victorian England: Portrait of an Age* (London 1937); Burn, W.L., *The Age of Equipoise* (London 1964); and Clark, Kitson, *The Making of Victorian England* (London 1962)
7 Horsburgh, E.L.S., *Bromley, Kent, from the Earliest Times to the Present Century* (London 1929)
8 The Baxter papers are in the Bromley Public Library

Chapter 2

1 The main sources for the childhood of Wells are his autobiography, his mother's diary, letters written to and by relatives and friends that are in the

Wells Archive, inquiries by Geoffrey West when he was writing *H.G.Wells: A Sketch for a Portrait* (London, 1930) with the direct help of Wells, and the Baxter papers.
2 Baxter papers
3 Frank Wells to William Baxter
4 Wells, H.G., *The Happy Turning*
5 Horsburgh, E.L.S., op. cit.
6 See Lowndes, G.A.N., *The Silent Social Revolution* (London 1969)
7 West, Geoffrey, op. cit.
8 Wells, H.G., *The Desert Daisy* edited, with an introduction by Ray, Gordon N. (Carbondale 1957)

Chapter 3
1 This letter is reproduced in facsimile in *Experiment in Autobiography*
2 Wells Archive
3 The information on the school at Wookey comes from the school's log-book
4 Pound, Reginald, *Arnold Bennett* (London 1952)
5 Wells Archive
6 ibid
7 Facsimile in *Experiment in Autobiography*
8 Wells Archive
9 ibid
10 ibid
11 ibid
12 ibid
13 ibid
14 ibid
15 Wells Collection, Bromley Public Library

Chapter 4
1 Wells, H.G., "Huxley" in *Royal College of Science Journal* (April 1901)
2 Armytage, W.H.G., *Sir Richard Gregory* (London 1967) contains many details of the lifelong friendship between Wells and Gregory, and prints a good deal of the correspondence between them. Other Gregory letters are in the Wells Archive.
3 See: Bibby, Cyril, *T.H.Huxley* (London 1969); Irvine, William, *Apes, Angels and Victorians* (Cleveland 1959); Lynd, Helen M., *England in the Eighteen-Eighties* (New York 1945); and Chadwick, Owen, *The Victorian Church* (London 1970)
4 Webb, Beatrice, *My Apprenticeship* (London 1926)
5 Huxley, T.H., "Evolution and Ethics". This celebrated Romanes Lecture at Oxford is reprinted in the *Works* (1893)
6 Wells, H.G., "Huxley", op. cit.

7 Published in *Mind*, New Series, Vol XIII, No 51: the quotation is from *Experiment in Autobiography*
8 Webb, Beatrice, op. cit.
9 Wells Archive
10 The letters to Elizabeth Healey are an important source, extending over fifty years
11 Armytage, W.H.G., op. cit.
12 Wells Archive
13 An ample bibliography on the Socialist movement is in McBriar, A.M., *Fabian Socialism and English Politics 1884–1918* (Cambridge 1962)
14 Wells Archive
15 ibid
16 This story and the first draft of *The Chronic Argonauts* are reprinted as appendices in Bergonzi, Bernard, *The Early H.G.Wells* (Manchester 1961)

Chapter 5

1 Wells Archive
2 ibid
3 ibid
4 ibid
5 ibid
6 ibid
7 ibid
8 ibid
9 ibid
10 ibid
11 West, Geoffrey, op. cit., gives an extended quotation
12 Wells Archive
13 ibid
14 ibid
15 ibid
16 ibid
17 ibid
18 Wells Archive
19 Reproduced in West, Geoffrey, op. cit.
20 Wells Archive
21 ibid
22 ibid
23 ibid
24 ibid
25 ibid
26 ibid

27 West, Geoffrey, op. cit., prints the whole letter
28 Wells Archive
29 ibid
30 Letter from T.Ormerod in *Manchester Guardian* (21 August 1946)
31 Wells Archive
32 Richards, Grant, *Memories of a Misspent Youth* (London 1932)
33 Harris, Frank, *Contemporary Portraits* (New York 1970, reprint)

Chapter 6

1 The letter is reproduced in *Experiment in Autobiography*
2 See, for example, Weekes, Robert P., "Disentanglement as a Theme in H. G.Wells's Fiction" in Papers of the Michigan Academy of Science, Arts and Letters, Vol xxxix, 1954
3 The diary of Sarah Wells
4 The cheque is in the Sussex county archive at Chichester
5 Reprinted in *Experiment in Autobiography*
6 ibid
7 Wells Archive
8 ibid
9 Reprinted in *Experiment in Autobiography*
10 Wells Archive
11 In *Experiment in Autobiography*
12 Wells Archive
13 ibid
14 Both in *Experiment in Autobiography*

Chapter 7

1 Jackson, Holbrook, *The Eighteen-Nineties* (London 1913)
2 Chesterton, G.K., *The Victorian Age in Literature* (London 1913)
3 Nordau, Max, *Degeneration* (London 1895)
4 See: Nowell-Smith, Simon (Ed.), *Edwardian England* (London 1964); Cecil, Robert, *Life in Edwardian England* (London 1969); Montgomery, John, *1900: The End of an Era* (London 1968); Chapple, J.A.V., *Documentary and Imaginative Literature 1880–1920* (London 1970); Lester, John A., *Journey Through Despair 1880–1914* (Princeton 1968); Le Galliene, Richard, *The Romantic Nineties* (London 1925)
5 Wells, H.G., Preface to *The Country of the Blind and Other Stories*
6 Unpublished letter in possession of the daughter of E.S.P.Haynes, Mrs Renée Tickell
7 Facsimile in *Experiment in Autobiography*
8 Wells Archive
9 Hind, Lewis, *Authors and I* (London 1920)

10 An appendix in West, Geoffrey, op. cit., gives an account of the various versions

11 Wells Archive

12 ibid

13 ibid

14 ibid

15 Richards, Grant, op. cit.

16 There is a description of this scene in *Experiment in Autobiography*. See also: Brome, Vincent, *Frank Harris* (London 1959)

17 Wells Archive

18 ibid

19 ibid

20 Addressee unknown: in Yale University Library

21 Raknem, Ingwald, *H.G.Wells and His Critics* (London 1964)

22 Wells Archive

23 Much of this correspondence is in the Wells Archive: William Burns has a specialist study of this matter in preparation

24 Reproduced in *Experiment in Autobiography*

25 ibid

26 Wells Archive

27 ibid

28 Richards, Grant, op. cit.

29 Reprinted in *Experiment in Autobiography*

Chapter 8

1 Ford, Ford Madox (Hueffer, F.M.) in *Saturday Review*, January 1898. See also his *Mightier than the Sword* (London 1938)

2 On the scientific romances see: Bergonzi, Bernard, op. cit., Hillegas, Mark, *The Future as Nightmare* (New York 1967); Parrinder, Patrick, *H.G.Wells* (Ed) (London 1972); and Wagar, Warren, *H.G.Wells and the World State* (New Haven 1961)

3 Wells, H.G., Preface to Collected Edition of the Scientific Romances (London 1933)

4 "Jules Verne Revisited", *T.P.'s Weekly*, 9 October 1903

5 Wells, H.G., Preface to *The Country of the Blind and Other Stories*

6 See Raknem, Ingwald on his indebtedness. Also Hughes, David, "H.G. Wells and the Charge of Plagiarism", *Nineteenth-Century Fiction*, June 1966

7 Reprinted in Wells, H.G., *Certain Personal Matters*

8 See: Buckley, J.H., *The Triumph of Time* (Cambridge, Mass. 1967)

9 Jean-Aubry, G., *Joseph Conrad: Life and Letters* (London 1927)

10 Huxley, T.H., op. cit.

11 Suvin, Darko, "A Grammar of Form and a Criticism of Fact: *The Time*

Machine as a Structural Model for Science Fiction". Paper delivered at Wells symposium, McGill University, 1971

12 *The Athenaeum*, 9 May 1896: *The Times*, 17 June 1896; the *Spectator*, 18 April 1896

13 *The Guardian*, 3 June 1896

14 Conversation with H.G.Wells, reported in West, Geoffrey, op. cit.

15 Toulmin, Stephen and Goodfield, June, *The Discovery of Time* (London 1965)

16 See: Cohn, Norman, *The Pursuit of the Millennium* (New York 1961); Kermode, Frank, *A Sense an of Ending* (New York 1967); Kermode, Frank, *Continuities* (London 1968); Hill Christopher, *Antichrist in England* (London 1970); Mannheim, Karl, *Ideology and Utopia* (London 1936); Miller, Hillis J., *The Disappearance of God* (Cambridge, Mass. 1963); and Miller, Perry, *Errand into the Wilderness* (New York 1964)

Chapter 9

1 Gettman, Royal A., *George Gissing and H.G.Wells* (London 1961). All following quotations from the Gissing-Wells correspondence are from this volume

2 Korg, Jacob, *George Gissing: A Critical Biography* (Seattle 1963)

3 *Monthly Review*, August 1904

4 Wells Archive

5 ibid

6 *Monthly Review*, op. cit.

7 Wells Archive

8 Jean-Aubry, G., op. cit.

9 Wells Archive

10 Wells Archive

11 ibid

12 Reproduced in *Experiment in Autobiography*

13 Wells Archive

14 ibid

15 Wells Archive

16 Jean-Aubry, G., op. cit.

17 ibid

18 ibid

19 Ford, Ford Madox, *Conrad* (London 1924)

20 Ford, Ford Madox, *Mightier than the Sword*, op. cit.

21 Ford, Ford Madox, *Conrad*, op. cit.

22 Jean-Aubry, G., op. cit.

23 ibid

24 Ford, Ford Madox, *Conrad*, op. cit.

25 Ford, Ford Madox, *Mightier than the Sword*, op. cit.

26 ibid

27 Unpublished letter to Mark Benney, 13 August 1940, Wells Archive

28 Edel, Leon and Ray, Gordon N., *Henry James and H.G.Wells* (London 1958)

29 Wells Archive

30 Ford, Ford Madox, *Mightier than the Sword*, op. cit.

31 ibid

32 Jean-Aubry, G., op. cit.

33 Gilkes, Lillian, *Cora Crane* (London 1962)

34 Ford, Ford Madox, *Mightier than the Sword*, op. cit.

35 Gilkes, Lillian, op. cit.

36 Hind, Lewis, op. cit.

37 Gilkes, Lillian, op. cit.

Chapter 10

1 Wilson, Harris, *Arnold Bennett and H.G.Wells* (London 1960)

2 Wells, H.G., *Anticipations*

3 Wells Archive

4 Gettman, Royal A., op. cit.

5 Wells Archive

6 ibid

7 The James letters are in Edel, L. and Ray, Gordon N. op. cit.

8 Wilson, Harris, op. cit.

9 For Bennett, see: Bennett, Arnold, *Letters* (London 1933); *Letters to His Nephew* (London 1936); *Letters to J.B.Pinker* (New York 1966); and Pound, Reginald, *Arnold Bennett* (London 1952)

10 Ford, Ford Madox, *Mightier than the Sword*, op. cit.

11 Wells Archive

12 ibid

13 Korg, Jacob, op. cit.

14 Edel, Leon and Ray, Gordon N., op. cit.

15 Wells Archive

16 ibid

Chapter 11

1 Wells Archive

2 ibid

3 Wilson, Harris, op. cit.

4 Wells, H.G., *Anticipations*

5 Wells Archive

6 ibid

7 Jean-Aubry, G., op. cit. This undated letter is wrongly attributed by Jean-Aubry to 1904

8 Wells Archive

9 Quoted in Kargalitski, J., *The Life and Thought of H.G.Wells* (London 1966)

10 See: Wiener, Martin J., *Between Two Worlds* (Oxford 1971); Kent, Frank, *Radical London* (London 1932); Smith, W.S., *The London Heretics* (London 1967); and Spiller, G., *The Ethical Movement in Great Britain* (London 1934)

11 Wells Archive

12 The manuscript of Beatrice Webb's diary is in the Passfield Papers at the London School of Economics. See: Webb, Beatrice, *My Apprenticeship* (London 1926); *Our Partnership* (London 1948); Cole, Margaret, Beatrice Webb's Diaries (2 vols) (London 1952 and 1956); Cole, Margaret, *Beatrice Webb* (London 1945); and Cole, Margaret (Ed.), *The Webbs and their Work* (London 1949)

13 Wells Archive

14 ibid

15 ibid

16 Beatrice Webb's diary, 19 April 1904

17 ibid, November 1902

18 Amery, L.S., *My Political Life* (London 1953)

19 On the Blands, see: Moore, Doris Langley Moore, *E.Nesbit* (London 1933); Bland, E.N., *Essays by Hubert Bland* (London 1914); and Ruck, Berta, *A Story-Teller Tells the Truth* (London n.d.)

20 On the Fabian Society, see: Pease, E.R., *The History of the Fabian Society* (London 1916); McBriar, A.M., op. cit.; Shaw, G.Bernard, *The Early History of the Fabian Society* (London 1892); and Cole, G.D.H., *Fabian Socialism* (London 1943)

21 Sinclair, Keith, *William Pember Reeves* (Oxford 1965)

22 Jean-Aubry, G., op. cit.

23 Ford, Ford Madox, *Mightier than the Sword*, op. cit.

24 ibid

25 Wells Archive

26 Wilson, Harris, op. cit.

27 Gettmann, Royal A., op. cit.

28 Wilson, Harris, op. cit.

29 Edel, Leon and Ray, Gordon N., op. cit.

30 Jean-Aubry, G., op. cit.

31 ibid

32 Wilson, Harris, op. cit.

33 Edel, Leon (Ed.), *Selected Letters of Henry James* (London 1956)

34 Wells Archive

35 ibid

36 ibid

37 ibid

Chapter 12

1 Wells, H.G.,*The Faults of the Fabian*. Reprinted as an appendix in Hynes, Samuel, *The Edwardian Frame of Mind* (London 1963)

2 See: Fremantle, Anne, *This Little Band of Prophets* (London 1960); Pelling, H., *The Origins of the Labour Party* (London 1954); Pelling, H. and Bealey, F., *Labour and Politics 1900–1906* (London 1958); and Poirier, P., *The Advent of the Labour Party* (London 1958)

3 The correspondence with Pease is in the Wells Archive. There are other letters by Pease in the Fabian Society papers in the Library of Nuffield College

4 Wells Archive

5 ibid

6 ibid

7 ibid

8 An extended account of the dealings between Wells and Sir Frederick Macmillan can be found in Dickson, Lovat, *H.G.Wells* (London 1969). Most of the letters are undated: the originals are now in the British Museum in the Macmillan papers

9 Bennett, Arnold, *Journal*, 29 July 1904

10 Laurence, Dan H., *Bernard Shaw: Collected Letters 1898–1910* (London 1972). This collection is not complete. Several letters from Shaw to Wells that are in the Wells Archive have been omitted

11 Chesterton, G.K., *Heretics* (London 1905)

12 Ford, Ford Madox, *Mightier than the Sword*, op. cit.

13 Wells Archive

14 ibid

15 Olivier, Margaret (Ed.), *Sydney Olivier: Letters and Selected Writings* (London 1948)

16 For the details of this manuscript see: Wells, H G., *The Wealth of Mr Waddy*, Wilson, Harris (Ed.), (Carbondale, Illinois 1969)

17 Wells Archive

18 Extracts and a summary of the omitted material can be found in Wilson, Harris, "The Death of Masterman: A Suppressed Episode in H.G.Wells's Kipps". PMLA Vol 86, No 1, January 1971

19 Wilson, Harris, *Arnold Bennett and H.G.Wells*, op. cit.

20 Edel, Leon and Ray, Gordon N., op. cit.

21 Laurence, Dan H., op. cit.

22 Ford, Ford Madox, op. cit.

23 Wells Archive

24 Laurence, Dan H., op. cit.

25 Wells Archive

26 ibid

27 ibid

28 ibid
29 ibid
30 ibid
31 Laurence, Dan H., op. cit.
32 Wells Archive

Chapter 13
1 Edel, Leon and Ray, Gordon N., op. cit.
2 Wells Archive
3 ibid
4 ibid
5 Wells, H.G., *The Future in America*
6 Wells Archive
7 Edel, Leon and Ray, Gordon N., op. cit.
8 Wells Archive
9 ibid
10 Beatrice Webb's diary, 15 July 1906
11 Quoted in Hynes, Samuel, op. cit.
12 Beatrice Webb's diary, 1 October 1906
13 Wells Archive
14 ibid
15 ibid
16 ibid
17 Laurence, Dan H., op. cit.
18 ibid
19 Wells Archive
20 Laurence, Dan H., op. cit.
21 Wells Archive
22 Laurence, Dan H., op. cit.
23 ibid
24 The Wells Archive and the Fabian Papers at Nuffield College both contain copies
25 Fabian Papers
26 Wells Archive
27 The meetings of 7 December and 14 December were reported at length in *Fabian News*, January 1907. The Wells speech at the 7 December meeting was printed immediately and circulated at the meeting of 14 December.
28 Fabian Papers
29 Laurence, Dan H., op. cit.
30 ibid
31 Beatrice Webb's diary, 15 December 1906
32 Laurence, Dan H., op. cit.

33 Wells Archive

34 Shaw, G.Bernard, "Mr. H.G.Wells and the Rest of Us", *The Christian Commonwealth*, 19 May 1909

Chapter 14

1 Wells Archive

2 ibid

3 There are other letters from J.W.Dunne in the Wells Archive

4 Wells Archive

5 Passfield Papers

6 Wells Archive

7 ibid

8 ibid

9 ibid

10 Mairet, Philip, *A.R.Orage* (London 1936)

11 The Violet Hunt letters are in Cornell University Library

12 Beatrice Webb's diary, September 1908

13 Wells Archive

14 ibid

15 The Wells Archive contains much repetitious material on this issue

16 Russell, Bertrand, *Portraits from Memory* (London 1956)

17 Masterman, Lucy, *C.F.G.Masterman* (London 1939)

18 The source for remarks by the servants, and for impressions of life in the Wells household in these years is Meyer, Mathilde, *H.G.Wells and His Family* (Edinburgh 1955)

19 Memories of this period at Sandgate can be found in Hunt, Violet, *The Flurried Years* (London n.d.) and also in Mizener, Alfred, *The Saddest Story* (London 1972). On Dorothy Richardson see: Trickett, P.M., "The Living Dead: Dorothy Richardson", and Brome, Vincent, "A Last Meeting with Dorothy Richardson", *London Magazine*, Vol 6, 1959

20 Masterman, Lucy, op. cit.

21 Laurence, Dan H., op. cit.

22 Wells Archive

23 Material on this controversy is in the Wells Archive

24 Salter, Arthur, *Personality in Politics* (London 1957)

25 *Fabian News* May 1908

26 Wells Archive

27 Keynes, Geoffrey (Ed.), *The Letters of Rupert Brooke* (London 1968)

28 See Dickson, Lovat, op. cit. for Macmillan correspondence

29 Wells Archive

Chapter 15

1 Salter, Arthur, op. cit.
2 Wells Archive
3 Edel, Leon and Ray, Gordon N., op. cit.
4 Hart-Davis, Rupert, *Hugh Walpole* (London 1952)
5 The letters which deal with this episode are in Ludwig, Richard, M. (Ed.), *Letters of Ford Madox Ford* (Princeton 1965)
6 Goldring, Douglas, *Reputations* (London 1920)
7 Ludwig, Richard M. op. cit.
8 Wells Archive
9 *Observer*, 14 February 1909
10 See the essay on *Tono-Bungay* in Lodge, David, *Language of Fiction* (London 1966)
11 See "The Scope of the Novel", reprinted in Edel, Leon and Ray, Gordon N., op. cit.
12 Beatrice Webb's diary, 24 February 1909
13 Wells Archive
14 Beatrice Webb's diary, March 1909
15 Fremantle, Anne, op. cit. contains one of the few references to this episode, which has often been confused with the later affair with Amber Reeves. This account has been based on personal statements to the authors, especially by Berta Ruck in 1972. Berta Ruck (Mrs Oliver) was a close friend of Edith Nesbit.
16 Wells Archive
17 ibid
18 ibid
19 Dickson, Lovat, op. cit.
20 Wells Archive

Chapter 16

1 Wells Archive
2 All statements attributed to Amber Reeves were made to the authors in interviews in 1971 and 1972
3 Beatrice Webb's diary, 27 September 1909
4 Wells Archive
5 Beatrice Webb's diary, 22 August 1909
6 Statement to authors
7 Statement to authors
8 This was G. Rivers Blanco White, a young lawyer who was an active member of the Fabian nursery
9 Beatrice Webb's diary, 27 September 1909
10 Wilson, Harris, op. cit.

11 Beatrice Webb's diary, 27 September 1909
12 Statement to authors
13 Wells Archive
14 ibid
15 ibid
16 The Shaw letter is in the Passfield Papers
17 Beatrice Webb's diary, 4 October 1909
18 The Vernon Lee letters are in Colby College Library. Some of them are printed in Gunn, Peter, *Vernon Lee (Violet Paget) 1856–1935* (London 1964). See also in Wells Archive
19 *Spectator*, 20 November 1909. See also: Hynes, Samuel, *The Edwardian Frame of Mind*, op. cit. on the "moral purity" campaign
20 Bennett, Arnold, *Journal*, op. cit.
21 Beatrice Webb's diary, 20 March 1910
22 Gunn, Peter, op. cit.
23 Wells Archive
24 Beatrice Webb's diary, 20 March 1910
25 Dunbar, Janet, *J.M.Barrie: The Man Behind the Image* (London 1970)
26 The letter is printed in full in Dickson, Lovat, op. cit.
27 Wells Archive
28 In the possession of Mrs Renée Tickell
29 "My Lucky Moment", *The View*, 29 April 1911

Chapter 17
1 Rothenstein, William, *Men and Memories* (London 1932)
2 Swinnerton, Frank, *An Autobiography* (London 1937)
3 Wells, H.G., *The Book of Catherine Wells* (London 1928)
4 ibid
5 ibid
6 Statement to authors 1972
7 Ross, Margery, *Robert Ross* (London 1952)
8 Wells Archive
9 Dickson, Lovat, op. cit.
10 Wells Archive
11 ibid
12 ibid
13 Beatrice Webb's, diary 5 November 1910
14 Wells Archive
15 Edel, Leon and Ray, Gordon N., op. cit.
16 Rothenstein, William, op. cit.
17 de Charms, Leslie, *Elizabeth of the German Garden* (London 1958). See also

the letter from Katherine Mansfield to Violet Schiff (undated) in *Adam 300* (London 1965)
18 Wells Archive
19 ibid
20 Blunden, Margaret, *The Countess of Warwick* (London 1967)
21 Wells Archive

Chapter 18

1 In Edel, Leon and Ray, Gordon N., op. cit.
2 Wells Archive
3 Wilson, Harris, op. cit.
4 This exchange is in Edel, Leon and Ray, Gordon N., op. cit.
5 ibid
6 Brooks, Van Wyck, *The World of H.G.Wells* (New York 1915)
7 Dickson, Lovat, op. cit.
8 Charteris, E., *The Life and Letters of Edmund Gosse* (London 1931)
9 Edel, Leon and Ray, Gordon N., op. cit.
10 ibid
11 This material and statements made by Rebecca West come from statements to the authors in 1971 and 1972
12 Hunt, Violet, op. cit.
13 Meyer, Mathilde, op. cit.
14 Swinnerton, Frank, op. cit.
15 West, Rebecca, *The Strange Necessity* (London 1928)
16 Wilson, Harris, op. cit.
17 Swinnerton, Frank, op. cit.
18 Wells Archive
19 Bennett, Arnold, *Letters to J.B.Pinker* (New York 1966)
20 Edel, Leon and Ray, Gordon N., op. cit.
21 Wells Archive
22 The remaining Wells-James correspondence is in Edel, Leon and Ray, Gordon N., op. cit.

Chapter 19

1 Statement to authors by Sir John Elliot (the son of R.D.Blumenfeld)
2 Wells, H.G., *Joan and Peter*
3 Preface in Atlantic Edition (London 1927)
4 Szilard, Leo, *Perspectives II* (Cambridge, Mass. 1968)
5 Wells, H.G., *The War That Will End War* (London 1914)
6 Gunn, Peter, op. cit.
7 *Daily Chronicle*, 31 December 1914
8 Wells Archive

9 Wells, H.G., *The War and the Future*
10 Statement to authors
11 Letter in possession of Mrs Renée Tickell
12 Wells Archive
13 Bennett, Arnold, *Journal* 18 March 1918
14 ibid 12 October 1915
15 Letter in possession of Mrs Guedalla
16 Swinnerton, Frank, op. cit.
17 Wells Archive
18 ibid
19 ibid
20 ibid
21 ibid
22 ibid
23 The letter to James Benard is quoted in West, Geoffrey, op. cit.
24 Wells Archive
25 Bennett, Arnold, *Journal*, April 1917
26 ibid 10 October 1917
27 Wells, H.G., *In the Fourth Year*
28 There is a copy in the Wells Archive
29 The letters to Northcliffe are in the Wells Archive
30 Wells Archive

Chapter 20
1 Gilbert Murray papers, Bodleian Library
2 Letter in possession of Mrs Guedalla
3 Wells Archive
4 Gilbert Murray papers
5 Broadcast by Frank Horrabin, 18 December 1949
6 *Today and Tomorrow*, September/October 1920
7 Toynbee, Arnold, *A Study of History*, Vol 1 (London 1934)
8 Letter from H.A.L.Fisher, 14 September 1920 in Wells Archive; and see Haynes, C.J.H., "The Other-Worldly Mr Wells" in *The Freeman* No 3, 1921
9 Dark, Sidney, *The Outline of Mr Wells* (London 1922)
10 Wilson, Harris, op. cit.
11 Wells Archive. Five letters from the exchange between Wells and Gorki were published in *Adam 300* (London 1965)
12 Trotsky's article was published in *Labour Monthly* July 1924
13 Brome, Vincent, *Six Studies in Quarrelling* (London 1958) contains an extended account of this controversy
14 There is a copy of the scheme in the Wells Archive
15 Wilson, Harris, op. cit.

16 Kennedy, D.M., *Birth Control in America* (New Haven 1970)
17 The letters exchanged with Margaret Sanger are in the Sophia Smith Collection at Smith College Library
18 Letter in possession of Mrs Renée Tickell
19 Wells Archive
20 Woolf, Leonard, *Downhill All the Way 1919–1939* (London 1967)
21 Statement to authors, 1972
22 Beatrice Webb's diary, July 1923

Chapter 21
1 Wells, H.G., "An Outbreak of Autobiography" in *A Year of Prophesying*
2 This, and following statements made to authors in interviews, 1971 and 1972
3 Chesterton, G.K., *Autobiography*, op. cit.
4 Statements made by Odette Keun to authors in 1971 and 1972
5 Sanger Papers
6 Wells Archive
7 ibid
8 ibid
9 Chaplin, C., *My Autobiography* (London 1964)
10 Bennett, Arnold, *Journal*, February 1927
11 Wells Archive, to Chevalley, 13 March 1927
12 Speaight, Robert, *The Life of Hilaire Belloc* (London 1957)
13 Brome, Vincent, *Six Studies in Quarrelling*, op. cit.
14 Wells Archive
15 See: Huxley, Julian, *Memories* (London 1970). This contains extracts from letters exchanged at this time, but the majority are in the Wells Archive
16 Wells Archive
17 Sanger Papers
18 The letters from Charlotte Shaw and G.Bernard Shaw are in the Wells Archive
19 Bennett, Arnold, *Journal* June 1927
20 Wilson, Harris, op. cit.
21 Wells Archive
22 Letter to Miss Butts: Wells Archive
23 Huxley, Julian, op. cit.
24 Wells Archive
25 Bennett, Arnold, *Journal* June 1927
26 Bennett, Arnold, *Letters to His Nephew*, op. cit.
27 Wells Archive
28 Dunbar, Janet, *Mrs G.B.S.* (New York 1963)

Chapter 22
1 Wells Archive
2 ibid
3 ibid
4 Letters in possession of Enid Bagnold
5 Huxley, Julian, op. cit. and Wells Archive
6 Wells Archive
7 ibid
8 Wells, H.G., *The Problem of the Troublesome Collaborator* (Limited private edition 1930). Copy in Wells Archive
9 Wells Archive
10 ibid
11 *The Problem of the Troublesome Collaborator* includes the following exchanges
12 Wells Archive
13 ibid
14 ibid
15 Bennett, Arnold, *Letters to J.B.Pinker*, op. cit.
16 Wells Archive
17 ibid
18 *Privy Council Reports* No 18, 1932
19 Chaplin, Charles, op. cit.
20 Letter in possession of Enid Bagnold
21 Wells Archive
22 Wilson, Harris, op. cit.
23 Letter in possession of Enid Bagnold
24 Wells Archive
25 ibid
26 ibid
27 ibid
28 ibid
29 Statement to authors
30 The letters are in the possession of Félicie Goletto, interviewed by the authors in September 1972

Chapter 23
1 Wells Archive
2 Wells, H.G., *The Shape of Things to Come*
3 *The New Statesman*, 27 October 1934: see also *Stalin-Wells-Shaw*, pamphlet published by *The New Statesman* 1934
4 Brome, Vincent, *Six Studies in Quarrelling*, op. cit.
5 Statement by Kingsley Martin to authors: see also the second volume of his autobiography, *Editor* (London 1968). His papers are in the University of Sussex

Library, and Kingsley, by Rolph, C.H. (London 1973) is based in part on these papers

6 Wells Archive

7 Kingsley Martin Papers

8 Wells Archive

9 ibid: the Roosevelt letter is dated 13 February 1935

10 ibid

11 Beatrice Webb's diary 25 October 1934

12 Keun, Odette, "H.G.Wells. The Player" *Time and Tide* 13, 20 and 27 October 1934

13 Wells Archive. Letter to Ellis Roberts, 23 October 1934

14 ibid

15 ibid

16 ibid

17 *The Bookseller*, 22 August 1946

18 Statement to authors, 1972

19 Maugham, W.Somerset, *The Vagrant Mood* (London 1952) and Chaplin, Charles, op. cit.

20 Bagnold, Enid, *Autobiography* (London 1970)

21 Statement to authors

22 Wells Archive

23 BBC Centenary broadcast,

24 Noyes, Alfred, *Two Worlds for Memory* (London 1953)

25 Statement to authors by Vincent Korda, 1971

26 Bliss, Arthur, *As I Remember* (London 1970)

27 Passfield Papers

28 Wells Archive

29 Walpole, Hugh, *Autobiography* (London 1952)

30 Chaplin, Charles, op. cit.

31 Wells Archive

32 ibid

33 ibid

34 ibid

35 Statement to authors, 1971

36 The printed report is in the Wells Archive

Chapter 24

1 Wells Archive

2 ibid

3 *Phoenix* (Imperial College of Science student journal) 1937

4 Wells Archive

5 ibid

6 Wells, H.G., *World Brain*

7 Armytage, W.H.G., op. cit. for further details on relations with Richard Gregory at this time

8 Sanger Papers

9 Wells Archive

10 ibid

11 ibid

12 Cantril, Hadley, *The Invasion from Mars* (Princeton 1940)

13 Wilson, Harris, *Life So Far* (London 1954); and Lord Snow, reported in *The Times*, 6 December 1966

14 Wells Archive

15 Wells, H.G., *Outlook for Homo Sapiens*

16 Wells, H.G., *Travels of a Republican Radical in Search of Hot Water* (London 1939)

17 Wells, H.G., *Outlook for Homo Sapiens*, op. cit.

18 ibid

19 Beatrice Webb's diary, 11 February 1949

20 ibid, 31 March 1939

21 Barker, Ernest, *Age and Youth* (London 1953)

Chapter 25

1 *Travels of a Republican Radical*, op. cit.

2 Reprinted in Wells, H.G., *The Rights of Man* (London 1940)

3 See Armytage, W.H.G., op. cit.: also statement to authors by Lord Ritchie-Calder

4 Maugham, W.Somerset, *The Vagrant Mood* (London 1952)

5 See: Laski, Harold J., *Reflections on the Revolution of Our Times* (London 1943); and Streit, Clarence, *Union Now* (London 1942)

6 Wells Archive

7 Wells, H.G., *Science and the World Mind* (London 1942)

8 The correspondence is in the Kingsley Martin Papers

9 See *The Listener*, 24 February 1972 and succeeding issues for letters from Inez Holden and others

10 Orwell, George, *Critical Essays* (London 1946)

11 *The Listener*, June 1942

12 Wells Archive

13 ibid

14 ibid

15 ibid

16 Wells, H.G., *'42 to '44*

17 Wells Archive

18 ibid

19 The exchange of letters with R.Palme Dutt is in the Wells Archive
20 Wells, H.G., *'42 to '44*
21 ibid
22 Wells Archive
23 ibid
24 ibid
25 Wells, H.G., *'42 to '44*
26 Papers of Professor Morris Ginsberg, in possession of Professor E.M. Eppel
27 Wells Archive
28 Sanger Papers
29 Wells Archive
30 ibid
31 ibid

Chapter 26
1 *Freethinker*, New York, May 1944
2 Sanger Papers
3 Sanger Papers. These contain the correspondence with Leo Lehman, the publisher,
4 ibid
5 Wells Archive
6 ibid
7 Wells, H.G., *Mind at the End of its Tether*
8 Wells Archive
9 ibid
10 Wells, G.P., *The Last Books of H.G.Wells* (London 1968)
11 Wells Archive
12 *Encounter*, February 1957
13 Mackenzie, Compton, *My Life and Times* (London 1963)
14 Wells Archive

BIBLIOGRAPHY

1 The Works of H.G.Wells

There is no complete bibliography of the books, pamphlets and articles of Wells. The following works contain extensive bibliographic material.

Chapell, F.A., *A Bibliography with a Prologue introducing Mr Wells to the Future* (London, 1924).

Connes, G., *A Dictionary of the Characters and Scenes in the Novels, Romances and Short Stories of H.G.Wells* (London, 1925).

Wells, Geoffrey, H., (Geoffrey West) *The Works of H.G.Wells 1887–1925* (London 1926).

Wells, H.G. A Comprehensive Bibliography, H.G.Wells Society (London, 1968). Additional bibliographic material has been published at intervals in *English Literature in Transition*, and Professors David Y. Hughes, Robert M. Philmus and J.P.Vernier have in preparation an annotated bibliography of the uncollected Wells articles and essays 1887–1920. In addition, Raknem, Ingvald, *H.G.Wells and his Critics* (London, 1962) has many references to reviews and critical articles about Wells and to other relevant books. Vernier, Jean-Pierre, *H.G.Wells et son Temps* (Rouen, 1972) has an excellent bibliography which should be consulted especially for the early journalism, for critical articles and for theses.

There is no complete edition of the novels and stories. *The Atlantic Edition of the Works of H.G.Wells* (London, 1924–1928) was printed only in an edition of 1670 copies, but it is important on account of the new prefaces that Wells contributed. *The Essex Edition of the Works of H.G.Wells* (London, 1926–1927) was published in twenty-four volumes, and *The Complete Short Stories of H.G. Wells* (London, 1927) is not, in fact, a complete collection.

The works are entered below under the year of first publication in London, with the name of the original publisher. This does not necessarily represent the order in which the books were written. Some books were held back by Wells; some encountered publishing delays; and some were first published in the United States. The date of publication was also affected by the arrangements for prior publication in serial form.

1893　*Text Book of Biology* 2 volumes (Clive)

　　　Honours Physiography Gregory, R.A. and Wells, H.G. (Hughes)

1895　*Select Conversations with an Uncle, Now Extinct, and Two Other Reminiscences*
(John Lane)
The Time Machine: An Invention (Heinemann)
The Wonderful Visit (Dent)
The Stolen Bacillus, and Other Incidents (Methuen)

1896　*The Island of Dr Moreau* (Heinemann)
The Wheels of Chance: A Cycling Holiday Adventure (Dent)

1897　*The Plattner Story, and Others* (Methuen)
The Invisible Man, A Grotesque Romance (Pearson)
Certain Personal Matters: A Collection of Material, Mainly Autobiographical
(Lawrence and Bullen)

1898　*The War of the Worlds* (Heinemann)

1899　*When the Sleeper Wakes: A Story of Years to Come* (Harper)
Tales of Space and Time (Harper)

1900　*Love and Mr Lewisham* (Harper)

1901　*The First Men in the Moon* (Newnes)
*Anticipations of the Reaction of Mechanical and Scientific Progress upon Human
Life and Thought* (Chapman & Hall)

1902　*The Discovery of the Future* (T. Fisher Unwin)
The Sea Lady: A Tissue of Moonshine (Methuen)

1903　*Mankind in the Making* (Chapman & Hall)
Twelve Stories and a Dream (Macmillan)

1904　*The Food of the Gods, and How It Came to Earth* (Macmillan)

1905　*A Modern Utopia* (Chapman & Hall)
Kipps: The Story of a Simple Soul (Macmillan)

1906　*In the Days of the Comet* (Macmillan)
The Future in America: A Search after Realities (Chapman & Hall)

1907　*This Misery of Boots* (Fabian Society)

1908　*New Worlds for Old* (Constable)
*The War in the Air, and Particularly How Mr Bert Smallways Fared While It
Lasted* (Bell)
First and Last Things: A Confession of Faith and Rule of Life (Constable)

1909　*Tono-Bungay* (Macmillan)
Ann Veronica (T. Fisher Unwin)

1910　*The History of Mr Polly* (Nelson)

1911　*The New Machiavelli* (John Lane)
The Country of the Blind and Other Stories (Nelson)
Floor Games (Palmer)

1912　*Marriage* (Macmillan)

1913　*Little Wars: A Game for Boys from Twelve Years of Age to One Hundred and
Fifty and for That More Intelligent Sort of Girls Who Like Boys' Games*
(Palmer)

The Passionate Friends (Macmillan)

1914   *An Englishman Looks at the World* (Cassell)
The World Set Free (Macmillan)
The Wife of Sir Isaac Harman (Macmillan)
The War that Will End War (Palmer)

1915   *Boon, the Mind of the Race, the Wild Asses of the Devil, and the Last Trump,*
Being a First Selection from the Literary Remains of George Boon, Appropriate
to the Times (T.Fisher Unwin)
Bealby: A Holiday (Methuen)
The Research Magnificent (Macmillan)

1916   *What is Coming: A Forecast of Things after the War* (Cassell)
Mr Britling Sees It Through (Cassell)

1917   *War and the Future* (Cassell)
God the Invisible King (Cassell)
The Soul of a Bishop (Cassell)

1918   *In the Fourth Year* (Chatto & Windus)
Joan and Peter: The Story of an Education (Cassell)

1919   *The Undying Fire* (Cassell)

1920   *The Outline of History* (Newnes)
Russia in the Shadows (Hodder & Stoughton)

1921   *The Salvaging of Civilization* (Cassell)

1922   *Washington and the Hope of Peace* (Collins)
The Secret Places of the Heart (Cassell)
A Short History of the World (Cassell)

1923   *Men Like Gods* (Cassell)

1924   *The Story of a Great Schoolmaster* (Chatto & Windus)
The Dream (Cape)
A Year of Prophesying (T.Fisher Unwin)

1925   *Christina Alberta's Father* (Cape)

1926   *The World of William Clissold* (Benn)
Mr Belloc Objects to the Outline of History (Watts)

1927   *Meanwhile* (Benn)
Democracy under Revision (Hogarth Press)

1928   *The Way the World is Going* (Benn)
The Open Conspiracy: Blue Prints for a World Revolution (Gollancz)
The Book of Amy Catherine Wells (Chatto & Windus)
Mr Blettsworthy on Rampole Island (Benn)

1929   *The King Who Was a King: The Book of a Film* (Benn)
The Common Sense of World Peace (Hogarth Press)
The Adventures of Tommy (Harrap)

1930   *The Autocracy of Mr Parham* (Heinemann)
The Science of Life: A Summary of Contemporary Knowledge about Life and its

Possibilities (Amalgamated Press)

1931 *What Are We To Do With Our Lives?* (Heinemann)

1932 *After Democracy* (Watts)
The Work, Wealth and Happiness of Mankind (Heinemann)
The Bulpington of Blup (Hutchinson)

1933 *The Shape of Things to Come: The Ultimate Revolution* (Hutchinson)

1934 *Experiment in Autobiography: Discoveries and Conclusions of a Very Ordinary Brain—Since 1866* (Gollancz and The Cresset Press)

1935 *The New America: The New World* (The Cresset Press)

1936 *The Anatomy of Frustration* (The Cresset Press)
The Croquet Player (Chatto & Windus)
The Idea of a World Encyclopaedia (Hogarth Press)

1937 *Star Begotten: A Biological Fantasia* (Chatto & Windus)
Brynhild (Methuen)
The Camford Visitation (Methuen)

1938 *The Brothers* (Chatto & Windus)
Apropos of Dolores (Cape)
Wild Brain (Methuen)

1939 *The Holy Terror* (Michael Joseph)
Travels of a Republican Radical in Search of Hot Water (Penguin Books)
The Fate of Homo Sapiens (Secker & Warburg)
The New World Order (Secker & Warburg)

1940 *The Rights of Man, or What Are We Fighting For?* (Penguin Books)
Babes in the Darkling Wood (Secker & Warburg)
The Common Sense of War and Peace: World Revolution or War Unending (Penguin Books)
All Aboard for Ararat (Secker & Warburg)

1941 *You Can't Be Too Careful* (Secker & Warburg)
Guide to the New World: A Handbook of Constructive Revolution (Gollancz)

1942 *The Outlook for Homo Sapiens* (Secker & Warburg)
Science and the World-Mind (New Europe Publishing Co.)
The Conquest of Time (Watts)
Phoenix: A Summary of the Inescapable Conditions of World Organisation (Secker & Warburg)
A Thesis on the Quality of Illusion in the Continuity of the Individual Life in the Higher Metazoa, with Particular Reference to the Species Homo Sapiens (Watts)
The Conquest of Time (Watts)

1943 *Crux Ansata. An Indictment of the Roman Catholic Church* (Penguin Books)

1944 *'42 to '44: A Contemporary Memoir* (Secker & Warburg)

1945 *The Happy Turning: A Dream of Life* (Heinemann)
Mind at the End of Its Tether (Heinemann)

Two books were published posthumously from original manuscripts.
The Desert Daisy (written in 1878) was published in Urbana, Illinois, in 1957, in an edition by Ray, Gordon N.
The Wealth of Mr Waddy (written after 1900) was published in Carbondale, Illinois, in 1969, in an edition by Wilson, Harris.

2 *Criticism and Biography*
Archer, William *God and Mr Wells* (London, 1917)
Barber, Otto *H.G.Wells's Verhältnis zum Darwinismus* (Leipzig, 1934)
Belgion, Montgomery *H.G.Wells* (London, 1953)
Belloc, Hilaire *A Companion to Mr Wells's Outline of History* (London, 1926)
Belloc, Hilaire *Mr Belloc Still Objects* (London, 1926)
Bergonzi, Bernard *The Early H.G.Wells* (Manchester, 1961)
Binns, L.E. *Mr Wells's Invisible King* (London, 1919)
Borrello, Alfred H. *H.G.Wells: Author in Agony* (Carbondale, 1972)
Braybrooke, Patrick *Some Aspects of H.G.Wells* (London, 1928)
Brome, Vincent *H.G.Wells* (London, 1951)
Brooks, Van Wyck *The World of H.G.Wells* (London, 1915)
Brown, Ivor *H.G.Wells* (London, 1923)
Chaplin, F.K. *H.G.Wells. An Outline* (London, 1961)
Connes, G. *Étude sur la pensée de Wells* (Paris, 1926)
Costa, R.H. *H.G.Wells* (New York, 1967)
Craufurd, A.H. *The Religion of H.G.Wells* (London, 1909)
Dark, Sydney *The Outline of H.G.Wells* (London, 1922)
Dickson, Lovat *H.G.Wells. His Turbulent Life and Times* (London, 1969)
Doughty, F.H. *H.G.Wells Educationalist* (London, 1926)
Downey, R. *Some Errors of H.G.Wells* (London, 1933)
Dudley, Owen F. *Human Happiness and H.G.Wells* (London, 1936)
Edel, L. and Ray, Gordon N. (Eds.) *Henry James and H.G.Wells* (London, 1959)
Gettman, Royal (Ed.) *George Gissing and H.G.Wells* (London, 1960)
Gomme, A.W. *Mr Wells as Historian* (Glasgow, 1921)
Guyot, Edouard *H.G.Wells* (Paris, 1920)
Hillegas, Mark R. *The Future as Nightmare, H.G.Wells and the Anti-Utopians* (New York, 1967)
Hopkins, R.T. *H.G.Wells: Personality, Character, Topography* (London, 1922)
Kargalitski, J. *The Life and Thought of H.G.Wells* (London, 1966)
Jones, H.A. *My Dear Wells: A Manual for the Haters of England* (London, 1921)
Lacey, T.A. *Mr Britling's Finite God* (London, 1917)
Lang, Hans Joachim *Herbert George Wells* (Hamburg, 1948)

BIBLIOGRAPHY

Levidov, I.M. and Partchevskaya, M. *Herbert George Wells. A Bibliography of Russian Translations and Literature on Wells in Russian* (Moscow, 1966)

Mattick, Heinz *H.G.Wells als Sozialreformer* (Leipzig, 1935)

Meyer, Mathilde *H.G.Wells and his family* (Edinburgh, 1956)

Nicholson, Norman *H.G.Wells* (London, 1950)

Newell, Kenneth B. *Structure in Four Novels by H.G.Wells* (The Hague, 1968)

Norton, Philip *I See Through Mr Britling* (London, 1918)

Parrinder, Patrick *H.G.Wells* (Edinburgh, 1970)

Parrinder, Patrick (Ed.) *H.G.Wells: The Critical Heritage* (London, 1972)

Raknem, Ingwald *H.G.Wells and His Critics* (London, 1962)

Sonnemann, U. *Der Soziale gedanke im Werk von H.G.Wells* (Berlin, 1935)

Vallentin, A. *H.G.Wells: Prophet of Our Day* (New York, 1950)

Wagar, W.Warren *H.G.Wells and the World State* (New Haven, 1961)

Wagar, W.Warren *H.G.Wells: Journalism and Prophecy 1893–1946* (Boston 1964)

West, Geoffrey *H.G.Wells: A Sketch for a Portrait* (London, 1930)

Wilson, Harris *Arnold Bennett and H.G.Wells* (London, 1960)

INDEX